MADAM & EVE
TWENTY

BY STEPHEN FRANCIS & RICO

Published in 2012 in South Africa by
Jacana Media
10 Orange Street, Auckland Park, 2092
PO Box 291784, Melville, 2109
www.jacana.co.za

ISBN 978-1-4314-0451-3
Job number 001873
Layout by squareart
Printed and bound by Ultra Litho (Pty) Ltd, Johannesburg

OTHER MADAM & EVE BOOKS

Madam & Eve Collection	(Rapid Phase, 1993, reprint 1999)
Free At Last	(Penguin Books, 1994)
All Aboard for the Gravy Train	(Penguin Books, 1995)
Somewhere over the Rainbow Nation	(Penguin Books, 1996)
Madam & Eve's Greatest Hits	(Penguin Books, 1997)
Madams are from Mars, Maids are from Venus	(Penguin Books, 1997)
It's a Jungle Out There	(David Philip, 1998)
International Maid of Mystery	(David Philip, 1999)
Has anyone seen my Vibrating Cellphone?	(interactive.Africa, 2000)
The Madams are Restless	(Rapid Phase, 2000)
Crouching Madam, Hidden Maid	(Rapid Phase, 2001)
Madam & Eve, 10 Wonderful Years	(Rapid Phase, 2002)
The Maidtrix	(Rapid Phase, 2003)
Gin & Tonic for the Soul	(Rapid Phase, 2004)
Desperate Housemaids	(Rapid Phase, 2005)
Madams of the Caribbean	(Rapid Phase, 2006)
Bring me my (new) Washing Machine	(Rapid Phase, 2007)
Madam & Eve Unplugged	(Rapid Phase, 2008)
Strike While The Iron Is Hot	(Jacana, 2009)
Twilight of the Vuvuzelas	(Jacana, 2010)
Mother Anderson's Secret Book of Wit & Wisdom	(Jacana, 2011)
The Pothole at the End of the Rainbow	(Jacana, 2011)
Jamen sort kaffe er pa mode nu, Madam!	(Gyldendal, Denmark, 1995)
Jeg gyver Mandela Skylden for det her!	(Gyldendal, Denmark, 1995)
Alt under kontrol I Sydafrika!	(Bogfabrikken, Denmark, 1997)
Men alla dricker kaffet svart nufortiden, Madam!	(Bokfabrikken, Sweden, 1998)
Madame & Eve, Enfin Libres!	(Vents D'Ouest, France, 1997)
Votez Madame & Eve	(Vents D'Ouest, France, 1997)
La coupe est pleine	(Vents D'Ouest, France, 1998)
Rennue-Ménage à deux	(Vents D'Ouest, France, 1999)
En voient de toutes les couleurs	(Vents D'Ouest, France, 2000)
Madame vient de Mars, Eve de Venus,	(Vents D'Ouest, France, 2000)
Madam & Eve	(LIKE, Finland, 2005)

MADAM & EVE APPEARS REGULARLY IN:
Mail & Guardian, The Star, Saturday Star, Sunday Times, Herald, Mercury, Witness, Daily Dispatch, Cape Times, Pretoria News, Diamond Fields Advertiser, Die Volksblad, EC Today, Kokstad Advertiser, The Namibian, iMaverick, Daily Maverick Online.

TO CONTACT MADAM & EVE:
PO Box 413667, Craighall 2024, Johannesburg, South Africa
madamandeve@rapidphase.co.za
www.madamandeve.co.za

HAPPY BIRTHDAY AND MANY MORE...

'A superb mix of sitcom, satire and South African stuff – our top comic strip by far.'

Zapiro

'Madam & Eve gets the wonderful absurdity of being South African in a way that's smart, witty and deadly funny – it's amazeballs!'

Lauren Beukes
Award-winning author of Zoo City

'There's something quintessentially South African about Madam & Eve.

I remember desperately trying to get them into Kimberley's Diamond Fields Advertiser when I worked there and being so chuffed when they agreed – almost twenty years ago.

Then when I came to Joburg, I fell in love with them all over again as I discovered the reality of a suburban afternoon rent asunder with a cry of 'mieeeeellies'.

It doesn't matter whether you live in Camps Bay, Kakamas or Craighall Park; Madam & Eve have captured the miracle of our transformation and the lunacy of our lives. I look forward to their next twenty years chronicling our lives.'

Kevin Ritchie
Deputy editor, The Star

'If you don't understand South Africa, read Madam & Eve. When you've stopped laughing you'll get it: tokoloshes, politics, class warfare, three-men-on-the-back-of-a-bakkie syndrome, and how to mix the perfect G&T. All you need to survive. PS: Eve is my choice for next president: we need a strong woman with clean hands.'

Margie Orford
Crime writer

'I love Madam & Eve. I remember when I first heard one of the servants call my mother "Madam" all those years ago. The "Eve" in question would later employ coarse Setswana in her responses, but only after many years of loyal service. Congratulations on your own twenty years of loyal service, Stephen and Rico. May you have twenty more.'

Gareth Cliff
5FM DJ and author

'Dear Madam & Eve

Thanks for bludgeoning my funny bone into submission. I would cry if I couldn't laugh.

Regards
Brett'

Brett Murray
Artist

'Things Madam & Eve has taught me:

1. Gin prevents visible ageing

2. Politicians don't have faces

3. Thandi doesn't grow very fast

Thanks, Steve and Rico. I know stuff now I wouldn't have thought important twenty years ago.'

Bruce Dennill
CitiVibe editor

'Madam & Eve were just dying to leap off the page and get a life!! I was fortunate as the creative producer to help them do just that with a wonderful cast including Val Donald Bell as Madam Tina, Jaxa as Eve and the late Pat Saunders as Mother Anderson. And of course great scripts from the writers! It was fun... Let's bring Madam & Eve back to life again and see what's cooking today!'

Roberta Durrant
Creative director/producer of Madam & Eve, the sitcom

'Damn – twenty short years! We've represented Madam (reluctantly), Eve (enthusiastically), Mother Anderson (worryingly), Steve and Rico (naggingly) and almost NEVER got paid. Even Max the Gorilla died before he paid us. But hell, at least we turned up in the strip, were judged, praised and accused and earned big kudos there! So thanks to our famous friends and characters at Madam & Eve and hope we're still featuring when you turn forty! Congratulations and please invite us to your 21st. Your lawyers, Mark and Dan.'

Mark Rosin and Dan Rosengarten

'I have been with Madam & Eve since day one. Well, I would have been if I had been born on day one! But Gwen, Edith, Thandi, Eve and their company of societal crazies have kept me laughing for fifteen years and made me into the man (!) I am today. Thanks Steve & Rico!!'

Matt Rosin
Madam & Eve fan

'On the wall of my corridor at home, just as you come in, on the left-hand side, beyond the infra-red alarm and the accordion security door, you will find a rare and much sought-after work of art. The very first Madam & Eve eight-panel colour cartoon in its original form.

I'm sure it's worth a small fortune now, because it's twenty years old, and as you may know, no-one inks cartoons by hand anymore; it's all done by computer these days. So an original like this, well, let's just say you don't come across it every day.

But the best thing about it is, I got it for absolutely nothing from Francis & Rico, back in the early '90s, when they were still young and innocent and relatively good-looking. And boy, were they stupid! To give me an original Madam & Eve colour cartoon for free! And not just any original Madam & Eve colour cartoon, but the very first one to be published!

Oh yes, I forgot to mention, I also have a very vicious dog, whose job is to sit in the corridor at home and look after my cartoon.

But thank you Rico and Stephen, for your characters, for your comedy, for the role you have played in helping us learn to laugh at ourselves... and most of all, for your naïve lack of appreciation for the value of original cartoon art. Ha!'

Gus Silber
Collector of original *Madam & Eve* cartoon art

'I don't believe it is twenty years. Next you'll be telling me I am over fifty-five! I remember the start and thinking Madam & Eve was such a boring predictable convention. How wrong can you be. It was funny from the beginning and the secret is in the mix. Big national topics are covered but on slow days there is the domestic situation to be exploited and we laugh just as much. Inevitably there was a period when the whole thing got a bit tired but, thankfully, it didn't last long. It was as though someone told the creators that they now were responsible for icons and icons must be protected. Madam & Eve is better than ever and no morning is complete without a look. Congratulations.'

John Robbie
Radio 702 presenter

'The duel between Eve and her madam and all the other hangers-on has been one of the most entertaining columns in South Africa over the years. I can't think there is anyone who has followed Madam & Eve over the years who hasn't crumpled into the foetal position with laughter and recognition at LEAST once a week since the column began. It's heightened the absurdity of our country and lampooned – with such grace and skill – some of the people who strut across our stage. Life in SA would be the poorer without Eve taking us into the future, sometimes yelling and kicking, but always with humour.'

Jenny Crwys-Williams
Book champion and Radio 702 presenter

'I grew up on Madam & Eve, it was in these panels where I discovered that SA was actually a really funny place.'

Kagiso Lediga
Stand-up comedian

'Twenty years ago, these three lunatics arrived at the Weekly Mail and proffered a cartoon called Madam & Eve. We said yes and ran it from that week. Now they ask me to write about why we said yes. But this time I say no, I won't make the same mistake twice. The first time we were desperadoes, out of money, ideas and hope, and we needed something new to keep our newspaper going. For years thereafter, we had to deal with these guys, and the fact that they had a huge following and were hard to get rid of. We had to go to their exhibitions, and book launches, and prize-givings. We had to live with the fact that people liked their cartoons better than our editorials. They were smarter, wittier and probably newsier. They became more famous than us. They got all the girls. They probably kept the paper alive. Even when we didn't pay them, they carried on, week after week. So, no, I have learnt to keep my mouth shut around these guys. It can only lead to another twenty years of trouble.'

Anton Harber
Joint founder, *Weekly Mail*

'Three big ugly guys trooped into the office. It takes three ugly guys to draw a cartoon? One did the jokes. One did the drawings. One did the blackmail. Buy this now or we give it to The Star. It was a winning line. Later a reader complained: There's a funny cartoon in the paper? You guys getting soft? But it was too late.'

Irwin Manoim
Joint founder, *Weekly Mail*

'Oh Shucks. I'm going to keep this Sweet and Short. Madam & Eve make me laugh lekker when I'm feeling Gatvol. Dankie, Stephen en Rico!'

Leon Schuster
Funny man

'Can't believe it's been twenty years. Madam & Eve still look the same age. They haven't aged a page!'

David Kau
Comedian

'Twenty years of daily joy.'

Amy J. Moore
Producer, *No. 1 Ladies' Detective Agency* TV series (HBO)

Introduction

I first met Rico when he was still Enrico Schacherl, an ardent young wannabe cartoonist. It was in the days of snail mail, and I was editing a funny little fanzine called *PAX* (Pre-Azanian Comix). Every couple of months, a fat A4 envelope would arrive from Enrico, jam-packed with rambling post-apocalyptic sci-fi comics. What made these stories special was that they weren't set in New York or Metropolis or on Mars, but in a parched and dusty future Africa, where raggedy armies scrapped over diminishing resources. They weren't funny, but they did speak volumes about how South Africans saw their future.

Then came 1990, the beaming Madiba walked free and an alternative future became the present. The bleak Afro-pessimism of Rico's sci-fi comics was banished, momentarily at least, by the euphoria of our new-found consensus. We stood, with dewy-eyed optimism, at the gates of the Rainbow Nation. At this exact moment, as if scripted in a Johannesburg-based remake of *The Odd Couple*, a funnyman walked into Rico's life.

Bouncing between possible careers in graphic design and architecture, Rico had heard a radio interview with up-and-coming humour writers Gus Silber and Arthur Goldstuck, about a new satirical magazine called *Laughing Stock*. He immediately went to their offices in search of them, but they weren't there. Instead he found Stephen Francis, a wisecracking Yank with a numb jaw.

Steve had just been to the dentist, and was still a bit spaced out from the Novacaine. Rico describes their brief encounter as 'surreal'. But it was one of those epoch-defining moments that become apocryphal. From the unlikely marriage of these two minds was born the funniest and most accurate cartoon satire that South Africans had ever seen.

Looking back at the earliest *Madam & Eve* strips collected in this book, it's easy to be swept away by the crazy energy of those days. It was a bipolar world of glorious optimism and suicidal pessimism. Everything hung in the balance. Balaclava-hooded gangsters ran wild in the streets, and in a classic *Madam & Eve* cartoon from 1996, we see them running off with a chunk of the Rainbow.

So what's changed? Everything still hangs in the balance. The balaclava-hooded gangsters have been promoted into cushy government jobs, and the *Madam & Eve* jokes about them just keep on rolling in. How do Steve and Rico do it, you might ask. And what is it exactly that makes *Madam & Eve* so funny?

It's a kind of alchemy. It's not just about the ability to write witty lines that capture the essence of our human condition or our peculiar South Africanness – an ability that Stephen Francis has in abundance. Nor is it just about the talent to render the visual complexities of suburb and township, character and expression in a few economical lines – a talent for which Rico is legendary. It's about the alchemic process that occurs when the base metals of good writing and precise artwork combine to produce gold – the truly funny strip that liberates a laugh from your belly and causes a smile to light up your face as you go about your day.

Striking this kind of gold is what cartoonists dream of, what they work towards with every fibre of their being. And it's as abundant in these pages as it once was in the seams of the Witwatersrand.

Madam & Eve has more to tell us about the reality of who we are and where we live than roomfuls of statistic-quoting experts could ever do. After all, when it comes to the special kinds of expertise that we as South Africans need in our quest to live together in harmony, there are no better experts than the redoubtable characters of *Madam & Eve*. And for that we can thank Stephen Francis and Rico, the unstoppable Odd Couple of South African cartooning.

Andy Mason, acclaimed cartoonist and the author of *What's So Funny? Under the Skin of South African Cartooning*

Thank you to all our readers and fans
for twenty years of laughter and support

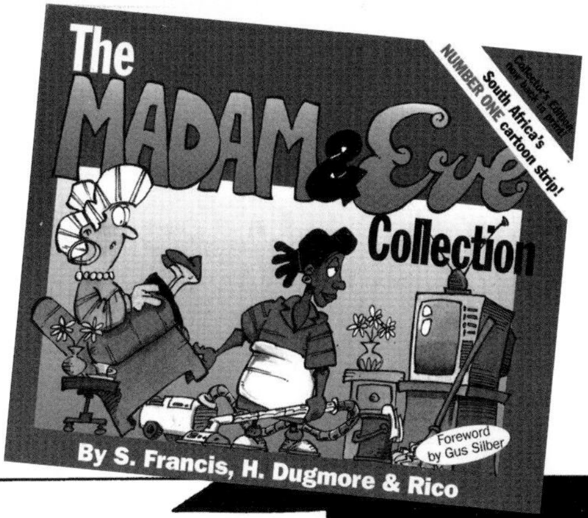
The MADAM & Eve Collection
South Africa's NUMBER ONE cartoon strip!
Foreword by Gus Silber
By S. Francis, H. Dugmore & Rico

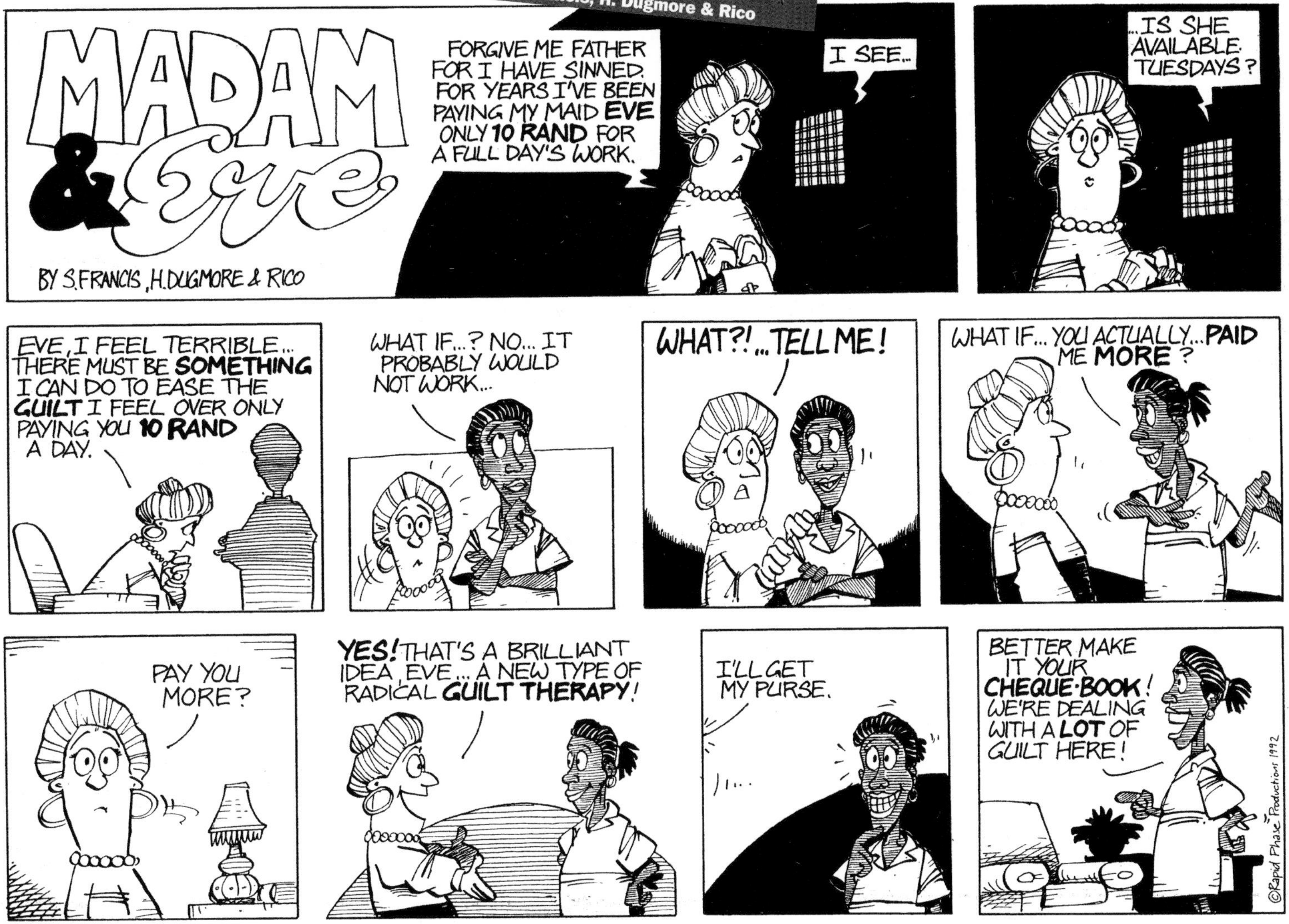
MADAM & Eve
BY S.FRANCIS, H.DUGMORE & RICO
FORGIVE ME FATHER FOR I HAVE SINNED. FOR YEARS I'VE BEEN PAYING MY MAID EVE ONLY 10 RAND FOR A FULL DAY'S WORK.
I SEE...
...IS SHE AVAILABLE TUESDAYS?
EVE, I FEEL TERRIBLE... THERE MUST BE SOMETHING I CAN DO TO EASE THE GUILT I FEEL OVER ONLY PAYING YOU 10 RAND A DAY.
WHAT IF...? NO... IT PROBABLY WOULD NOT WORK...
WHAT?!...TELL ME!
WHAT IF... YOU ACTUALLY... PAID ME MORE?
PAY YOU MORE?
YES! THAT'S A BRILLIANT IDEA, EVE... A NEW TYPE OF RADICAL GUILT THERAPY!
I'LL GET MY PURSE.
BETTER MAKE IT YOUR CHEQUE·BOOK! WE'RE DEALING WITH A LOT OF GUILT HERE!
©Rapid Phase Productions 1992

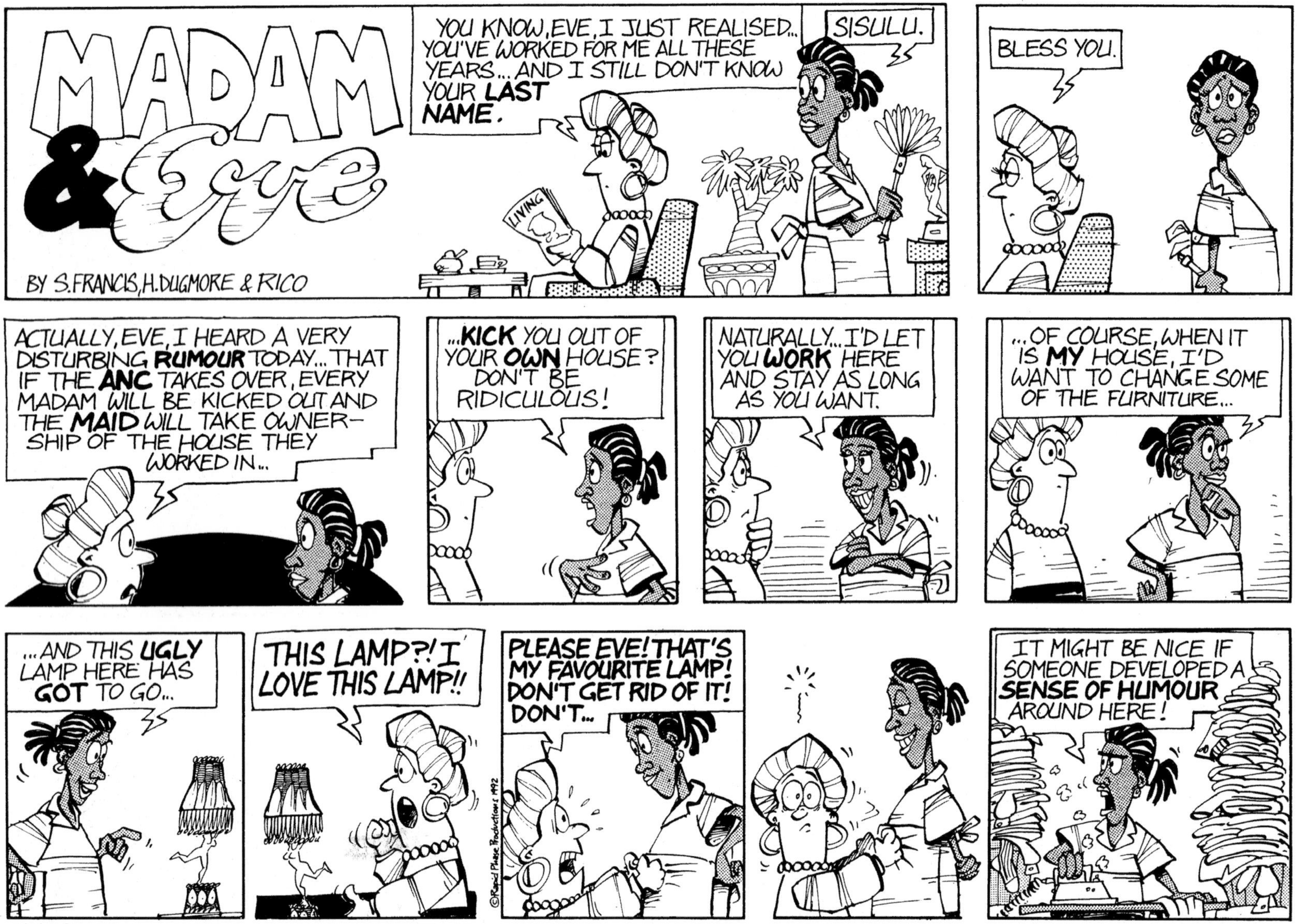
MADAM & Eve
BY S.FRANCIS, H.DUGMORE & RICO
YOU KNOW, EVE, I JUST REALISED... YOU'VE WORKED FOR ME ALL THESE YEARS... AND I STILL DON'T KNOW YOUR **LAST NAME**.
SISULU.
LIVING
BLESS YOU.
ACTUALLY, EVE, I HEARD A VERY DISTURBING **RUMOUR** TODAY... THAT IF THE **ANC** TAKES OVER, EVERY MADAM WILL BE KICKED OUT AND THE **MAID** WILL TAKE OWNERSHIP OF THE HOUSE THEY WORKED IN...
...**KICK** YOU OUT OF YOUR **OWN** HOUSE? DON'T BE RIDICULOUS!
NATURALLY... I'D LET YOU **WORK** HERE AND STAY AS LONG AS YOU WANT.
...OF COURSE, WHEN IT IS **MY** HOUSE, I'D WANT TO CHANGE SOME OF THE FURNITURE...
...AND THIS **UGLY** LAMP HERE HAS **GOT** TO GO...
THIS LAMP?! I LOVE THIS LAMP!!
©Rapid Phase Productions 1992
PLEASE EVE! THAT'S MY FAVOURITE LAMP! DON'T GET RID OF IT! DON'T...
IT MIGHT BE NICE IF SOMEONE DEVELOPED A **SENSE OF HUMOUR** AROUND HERE!

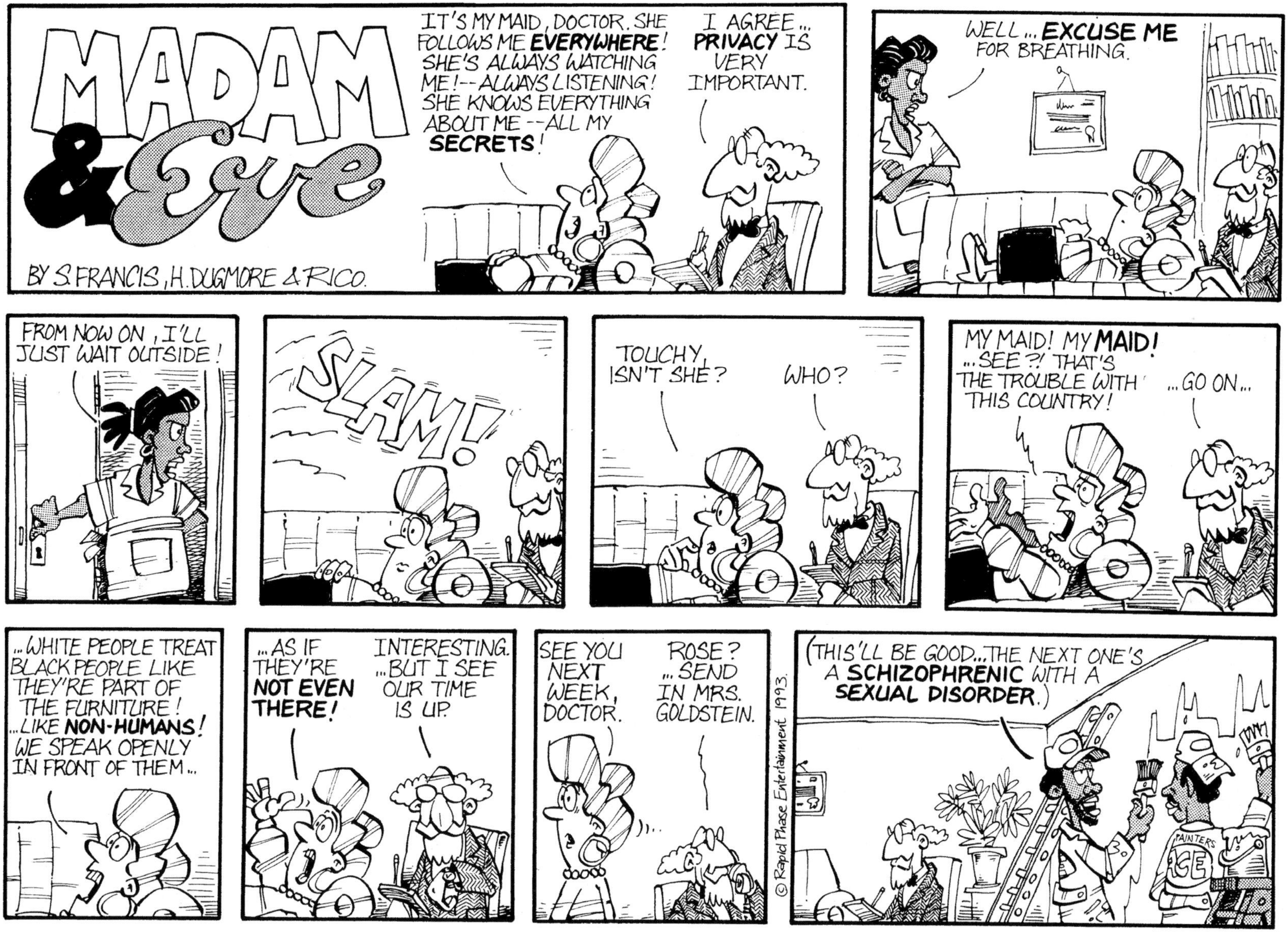
MADAM & Eve
BY S. FRANCIS, H. DUGMORE & RICO.
IT'S MY MAID, DOCTOR. SHE FOLLOWS ME EVERYWHERE! SHE'S ALWAYS WATCHING ME!--ALWAYS LISTENING! SHE KNOWS EVERYTHING ABOUT ME --ALL MY SECRETS!
I AGREE... PRIVACY IS VERY IMPORTANT.
WELL... EXCUSE ME FOR BREATHING.
FROM NOW ON, I'LL JUST WAIT OUTSIDE!
SLAM!
TOUCHY, ISN'T SHE?
WHO?
MY MAID! MY MAID! ...SEE?! THAT'S THE TROUBLE WITH THIS COUNTRY!
...GO ON...
...WHITE PEOPLE TREAT BLACK PEOPLE LIKE THEY'RE PART OF THE FURNITURE! ...LIKE NON-HUMANS! WE SPEAK OPENLY IN FRONT OF THEM...
...AS IF THEY'RE NOT EVEN THERE!
INTERESTING. ...BUT I SEE OUR TIME IS UP.
SEE YOU NEXT WEEK, DOCTOR.
ROSE? ...SEND IN MRS. GOLDSTEIN.
© Rapid Phase Entertainment 1993.
(THIS'LL BE GOOD... THE NEXT ONE'S A SCHIZOPHRENIC WITH A SEXUAL DISORDER.)
PAINTERS
ACE

EVE... THIS IS MY MOTHER FROM ENGLAND. SHE'LL BE VISITING US FOR A WHOLE WEEK. ISN'T THAT NICE?
There's a black person in the room.
I know, Mom. She's my maid.
© Rapid Phase Entertainment · 1993
JUST ONE WEEK. I CAN DO THIS. JUST ONE WEEK...

MOTHER, EVE -- I WANT YOU TWO TO GET TO KNOW EACH OTHER. YOU PROBABLY HAVE A LOT IN COMMON.
© Rapid Phase Entertainment · 1993

AND NOW, FOR THE FIRST TIME ANYWHERE, WHITE SOUTH AFRICANS WILL ACTUALLY SEE THE INSIDE OF A REAL MAID'S LIVING QUARTERS.
EVE... IS IT ALMOST... YES! THE DOOR IS OPEN! WE'RE GOING INSIDE!
EVE -- WHAT ARE THESE HUGE PILES ON THE FLOOR?
COFFEE AND SUGAR, GILLIAN. I'VE BEEN STEALING A LITTLE EACH WEEK SINCE 1975.
© Rapid Phase Entertainment · 1993 1-61
I KNEW IT! I KNEW IT!

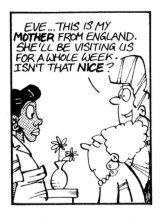

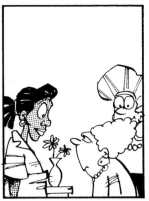

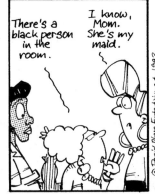

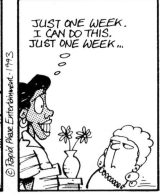

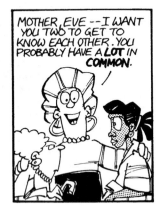

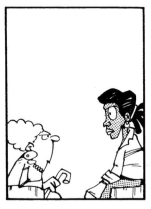

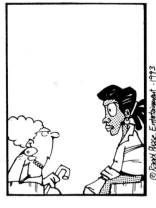

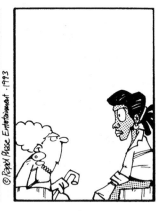

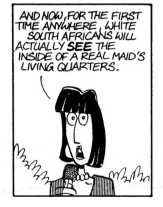

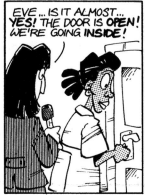

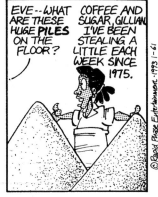

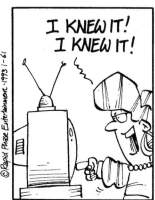

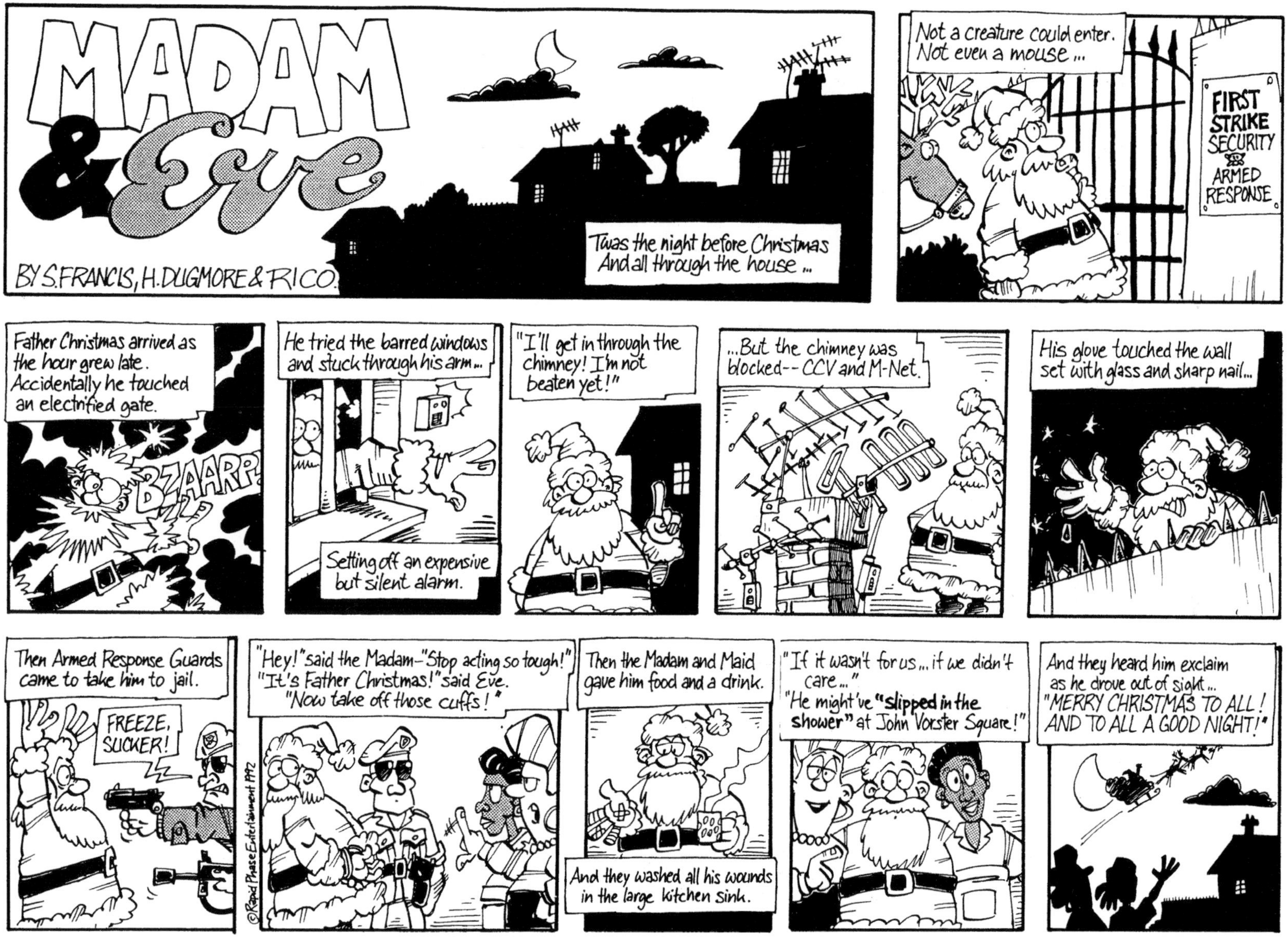
MADAM & Eve
BY S.FRANCIS, H.DUGMORE & RICO.
Twas the night before Christmas
And all through the house...
Not a creature could enter.
Not even a mouse...
FIRST STRIKE SECURITY
ARMED RESPONSE
Father Christmas arrived as the hour grew late. Accidentally he touched an electrified gate.
BZAARP!
He tried the barred windows and stuck through his arm...
Setting off an expensive but silent alarm.
"I'll get in through the chimney! I'm not beaten yet!"
...But the chimney was blocked-- CCV and M-Net.
His glove touched the wall set with glass and sharp nail...
Then Armed Response Guards came to take him to jail.
FREEZE, SUCKER!
©Rapid Phase Entertainment 1992
"Hey!" said the Madam- "Stop acting so tough!"
"It's Father Christmas!" said Eve.
"Now take off those cuffs!"
Then the Madam and Maid gave him food and a drink.
And they washed all his wounds in the large kitchen sink.
"If it wasn't for us... if we didn't care..."
"He might've "slipped in the shower" at John Vorster Square!"
And they heard him exclaim as he drove out of sight...
"MERRY CHRISTMAS TO ALL! AND TO ALL A GOOD NIGHT!"

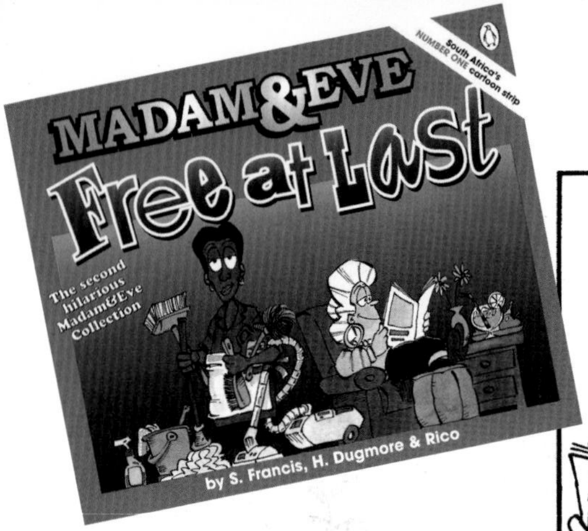

MADAM&EVE
Free at Last
South Africa's NUMBER ONE cartoon strip
The second hilarious Madam&Eve Collection
by S. Francis, H. Dugmore & Rico

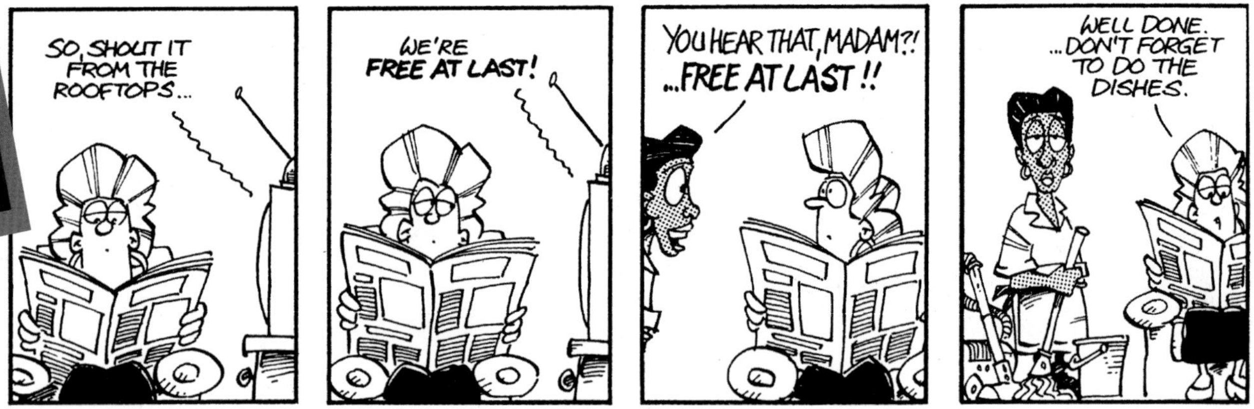

SO, SHOUT IT FROM THE ROOFTOPS...
WE'RE FREE AT LAST!
YOU HEAR THAT, MADAM?! ...FREE AT LAST!!
WELL DONE. ...DON'T FORGET TO DO THE DISHES.

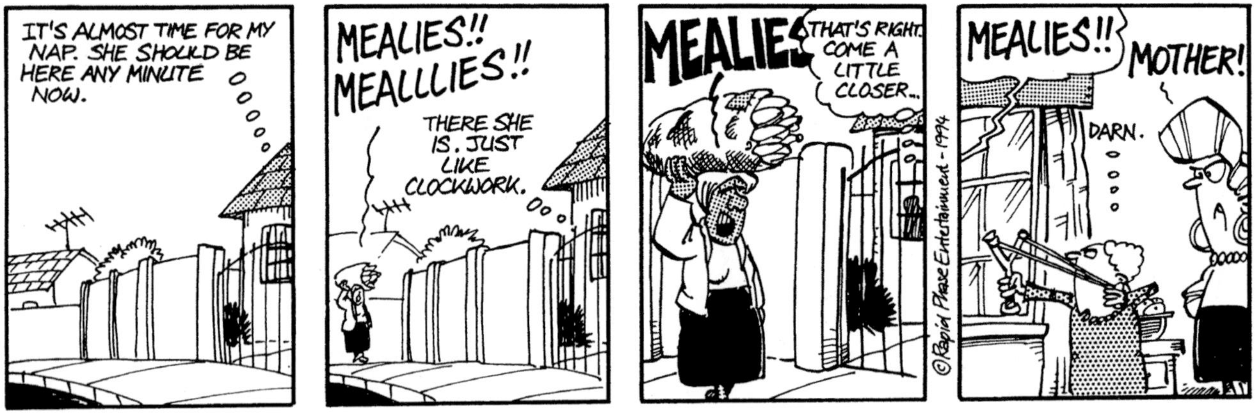

IT'S ALMOST TIME FOR MY NAP. SHE SHOULD BE HERE ANY MINUTE NOW.
MEALIES!! MEALLLIES!!
THERE SHE IS. JUST LIKE CLOCKWORK.
MEALIES
THAT'S RIGHT. COME A LITTLE CLOSER...
© Rapid Phase Entertainment - 1994
MEALIES!!
MOTHER!
DARN.

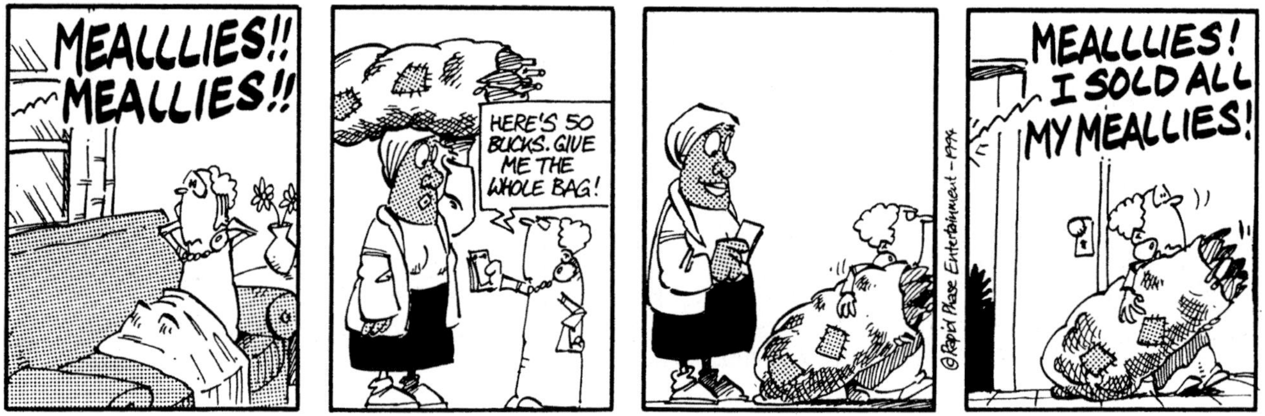

MEALLLIES!! MEALLIES!!
HERE'S 50 BUCKS. GIVE ME THE WHOLE BAG!
© Rapid Phase Entertainment - 1994
MEALLLIES! I SOLD ALL MY MEALLIES!

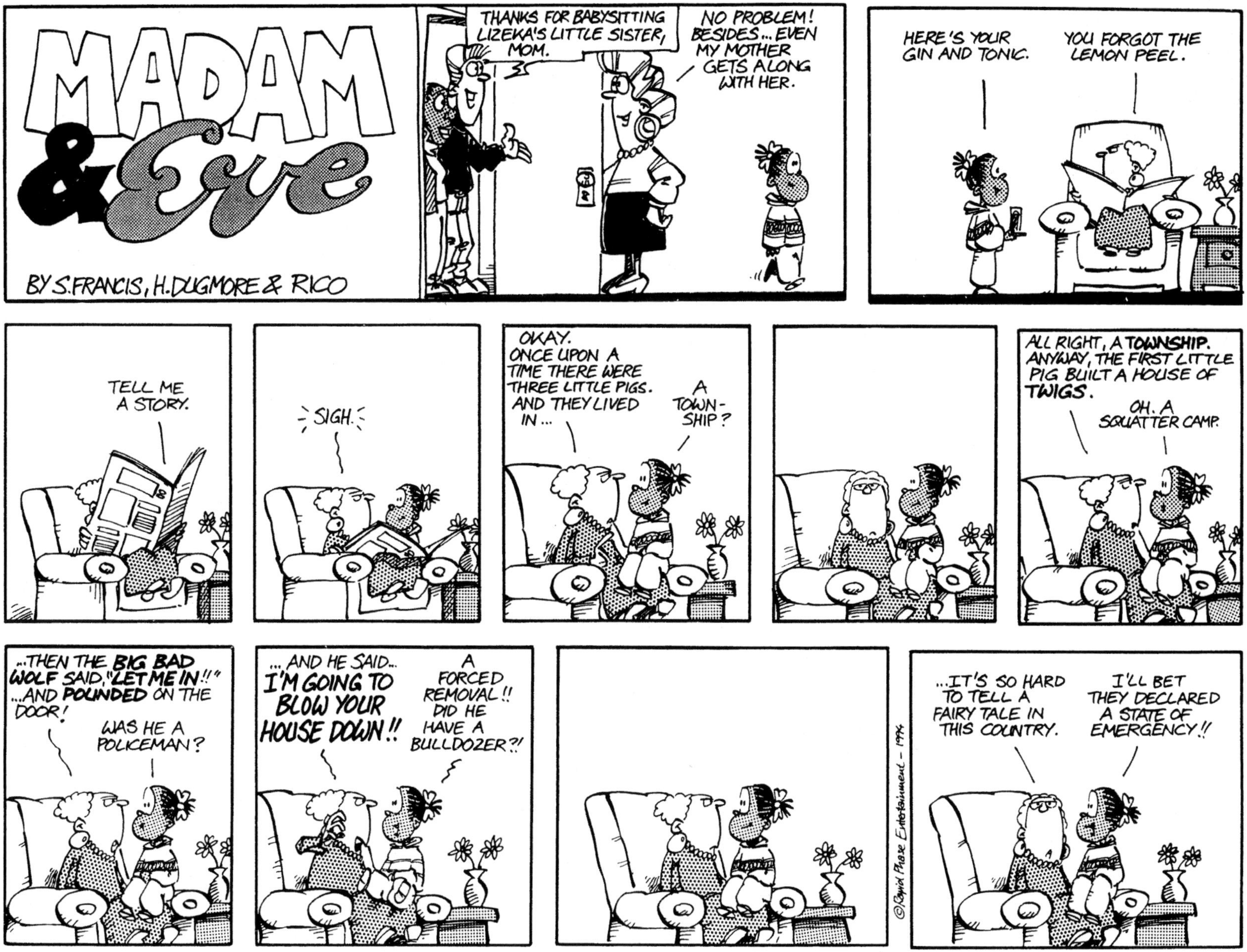
MADAM & Eve
BY S.FRANCIS, H.DUGMORE & RICO
THANKS FOR BABYSITTING LIZEKA'S LITTLE SISTER, MOM.
NO PROBLEM! BESIDES... EVEN MY MOTHER GETS ALONG WITH HER.
HERE'S YOUR GIN AND TONIC.
YOU FORGOT THE LEMON PEEL.
TELL ME A STORY.
SIGH.
OKAY. ONCE UPON A TIME THERE WERE THREE LITTLE PIGS. AND THEY LIVED IN...
A TOWN-SHIP?
ALL RIGHT, A TOWNSHIP. ANYWAY, THE FIRST LITTLE PIG BUILT A HOUSE OF TWIGS.
OH. A SQUATTER CAMP.
...THEN THE BIG BAD WOLF SAID, "LET ME IN!!" ...AND POUNDED ON THE DOOR!
WAS HE A POLICEMAN?
...AND HE SAID... I'M GOING TO BLOW YOUR HOUSE DOWN!!
A FORCED REMOVAL!! DID HE HAVE A BULLDOZER?!
...IT'S SO HARD TO TELL A FAIRY TALE IN THIS COUNTRY.
I'LL BET THEY DECLARED A STATE OF EMERGENCY!!
©Rapid Phase Entertainment - 1994

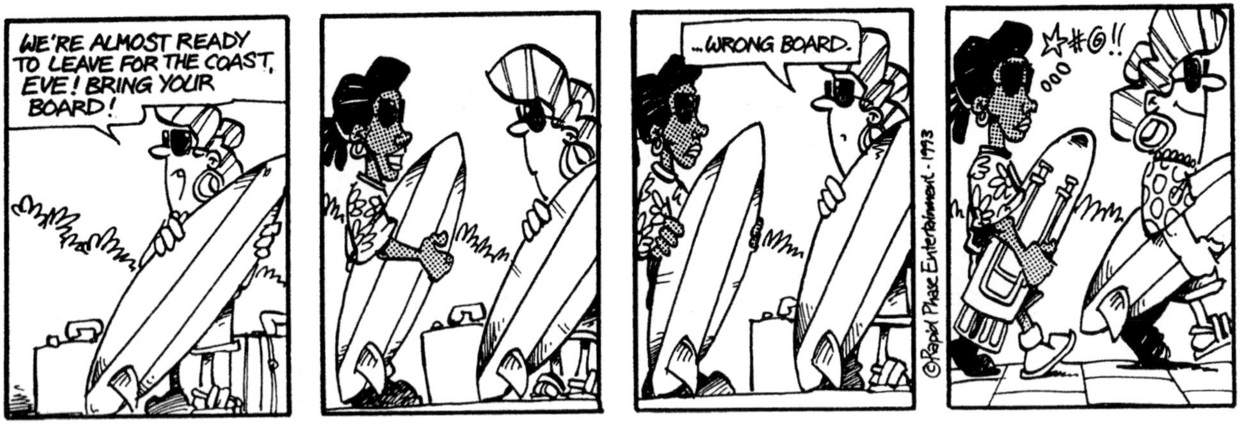
WE'RE ALMOST READY TO LEAVE FOR THE COAST, EVE! BRING YOUR BOARD!
...WRONG BOARD.
©Rapid Phase Entertainment · 1993

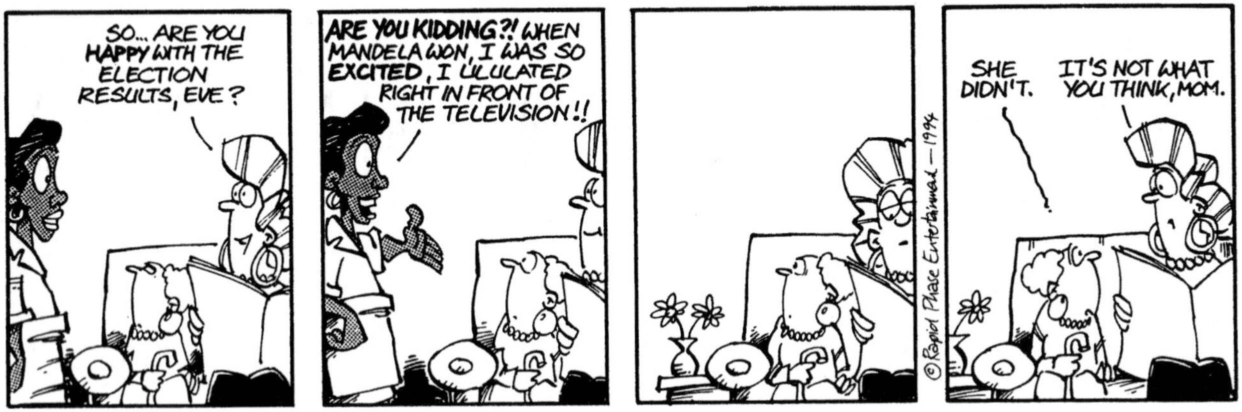
SO... ARE YOU HAPPY WITH THE ELECTION RESULTS, EVE?
ARE YOU KIDDING?! WHEN MANDELA WON, I WAS SO EXCITED, I ULULATED RIGHT IN FRONT OF THE TELEVISION!!
©Rapid Phase Entertainment — 1994
SHE DIDN'T.
IT'S NOT WHAT YOU THINK, MOM.

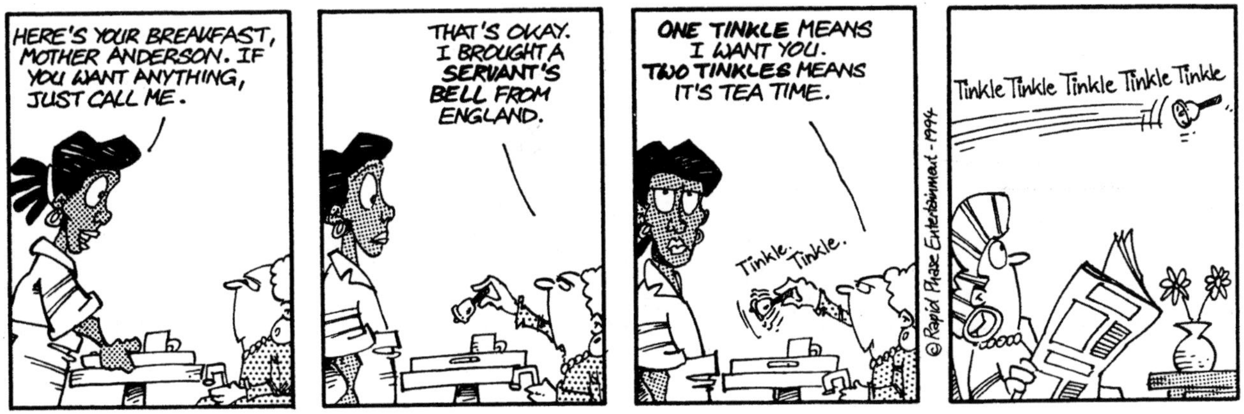
HERE'S YOUR BREAKFAST, MOTHER ANDERSON. IF YOU WANT ANYTHING, JUST CALL ME.
THAT'S OKAY. I BROUGHT A SERVANT'S BELL FROM ENGLAND.
ONE TINKLE MEANS I WANT YOU. TWO TINKLES MEANS IT'S TEA TIME.
Tinkle. Tinkle.
©Rapid Phase Entertainment · 1994
Tinkle Tinkle Tinkle Tinkle Tinkle

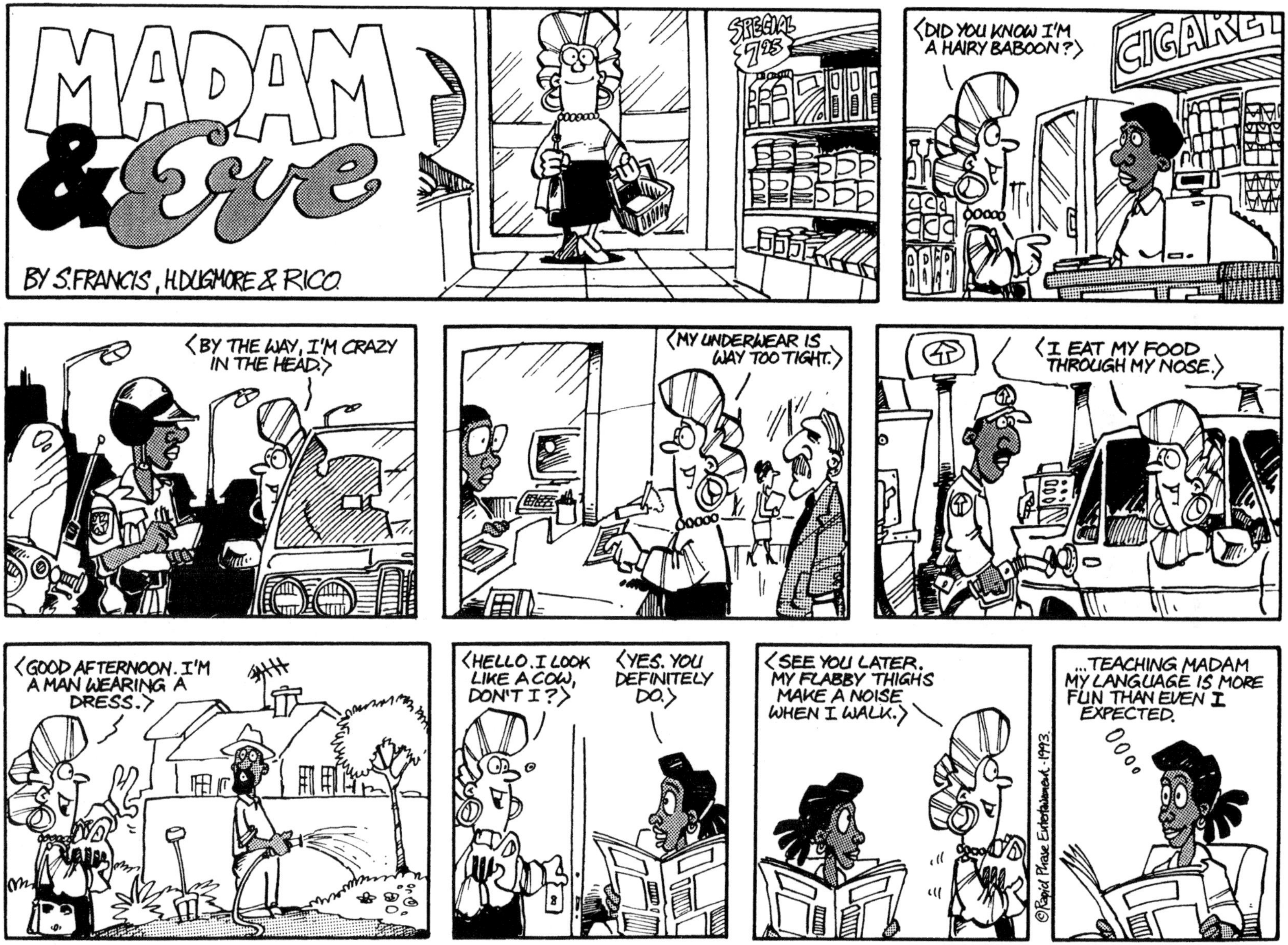
MADAM & Eve
BY S.FRANCIS, H.DUGMORE & RICO.
SPECIAL 7.95
‹DID YOU KNOW I'M A HAIRY BABOON?›
CIGARE
‹BY THE WAY, I'M CRAZY IN THE HEAD.›
‹MY UNDERWEAR IS WAY TOO TIGHT.›
‹I EAT MY FOOD THROUGH MY NOSE.›
‹GOOD AFTERNOON. I'M A MAN WEARING A DRESS.›
‹HELLO. I LOOK LIKE A COW, DON'T I?›
‹YES. YOU DEFINITELY DO.›
‹SEE YOU LATER. MY FLABBY THIGHS MAKE A NOISE WHEN I WALK.›
©Rapid Phase Entertainment · 1993.
...TEACHING MADAM MY LANGUAGE IS MORE FUN THAN EVEN I EXPECTED.

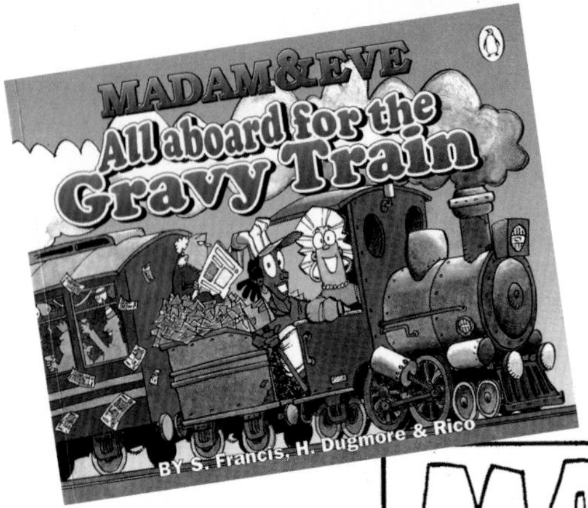
MADAM&EVE
All aboard for the Gravy Train
BY S. Francis, H. Dugmore & Rico

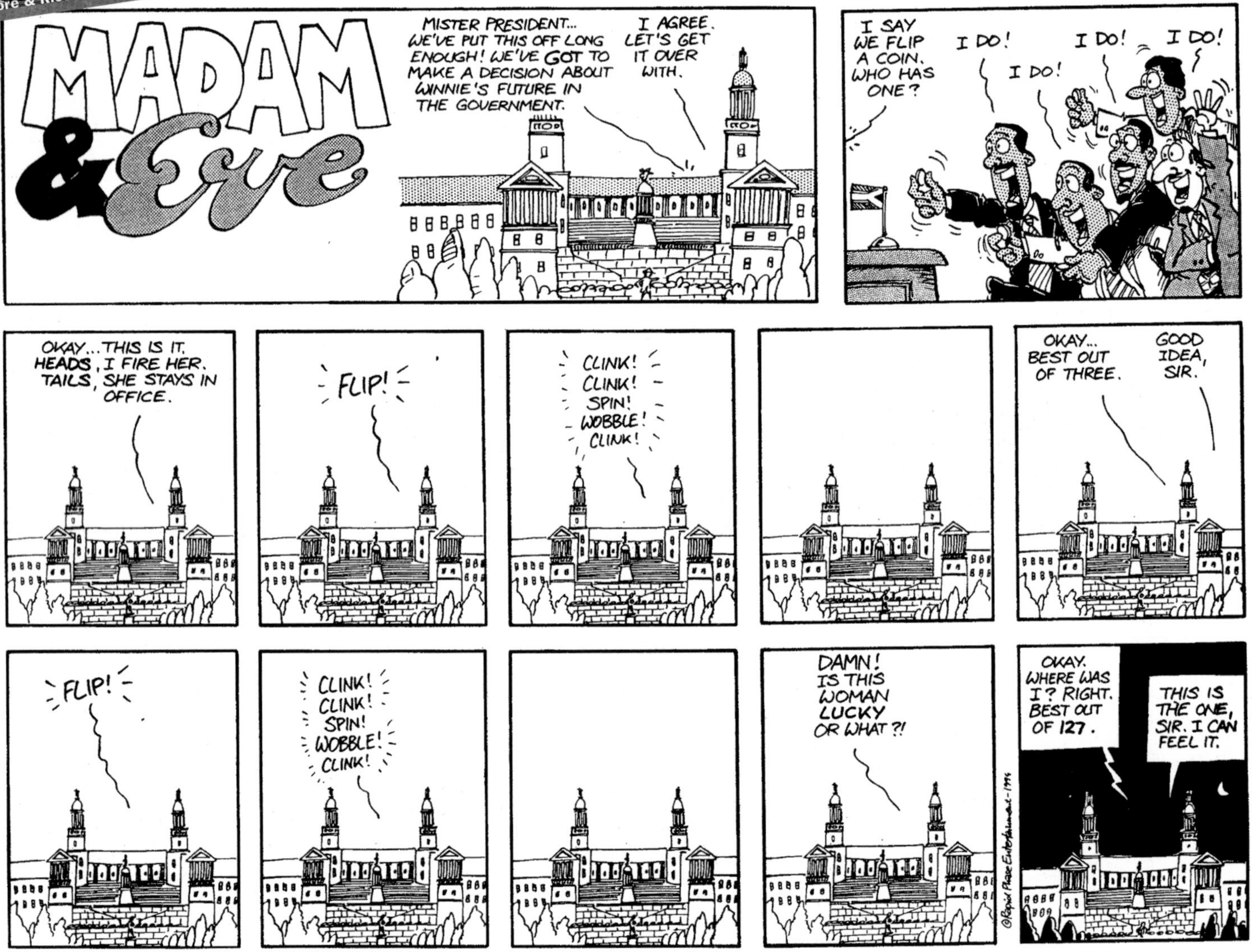
MADAM & Eve
MISTER PRESIDENT... WE'VE PUT THIS OFF LONG ENOUGH! WE'VE GOT TO MAKE A DECISION ABOUT WINNIE'S FUTURE IN THE GOVERNMENT.
I AGREE. LET'S GET IT OVER WITH.
I SAY WE FLIP A COIN. WHO HAS ONE?
I DO!
I DO!
I DO!
I DO!
OKAY... THIS IS IT. HEADS, I FIRE HER. TAILS, SHE STAYS IN OFFICE.
FLIP!
CLINK! CLINK! SPIN! WOBBLE! CLINK!
OKAY... BEST OUT OF THREE.
GOOD IDEA, SIR.
FLIP!
CLINK! CLINK! SPIN! WOBBLE! CLINK!
DAMN! IS THIS WOMAN LUCKY OR WHAT?!
OKAY. WHERE WAS I? RIGHT. BEST OUT OF 127.
THIS IS THE ONE, SIR. I CAN FEEL IT.

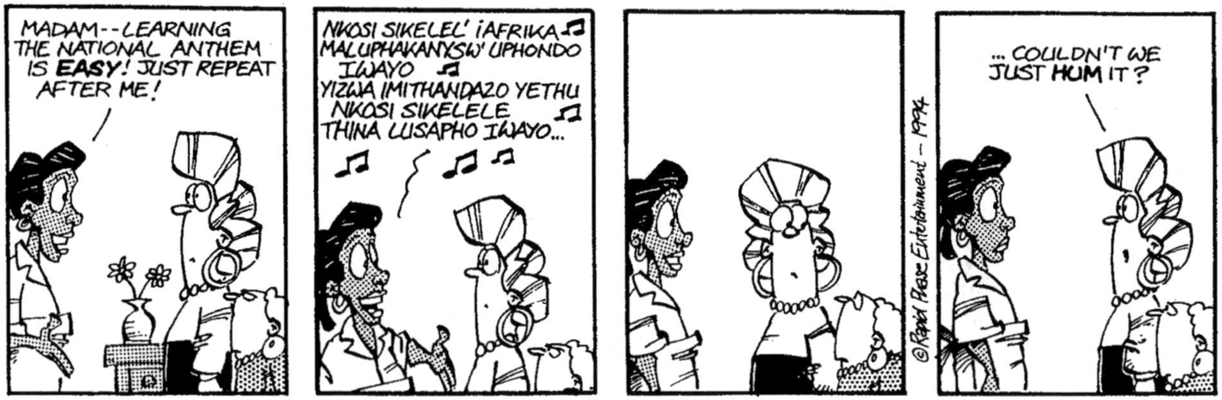
MADAM--LEARNING THE NATIONAL ANTHEM IS EASY! JUST REPEAT AFTER ME!
NKOSI SIKELEL' iAFRIKA
MALUPHAKANYSW' UPHONDO IWAYO
YIZWA IMITHANDAZO YETHU
NKOSI SIKELELE
THINA LUSAPHO IWAYO...
... COULDN'T WE JUST HUM IT?
© Rapid Phase Entertainment – 1994

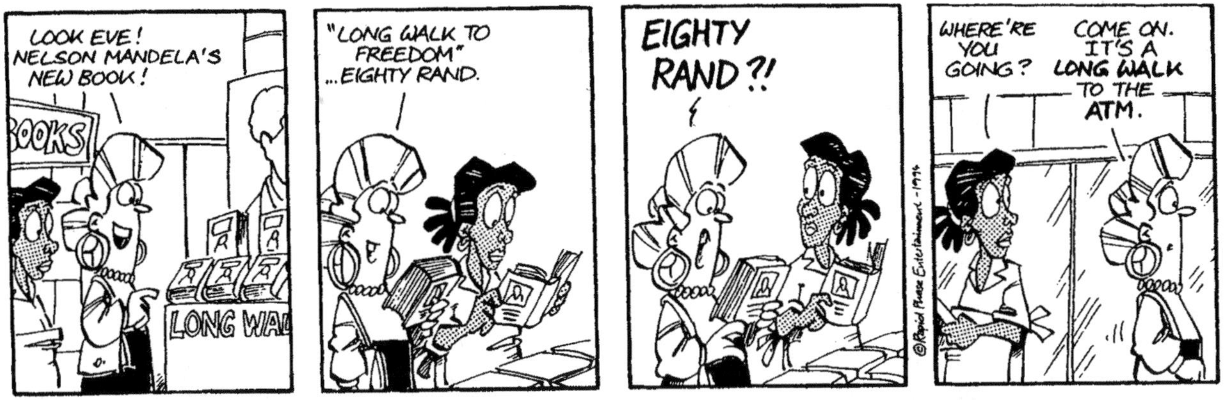
LOOK EVE! NELSON MANDELA'S NEW BOOK!
BOOKS
LONG WAL
"LONG WALK TO FREEDOM" ... EIGHTY RAND.
EIGHTY RAND?!
WHERE'RE YOU GOING?
COME ON. IT'S A LONG WALK TO THE ATM.
© Rapid Phase Entertainment - 1996

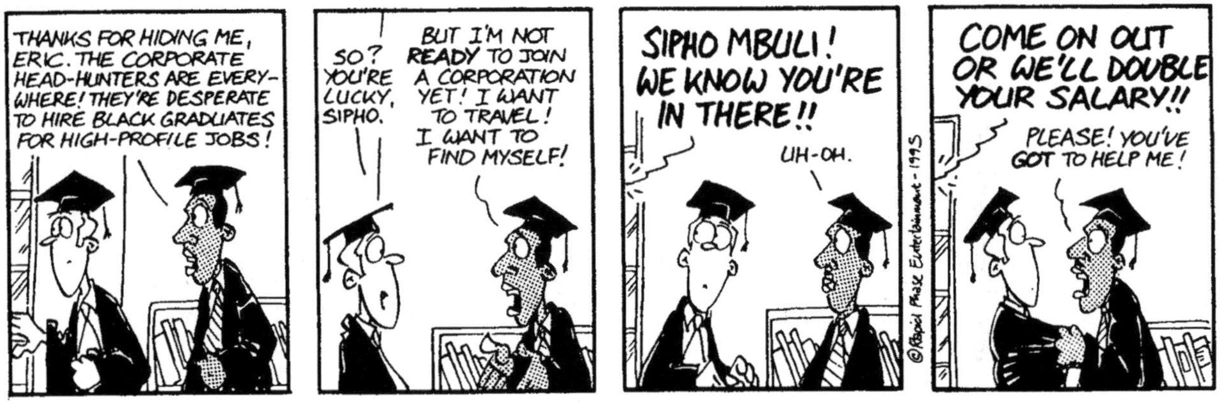
THANKS FOR HIDING ME, ERIC. THE CORPORATE HEAD-HUNTERS ARE EVERYWHERE! THEY'RE DESPERATE TO HIRE BLACK GRADUATES FOR HIGH-PROFILE JOBS!
SO? YOU'RE LUCKY, SIPHO.
BUT I'M NOT READY TO JOIN A CORPORATION YET! I WANT TO TRAVEL! I WANT TO FIND MYSELF!
SIPHO MBULI! WE KNOW YOU'RE IN THERE!!
UH-OH.
COME ON OUT OR WE'LL DOUBLE YOUR SALARY!!
PLEASE! YOU'VE GOT TO HELP ME!
© Rapid Phase Entertainment - 1995

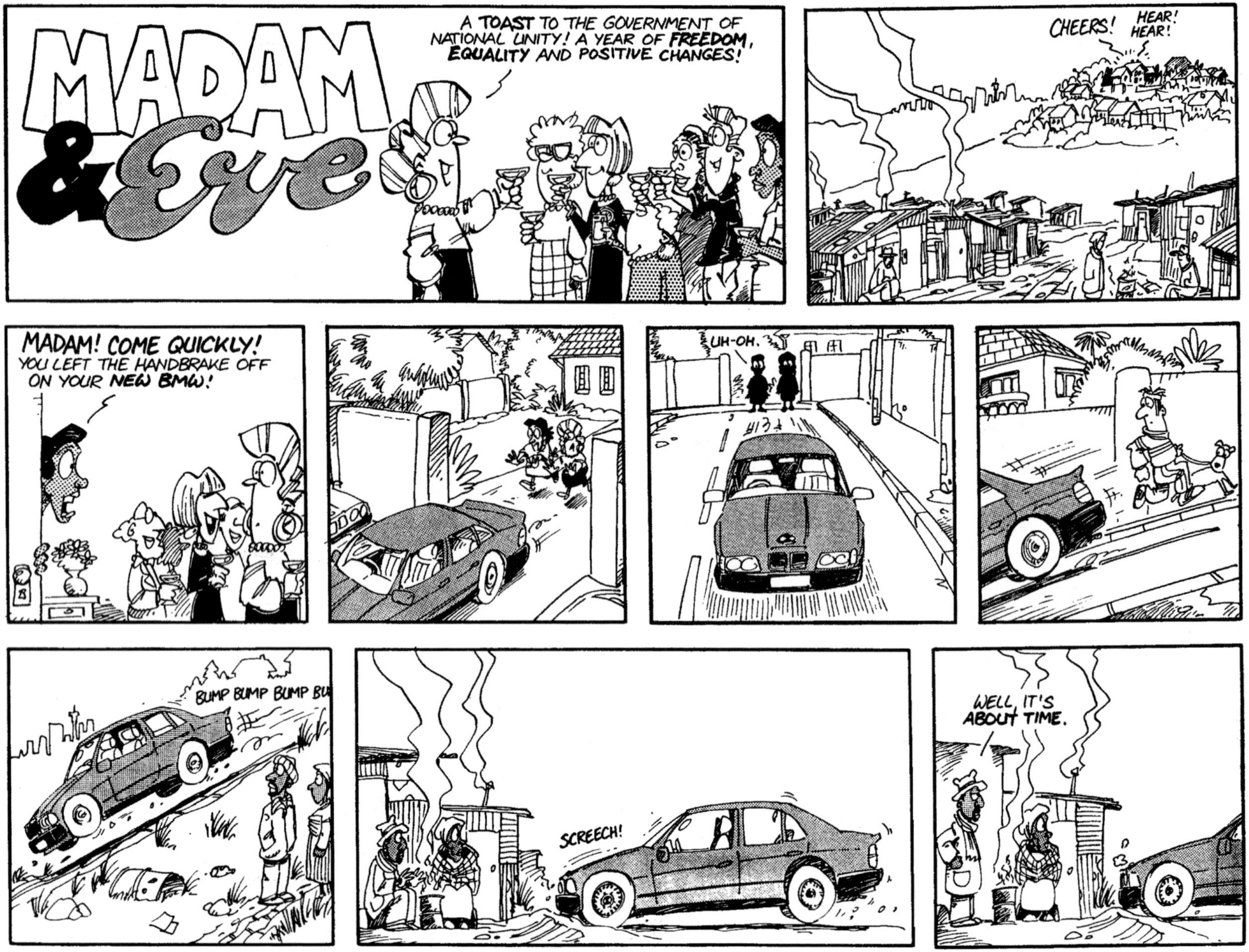
MADAM & Eve
A TOAST TO THE GOVERNMENT OF NATIONAL UNITY! A YEAR OF FREEDOM, EQUALITY AND POSITIVE CHANGES!
CHEERS!
HEAR! HEAR!
MADAM! COME QUICKLY! YOU LEFT THE HANDBRAKE OFF ON YOUR NEW BMW!
UH-OH.
BUMP BUMP BUMP BU
SCREECH!
WELL, IT'S ABOUT TIME.

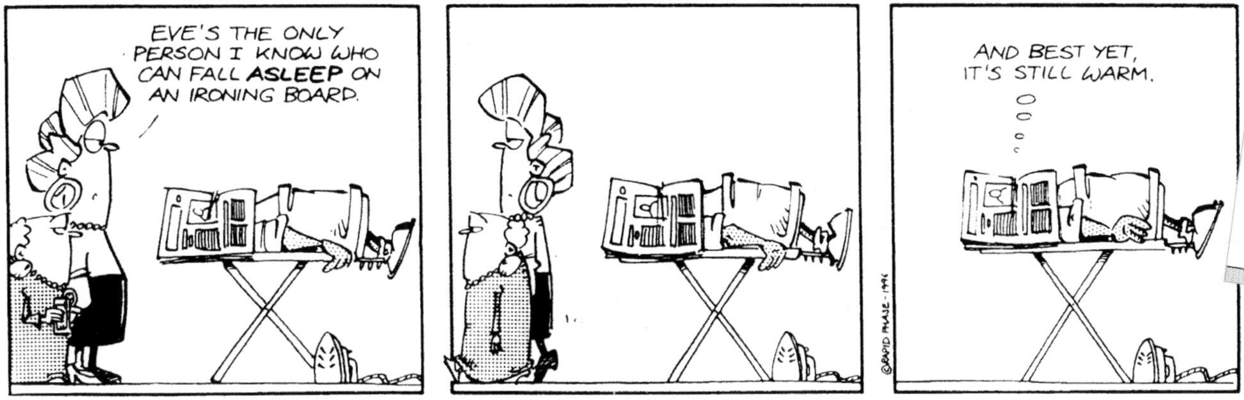
EVE'S THE ONLY PERSON I KNOW WHO CAN FALL **ASLEEP** ON AN IRONING BOARD.
AND BEST YET, IT'S STILL WARM.

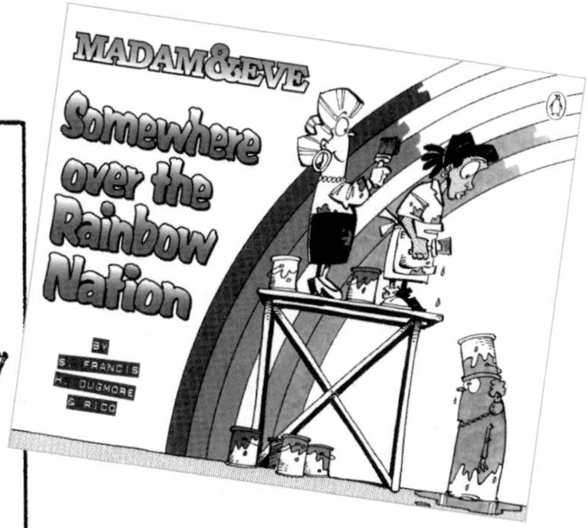
MADAM&EVE
Somewhere over the Rainbow Nation
BY
S. FRANCIS
H. DUGMORE
& RICO

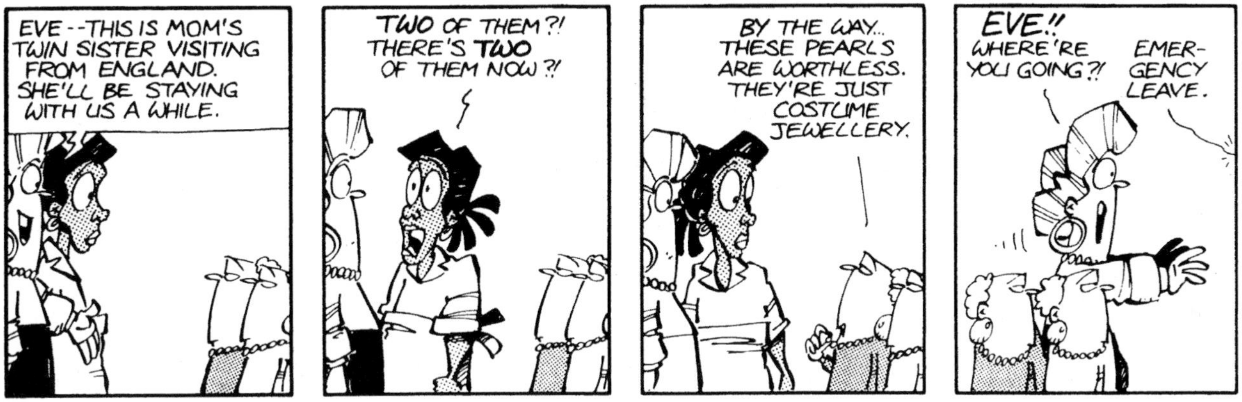
EVE--THIS IS MOM'S TWIN SISTER VISITING FROM ENGLAND. SHE'LL BE STAYING WITH US A WHILE.
TWO OF THEM?! THERE'S **TWO** OF THEM NOW?!
BY THE WAY... THESE PEARLS ARE WORTHLESS. THEY'RE JUST COSTUME JEWELLERY.
EVE!! WHERE'RE YOU GOING?!
EMER-GENCY LEAVE.

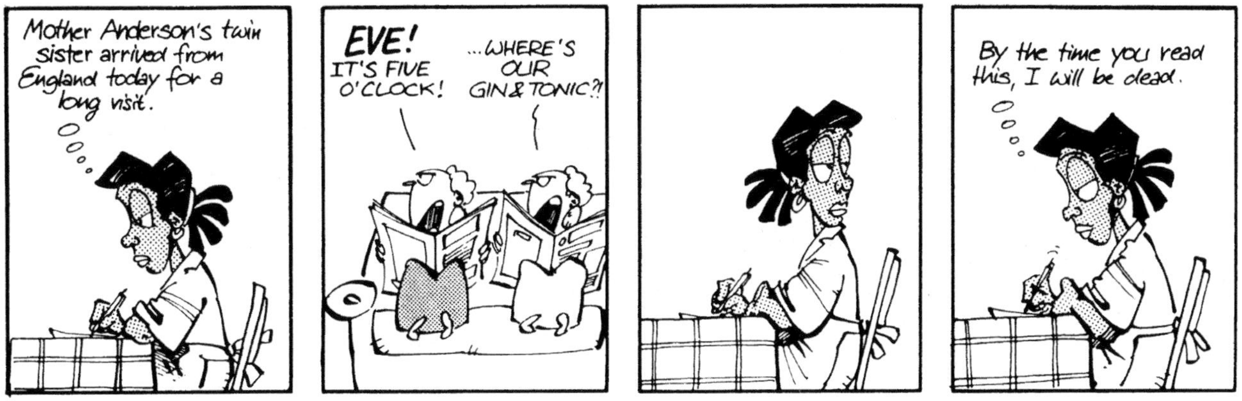
Mother Anderson's twin sister arrived from England today for a long visit.
EVE! IT'S FIVE O'CLOCK!
...WHERE'S OUR GIN & TONIC?!
By the time you read this, I will be dead.

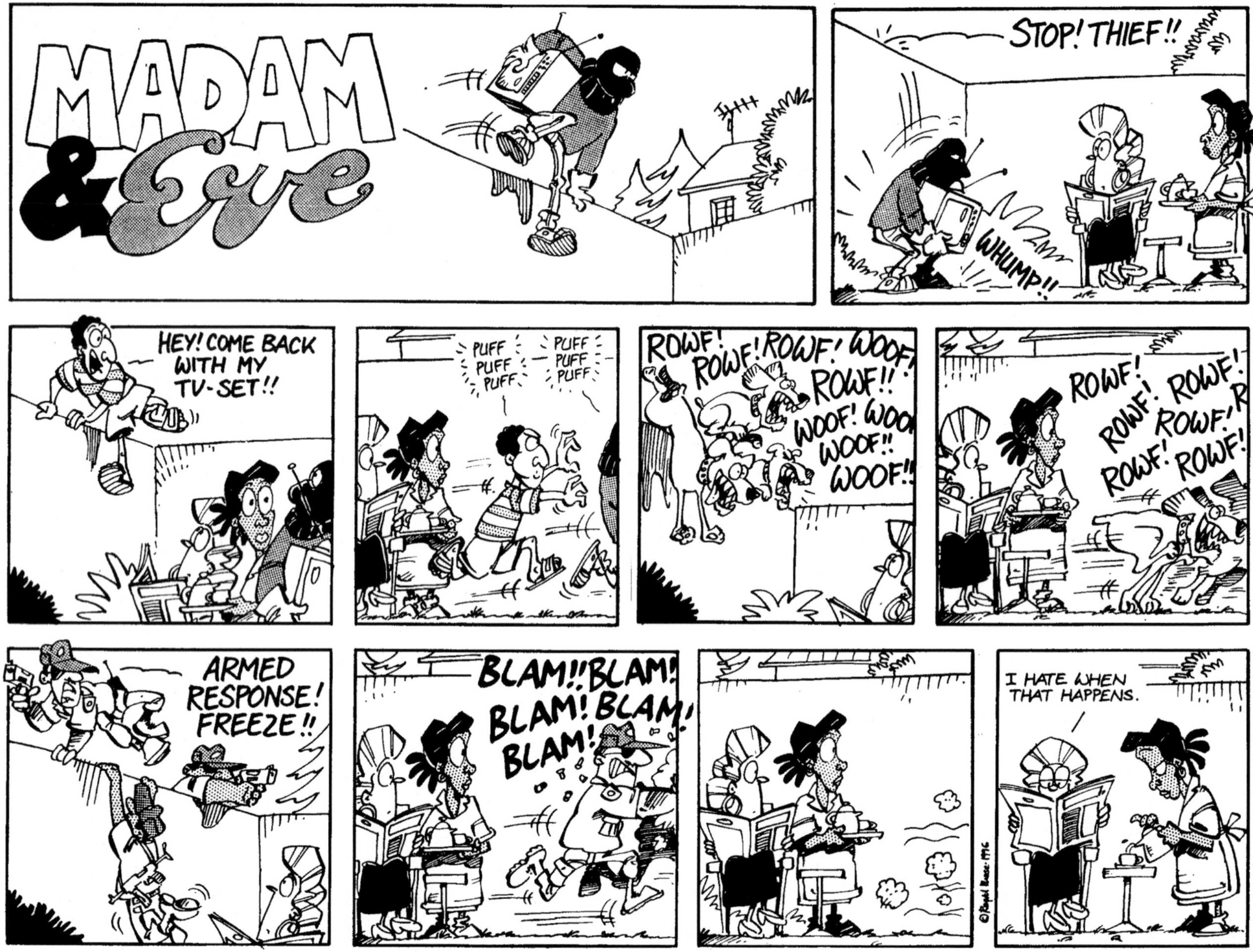

MADAM
&Eve
STOP! THIEF!!
WHUMP!!
HEY! COME BACK WITH MY TV-SET!!
PUFF PUFF PUFF
PUFF PUFF PUFF
ROWF! ROWF! ROWF!
ROWF!!
WOOF!
WOOF!!
WOOF!!
ROWF! ROWF! ROWF! ROWF! ROWF! ROWF!
ARMED RESPONSE! FREEZE!!
BLAM!! BLAM! BLAM! BLAM! BLAM!
I HATE WHEN THAT HAPPENS.

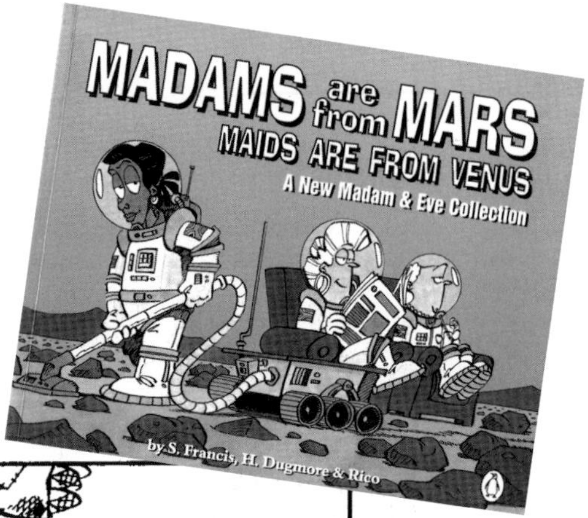
MADAMS are from MARS
MAIDS ARE FROM VENUS
A New Madam & Eve Collection
by S. Francis, H. Dugmore & Rico

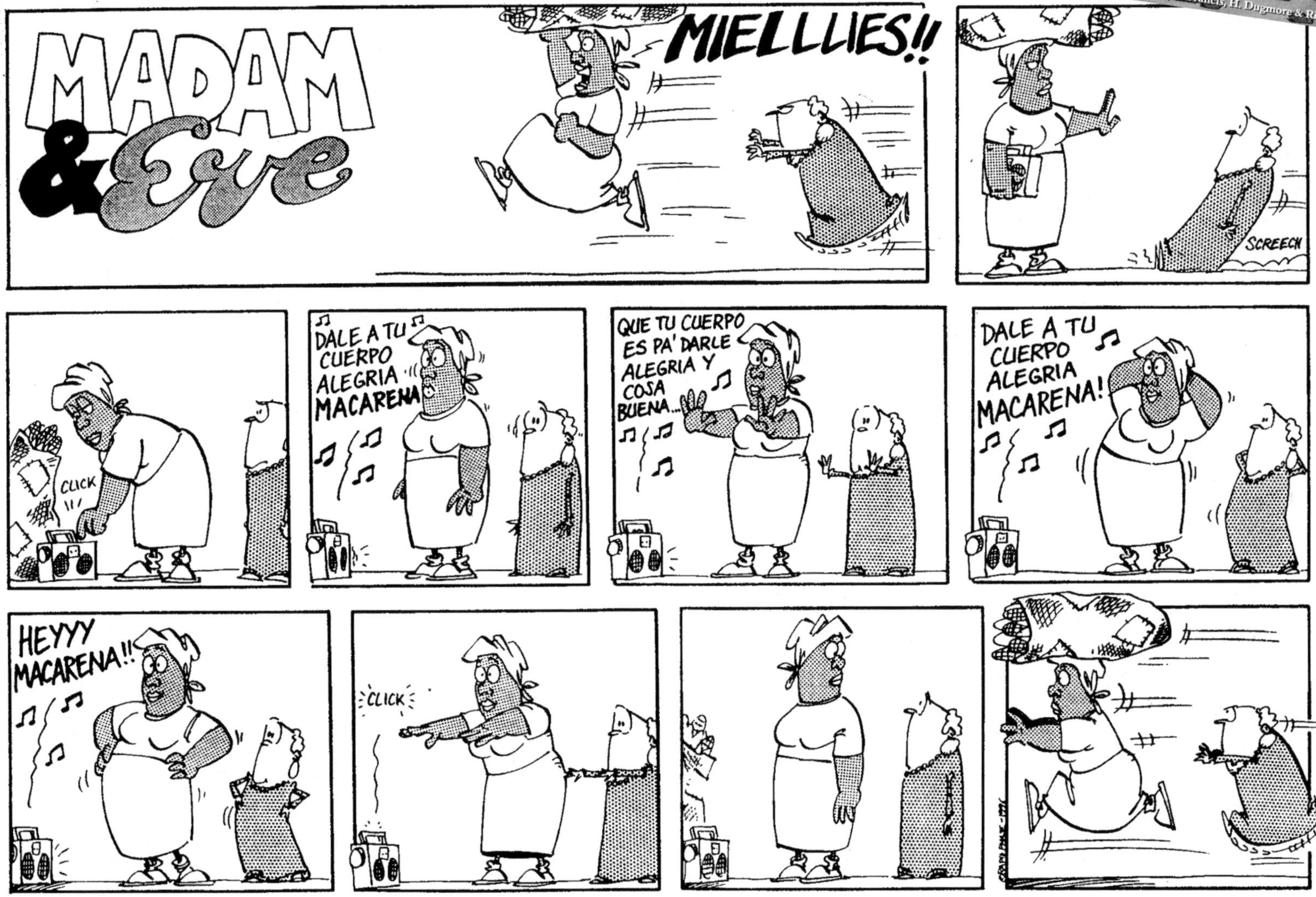
MADAM & Eve
MIELLLIES!!
SCREECH
CLICK
DALE A TU CUERPO ALEGRIA MACARENA
QUE TU CUERPO ES PA' DARLE ALEGRIA Y COSA BUENA...
DALE A TU CUERPO ALEGRIA MACARENA!
HEYYY MACARENA!!
CLICK

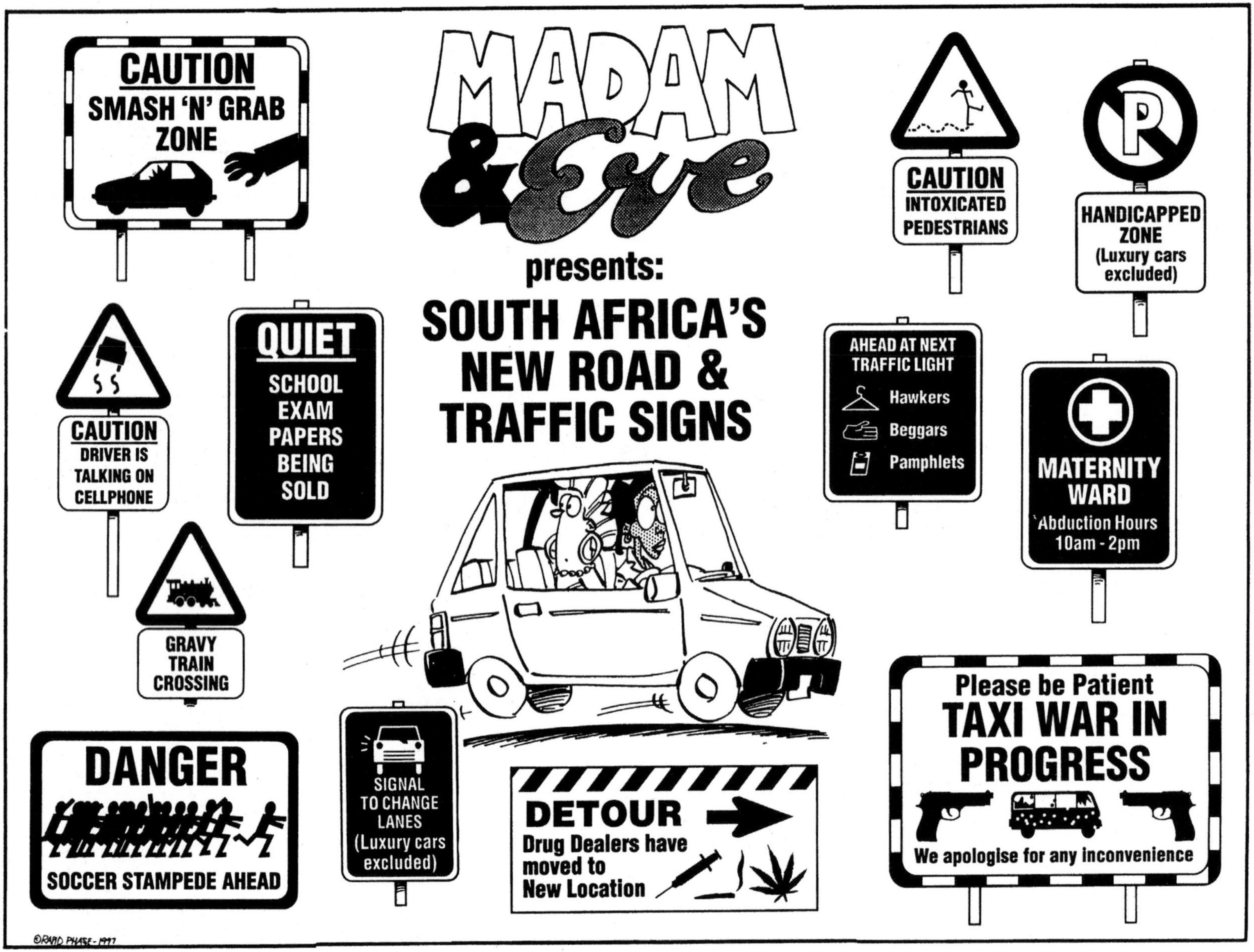
CAUTION
SMASH 'N' GRAB ZONE
MADAM & Eve
presents:
SOUTH AFRICA'S NEW ROAD & TRAFFIC SIGNS
CAUTION
INTOXICATED PEDESTRIANS
HANDICAPPED ZONE
(Luxury cars excluded)
CAUTION
DRIVER IS TALKING ON CELLPHONE
QUIET
SCHOOL EXAM PAPERS BEING SOLD
AHEAD AT NEXT TRAFFIC LIGHT
Hawkers
Beggars
Pamphlets
MATERNITY WARD
Abduction Hours
10am - 2pm
GRAVY TRAIN CROSSING
DANGER
SOCCER STAMPEDE AHEAD
SIGNAL TO CHANGE LANES
(Luxury cars excluded)
DETOUR
Drug Dealers have moved to New Location
Please be Patient
TAXI WAR IN PROGRESS
We apologise for any inconvenience
©RAPID PHASE-1997

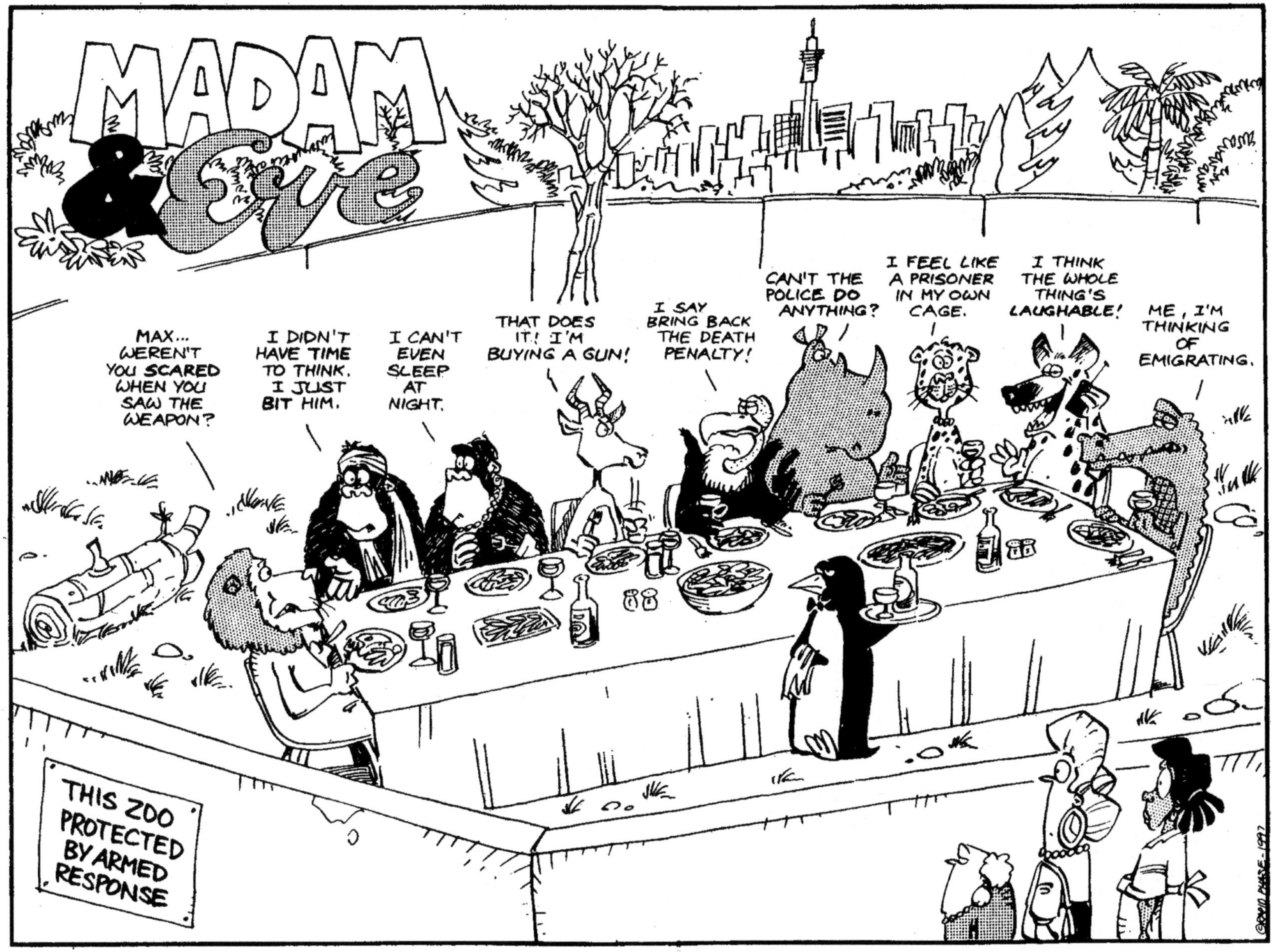
MADAM & Eve
MAX... WEREN'T YOU SCARED WHEN YOU SAW THE WEAPON?
I DIDN'T HAVE TIME TO THINK. I JUST BIT HIM.
I CAN'T EVEN SLEEP AT NIGHT.
THAT DOES IT! I'M BUYING A GUN!
I SAY BRING BACK THE DEATH PENALTY!
CAN'T THE POLICE DO ANYTHING?
I FEEL LIKE A PRISONER IN MY OWN CAGE.
I THINK THE WHOLE THING'S LAUGHABLE!
ME, I'M THINKING OF EMIGRATING.
THIS ZOO PROTECTED BY ARMED RESPONSE

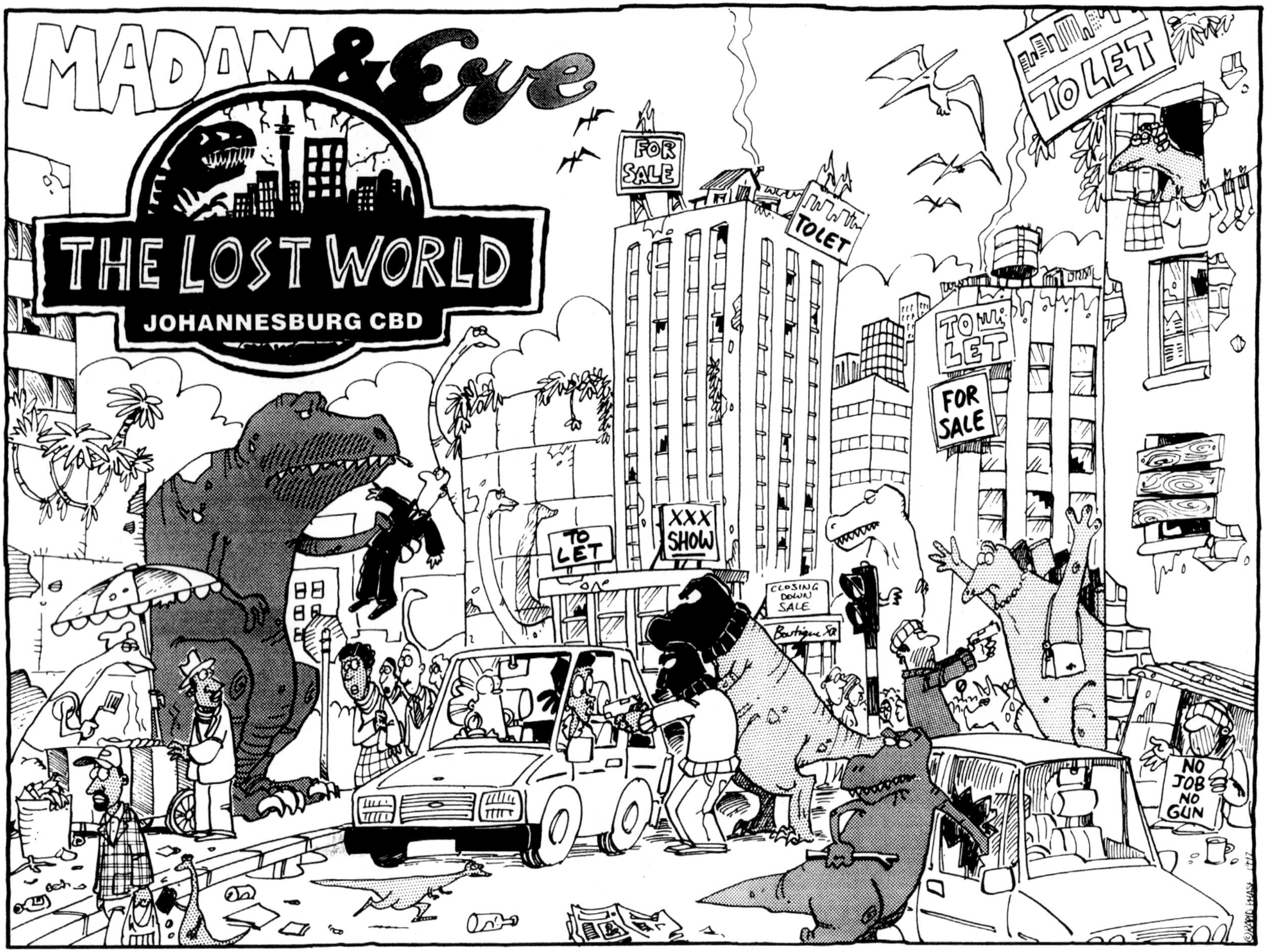
MADAM & Eve
THE LOST WORLD
JOHANNESBURG CBD
FOR SALE
TO LET
TO LET
FOR SALE
TO LET
XXX SHOW
TO LET
CLOSING DOWN SALE
NO JOB NO GUN

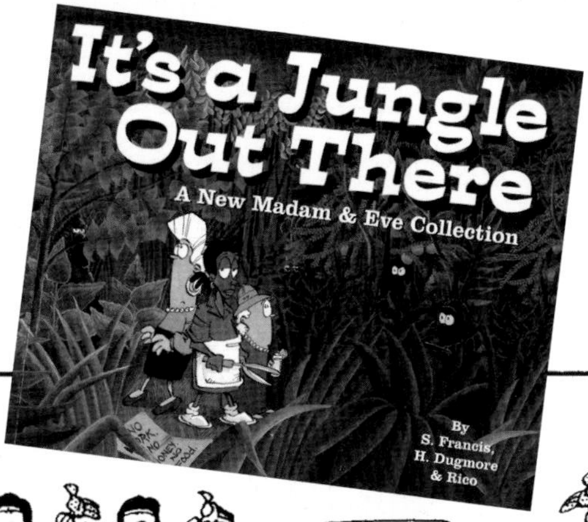
It's a Jungle Out There
A New Madam & Eve Collection
By
S. Francis,
H. Dugmore
& Rico

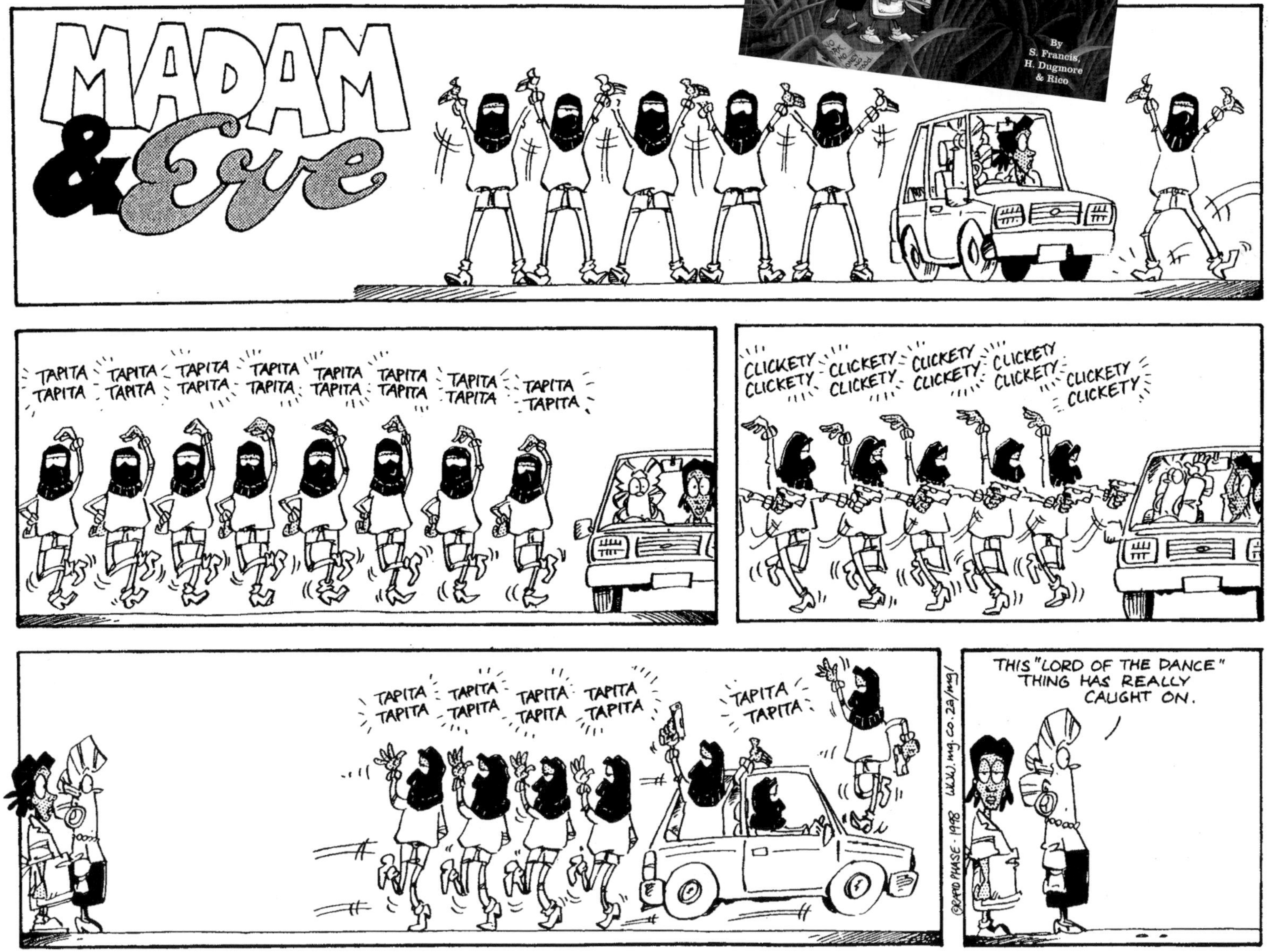
MADAM & Eve
TAPITA TAPITA
TAPITA TAPITA
TAPITA TAPITA
TAPITA TAPITA
TAPITA TAPITA
TAPITA TAPITA
TAPITA TAPITA
TAPITA TAPITA
CLICKETY CLICKETY
CLICKETY CLICKETY
CLICKETY CLICKETY
CLICKETY CLICKETY
CLICKETY CLICKETY
TAPITA TAPITA
TAPITA TAPITA
TAPITA TAPITA
TAPITA TAPITA
TAPITA TAPITA
©RAPID PHASE · 1998 www.mg.co.za/mg/
THIS "LORD OF THE DANCE" THING HAS REALLY CAUGHT ON.

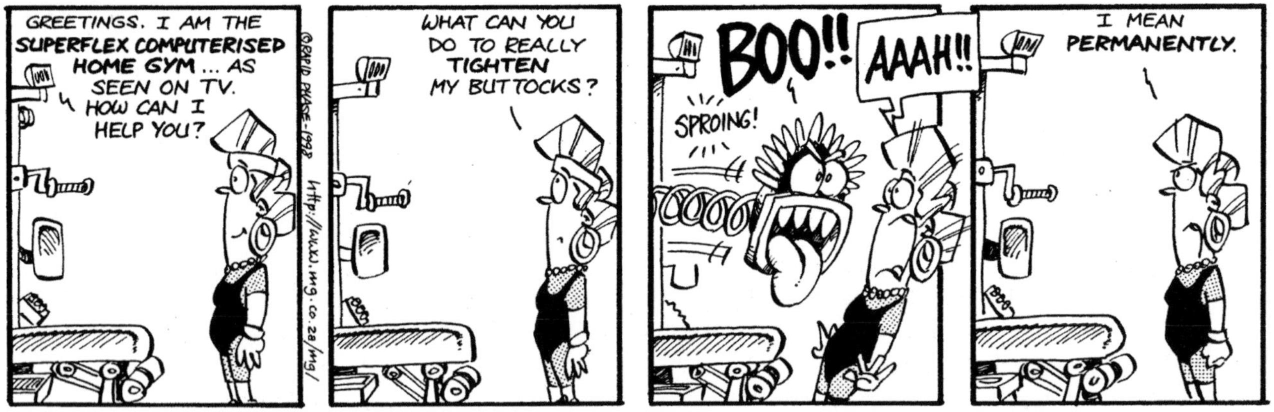
GREETINGS. I AM THE SUPERFLEX COMPUTERISED HOME GYM ... AS SEEN ON TV. HOW CAN I HELP YOU?
©RAPID PHASE-1998
http://www.mg.co.za/mg/
WHAT CAN YOU DO TO REALLY TIGHTEN MY BUTTOCKS?
BOO!!
SPROING!
AAAH!!
I MEAN PERMANENTLY.

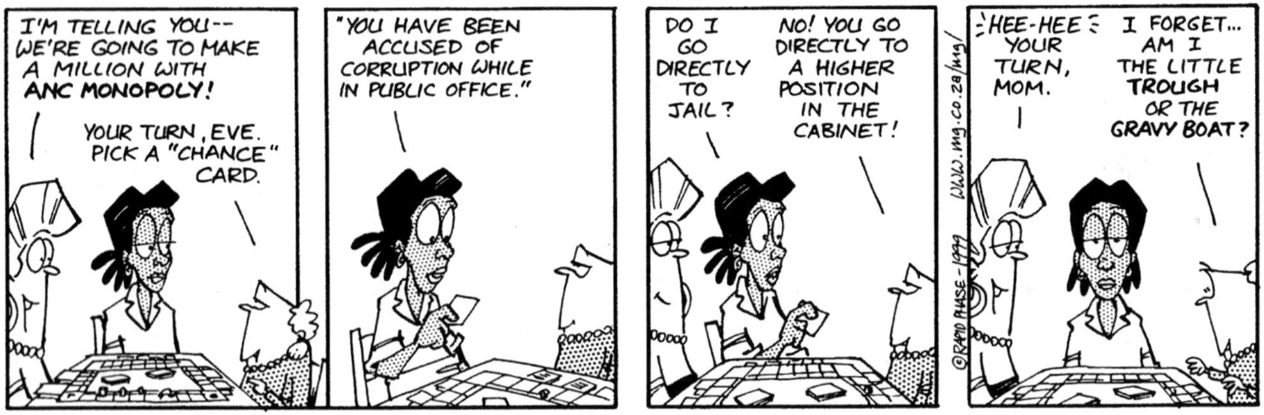
I'M TELLING YOU-- WE'RE GOING TO MAKE A MILLION WITH ANC MONOPOLY!
YOUR TURN, EVE. PICK A "CHANCE" CARD.
"YOU HAVE BEEN ACCUSED OF CORRUPTION WHILE IN PUBLIC OFFICE."
DO I GO DIRECTLY TO JAIL?
NO! YOU GO DIRECTLY TO A HIGHER POSITION IN THE CABINET!
www.mg.co.za/mg/
©RAPID PHASE-1999
HEE-HEE YOUR TURN, MOM.
I FORGET... AM I THE LITTLE TROUGH OR THE GRAVY BOAT?

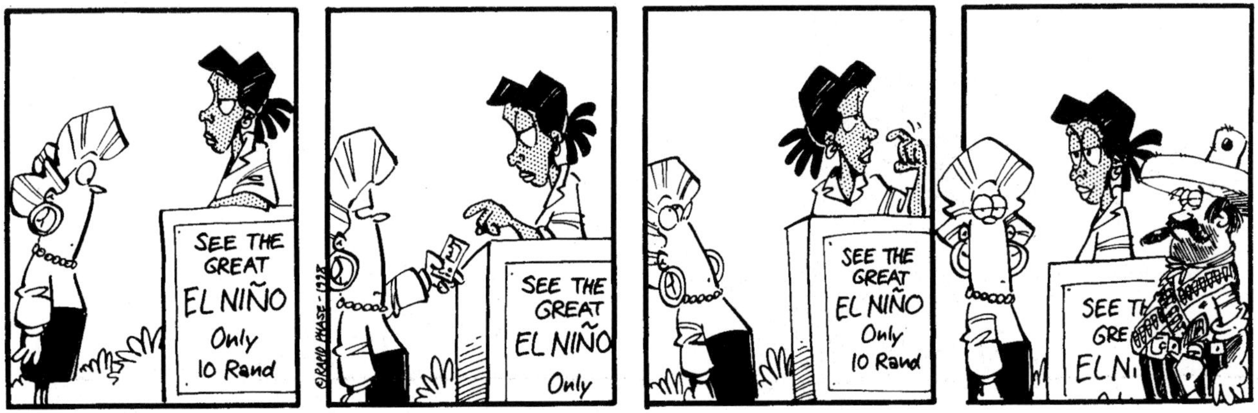
SEE THE GREAT EL NIÑO Only 10 Rand
©RAPID PHASE-1998
SEE THE GREAT EL NIÑO Only
SEE THE GREAT EL NIÑO Only 10 Rand

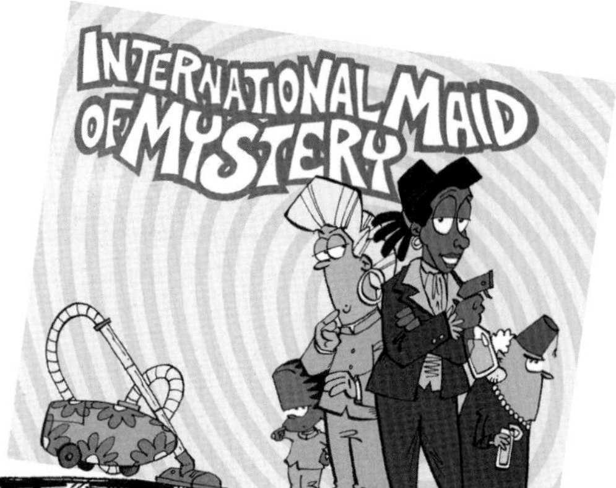
INTERNATIONAL MAID OF MYSTERY

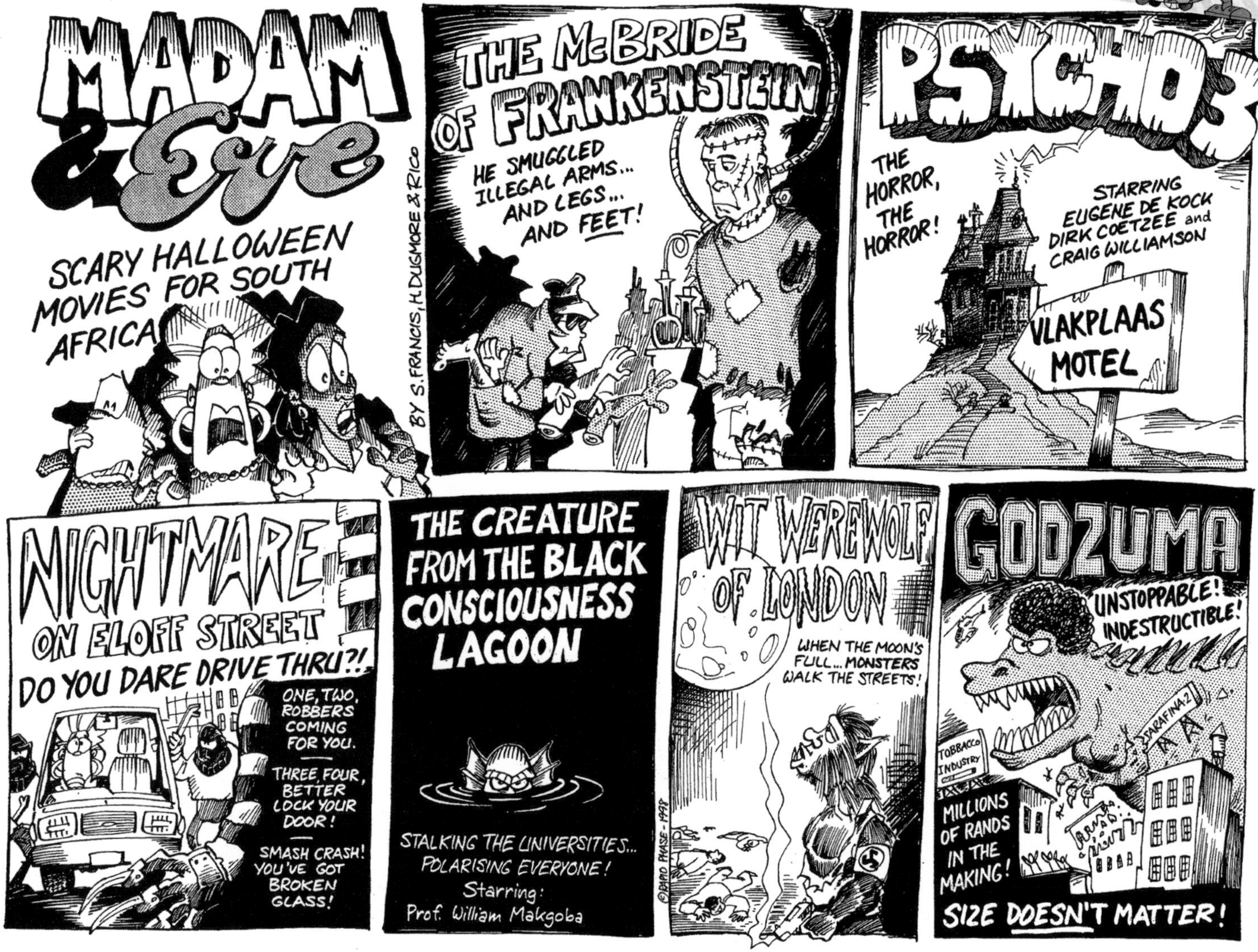
MADAM & Eve
SCARY HALLOWEEN MOVIES FOR SOUTH AFRICA
BY S. FRANCIS, H. DUGMORE & RICO
THE McBRIDE OF FRANKENSTEIN
HE SMUGGLED ILLEGAL ARMS... AND LEGS... AND FEET!
PSYCHO 3
THE HORROR, THE HORROR!
STARRING EUGENE DE KOCK DIRK COETZEE and CRAIG WILLIAMSON
VLAKPLAAS MOTEL
NIGHTMARE ON ELOFF STREET
DO YOU DARE DRIVE THRU?!
ONE, TWO, ROBBERS COMING FOR YOU.
THREE, FOUR, BETTER LOCK YOUR DOOR!
SMASH CRASH! YOU'VE GOT BROKEN GLASS!
THE CREATURE FROM THE BLACK CONSCIOUSNESS LAGOON
STALKING THE UNIVERSITIES... POLARISING EVERYONE!
Starring: Prof. William Makgoba
WIT WEREWOLF OF LONDON
WHEN THE MOON'S FULL... MONSTERS WALK THE STREETS!
GODZUMA
UNSTOPPABLE! INDESTRUCTIBLE!
TOBBACCO INDUSTRY
SARAFINA 2
MILLIONS OF RANDS IN THE MAKING!
SIZE DOESN'T MATTER!

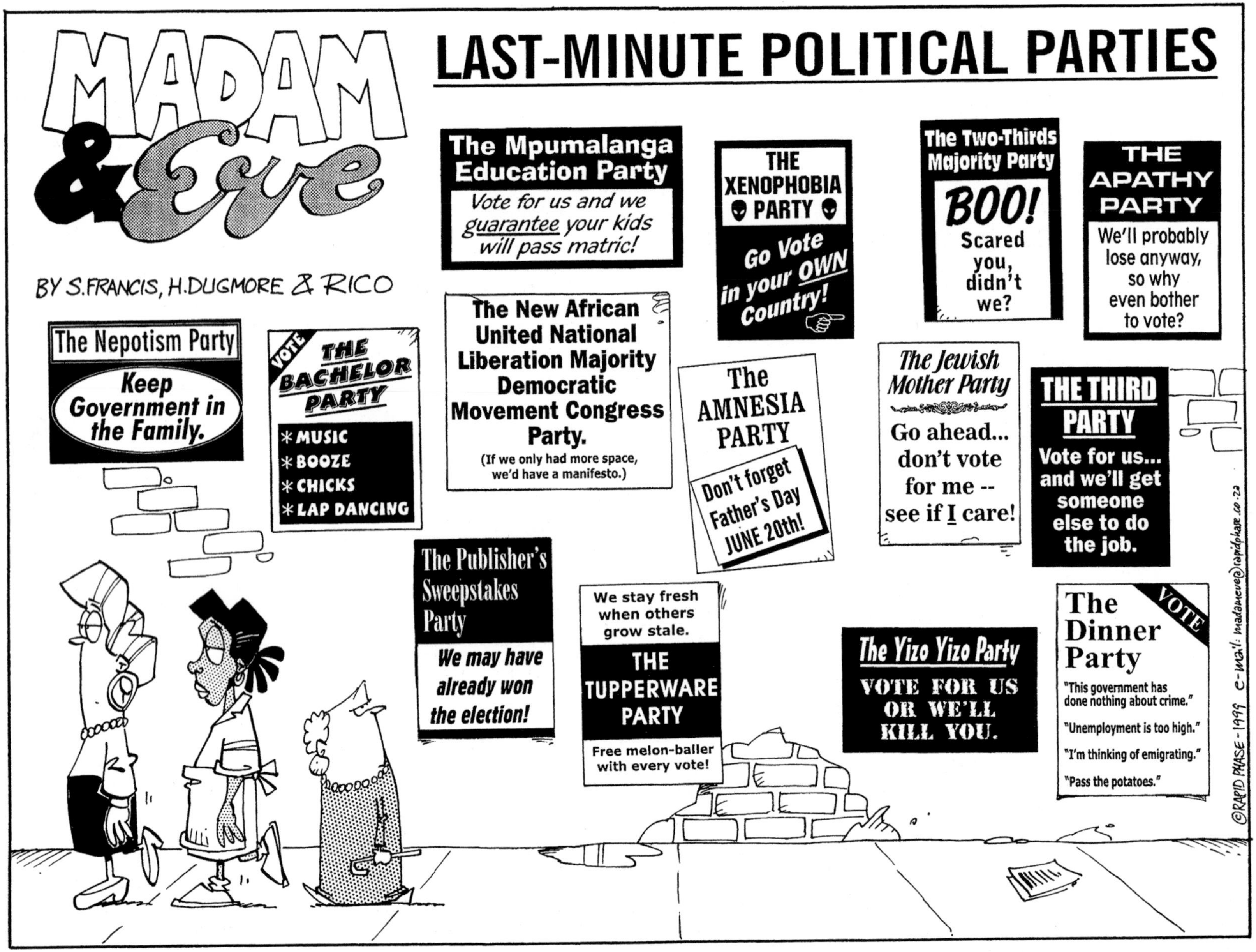
MADAM & Eve
BY S.FRANCIS, H.DUGMORE & RICO
LAST-MINUTE POLITICAL PARTIES
The Mpumalanga Education Party
Vote for us and we guarantee your kids will pass matric!
THE XENOPHOBIA PARTY
Go Vote in your OWN Country!
The Two-Thirds Majority Party
BOO! Scared you, didn't we?
THE APATHY PARTY
We'll probably lose anyway, so why even bother to vote?
The Nepotism Party
Keep Government in the Family.
VOTE
THE BACHELOR PARTY
*MUSIC
*BOOZE
*CHICKS
*LAP DANCING
The New African United National Liberation Majority Democratic Movement Congress Party.
(If we only had more space, we'd have a manifesto.)
The AMNESIA PARTY
Don't forget Father's Day JUNE 20th!
The Jewish Mother Party
Go ahead... don't vote for me -- see if I care!
THE THIRD PARTY
Vote for us... and we'll get someone else to do the job.
The Publisher's Sweepstakes Party
We may have already won the election!
We stay fresh when others grow stale.
THE TUPPERWARE PARTY
Free melon-baller with every vote!
The Yizo Yizo Party
VOTE FOR US OR WE'LL KILL YOU.
VOTE
The Dinner Party
"This government has done nothing about crime."
"Unemployment is too high."
"I'm thinking of emigrating."
"Pass the potatoes."
©RAPID PHASE-1999 e-mail: madameve@rapidphase.co.za

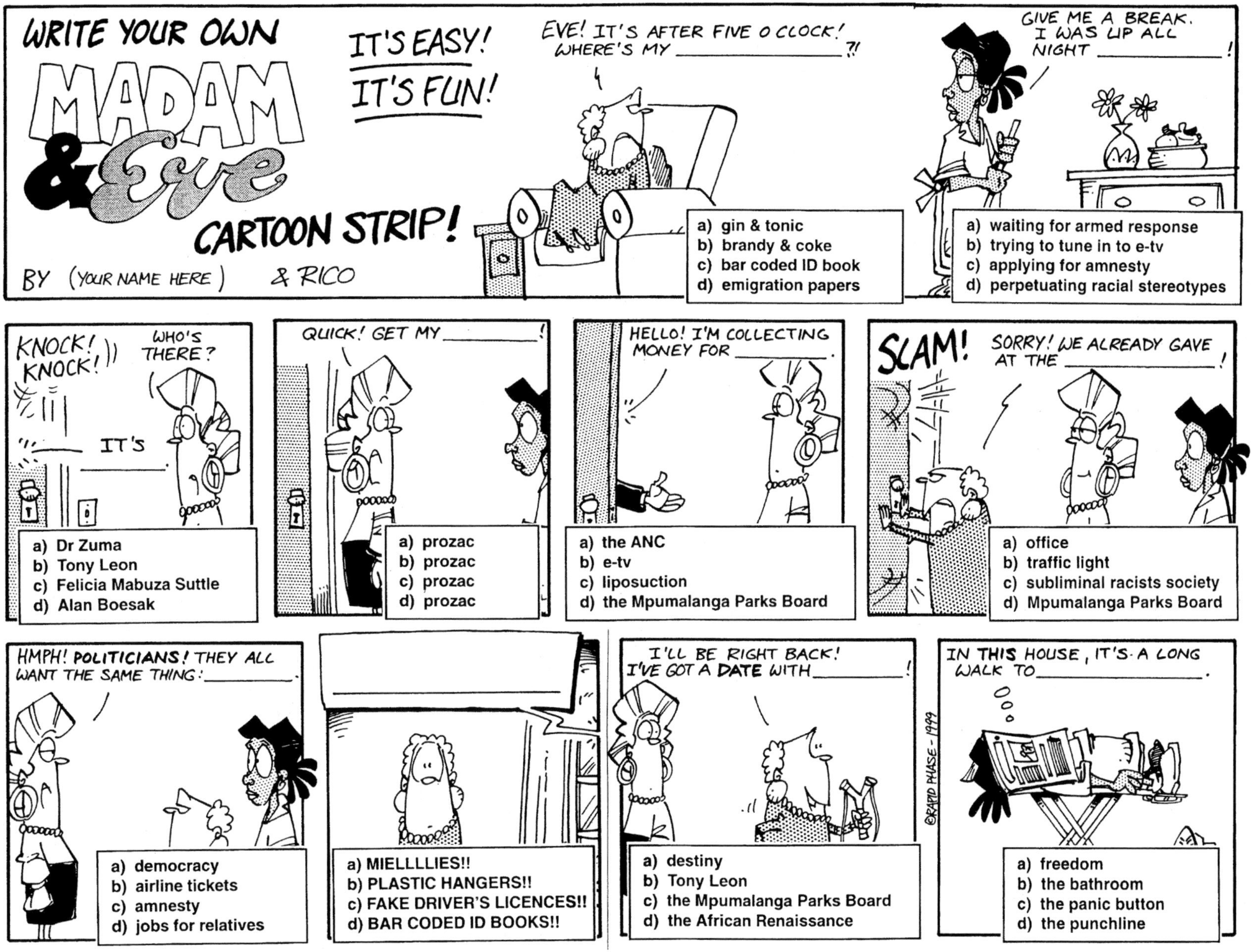
WRITE YOUR OWN
MADAM & Eve
CARTOON STRIP!
IT'S EASY!
IT'S FUN!
BY (YOUR NAME HERE) & RICO
EVE! IT'S AFTER FIVE O CLOCK! WHERE'S MY ________?!
a) gin & tonic
b) brandy & coke
c) bar coded ID book
d) emigration papers
GIVE ME A BREAK. I WAS UP ALL NIGHT ________!
a) waiting for armed response
b) trying to tune in to e-tv
c) applying for amnesty
d) perpetuating racial stereotypes
KNOCK! KNOCK!
WHO'S THERE?
IT'S ________.
a) Dr Zuma
b) Tony Leon
c) Felicia Mabuza Suttle
d) Alan Boesak
QUICK! GET MY ________!
a) prozac
b) prozac
c) prozac
d) prozac
HELLO! I'M COLLECTING MONEY FOR ________.
a) the ANC
b) e-tv
c) liposuction
d) the Mpumalanga Parks Board
SLAM!
SORRY! WE ALREADY GAVE AT THE ________!
a) office
b) traffic light
c) subliminal racists society
d) Mpumalanga Parks Board
HMPH! POLITICIANS! THEY ALL WANT THE SAME THING: ________.
a) democracy
b) airline tickets
c) amnesty
d) jobs for relatives
____
a) MIELLLLIES!!
b) PLASTIC HANGERS!!
c) FAKE DRIVER'S LICENCES!!
d) BAR CODED ID BOOKS!!
I'LL BE RIGHT BACK! I'VE GOT A DATE WITH ________!
a) destiny
b) Tony Leon
c) the Mpumalanga Parks Board
d) the African Renaissance
©RAPID PHASE - 1999
IN THIS HOUSE, IT'S A LONG WALK TO ________.
a) freedom
b) the bathroom
c) the panic button
d) the punchline

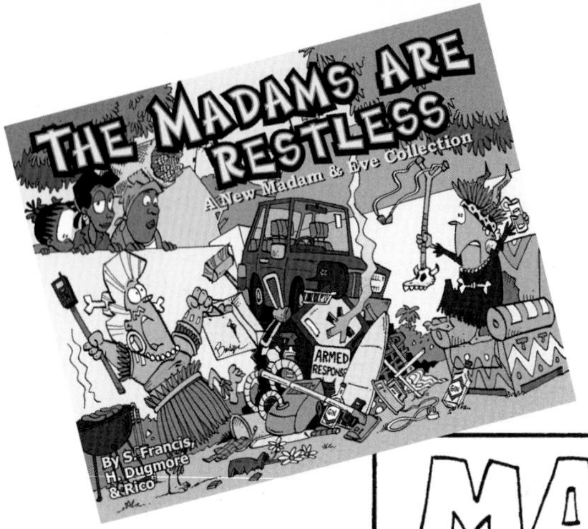
THE MADAMS ARE RESTLESS
A New Madam & Eve Collection
ARMED RESPONSE
By S. Francis, H. Dugmore & Rico

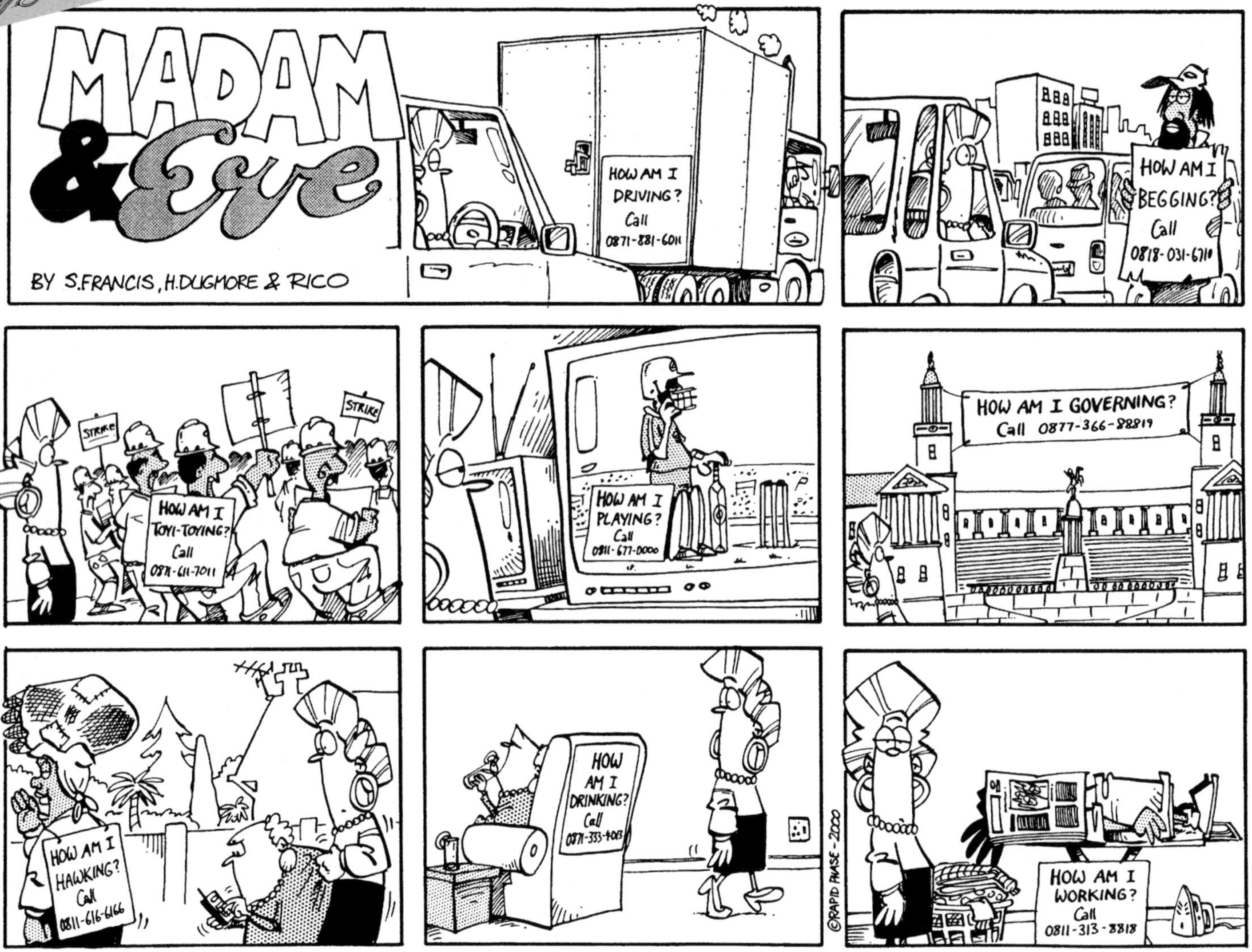
MADAM & Eve
BY S.FRANCIS, H.DUGMORE & RICO
HOW AM I DRIVING? Call 0871-881-6011
HOW AM I BEGGING? Call 0818-031-6710
STRIKE
STRIKE
HOW AM I TOYI-TOYING? Call 0871-611-7011
HOW AM I PLAYING? Call 0811-677-0000
HOW AM I GOVERNING? Call 0877-366-88819
HOW AM I HAWKING? Call 0811-616-6166
HOW AM I DRINKING? Call 0871-333-4013
©RAPID PHASE-2000
HOW AM I WORKING? Call 0811-313-8818

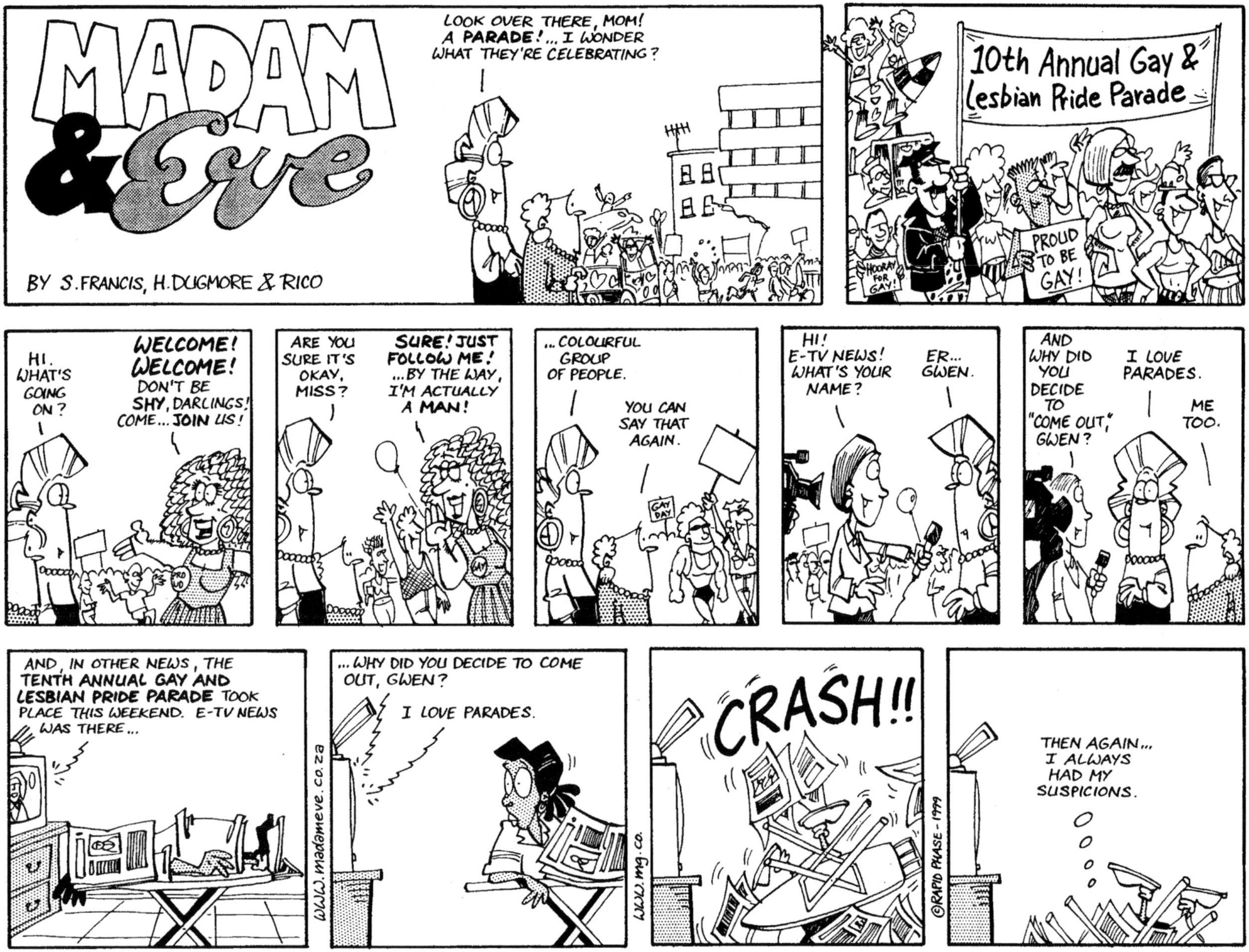
MADAM & Eve
BY S. FRANCIS, H. DUGMORE & RICO
LOOK OVER THERE, MOM! A PARADE! ... I WONDER WHAT THEY'RE CELEBRATING?
10th Annual Gay & Lesbian Pride Parade
HOORAY FOR GAY!
PROUD TO BE GAY!
HI. WHAT'S GOING ON?
WELCOME! WELCOME! DON'T BE SHY, DARLINGS! COME... JOIN US!
ARE YOU SURE IT'S OKAY, MISS?
SURE! JUST FOLLOW ME! ...BY THE WAY, I'M ACTUALLY A MAN!
... COLOURFUL GROUP OF PEOPLE.
YOU CAN SAY THAT AGAIN.
GAY DAY
HI! E-TV NEWS! WHAT'S YOUR NAME?
ER... GWEN.
AND WHY DID YOU DECIDE TO "COME OUT," GWEN?
I LOVE PARADES.
ME TOO.
AND, IN OTHER NEWS, THE TENTH ANNUAL GAY AND LESBIAN PRIDE PARADE TOOK PLACE THIS WEEKEND. E-TV NEWS WAS THERE...
www.madameve.co.za
... WHY DID YOU DECIDE TO COME OUT, GWEN?
I LOVE PARADES.
www.mg.co.
CRASH!!
©RAPID PHASE - 1999
THEN AGAIN... I ALWAYS HAD MY SUSPICIONS.

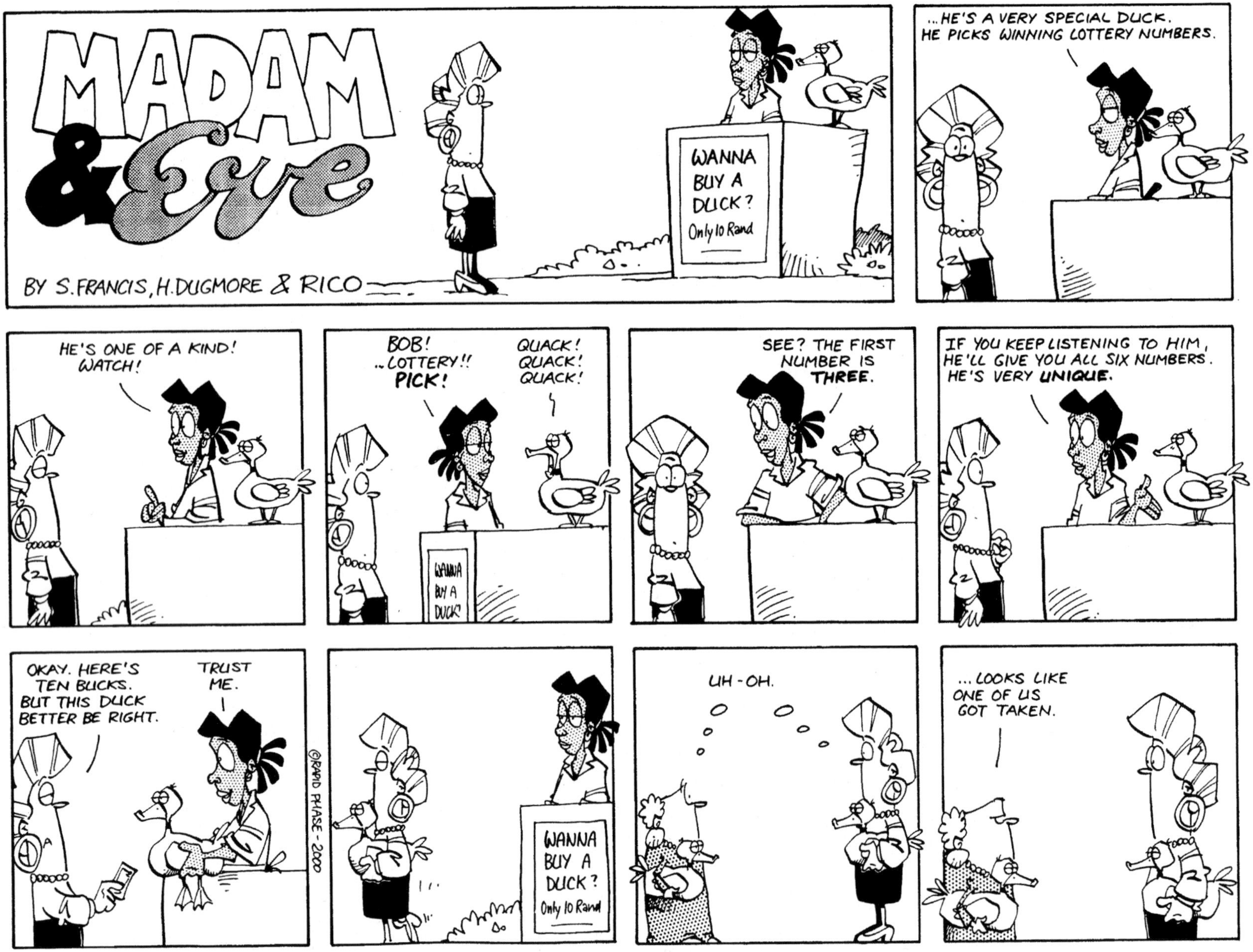
MADAM & Eve
BY S. FRANCIS, H. DUGMORE & RICO
WANNA BUY A DUCK? Only 10 Rand
...HE'S A VERY SPECIAL DUCK. HE PICKS WINNING LOTTERY NUMBERS.
HE'S ONE OF A KIND! WATCH!
BOB! ..LOTTERY!! PICK!
QUACK! QUACK! QUACK!
WANNA BUY A DUCK?
SEE? THE FIRST NUMBER IS THREE.
IF YOU KEEP LISTENING TO HIM, HE'LL GIVE YOU ALL SIX NUMBERS. HE'S VERY UNIQUE.
OKAY. HERE'S TEN BUCKS. BUT THIS DUCK BETTER BE RIGHT.
TRUST ME.
©RAPID PHASE - 2000
WANNA BUY A DUCK? Only 10 Rand
UH-OH.
...LOOKS LIKE ONE OF US GOT TAKEN.

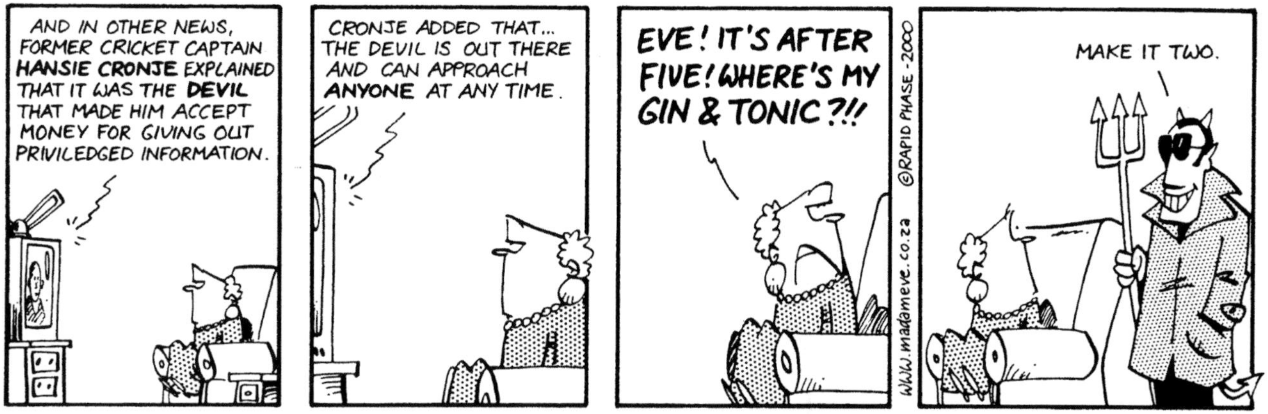
AND IN OTHER NEWS, FORMER CRICKET CAPTAIN HANSIE CRONJE EXPLAINED THAT IT WAS THE DEVIL THAT MADE HIM ACCEPT MONEY FOR GIVING OUT PRIVILEDGED INFORMATION.
CRONJE ADDED THAT... THE DEVIL IS OUT THERE AND CAN APPROACH ANYONE AT ANY TIME.
EVE! IT'S AFTER FIVE! WHERE'S MY GIN & TONIC?!!
©RAPID PHASE - 2000
www.madameve.co.za
MAKE IT TWO.

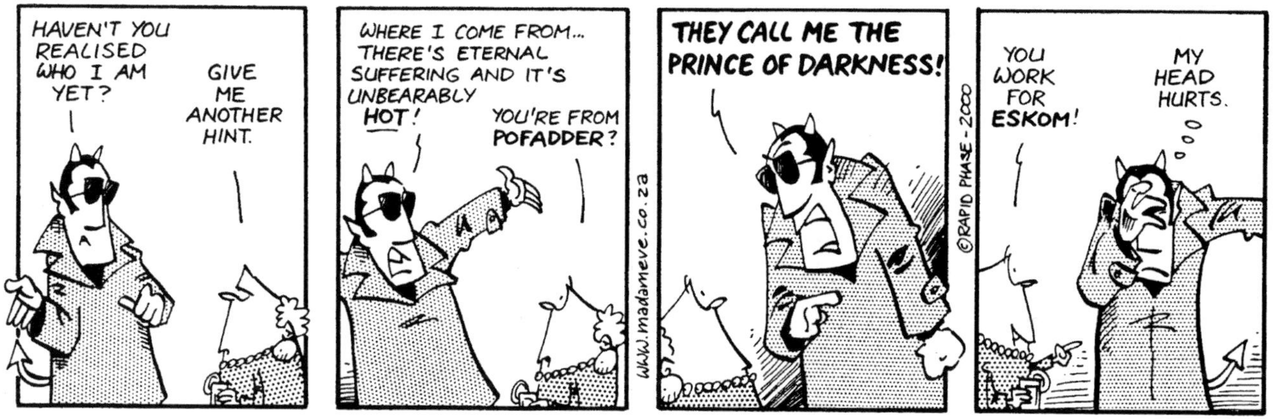
HAVEN'T YOU REALISED WHO I AM YET?
GIVE ME ANOTHER HINT.
WHERE I COME FROM... THERE'S ETERNAL SUFFERING AND IT'S UNBEARABLY HOT!
YOU'RE FROM POFADDER?
www.madameve.co.za
THEY CALL ME THE PRINCE OF DARKNESS!
©RAPID PHASE - 2000
YOU WORK FOR ESKOM!
MY HEAD HURTS.

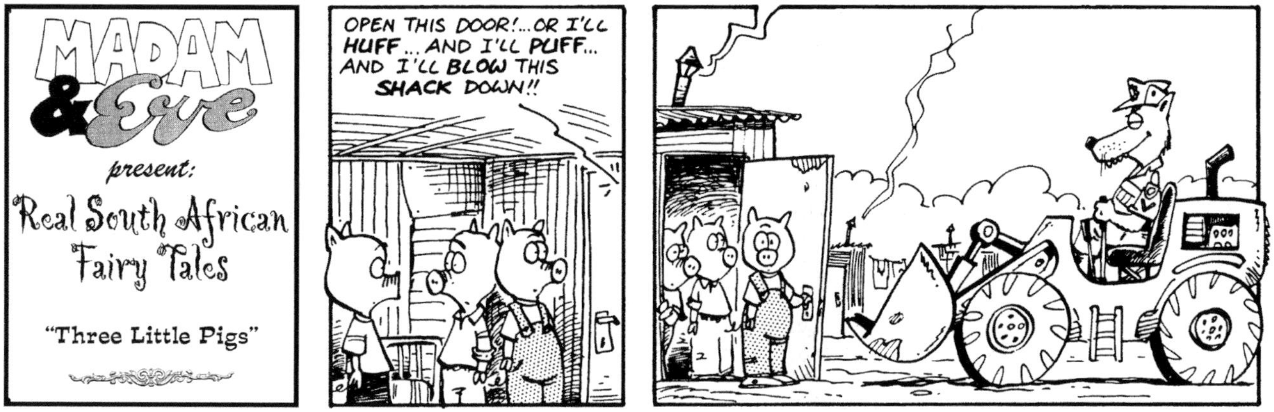
MADAM & Eve
present:
Real South African Fairy Tales
"Three Little Pigs"
OPEN THIS DOOR!...OR I'LL HUFF... AND I'LL PUFF... AND I'LL BLOW THIS SHACK DOWN!!

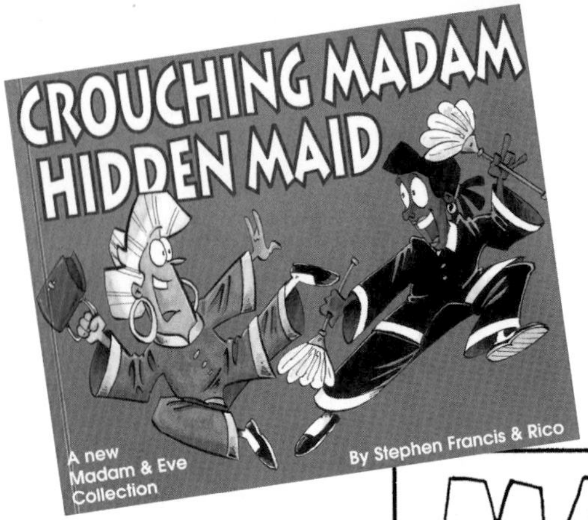
CROUCHING MADAM
HIDDEN MAID
A new
Madam & Eve
Collection
By Stephen Francis & Rico

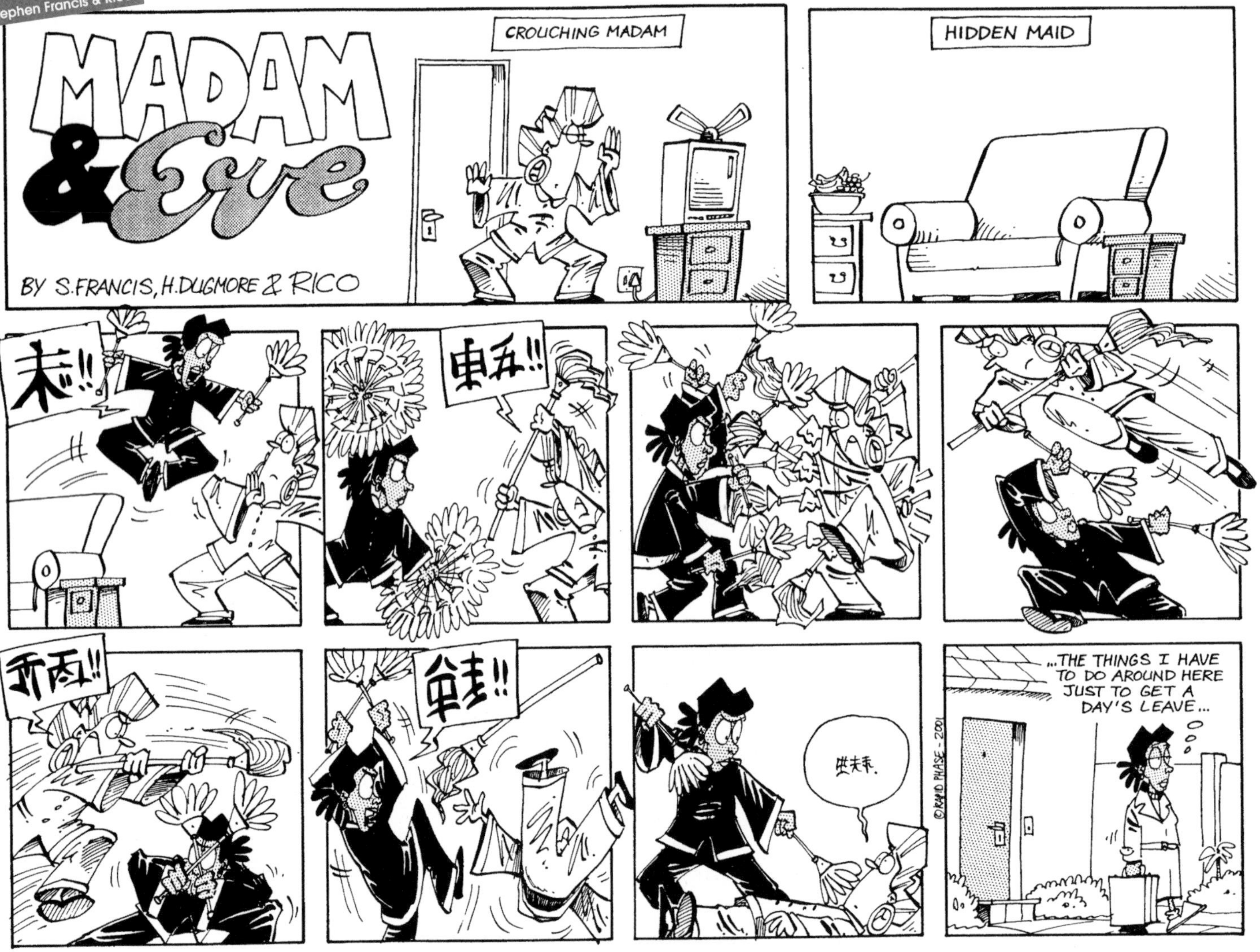
MADAM & Eve
BY S.FRANCIS, H.DUGMORE & RICO
CROUCHING MADAM
HIDDEN MAID
© RAPID PHASE · 2001
...THE THINGS I HAVE TO DO AROUND HERE JUST TO GET A DAY'S LEAVE...

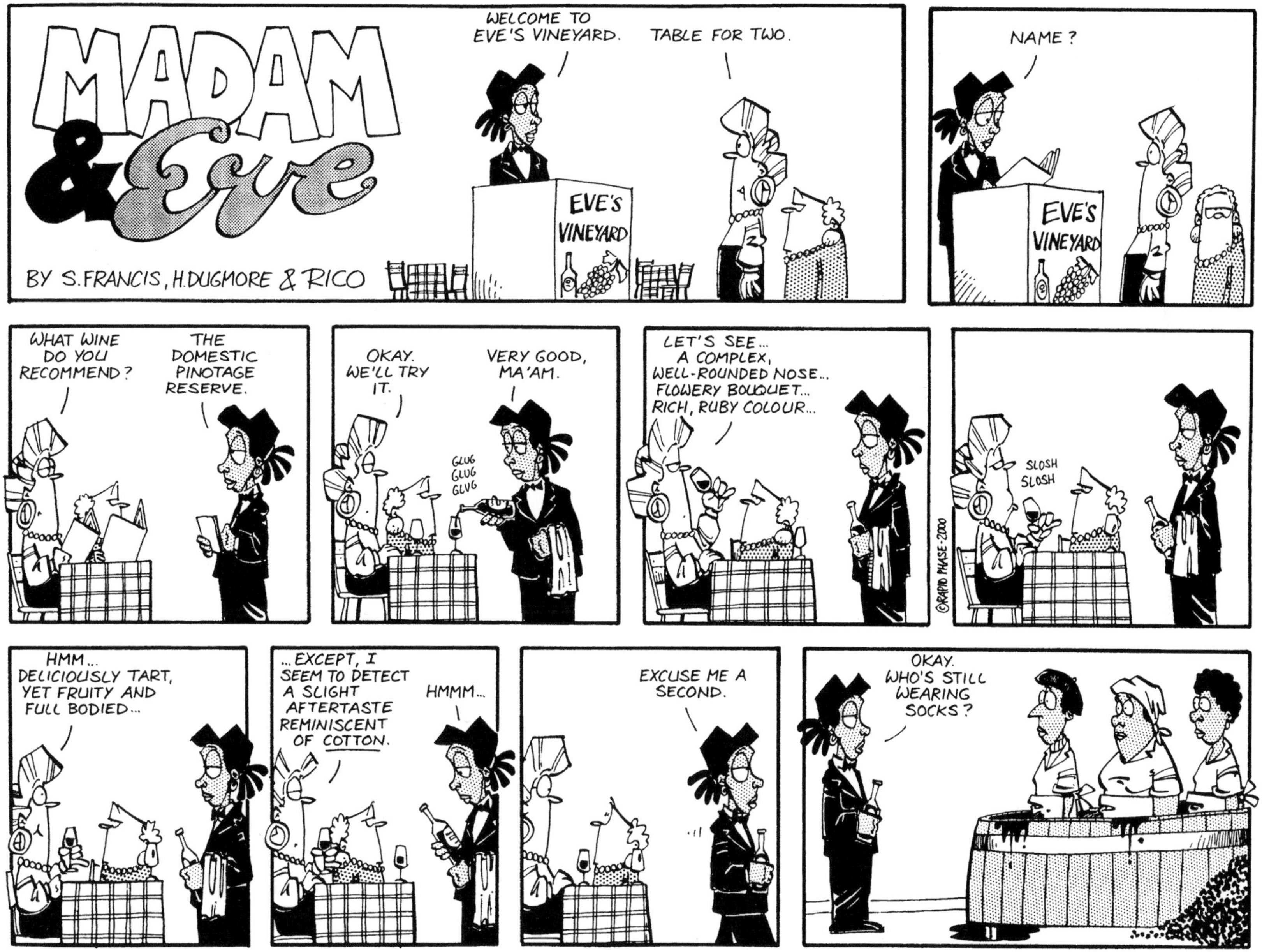
MADAM & Eve
BY S.FRANCIS, H.DUGMORE & RICO
WELCOME TO EVE'S VINEYARD.
TABLE FOR TWO.
EVE'S VINEYARD
NAME ?
EVE'S VINEYARD
WHAT WINE DO YOU RECOMMEND ?
THE DOMESTIC PINOTAGE RESERVE.
OKAY. WE'LL TRY IT.
VERY GOOD, MA'AM.
GLUG GLUG GLUG
LET'S SEE... A COMPLEX, WELL-ROUNDED NOSE... FLOWERY BOUQUET... RICH, RUBY COLOUR...
SLOSH SLOSH
©RAPID PHASE·2000
HMM... DELICIOUSLY TART, YET FRUITY AND FULL BODIED...
...EXCEPT, I SEEM TO DETECT A SLIGHT AFTERTASTE REMINISCENT OF COTTON.
HMMM...
EXCUSE ME A SECOND.
OKAY. WHO'S STILL WEARING SOCKS ?

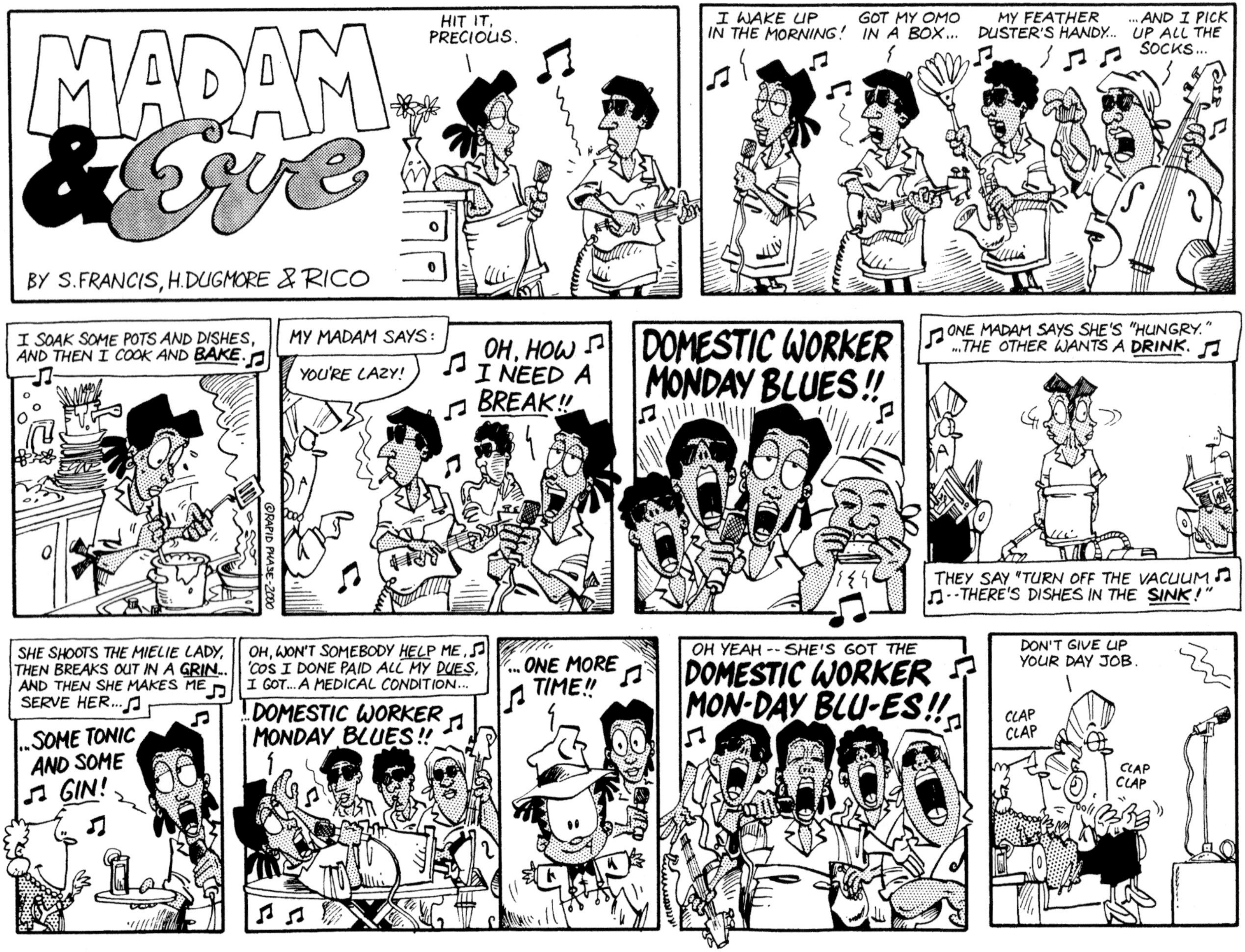
MADAM & Eve
BY S.FRANCIS, H.DUGMORE & RICO
HIT IT, PRECIOUS.
I WAKE UP IN THE MORNING!
GOT MY OMO IN A BOX...
MY FEATHER DUSTER'S HANDY...
...AND I PICK UP ALL THE SOCKS...
I SOAK SOME POTS AND DISHES, AND THEN I COOK AND BAKE.
©RAPID PHASE-2000
MY MADAM SAYS:
YOU'RE LAZY!
OH, HOW I NEED A BREAK!!
DOMESTIC WORKER MONDAY BLUES!!
ONE MADAM SAYS SHE'S "HUNGRY." ...THE OTHER WANTS A DRINK.
THEY SAY "TURN OFF THE VACUUM --THERE'S DISHES IN THE SINK!"
SHE SHOOTS THE MIELIE LADY, THEN BREAKS OUT IN A GRIN... AND THEN SHE MAKES ME SERVE HER...
...SOME TONIC AND SOME GIN!
OH, WON'T SOMEBODY HELP ME, 'COS I DONE PAID ALL MY DUES, I GOT... A MEDICAL CONDITION...
...DOMESTIC WORKER MONDAY BLUES!!
...ONE MORE TIME!!
OH YEAH -- SHE'S GOT THE DOMESTIC WORKER MON-DAY BLU-ES!!
DON'T GIVE UP YOUR DAY JOB.
CLAP CLAP
CLAP CLAP

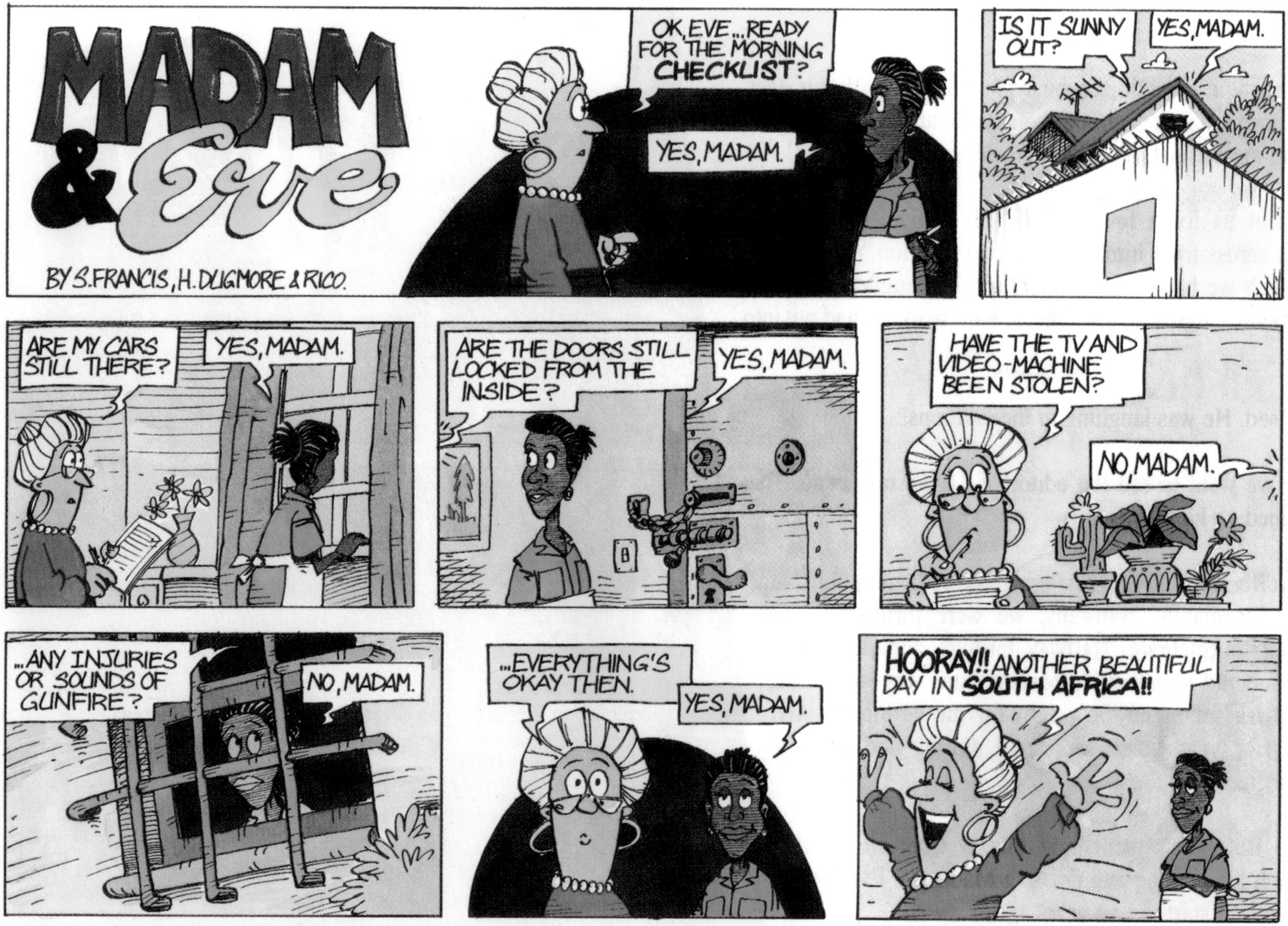
MADAM & Eve
BY S.FRANCIS, H.DUGMORE & RICO.
OK, EVE... READY FOR THE MORNING CHECKLIST?
YES, MADAM.
IS IT SUNNY OUT?
YES, MADAM.
ARE MY CARS STILL THERE?
YES, MADAM.
ARE THE DOORS STILL LOCKED FROM THE INSIDE?
YES, MADAM.
HAVE THE TV AND VIDEO-MACHINE BEEN STOLEN?
NO, MADAM.
...ANY INJURIES OR SOUNDS OF GUNFIRE?
NO, MADAM.
...EVERYTHING'S OKAY THEN.
YES, MADAM.
HOORAY!! ANOTHER BEAUTIFUL DAY IN SOUTH AFRICA!!

MADAM & Eve

ART APPRECIATION

BY S.FRANCIS, H.DUGMORE & RICO

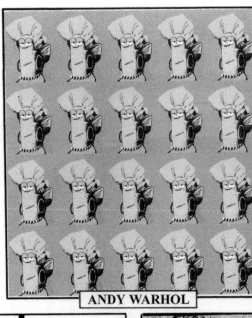

ANDY WARHOL

SALVADOR DALI

EDVARD MUNCH

PIET MONDRIAN

JACKSON POLLOCK

GOOD MORNING, MADAM.

PABLO PICASSO

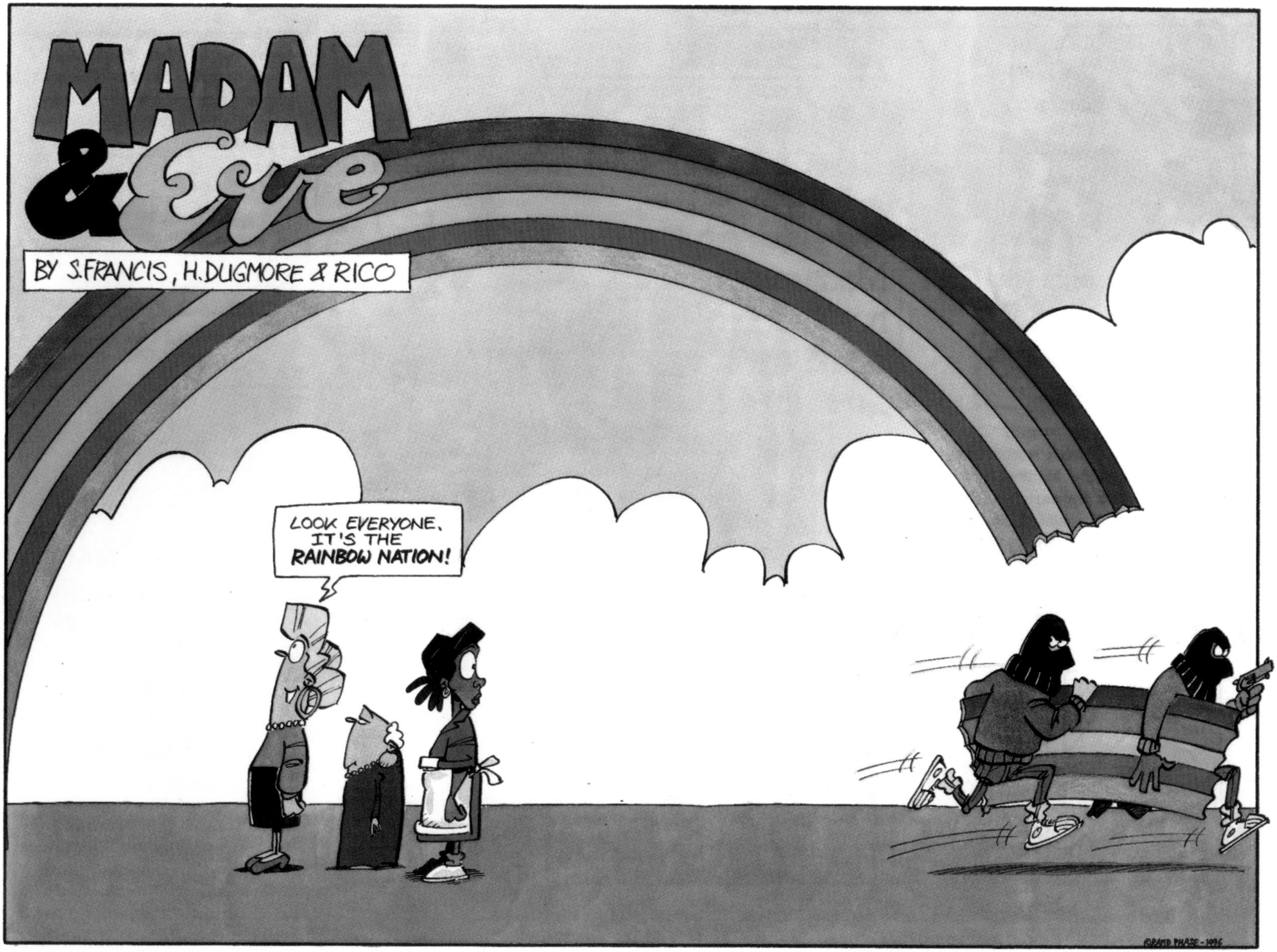
MADAM & Eve
BY S.FRANCIS, H.DUGMORE & RICO
LOOK EVERYONE. IT'S THE RAINBOW NATION!

MADAM & Eve Art Appreciation II

BY S. FRANCIS, H. DUGMORE & RICO

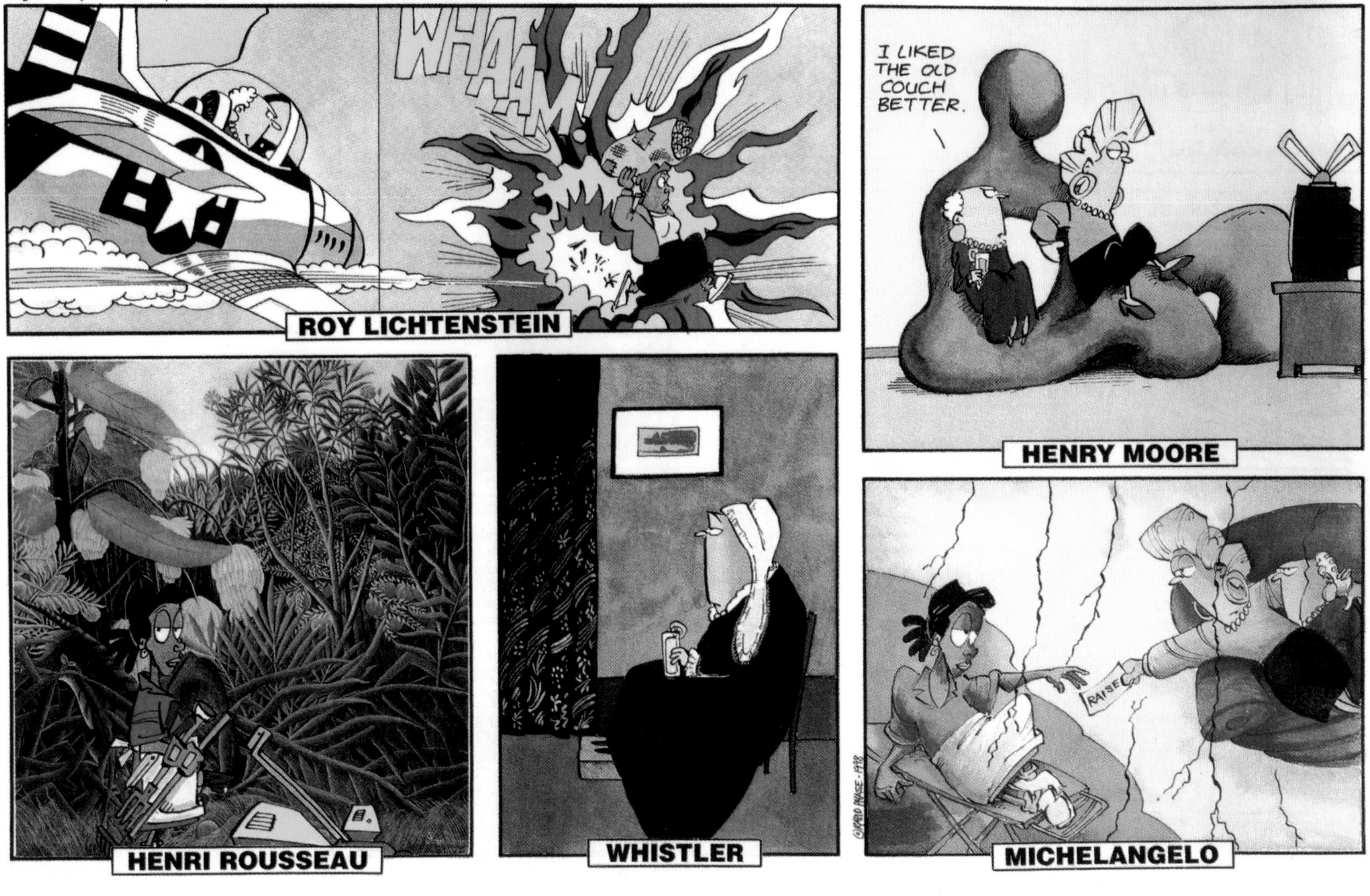

WHAAM!
ROY LICHTENSTEIN
I LIKED THE OLD COUCH BETTER.
HENRY MOORE
HENRI ROUSSEAU
WHISTLER
RAISE
MICHELANGELO

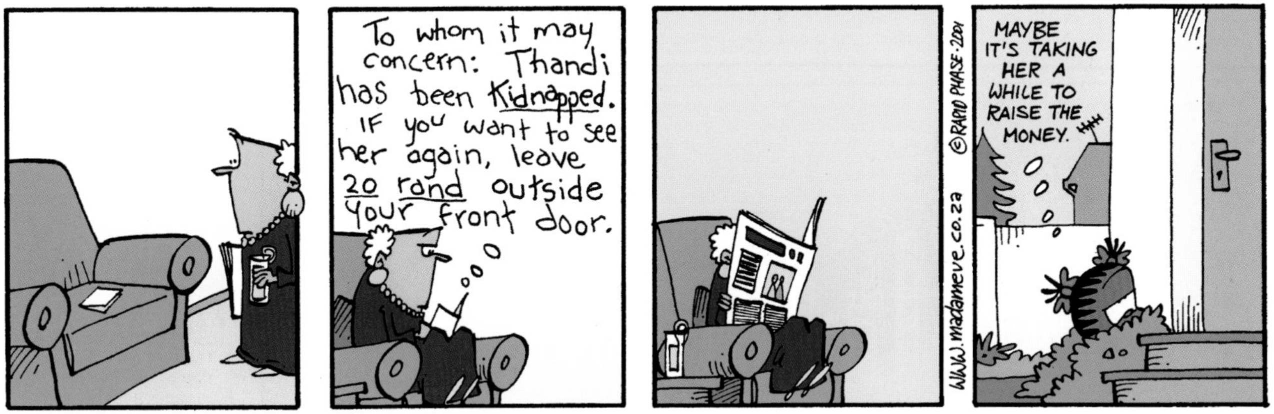
To whom it may concern: Thandi has been Kidnapped. IF you want to see her again, leave 20 rand outside your front door.
©RAPID PHASE · 2001
www.madameve.co.za
MAYBE IT'S TAKING HER A WHILE TO RAISE THE MONEY.

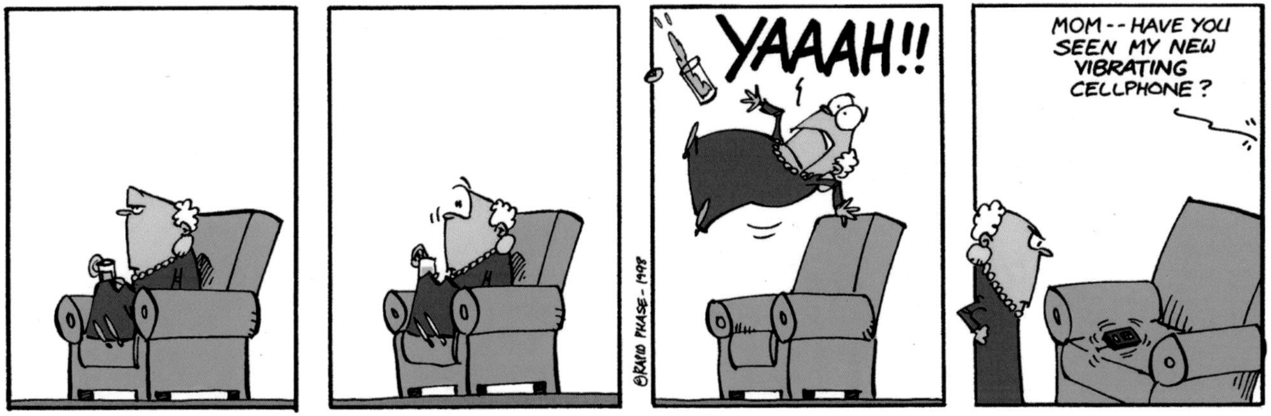
©RAPID PHASE - 1998
YAAAH!!
MOM -- HAVE YOU SEEN MY NEW VIBRATING CELLPHONE?

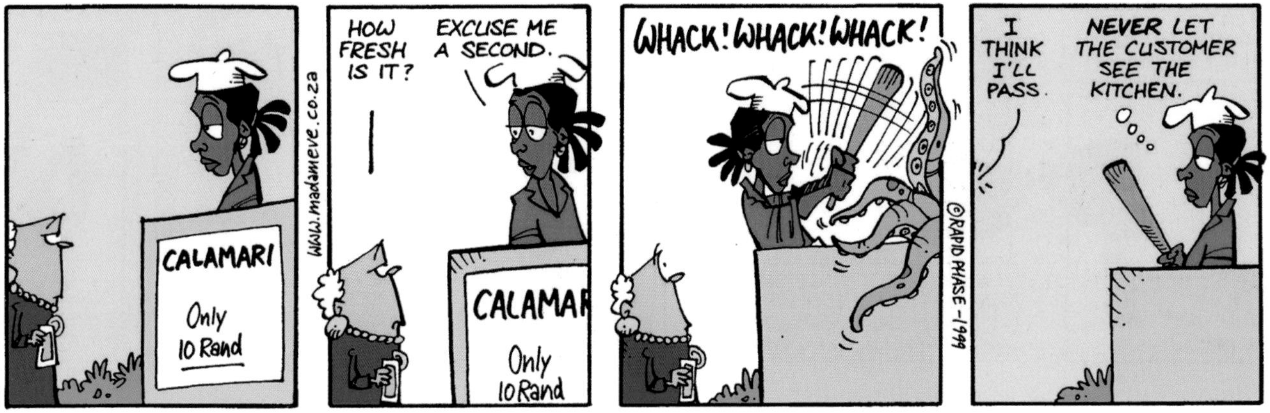
CALAMARI
Only 10 Rand
www.madameve.co.za
HOW FRESH IS IT?
EXCUSE ME A SECOND.
CALAMAR
Only 10 Rand
WHACK! WHACK! WHACK!
©RAPID PHASE - 1999
I THINK I'LL PASS.
NEVER LET THE CUSTOMER SEE THE KITCHEN.

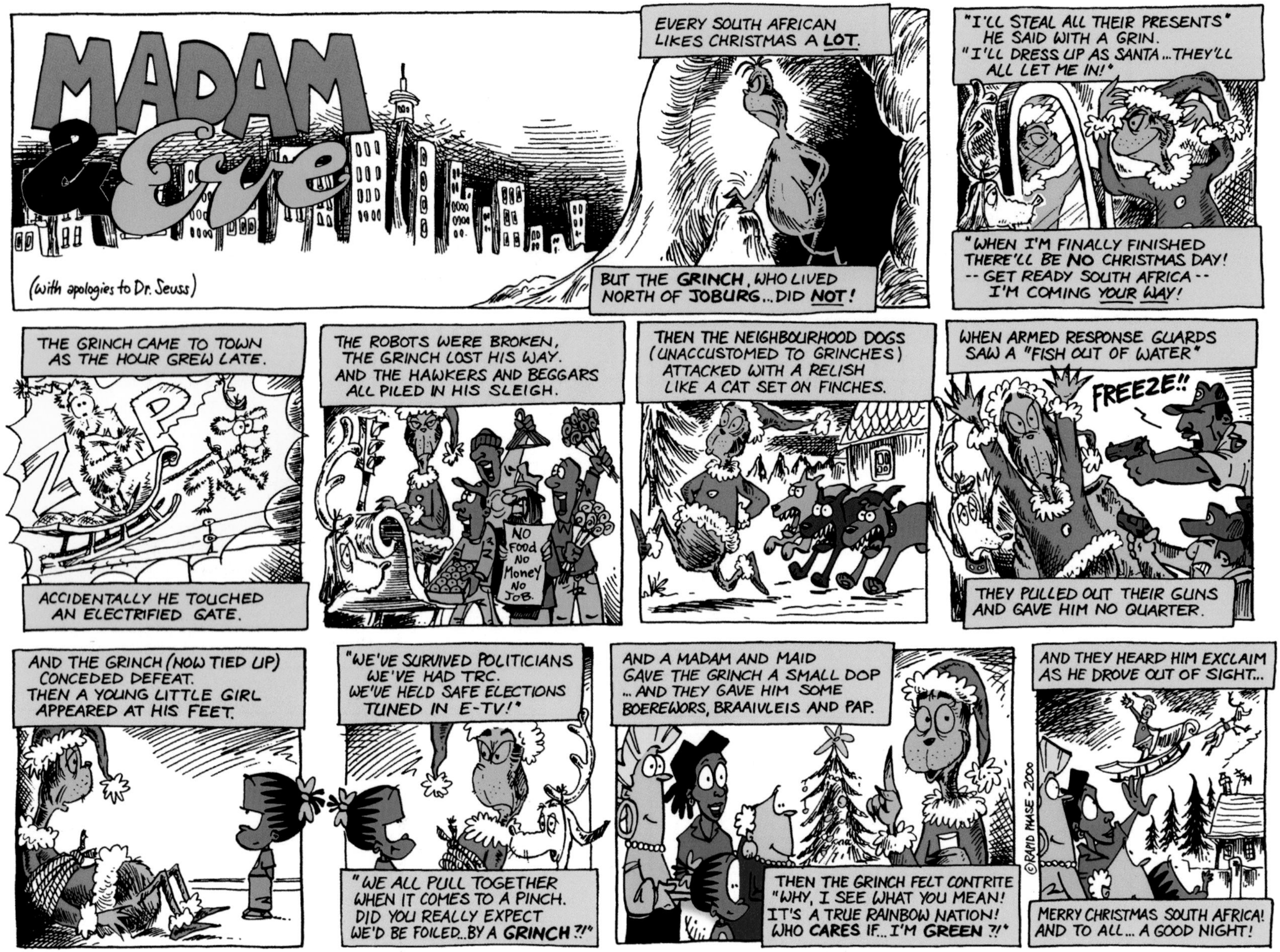
MADAM & Eve
(with apologies to Dr. Seuss)
EVERY SOUTH AFRICAN LIKES CHRISTMAS A LOT.
BUT THE GRINCH, WHO LIVED NORTH OF JOBURG... DID NOT!
"I'LL STEAL ALL THEIR PRESENTS" HE SAID WITH A GRIN. "I'LL DRESS UP AS SANTA... THEY'LL ALL LET ME IN!"
"WHEN I'M FINALLY FINISHED THERE'LL BE NO CHRISTMAS DAY! -- GET READY SOUTH AFRICA -- I'M COMING YOUR WAY!
THE GRINCH CAME TO TOWN AS THE HOUR GREW LATE.
ZAP
ACCIDENTALLY HE TOUCHED AN ELECTRIFIED GATE.
THE ROBOTS WERE BROKEN, THE GRINCH LOST HIS WAY. AND THE HAWKERS AND BEGGARS ALL PILED IN HIS SLEIGH.
NO Food NO Money NO JOB.
THEN THE NEIGHBOURHOOD DOGS (UNACCUSTOMED TO GRINCHES) ATTACKED WITH A RELISH LIKE A CAT SET ON FINCHES.
WHEN ARMED RESPONSE GUARDS SAW A "FISH OUT OF WATER"
FREEZE!!
THEY PULLED OUT THEIR GUNS AND GAVE HIM NO QUARTER.
AND THE GRINCH (NOW TIED UP) CONCEDED DEFEAT. THEN A YOUNG LITTLE GIRL APPEARED AT HIS FEET.
"WE'VE SURVIVED POLITICIANS WE'VE HAD TRC. WE'VE HELD SAFE ELECTIONS TUNED IN E-TV!"
"WE ALL PULL TOGETHER WHEN IT COMES TO A PINCH. DID YOU REALLY EXPECT WE'D BE FOILED... BY A GRINCH?!"
AND A MADAM AND MAID GAVE THE GRINCH A SMALL DOP ... AND THEY GAVE HIM SOME BOEREWORS, BRAAIVLEIS AND PAP.
THEN THE GRINCH FELT CONTRITE "WHY, I SEE WHAT YOU MEAN! IT'S A TRUE RAINBOW NATION! WHO CARES IF... I'M GREEN?!"
©RAPID PHASE - 2000
AND THEY HEARD HIM EXCLAIM AS HE DROVE OUT OF SIGHT...
MERRY CHRISTMAS SOUTH AFRICA! AND TO ALL... A GOOD NIGHT!

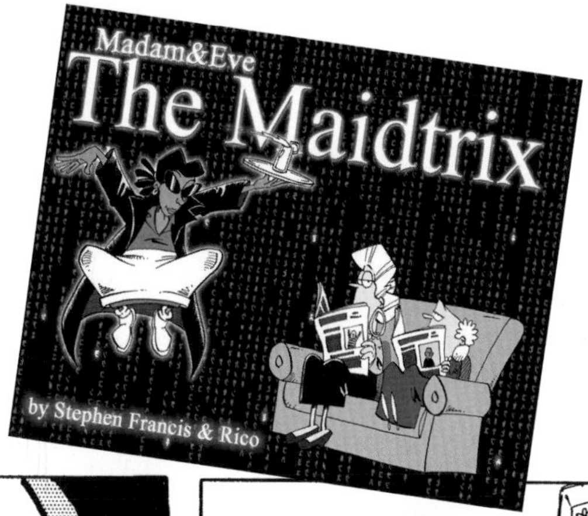
Madam&Eve
The Maidtrix
by Stephen Francis & Rico

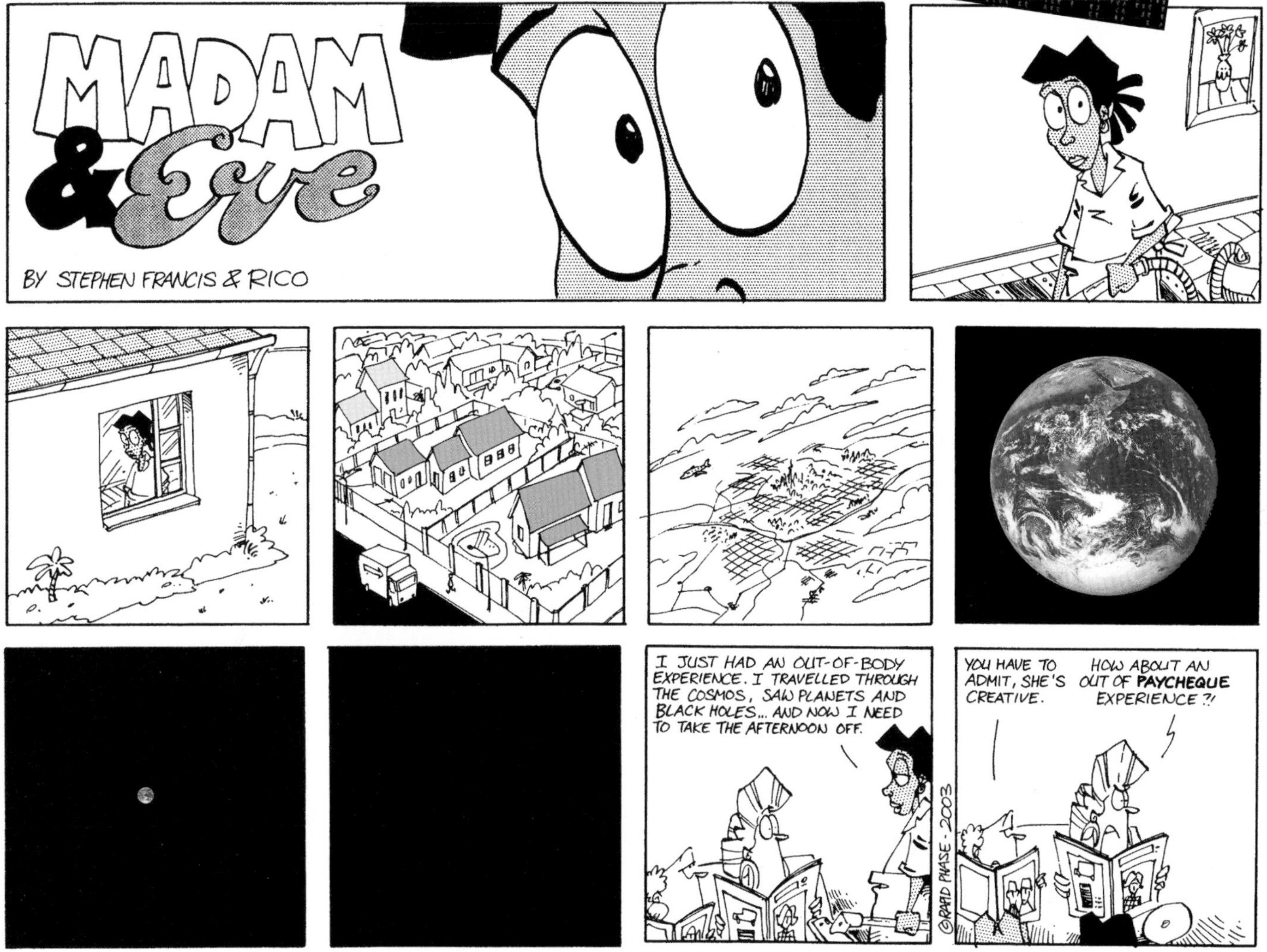
MADAM
&Eve
BY STEPHEN FRANCIS & RICO
I JUST HAD AN OUT-OF-BODY EXPERIENCE. I TRAVELLED THROUGH THE COSMOS, SAW PLANETS AND BLACK HOLES... AND NOW I NEED TO TAKE THE AFTERNOON OFF.
©RAPID PHASE · 2003
YOU HAVE TO ADMIT, SHE'S CREATIVE.
HOW ABOUT AN OUT OF **PAYCHEQUE** EXPERIENCE ?!

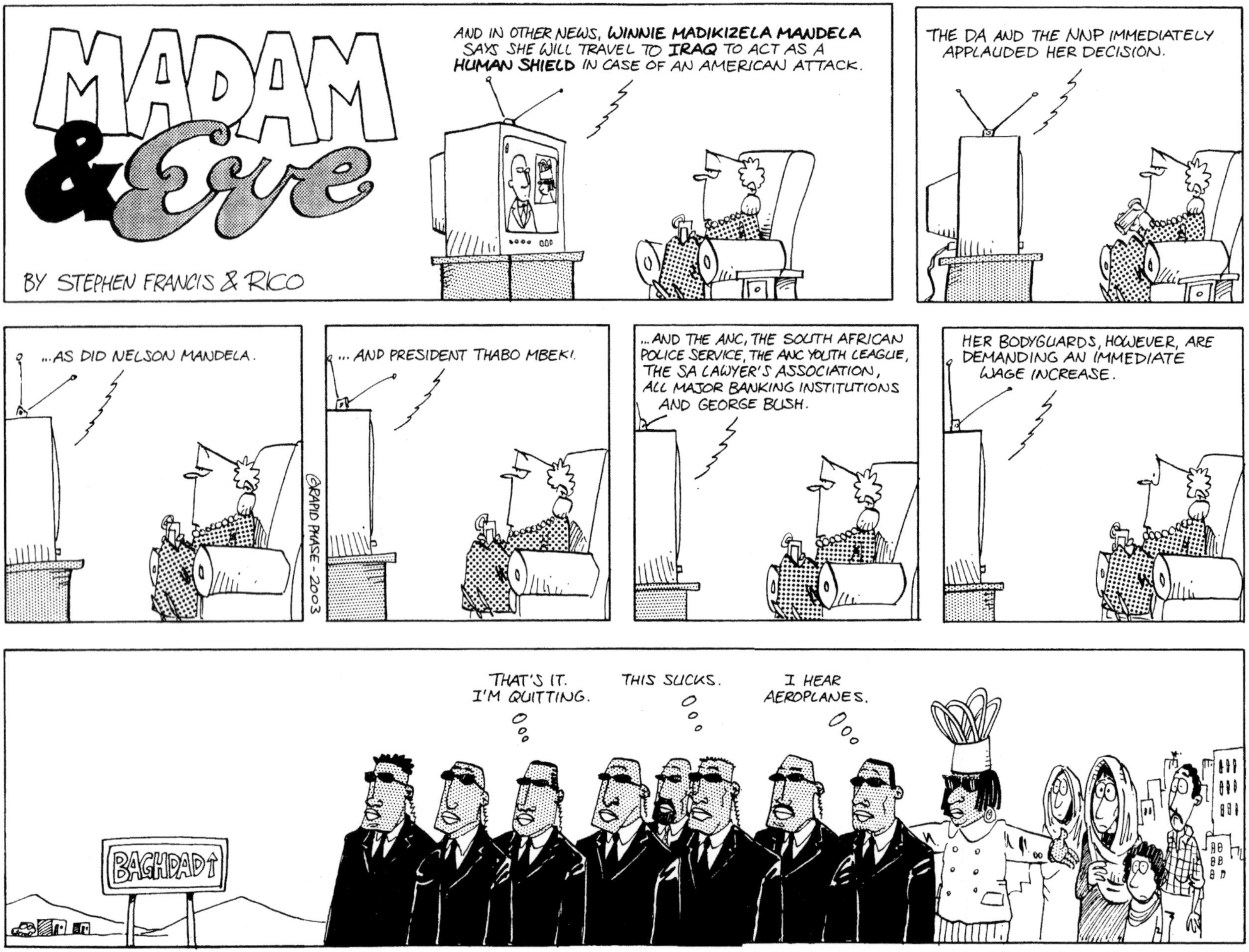
MADAM & Eve
BY STEPHEN FRANCIS & RICO
AND IN OTHER NEWS, WINNIE MADIKIZELA MANDELA SAYS SHE WILL TRAVEL TO IRAQ TO ACT AS A HUMAN SHIELD IN CASE OF AN AMERICAN ATTACK.
THE DA AND THE NNP IMMEDIATELY APPLAUDED HER DECISION.
...AS DID NELSON MANDELA.
©RAPID PHASE - 2003
...AND PRESIDENT THABO MBEKI.
...AND THE ANC, THE SOUTH AFRICAN POLICE SERVICE, THE ANC YOUTH LEAGUE, THE SA LAWYER'S ASSOCIATION, ALL MAJOR BANKING INSTITUTIONS AND GEORGE BUSH.
HER BODYGUARDS, HOWEVER, ARE DEMANDING AN IMMEDIATE WAGE INCREASE.
THAT'S IT. I'M QUITTING.
THIS SUCKS.
I HEAR AEROPLANES.
BAGHDAD

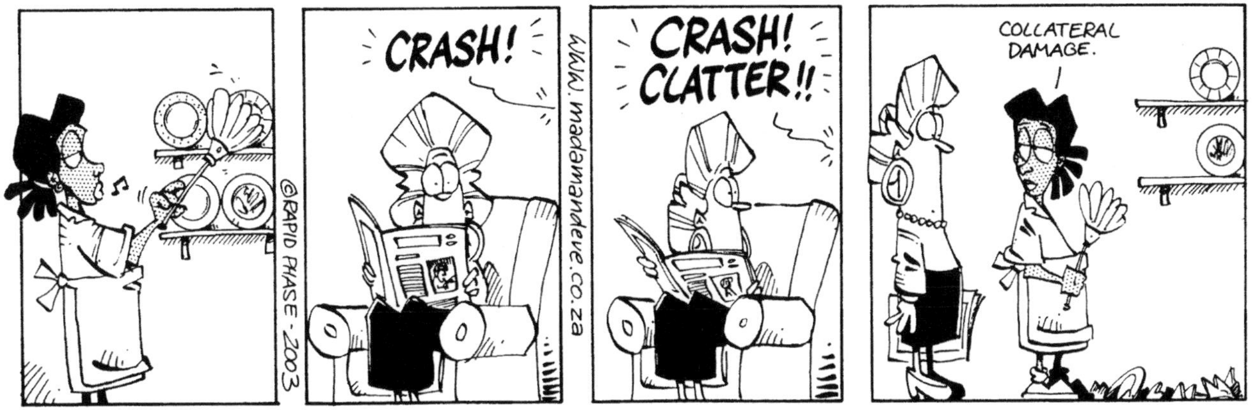
©RAPID PHASE - 2003
CRASH!
www.madamandeve.co.za
CRASH! CLATTER!!
COLLATERAL DAMAGE.

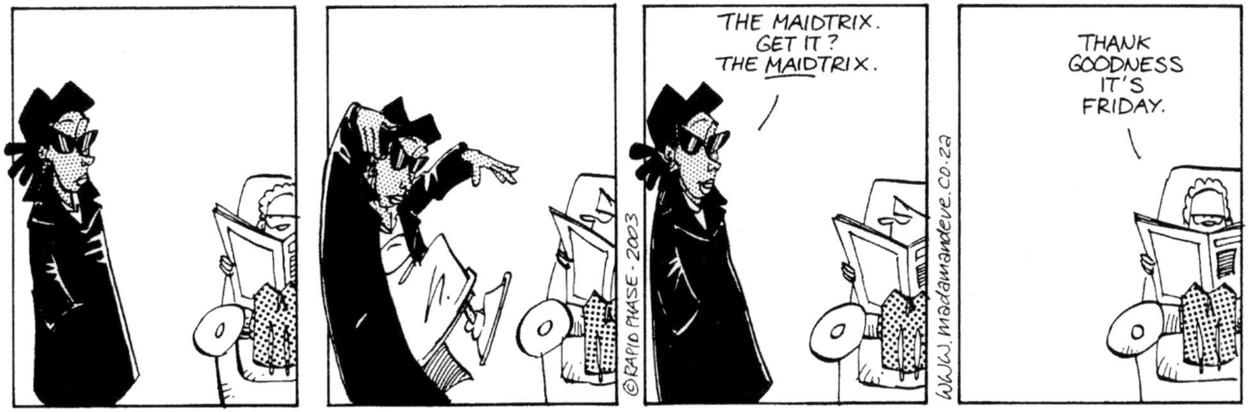
©RAPID PHASE - 2003
THE MAIDTRIX. GET IT? THE MAIDTRIX.
www.madamandeve.co.za
THANK GOODNESS IT'S FRIDAY.

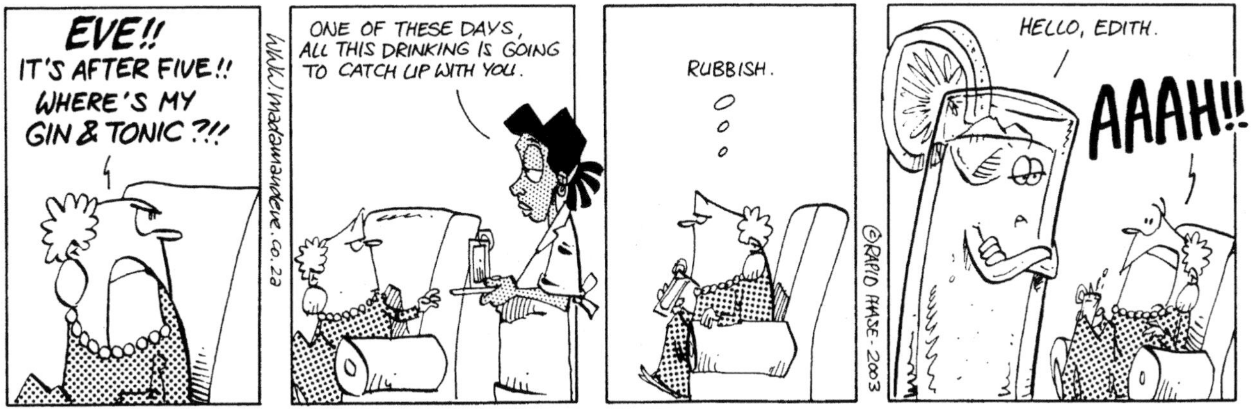
EVE!! IT'S AFTER FIVE!! WHERE'S MY GIN & TONIC?!!
www.madamandeve.co.za
ONE OF THESE DAYS, ALL THIS DRINKING IS GOING TO CATCH UP WITH YOU.
RUBBISH.
©RAPID PHASE - 2003
HELLO, EDITH.
AAAH!!

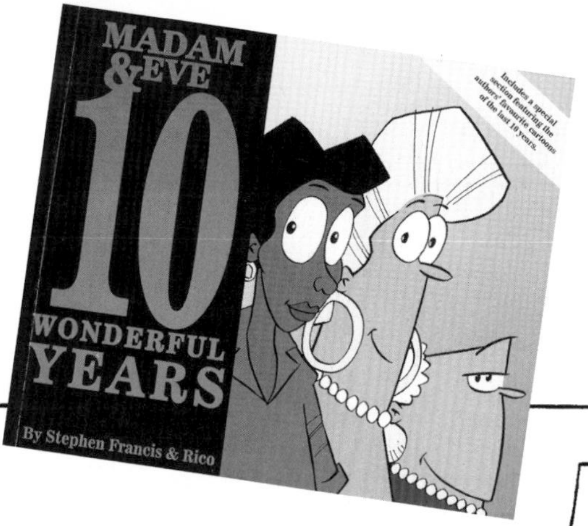
MADAM & EVE
10
WONDERFUL YEARS
By Stephen Francis & Rico
Includes a special section featuring the authors' favourite cartoons of the last 10 years.

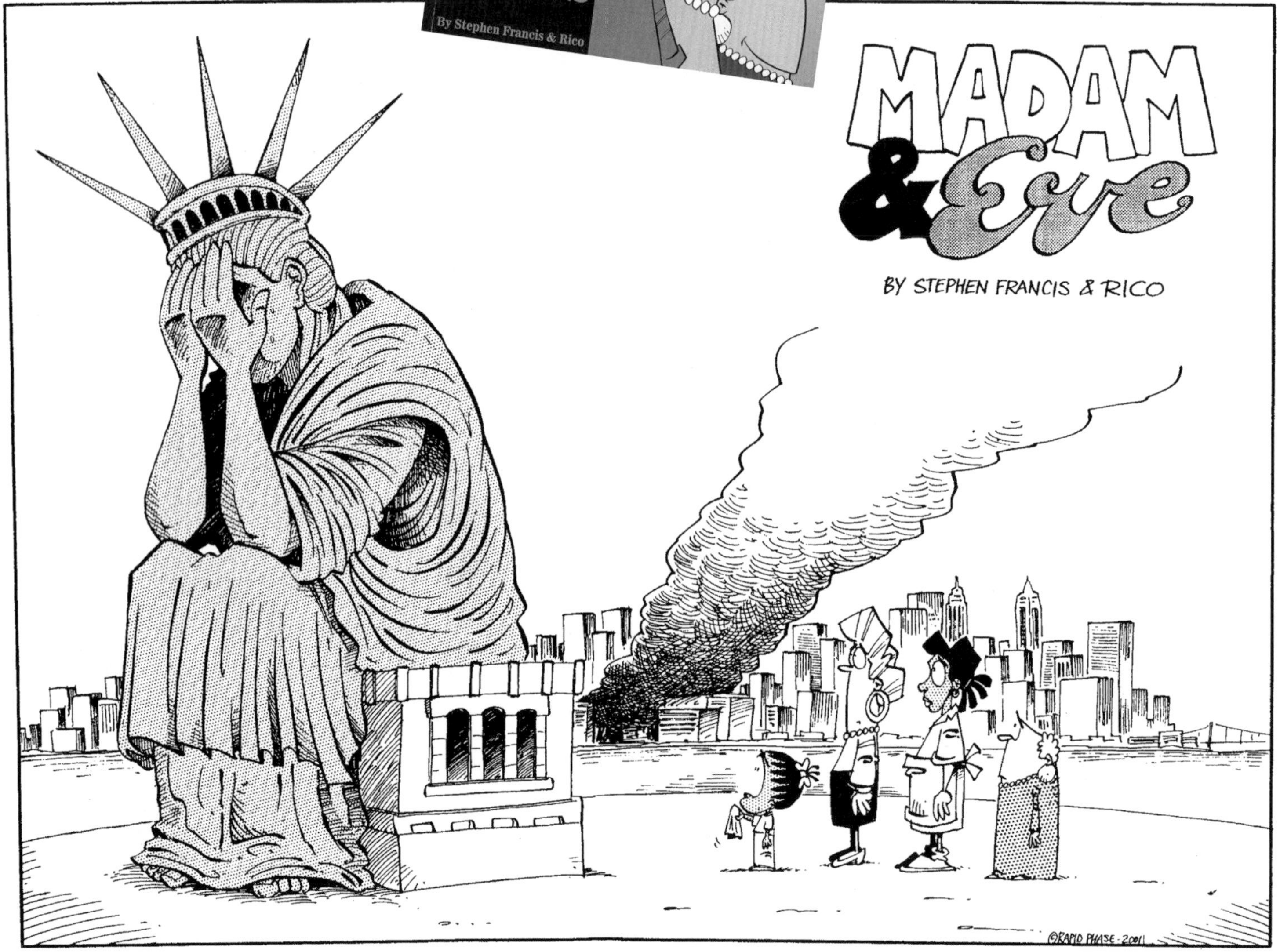
MADAM & Eve
BY STEPHEN FRANCIS & RICO
©RAPID PHASE·2001

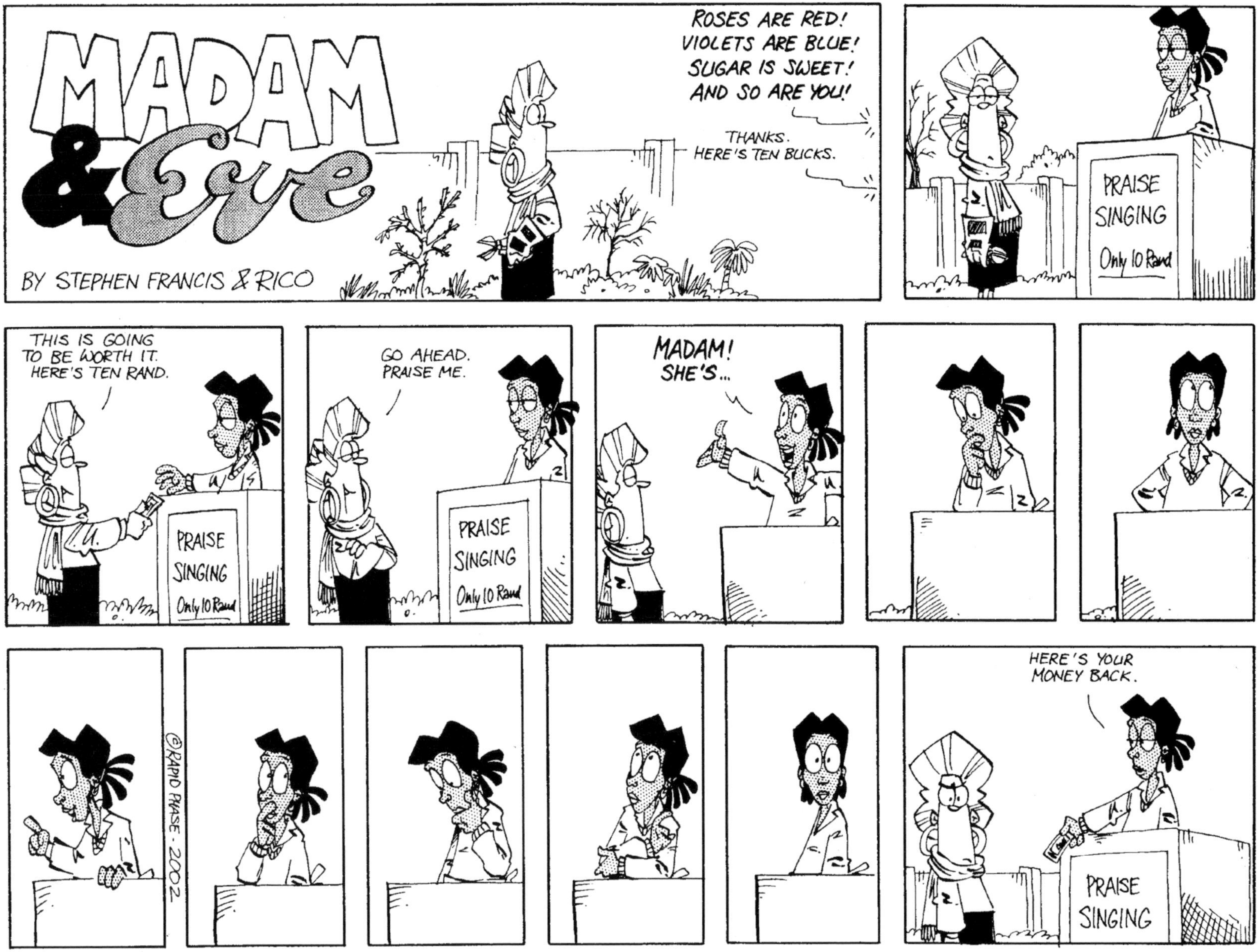
MADAM & Eve
BY STEPHEN FRANCIS & RICO
ROSES ARE RED! VIOLETS ARE BLUE! SUGAR IS SWEET! AND SO ARE YOU!
THANKS. HERE'S TEN BUCKS.
PRAISE SINGING Only 10 Rand
THIS IS GOING TO BE WORTH IT. HERE'S TEN RAND.
PRAISE SINGING Only 10 Rand
GO AHEAD. PRAISE ME.
PRAISE SINGING Only 10 Rand
MADAM! SHE'S...
©RAPID PHASE · 2002
HERE'S YOUR MONEY BACK.
PRAISE SINGING

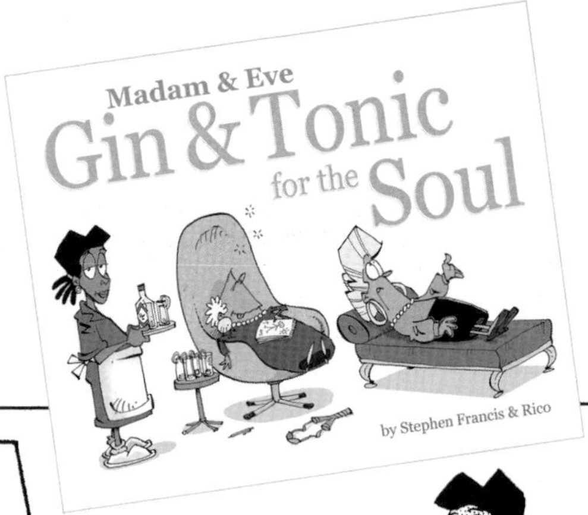
Madam & Eve
Gin & Tonic for the Soul
by Stephen Francis & Rico

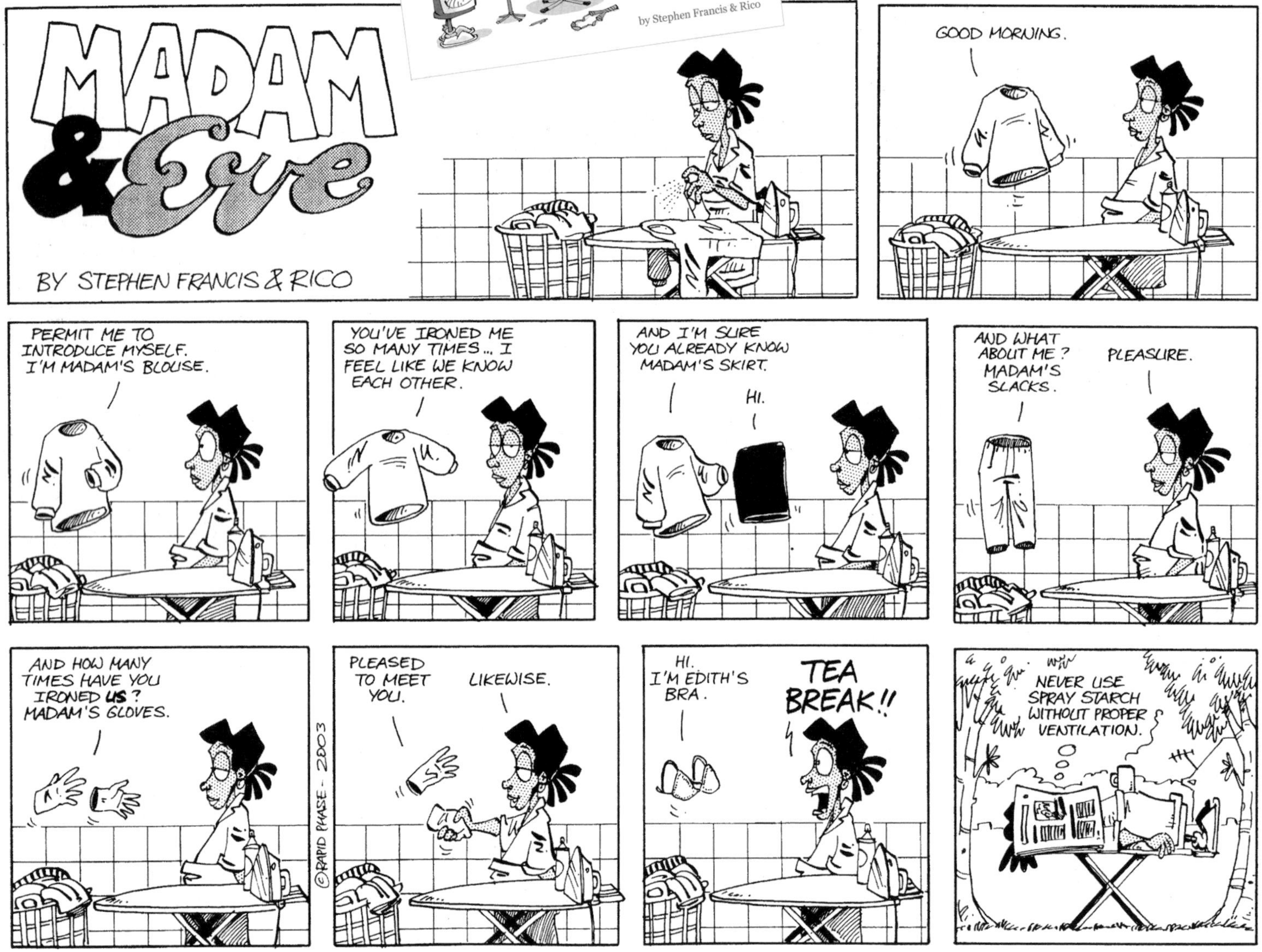
MADAM & Eve
BY STEPHEN FRANCIS & RICO
GOOD MORNING.
PERMIT ME TO INTRODUCE MYSELF. I'M MADAM'S BLOUSE.
YOU'VE IRONED ME SO MANY TIMES... I FEEL LIKE WE KNOW EACH OTHER.
AND I'M SURE YOU ALREADY KNOW MADAM'S SKIRT.
HI.
AND WHAT ABOUT ME? MADAM'S SLACKS.
PLEASURE.
AND HOW MANY TIMES HAVE YOU IRONED US? MADAM'S GLOVES.
©RAPID PHASE - 2003
PLEASED TO MEET YOU.
LIKEWISE.
HI. I'M EDITH'S BRA.
TEA BREAK!!
NEVER USE SPRAY STARCH WITHOUT PROPER VENTILATION.

MADAM & Eve
BY STEPHEN FRANCIS & RICO
WHIRRRR
©RAPID PHASE - 2004
JUST ONCE I'D LIKE TO KNOW WHERE ALL THESE PLASTIC HANGER GUYS COME FROM.

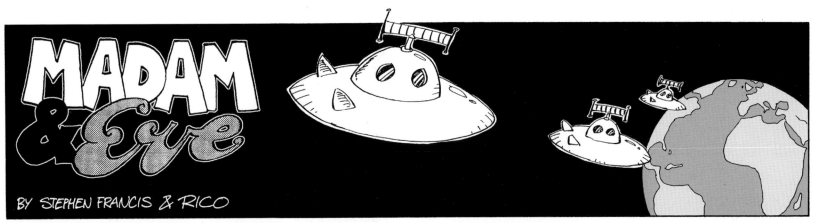

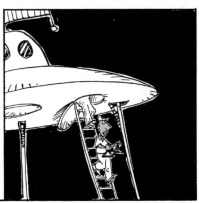

MADAM & Eve

BY STEPHEN FRANCIS & RICO

THE ICY WATERS OF THE ATLANTIC OCEAN, SOMEWHERE OFF THE COAST OF CAPE TOWN.

WHEN SUDDENLY A LARGE LOOMING SHADOW APPEARS...

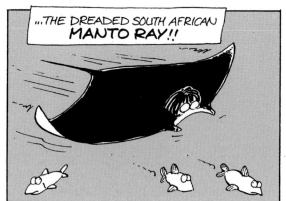

...THE DREADED SOUTH AFRICAN **MANTO RAY!!**

TRAVELLING WITH SEVERAL "BODYGUARD FISH", THE UNFATHOMABLE **MANTO** IS OFTEN WAY OUT OF ITS DEPTH.

UNPREDICTABLE AND OFTEN IRRATIONAL, THIS UNSTOPPABLE BEHEMOTH BARGES THROUGH WATERS WITH IMPUNITY.

ACME PHARMACEUTICALS

OW!!

BONK!!

ITS PECULIAR DIET CONSISTS OF SEA GARLIC, BEETROOT AND AFRICAN POTATOES.

CHOMP CHOMP

PREDATORS LIKE THE LEON FISH AVOID THE MANTO, AS IT IS OFTEN PROTECTED BY THE POWERFUL GIANT THABO TURTLE.

DA

AMPHIBIOUS BY NATURE, THE MANTO IS ABLE TO EXIST OUT OF WATER FOR LONG PERIODS OF TIME.

MEANWHILE... AT A CAPE TOWN RESTAURANT, A SMALL PUFF OF SECOND-HAND **SMOKE** WAFTS THROUGH THE BACK DOOR...

©RAPID PHASE - 2004

THE MANTO **STRIKES!!**

AAAAH!!

WAIT A MINUTE. ARE YOU **SURE** YOU SAW THIS ON THE DISCOVERY CHANNEL?

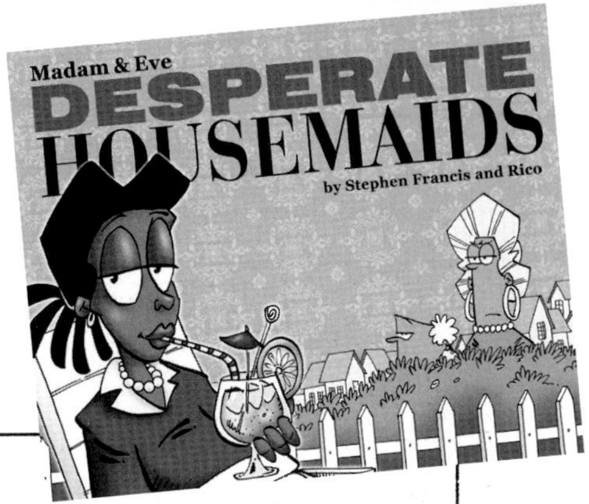
Madam & Eve
DESPERATE
HOUSEMAIDS
by Stephen Francis and Rico

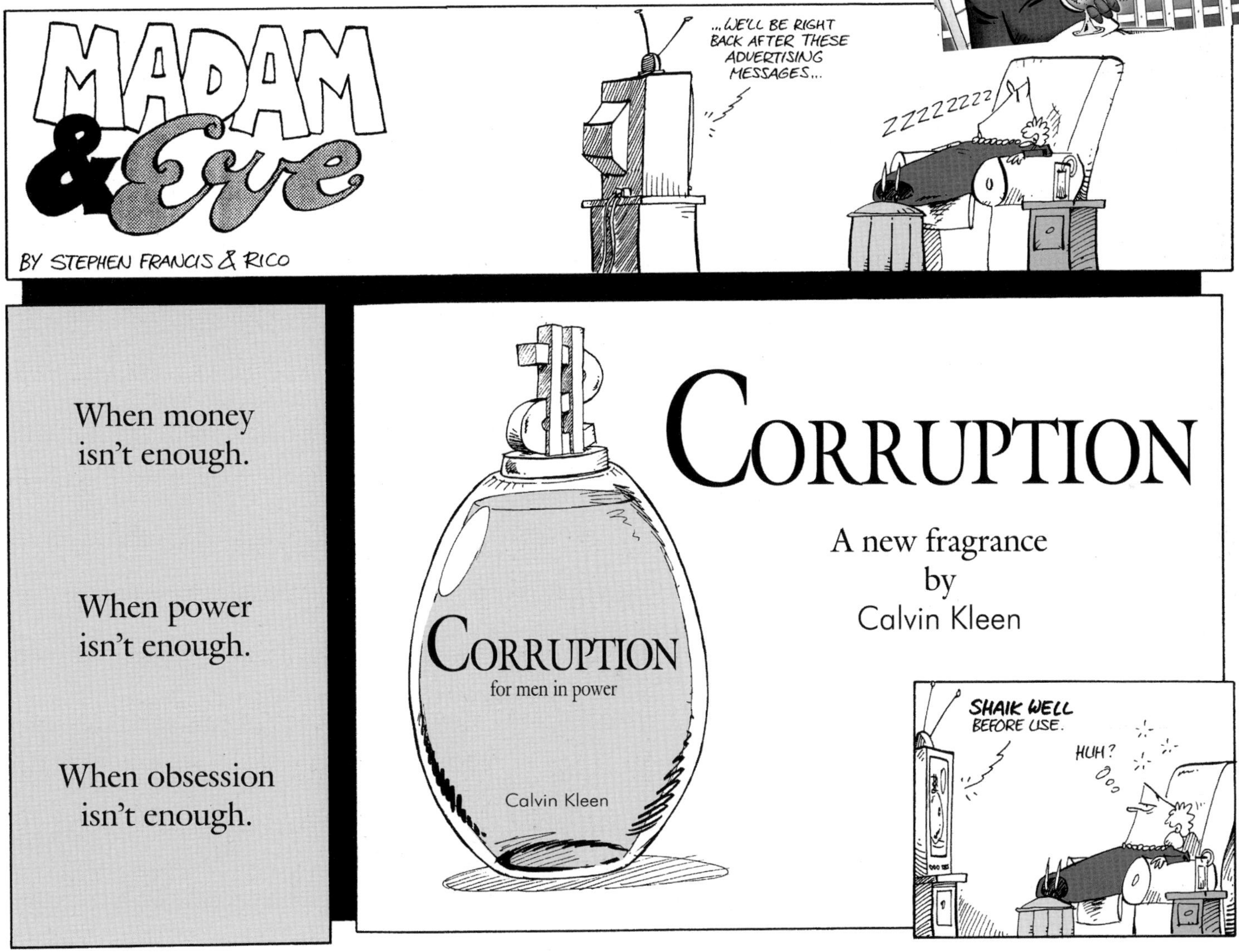
MADAM & Eve
BY STEPHEN FRANCIS & RICO
...WE'LL BE RIGHT BACK AFTER THESE ADVERTISING MESSAGES...
ZZZZZZZZ
When money isn't enough.
When power isn't enough.
When obsession isn't enough.
CORRUPTION
for men in power
Calvin Kleen
CORRUPTION
A new fragrance by Calvin Kleen
SHAIK WELL BEFORE USE.
HUH?

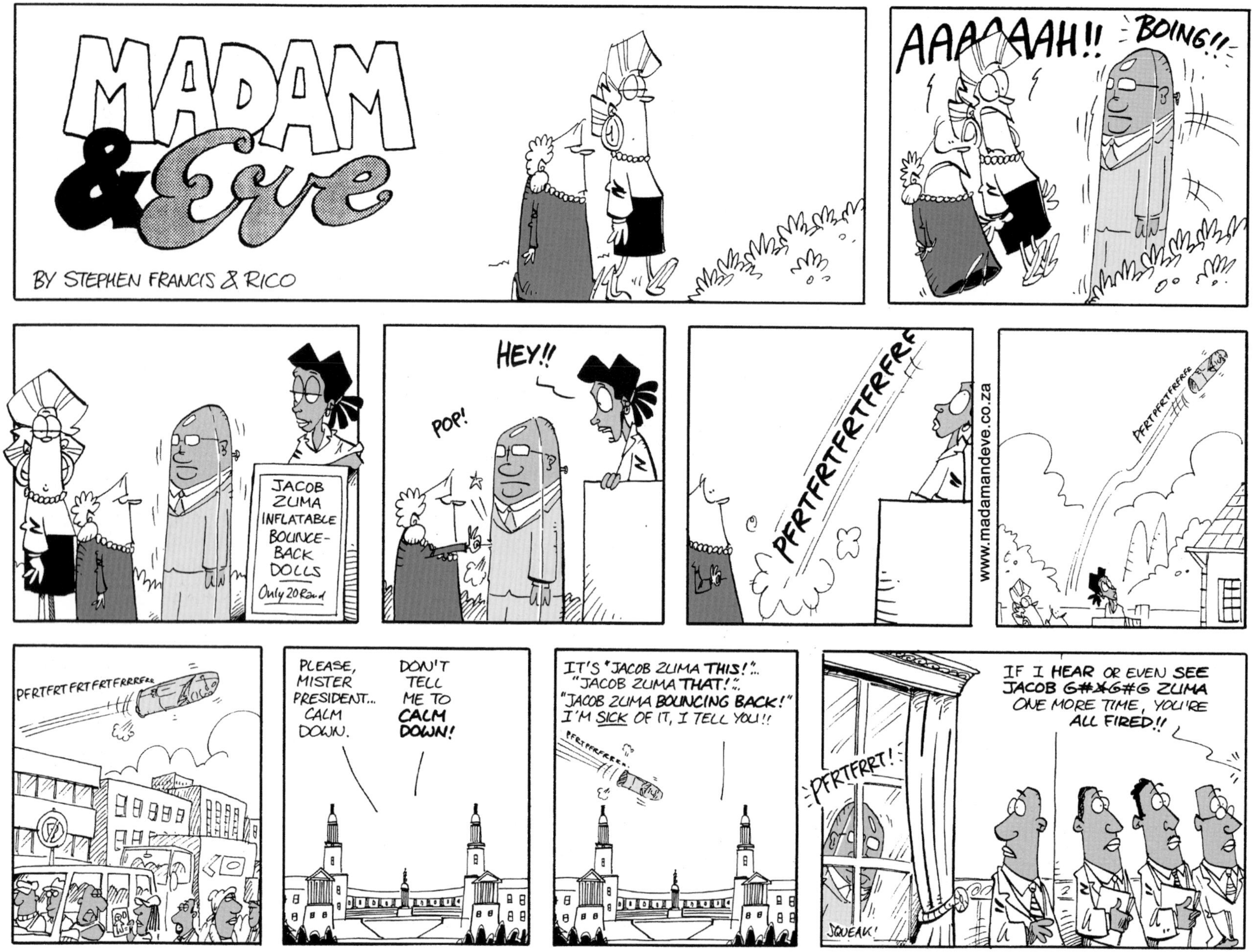
MADAM & Eve
BY STEPHEN FRANCIS & RICO
AAAAAAH!!
BOING!!
JACOB ZUMA INFLATABLE BOUNCE-BACK DOLLS
Only 20 Rand
POP!
HEY!!
PFRTFRTFRTFRFRF
www.madamandeve.co.za
PFRTPFRTFRFRF
PFRTFRTFRTFRTFRRRFRRR
PLEASE, MISTER PRESIDENT... CALM DOWN.
DON'T TELL ME TO CALM DOWN!
IT'S "JACOB ZUMA THIS!"... "JACOB ZUMA THAT!"... "JACOB ZUMA BOUNCING BACK!" I'M SICK OF IT, I TELL YOU!!
PFRTPFRFRRR
PFRTFRRT!
SQUEAK!
IF I HEAR OR EVEN SEE JACOB G#%G#G ZUMA ONE MORE TIME, YOU'RE ALL FIRED!!

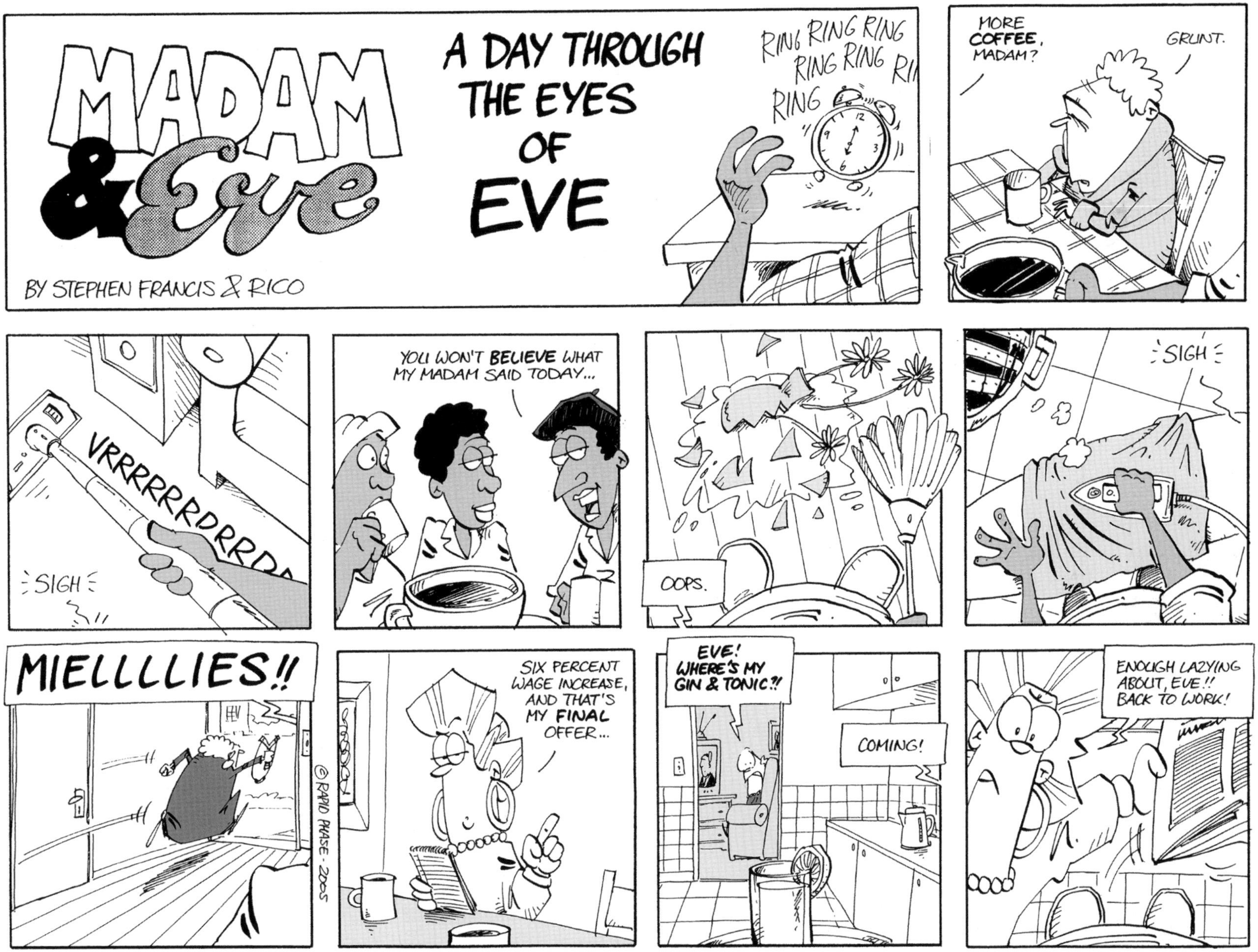
MADAM & Eve
A DAY THROUGH THE EYES OF EVE
BY STEPHEN FRANCIS & RICO
RING RING RING RING RING RI RING
MORE COFFEE, MADAM?
GRUNT.
VRRRRRRDRRRD
SIGH
YOU WON'T BELIEVE WHAT MY MADAM SAID TODAY...
OOPS.
SIGH
MIELLLLIES!!
© RAPID PHASE · 2005
SIX PERCENT WAGE INCREASE, AND THAT'S MY FINAL OFFER...
EVE! WHERE'S MY GIN & TONIC?!
COMING!
ENOUGH LAZYING ABOUT, EVE!! BACK TO WORK!

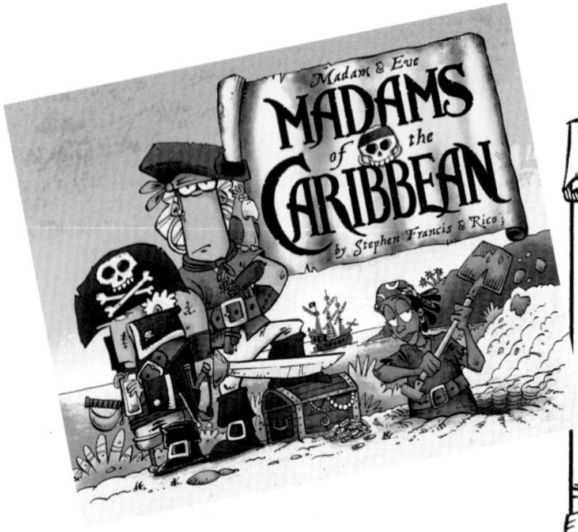
Madam & Eve
MADAMS of the CARIBBEAN
by Stephen Francis & Rico

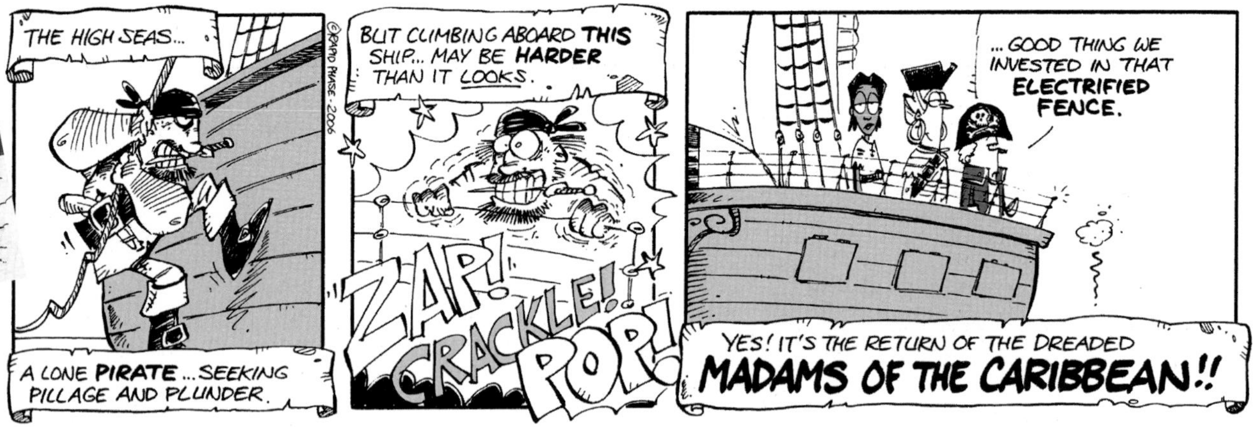
THE HIGH SEAS...
A LONE PIRATE... SEEKING PILLAGE AND PLUNDER.
©RAPID PHASE · 2006
BUT CLIMBING ABOARD THIS SHIP... MAY BE HARDER THAN IT LOOKS.
ZAP! CRACKLE! POP!
...GOOD THING WE INVESTED IN THAT ELECTRIFIED FENCE.
YES! IT'S THE RETURN OF THE DREADED
MADAMS OF THE CARIBBEAN!!

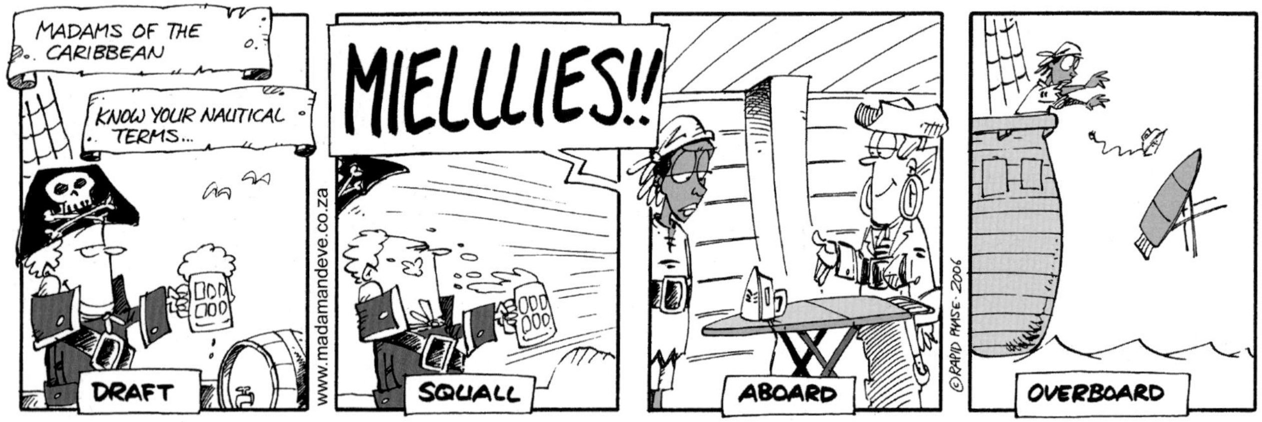
MADAMS OF THE CARIBBEAN
KNOW YOUR NAUTICAL TERMS...
DRAFT
www.madamandeve.co.za
MIELLLIES!!
SQUALL
ABOARD
©RAPID PHASE · 2006
OVERBOARD

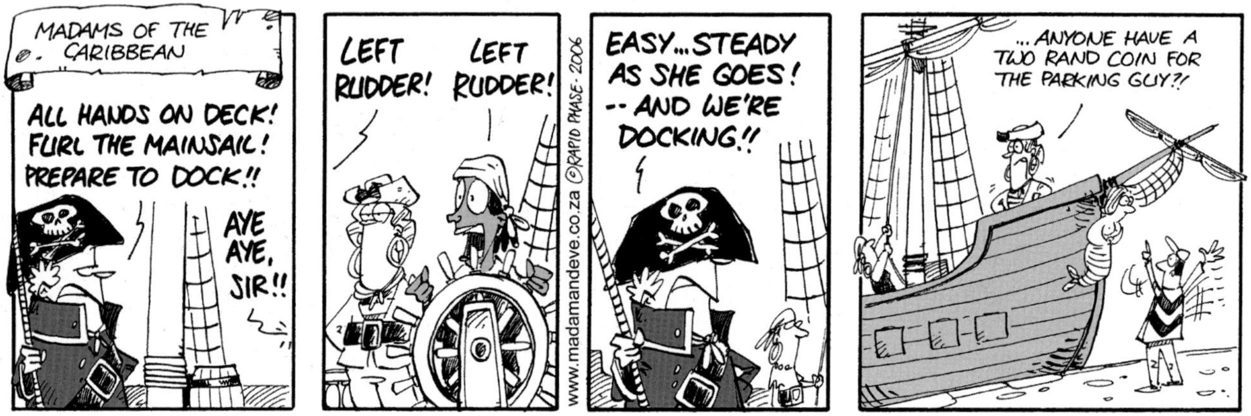
MADAMS OF THE CARIBBEAN
ALL HANDS ON DECK! FURL THE MAINSAIL! PREPARE TO DOCK!!
AYE AYE, SIR!!
LEFT RUDDER!
LEFT RUDDER!
©RAPID PHASE · 2006
www.madamandeve.co.za
EASY...STEADY AS SHE GOES! -- AND WE'RE DOCKING!!
...ANYONE HAVE A TWO RAND COIN FOR THE PARKING GUY?!

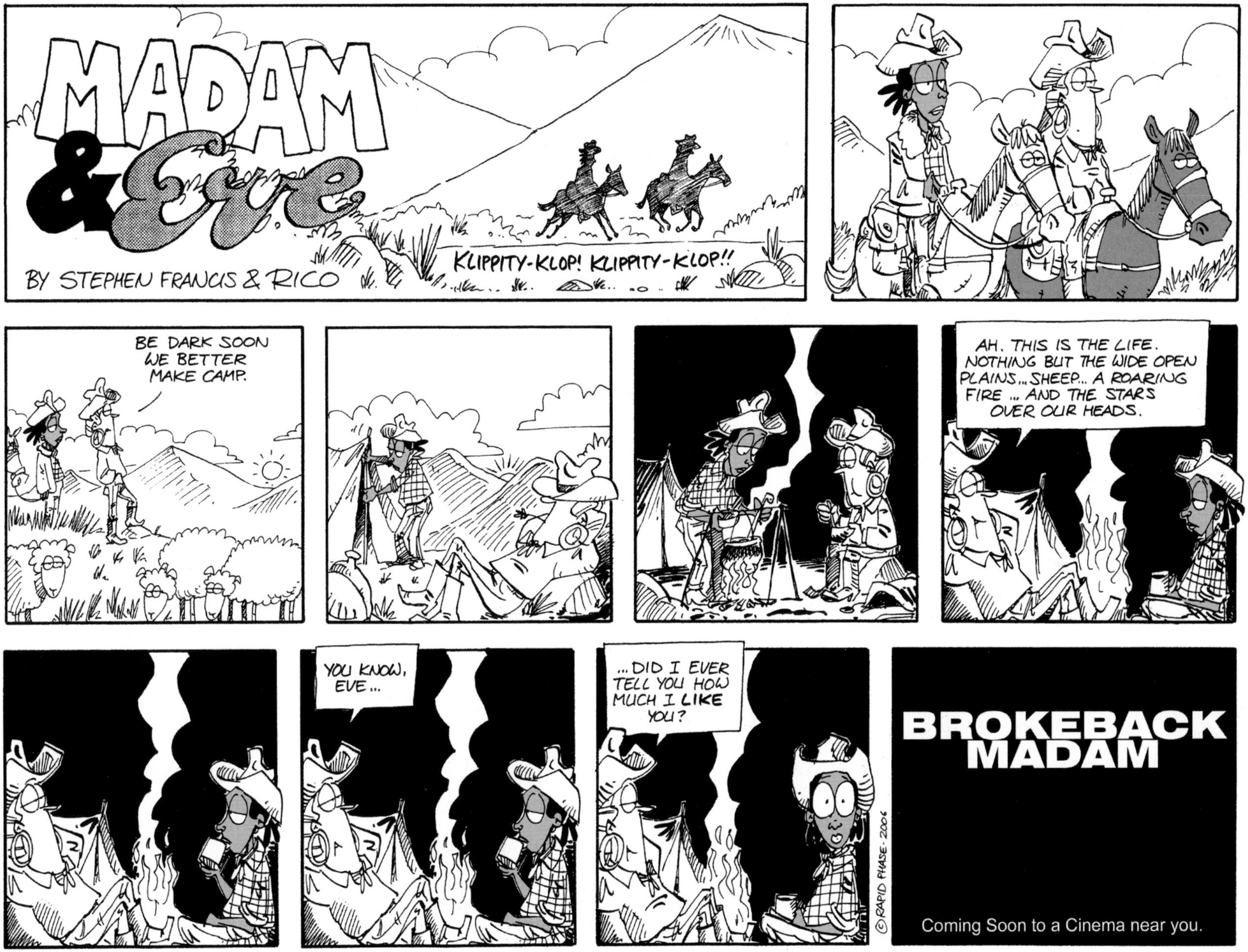
MADAM & Eve
BY STEPHEN FRANCIS & RICO
KLIPPITY-KLOP! KLIPPITY-KLOP!!
BE DARK SOON WE BETTER MAKE CAMP.
AH. THIS IS THE LIFE. NOTHING BUT THE WIDE OPEN PLAINS... SHEEP... A ROARING FIRE ... AND THE STARS OVER OUR HEADS.
YOU KNOW, EVE...
...DID I EVER TELL YOU HOW MUCH I LIKE YOU?
© RAPID PHASE 2006
BROKEBACK MADAM
Coming Soon to a Cinema near you.

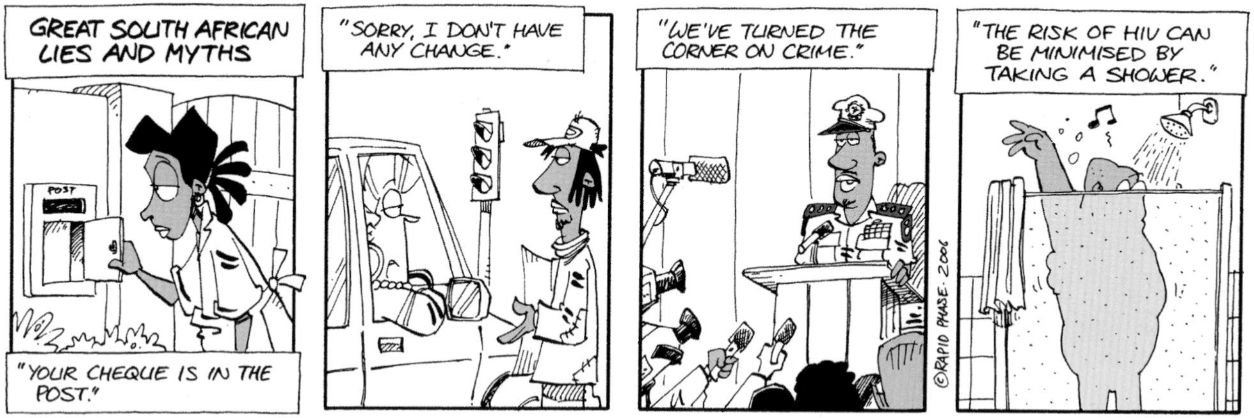

GREAT SOUTH AFRICAN LIES AND MYTHS
"YOUR CHEQUE IS IN THE POST."
"SORRY, I DON'T HAVE ANY CHANGE."
"WE'VE TURNED THE CORNER ON CRIME."
©RAPID PHASE - 2006
"THE RISK OF HIV CAN BE MINIMISED BY TAKING A SHOWER."

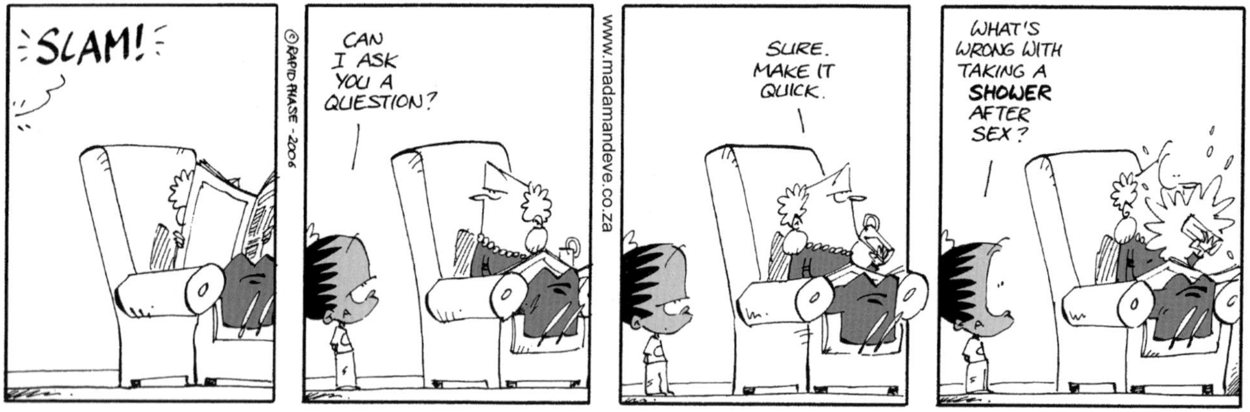

SLAM!
© RAPID PHASE - 2006
CAN I ASK YOU A QUESTION?
www.madamandeve.co.za
SURE. MAKE IT QUICK.
WHAT'S WRONG WITH TAKING A SHOWER AFTER SEX?

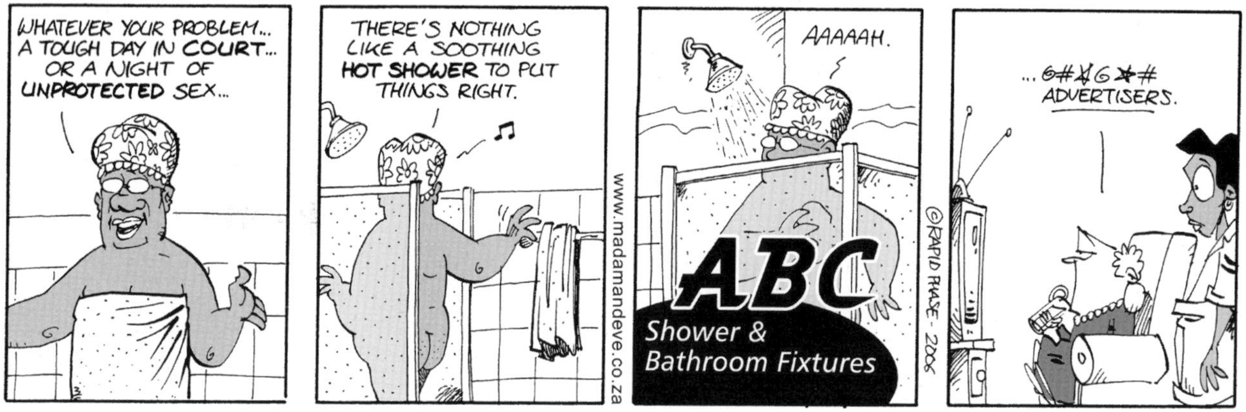

WHATEVER YOUR PROBLEM... A TOUGH DAY IN COURT... OR A NIGHT OF UNPROTECTED SEX...
THERE'S NOTHING LIKE A SOOTHING HOT SHOWER TO PUT THINGS RIGHT.
www.madamandeve.co.za
AAAAAH.
ABC
Shower & Bathroom Fixtures
©RAPID PHASE - 2006
ADVERTISERS.

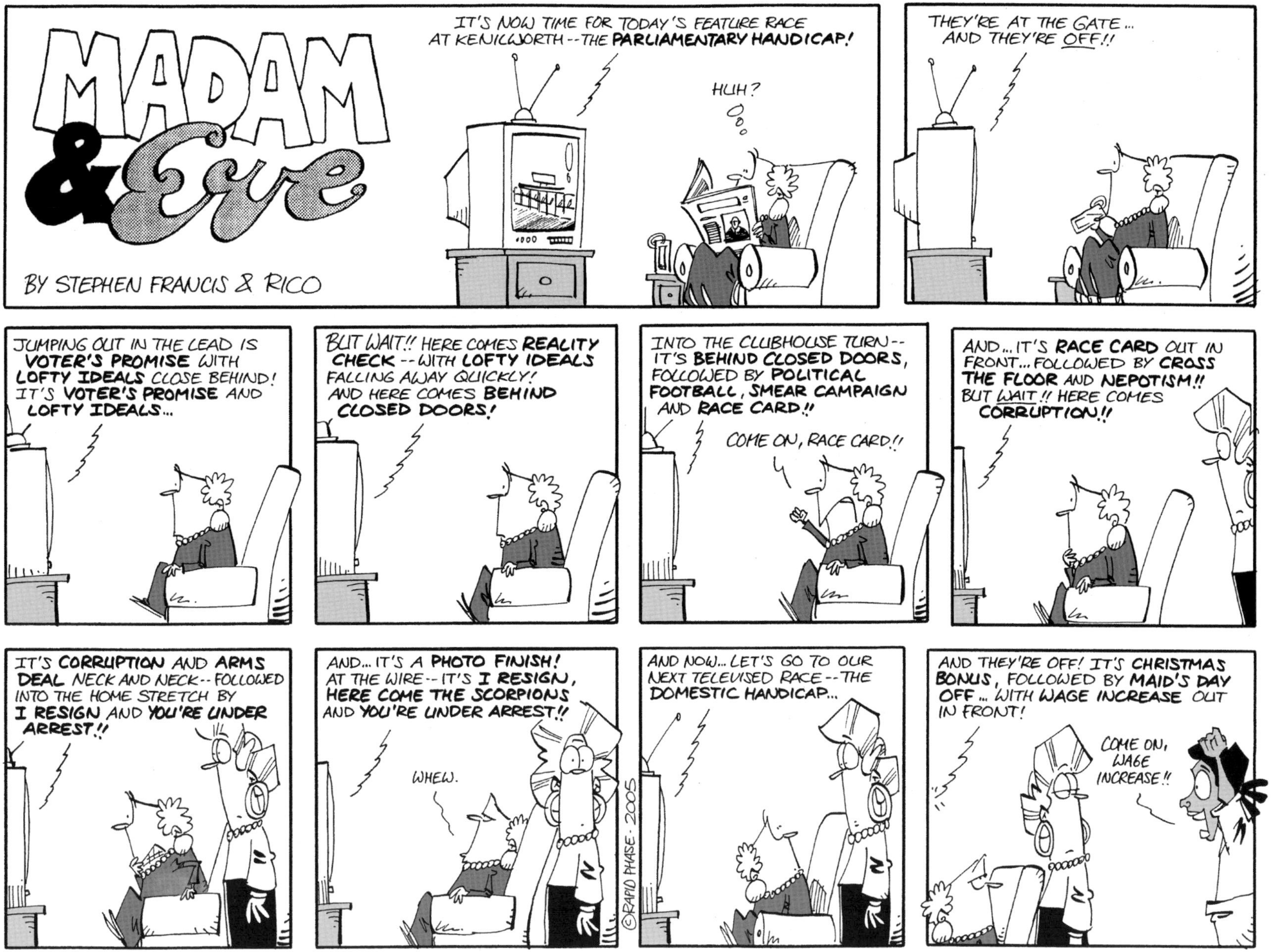
MADAM & Eve
BY STEPHEN FRANCIS & RICO
IT'S NOW TIME FOR TODAY'S FEATURE RACE AT KENILWORTH -- THE PARLIAMENTARY HANDICAP!
HUH?
THEY'RE AT THE GATE... AND THEY'RE OFF!!
JUMPING OUT IN THE LEAD IS VOTER'S PROMISE WITH LOFTY IDEALS CLOSE BEHIND! IT'S VOTER'S PROMISE AND LOFTY IDEALS...
BUT WAIT!! HERE COMES REALITY CHECK -- WITH LOFTY IDEALS FALLING AWAY QUICKLY! AND HERE COMES BEHIND CLOSED DOORS!
INTO THE CLUBHOUSE TURN -- IT'S BEHIND CLOSED DOORS, FOLLOWED BY POLITICAL FOOTBALL, SMEAR CAMPAIGN AND RACE CARD!!
COME ON, RACE CARD!!
AND... IT'S RACE CARD OUT IN FRONT... FOLLOWED BY CROSS THE FLOOR AND NEPOTISM!! BUT WAIT!! HERE COMES CORRUPTION!!
IT'S CORRUPTION AND ARMS DEAL NECK AND NECK -- FOLLOWED INTO THE HOME STRETCH BY I RESIGN AND YOU'RE UNDER ARREST!!
AND... IT'S A PHOTO FINISH! AT THE WIRE -- IT'S I RESIGN, HERE COME THE SCORPIONS AND YOU'RE UNDER ARREST!!
WHEW.
©RAPID PHASE · 2005
AND NOW... LET'S GO TO OUR NEXT TELEVISED RACE -- THE DOMESTIC HANDICAP...
AND THEY'RE OFF! IT'S CHRISTMAS BONUS, FOLLOWED BY MAID'S DAY OFF... WITH WAGE INCREASE OUT IN FRONT!
COME ON, WAGE INCREASE!!

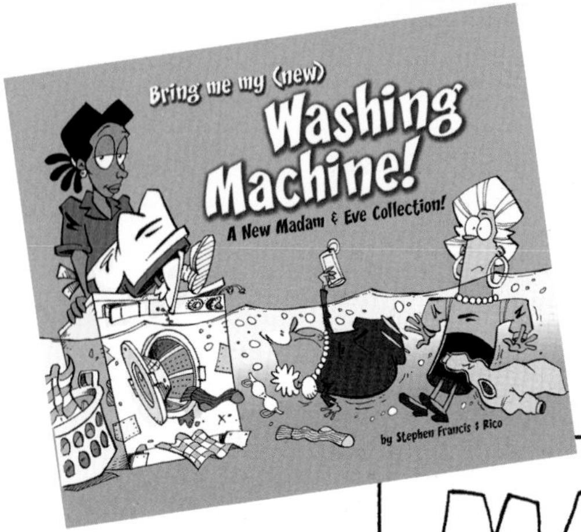
Bring me my (new)
Washing Machine!
A New Madam & Eve Collection!
by Stephen Francis & Rico

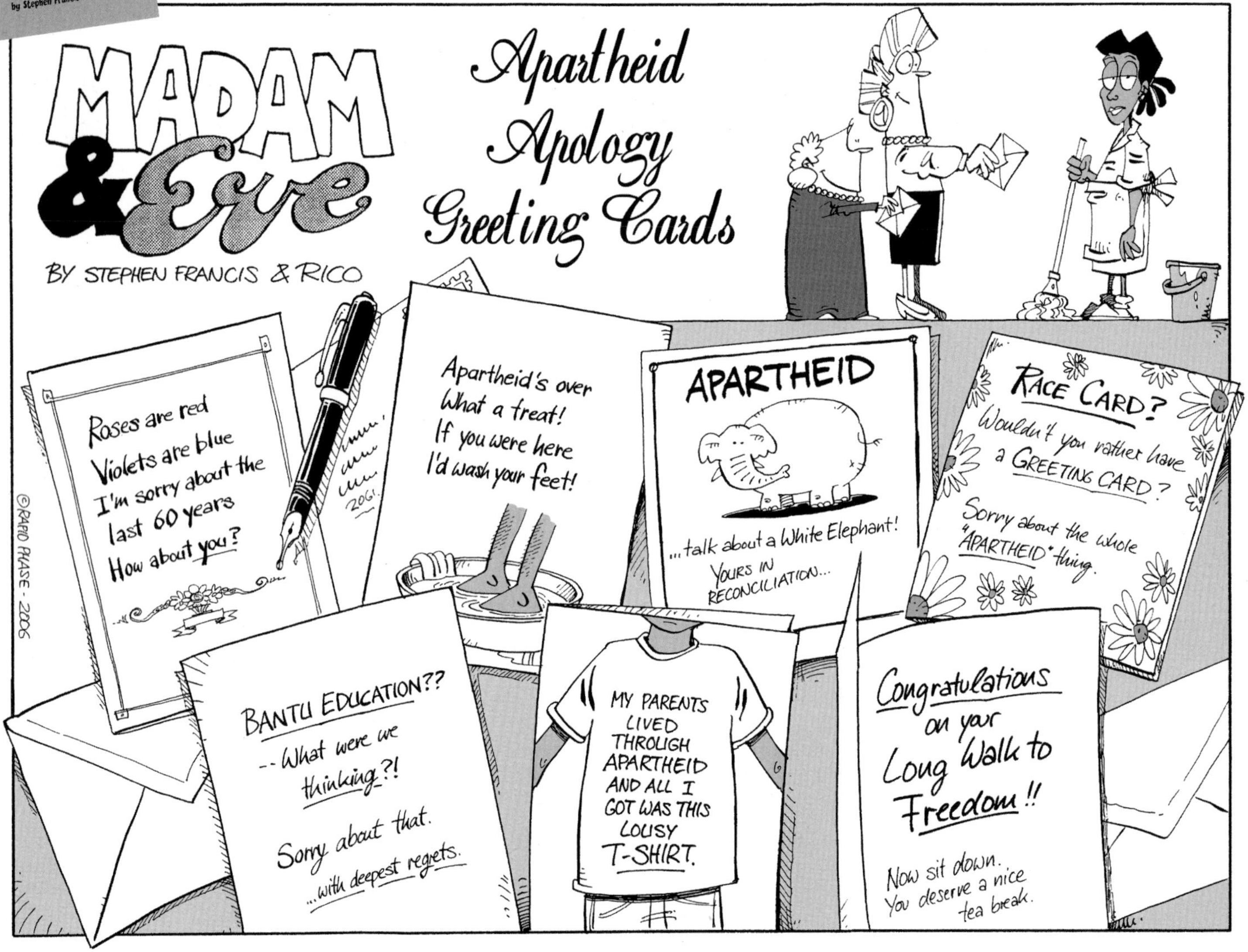
MADAM & Eve
BY STEPHEN FRANCIS & RICO
Apartheid Apology Greeting Cards
Roses are red
Violets are blue
I'm sorry about the
last 60 years
How about you?
©RAPID PHASE · 2006
Apartheid's over
What a treat!
If you were here
I'd wash your feet!
APARTHEID
...talk about a White Elephant!
YOURS IN RECONCILIATION...
RACE CARD?
Wouldn't you rather have a GREETING CARD?
Sorry about the whole "APARTHEID" thing.
BANTU EDUCATION??
-- What were we thinking?!
Sorry about that.
...with deepest regrets.
MY PARENTS LIVED THROUGH APARTHEID AND ALL I GOT WAS THIS LOUSY T-SHIRT.
Congratulations on your Long Walk to Freedom!!
Now sit down. You deserve a nice tea break.

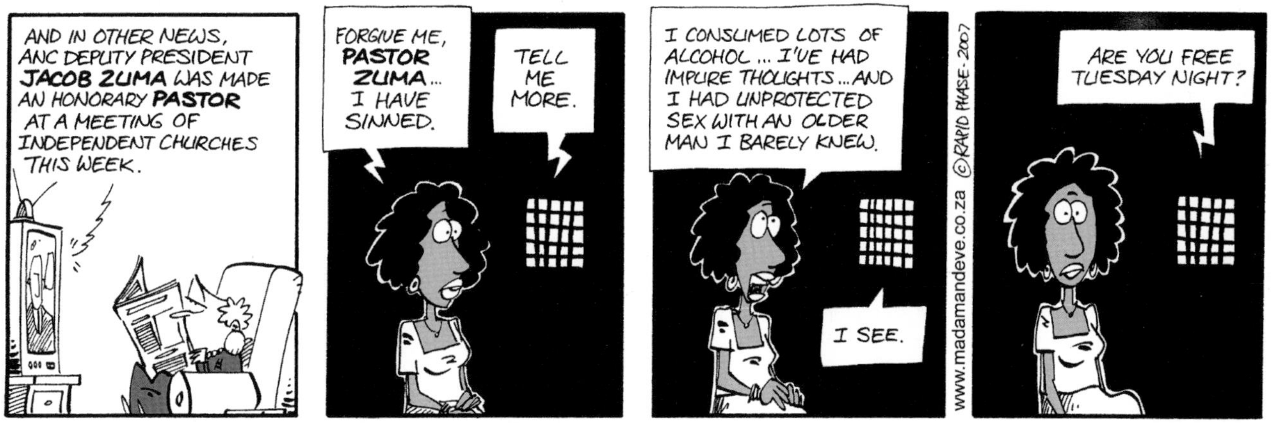
AND IN OTHER NEWS, ANC DEPUTY PRESIDENT **JACOB ZUMA** WAS MADE AN HONORARY **PASTOR** AT A MEETING OF INDEPENDENT CHURCHES THIS WEEK.
FORGIVE ME, **PASTOR ZUMA**... I HAVE SINNED.
TELL ME MORE.
I CONSUMED LOTS OF ALCOHOL ... I'VE HAD IMPURE THOUGHTS ... AND I HAD UNPROTECTED SEX WITH AN OLDER MAN I BARELY KNEW.
I SEE.
www.madamandeve.co.za ©RAPID PHASE 2007
ARE YOU FREE TUESDAY NIGHT?

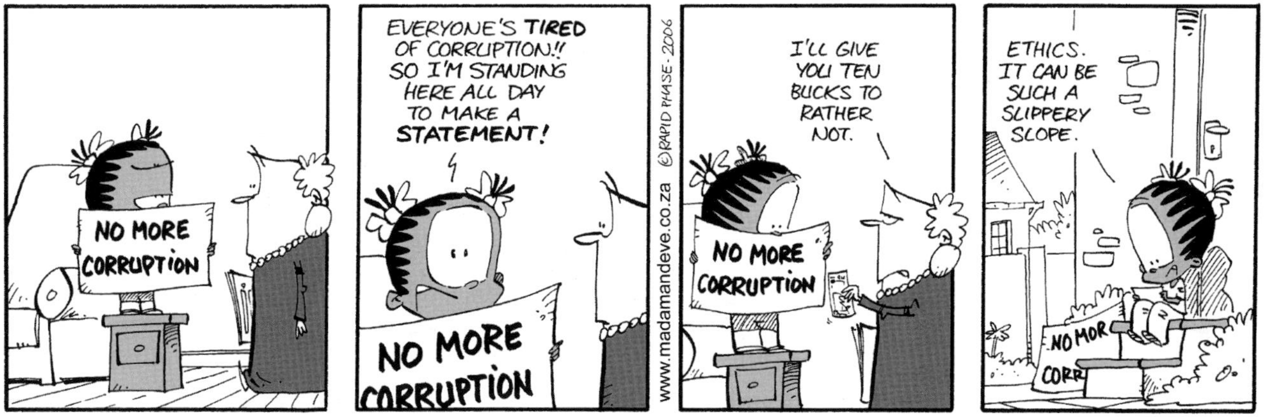
NO MORE CORRUPTION
EVERYONE'S **TIRED** OF CORRUPTION!! SO I'M STANDING HERE ALL DAY TO MAKE A **STATEMENT!**
NO MORE CORRUPTION
www.madamandeve.co.za ©RAPID PHASE 2006
I'LL GIVE YOU TEN BUCKS TO RATHER NOT.
NO MORE CORRUPTION
ETHICS. IT CAN BE SUCH A SLIPPERY SLOPE.
NO MOR CORR

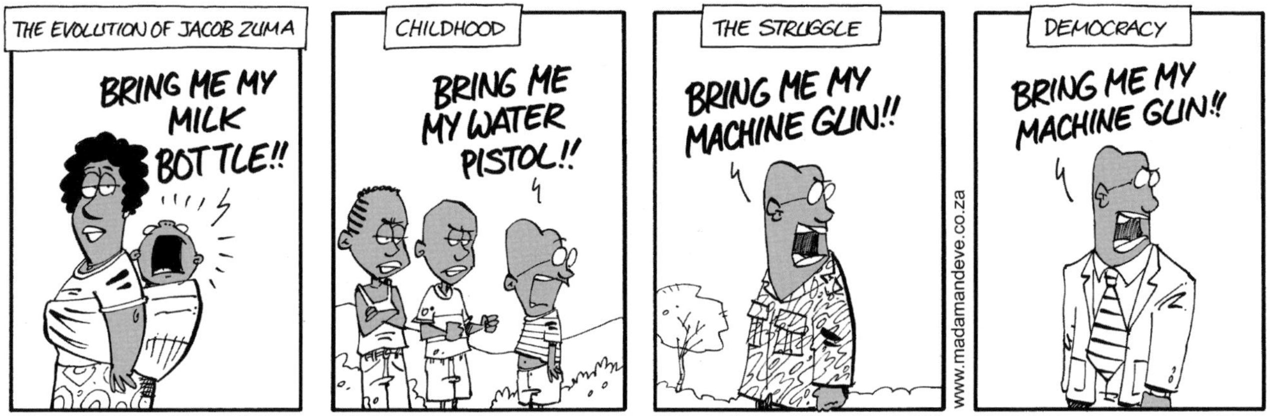
THE EVOLUTION OF JACOB ZUMA
BRING ME MY MILK BOTTLE!!
CHILDHOOD
BRING ME MY WATER PISTOL!!
THE STRUGGLE
BRING ME MY MACHINE GUN!!
www.madamandeve.co.za
DEMOCRACY
BRING ME MY MACHINE GUN!!

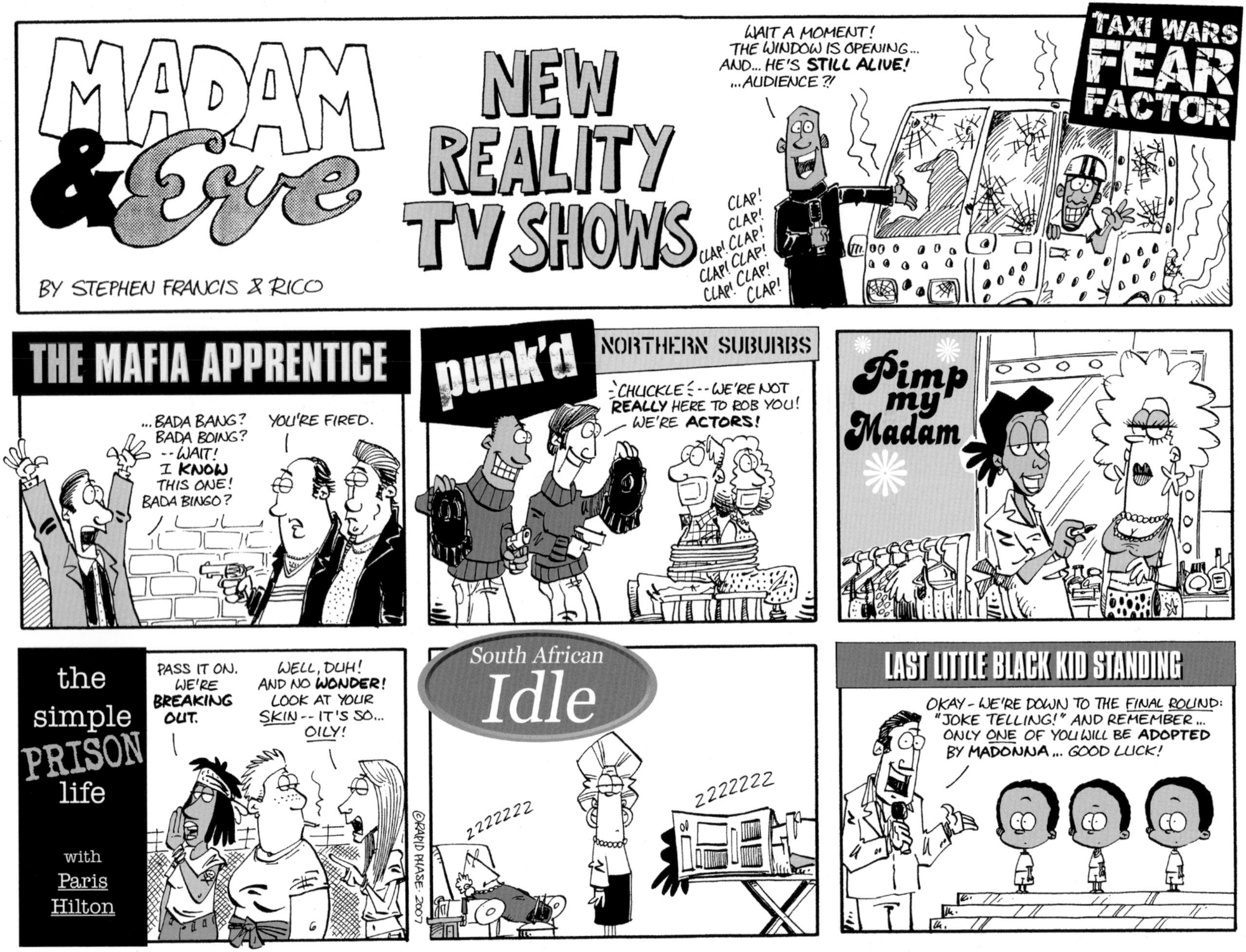
MADAM & Eve
NEW REALITY TV SHOWS
BY STEPHEN FRANCIS & RICO
WAIT A MOMENT! THE WINDOW IS OPENING... AND... HE'S STILL ALIVE! ...AUDIENCE?!
CLAP! CLAP! CLAP! CLAP! CLAP! CLAP! CLAP! CLAP! CLAP!
TAXI WARS FEAR FACTOR
THE MAFIA APPRENTICE
...BADA BANG? BADA BOING? --WAIT! I KNOW THIS ONE! BADA BINGO?
YOU'RE FIRED.
punk'd
NORTHERN SUBURBS
CHUCKLE --WE'RE NOT REALLY HERE TO ROB YOU! WE'RE ACTORS!
Pimp my Madam
the simple PRISON life with Paris Hilton
PASS IT ON. WE'RE BREAKING OUT.
WELL, DUH! AND NO WONDER! LOOK AT YOUR SKIN--IT'S SO... OILY!
©RAPID PHASE 2007
South African Idle
ZZZZZZZ
ZZZZZZZ
LAST LITTLE BLACK KID STANDING
OKAY-WE'RE DOWN TO THE FINAL ROUND: "JOKE TELLING!" AND REMEMBER... ONLY ONE OF YOU WILL BE ADOPTED BY MADONNA... GOOD LUCK!

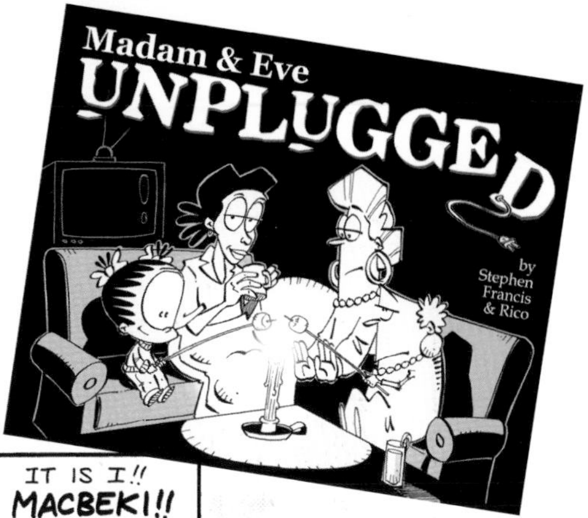
Madam & Eve
UNPLUGGED
by Stephen Francis & Rico

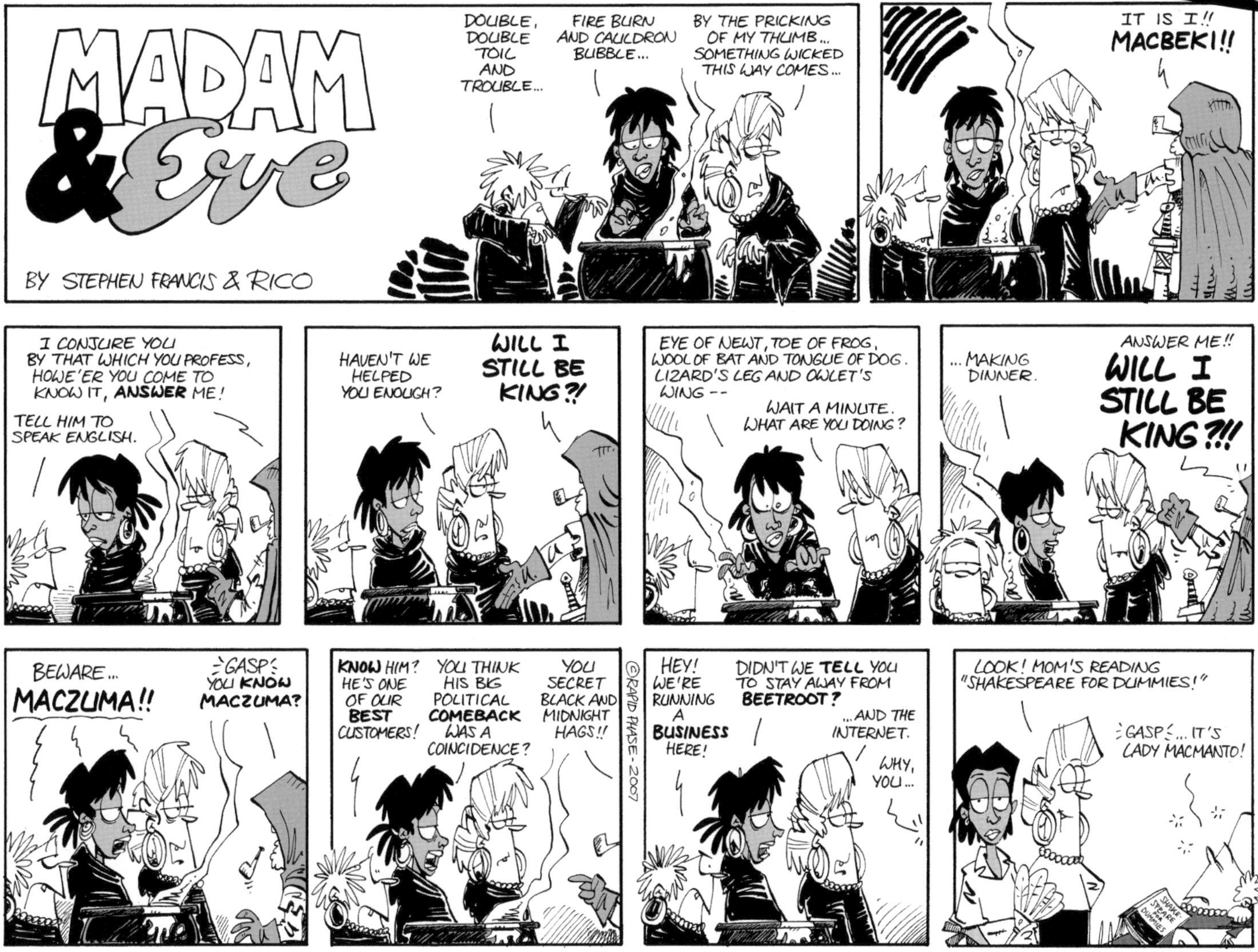
MADAM & Eve
BY STEPHEN FRANCIS & RICO
DOUBLE, DOUBLE TOIL AND TROUBLE...
FIRE BURN AND CAULDRON BUBBLE...
BY THE PRICKING OF MY THUMB... SOMETHING WICKED THIS WAY COMES...
IT IS I!! MACBEKI!!
I CONJURE YOU BY THAT WHICH YOU PROFESS, HOWE'ER YOU COME TO KNOW IT, ANSWER ME!
TELL HIM TO SPEAK ENGLISH.
HAVEN'T WE HELPED YOU ENOUGH?
WILL I STILL BE KING?!
EYE OF NEWT, TOE OF FROG, WOOL OF BAT AND TONGUE OF DOG. LIZARD'S LEG AND OWLET'S WING --
WAIT A MINUTE. WHAT ARE YOU DOING?
...MAKING DINNER.
ANSWER ME!! WILL I STILL BE KING?!!
BEWARE... MACZUMA!!
GASP YOU KNOW MACZUMA?
KNOW HIM? HE'S ONE OF OUR BEST CUSTOMERS!
YOU THINK HIS BIG POLITICAL COMEBACK WAS A COINCIDENCE?
YOU SECRET BLACK AND MIDNIGHT HAGS!!
©RAPID PHASE·2007
HEY! WE'RE RUNNING A BUSINESS HERE!
DIDN'T WE TELL YOU TO STAY AWAY FROM BEETROOT?
...AND THE INTERNET.
WHY, YOU...
LOOK! MOM'S READING "SHAKESPEARE FOR DUMMIES!"
GASP... IT'S LADY MACMANTO!
SHAKESPEARE FOR DUMMIES

MADAM & EVE

BY STEPHEN FRANCIS & RICO

THE TRIBE HAVE MADE THEIR DECISION! THE PERSON WHO WILL BE LEAVING THE ISLAND IS...

...ROBERT MUGABE!

...WHO, ME?!

SORRY, BOB. THE TRIBE HAS SPOKEN. YOU'VE BEEN VOTED OUT.

NO I HAVEN'T.

WE'RE REALLY SORRY, BOB. BUT WE ALL WANT YOU TO LEAVE THE ISLAND.

NO YOU DON'T.

BOB-- SEE FOR YOURSELF! LOOK AT THE VOTING RESULTS! YOU'RE HISTORY!!

NO I'M NOT.

YOU'RE OUT, BOB! IT'S PRACTICALLY UNANIMOUS!!

NO IT ISN'T.

©RICO PHASE · 2008

DAMMIT BOB!! YOU'VE GOT TO FACE REALITY!!

NO I DON'T.

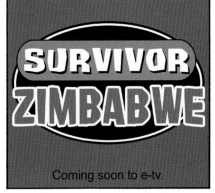

SURVIVOR ZIMBABWE

Coming soon to e-tv.

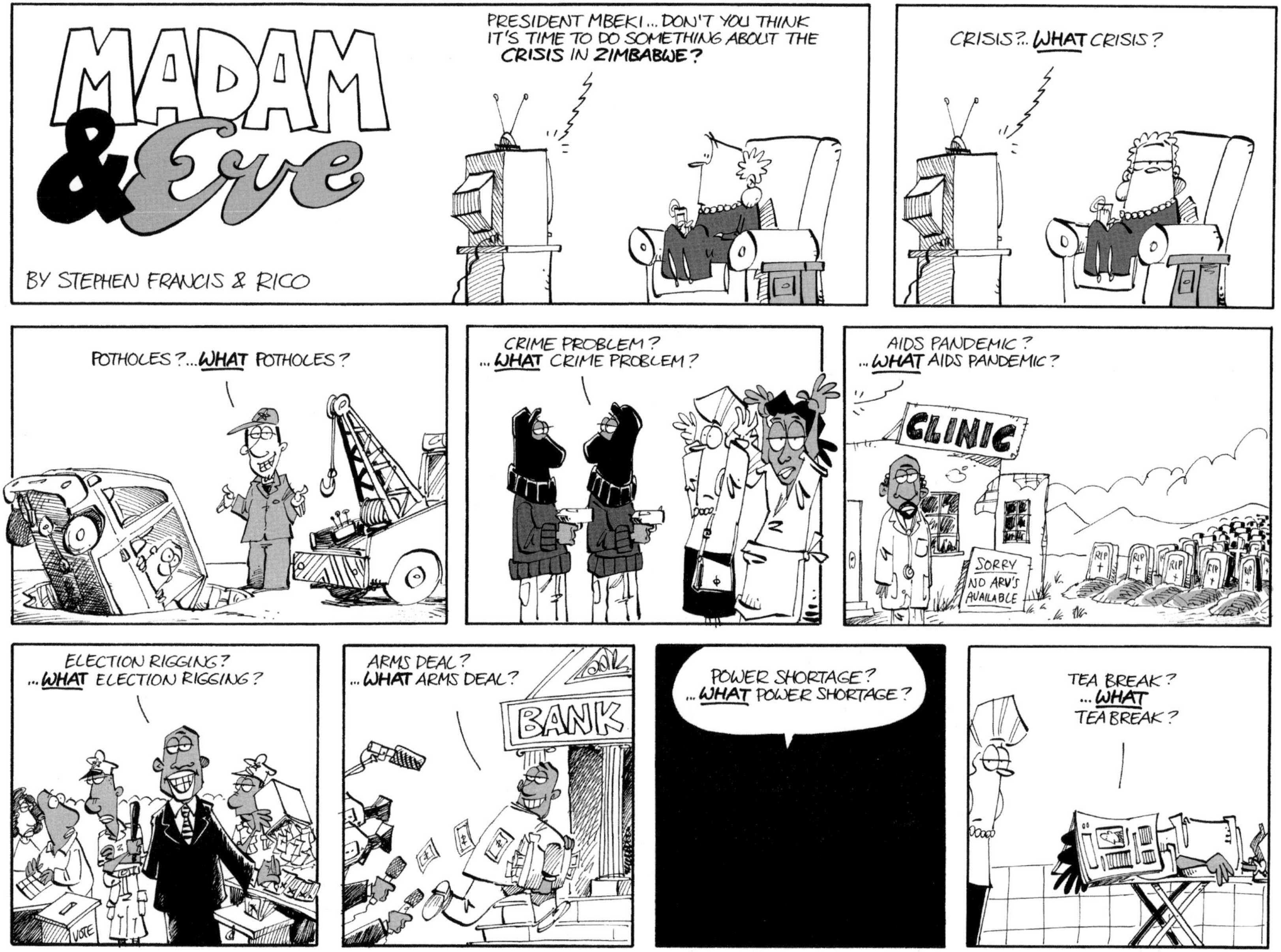
MADAM & Eve
BY STEPHEN FRANCIS & RICO
PRESIDENT MBEKI... DON'T YOU THINK IT'S TIME TO DO SOMETHING ABOUT THE CRISIS IN ZIMBABWE?
CRISIS?.. WHAT CRISIS?
POTHOLES?... WHAT POTHOLES?
CRIME PROBLEM? ... WHAT CRIME PROBLEM?
AIDS PANDEMIC? ... WHAT AIDS PANDEMIC?
CLINIC
SORRY NO ARV'S AVAILABLE
ELECTION RIGGING? ... WHAT ELECTION RIGGING?
VOTE
ARMS DEAL? ... WHAT ARMS DEAL?
BANK
POWER SHORTAGE? ... WHAT POWER SHORTAGE?
TEA BREAK? ... WHAT TEA BREAK?

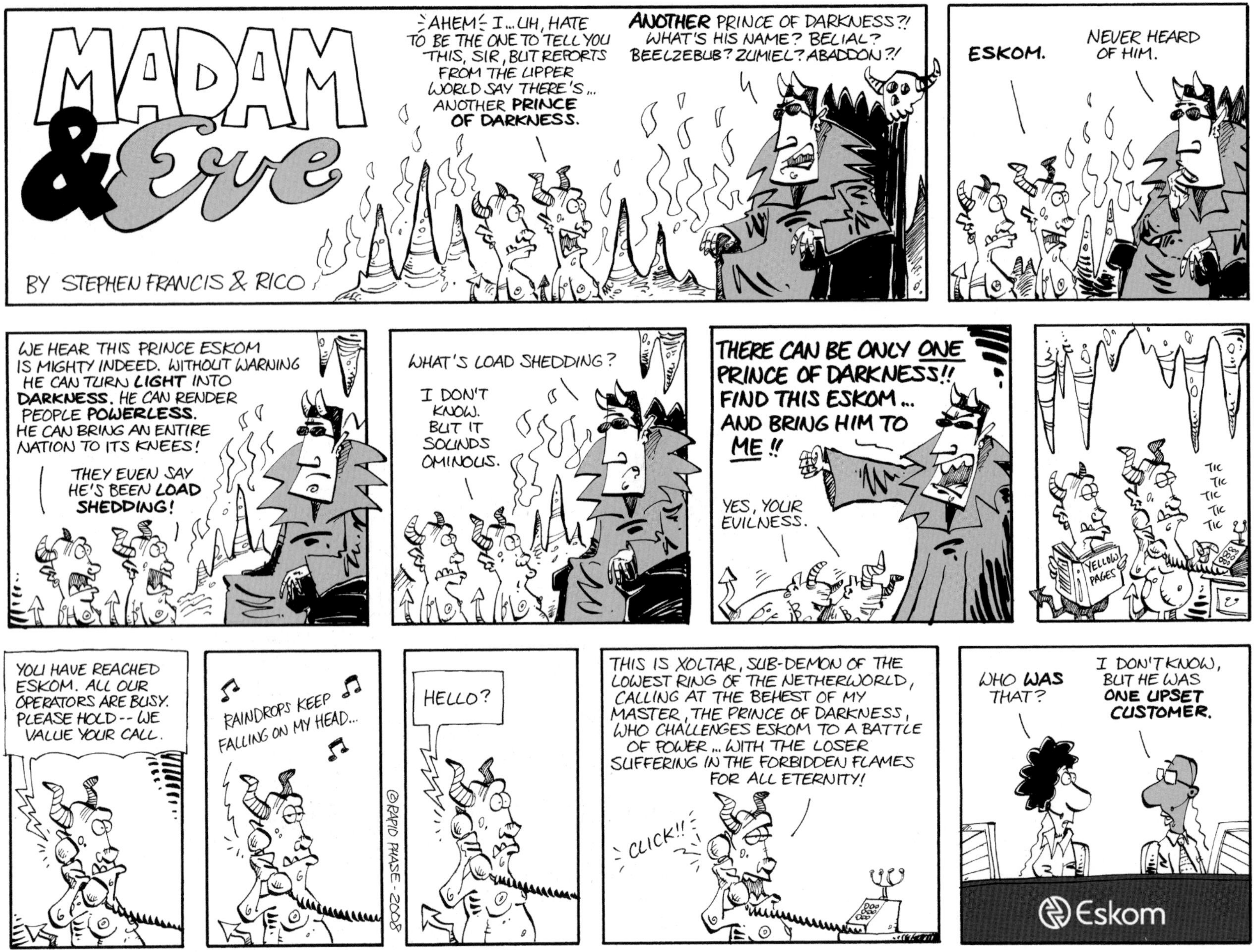
MADAM & Eve
BY STEPHEN FRANCIS & RICO
-AHEM- I... UH, HATE TO BE THE ONE TO TELL YOU THIS, SIR, BUT REPORTS FROM THE UPPER WORLD SAY THERE'S... ANOTHER PRINCE OF DARKNESS.
ANOTHER PRINCE OF DARKNESS?! WHAT'S HIS NAME? BELIAL? BEELZEBUB? ZUMIEL? ABADDON?!
ESKOM.
NEVER HEARD OF HIM.
WE HEAR THIS PRINCE ESKOM IS MIGHTY INDEED. WITHOUT WARNING HE CAN TURN LIGHT INTO DARKNESS. HE CAN RENDER PEOPLE POWERLESS. HE CAN BRING AN ENTIRE NATION TO ITS KNEES!
THEY EVEN SAY HE'S BEEN LOAD SHEDDING!
WHAT'S LOAD SHEDDING?
I DON'T KNOW. BUT IT SOUNDS OMINOUS.
THERE CAN BE ONLY ONE PRINCE OF DARKNESS!! FIND THIS ESKOM... AND BRING HIM TO ME!!
YES, YOUR EVILNESS.
YELLOW PAGES
TIC TIC TIC TIC TIC
YOU HAVE REACHED ESKOM. ALL OUR OPERATORS ARE BUSY. PLEASE HOLD -- WE VALUE YOUR CALL.
RAINDROPS KEEP FALLING ON MY HEAD...
©RAPID PHASE - 2008
HELLO?
THIS IS XOLTAR, SUB-DEMON OF THE LOWEST RING OF THE NETHERWORLD, CALLING AT THE BEHEST OF MY MASTER, THE PRINCE OF DARKNESS, WHO CHALLENGES ESKOM TO A BATTLE OF POWER... WITH THE LOSER SUFFERING IN THE FORBIDDEN FLAMES FOR ALL ETERNITY!
CLICK!!
WHO WAS THAT?
I DON'T KNOW, BUT HE WAS ONE UPSET CUSTOMER.
Eskom

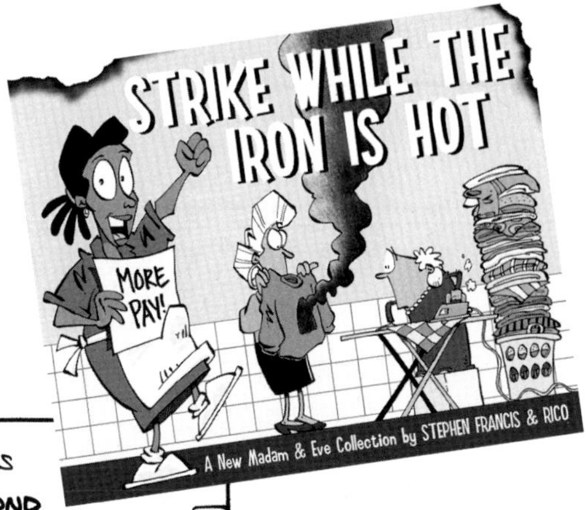
STRIKE WHILE THE IRON IS HOT
MORE PAY!
A New Madam & Eve Collection by STEPHEN FRANCIS & RICO

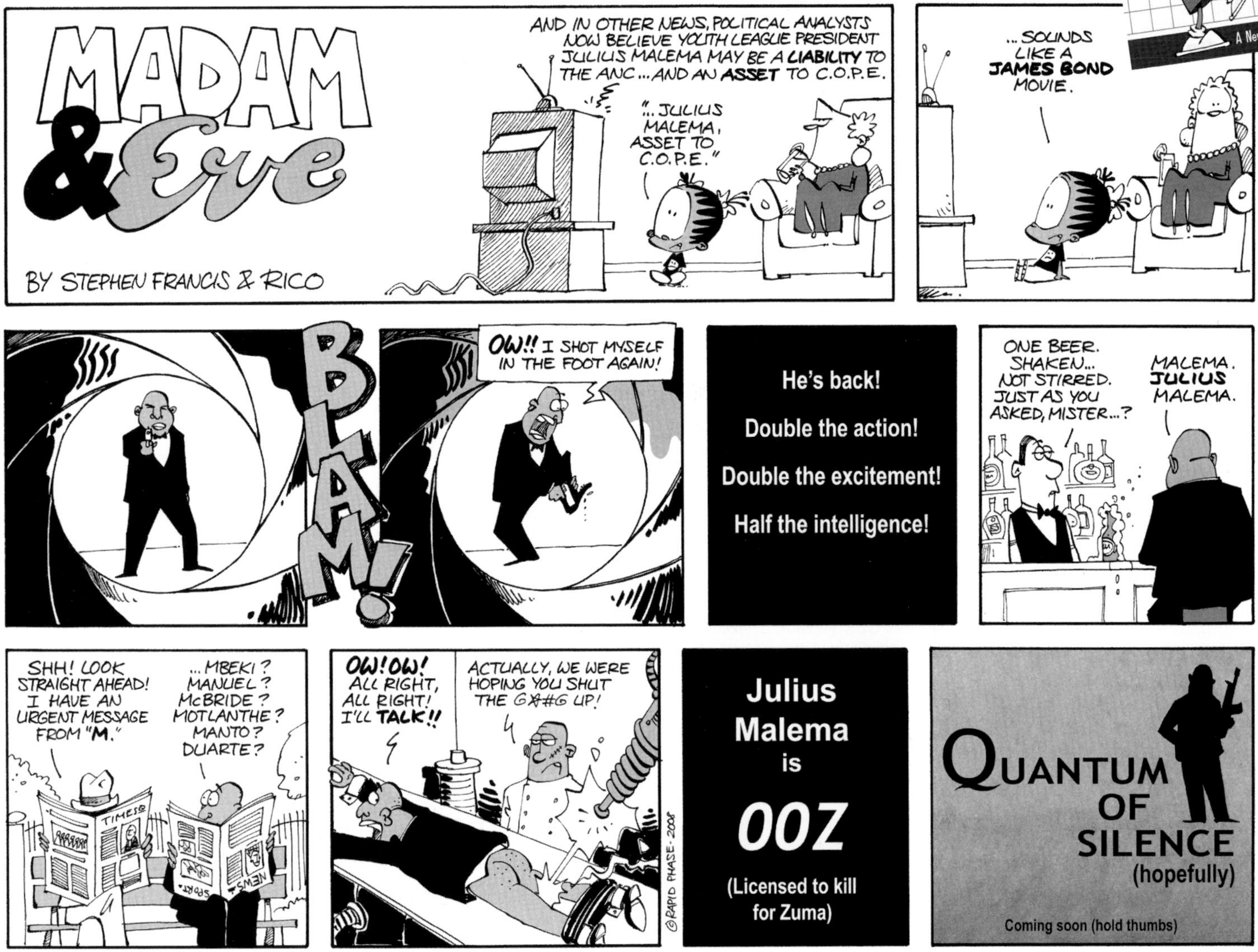
MADAM & Eve
BY STEPHEN FRANCIS & RICO
AND IN OTHER NEWS, POLITICAL ANALYSTS NOW BELIEVE YOUTH LEAGUE PRESIDENT JULIUS MALEMA MAY BE A LIABILITY TO THE ANC ... AND AN ASSET TO C.O.P.E.
"... JULIUS MALEMA, ASSET TO C.O.P.E."
... SOUNDS LIKE A JAMES BOND MOVIE.
BLAM!
OW!! I SHOT MYSELF IN THE FOOT AGAIN!
He's back!
Double the action!
Double the excitement!
Half the intelligence!
ONE BEER. SHAKEN... NOT STIRRED. JUST AS YOU ASKED, MISTER...?
MALEMA. JULIUS MALEMA.
SHH! LOOK STRAIGHT AHEAD! I HAVE AN URGENT MESSAGE FROM "M."
... MBEKI? MANUEL? McBRIDE? MOTLANTHE? MANTO? DUARTE?
TIMES
NEWS
SPORT
OW! OW! ALL RIGHT, ALL RIGHT! I'LL TALK!!
ACTUALLY, WE WERE HOPING YOU SHUT THE G✗#G UP!
© RAPID PHASE · 2008
Julius Malema is 00Z
(Licensed to kill for Zuma)
QUANTUM OF SILENCE
(hopefully)
Coming soon (hold thumbs)

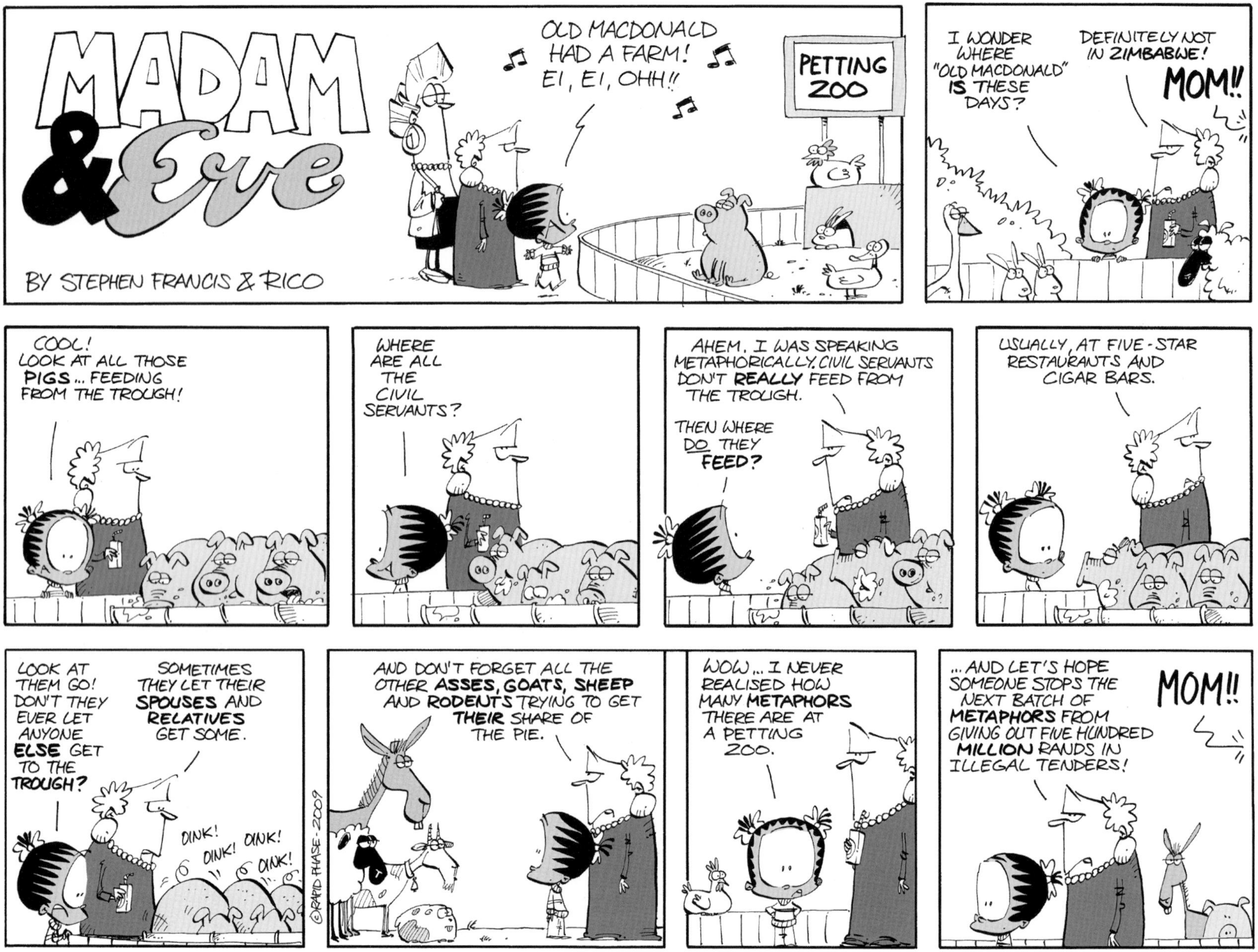
MADAM & Eve
BY STEPHEN FRANCIS & RICO
OLD MACDONALD HAD A FARM! EI, EI, OHH!!
PETTING ZOO
I WONDER WHERE "OLD MACDONALD" IS THESE DAYS?
DEFINITELY NOT IN ZIMBABWE!
MOM!!
COOL! LOOK AT ALL THOSE PIGS... FEEDING FROM THE TROUGH!
WHERE ARE ALL THE CIVIL SERVANTS?
AHEM. I WAS SPEAKING METAPHORICALLY. CIVIL SERVANTS DON'T REALLY FEED FROM THE TROUGH.
THEN WHERE DO THEY FEED?
USUALLY, AT FIVE-STAR RESTAURANTS AND CIGAR BARS.
LOOK AT THEM GO! DON'T THEY EVER LET ANYONE ELSE GET TO THE TROUGH?
SOMETIMES THEY LET THEIR SPOUSES AND RELATIVES GET SOME.
OINK! OINK! OINK! OINK!
©RAPID PHASE-2009
AND DON'T FORGET ALL THE OTHER ASSES, GOATS, SHEEP AND RODENTS TRYING TO GET THEIR SHARE OF THE PIE.
WOW... I NEVER REALISED HOW MANY METAPHORS THERE ARE AT A PETTING ZOO.
...AND LET'S HOPE SOMEONE STOPS THE NEXT BATCH OF METAPHORS FROM GIVING OUT FIVE HUNDRED MILLION RANDS IN ILLEGAL TENDERS!
MOM!!

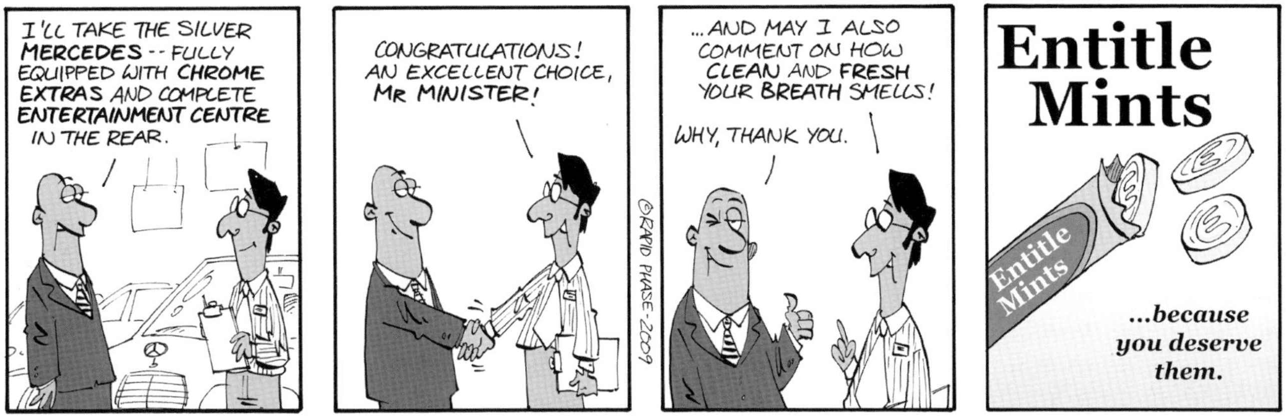
I'LL TAKE THE SILVER MERCEDES -- FULLY EQUIPPED WITH CHROME EXTRAS AND COMPLETE ENTERTAINMENT CENTRE IN THE REAR.
CONGRATULATIONS! AN EXCELLENT CHOICE, MR MINISTER!
©RAPID PHASE-2009
...AND MAY I ALSO COMMENT ON HOW CLEAN AND FRESH YOUR BREATH SMELLS!
WHY, THANK YOU.
Entitle Mints
Entitle Mints
...because you deserve them.

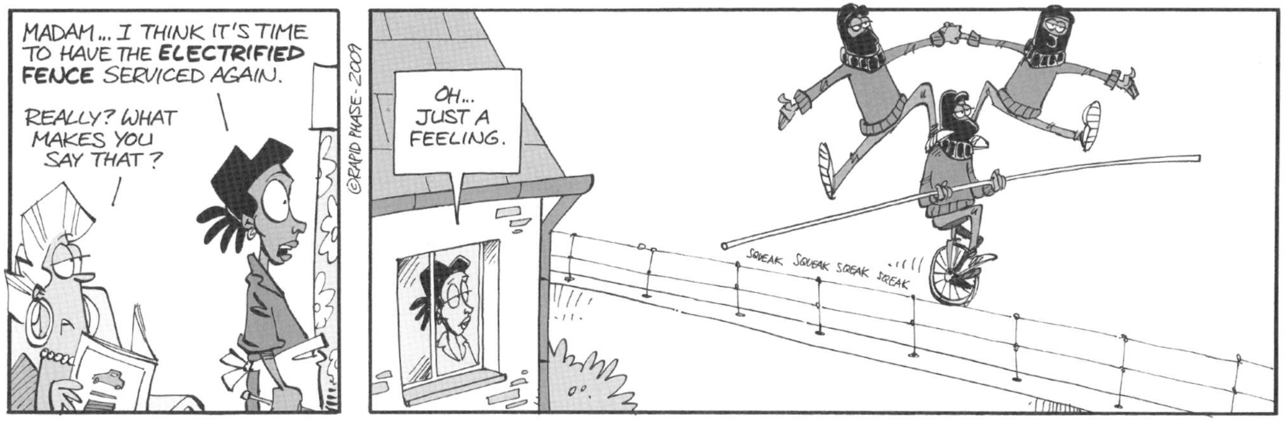
MADAM... I THINK IT'S TIME TO HAVE THE ELECTRIFIED FENCE SERVICED AGAIN.
REALLY? WHAT MAKES YOU SAY THAT?
©RAPID PHASE-2009
OH... JUST A FEELING.
SQUEAK SQUEAK SQEAK SQEAK

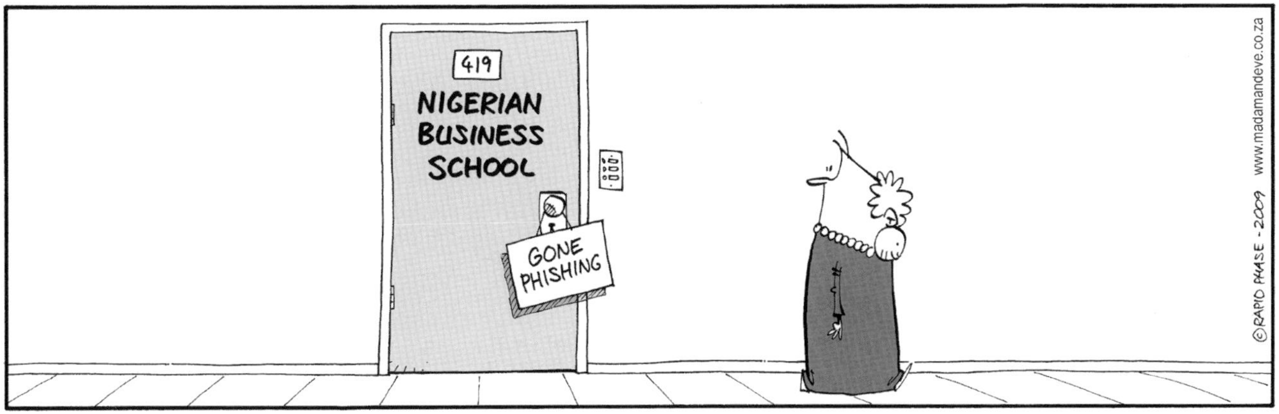
419
NIGERIAN BUSINESS SCHOOL
GONE PHISHING
©RAPID PHASE-2009 www.madamandeve.co.za

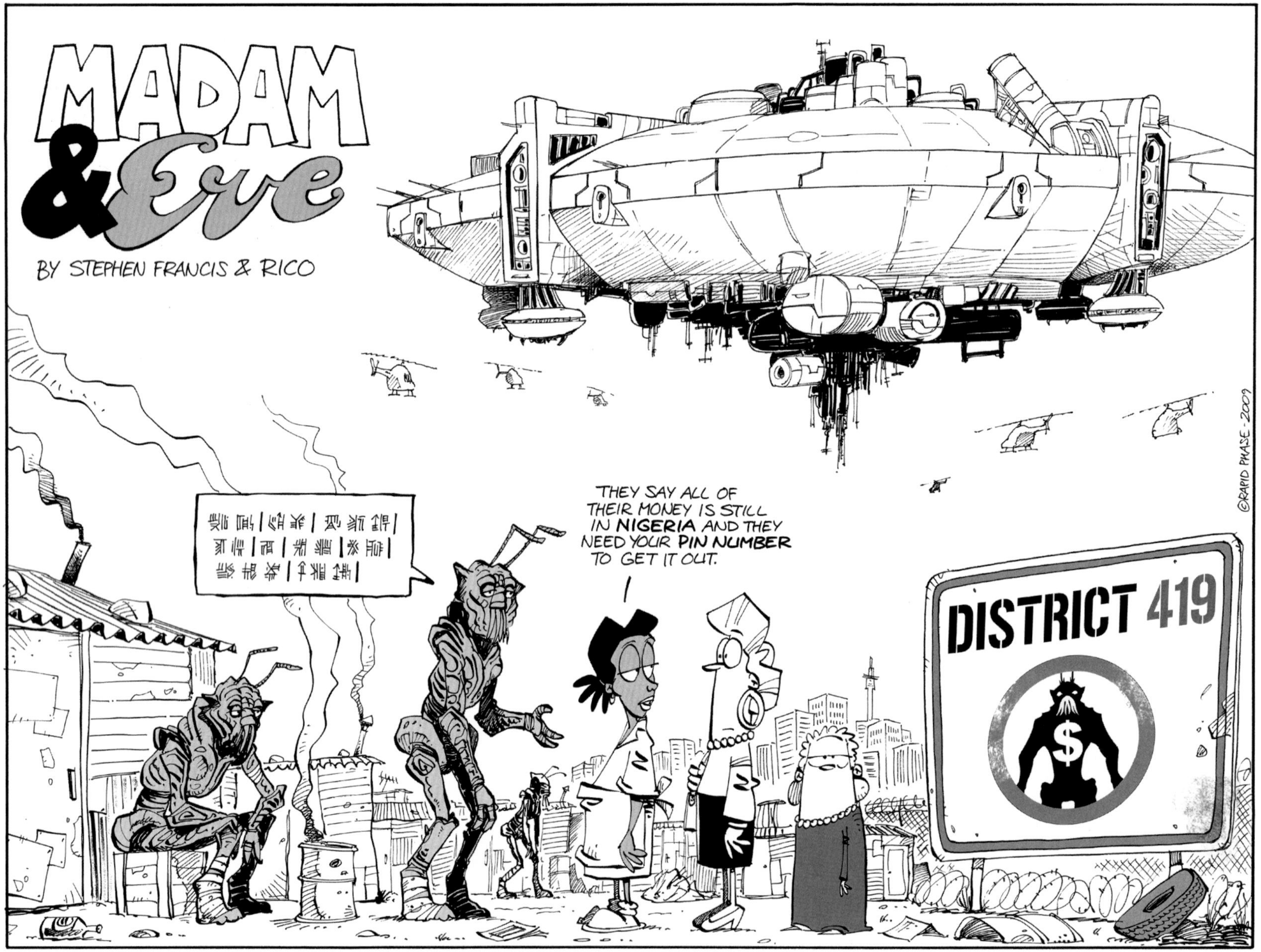
MADAM & Eve
BY STEPHEN FRANCIS & RICO
THEY SAY ALL OF THEIR MONEY IS STILL IN NIGERIA AND THEY NEED YOUR PIN NUMBER TO GET IT OUT.
DISTRICT 419
$
©RAPID PHASE · 2009

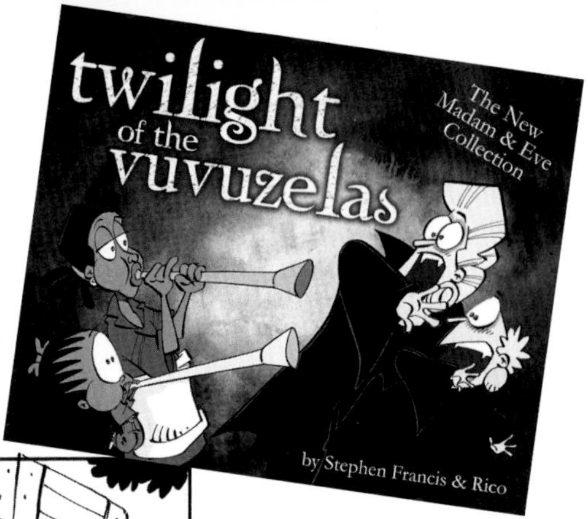
twilight of the vuvuzelas
The New Madam & Eve Collection
by Stephen Francis & Rico

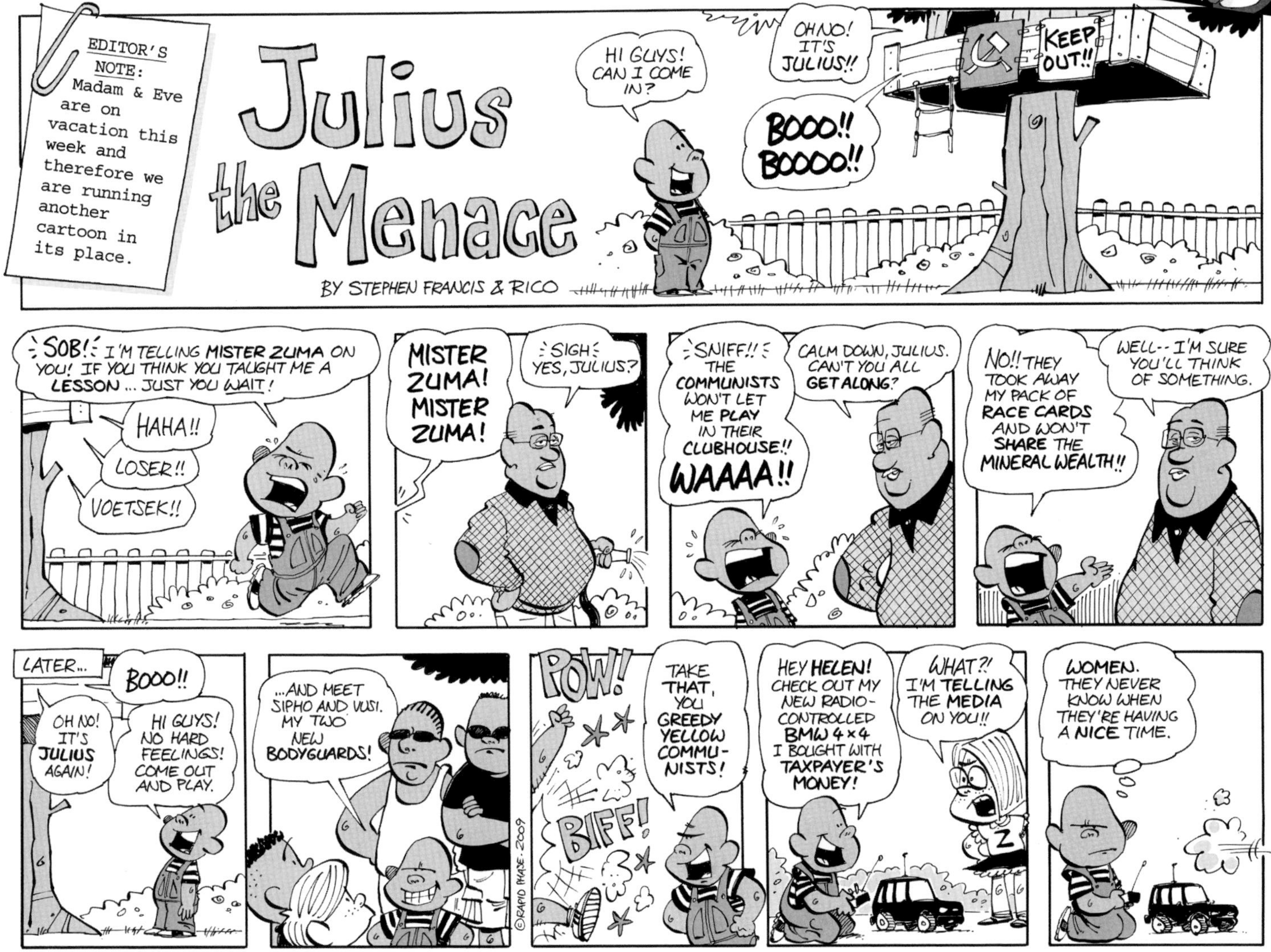
EDITOR'S NOTE: Madam & Eve are on vacation this week and therefore we are running another cartoon in its place.
Julius the Menace
BY STEPHEN FRANCIS & RICO
HI GUYS! CAN I COME IN?
OH NO! IT'S JULIUS!!
KEEP OUT!!
BOOO!! BOOOO!!
SOB! I'M TELLING MISTER ZUMA ON YOU! IF YOU THINK YOU TAUGHT ME A LESSON ... JUST YOU WAIT!
HAHA!!
LOSER!!
VOETSEK!!
MISTER ZUMA! MISTER ZUMA!
SIGH YES, JULIUS?
SNIFF!! THE COMMUNISTS WON'T LET ME PLAY IN THEIR CLUBHOUSE!! WAAAA!!
CALM DOWN, JULIUS. CAN'T YOU ALL GET ALONG?
NO!! THEY TOOK AWAY MY PACK OF RACE CARDS AND WON'T SHARE THE MINERAL WEALTH!!
WELL-- I'M SURE YOU'LL THINK OF SOMETHING.
LATER...
BOOO!!
OH NO! IT'S JULIUS AGAIN!
HI GUYS! NO HARD FEELINGS! COME OUT AND PLAY.
...AND MEET SIPHO AND VUSI. MY TWO NEW BODYGUARDS!
©RAPID PHASE · 2009
POW!
BIFF!
TAKE THAT, YOU GREEDY YELLOW COMMUNISTS!
HEY HELEN! CHECK OUT MY NEW RADIO-CONTROLLED BMW 4×4 I BOUGHT WITH TAXPAYER'S MONEY!
WHAT?! I'M TELLING THE MEDIA ON YOU!!
WOMEN. THEY NEVER KNOW WHEN THEY'RE HAVING A NICE TIME.

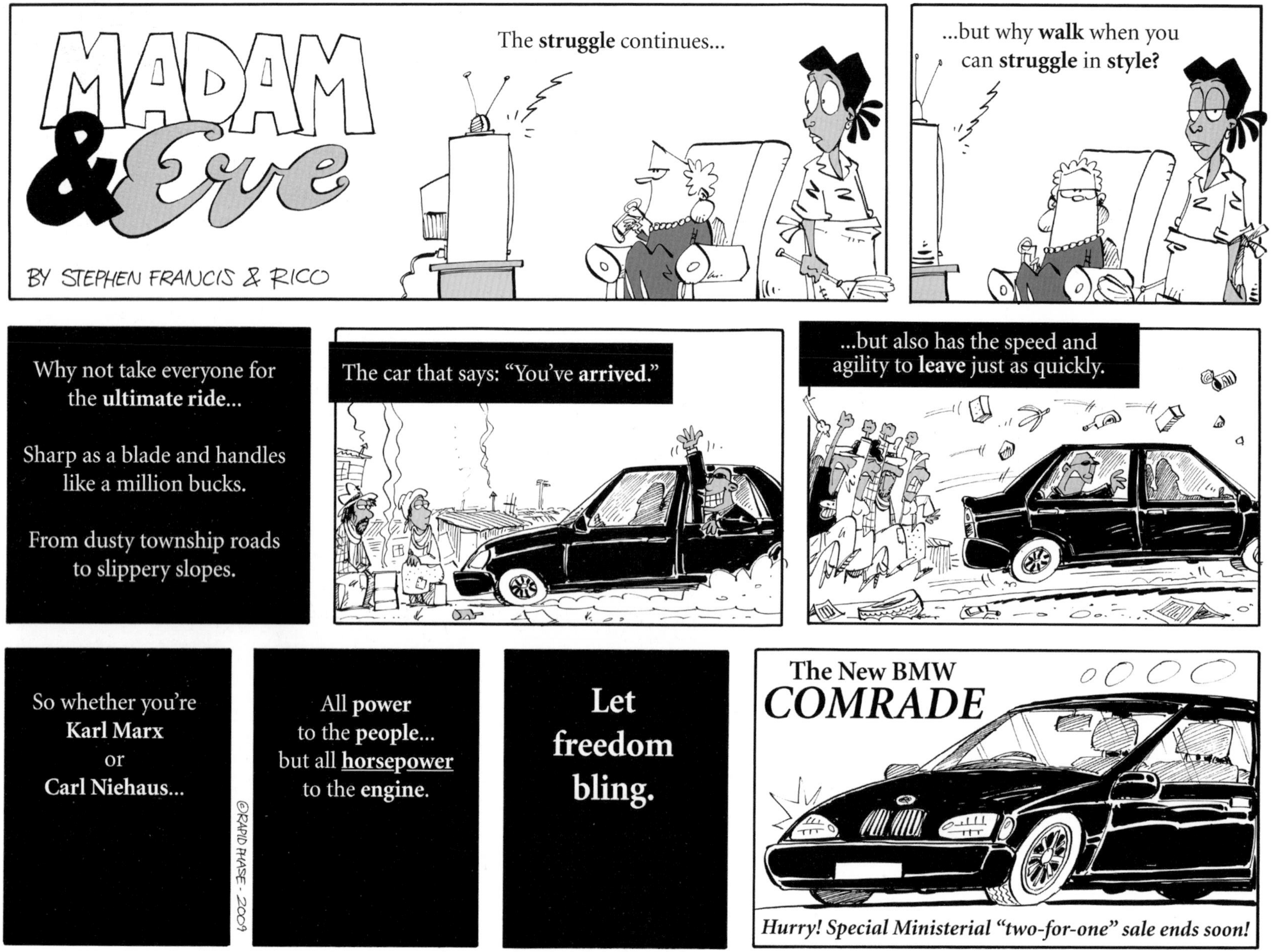

MADAM & Eve
BY STEPHEN FRANCIS & RICO
The struggle continues...
...but why walk when you can struggle in style?
Why not take everyone for the ultimate ride...
Sharp as a blade and handles like a million bucks.
From dusty township roads to slippery slopes.
The car that says: "You've arrived."
...but also has the speed and agility to leave just as quickly.
So whether you're Karl Marx or Carl Niehaus...
©RAPID PHASE - 2009
All power to the people... but all horsepower to the engine.
Let freedom bling.
The New BMW COMRADE
Hurry! Special Ministerial "two-for-one" sale ends soon!

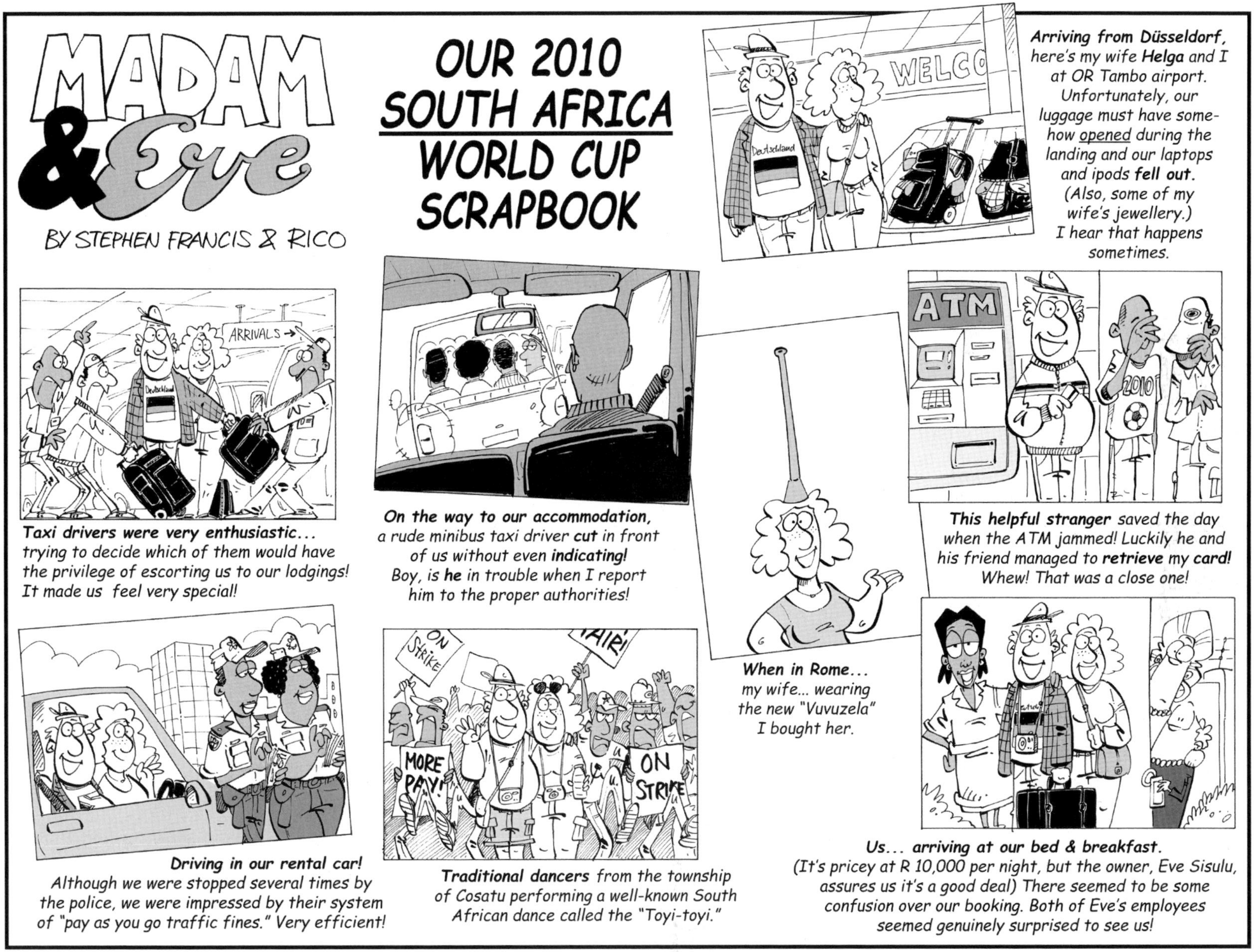
MADAM & Eve
BY STEPHEN FRANCIS & RICO
OUR 2010 SOUTH AFRICA WORLD CUP SCRAPBOOK
WELCO
Deutschland
Arriving from Düsseldorf, here's my wife Helga and I at OR Tambo airport. Unfortunately, our luggage must have somehow opened during the landing and our laptops and ipods fell out. (Also, some of my wife's jewellery.) I hear that happens sometimes.
ARRIVALS →
Taxi drivers were very enthusiastic... trying to decide which of them would have the privilege of escorting us to our lodgings! It made us feel very special!
On the way to our accommodation, a rude minibus taxi driver cut in front of us without even indicating! Boy, is he in trouble when I report him to the proper authorities!
ATM
2010
This helpful stranger saved the day when the ATM jammed! Luckily he and his friend managed to retrieve my card! Whew! That was a close one!
When in Rome... my wife... wearing the new "Vuvuzela" I bought her.
Driving in our rental car! Although we were stopped several times by the police, we were impressed by their system of "pay as you go traffic fines." Very efficient!
ON STRIKE
FAIR!
MORE PAY!
ON STRIKE
Traditional dancers from the township of Cosatu performing a well-known South African dance called the "Toyi-toyi."
Us... arriving at our bed & breakfast. (It's pricey at R 10,000 per night, but the owner, Eve Sisulu, assures us it's a good deal) There seemed to be some confusion over our booking. Both of Eve's employees seemed genuinely surprised to see us!

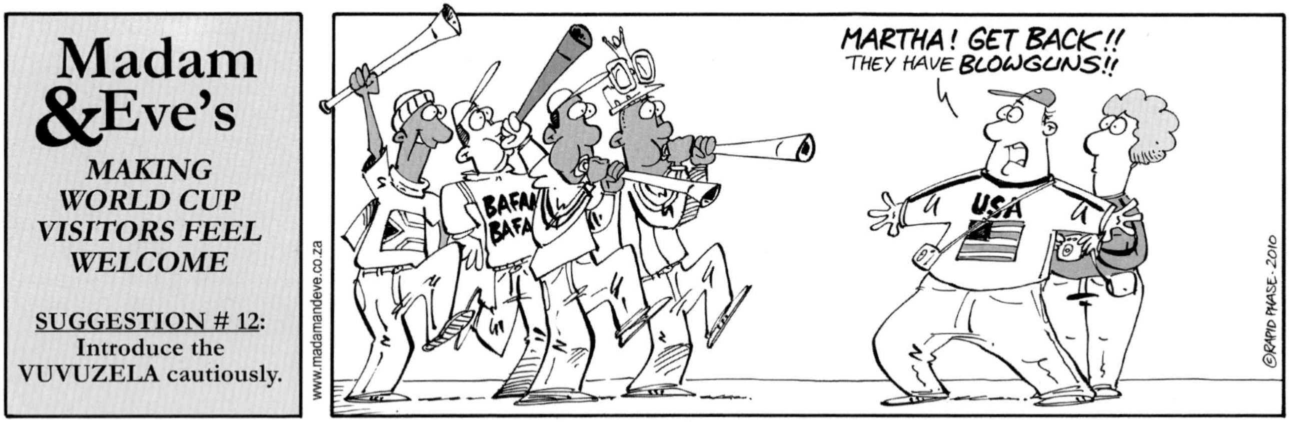
Madam &Eve's
MAKING WORLD CUP VISITORS FEEL WELCOME
SUGGESTION # 12: Introduce the VUVUZELA cautiously.
www.madamandeve.co.za
BAFANA BAFANA
MARTHA! GET BACK!! THEY HAVE BLOWGUNS!!
USA
©RAPID PHASE - 2010

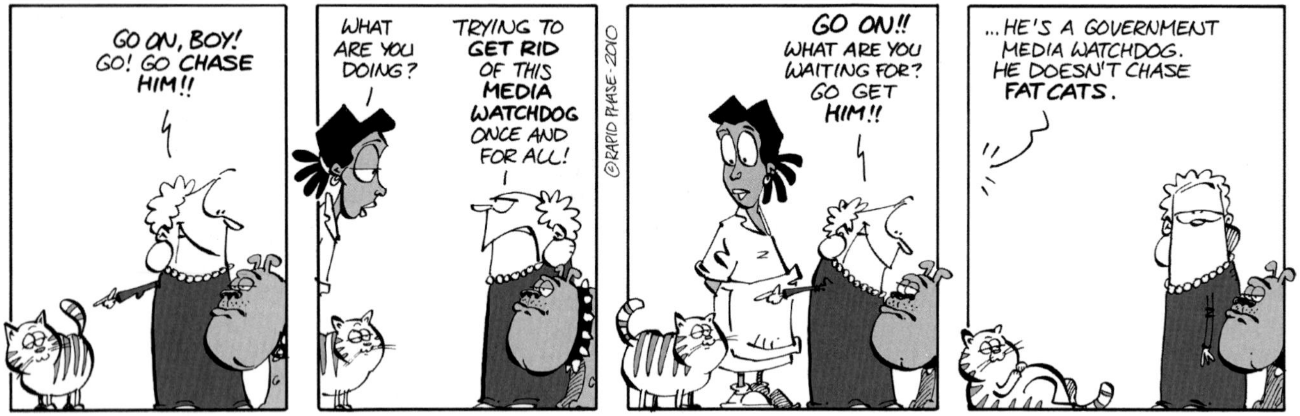
GO ON, BOY! GO! GO CHASE HIM!!
WHAT ARE YOU DOING?
TRYING TO GET RID OF THIS MEDIA WATCHDOG ONCE AND FOR ALL!
©RAPID PHASE - 2010
GO ON!! WHAT ARE YOU WAITING FOR? GO GET HIM!!
...HE'S A GOVERNMENT MEDIA WATCHDOG. HE DOESN'T CHASE FAT CATS.

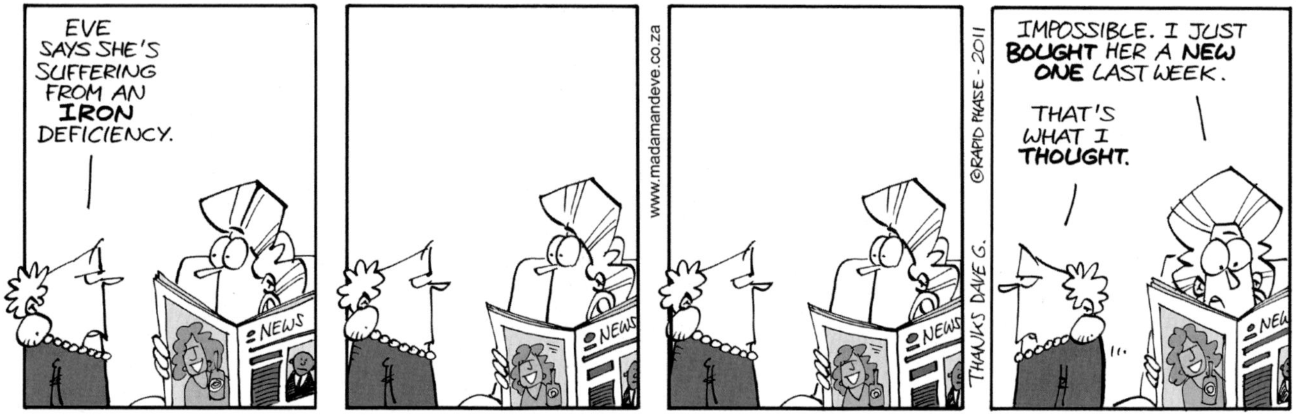
EVE SAYS SHE'S SUFFERING FROM AN IRON DEFICIENCY.
NEWS
www.madamandeve.co.za
©RAPID PHASE - 2011
THANKS DAVE G.
IMPOSSIBLE. I JUST BOUGHT HER A NEW ONE LAST WEEK.
THAT'S WHAT I THOUGHT.

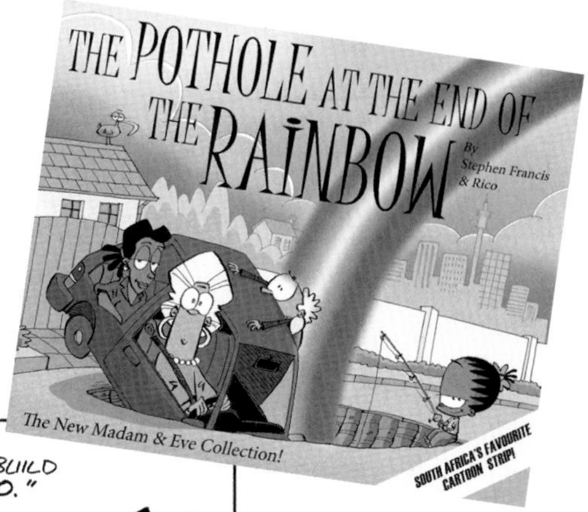
THE POTHOLE AT THE END OF THE RAINBOW
By Stephen Francis & Rico
The New Madam & Eve Collection!
SOUTH AFRICA'S FAVOURITE CARTOON STRIP!

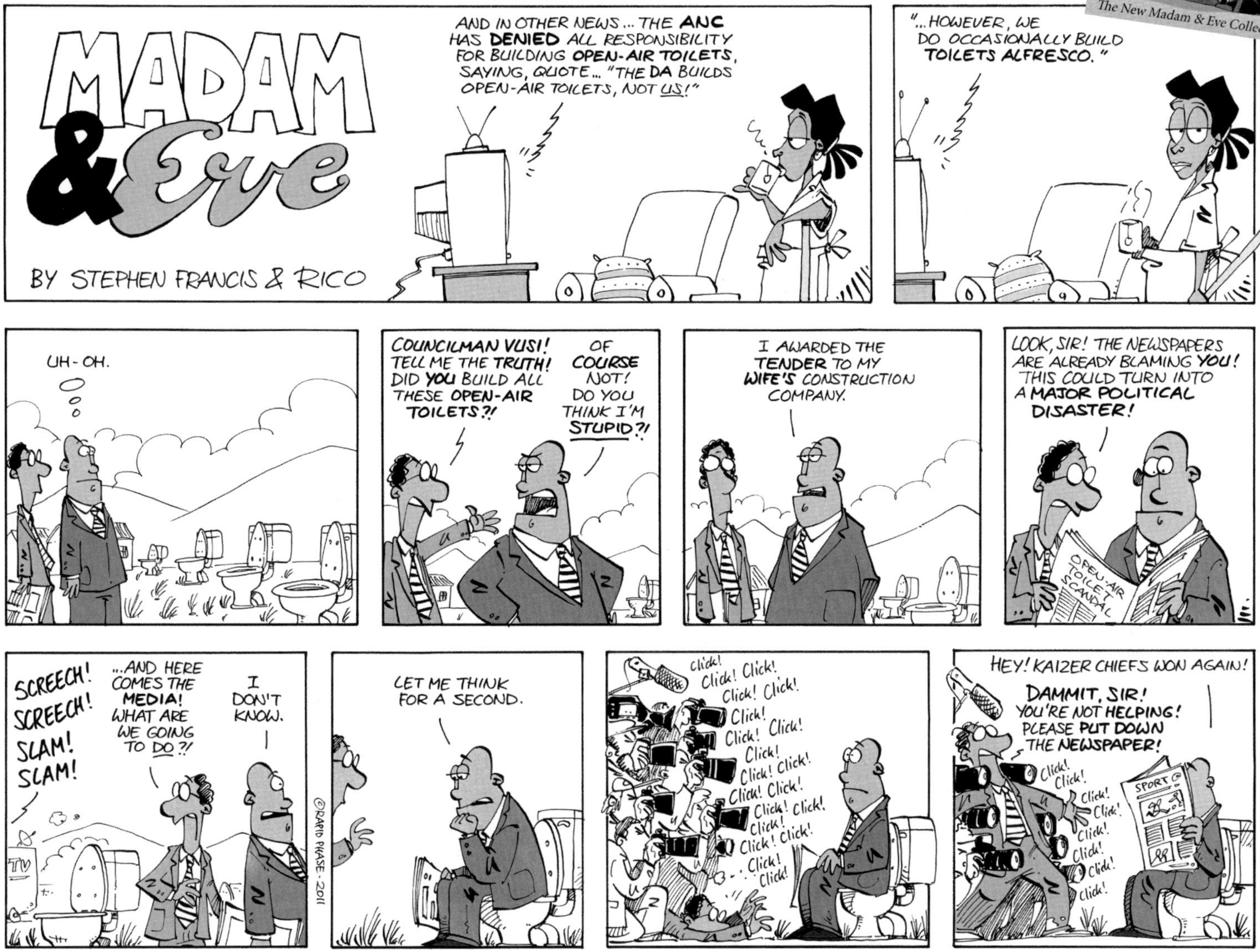
MADAM & Eve
BY STEPHEN FRANCIS & RICO
AND IN OTHER NEWS... THE ANC HAS DENIED ALL RESPONSIBILITY FOR BUILDING OPEN-AIR TOILETS, SAYING, QUOTE... "THE DA BUILDS OPEN-AIR TOILETS, NOT US!"
"...HOWEVER, WE DO OCCASIONALLY BUILD TOILETS ALFRESCO."
UH-OH.
COUNCILMAN VUSI! TELL ME THE TRUTH! DID YOU BUILD ALL THESE OPEN-AIR TOILETS?!
OF COURSE NOT! DO YOU THINK I'M STUPID?!
I AWARDED THE TENDER TO MY WIFE'S CONSTRUCTION COMPANY.
LOOK, SIR! THE NEWSPAPERS ARE ALREADY BLAMING YOU! THIS COULD TURN INTO A MAJOR POLITICAL DISASTER!
OPEN-AIR TOILET SCANDAL
SCREECH! SCREECH! SLAM! SLAM!
...AND HERE COMES THE MEDIA! WHAT ARE WE GOING TO DO?!
I DON'T KNOW.
TV
©RAPID PHASE · 2011
LET ME THINK FOR A SECOND.
Click! Click! Click! Click! Click! Click! Click! Click! Click! Click! Click! Click! Click! Click! Click! Click! Click! Click!
HEY! KAIZER CHIEFS WON AGAIN!
DAMMIT, SIR! YOU'RE NOT HELPING! PLEASE PUT DOWN THE NEWSPAPER!
Click! Click! Click! Click! Click! Click! Click! Click!
SPORT

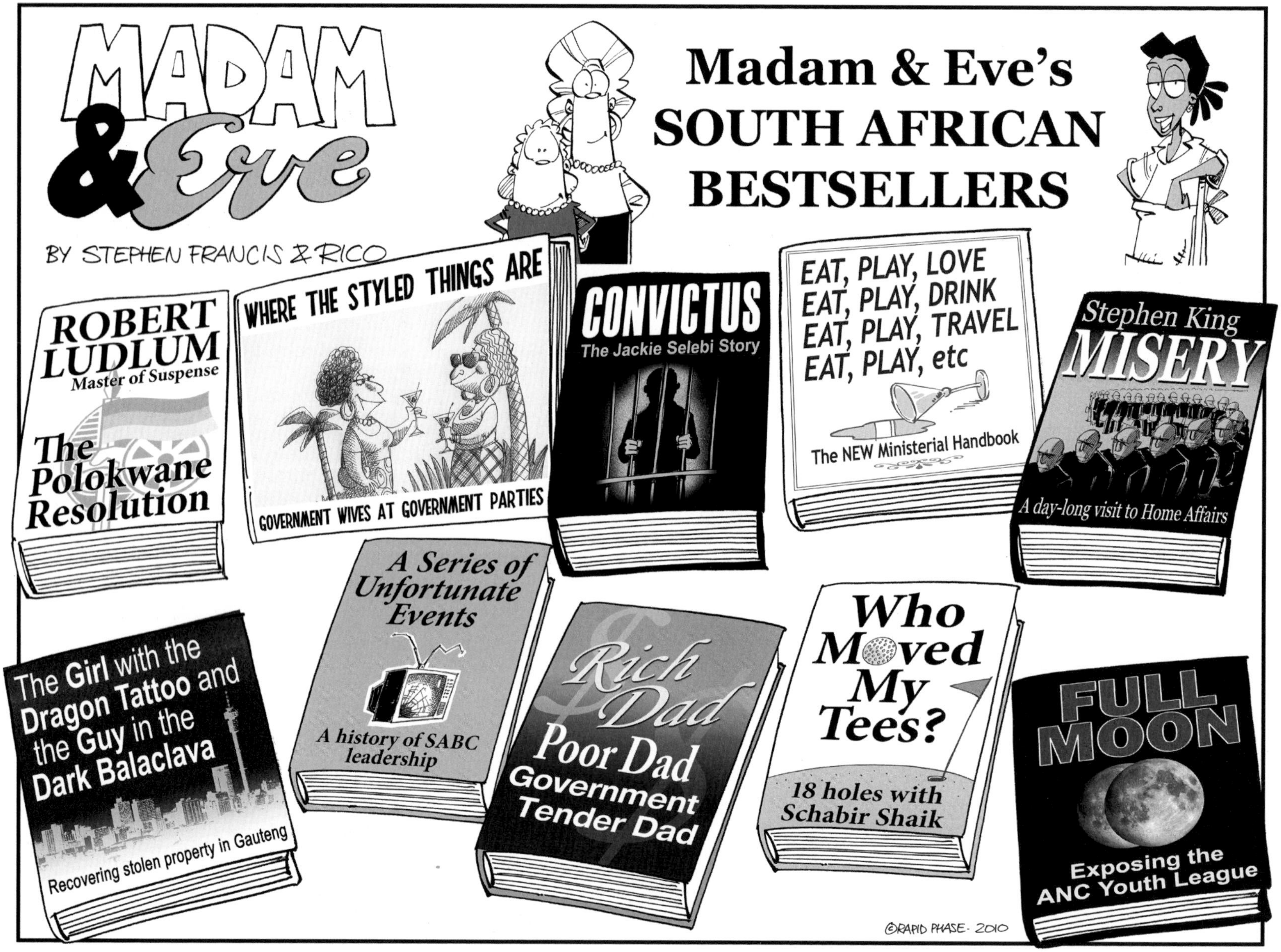
MADAM & Eve
BY STEPHEN FRANCIS & RICO
Madam & Eve's SOUTH AFRICAN BESTSELLERS
ROBERT LUDLUM
Master of Suspense
The Polokwane Resolution
WHERE THE STYLED THINGS ARE
GOVERNMENT WIVES AT GOVERNMENT PARTIES
CONVICTUS
The Jackie Selebi Story
EAT, PLAY, LOVE
EAT, PLAY, DRINK
EAT, PLAY, TRAVEL
EAT, PLAY, etc
The NEW Ministerial Handbook
Stephen King
MISERY
A day-long visit to Home Affairs
The Girl with the Dragon Tattoo and the Guy in the Dark Balaclava
Recovering stolen property in Gauteng
A Series of Unfortunate Events
A history of SABC leadership
Rich Dad Poor Dad
Government Tender Dad
Who Moved My Tees?
18 holes with Schabir Shaik
FULL MOON
Exposing the ANC Youth League
©RAPID PHASE- 2010

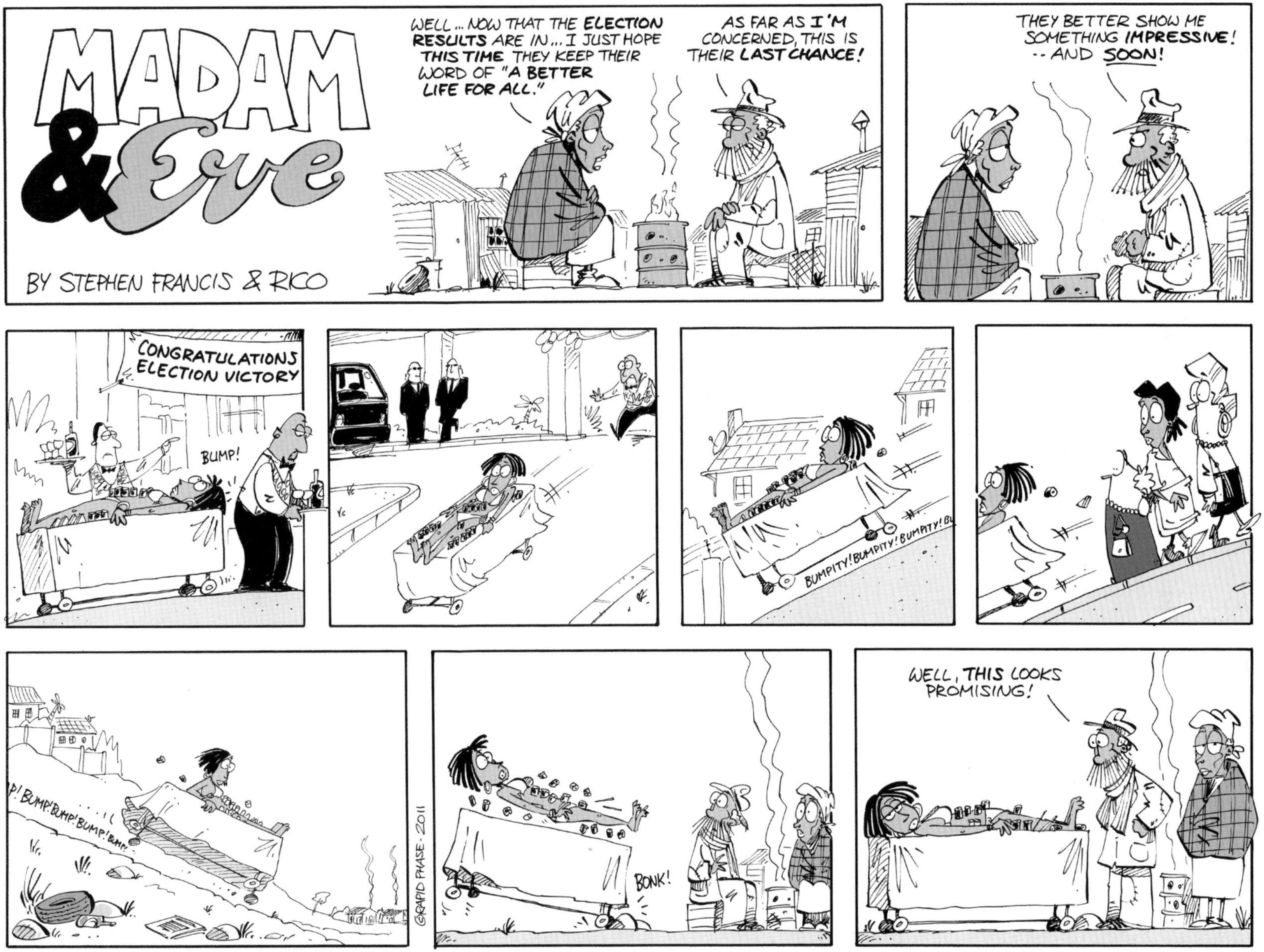
MADAM & Eve
BY STEPHEN FRANCIS & RICO
WELL... NOW THAT THE ELECTION RESULTS ARE IN... I JUST HOPE THIS TIME THEY KEEP THEIR WORD OF "A BETTER LIFE FOR ALL."
AS FAR AS I'M CONCERNED, THIS IS THEIR LAST CHANCE!
THEY BETTER SHOW ME SOMETHING IMPRESSIVE! --AND SOON!
CONGRATULATIONS ELECTION VICTORY
BUMP!
BUMPITY! BUMPITY! BUMPITY! BU
P! BUMP! BUMP! BUMP! BUMP!
©RAPID PHASE - 2011
BONK!
WELL, THIS LOOKS PROMISING!

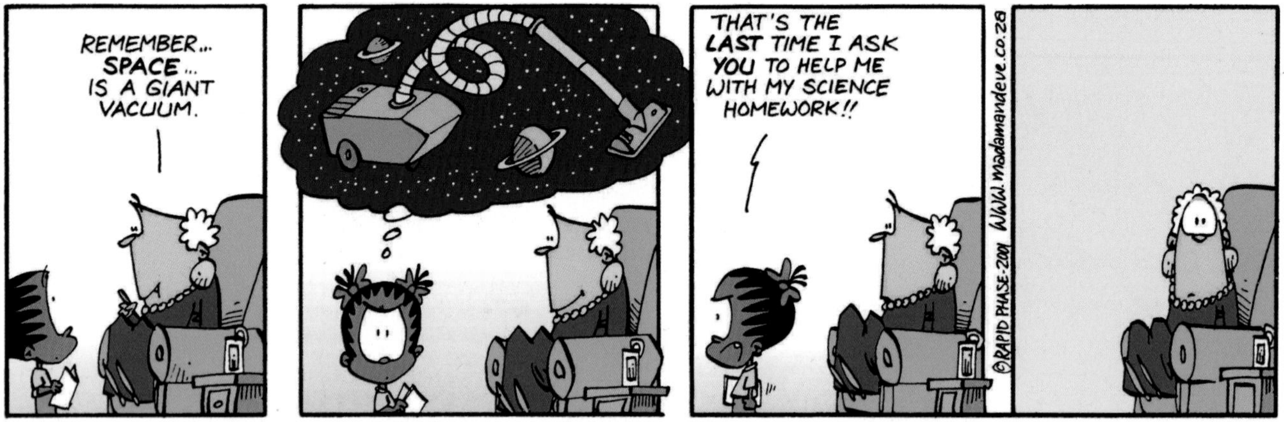
REMEMBER... SPACE... IS A GIANT VACUUM.
THAT'S THE LAST TIME I ASK YOU TO HELP ME WITH MY SCIENCE HOMEWORK!!
©RAPID PHASE·2001 WWW.madamandeve.co.za

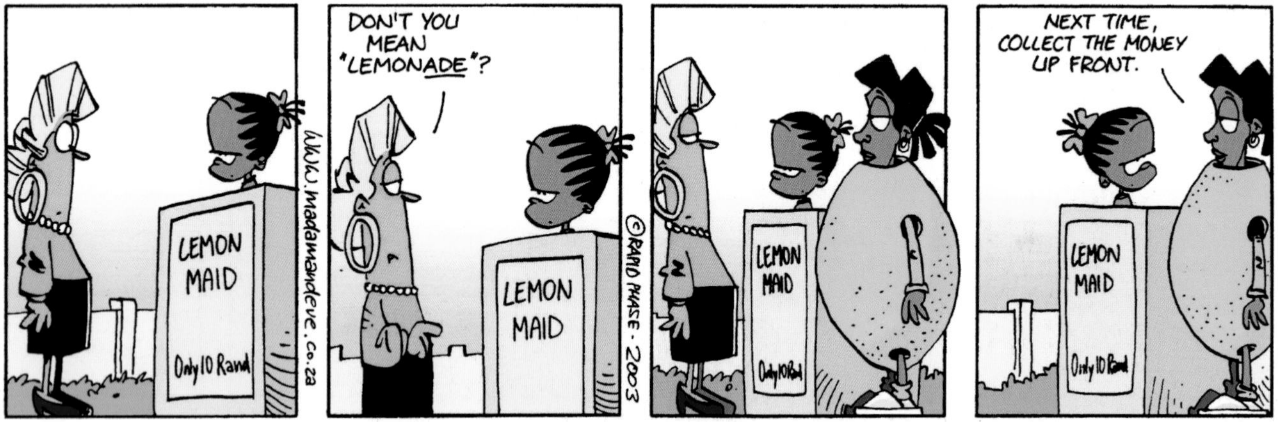
LEMON MAID
Only 10 Rand
WWW.madamandeve.co.za
DON'T YOU MEAN "LEMONADE"?
©RAPID PHASE·2003
NEXT TIME, COLLECT THE MONEY UP FRONT.

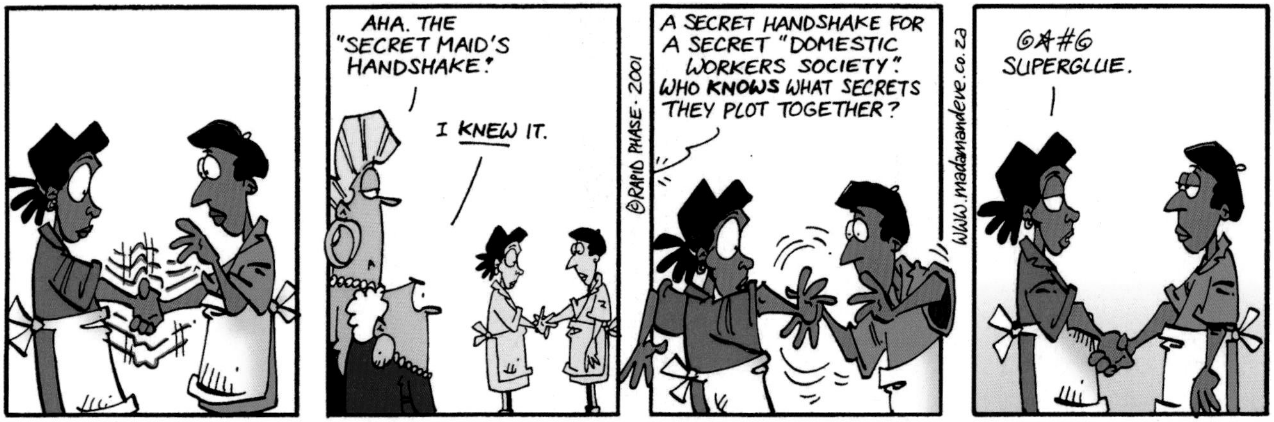
AHA. THE "SECRET MAID'S HANDSHAKE."
I KNEW IT.
©RAPID PHASE·2001
A SECRET HANDSHAKE FOR A SECRET "DOMESTIC WORKERS SOCIETY." WHO KNOWS WHAT SECRETS THEY PLOT TOGETHER?
WWW.madamandeve.co.za
@☆#@ SUPERGLUE.

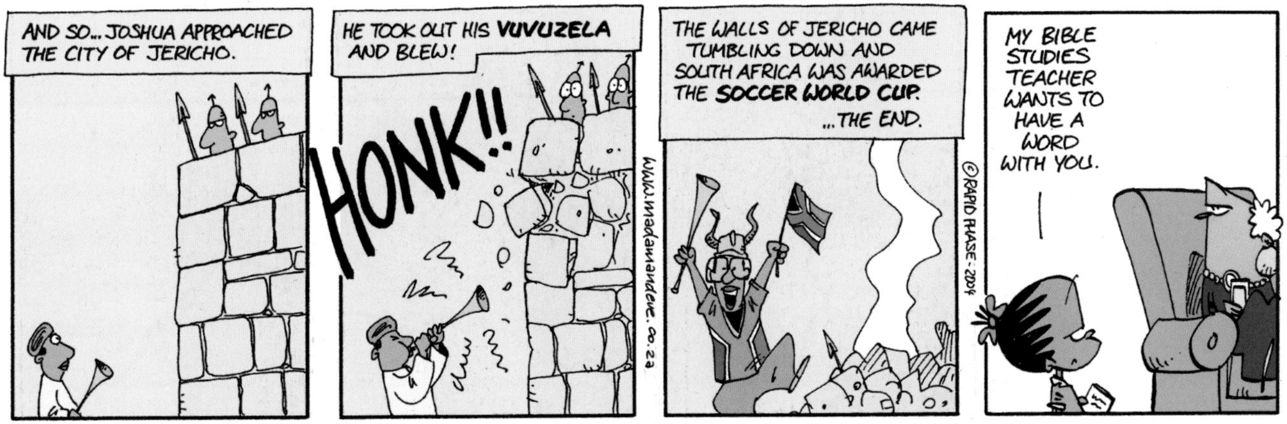
AND SO... JOSHUA APPROACHED THE CITY OF JERICHO.
HE TOOK OUT HIS **VUVUZELA** AND BLEW!
HONK!!
www.madamandeve.co.za
THE WALLS OF JERICHO CAME TUMBLING DOWN AND SOUTH AFRICA WAS AWARDED THE **SOCCER WORLD CUP**.
...THE END.
© RAPID PHASE · 2004
MY BIBLE STUDIES TEACHER WANTS TO HAVE A WORD WITH YOU.

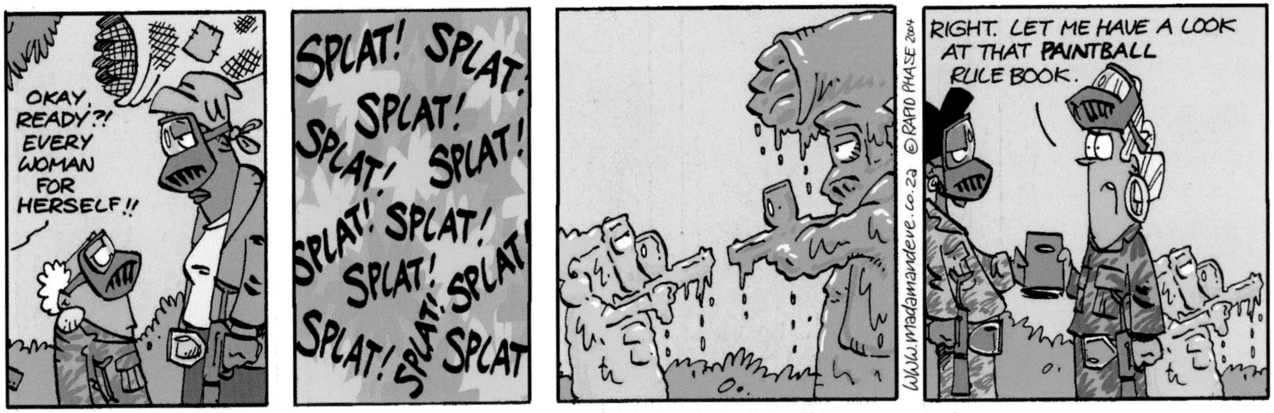
OKAY, READY?! EVERY WOMAN FOR HERSELF!!
SPLAT! SPLAT! SPLAT! SPLAT! SPLAT! SPLAT! SPLAT! SPLAT! SPLAT! SPLAT! SPLAT! SPLAT! SPLAT
© RAPID PHASE 2004
www.madamandeve.co.za
RIGHT. LET ME HAVE A LOOK AT THAT **PAINTBALL** RULE BOOK.

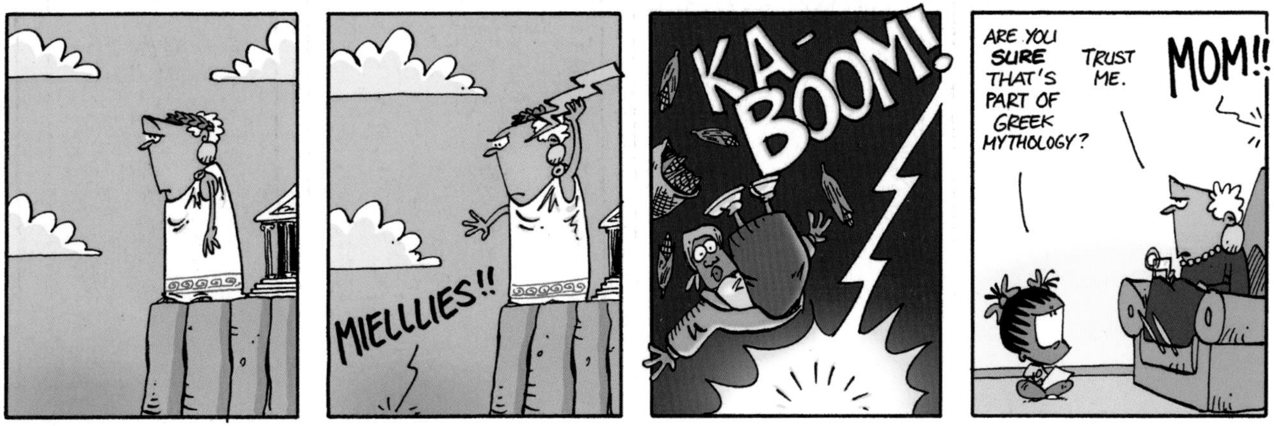
MIELLLIES!!
KA-BOOM!
ARE YOU **SURE** THAT'S PART OF GREEK MYTHOLOGY?
TRUST ME.
MOM!!

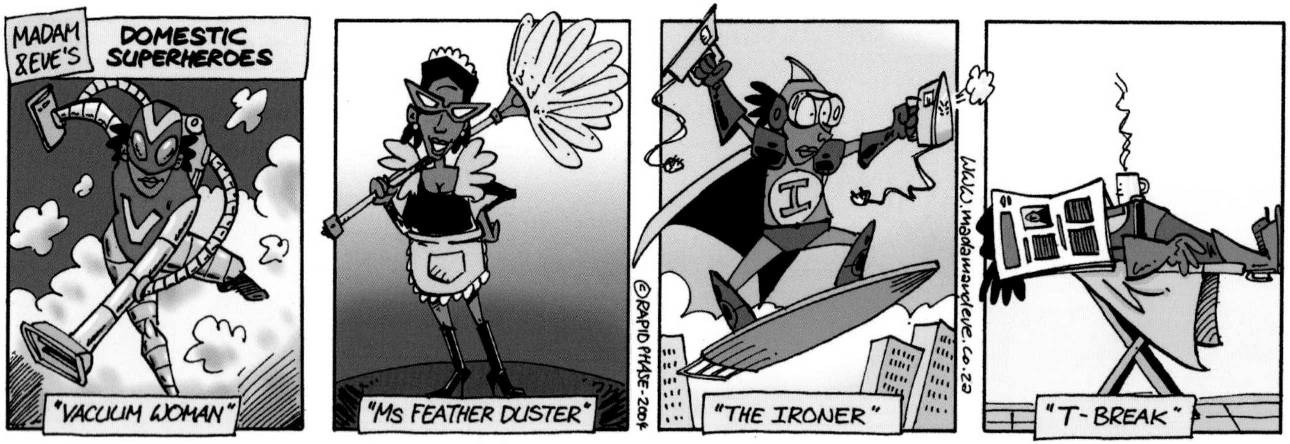
MADAM & EVE'S
DOMESTIC SUPERHEROES
"VACUUM WOMAN"
"MS FEATHER DUSTER"
©RAPID PHASE-2006
"THE IRONER"
www.madamandeve.co.za
"T-BREAK"

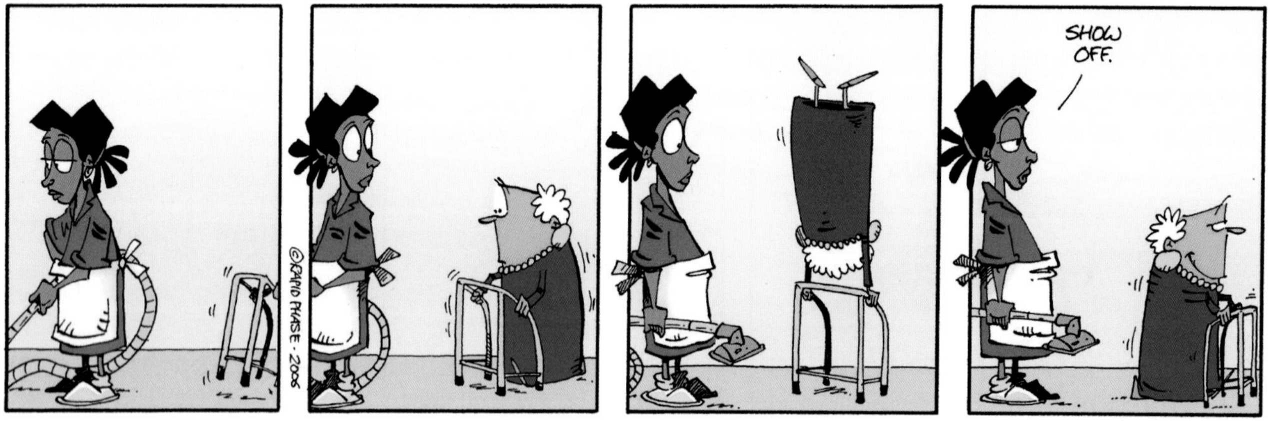
©RAPID PHASE-2006
SHOW OFF.

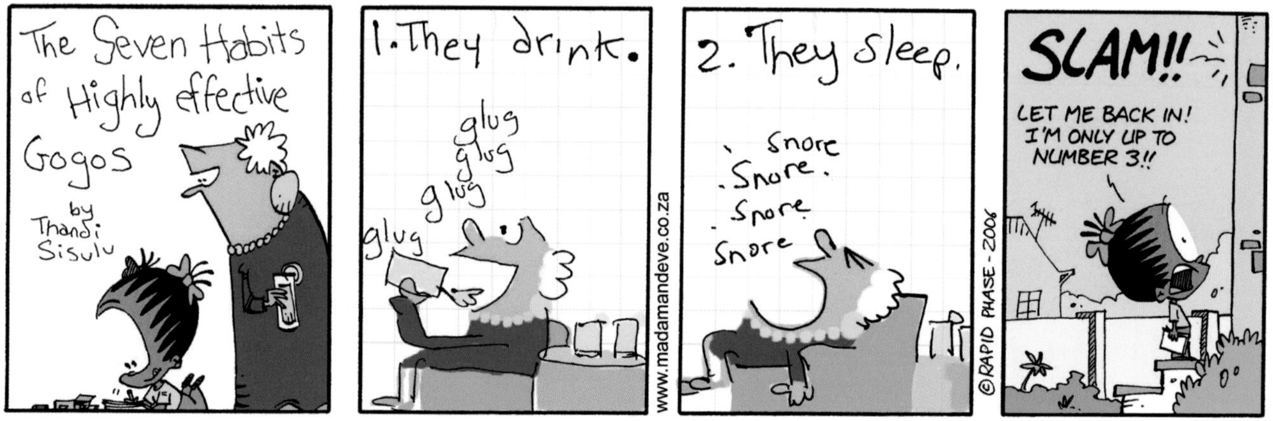
The Seven Habits of Highly effective Gogos
by Thandi Sisulu
1. They drink.
glug glug glug glug
www.madamandeve.co.za
2. They sleep.
snore snore snore snore
©RAPID PHASE-2006
SLAM!!
LET ME BACK IN! I'M ONLY UP TO NUMBER 3!!

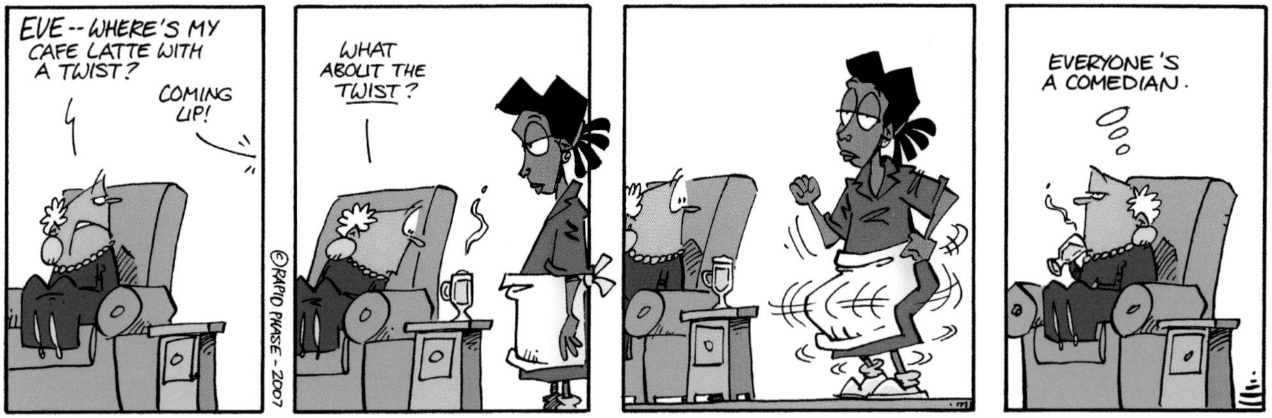
EVE -- WHERE'S MY CAFE LATTE WITH A TWIST?
COMING UP!
WHAT ABOUT THE TWIST?
EVERYONE'S A COMEDIAN.
©RAPID PHASE - 2007

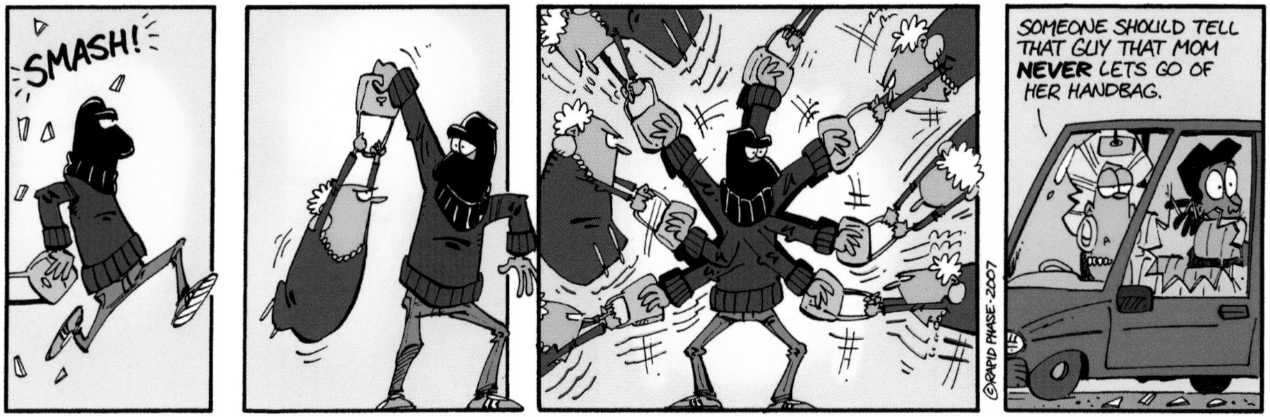
SMASH!
SOMEONE SHOULD TELL THAT GUY THAT MOM NEVER LETS GO OF HER HANDBAG.
©RAPID PHASE - 2007

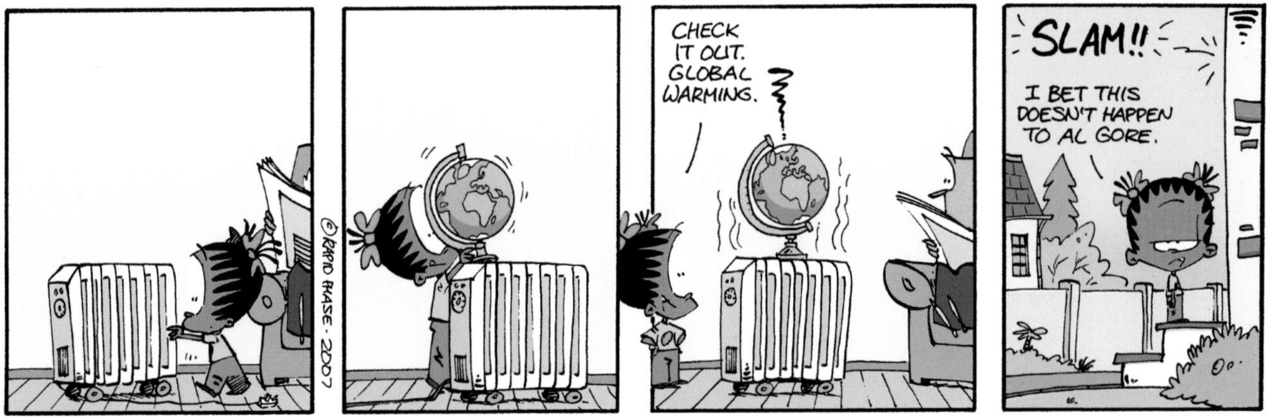
CHECK IT OUT. GLOBAL WARMING.
SLAM!!
I BET THIS DOESN'T HAPPEN TO AL GORE.
©RAPID PHASE - 2007

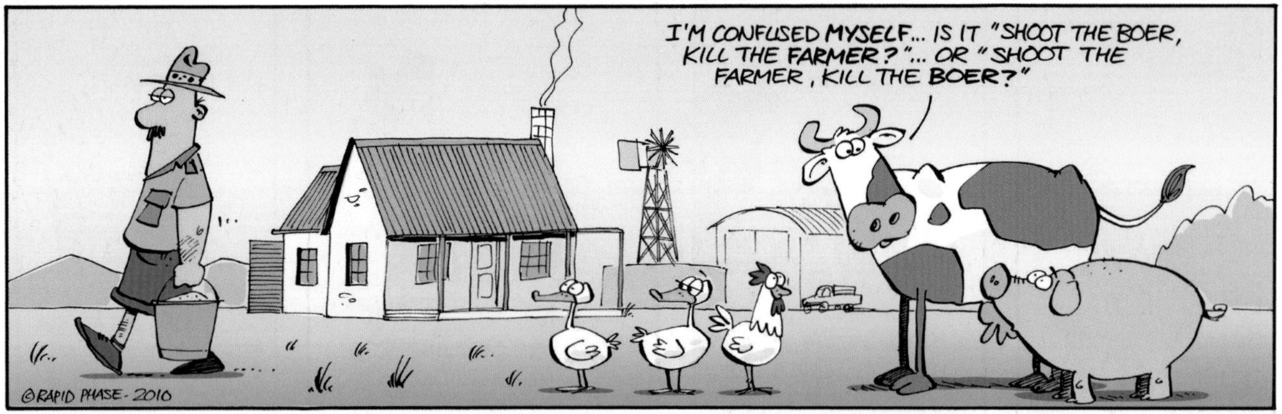
I'M CONFUSED MYSELF... IS IT "SHOOT THE BOER, KILL THE FARMER?"... OR "SHOOT THE FARMER, KILL THE BOER?"
©RAPID PHASE-2010

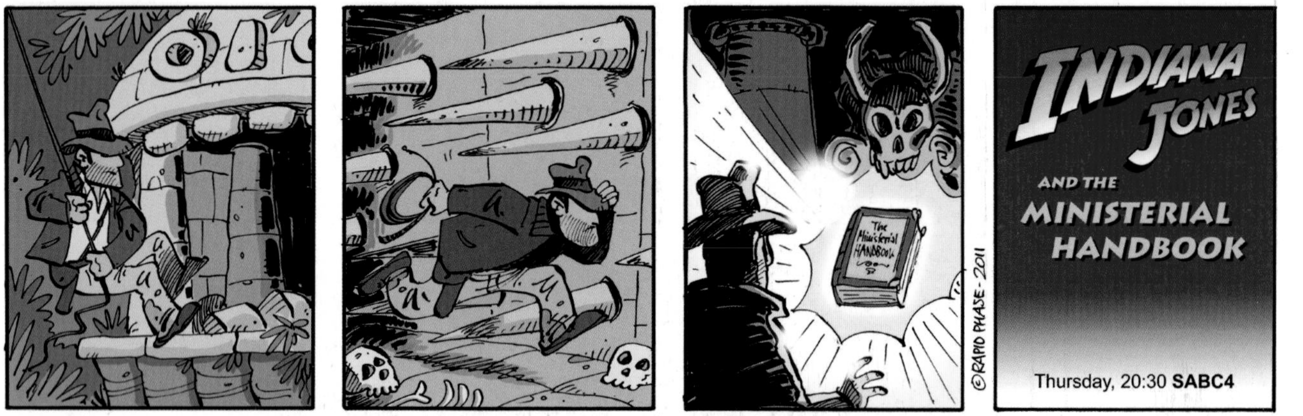
The Ministerial HANDBOOK
©RAPID PHASE-2011
INDIANA JONES
AND THE
MINISTERIAL HANDBOOK
Thursday, 20:30 SABC4

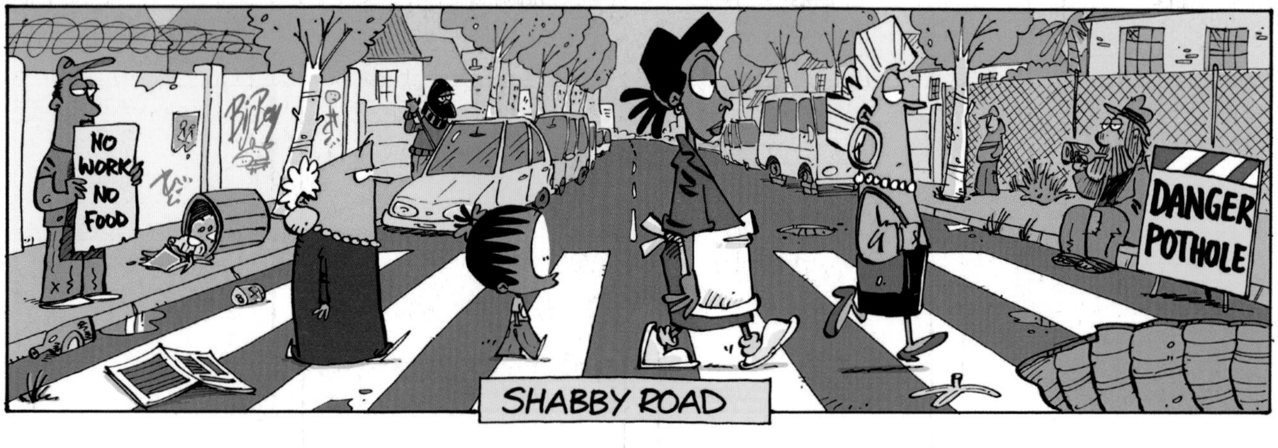
NO WORK NO FOOD
DANGER POTHOLE
SHABBY ROAD

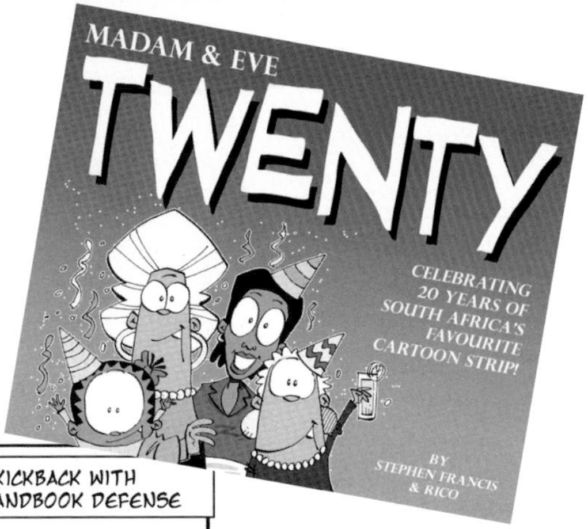
MADAM & EVE
TWENTY
CELEBRATING 20 YEARS OF SOUTH AFRICA'S FAVOURITE CARTOON STRIP!
BY STEPHEN FRANCIS & RICO

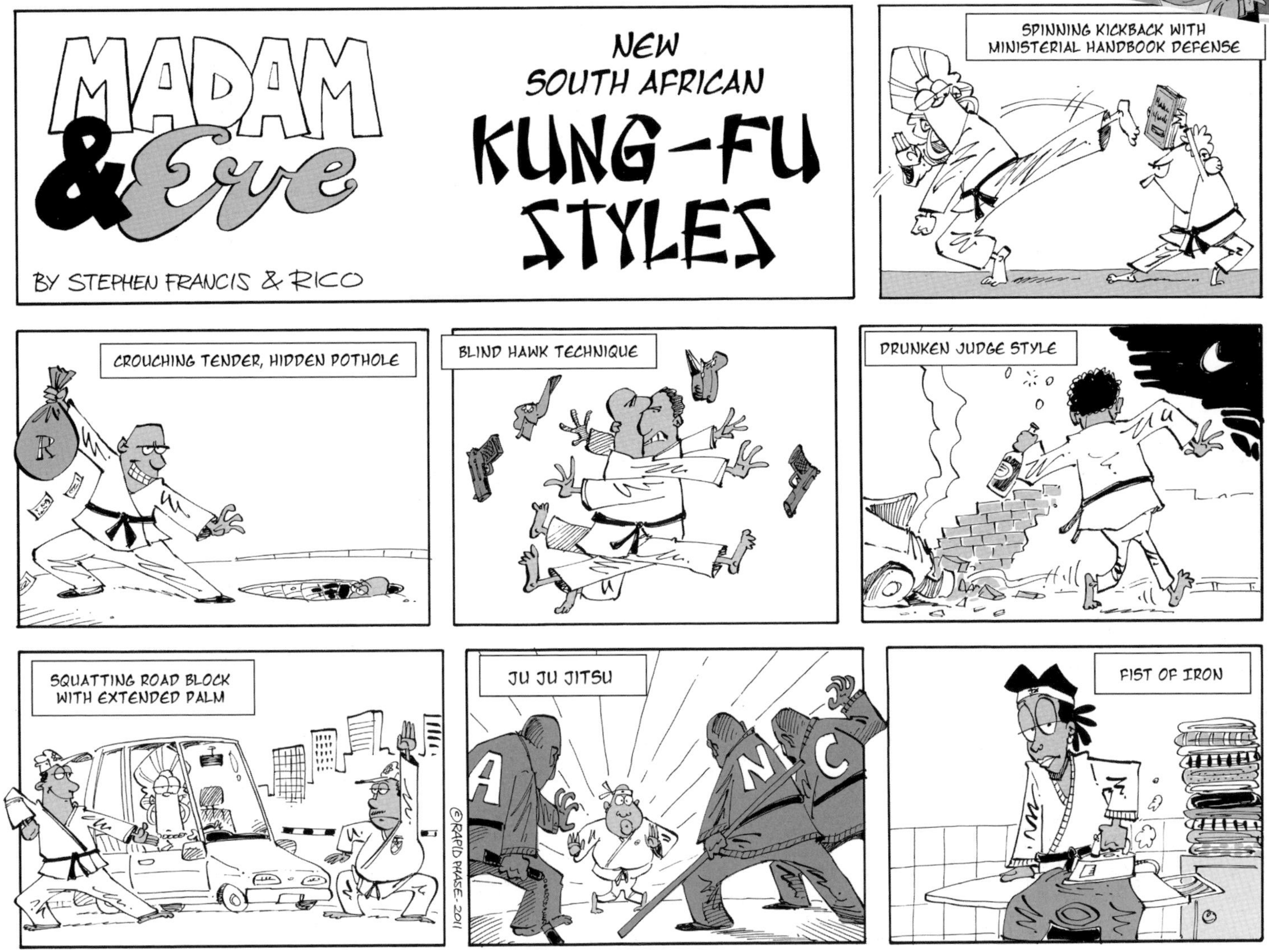
MADAM & Eve
BY STEPHEN FRANCIS & RICO
NEW SOUTH AFRICAN
KUNG-FU STYLES
SPINNING KICKBACK WITH MINISTERIAL HANDBOOK DEFENSE
CROUCHING TENDER, HIDDEN POTHOLE
R
BLIND HAWK TECHNIQUE
DRUNKEN JUDGE STYLE
SQUATTING ROAD BLOCK WITH EXTENDED PALM
JU JU JITSU
A
N
C
FIST OF IRON
© RAPID PHASE - 2011

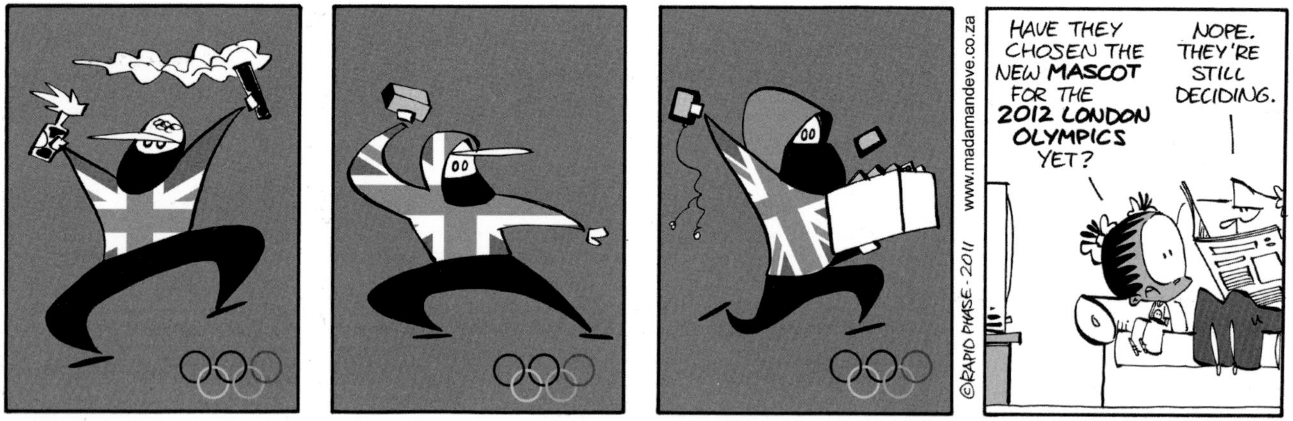

www.madamandeve.co.za
©RAPID PHASE · 2011
HAVE THEY CHOSEN THE NEW MASCOT FOR THE 2012 LONDON OLYMPICS YET?
NOPE. THEY'RE STILL DECIDING.

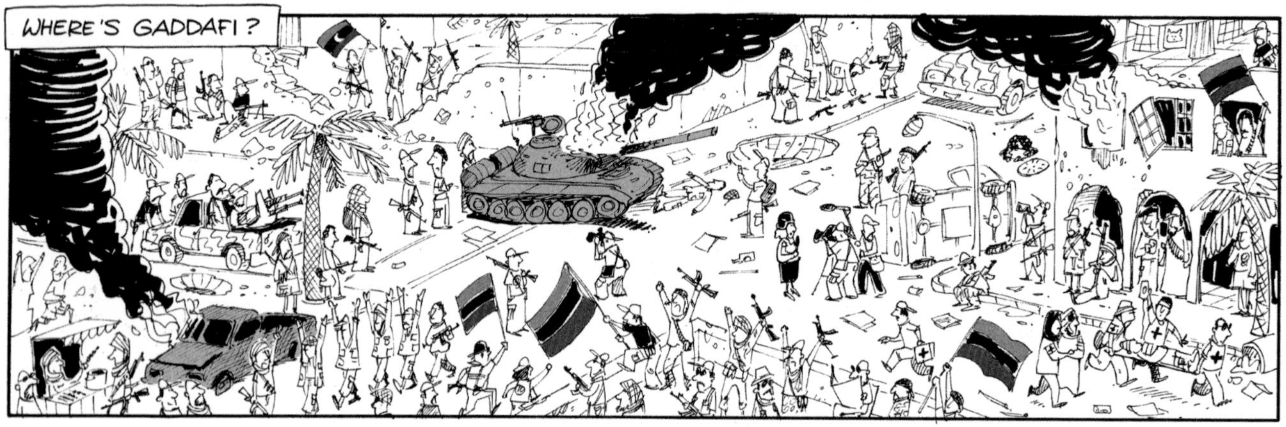

WHERE'S GADDAFI?

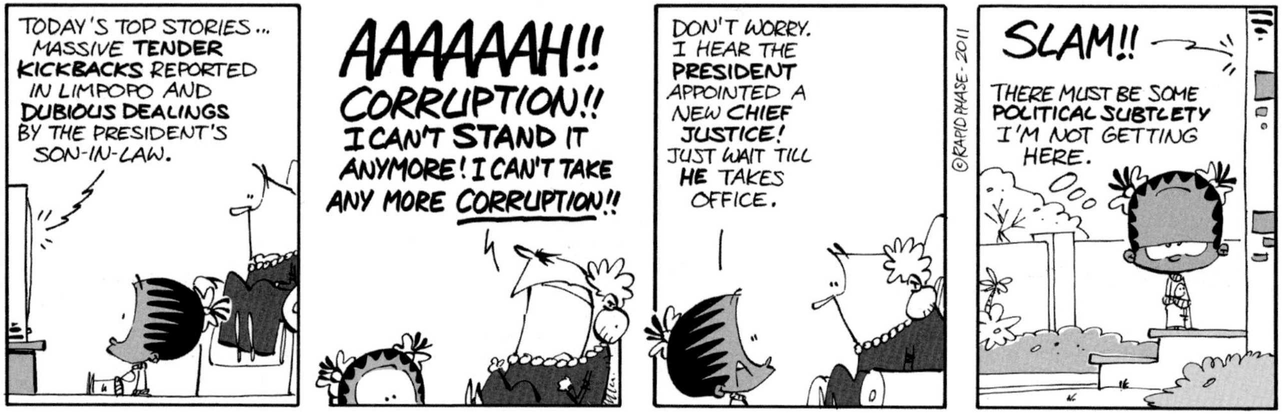

TODAY'S TOP STORIES... MASSIVE TENDER KICKBACKS REPORTED IN LIMPOPO AND DUBIOUS DEALINGS BY THE PRESIDENT'S SON-IN-LAW.
AAAAAAH!! CORRUPTION!! I CAN'T STAND IT ANYMORE! I CAN'T TAKE ANY MORE CORRUPTION!!
DON'T WORRY. I HEAR THE PRESIDENT APPOINTED A NEW CHIEF JUSTICE! JUST WAIT TILL HE TAKES OFFICE.
©RAPID PHASE · 2011
SLAM!!
THERE MUST BE SOME POLITICAL SUBTLETY I'M NOT GETTING HERE.

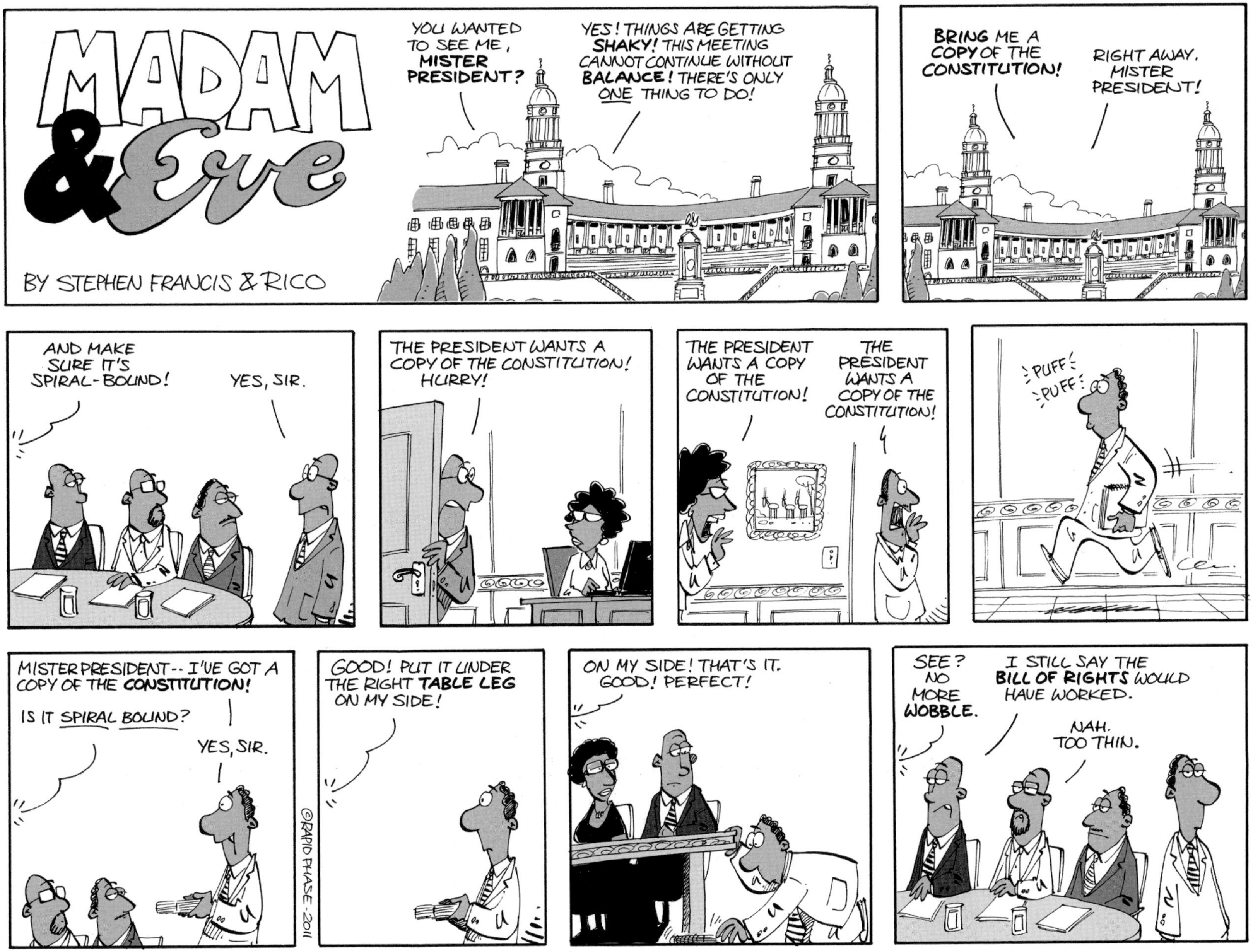
MADAM & Eve
BY STEPHEN FRANCIS & RICO
YOU WANTED TO SEE ME, **MISTER PRESIDENT?**
YES! THINGS ARE GETTING **SHAKY!** THIS MEETING CANNOT CONTINUE WITHOUT **BALANCE!** THERE'S ONLY ONE THING TO DO!
BRING ME A **COPY** OF THE **CONSTITUTION!**
RIGHT AWAY, MISTER PRESIDENT!
AND MAKE SURE IT'S SPIRAL-BOUND!
YES, SIR.
THE PRESIDENT WANTS A COPY OF THE CONSTITUTION! HURRY!
THE PRESIDENT WANTS A COPY OF THE CONSTITUTION!
THE PRESIDENT WANTS A COPY OF THE CONSTITUTION!
PUFF
PUFF
MISTER PRESIDENT-- I'VE GOT A COPY OF THE **CONSTITUTION!**
IS IT SPIRAL BOUND?
YES, SIR.
©RAPID PHASE-2011
GOOD! PUT IT UNDER THE RIGHT **TABLE LEG** ON MY SIDE!
ON MY SIDE! THAT'S IT. GOOD! PERFECT!
SEE? NO MORE **WOBBLE.**
I STILL SAY THE **BILL OF RIGHTS** WOULD HAVE WORKED.
NAH. TOO THIN.

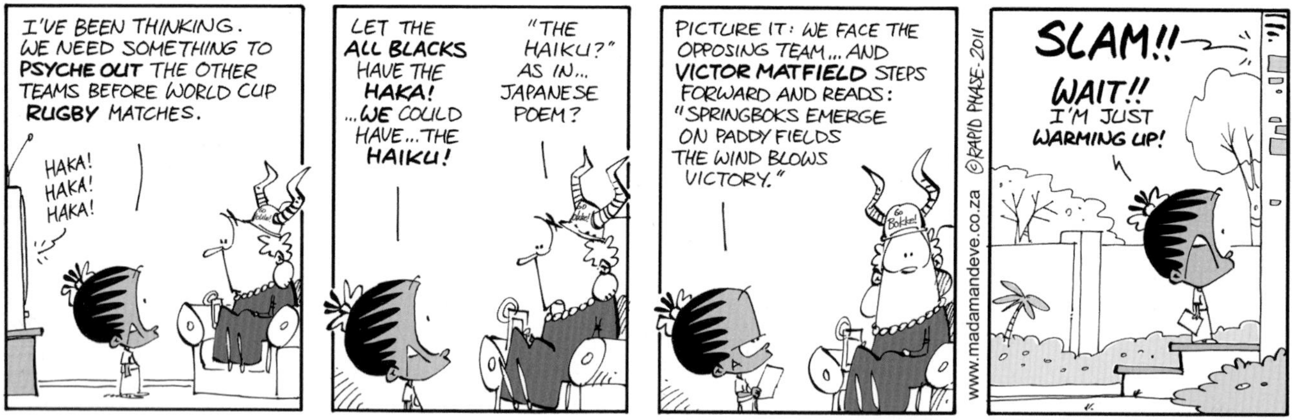
I'VE BEEN THINKING. WE NEED SOMETHING TO PSYCHE OUT THE OTHER TEAMS BEFORE WORLD CUP RUGBY MATCHES.
HAKA! HAKA! HAKA!
LET THE ALL BLACKS HAVE THE HAKA! ...WE COULD HAVE... THE HAIKU!
"THE HAIKU?" AS IN... JAPANESE POEM?
PICTURE IT: WE FACE THE OPPOSING TEAM... AND VICTOR MATFIELD STEPS FORWARD AND READS: "SPRINGBOKS EMERGE ON PADDY FIELDS THE WIND BLOWS VICTORY."
www.madamandeve.co.za ©RAPID PHASE-2011
SLAM!!
WAIT!! I'M JUST WARMING UP!

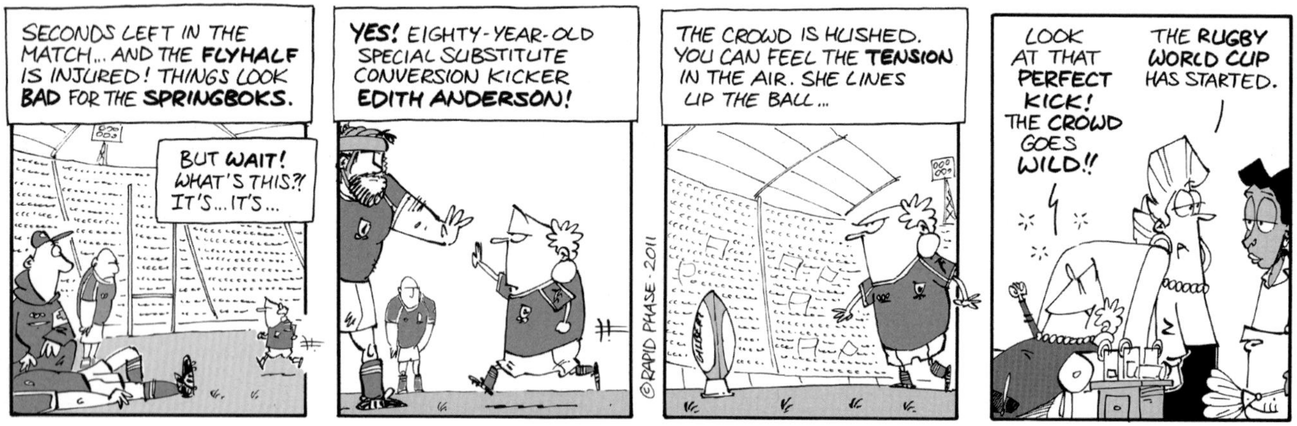
SECONDS LEFT IN THE MATCH... AND THE FLYHALF IS INJURED! THINGS LOOK BAD FOR THE SPRINGBOKS.
BUT WAIT! WHAT'S THIS?! IT'S... IT'S...
YES! EIGHTY-YEAR-OLD SPECIAL SUBSTITUTE CONVERSION KICKER EDITH ANDERSON!
©RAPID PHASE-2011
THE CROWD IS HUSHED. YOU CAN FEEL THE TENSION IN THE AIR. SHE LINES UP THE BALL...
LOOK AT THAT PERFECT KICK! THE CROWD GOES WILD!!
THE RUGBY WORLD CUP HAS STARTED.

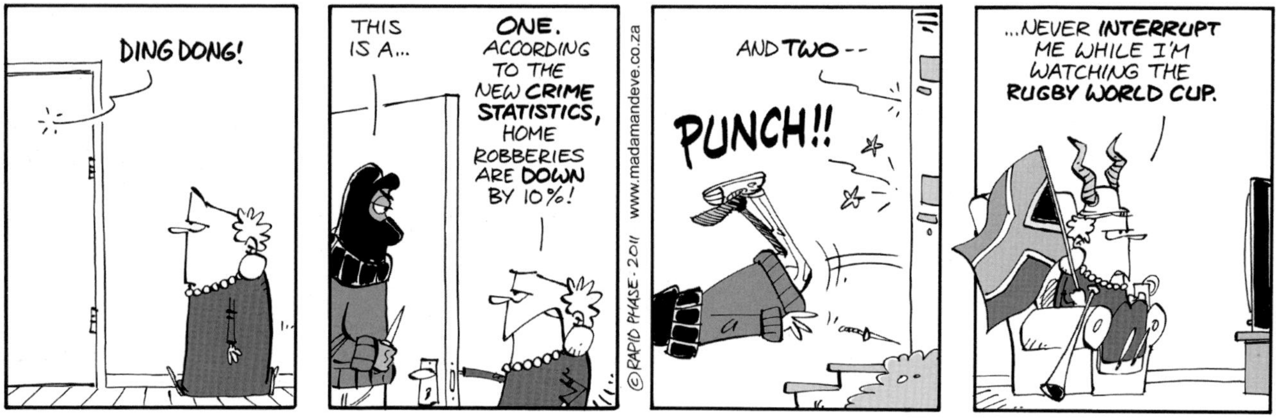
DING DONG!
THIS IS A...
ONE. ACCORDING TO THE NEW CRIME STATISTICS, HOME ROBBERIES ARE DOWN BY 10%!
©RAPID PHASE-2011 www.madamandeve.co.za
AND TWO--
PUNCH!!
...NEVER INTERRUPT ME WHILE I'M WATCHING THE RUGBY WORLD CUP.

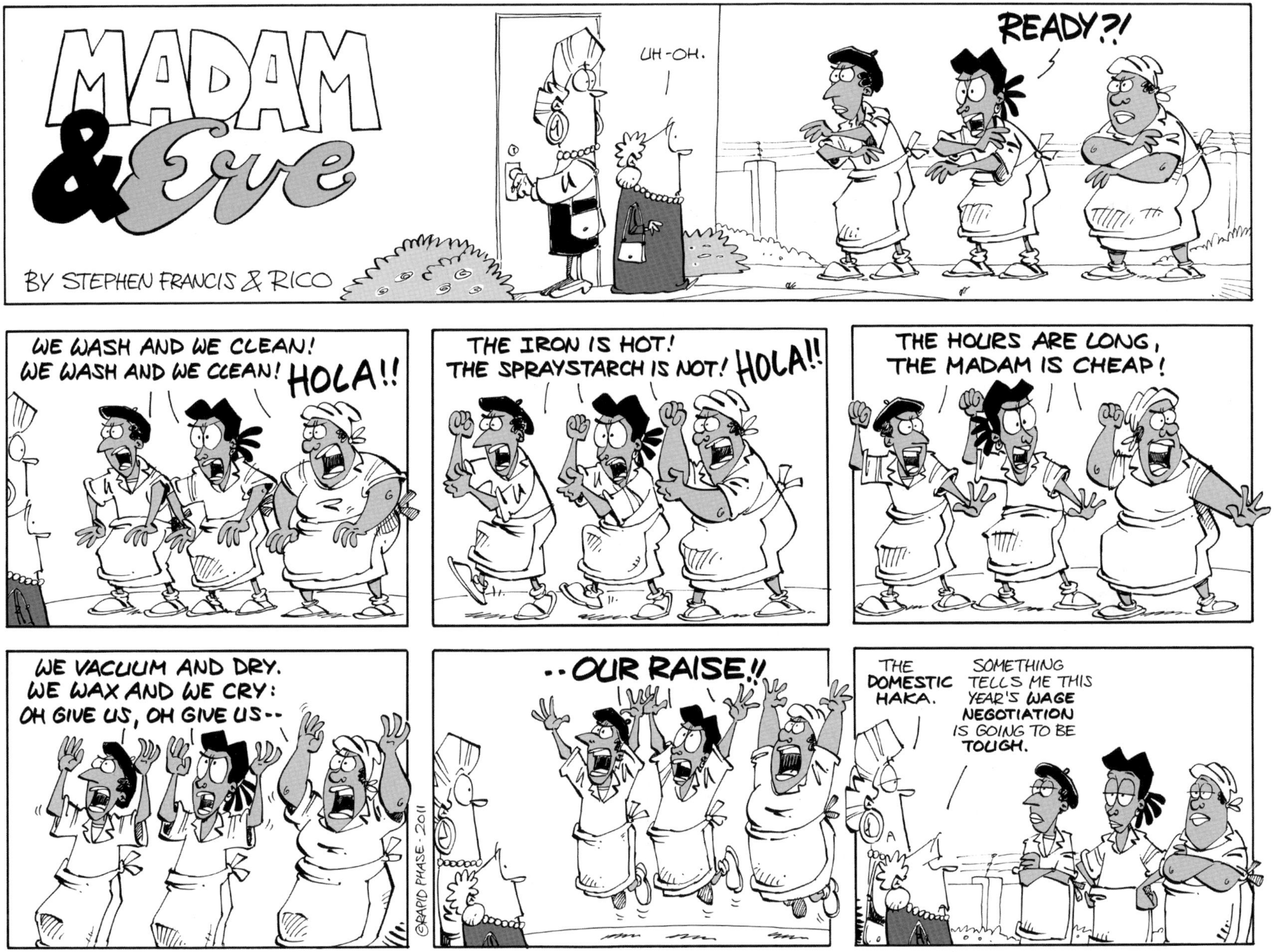
MADAM & Eve
BY STEPHEN FRANCIS & RICO
UH-OH.
READY?!
WE WASH AND WE CLEAN!
WE WASH AND WE CLEAN! HOLA!!
THE IRON IS HOT!
THE SPRAYSTARCH IS NOT! HOLA!!
THE HOURS ARE LONG,
THE MADAM IS CHEAP!
WE VACUUM AND DRY.
WE WAX AND WE CRY:
OH GIVE US, OH GIVE US--
©RAPID PHASE · 2011
..OUR RAISE!!
THE DOMESTIC HAKA.
SOMETHING TELLS ME THIS YEAR'S WAGE NEGOTIATION IS GOING TO BE TOUGH.

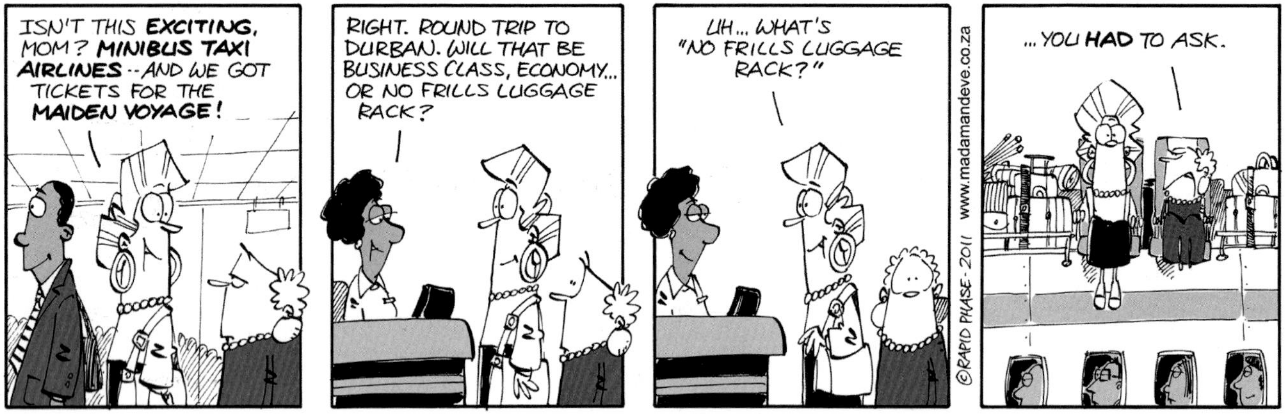
ISN'T THIS EXCITING, MOM? MINIBUS TAXI AIRLINES -- AND WE GOT TICKETS FOR THE MAIDEN VOYAGE!
RIGHT. ROUND TRIP TO DURBAN. WILL THAT BE BUSINESS CLASS, ECONOMY... OR NO FRILLS LUGGAGE RACK?
UH... WHAT'S "NO FRILLS LUGGAGE RACK?"
©RAPID PHASE-2011 www.madamandeve.co.za
...YOU HAD TO ASK.

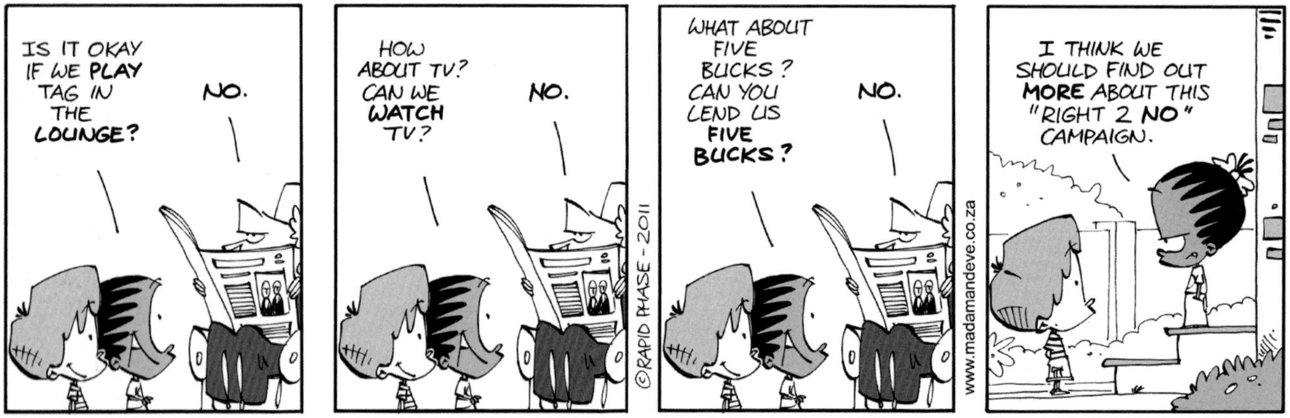
IS IT OKAY IF WE PLAY TAG IN THE LOUNGE?
NO.
HOW ABOUT TV? CAN WE WATCH TV?
NO.
©RAPID PHASE-2011
WHAT ABOUT FIVE BUCKS? CAN YOU LEND US FIVE BUCKS?
NO.
www.madamandeve.co.za
I THINK WE SHOULD FIND OUT MORE ABOUT THIS "RIGHT 2 NO" CAMPAIGN.

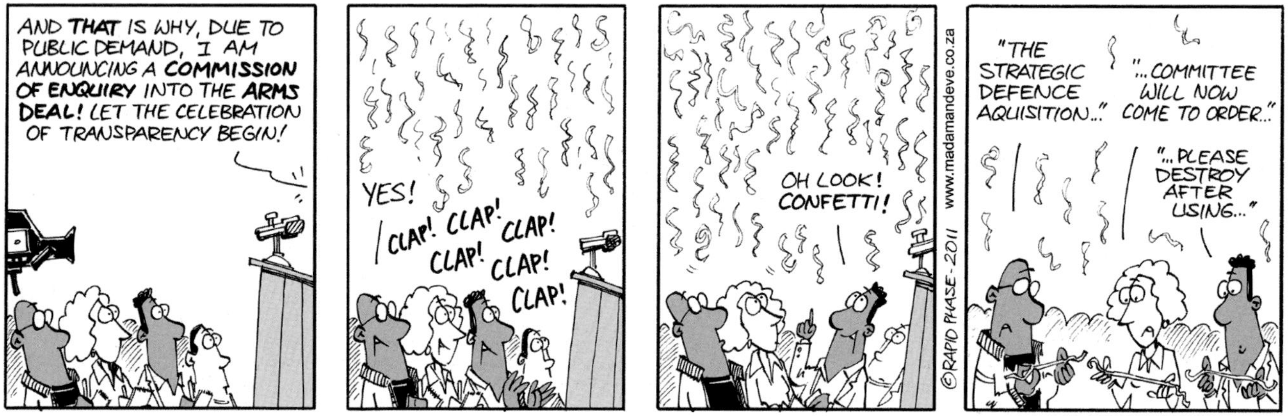
AND THAT IS WHY, DUE TO PUBLIC DEMAND, I AM ANNOUNCING A COMMISSION OF ENQUIRY INTO THE ARMS DEAL! LET THE CELEBRATION OF TRANSPARENCY BEGIN!
YES!
CLAP! CLAP! CLAP! CLAP! CLAP! CLAP!
OH LOOK! CONFETTI!
©RAPID PHASE-2011 www.madamandeve.co.za
"THE STRATEGIC DEFENCE AQUISITION..."
"...COMMITTEE WILL NOW COME TO ORDER..."
"...PLEASE DESTROY AFTER USING..."

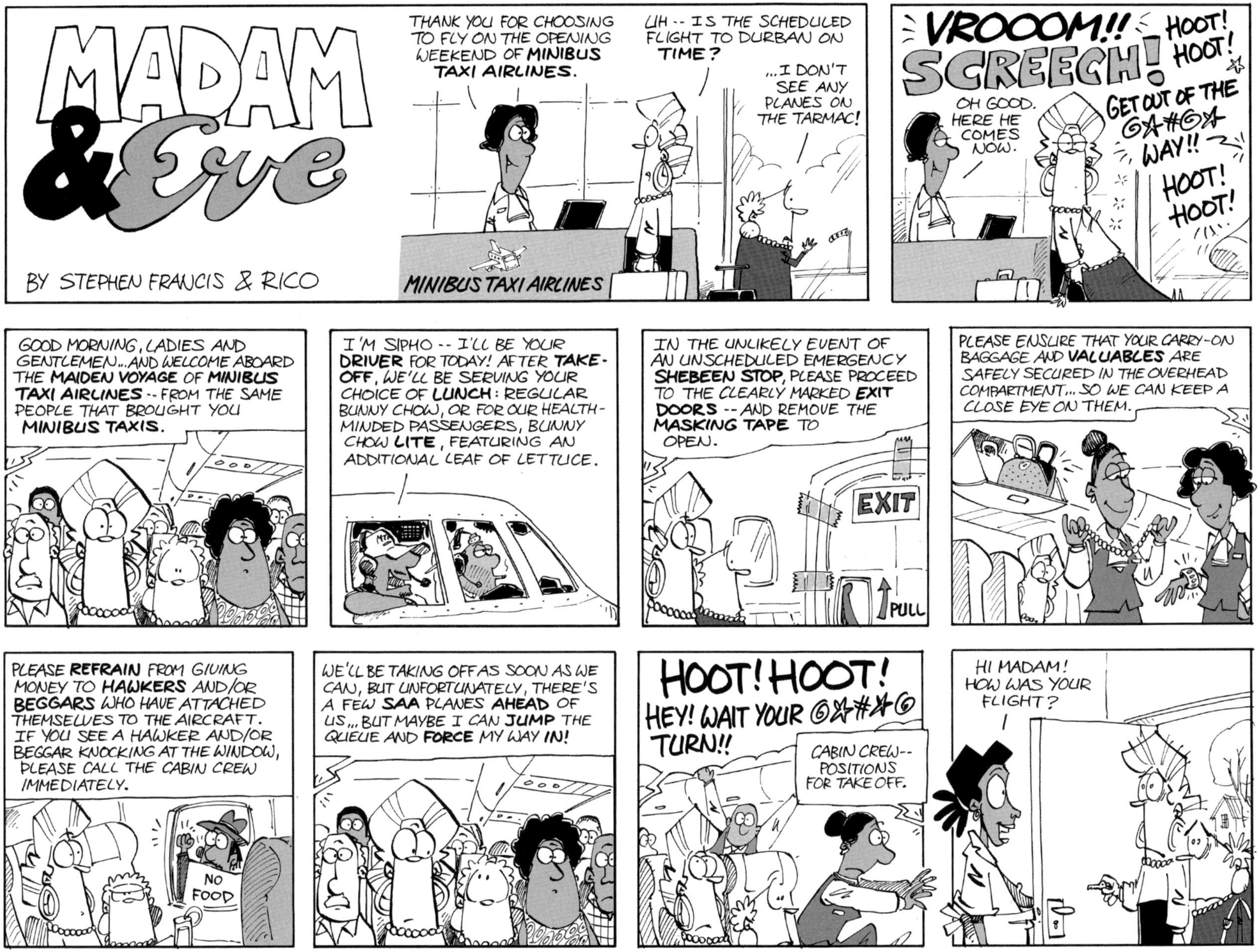
MADAM & Eve
BY STEPHEN FRANCIS & RICO
THANK YOU FOR CHOOSING TO FLY ON THE OPENING WEEKEND OF MINIBUS TAXI AIRLINES.
UH -- IS THE SCHEDULED FLIGHT TO DURBAN ON TIME?
...I DON'T SEE ANY PLANES ON THE TARMAC!
MINIBUS TAXI AIRLINES
VROOOM!!
SCREECH!
HOOT! HOOT!
OH GOOD. HERE HE COMES NOW.
GET OUT OF THE @#@# WAY!!
HOOT! HOOT!
GOOD MORNING, LADIES AND GENTLEMEN... AND WELCOME ABOARD THE MAIDEN VOYAGE OF MINIBUS TAXI AIRLINES -- FROM THE SAME PEOPLE THAT BROUGHT YOU MINIBUS TAXIS.
I'M SIPHO -- I'LL BE YOUR DRIVER FOR TODAY! AFTER TAKE-OFF, WE'LL BE SERVING YOUR CHOICE OF LUNCH: REGULAR BUNNY CHOW, OR FOR OUR HEALTH-MINDED PASSENGERS, BUNNY CHOW LITE, FEATURING AN ADDITIONAL LEAF OF LETTUCE.
IN THE UNLIKELY EVENT OF AN UNSCHEDULED EMERGENCY SHEBEEN STOP, PLEASE PROCEED TO THE CLEARLY MARKED EXIT DOORS -- AND REMOVE THE MASKING TAPE TO OPEN.
EXIT
PULL
PLEASE ENSURE THAT YOUR CARRY-ON BAGGAGE AND VALUABLES ARE SAFELY SECURED IN THE OVERHEAD COMPARTMENT... SO WE CAN KEEP A CLOSE EYE ON THEM.
PLEASE REFRAIN FROM GIVING MONEY TO HAWKERS AND/OR BEGGARS WHO HAVE ATTACHED THEMSELVES TO THE AIRCRAFT. IF YOU SEE A HAWKER AND/OR BEGGAR KNOCKING AT THE WINDOW, PLEASE CALL THE CABIN CREW IMMEDIATELY.
NO FOOD
WE'LL BE TAKING OFF AS SOON AS WE CAN, BUT UNFORTUNATELY, THERE'S A FEW SAA PLANES AHEAD OF US... BUT MAYBE I CAN JUMP THE QUEUE AND FORCE MY WAY IN!
HOOT! HOOT!
HEY! WAIT YOUR @#@ TURN!!
CABIN CREW-- POSITIONS FOR TAKE OFF.
HI MADAM! HOW WAS YOUR FLIGHT?

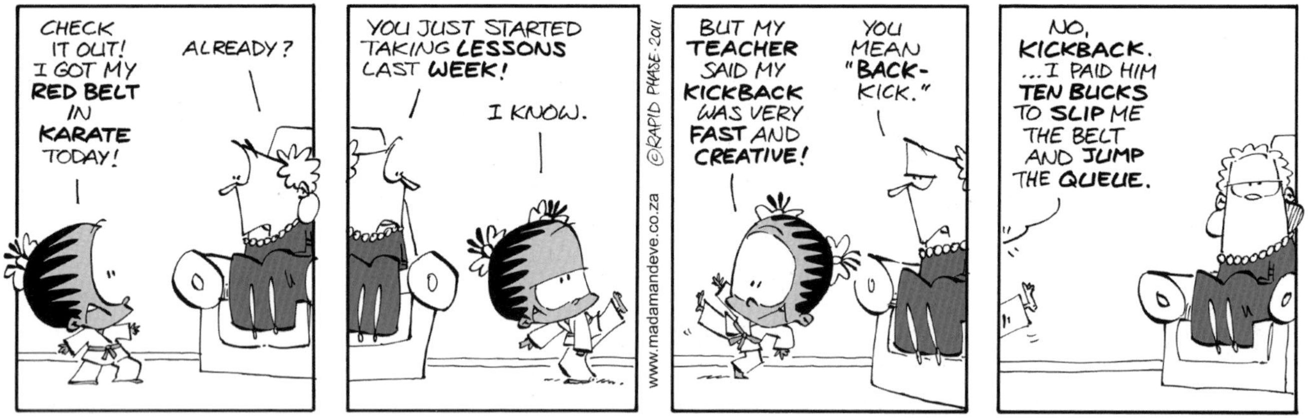
CHECK IT OUT! I GOT MY RED BELT IN KARATE TODAY!
ALREADY?
YOU JUST STARTED TAKING LESSONS LAST WEEK!
I KNOW.
©RAPID PHASE · 2011 www.madamandeve.co.za
BUT MY TEACHER SAID MY KICKBACK WAS VERY FAST AND CREATIVE!
YOU MEAN "BACK-KICK."
NO, KICKBACK. ...I PAID HIM TEN BUCKS TO SLIP ME THE BELT AND JUMP THE QUEUE.

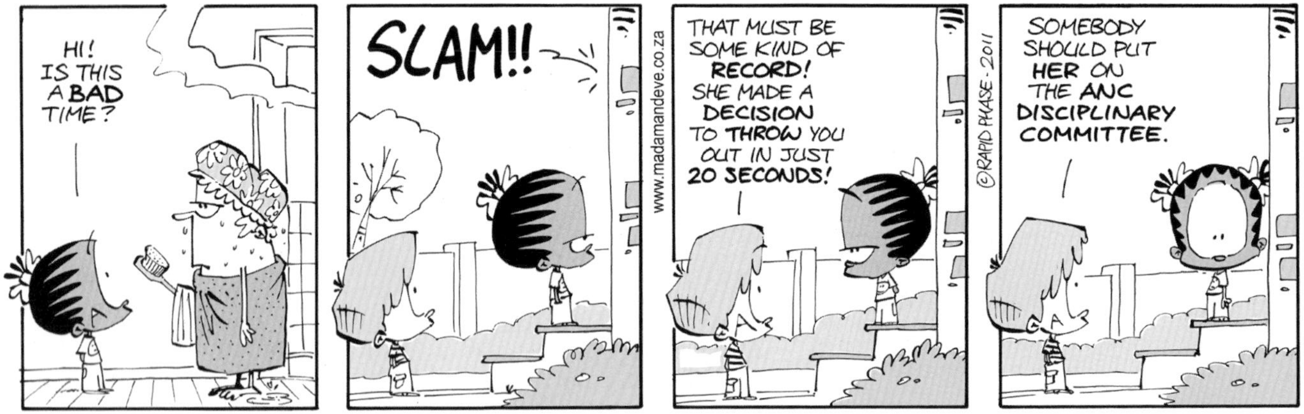
HI! IS THIS A BAD TIME?
SLAM!!
www.madamandeve.co.za
THAT MUST BE SOME KIND OF RECORD! SHE MADE A DECISION TO THROW YOU OUT IN JUST 20 SECONDS!
©RAPID PHASE · 2011
SOMEBODY SHOULD PUT HER ON THE ANC DISCIPLINARY COMMITTEE.

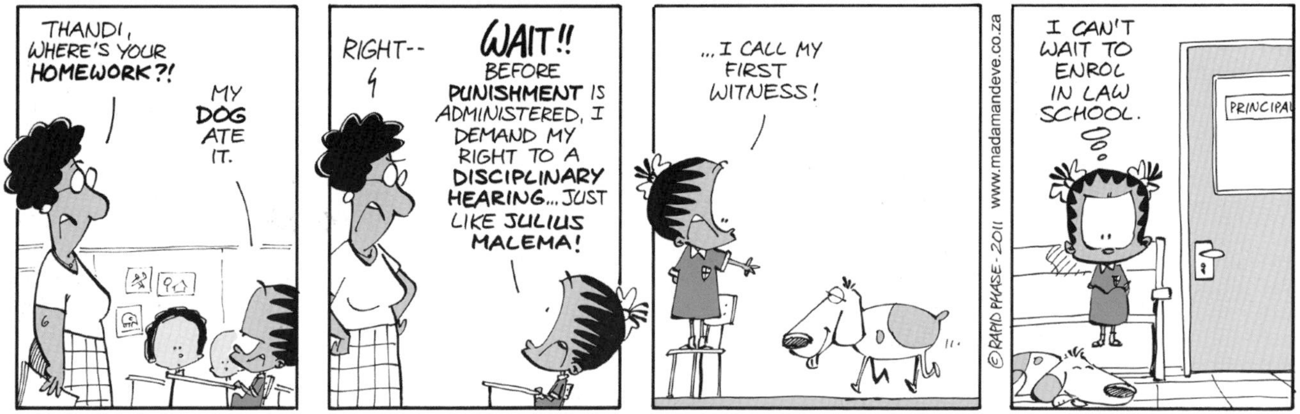
THANDI, WHERE'S YOUR HOMEWORK?!
MY DOG ATE IT.
RIGHT--
WAIT!! BEFORE PUNISHMENT IS ADMINISTERED, I DEMAND MY RIGHT TO A DISCIPLINARY HEARING... JUST LIKE JULIUS MALEMA!
...I CALL MY FIRST WITNESS!
©RAPID PHASE · 2011 www.madamandeve.co.za
I CAN'T WAIT TO ENROL IN LAW SCHOOL.
PRINCIPAL

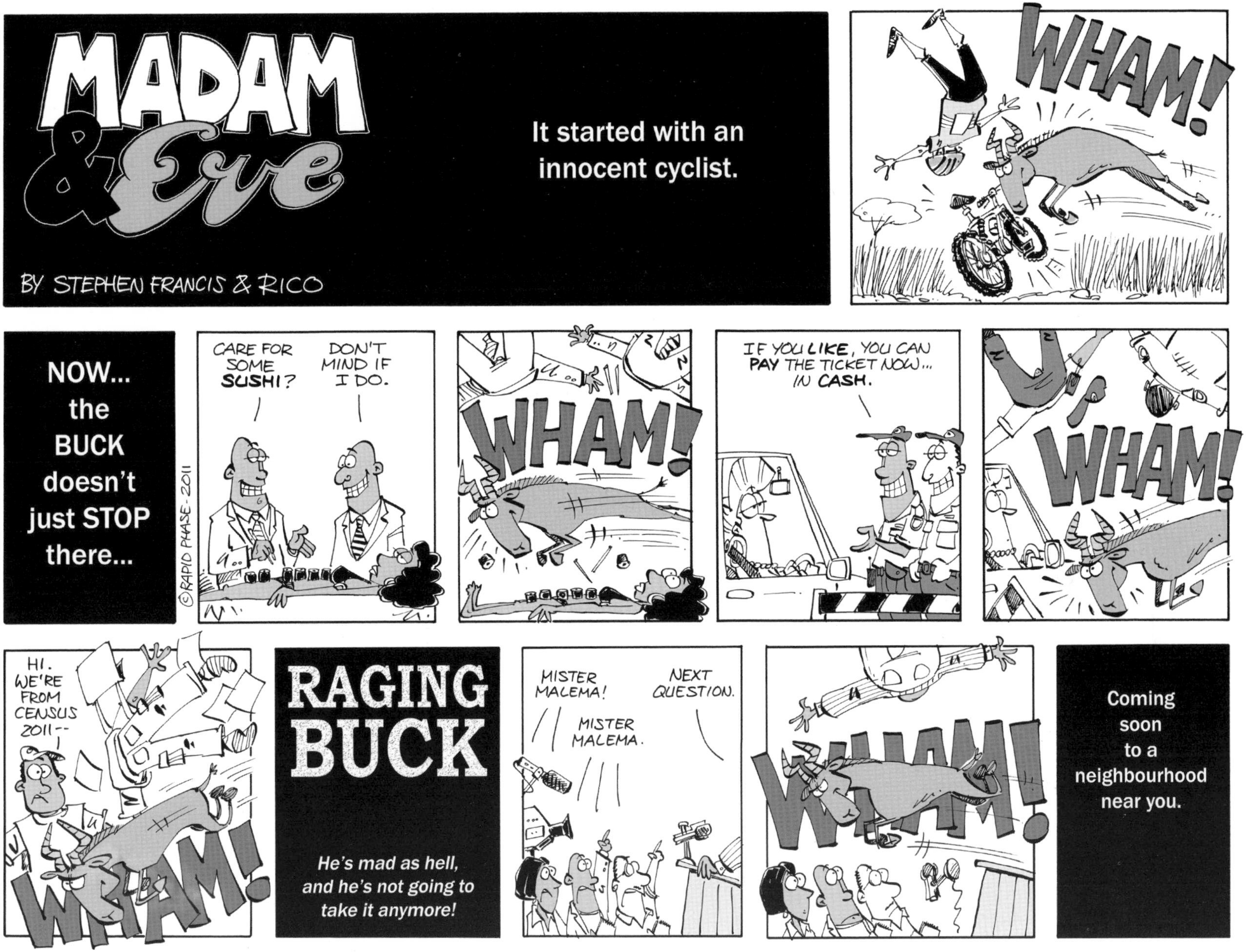
MADAM & Eve
BY STEPHEN FRANCIS & RICO
It started with an innocent cyclist.
WHAM!
NOW... the BUCK doesn't just STOP there...
CARE FOR SOME SUSHI?
DON'T MIND IF I DO.
©RAPID PHASE-2011
WHAM!
IF YOU LIKE, YOU CAN PAY THE TICKET NOW... IN CASH.
WHAM!
HI. WE'RE FROM CENSUS 2011--
WHAM!
RAGING BUCK
He's mad as hell, and he's not going to take it anymore!
MISTER MALEMA!
MISTER MALEMA.
NEXT QUESTION.
WHAM!
Coming soon to a neighbourhood near you.

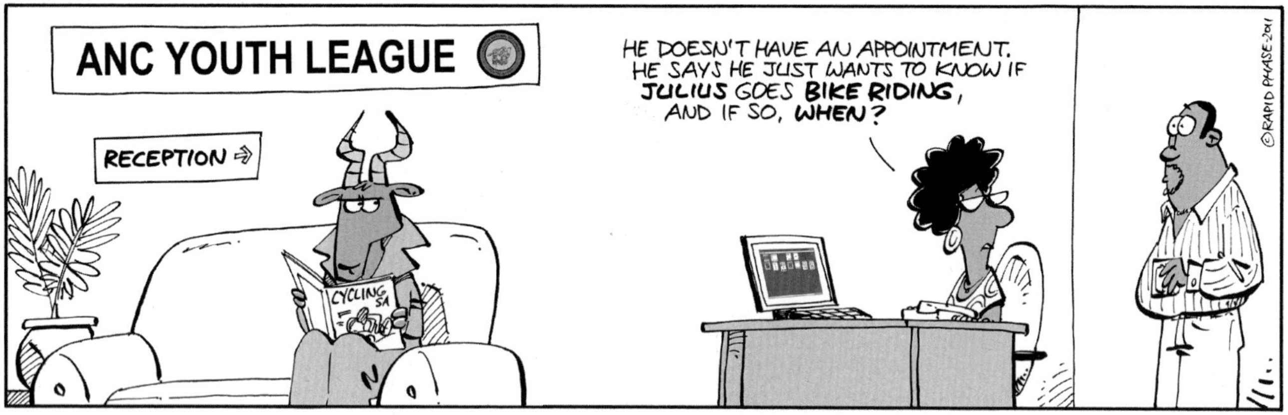
ANC YOUTH LEAGUE
RECEPTION
CYCLING SA
HE DOESN'T HAVE AN APPOINTMENT. HE SAYS HE JUST WANTS TO KNOW IF **JULIUS** GOES **BIKE RIDING**, AND IF SO, **WHEN?**
©RAPID PHASE 2011

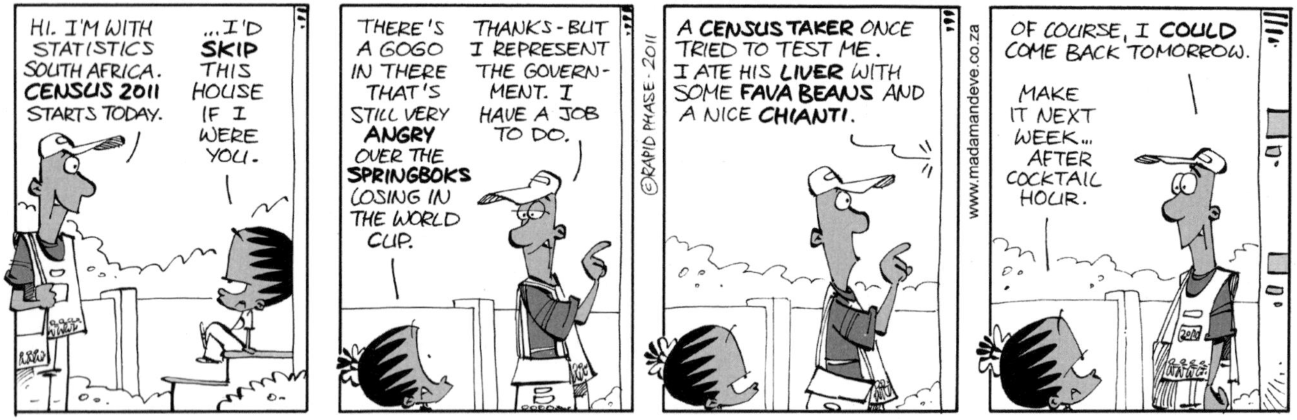
HI. I'M WITH STATISTICS SOUTH AFRICA. **CENSUS 2011** STARTS TODAY.
...I'D **SKIP** THIS HOUSE IF I WERE YOU.
THERE'S A GOGO IN THERE THAT'S STILL VERY **ANGRY** OVER THE **SPRINGBOKS** LOSING IN THE WORLD CUP.
THANKS - BUT I REPRESENT THE GOVERNMENT. I HAVE A JOB TO DO.
©RAPID PHASE 2011
A **CENSUS TAKER** ONCE TRIED TO TEST ME. I ATE HIS **LIVER** WITH SOME **FAVA BEANS** AND A NICE **CHIANTI**.
www.madamandeve.co.za
OF COURSE, I **COULD** COME BACK TOMORROW.
MAKE IT NEXT WEEK... AFTER COCKTAIL HOUR.

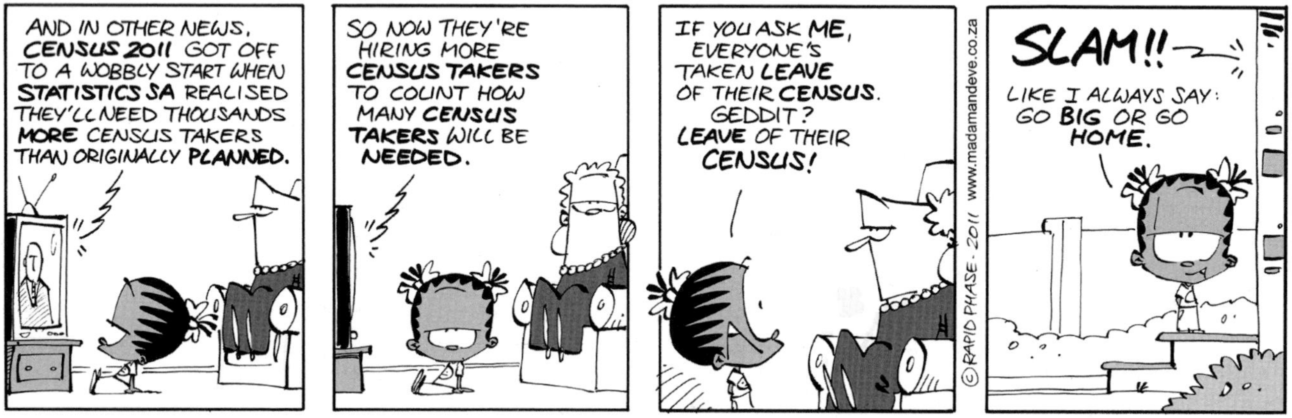
AND IN OTHER NEWS, **CENSUS 2011** GOT OFF TO A WOBBLY START WHEN **STATISTICS SA** REALISED THEY'LL NEED THOUSANDS **MORE** CENSUS TAKERS THAN ORIGINALLY **PLANNED**.
SO NOW THEY'RE HIRING MORE **CENSUS TAKERS** TO COUNT HOW MANY **CENSUS TAKERS** WILL BE **NEEDED**.
IF YOU ASK **ME**, EVERYONE'S TAKEN **LEAVE** OF THEIR **CENSUS**. GEDDIT? **LEAVE** OF THEIR **CENSUS**!
©RAPID PHASE 2011 www.madamandeve.co.za
SLAM!!
LIKE I ALWAYS SAY: GO **BIG** OR GO **HOME**.

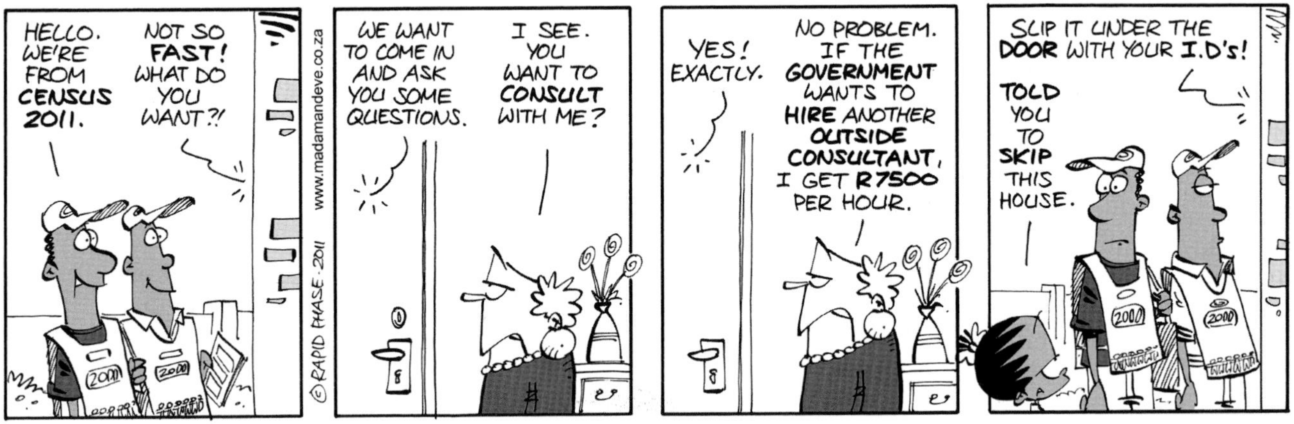
HELLO. WE'RE FROM CENSUS 2011.
NOT SO FAST! WHAT DO YOU WANT?!
© RAPID PHASE · 2011 www.madamandeve.co.za
WE WANT TO COME IN AND ASK YOU SOME QUESTIONS.
I SEE. YOU WANT TO CONSULT WITH ME?
YES! EXACTLY.
NO PROBLEM. IF THE GOVERNMENT WANTS TO HIRE ANOTHER OUTSIDE CONSULTANT, I GET R7500 PER HOUR.
SLIP IT UNDER THE DOOR WITH YOUR I.D's!
TOLD YOU TO SKIP THIS HOUSE.

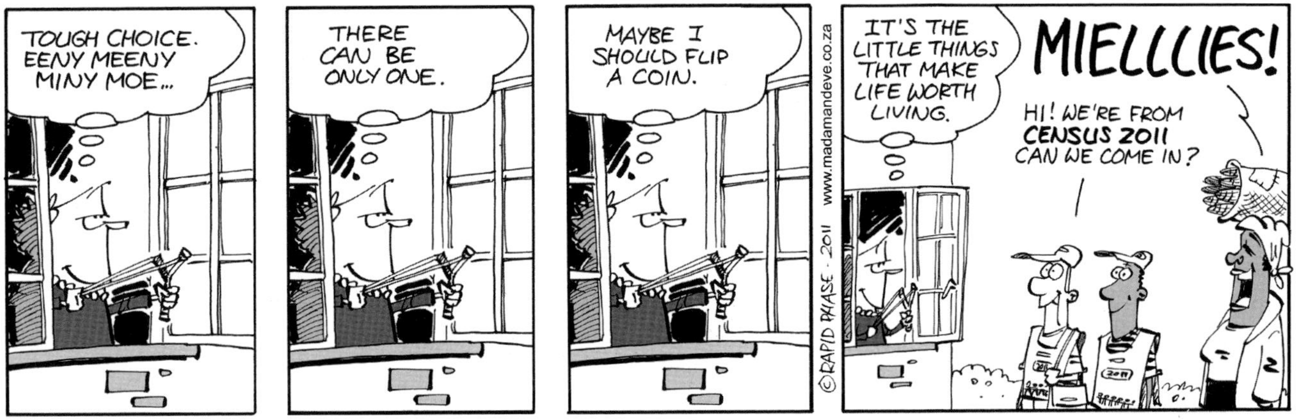
TOUGH CHOICE. EENY MEENY MINY MOE...
THERE CAN BE ONLY ONE.
MAYBE I SHOULD FLIP A COIN.
© RAPID PHASE · 2011 www.madamandeve.co.za
IT'S THE LITTLE THINGS THAT MAKE LIFE WORTH LIVING.
MIELLLIES!
HI! WE'RE FROM CENSUS 2011 CAN WE COME IN?

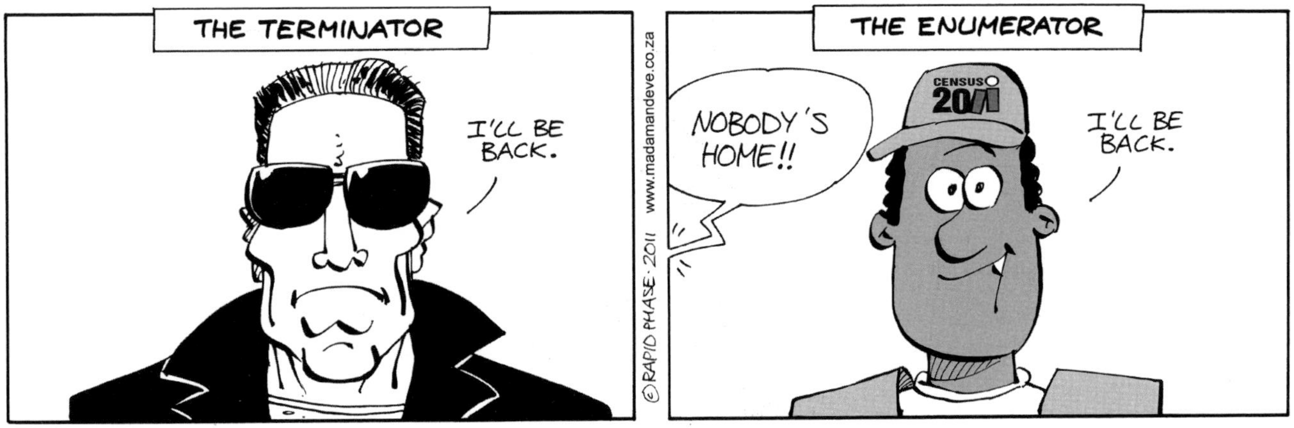
THE TERMINATOR
I'LL BE BACK.
© RAPID PHASE · 2011 www.madamandeve.co.za
THE ENUMERATOR
NOBODY'S HOME!!
CENSUS 2011
I'LL BE BACK.

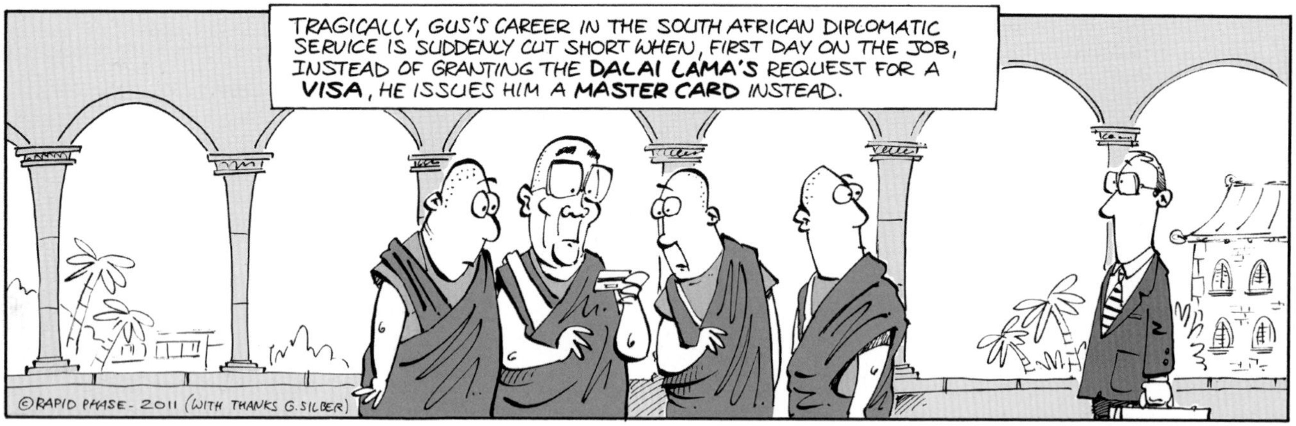
TRAGICALLY, GUS'S CAREER IN THE SOUTH AFRICAN DIPLOMATIC SERVICE IS SUDDENLY CUT SHORT WHEN, FIRST DAY ON THE JOB, INSTEAD OF GRANTING THE **DALAI LAMA'S** REQUEST FOR A **VISA**, HE ISSUES HIM A **MASTER CARD** INSTEAD.
©RAPID PHASE - 2011 (WITH THANKS G. SILBER)

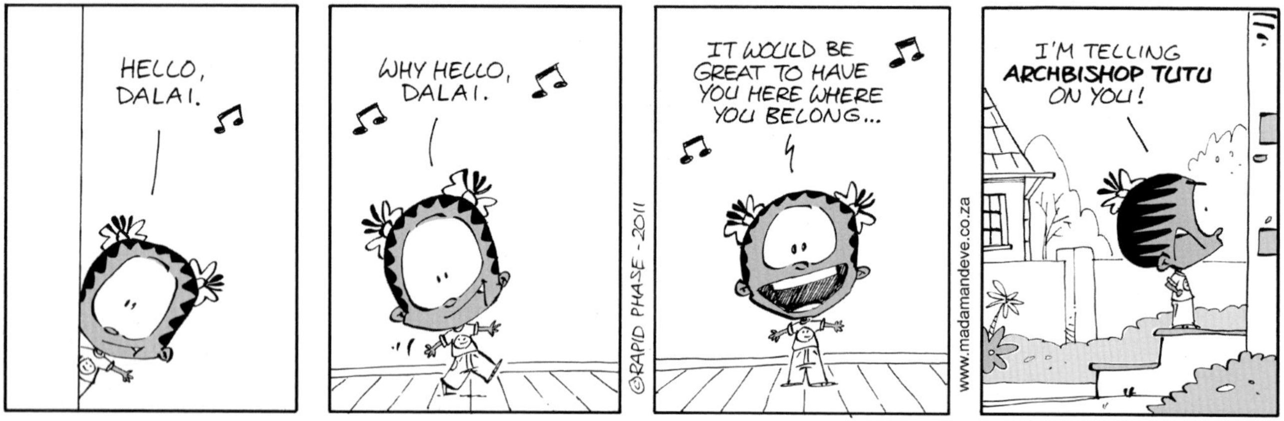
HELLO, DALAI.
WHY HELLO, DALAI.
IT WOULD BE GREAT TO HAVE YOU HERE WHERE YOU BELONG...
©RAPID PHASE - 2011
www.madamandeve.co.za
I'M TELLING **ARCHBISHOP TUTU** ON YOU!

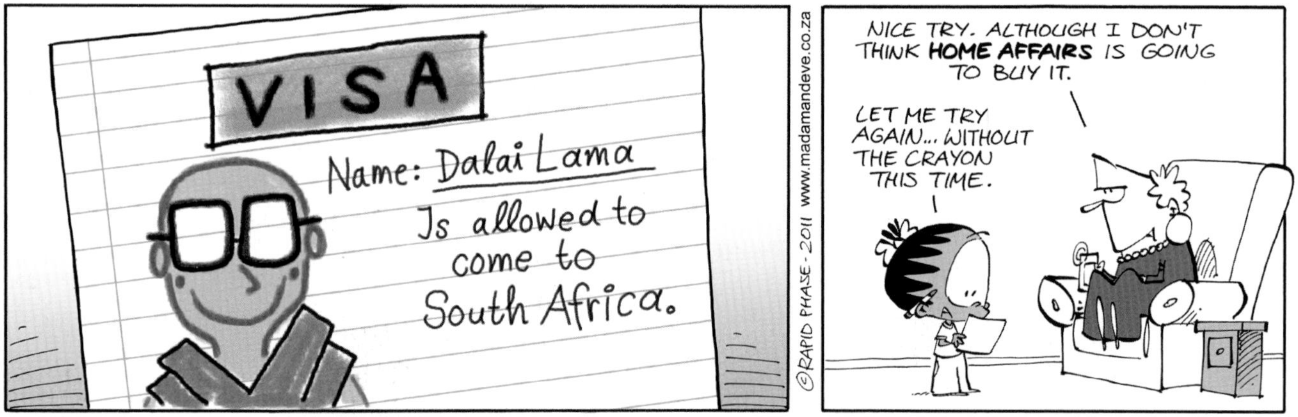
VISA
Name: Dalai Lama
Is allowed to come to South Africa.
©RAPID PHASE - 2011 www.madamandeve.co.za
NICE TRY. ALTHOUGH I DON'T THINK **HOME AFFAIRS** IS GOING TO BUY IT.
LET ME TRY AGAIN... WITHOUT THE CRAYON THIS TIME.

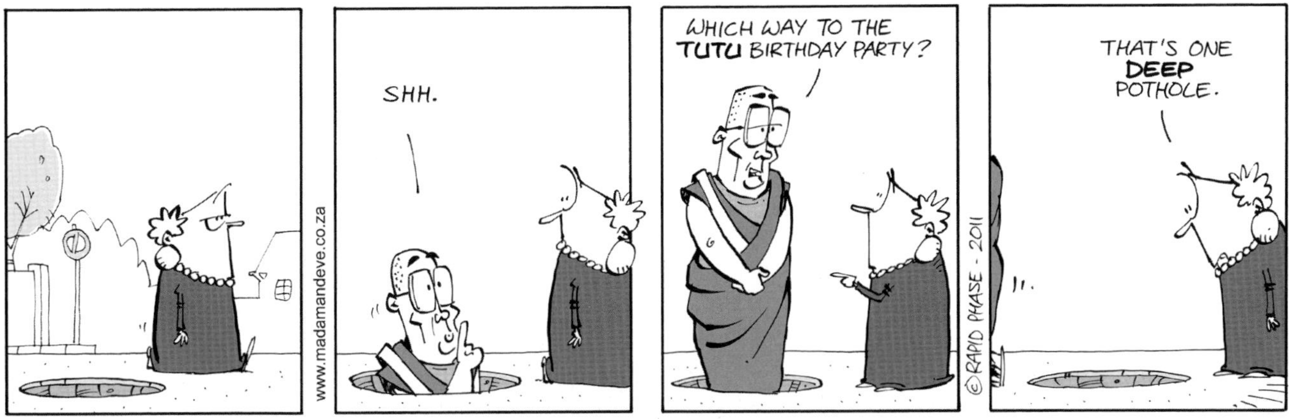
SHH.
www.madamandeve.co.za
WHICH WAY TO THE TUTU BIRTHDAY PARTY?
© RAPID PHASE · 2011
THAT'S ONE DEEP POTHOLE.

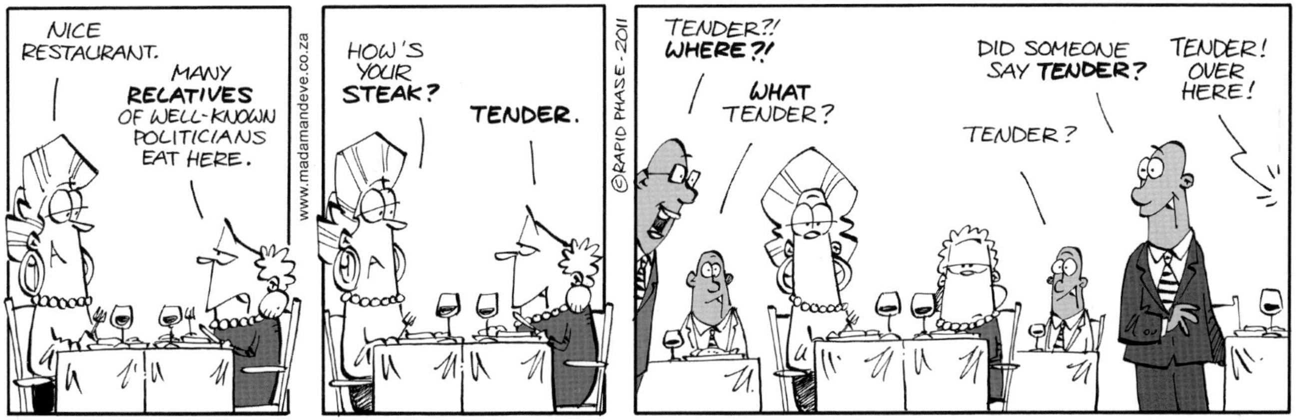
NICE RESTAURANT.
MANY RELATIVES OF WELL-KNOWN POLITICIANS EAT HERE.
www.madamandeve.co.za
HOW'S YOUR STEAK?
TENDER.
© RAPID PHASE · 2011
TENDER?! WHERE?!
WHAT TENDER?
TENDER?
DID SOMEONE SAY TENDER?
TENDER! OVER HERE!

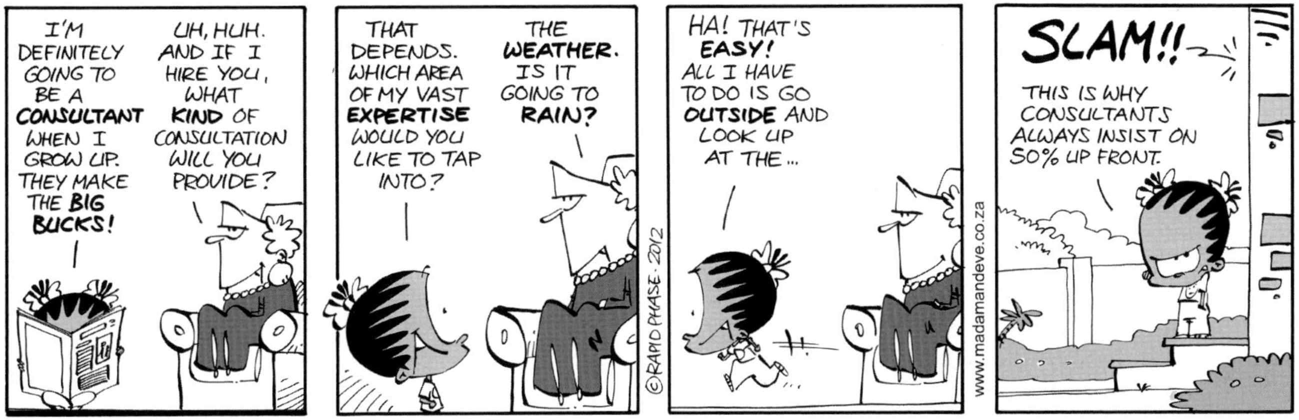
I'M DEFINITELY GOING TO BE A CONSULTANT WHEN I GROW UP. THEY MAKE THE BIG BUCKS!
UH, HUH. AND IF I HIRE YOU, WHAT KIND OF CONSULTATION WILL YOU PROVIDE?
THAT DEPENDS. WHICH AREA OF MY VAST EXPERTISE WOULD YOU LIKE TO TAP INTO?
THE WEATHER. IS IT GOING TO RAIN?
© RAPID PHASE · 2012
HA! THAT'S EASY! ALL I HAVE TO DO IS GO OUTSIDE AND LOOK UP AT THE...
www.madamandeve.co.za
SLAM!!
THIS IS WHY CONSULTANTS ALWAYS INSIST ON 50% UP FRONT.

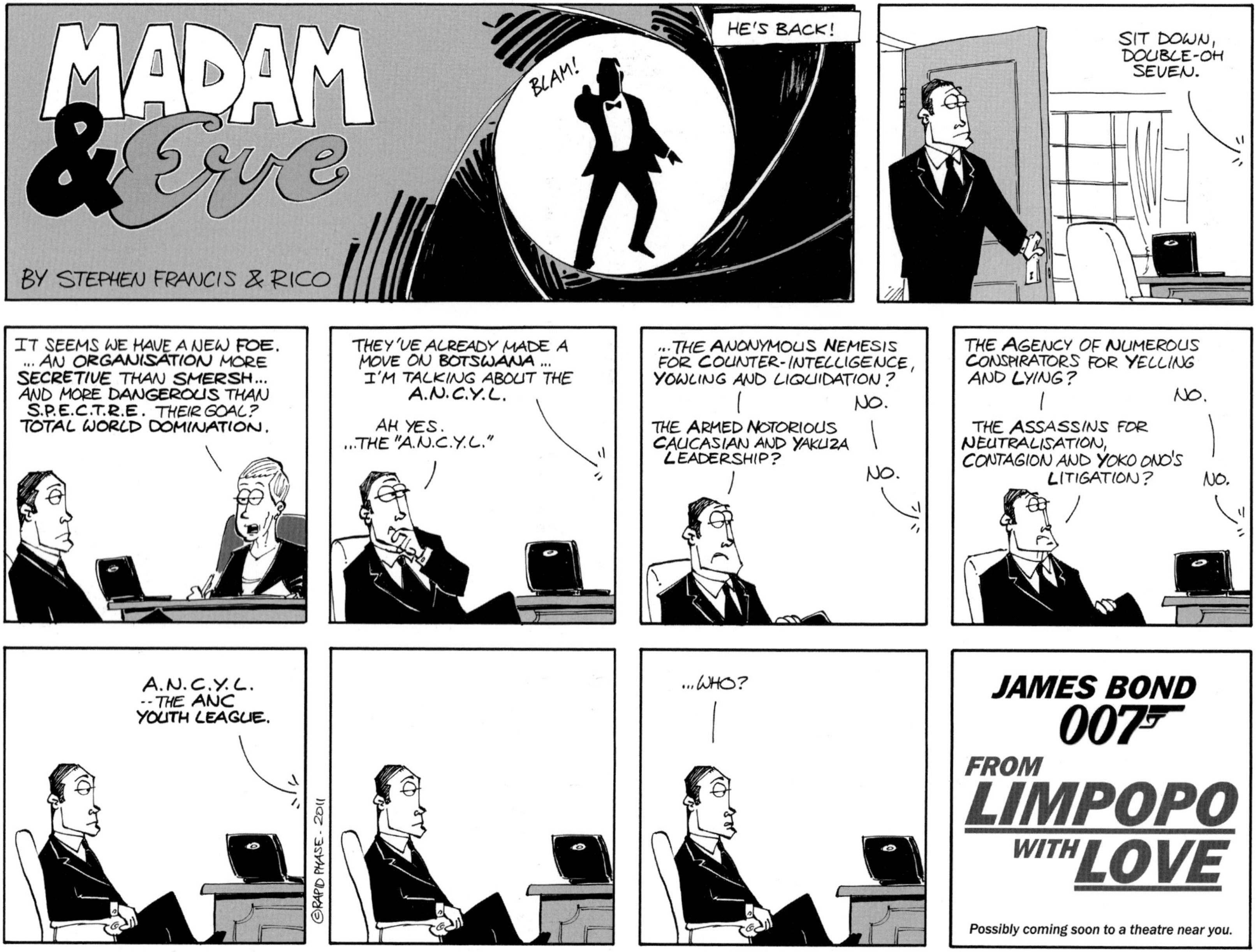
MADAM & Eve
BY STEPHEN FRANCIS & RICO
BLAM!
HE'S BACK!
SIT DOWN, DOUBLE-OH SEVEN.
IT SEEMS WE HAVE A NEW FOE. ... AN ORGANISATION MORE SECRETIVE THAN SMERSH... AND MORE DANGEROUS THAN S.P.E.C.T.R.E. THEIR GOAL? TOTAL WORLD DOMINATION.
THEY'VE ALREADY MADE A MOVE ON BOTSWANA ... I'M TALKING ABOUT THE A.N.C.Y.L.
AH YES. ...THE "A.N.C.Y.L."
...THE ANONYMOUS NEMESIS FOR COUNTER-INTELLIGENCE, YOWLING AND LIQUIDATION?
NO.
THE ARMED NOTORIOUS CAUCASIAN AND YAKUZA LEADERSHIP?
NO.
THE AGENCY OF NUMEROUS CONSPIRATORS FOR YELLING AND LYING?
NO.
THE ASSASSINS FOR NEUTRALISATION, CONTAGION AND YOKO ONO'S LITIGATION?
NO.
A.N.C.Y.L. --THE ANC YOUTH LEAGUE.
©RAPID PHASE - 2011
...WHO?
JAMES BOND 007
FROM LIMPOPO WITH LOVE
Possibly coming soon to a theatre near you.

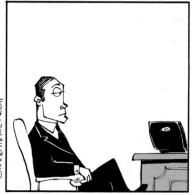

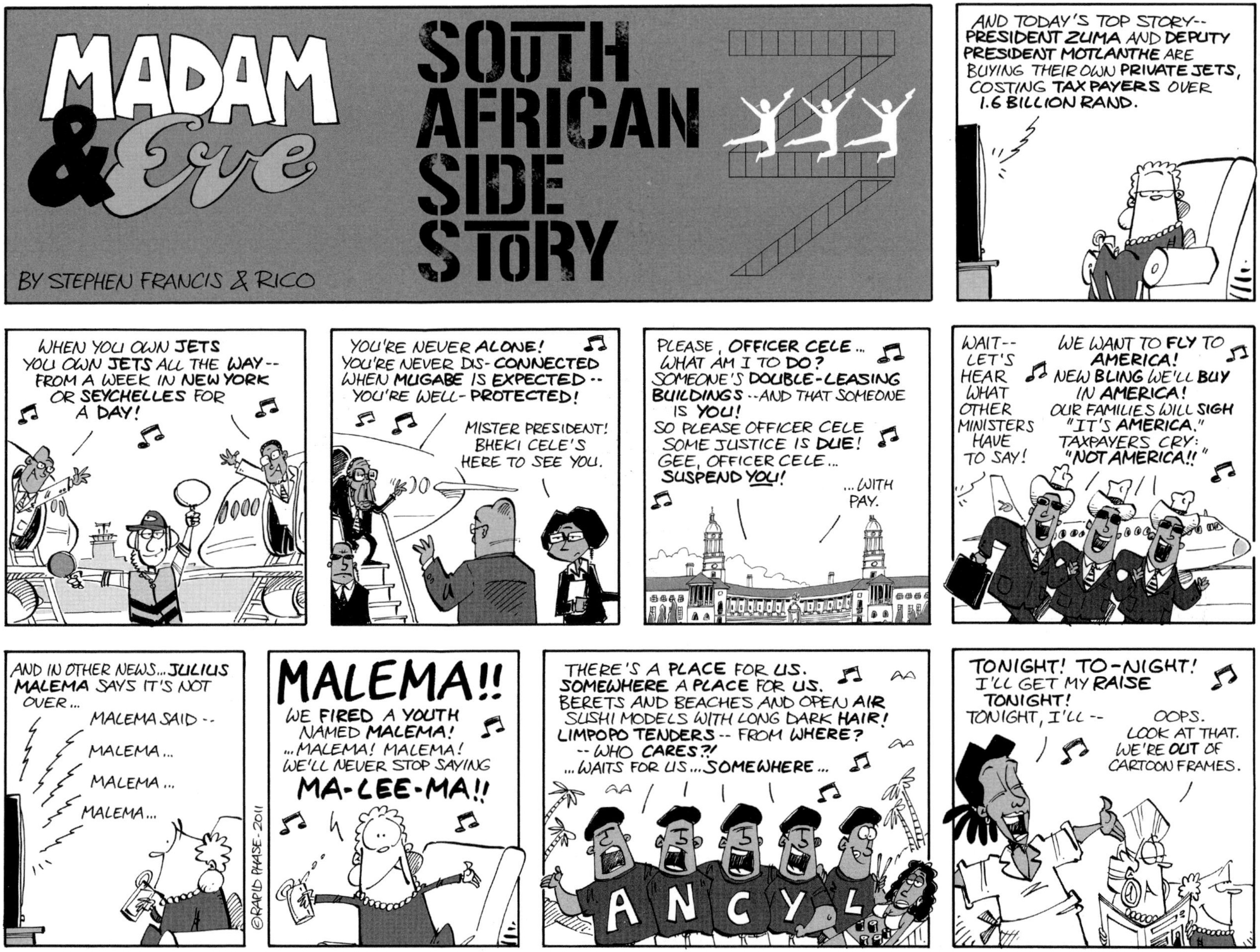
MADAM & Eve
SOUTH AFRICAN SIDE STORY
BY STEPHEN FRANCIS & RICO
AND TODAY'S TOP STORY-- PRESIDENT ZUMA AND DEPUTY PRESIDENT MOTLANTHE ARE BUYING THEIR OWN PRIVATE JETS, COSTING TAX PAYERS OVER 1.6 BILLION RAND.
WHEN YOU OWN JETS YOU OWN JETS ALL THE WAY-- FROM A WEEK IN NEW YORK OR SEYCHELLES FOR A DAY!
YOU'RE NEVER ALONE! YOU'RE NEVER DIS-CONNECTED WHEN MUGABE IS EXPECTED -- YOU'RE WELL-PROTECTED!
MISTER PRESIDENT! BHEKI CELE'S HERE TO SEE YOU.
PLEASE, OFFICER CELE... WHAT AM I TO DO? SOMEONE'S DOUBLE-LEASING BUILDINGS --AND THAT SOMEONE IS YOU! SO PLEASE OFFICER CELE SOME JUSTICE IS DUE! GEE, OFFICER CELE... SUSPEND YOU!
...WITH PAY.
WAIT-- LET'S HEAR WHAT OTHER MINISTERS HAVE TO SAY!
WE WANT TO FLY TO AMERICA! NEW BLING WE'LL BUY IN AMERICA! OUR FAMILIES WILL SIGH "IT'S AMERICA." TAXPAYERS CRY: "NOT AMERICA!!"
AND IN OTHER NEWS... JULIUS MALEMA SAYS IT'S NOT OVER...
MALEMA SAID --
MALEMA...
MALEMA...
MALEMA...
©RAPID PHASE · 2011
MALEMA!!
WE FIRED A YOUTH NAMED MALEMA! ...MALEMA! MALEMA! WE'LL NEVER STOP SAYING
MA-LEE-MA!!
THERE'S A PLACE FOR US. SOMEWHERE A PLACE FOR US. BERETS AND BEACHES AND OPEN AIR SUSHI MODELS WITH LONG DARK HAIR! LIMPOPO TENDERS -- FROM WHERE? -- WHO CARES?! ...WAITS FOR US... SOMEWHERE...
A N C Y L
TONIGHT! TO-NIGHT! I'LL GET MY RAISE TONIGHT! TONIGHT, I'LL --
OOPS. LOOK AT THAT. WE'RE OUT OF CARTOON FRAMES.

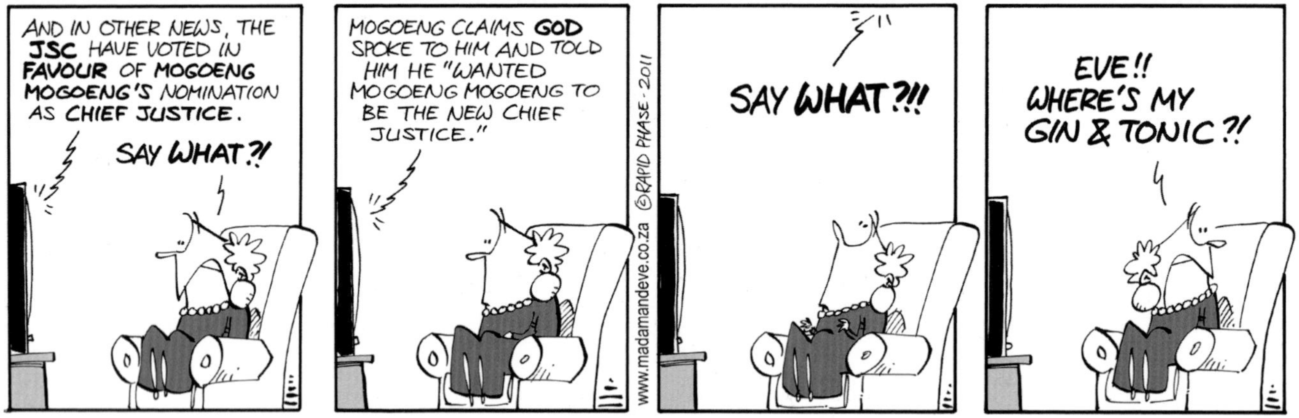
AND IN OTHER NEWS, THE JSC HAVE VOTED IN FAVOUR OF MOGOENG MOGOENG'S NOMINATION AS CHIEF JUSTICE.
SAY WHAT?!
MOGOENG CLAIMS GOD SPOKE TO HIM AND TOLD HIM HE "WANTED MOGOENG MOGOENG TO BE THE NEW CHIEF JUSTICE."
© RAPID PHASE · 2011
www.madamandeve.co.za
SAY WHAT?!!
EVE!! WHERE'S MY GIN & TONIC?!

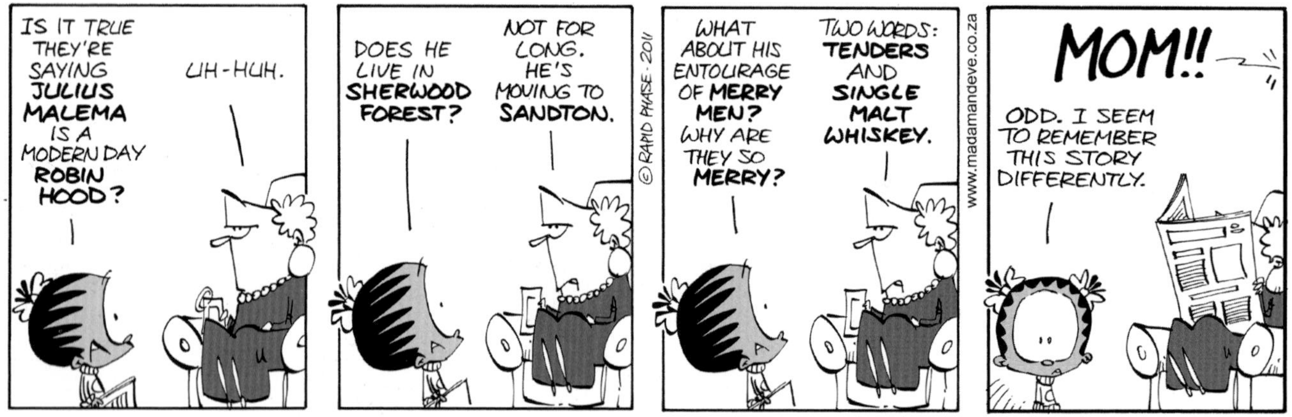
IS IT TRUE THEY'RE SAYING JULIUS MALEMA IS A MODERN DAY ROBIN HOOD?
UH-HUH.
DOES HE LIVE IN SHERWOOD FOREST?
NOT FOR LONG. HE'S MOVING TO SANDTON.
© RAPID PHASE · 2011
WHAT ABOUT HIS ENTOURAGE OF MERRY MEN? WHY ARE THEY SO MERRY?
TWO WORDS: TENDERS AND SINGLE MALT WHISKEY.
www.madamandeve.co.za
MOM!!
ODD. I SEEM TO REMEMBER THIS STORY DIFFERENTLY.

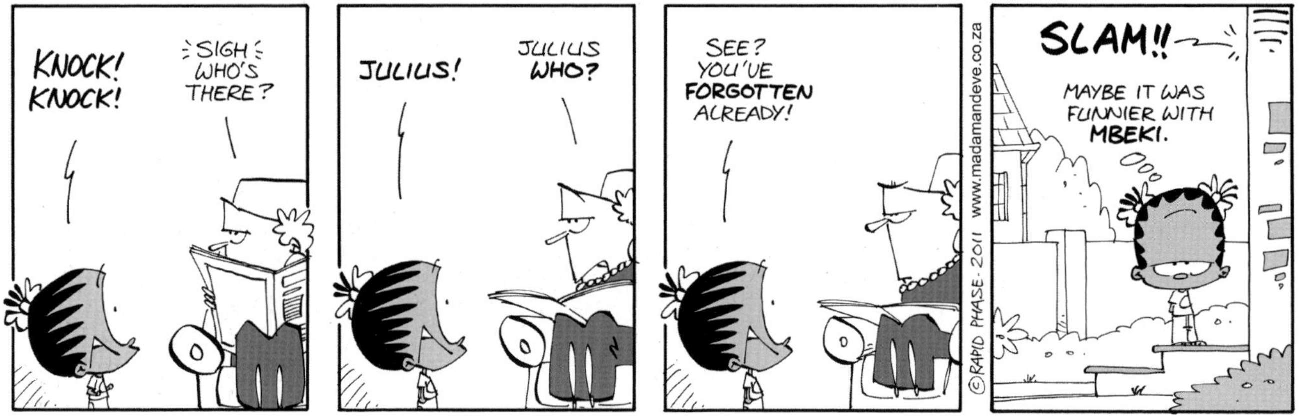
KNOCK! KNOCK!
SIGH WHO'S THERE?
JULIUS!
JULIUS WHO?
SEE? YOU'VE FORGOTTEN ALREADY!
© RAPID PHASE · 2011 www.madamandeve.co.za
SLAM!!
MAYBE IT WAS FUNNIER WITH MBEKI.

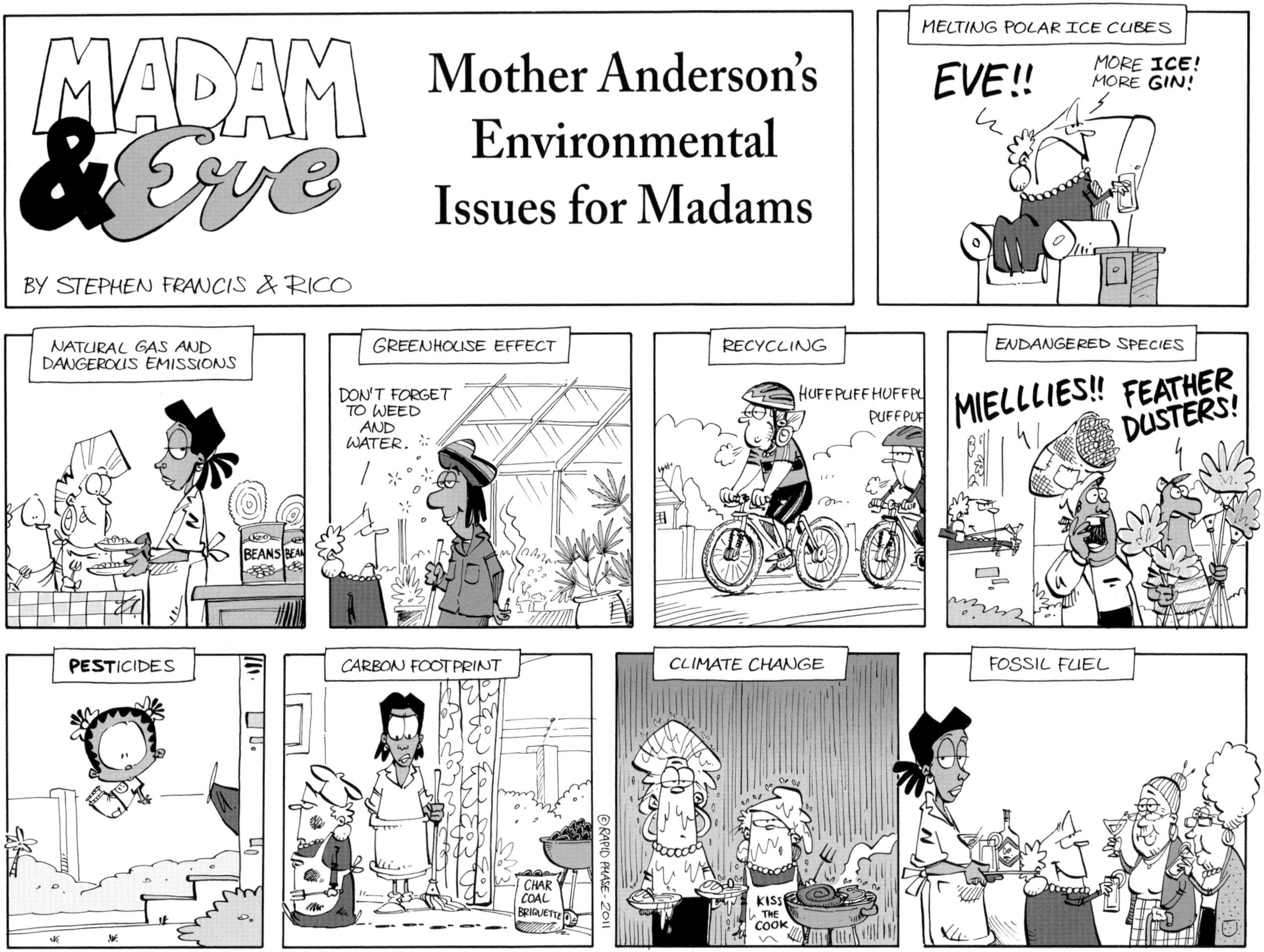
MADAM & Eve
Mother Anderson's Environmental Issues for Madams
BY STEPHEN FRANCIS & RICO
MELTING POLAR ICE CUBES
EVE!!
MORE ICE! MORE GIN!
NATURAL GAS AND DANGEROUS EMISSIONS
BEANS
GREENHOUSE EFFECT
DON'T FORGET TO WEED AND WATER.
RECYCLING
HUFFPUFFHUFFPU
PUFFPUF
ENDANGERED SPECIES
MIELLLIES!!
FEATHER DUSTERS!
PESTICIDES
CARBON FOOTPRINT
CHAR COAL BRIQUETTE
©RAPID PHASE-2011
CLIMATE CHANGE
KISS THE COOK
FOSSIL FUEL

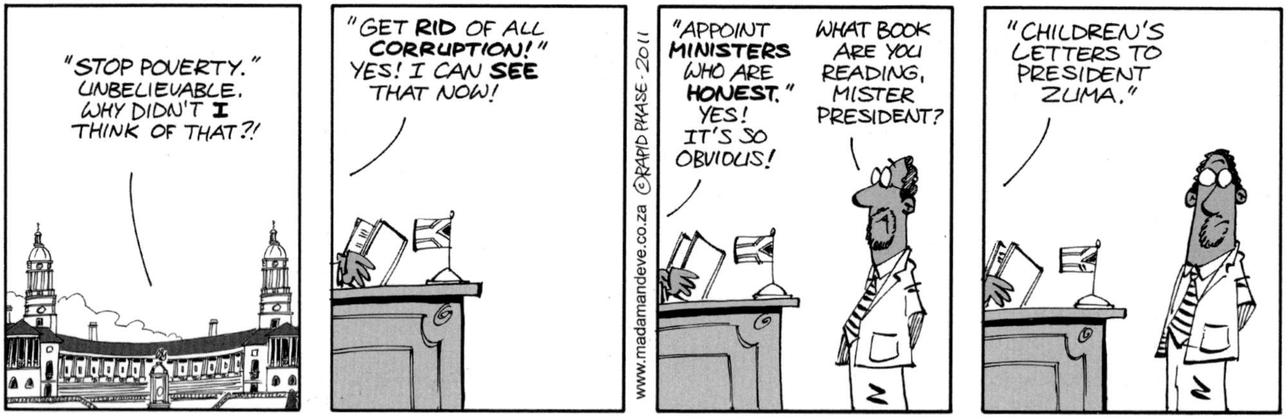
"STOP POVERTY." UNBELIEVABLE. WHY DIDN'T I THINK OF THAT?!
"GET RID OF ALL CORRUPTION!" YES! I CAN SEE THAT NOW!
www.madamandeve.co.za ©RAPID PHASE · 2011
"APPOINT MINISTERS WHO ARE HONEST." YES! IT'S SO OBVIOUS!
WHAT BOOK ARE YOU READING, MISTER PRESIDENT?
"CHILDREN'S LETTERS TO PRESIDENT ZUMA."

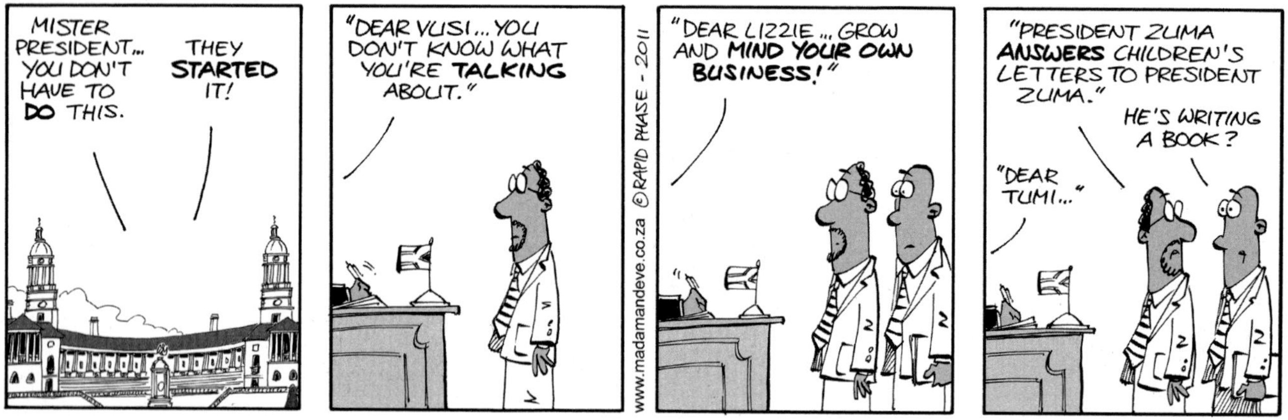
MISTER PRESIDENT... YOU DON'T HAVE TO DO THIS.
THEY STARTED IT!
"DEAR VUSI... YOU DON'T KNOW WHAT YOU'RE TALKING ABOUT."
www.madamandeve.co.za ©RAPID PHASE - 2011
"DEAR LIZZIE... GROW AND MIND YOUR OWN BUSINESS!"
"PRESIDENT ZUMA ANSWERS CHILDREN'S LETTERS TO PRESIDENT ZUMA."
HE'S WRITING A BOOK?
"DEAR TUMI..."

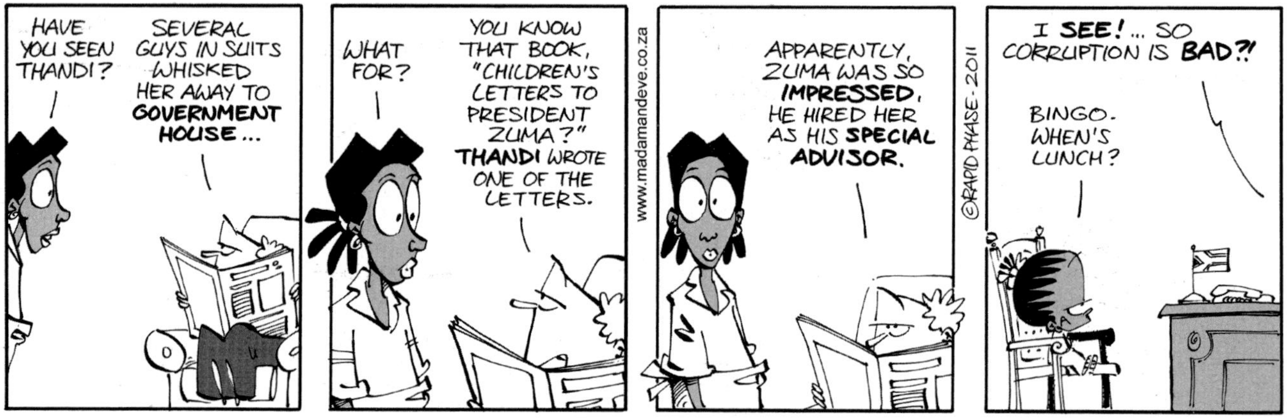
HAVE YOU SEEN THANDI?
SEVERAL GUYS IN SUITS WHISKED HER AWAY TO GOVERNMENT HOUSE...
WHAT FOR?
YOU KNOW THAT BOOK, "CHILDREN'S LETTERS TO PRESIDENT ZUMA?" THANDI WROTE ONE OF THE LETTERS.
www.madamandeve.co.za
APPARENTLY, ZUMA WAS SO IMPRESSED, HE HIRED HER AS HIS SPECIAL ADVISOR.
©RAPID PHASE · 2011
I SEE!... SO CORRUPTION IS BAD?!
BINGO. WHEN'S LUNCH?

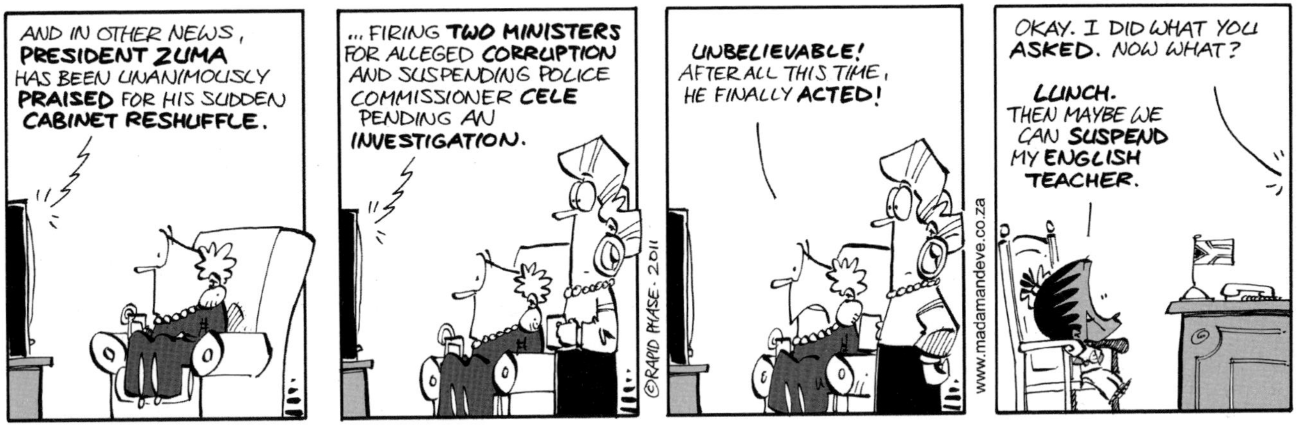
AND IN OTHER NEWS, PRESIDENT ZUMA HAS BEEN UNANIMOUSLY PRAISED FOR HIS SUDDEN CABINET RESHUFFLE.
... FIRING TWO MINISTERS FOR ALLEGED CORRUPTION AND SUSPENDING POLICE COMMISSIONER CELE PENDING AN INVESTIGATION.
©RAPID PHASE-2011
UNBELIEVABLE! AFTER ALL THIS TIME, HE FINALLY ACTED!
www.madamandeve.co.za
OKAY. I DID WHAT YOU ASKED. NOW WHAT?
LUNCH. THEN MAYBE WE CAN SUSPEND MY ENGLISH TEACHER.

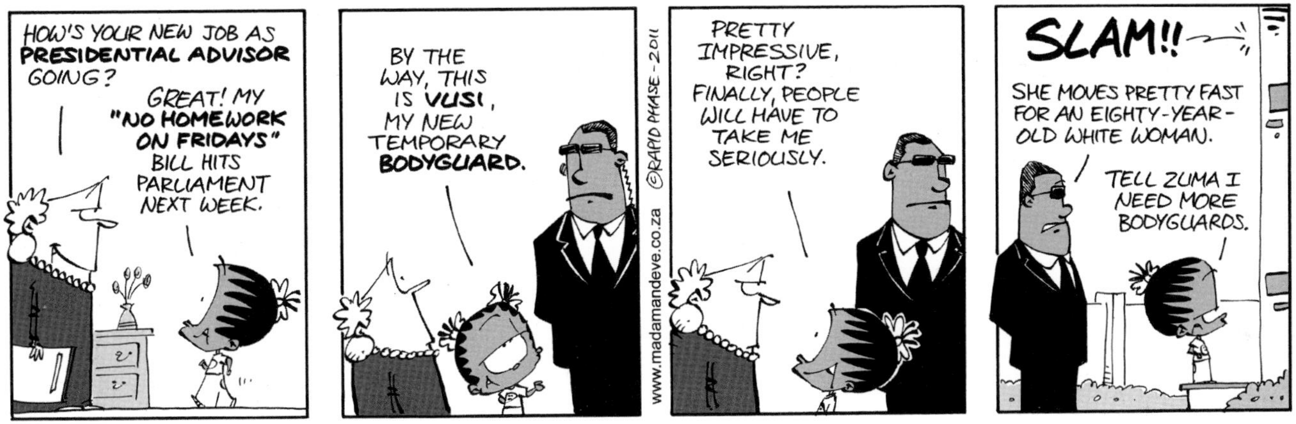
HOW'S YOUR NEW JOB AS PRESIDENTIAL ADVISOR GOING?
GREAT! MY "NO HOMEWORK ON FRIDAYS" BILL HITS PARLIAMENT NEXT WEEK.
BY THE WAY, THIS IS VUSI, MY NEW TEMPORARY BODYGUARD.
©RAPID PHASE-2011
www.madamandeve.co.za
PRETTY IMPRESSIVE, RIGHT? FINALLY, PEOPLE WILL HAVE TO TAKE ME SERIOUSLY.
SLAM!!
SHE MOVES PRETTY FAST FOR AN EIGHTY-YEAR-OLD WHITE WOMAN.
TELL ZUMA I NEED MORE BODYGUARDS.

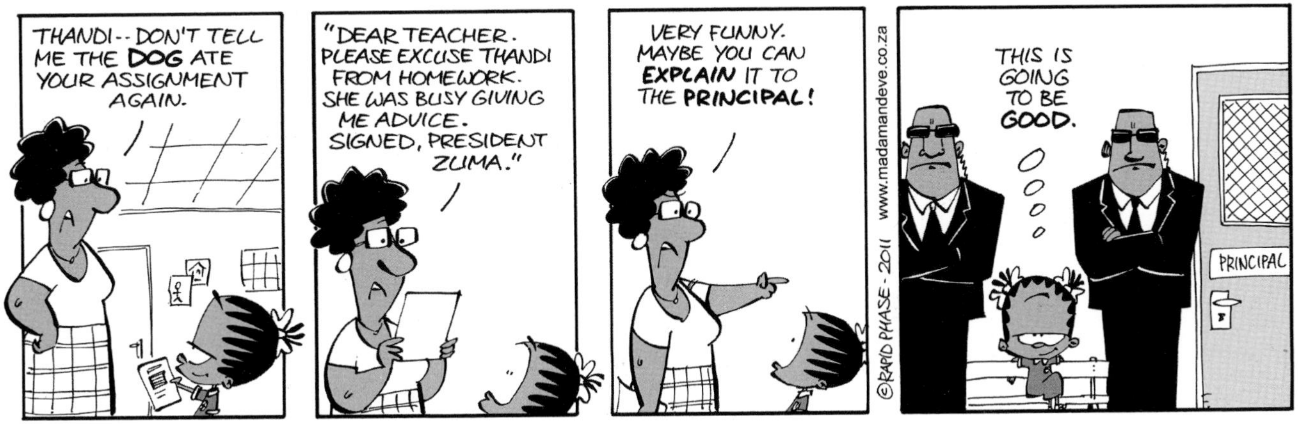
THANDI-- DON'T TELL ME THE DOG ATE YOUR ASSIGNMENT AGAIN.
"DEAR TEACHER. PLEASE EXCUSE THANDI FROM HOMEWORK. SHE WAS BUSY GIVING ME ADVICE. SIGNED, PRESIDENT ZUMA."
VERY FUNNY. MAYBE YOU CAN EXPLAIN IT TO THE PRINCIPAL!
©RAPID PHASE-2011 www.madamandeve.co.za
THIS IS GOING TO BE GOOD.
PRINCIPAL

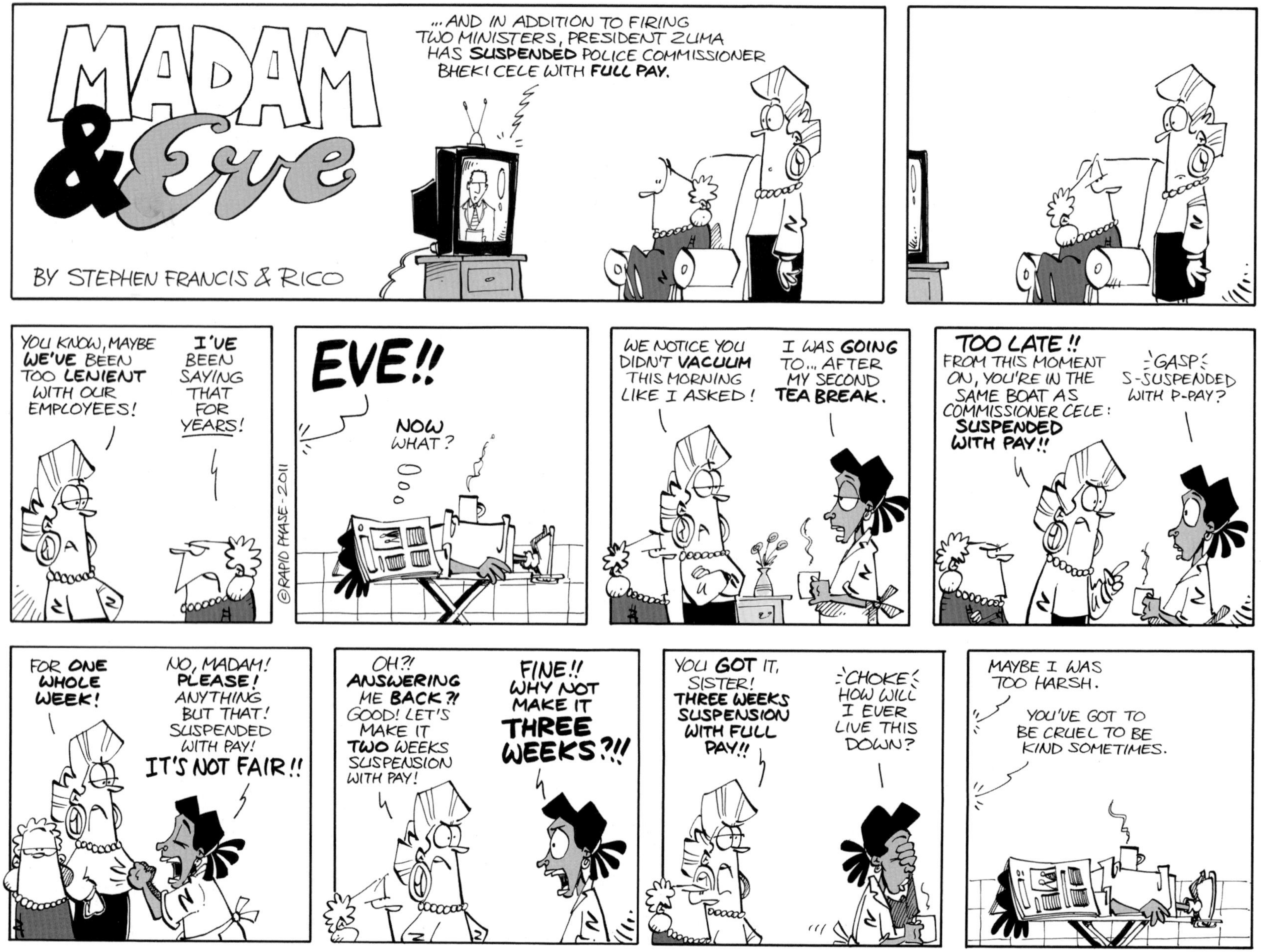
MADAM & Eve
BY STEPHEN FRANCIS & RICO
...AND IN ADDITION TO FIRING TWO MINISTERS, PRESIDENT ZUMA HAS SUSPENDED POLICE COMMISSIONER BHEKI CELE WITH FULL PAY.
YOU KNOW, MAYBE WE'VE BEEN TOO LENIENT WITH OUR EMPLOYEES!
I'VE BEEN SAYING THAT FOR YEARS!
©RAPID PHASE-2011
EVE!!
NOW WHAT?
WE NOTICE YOU DIDN'T VACUUM THIS MORNING LIKE I ASKED!
I WAS GOING TO... AFTER MY SECOND TEA BREAK.
TOO LATE!! FROM THIS MOMENT ON, YOU'RE IN THE SAME BOAT AS COMMISSIONER CELE: SUSPENDED WITH PAY!!
GASP S-SUSPENDED WITH P-PAY?
FOR ONE WHOLE WEEK!
NO, MADAM! PLEASE! ANYTHING BUT THAT! SUSPENDED WITH PAY! IT'S NOT FAIR!!
OH?! ANSWERING ME BACK?! GOOD! LET'S MAKE IT TWO WEEKS SUSPENSION WITH PAY!
FINE!! WHY NOT MAKE IT THREE WEEKS?!!
YOU GOT IT, SISTER! THREE WEEKS SUSPENSION WITH FULL PAY!!
CHOKE HOW WILL I EVER LIVE THIS DOWN?
MAYBE I WAS TOO HARSH.
YOU'VE GOT TO BE CRUEL TO BE KIND SOMETIMES.

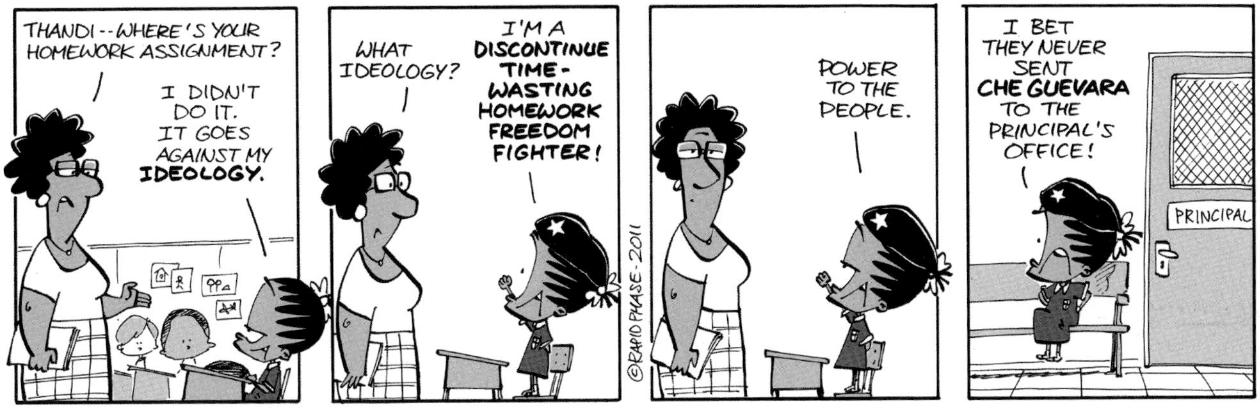
THANDI--WHERE'S YOUR HOMEWORK ASSIGNMENT?
I DIDN'T DO IT. IT GOES AGAINST MY **IDEOLOGY.**
WHAT IDEOLOGY?
I'M A **DISCONTINUE TIME-WASTING HOMEWORK FREEDOM FIGHTER!**
©RAPID PHASE·2011
POWER TO THE PEOPLE.
I BET THEY NEVER SENT **CHE GUEVARA** TO THE PRINCIPAL'S OFFICE!
PRINCIPAL

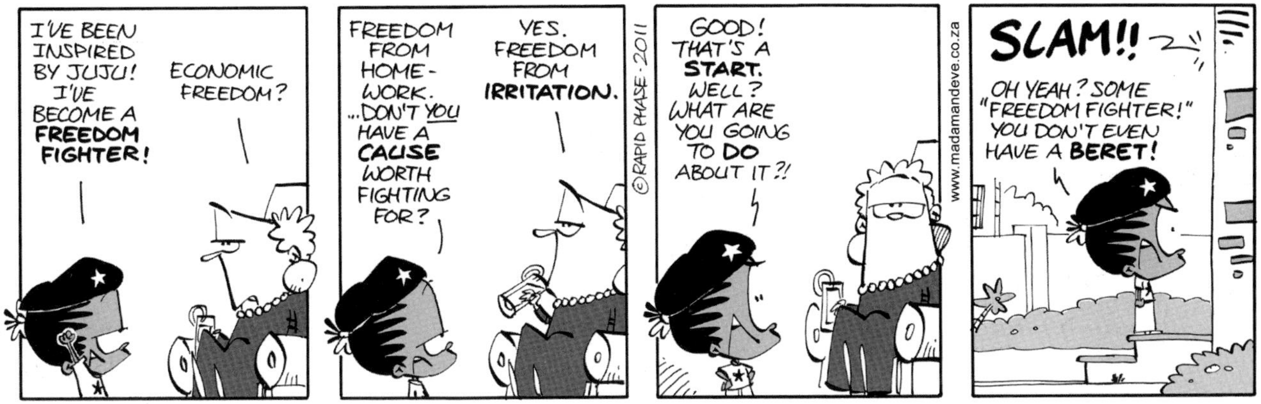
I'VE BEEN INSPIRED BY JUJU! I'VE BECOME A **FREEDOM FIGHTER!**
ECONOMIC FREEDOM?
FREEDOM FROM HOME-WORK. ...DON'T YOU HAVE A **CAUSE** WORTH FIGHTING FOR?
YES. FREEDOM FROM **IRRITATION.**
©RAPID PHASE·2011
GOOD! THAT'S A **START.** WELL? WHAT ARE YOU GOING TO **DO** ABOUT IT?!
www.madamandeve.co.za
SLAM!!
OH YEAH? SOME "FREEDOM FIGHTER!" YOU DON'T EVEN HAVE A **BERET!**

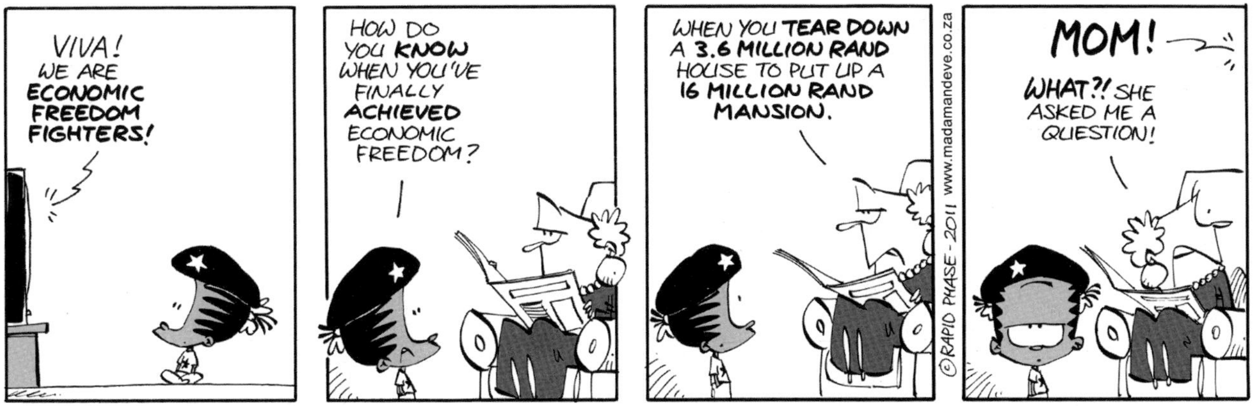
VIVA! WE ARE **ECONOMIC FREEDOM FIGHTERS!**
HOW DO YOU **KNOW** WHEN YOU'VE FINALLY **ACHIEVED** ECONOMIC FREEDOM?
WHEN YOU **TEAR DOWN** A **3.6 MILLION RAND** HOUSE TO PUT UP A **16 MILLION RAND MANSION.**
©RAPID PHASE·2011 www.madamandeve.co.za
MOM!
WHAT?! SHE ASKED ME A QUESTION!

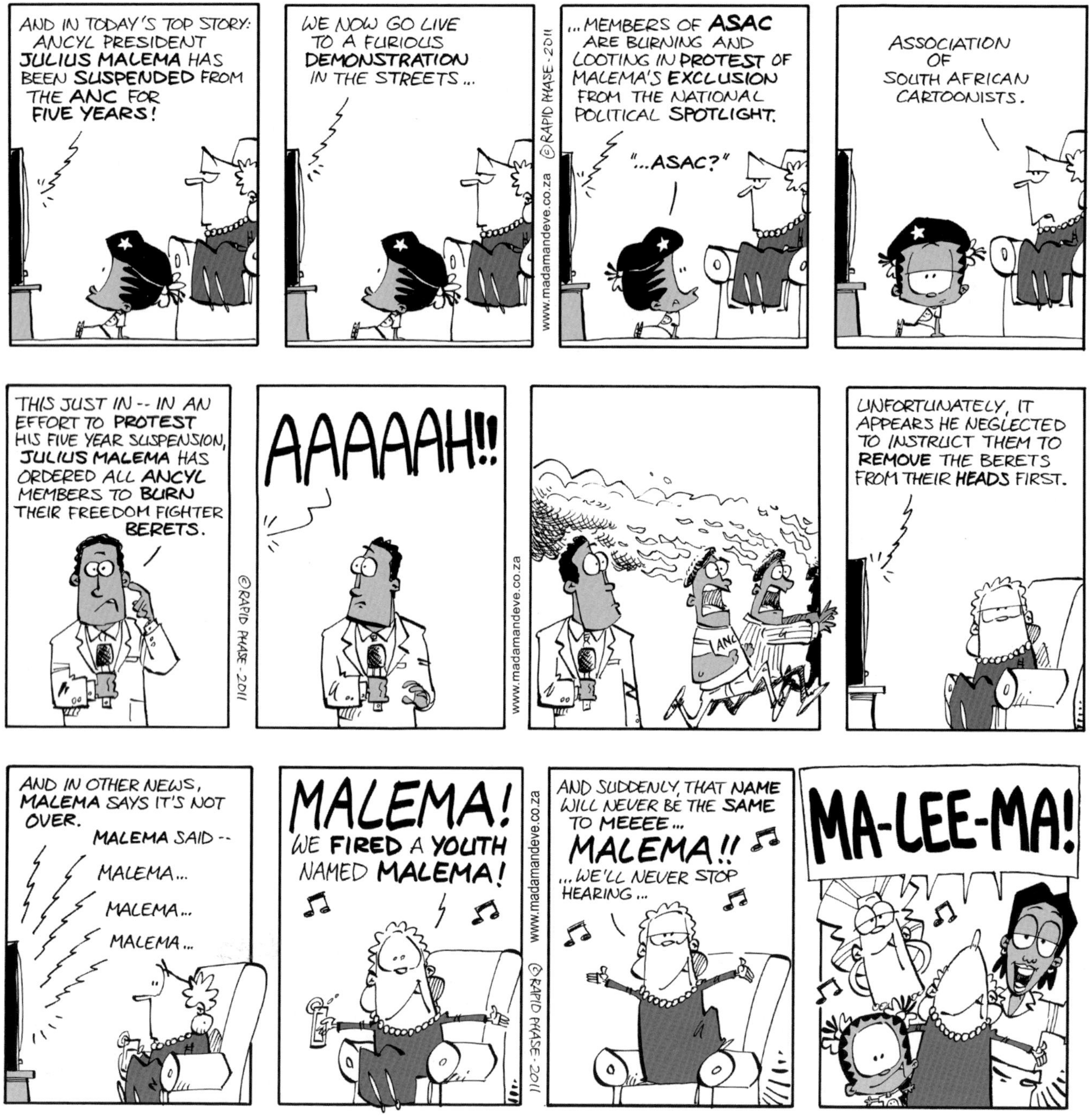
AND IN TODAY'S TOP STORY: ANCYL PRESIDENT JULIUS MALEMA HAS BEEN SUSPENDED FROM THE ANC FOR FIVE YEARS!
WE NOW GO LIVE TO A FURIOUS DEMONSTRATION IN THE STREETS...
© RAPID PHASE · 2011
www.madamandeve.co.za
...MEMBERS OF ASAC ARE BURNING AND LOOTING IN PROTEST OF MALEMA'S EXCLUSION FROM THE NATIONAL POLITICAL SPOTLIGHT.
"...ASAC?"
ASSOCIATION OF SOUTH AFRICAN CARTOONISTS.
THIS JUST IN -- IN AN EFFORT TO PROTEST HIS FIVE YEAR SUSPENSION, JULIUS MALEMA HAS ORDERED ALL ANCYL MEMBERS TO BURN THEIR FREEDOM FIGHTER BERETS.
© RAPID PHASE · 2011
AAAAAH!!
www.madamandeve.co.za
ANC
UNFORTUNATELY, IT APPEARS HE NEGLECTED TO INSTRUCT THEM TO REMOVE THE BERETS FROM THEIR HEADS FIRST.
AND IN OTHER NEWS, MALEMA SAYS IT'S NOT OVER.
MALEMA SAID --
MALEMA...
MALEMA...
MALEMA...
MALEMA!
WE FIRED A YOUTH NAMED MALEMA!
www.madamandeve.co.za
© RAPID PHASE · 2011
AND SUDDENLY, THAT NAME WILL NEVER BE THE SAME TO MEEEE...
MALEMA!!
...WE'LL NEVER STOP HEARING...
MA-LEE-MA!

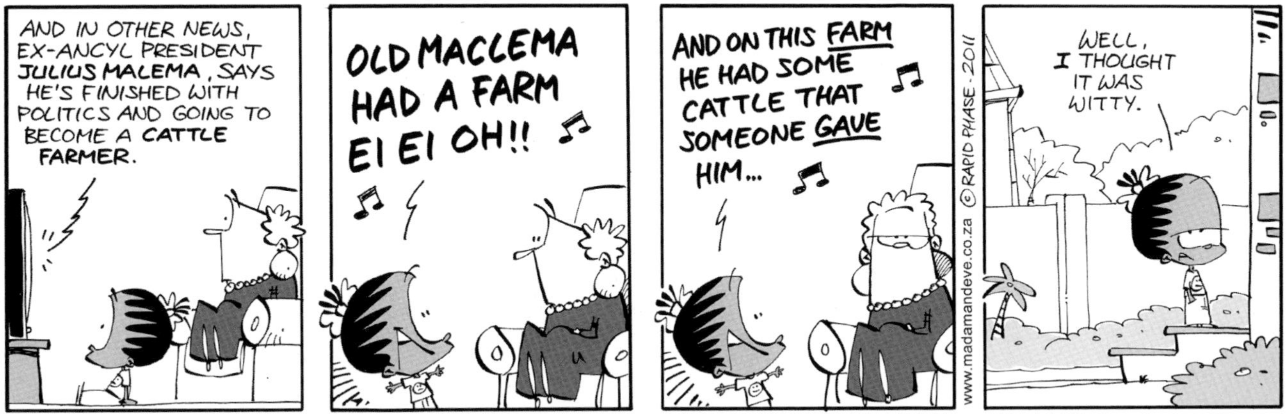
AND IN OTHER NEWS, EX-ANCYL PRESIDENT JULIUS MALEMA, SAYS HE'S FINISHED WITH POLITICS AND GOING TO BECOME A CATTLE FARMER.
OLD MACLEMA HAD A FARM EI EI OH!!
AND ON THIS FARM HE HAD SOME CATTLE THAT SOMEONE GAVE HIM...
www.madamandeve.co.za © RAPID PHASE - 2011
WELL, I THOUGHT IT WAS WITTY.

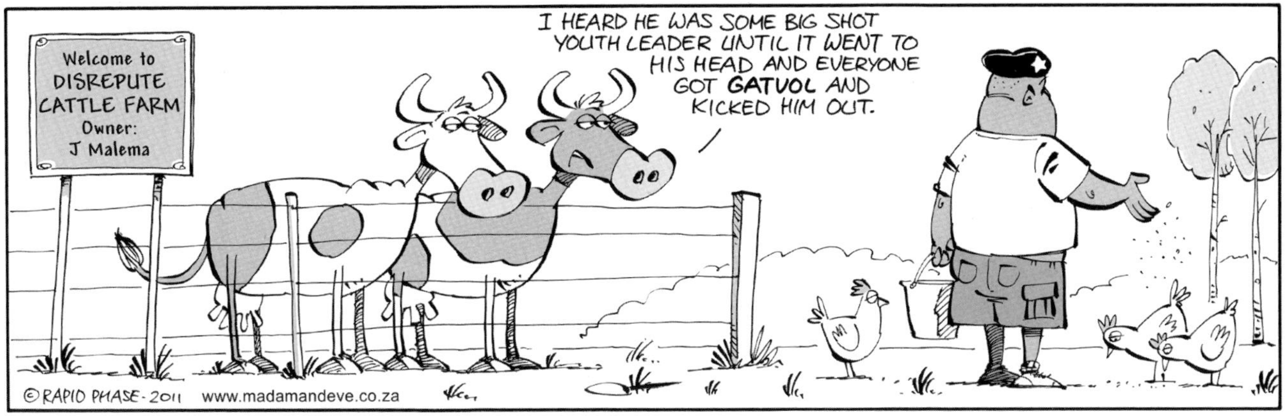
Welcome to DISREPUTE CATTLE FARM Owner: J Malema
I HEARD HE WAS SOME BIG SHOT YOUTH LEADER UNTIL IT WENT TO HIS HEAD AND EVERYONE GOT GATVOL AND KICKED HIM OUT.
© RAPID PHASE - 2011 www.madamandeve.co.za

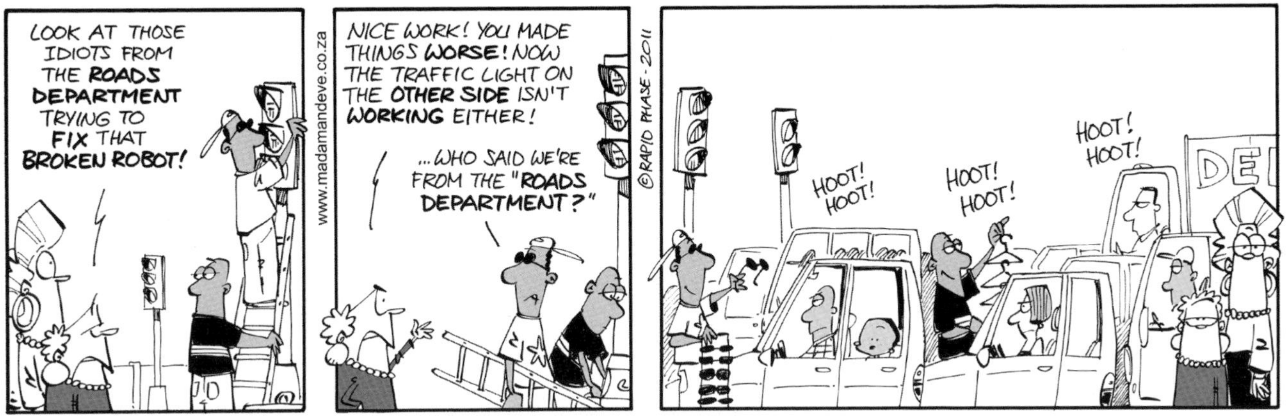
LOOK AT THOSE IDIOTS FROM THE ROADS DEPARTMENT TRYING TO FIX THAT BROKEN ROBOT!
www.madamandeve.co.za
NICE WORK! YOU MADE THINGS WORSE! NOW THE TRAFFIC LIGHT ON THE OTHER SIDE ISN'T WORKING EITHER!
...WHO SAID WE'RE FROM THE "ROADS DEPARTMENT?"
© RAPID PHASE - 2011
HOOT! HOOT!
HOOT! HOOT!
HOOT! HOOT!

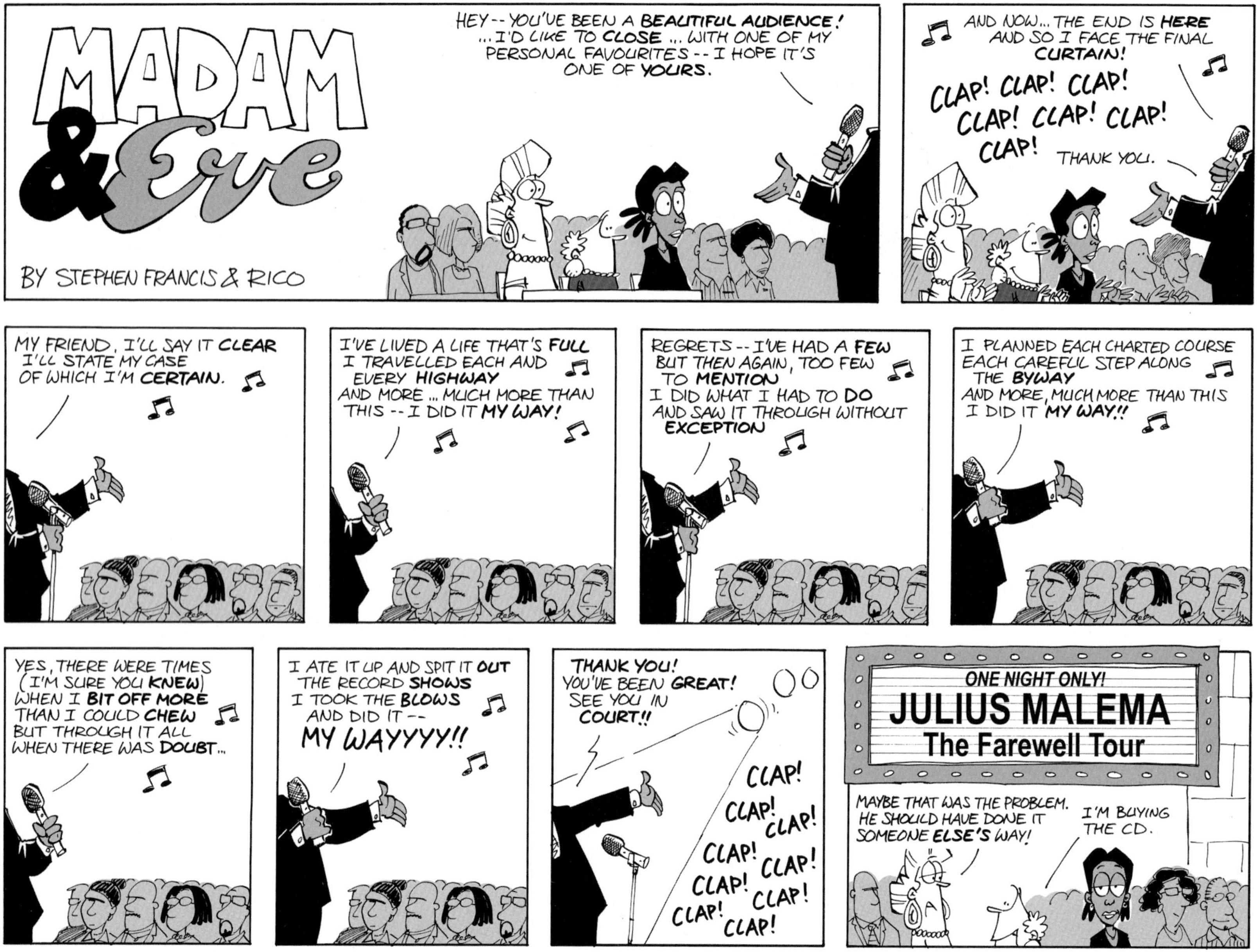
MADAM & Eve
BY STEPHEN FRANCIS & RICO
HEY -- YOU'VE BEEN A BEAUTIFUL AUDIENCE! ... I'D LIKE TO CLOSE ... WITH ONE OF MY PERSONAL FAVOURITES -- I HOPE IT'S ONE OF YOURS.
AND NOW... THE END IS HERE AND SO I FACE THE FINAL CURTAIN!
CLAP! CLAP! CLAP! CLAP! CLAP! CLAP! CLAP!
THANK YOU.
MY FRIEND, I'LL SAY IT CLEAR I'LL STATE MY CASE OF WHICH I'M CERTAIN.
I'VE LIVED A LIFE THAT'S FULL I TRAVELLED EACH AND EVERY HIGHWAY AND MORE ... MUCH MORE THAN THIS -- I DID IT MY WAY!
REGRETS -- I'VE HAD A FEW BUT THEN AGAIN, TOO FEW TO MENTION I DID WHAT I HAD TO DO AND SAW IT THROUGH WITHOUT EXCEPTION
I PLANNED EACH CHARTED COURSE EACH CAREFUL STEP ALONG THE BYWAY AND MORE, MUCH MORE THAN THIS I DID IT MY WAY!!
YES, THERE WERE TIMES (I'M SURE YOU KNEW) WHEN I BIT OFF MORE THAN I COULD CHEW BUT THROUGH IT ALL WHEN THERE WAS DOUBT...
I ATE IT UP AND SPIT IT OUT THE RECORD SHOWS I TOOK THE BLOWS AND DID IT --
MY WAYYYY!!
THANK YOU! YOU'VE BEEN GREAT! SEE YOU IN COURT!!
CLAP! CLAP! CLAP! CLAP! CLAP! CLAP! CLAP! CLAP! CLAP!
ONE NIGHT ONLY!
JULIUS MALEMA
The Farewell Tour
MAYBE THAT WAS THE PROBLEM. HE SHOULD HAVE DONE IT SOMEONE ELSE'S WAY!
I'M BUYING THE CD.

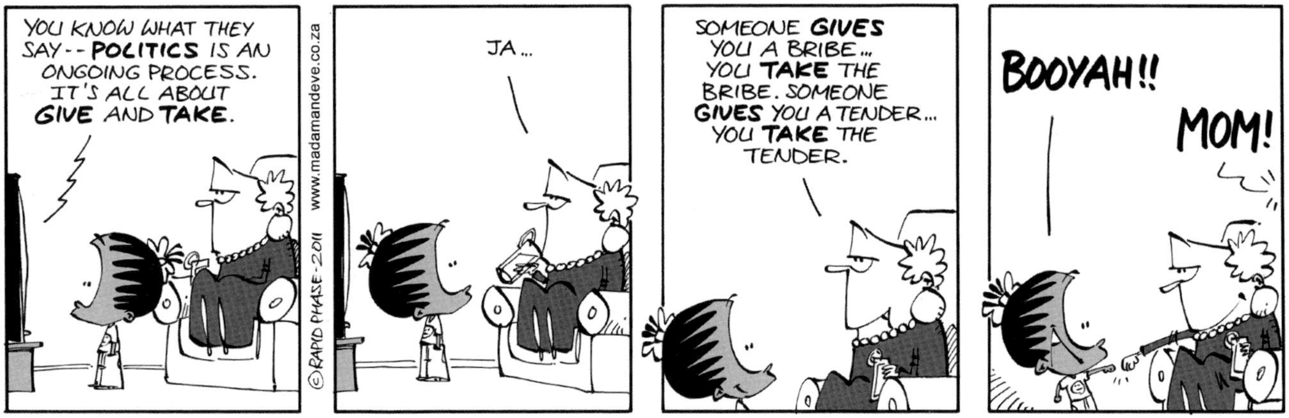
YOU KNOW WHAT THEY SAY -- POLITICS IS AN ONGOING PROCESS. IT'S ALL ABOUT GIVE AND TAKE.
©RAPID PHASE · 2011 www.madamandeve.co.za
JA ...
SOMEONE GIVES YOU A BRIBE... YOU TAKE THE BRIBE. SOMEONE GIVES YOU A TENDER... YOU TAKE THE TENDER.
BOOYAH!!
MOM!

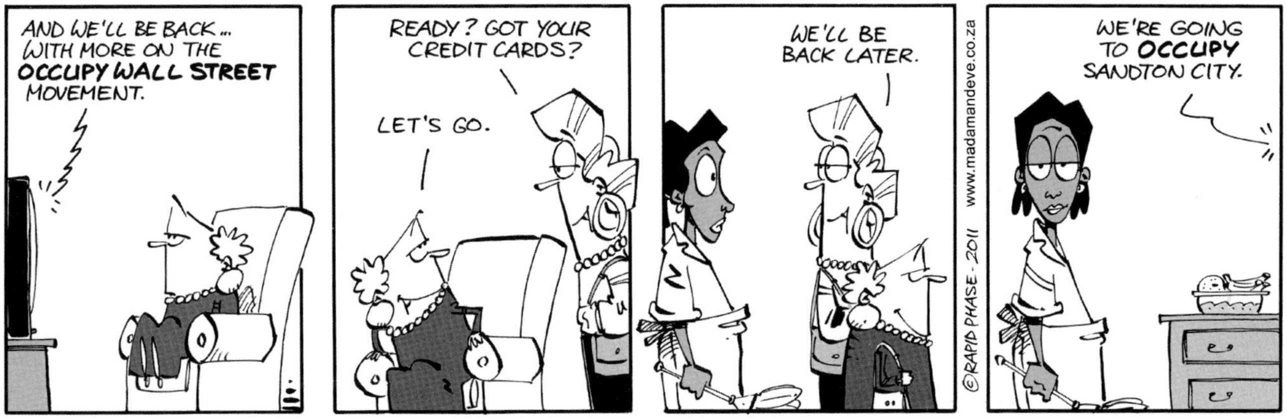
AND WE'LL BE BACK... WITH MORE ON THE OCCUPY WALL STREET MOVEMENT.
READY? GOT YOUR CREDIT CARDS?
LET'S GO.
WE'LL BE BACK LATER.
©RAPID PHASE · 2011 www.madamandeve.co.za
WE'RE GOING TO OCCUPY SANDTON CITY.

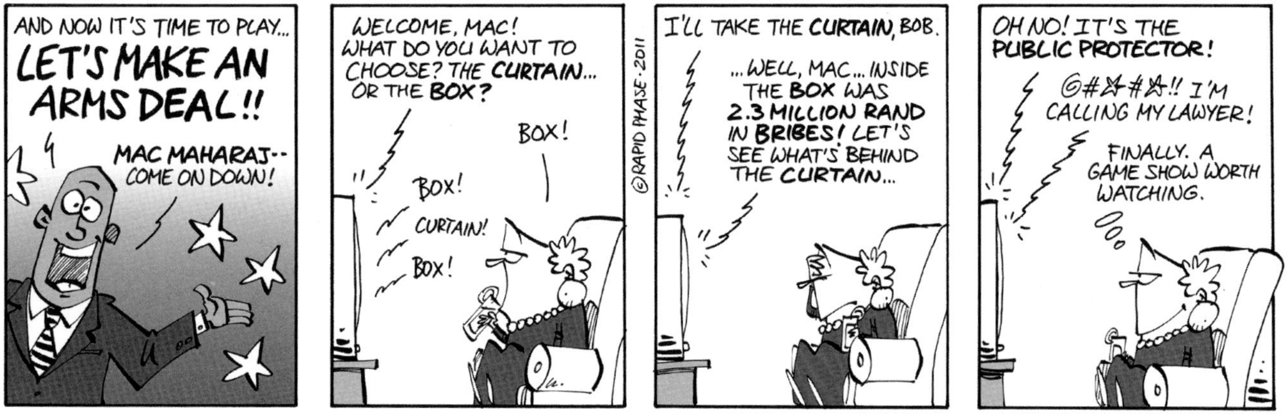
AND NOW IT'S TIME TO PLAY...
LET'S MAKE AN ARMS DEAL!!
MAC MAHARAJ-- COME ON DOWN!
WELCOME, MAC! WHAT DO YOU WANT TO CHOOSE? THE CURTAIN... OR THE BOX?
BOX!
BOX!
CURTAIN!
BOX!
©RAPID PHASE · 2011
I'LL TAKE THE CURTAIN, BOB.
...WELL, MAC... INSIDE THE BOX WAS 2.3 MILLION RAND IN BRIBES! LET'S SEE WHAT'S BEHIND THE CURTAIN...
OH NO! IT'S THE PUBLIC PROTECTOR!
@#☆#☆!! I'M CALLING MY LAWYER!
FINALLY. A GAME SHOW WORTH WATCHING.

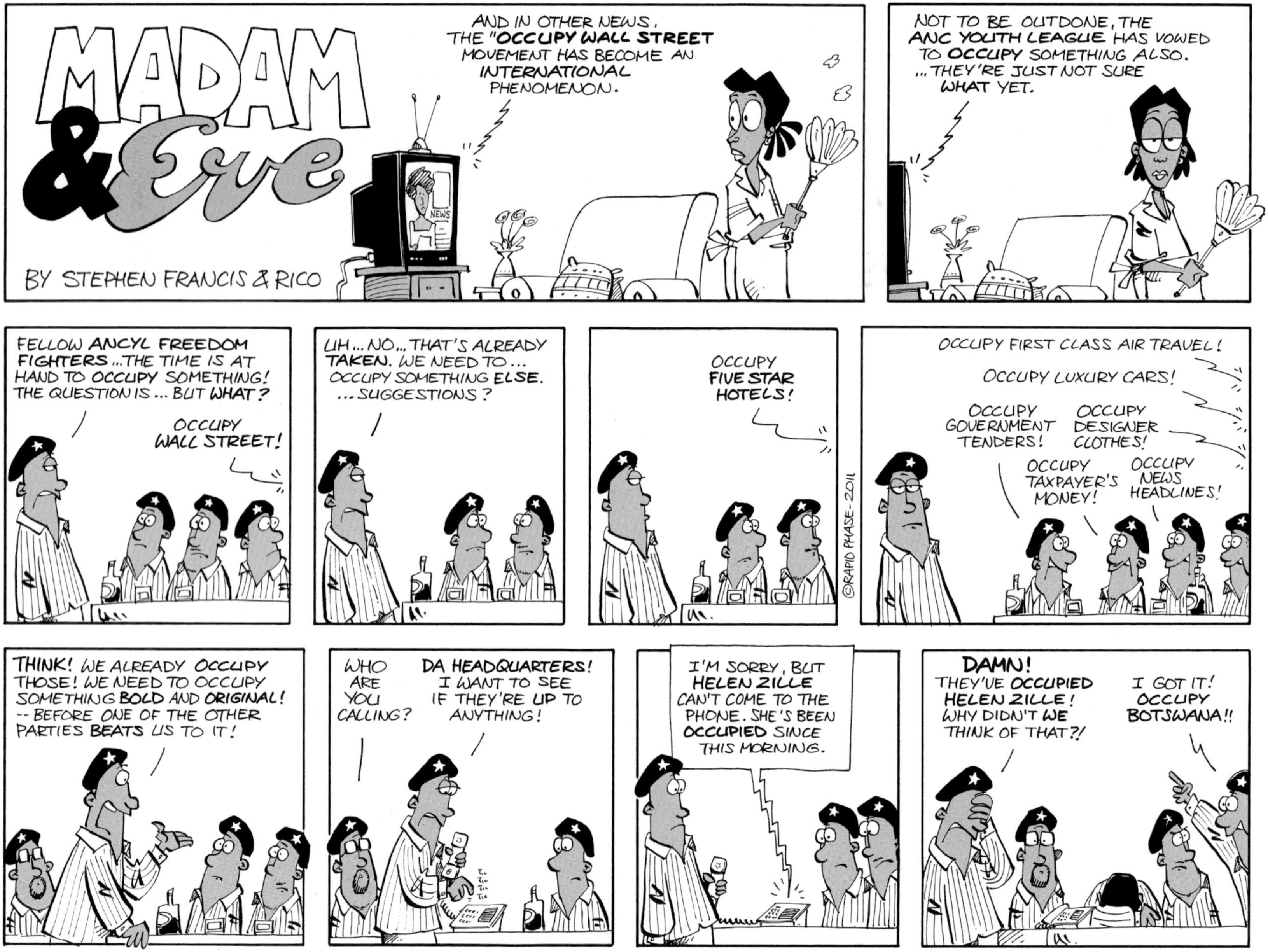
MADAM & Eve
BY STEPHEN FRANCIS & RICO
AND IN OTHER NEWS, THE "OCCUPY WALL STREET MOVEMENT HAS BECOME AN INTERNATIONAL PHENOMENON.
NEWS
NOT TO BE OUTDONE, THE ANC YOUTH LEAGUE HAS VOWED TO OCCUPY SOMETHING ALSO. ...THEY'RE JUST NOT SURE WHAT YET.
FELLOW ANCYL FREEDOM FIGHTERS...THE TIME IS AT HAND TO OCCUPY SOMETHING! THE QUESTION IS ... BUT WHAT?
OCCUPY WALL STREET!
UH...NO...THAT'S ALREADY TAKEN. WE NEED TO... OCCUPY SOMETHING ELSE. ...SUGGESTIONS?
OCCUPY FIVE STAR HOTELS!
©RAPID PHASE-2011
OCCUPY FIRST CLASS AIR TRAVEL!
OCCUPY LUXURY CARS!
OCCUPY GOVERNMENT TENDERS!
OCCUPY DESIGNER CLOTHES!
OCCUPY TAXPAYER'S MONEY!
OCCUPY NEWS HEADLINES!
THINK! WE ALREADY OCCUPY THOSE! WE NEED TO OCCUPY SOMETHING BOLD AND ORIGINAL! --BEFORE ONE OF THE OTHER PARTIES BEATS US TO IT!
WHO ARE YOU CALLING?
DA HEADQUARTERS! I WANT TO SEE IF THEY'RE UP TO ANYTHING!
I'M SORRY, BUT HELEN ZILLE CAN'T COME TO THE PHONE. SHE'S BEEN OCCUPIED SINCE THIS MORNING.
DAMN! THEY'VE OCCUPIED HELEN ZILLE! WHY DIDN'T WE THINK OF THAT?!
I GOT IT! OCCUPY BOTSWANA!!

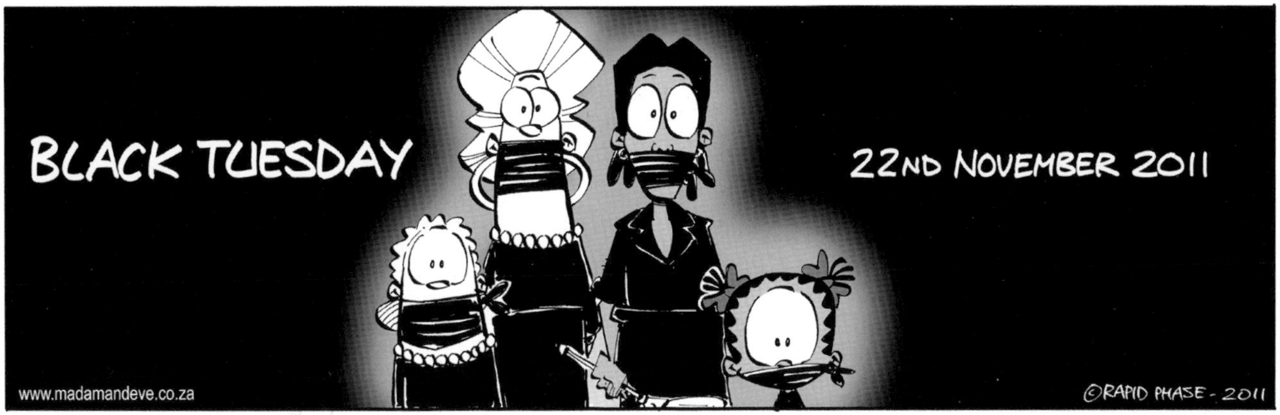
BLACK TUESDAY
22ND NOVEMBER 2011
www.madamandeve.co.za
©RAPID PHASE - 2011

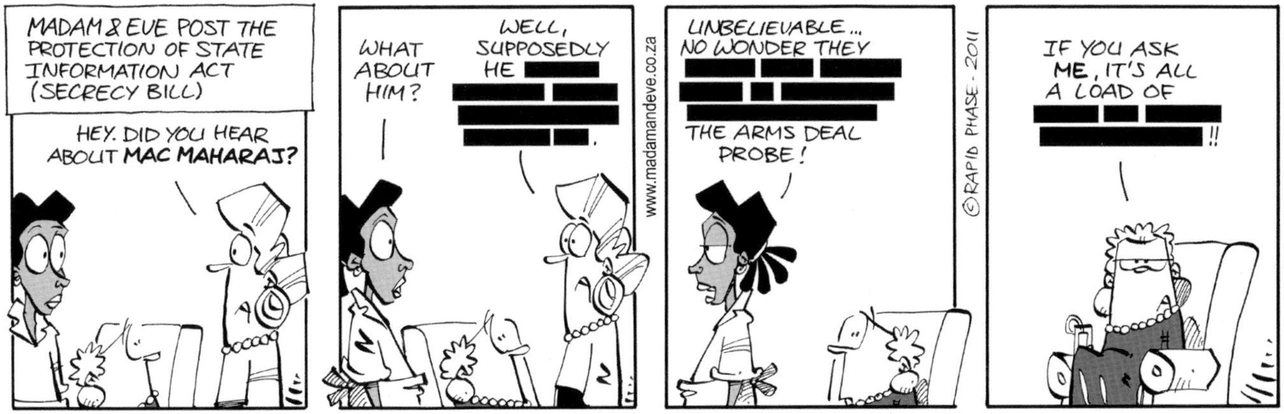
MADAM & EVE POST THE PROTECTION OF STATE INFORMATION ACT (SECRECY BILL)
HEY. DID YOU HEAR ABOUT MAC MAHARAJ?
WHAT ABOUT HIM?
WELL, SUPPOSEDLY HE [redacted].
www.madamandeve.co.za
UNBELIEVABLE... NO WONDER THEY [redacted] THE ARMS DEAL PROBE!
©RAPID PHASE - 2011
IF YOU ASK ME, IT'S ALL A LOAD OF [redacted]!!

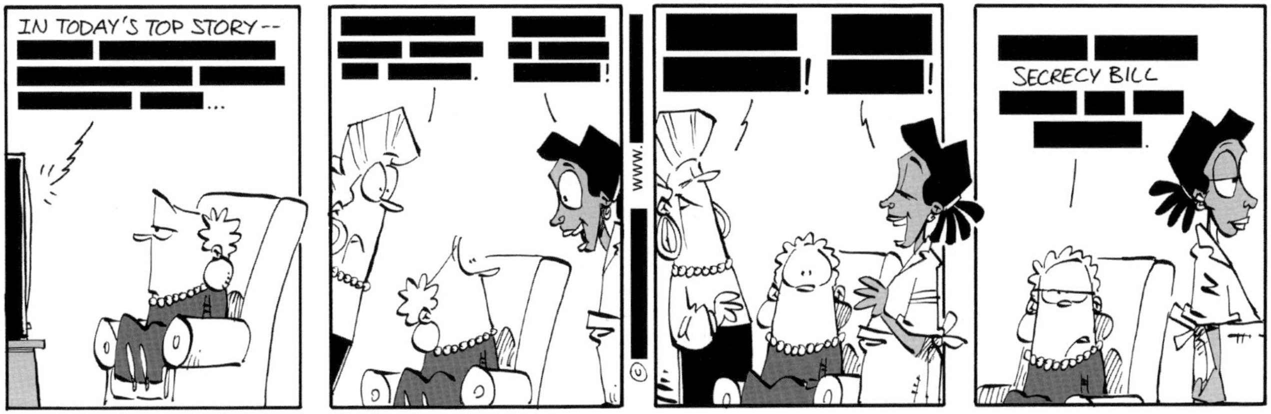
IN TODAY'S TOP STORY -- [redacted]...
[redacted].
[redacted]!
www. [redacted]
©
[redacted]!
[redacted]!
[redacted]
SECRECY BILL
[redacted].

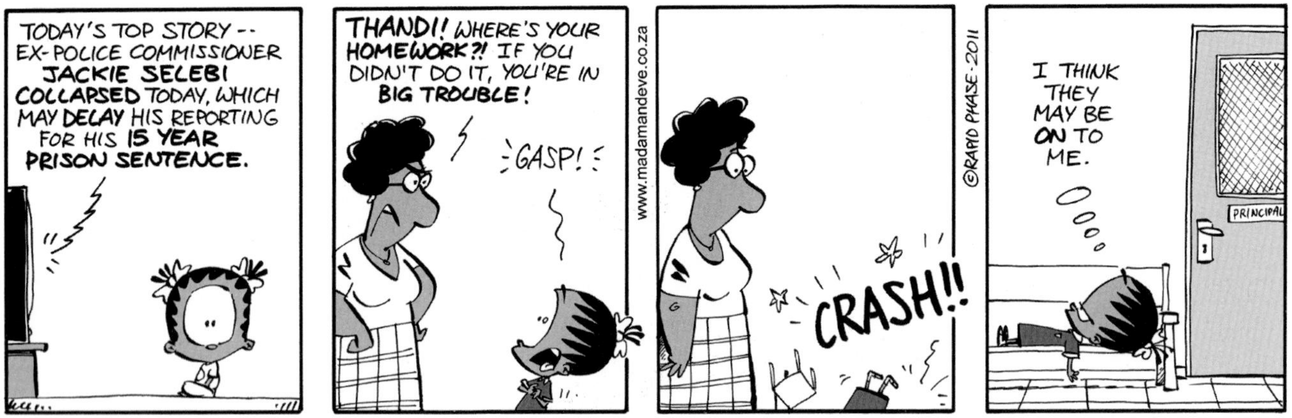
TODAY'S TOP STORY -- EX-POLICE COMMISSIONER JACKIE SELEBI COLLAPSED TODAY, WHICH MAY DELAY HIS REPORTING FOR HIS 15 YEAR PRISON SENTENCE.
THANDI! WHERE'S YOUR HOMEWORK?! IF YOU DIDN'T DO IT, YOU'RE IN BIG TROUBLE!
GASP!
www.madamandeve.co.za
CRASH!!
©RAPID PHASE·2011
I THINK THEY MAY BE ON TO ME.
PRINCIPAL

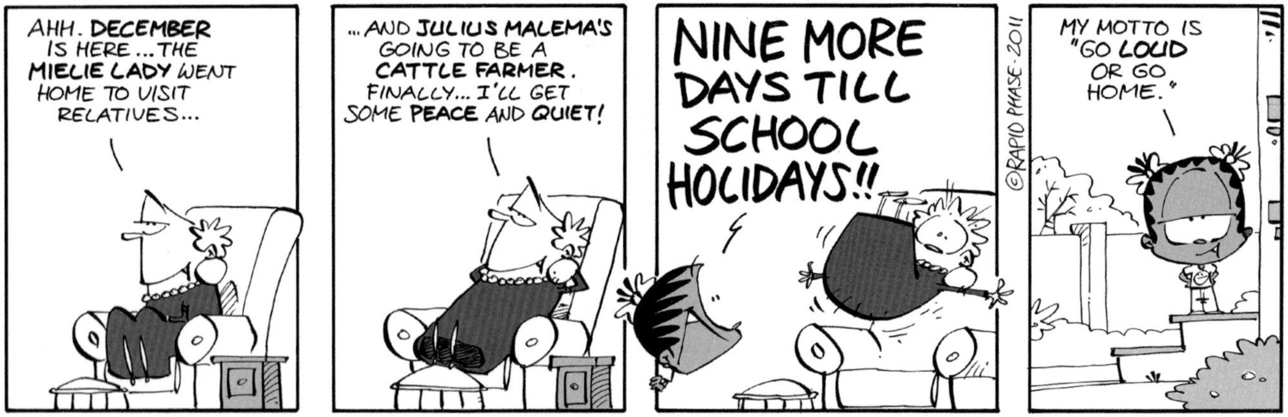
AHH. DECEMBER IS HERE ... THE MIELIE LADY WENT HOME TO VISIT RELATIVES...
... AND JULIUS MALEMA'S GOING TO BE A CATTLE FARMER. FINALLY... I'LL GET SOME PEACE AND QUIET!
NINE MORE DAYS TILL SCHOOL HOLIDAYS!!
©RAPID PHASE·2011
MY MOTTO IS "GO LOUD OR GO HOME."

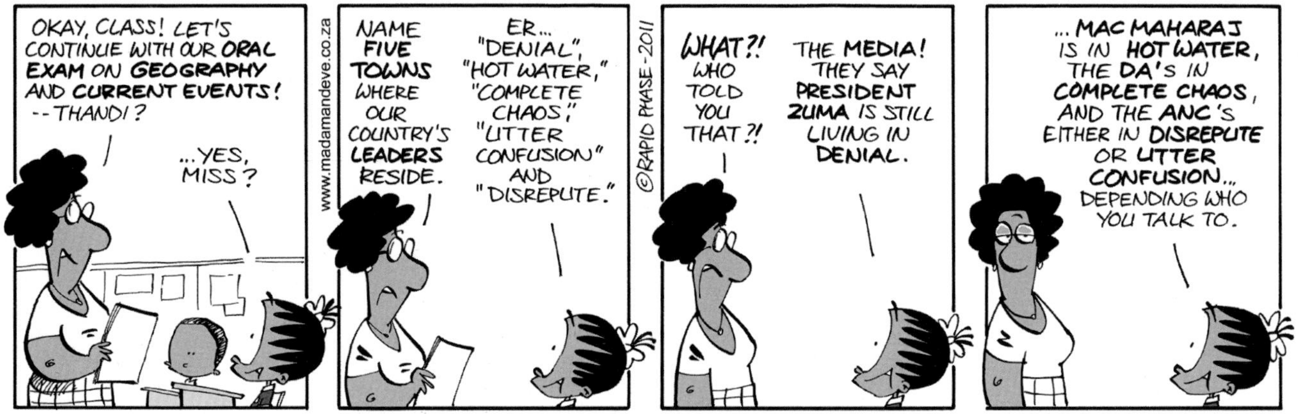
OKAY, CLASS! LET'S CONTINUE WITH OUR ORAL EXAM ON GEOGRAPHY AND CURRENT EVENTS! -- THANDI?
...YES, MISS?
www.madamandeve.co.za
NAME FIVE TOWNS WHERE OUR COUNTRY'S LEADERS RESIDE.
ER... "DENIAL", "HOT WATER," "COMPLETE CHAOS," "UTTER CONFUSION" AND "DISREPUTE."
©RAPID PHASE·2011
WHAT?! WHO TOLD YOU THAT?!
THE MEDIA! THEY SAY PRESIDENT ZUMA IS STILL LIVING IN DENIAL.
... MAC MAHARAJ IS IN HOT WATER, THE DA'S IN COMPLETE CHAOS, AND THE ANC'S EITHER IN DISREPUTE OR UTTER CONFUSION... DEPENDING WHO YOU TALK TO.

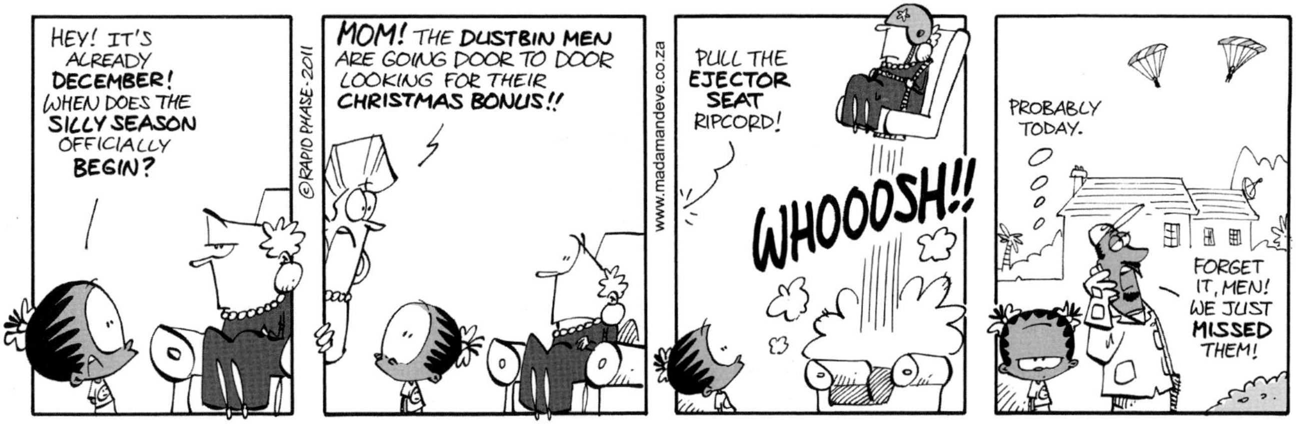
HEY! IT'S ALREADY DECEMBER! WHEN DOES THE SILLY SEASON OFFICIALLY BEGIN?
©RAPID PHASE - 2011
MOM! THE DUSTBIN MEN ARE GOING DOOR TO DOOR LOOKING FOR THEIR CHRISTMAS BONUS!!
www.madamandeve.co.za
PULL THE EJECTOR SEAT RIPCORD!
WHOOOSH!!
PROBABLY TODAY.
FORGET IT, MEN! WE JUST MISSED THEM!

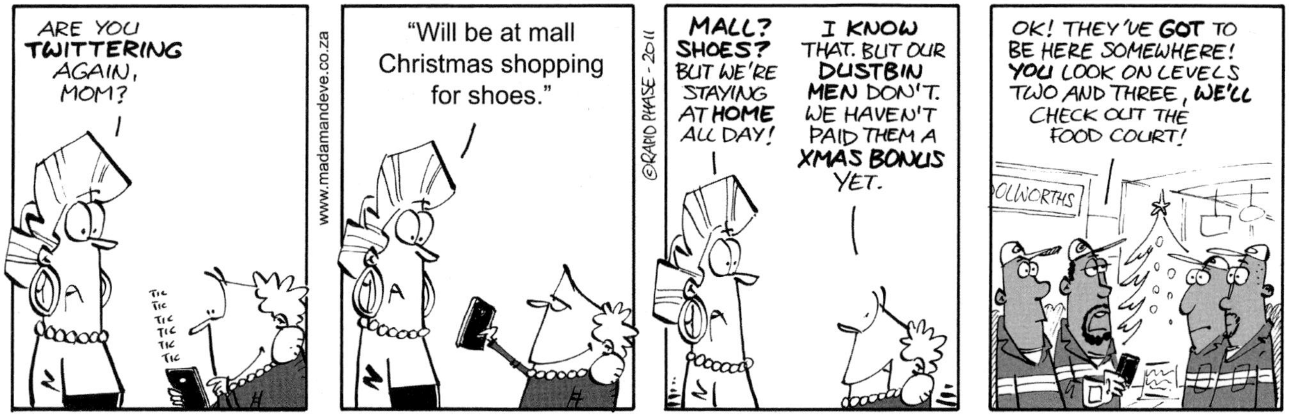
ARE YOU TWITTERING AGAIN, MOM?
TIC TIC TIC TIC TIC TIC
www.madamandeve.co.za
"Will be at mall Christmas shopping for shoes."
©RAPID PHASE - 2011
MALL? SHOES? BUT WE'RE STAYING AT HOME ALL DAY!
I KNOW THAT. BUT OUR DUSTBIN MEN DON'T. WE HAVEN'T PAID THEM A XMAS BONUS YET.
OK! THEY'VE GOT TO BE HERE SOMEWHERE! YOU LOOK ON LEVELS TWO AND THREE, WE'LL CHECK OUT THE FOOD COURT!
OLWORTHS

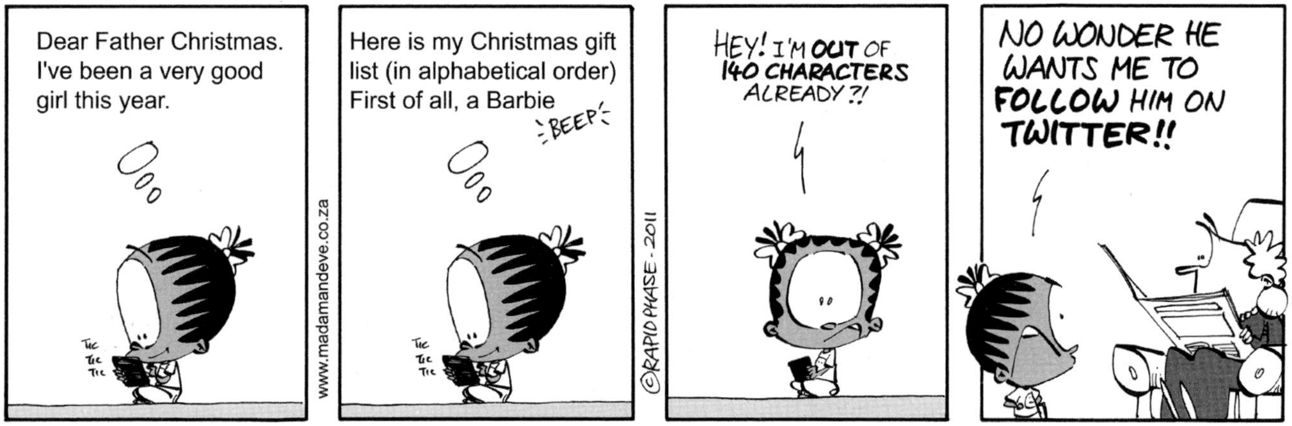
Dear Father Christmas. I've been a very good girl this year.
TIC TIC TIC
www.madamandeve.co.za
Here is my Christmas gift list (in alphabetical order) First of all, a Barbie
BEEP
TIC TIC TIC
©RAPID PHASE - 2011
HEY! I'M OUT OF 140 CHARACTERS ALREADY?!
NO WONDER HE WANTS ME TO FOLLOW HIM ON TWITTER!!

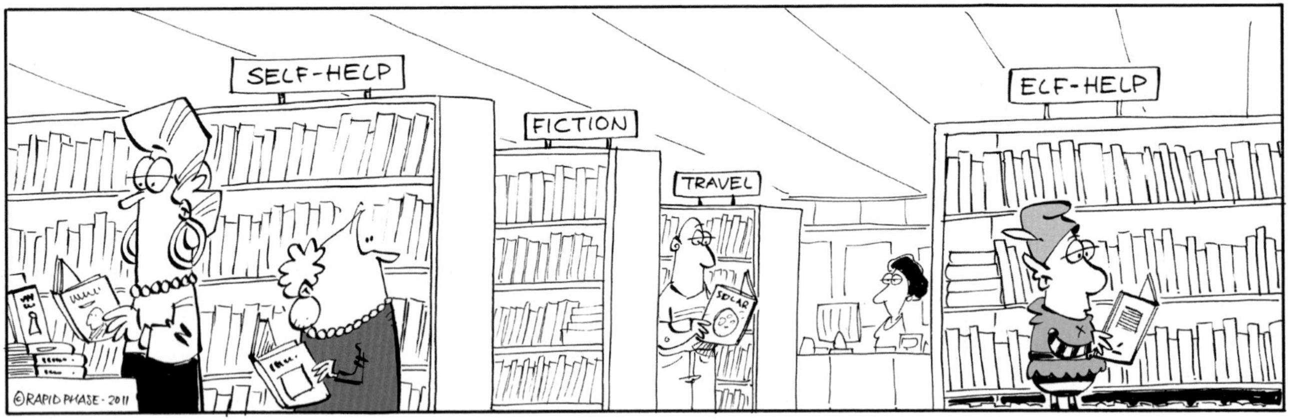
SELF-HELP
FICTION
TRAVEL
ELF-HELP
©RAPID PHASE · 2011

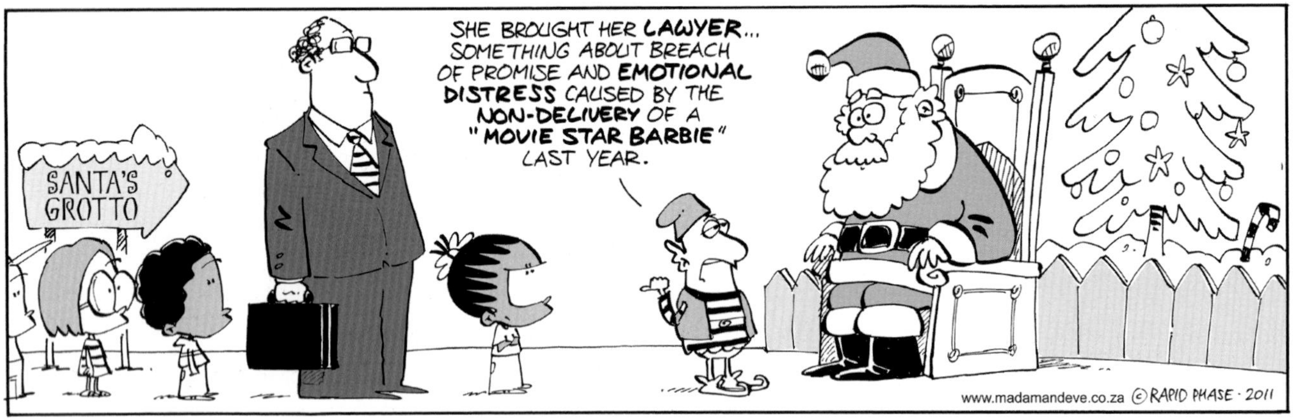
SANTA'S GROTTO
SHE BROUGHT HER LAWYER... SOMETHING ABOUT BREACH OF PROMISE AND EMOTIONAL DISTRESS CAUSED BY THE NON-DELIVERY OF A "MOVIE STAR BARBIE" LAST YEAR.
www.madamandeve.co.za ©RAPID PHASE · 2011

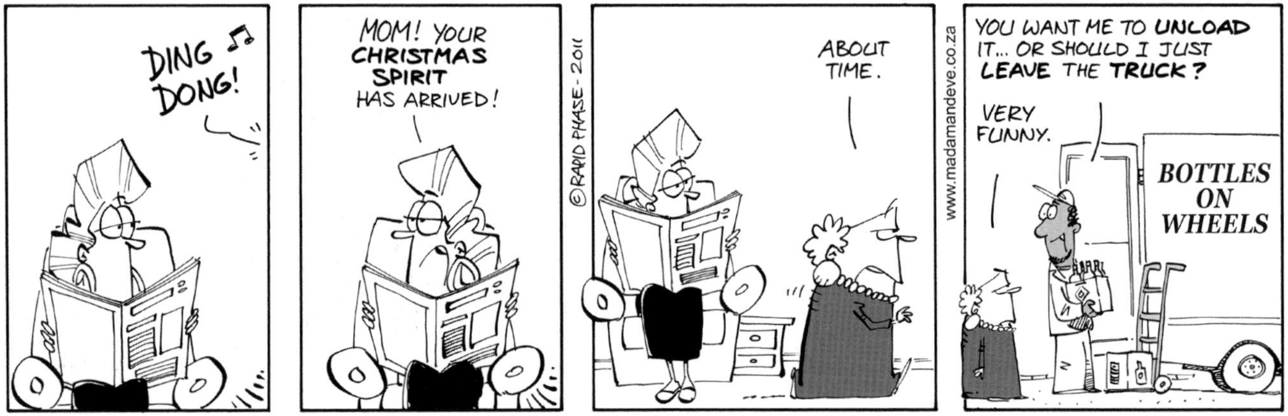
DING DONG!
MOM! YOUR CHRISTMAS SPIRIT HAS ARRIVED!
©RAPID PHASE · 2011
ABOUT TIME.
www.madamandeve.co.za
YOU WANT ME TO UNLOAD IT... OR SHOULD I JUST LEAVE THE TRUCK?
VERY FUNNY.
BOTTLES ON WHEELS

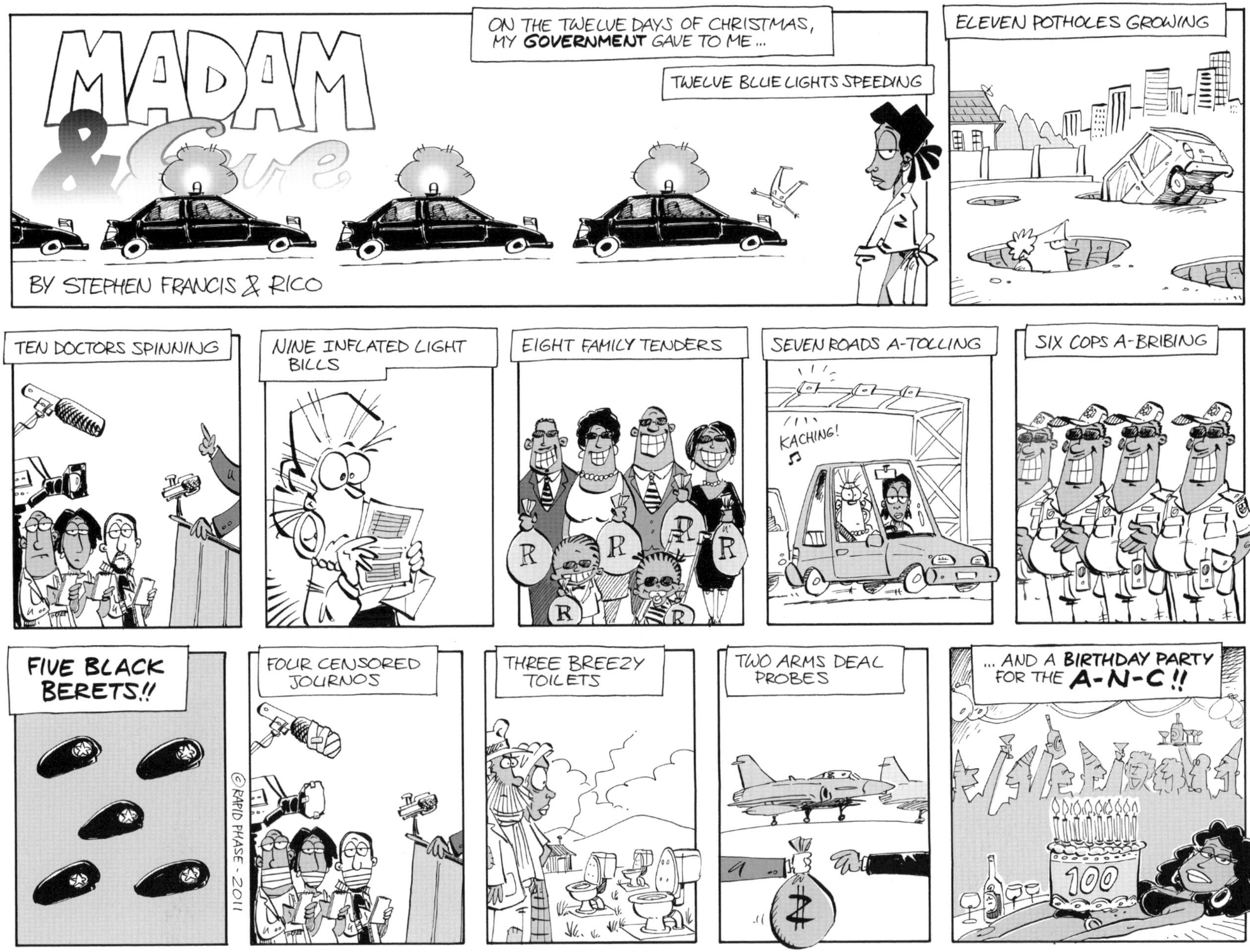
MADAM & Eve
ON THE TWELVE DAYS OF CHRISTMAS, MY GOVERNMENT GAVE TO ME ...
TWELVE BLUE LIGHTS SPEEDING
BY STEPHEN FRANCIS & RICO
ELEVEN POTHOLES GROWING
TEN DOCTORS SPINNING
NINE INFLATED LIGHT BILLS
EIGHT FAMILY TENDERS
SEVEN ROADS A-TOLLING
KACHING!
SIX COPS A-BRIBING
FIVE BLACK BERETS!!
© RAPID PHASE - 2011
FOUR CENSORED JOURNOS
THREE BREEZY TOILETS
TWO ARMS DEAL PROBES
... AND A BIRTHDAY PARTY FOR THE A-N-C!!
100

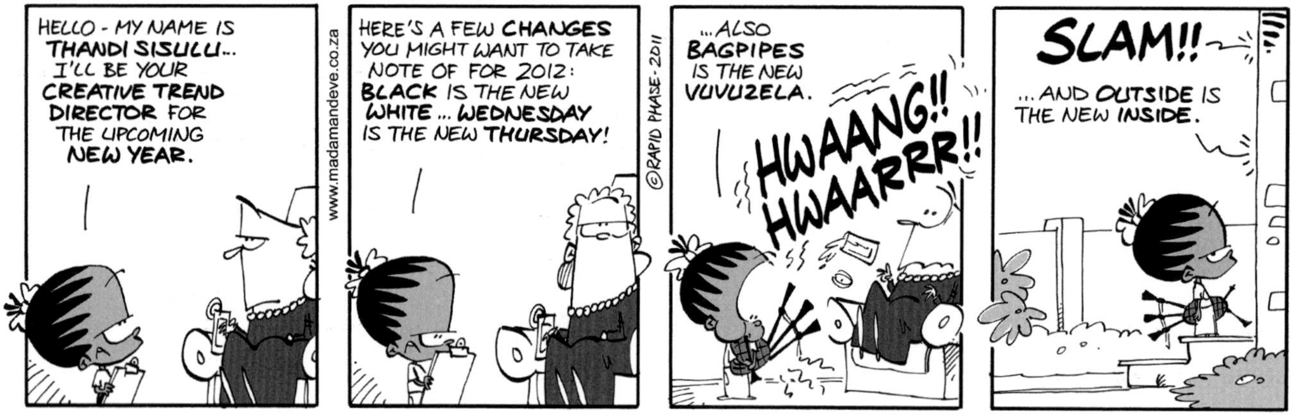
HELLO - MY NAME IS THANDI SISULU... I'LL BE YOUR CREATIVE TREND DIRECTOR FOR THE UPCOMING NEW YEAR.
www.madamandeve.co.za
HERE'S A FEW CHANGES YOU MIGHT WANT TO TAKE NOTE OF FOR 2012: BLACK IS THE NEW WHITE ... WEDNESDAY IS THE NEW THURSDAY!
©RAPID PHASE · 2011
...ALSO BAGPIPES IS THE NEW VUVUZELA.
HWAANG!! HWAARRR!!
SLAM!!
...AND OUTSIDE IS THE NEW INSIDE.

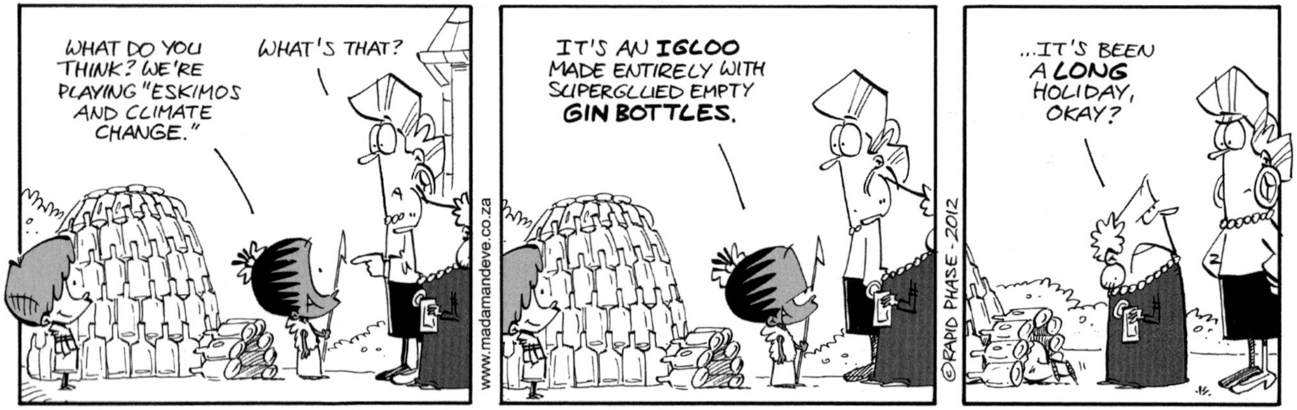
WHAT DO YOU THINK? WE'RE PLAYING "ESKIMOS AND CLIMATE CHANGE."
WHAT'S THAT?
www.madamandeve.co.za
IT'S AN IGLOO MADE ENTIRELY WITH SUPERGLUED EMPTY GIN BOTTLES.
©RAPID PHASE · 2012
...IT'S BEEN A LONG HOLIDAY, OKAY?

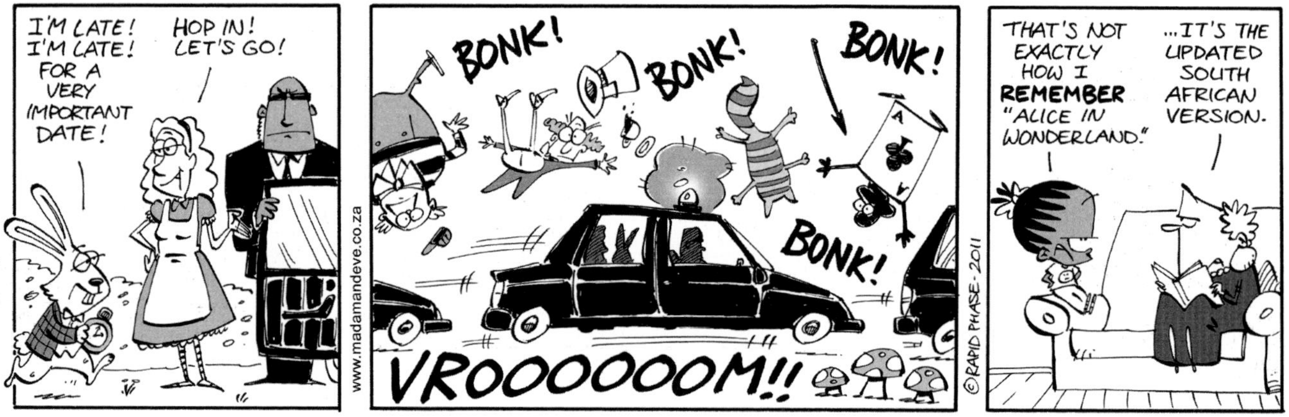
I'M LATE! I'M LATE! FOR A VERY IMPORTANT DATE!
HOP IN! LET'S GO!
www.madamandeve.co.za
BONK!
BONK!
BONK!
BONK!
VROOOOOOM!!
©RAPID PHASE · 2011
THAT'S NOT EXACTLY HOW I REMEMBER "ALICE IN WONDERLAND."
...IT'S THE UPDATED SOUTH AFRICAN VERSION.

MADAM & Eve

BY STEPHEN FRANCIS & RICO

❧ *EVE SISULU'S* ☙

8 STAGES of dealing with
returning to work
after the long holidays

DENIAL	DISBELIEF	ANGER	ISOLATION

DESPAIR	BARGAINING	GUILT	ACCEPTANCE

© RAPID PHASE - 2012

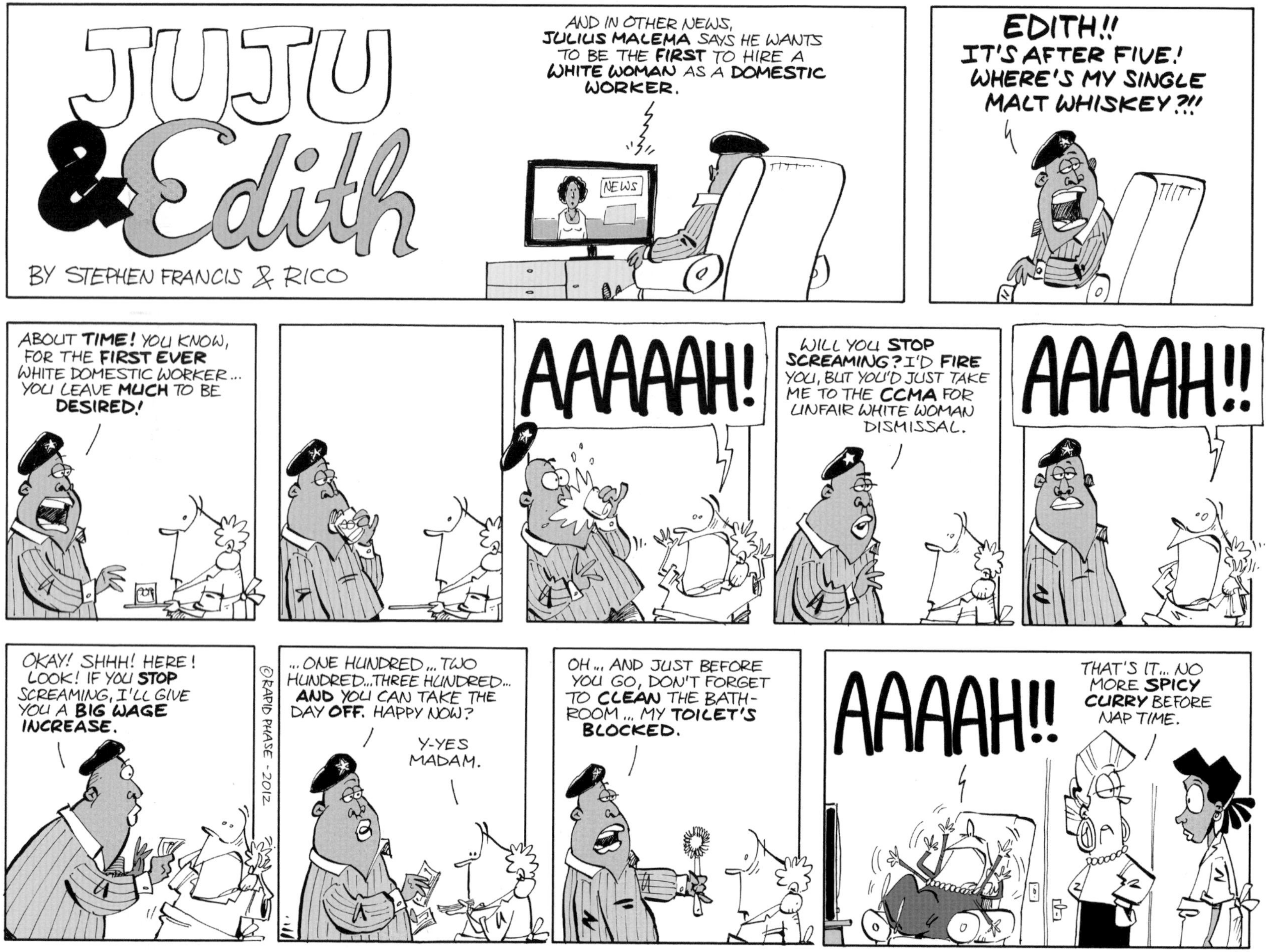
JUJU & Edith
BY STEPHEN FRANCIS & RICO
AND IN OTHER NEWS, JULIUS MALEMA SAYS HE WANTS TO BE THE FIRST TO HIRE A WHITE WOMAN AS A DOMESTIC WORKER.
NEWS
EDITH!! IT'S AFTER FIVE! WHERE'S MY SINGLE MALT WHISKEY?!!
ABOUT TIME! YOU KNOW, FOR THE FIRST EVER WHITE DOMESTIC WORKER... YOU LEAVE MUCH TO BE DESIRED!
AAAAAH!
WILL YOU STOP SCREAMING? I'D FIRE YOU, BUT YOU'D JUST TAKE ME TO THE CCMA FOR UNFAIR WHITE WOMAN DISMISSAL.
AAAAH!!
OKAY! SHHH! HERE! LOOK! IF YOU STOP SCREAMING, I'LL GIVE YOU A BIG WAGE INCREASE.
© RAPID PHASE - 2012
...ONE HUNDRED... TWO HUNDRED...THREE HUNDRED... AND YOU CAN TAKE THE DAY OFF. HAPPY NOW?
Y-YES MADAM.
OH... AND JUST BEFORE YOU GO, DON'T FORGET TO CLEAN THE BATH-ROOM... MY TOILET'S BLOCKED.
AAAAH!!
THAT'S IT... NO MORE SPICY CURRY BEFORE NAP TIME.

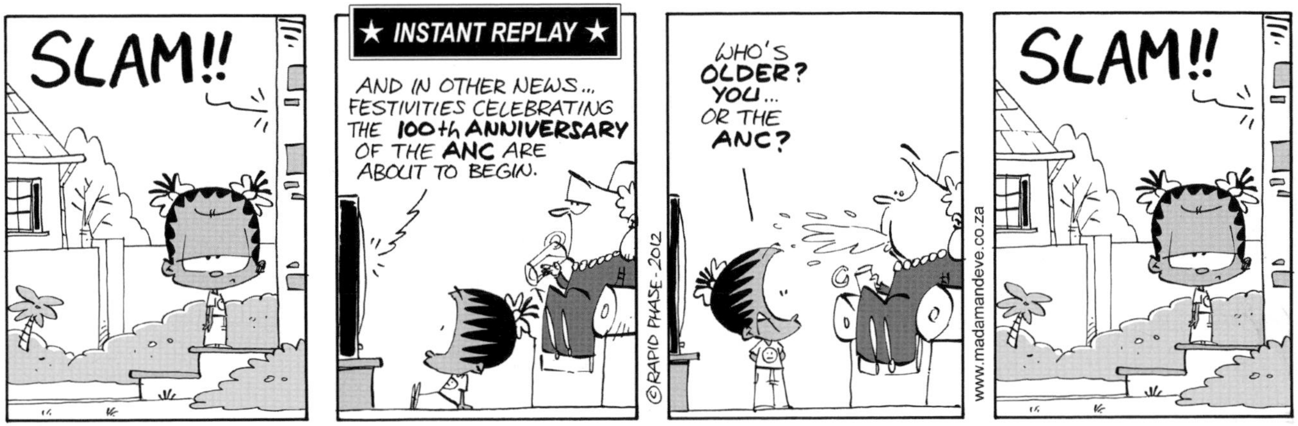
SLAM!!
★ INSTANT REPLAY ★
AND IN OTHER NEWS... FESTIVITIES CELEBRATING THE 100th ANNIVERSARY OF THE ANC ARE ABOUT TO BEGIN.
©RAPID PHASE-2012
WHO'S OLDER? YOU... OR THE ANC?
www.madamandeve.co.za
SLAM!!

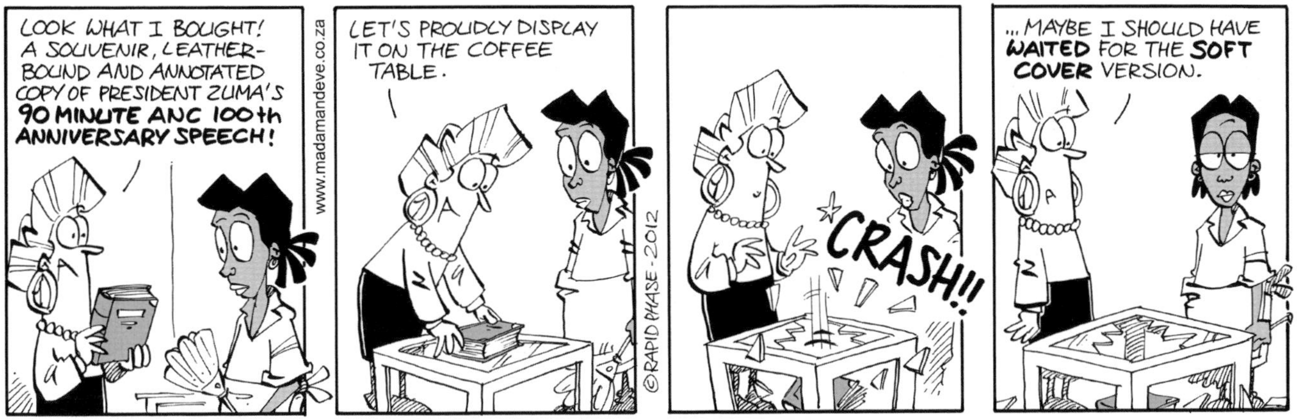
LOOK WHAT I BOUGHT! A SOUVENIR, LEATHER-BOUND AND ANNOTATED COPY OF PRESIDENT ZUMA'S 90 MINUTE ANC 100th ANNIVERSARY SPEECH!
www.madamandeve.co.za
LET'S PROUDLY DISPLAY IT ON THE COFFEE TABLE.
©RAPID PHASE-2012
CRASH!!
...MAYBE I SHOULD HAVE WAITED FOR THE SOFT COVER VERSION.

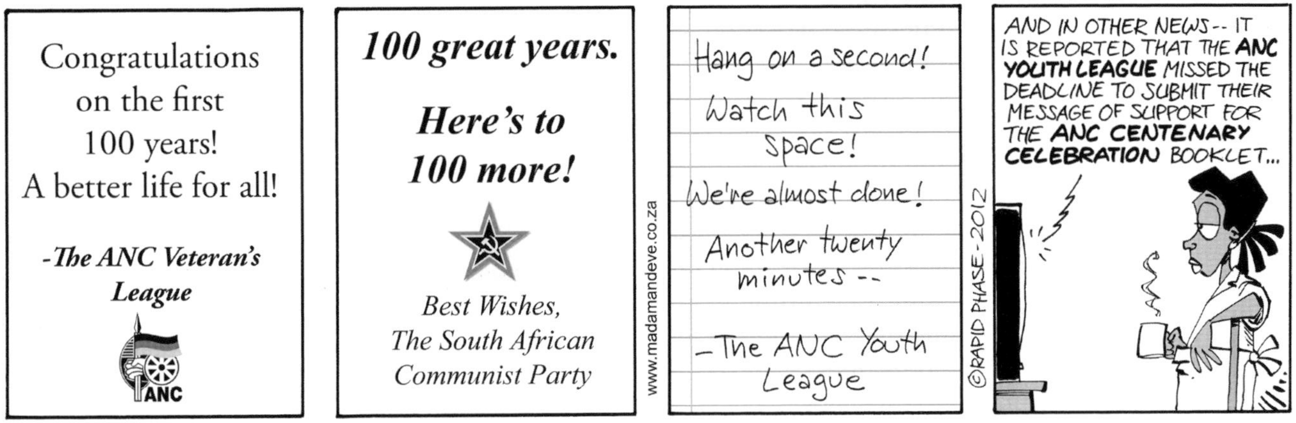
Congratulations on the first 100 years! A better life for all!
-The ANC Veteran's League
ANC
100 great years.
Here's to 100 more!
Best Wishes, The South African Communist Party
www.madamandeve.co.za
Hang on a second!
Watch this space!
We're almost done!
Another twenty minutes --
-The ANC Youth League
©RAPID PHASE-2012
AND IN OTHER NEWS-- IT IS REPORTED THAT THE ANC YOUTH LEAGUE MISSED THE DEADLINE TO SUBMIT THEIR MESSAGE OF SUPPORT FOR THE ANC CENTENARY CELEBRATION BOOKLET...

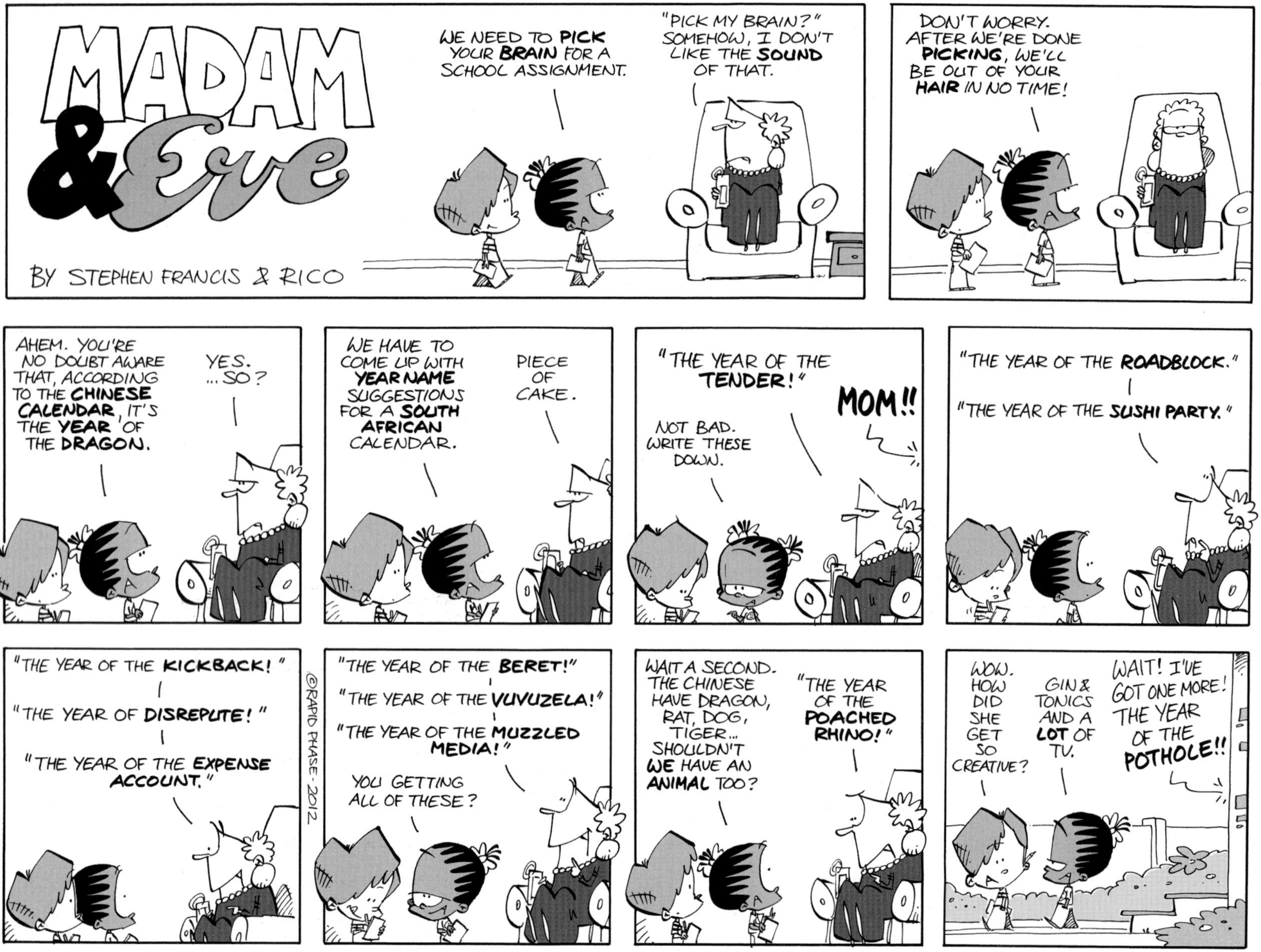
MADAM & Eve
BY STEPHEN FRANCIS & RICO
WE NEED TO PICK YOUR BRAIN FOR A SCHOOL ASSIGNMENT.
"PICK MY BRAIN?" SOMEHOW, I DON'T LIKE THE SOUND OF THAT.
DON'T WORRY. AFTER WE'RE DONE PICKING, WE'LL BE OUT OF YOUR HAIR IN NO TIME!
AHEM. YOU'RE NO DOUBT AWARE THAT, ACCORDING TO THE CHINESE CALENDAR, IT'S THE YEAR OF THE DRAGON.
YES. ...SO?
WE HAVE TO COME UP WITH YEAR NAME SUGGESTIONS FOR A SOUTH AFRICAN CALENDAR.
PIECE OF CAKE.
"THE YEAR OF THE TENDER!"
MOM!!
NOT BAD. WRITE THESE DOWN.
"THE YEAR OF THE ROADBLOCK."
"THE YEAR OF THE SUSHI PARTY."
"THE YEAR OF THE KICKBACK!"
"THE YEAR OF DISREPUTE!"
"THE YEAR OF THE EXPENSE ACCOUNT."
©RAPID PHASE·2012
"THE YEAR OF THE BERET!"
"THE YEAR OF THE VUVUZELA!"
"THE YEAR OF THE MUZZLED MEDIA!"
YOU GETTING ALL OF THESE?
WAIT A SECOND. THE CHINESE HAVE DRAGON, RAT, DOG, TIGER... SHOULDN'T WE HAVE AN ANIMAL TOO?
"THE YEAR OF THE POACHED RHINO!"
WOW. HOW DID SHE GET SO CREATIVE?
GIN & TONICS AND A LOT OF TV.
WAIT! I'VE GOT ONE MORE! THE YEAR OF THE POTHOLE!!

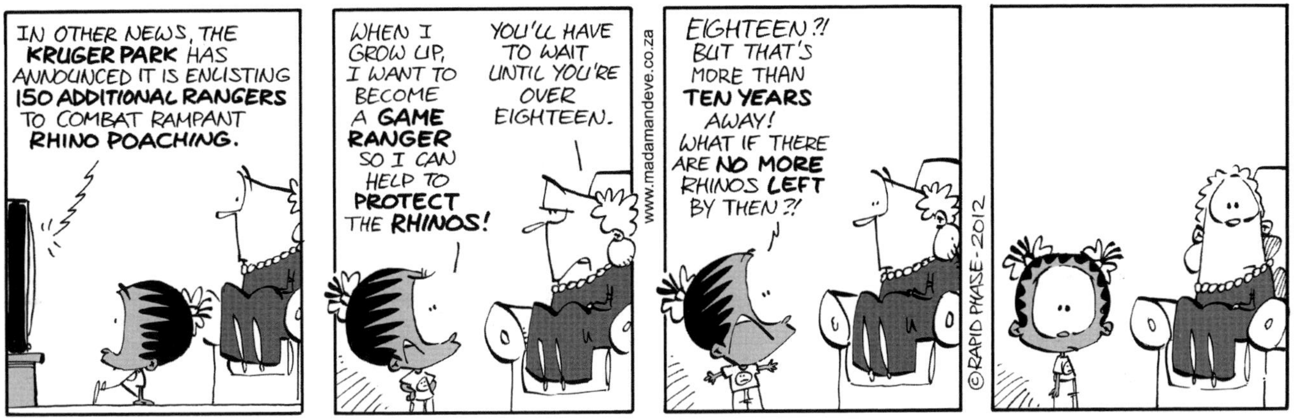
IN OTHER NEWS, THE KRUGER PARK HAS ANNOUNCED IT IS ENLISTING 150 ADDITIONAL RANGERS TO COMBAT RAMPANT RHINO POACHING.
WHEN I GROW UP, I WANT TO BECOME A GAME RANGER SO I CAN HELP TO PROTECT THE RHINOS!
YOU'LL HAVE TO WAIT UNTIL YOU'RE OVER EIGHTEEN.
www.madamandeve.co.za
EIGHTEEN?! BUT THAT'S MORE THAN TEN YEARS AWAY! WHAT IF THERE ARE NO MORE RHINOS LEFT BY THEN?!
©RAPID PHASE-2012

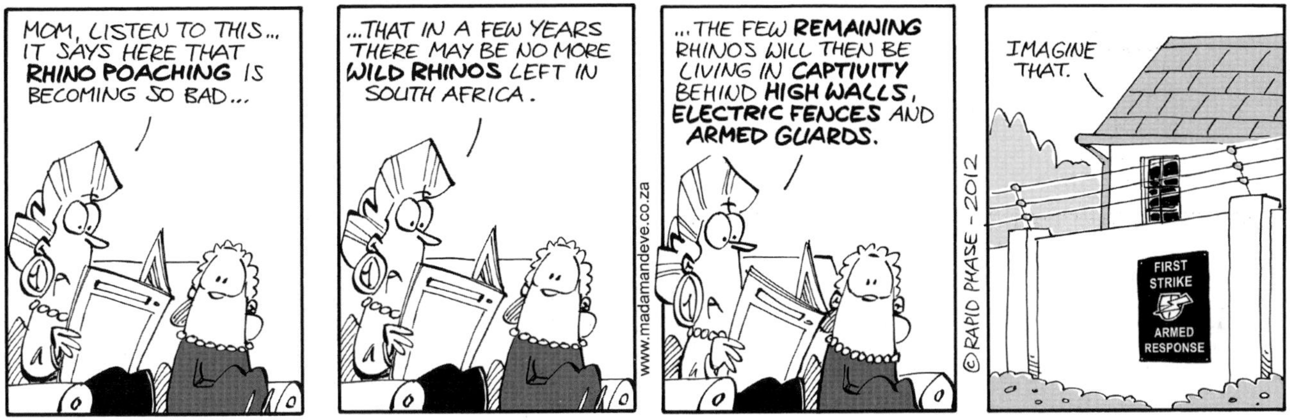
MOM, LISTEN TO THIS... IT SAYS HERE THAT RHINO POACHING IS BECOMING SO BAD...
...THAT IN A FEW YEARS THERE MAY BE NO MORE WILD RHINOS LEFT IN SOUTH AFRICA.
www.madamandeve.co.za
...THE FEW REMAINING RHINOS WILL THEN BE LIVING IN CAPTIVITY BEHIND HIGH WALLS, ELECTRIC FENCES AND ARMED GUARDS.
©RAPID PHASE-2012
IMAGINE THAT.
FIRST STRIKE
ARMED RESPONSE

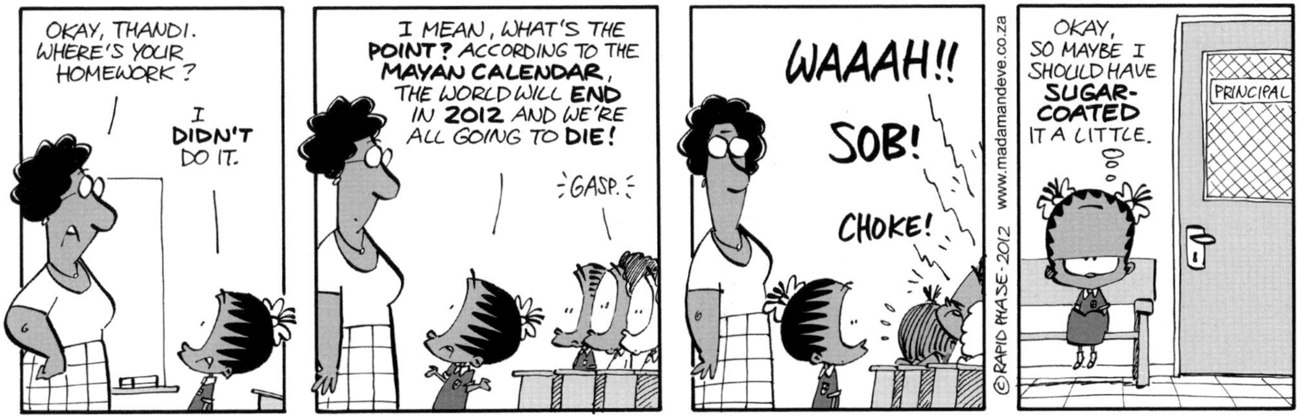
OKAY, THANDI. WHERE'S YOUR HOMEWORK?
I DIDN'T DO IT.
I MEAN, WHAT'S THE POINT? ACCORDING TO THE MAYAN CALENDAR, THE WORLD WILL END IN 2012 AND WE'RE ALL GOING TO DIE!
GASP.
WAAAH!!
SOB!
CHOKE!
www.madamandeve.co.za
©RAPID PHASE-2012
OKAY, SO MAYBE I SHOULD HAVE SUGAR-COATED IT A LITTLE.
PRINCIPAL

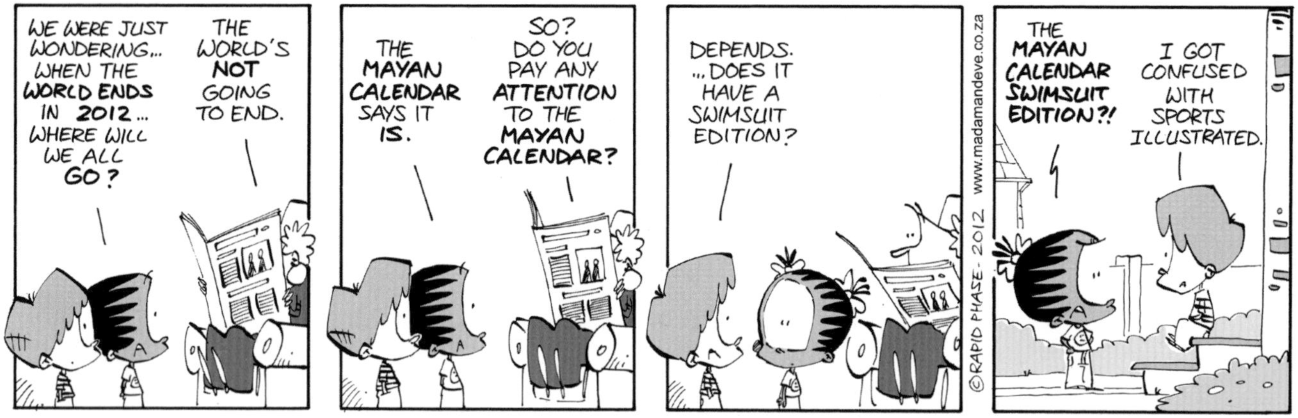
WE WERE JUST WONDERING... WHEN THE WORLD ENDS IN 2012... WHERE WILL WE ALL GO?
THE WORLD'S NOT GOING TO END.
THE MAYAN CALENDAR SAYS IT IS.
SO? DO YOU PAY ANY ATTENTION TO THE MAYAN CALENDAR?
DEPENDS. ...DOES IT HAVE A SWIMSUIT EDITION?
www.madamandeve.co.za ©RAPID PHASE - 2012
THE MAYAN CALENDAR SWIMSUIT EDITION?!
I GOT CONFUSED WITH SPORTS ILLUSTRATED.

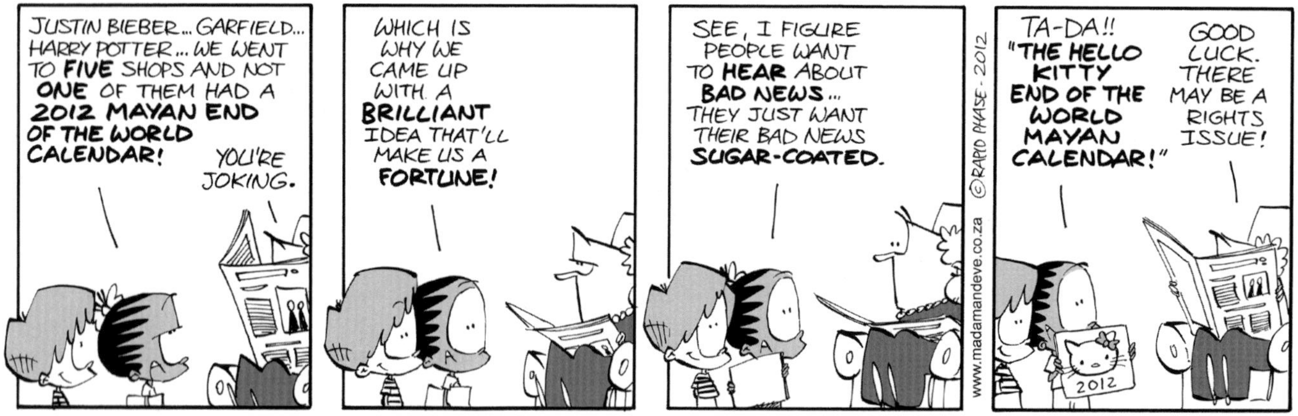
JUSTIN BIEBER... GARFIELD... HARRY POTTER... WE WENT TO FIVE SHOPS AND NOT ONE OF THEM HAD A 2012 MAYAN END OF THE WORLD CALENDAR!
YOU'RE JOKING.
WHICH IS WHY WE CAME UP WITH A BRILLIANT IDEA THAT'LL MAKE US A FORTUNE!
SEE, I FIGURE PEOPLE WANT TO HEAR ABOUT BAD NEWS... THEY JUST WANT THEIR BAD NEWS SUGAR-COATED.
www.madamandeve.co.za ©RAPID PHASE - 2012
TA-DA!! "THE HELLO KITTY END OF THE WORLD MAYAN CALENDAR!"
GOOD LUCK. THERE MAY BE A RIGHTS ISSUE!
2012

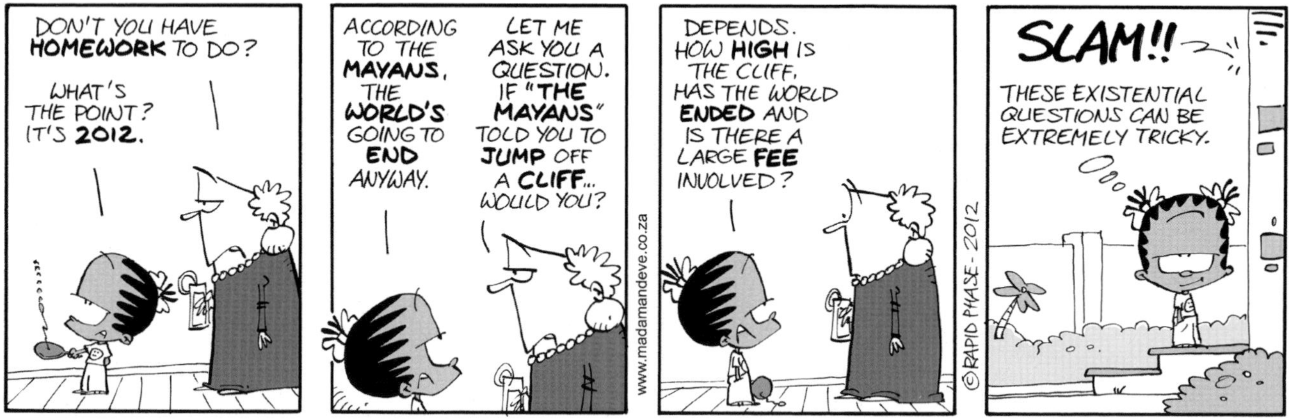
DON'T YOU HAVE HOMEWORK TO DO?
WHAT'S THE POINT? IT'S 2012.
ACCORDING TO THE MAYANS, THE WORLD'S GOING TO END ANYWAY.
LET ME ASK YOU A QUESTION. IF "THE MAYANS" TOLD YOU TO JUMP OFF A CLIFF... WOULD YOU?
www.madamandeve.co.za
DEPENDS. HOW HIGH IS THE CLIFF, HAS THE WORLD ENDED AND IS THERE A LARGE FEE INVOLVED?
©RAPID PHASE - 2012
SLAM!!
THESE EXISTENTIAL QUESTIONS CAN BE EXTREMELY TRICKY.

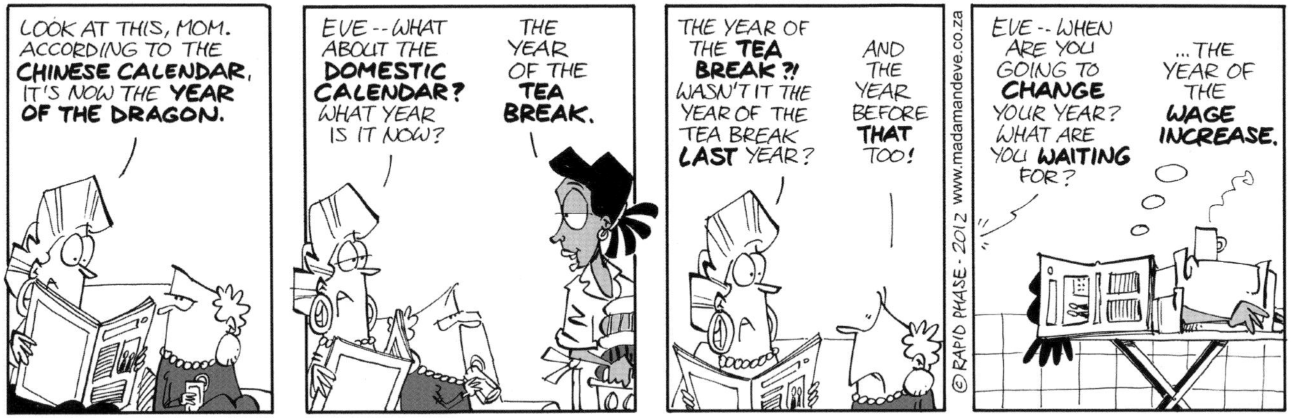
LOOK AT THIS, MOM. ACCORDING TO THE **CHINESE CALENDAR**, IT'S NOW THE **YEAR OF THE DRAGON.**
EVE -- WHAT ABOUT THE **DOMESTIC CALENDAR?** WHAT YEAR IS IT NOW?
THE YEAR OF THE **TEA BREAK.**
THE YEAR OF THE **TEA BREAK?!** WASN'T IT THE YEAR OF THE TEA BREAK **LAST** YEAR?
AND THE YEAR BEFORE **THAT** TOO!
© RAPID PHASE - 2012 www.madamandeve.co.za
EVE -- WHEN ARE YOU GOING TO **CHANGE** YOUR YEAR? WHAT ARE YOU **WAITING** FOR?
...THE YEAR OF THE **WAGE INCREASE.**

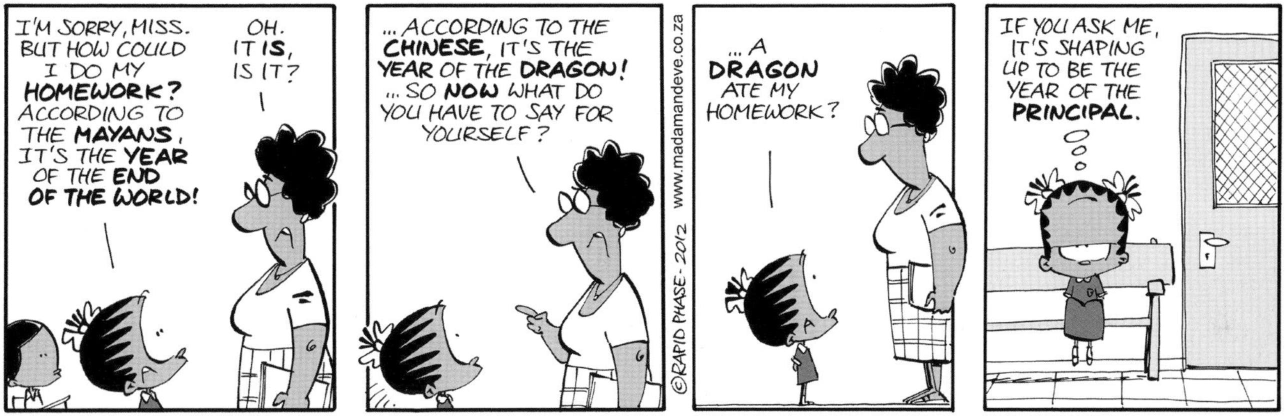
I'M SORRY, MISS. BUT HOW COULD I DO MY **HOMEWORK?** ACCORDING TO THE **MAYANS**, IT'S THE **YEAR** OF THE **END OF THE WORLD!**
OH. IT **IS**, IS IT?
...ACCORDING TO THE **CHINESE**, IT'S THE **YEAR** OF THE **DRAGON!** ...SO **NOW** WHAT DO YOU HAVE TO SAY FOR YOURSELF?
© RAPID PHASE - 2012 www.madamandeve.co.za
...A **DRAGON** ATE MY HOMEWORK?
IF YOU ASK ME, IT'S SHAPING UP TO BE THE YEAR OF THE **PRINCIPAL.**

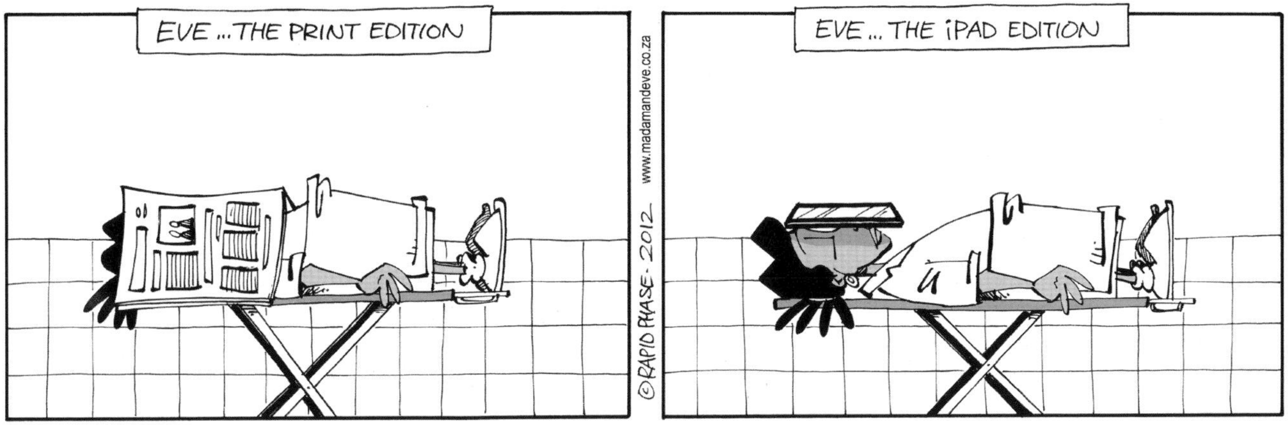
EVE ... THE PRINT EDITION
© RAPID PHASE - 2012 www.madamandeve.co.za
EVE ... THE iPAD EDITION

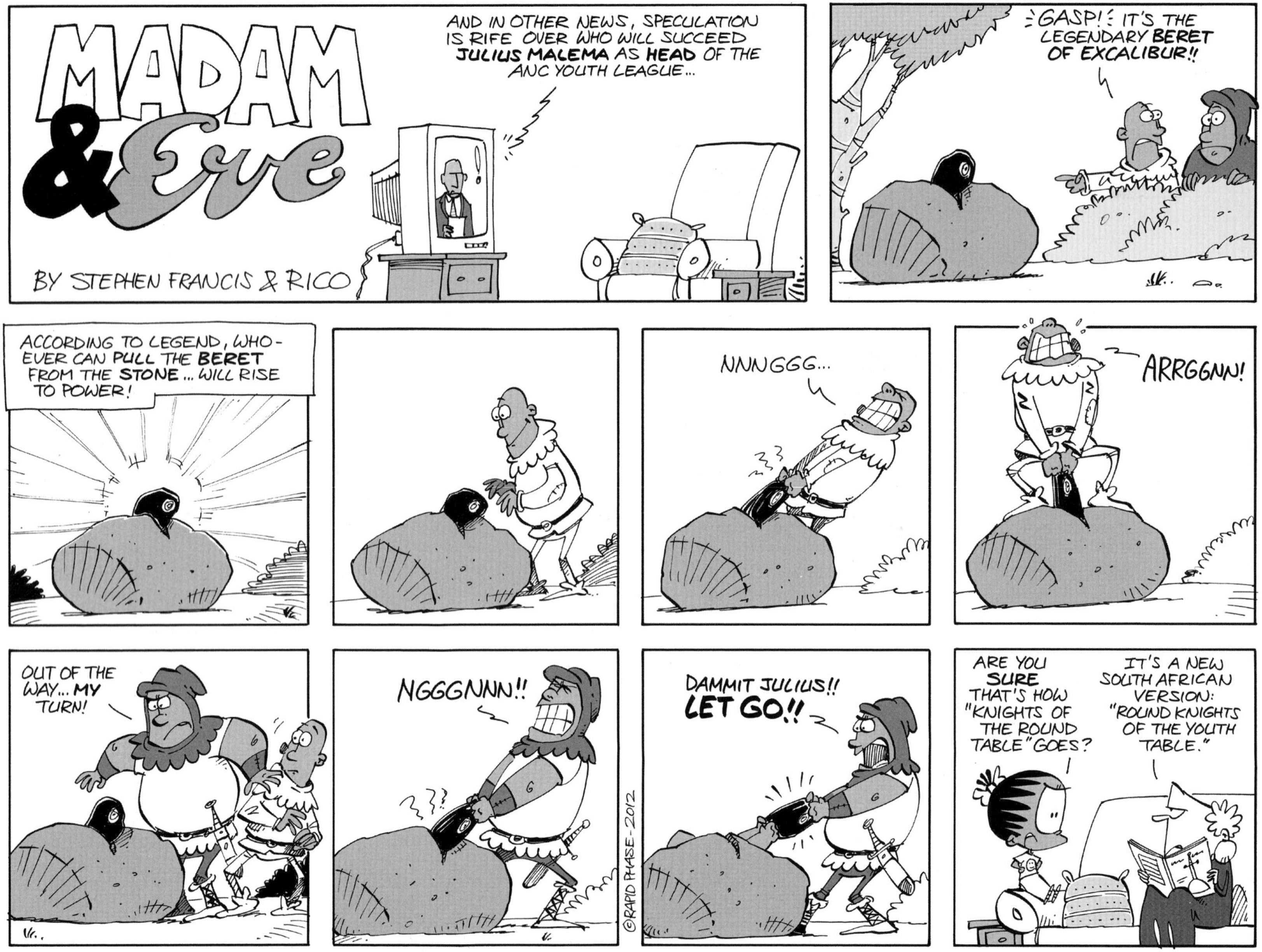
MADAM & Eve
BY STEPHEN FRANCIS & RICO
AND IN OTHER NEWS, SPECULATION IS RIFE OVER WHO WILL SUCCEED JULIUS MALEMA AS HEAD OF THE ANC YOUTH LEAGUE...
GASP! IT'S THE LEGENDARY BERET OF EXCALIBUR!!
ACCORDING TO LEGEND, WHOEVER CAN PULL THE BERET FROM THE STONE... WILL RISE TO POWER!
NNNGGG...
ARRGGNN!
OUT OF THE WAY... MY TURN!
NGGGNNN!!
©RAPID PHASE-2012
DAMMIT JULIUS!! LET GO!!
ARE YOU SURE THAT'S HOW "KNIGHTS OF THE ROUND TABLE" GOES?
IT'S A NEW SOUTH AFRICAN VERSION: "ROUND KNIGHTS OF THE YOUTH TABLE."

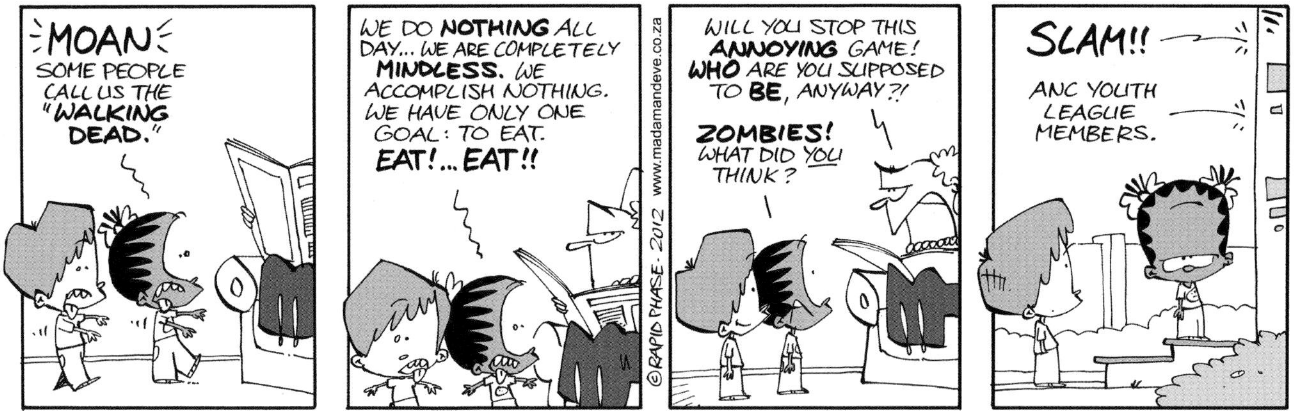
MOAN
SOME PEOPLE CALL US THE "WALKING DEAD."
WE DO NOTHING ALL DAY... WE ARE COMPLETELY MINDLESS. WE ACCOMPLISH NOTHING. WE HAVE ONLY ONE GOAL: TO EAT.
EAT!... EAT!!
www.madamandeve.co.za
©RAPID PHASE - 2012
WILL YOU STOP THIS ANNOYING GAME! WHO ARE YOU SUPPOSED TO BE, ANYWAY?!
ZOMBIES! WHAT DID YOU THINK?
SLAM!!
ANC YOUTH LEAGUE MEMBERS.

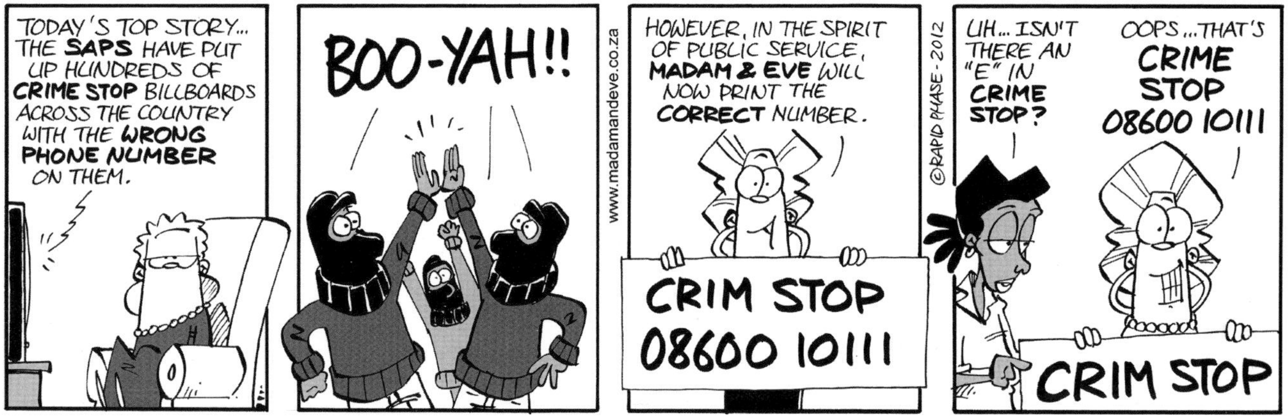
TODAY'S TOP STORY... THE SAPS HAVE PUT UP HUNDREDS OF CRIME STOP BILLBOARDS ACROSS THE COUNTRY WITH THE WRONG PHONE NUMBER ON THEM.
BOO-YAH!!
www.madamandeve.co.za
HOWEVER, IN THE SPIRIT OF PUBLIC SERVICE, MADAM & EVE WILL NOW PRINT THE CORRECT NUMBER.
CRIM STOP 08600 10111
©RAPID PHASE - 2012
UH... ISN'T THERE AN "E" IN CRIME STOP?
OOPS... THAT'S CRIME STOP 08600 10111
CRIM STOP

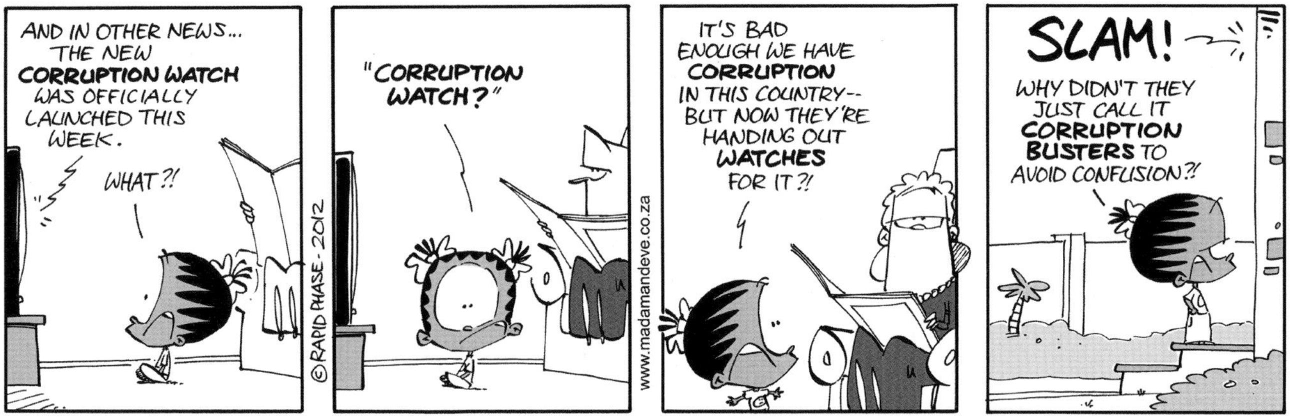
AND IN OTHER NEWS... THE NEW CORRUPTION WATCH WAS OFFICIALLY LAUNCHED THIS WEEK.
WHAT?!
©RAPID PHASE - 2012
"CORRUPTION WATCH?"
www.madamandeve.co.za
IT'S BAD ENOUGH WE HAVE CORRUPTION IN THIS COUNTRY-- BUT NOW THEY'RE HANDING OUT WATCHES FOR IT?!
SLAM!
WHY DIDN'T THEY JUST CALL IT CORRUPTION BUSTERS TO AVOID CONFUSION?!

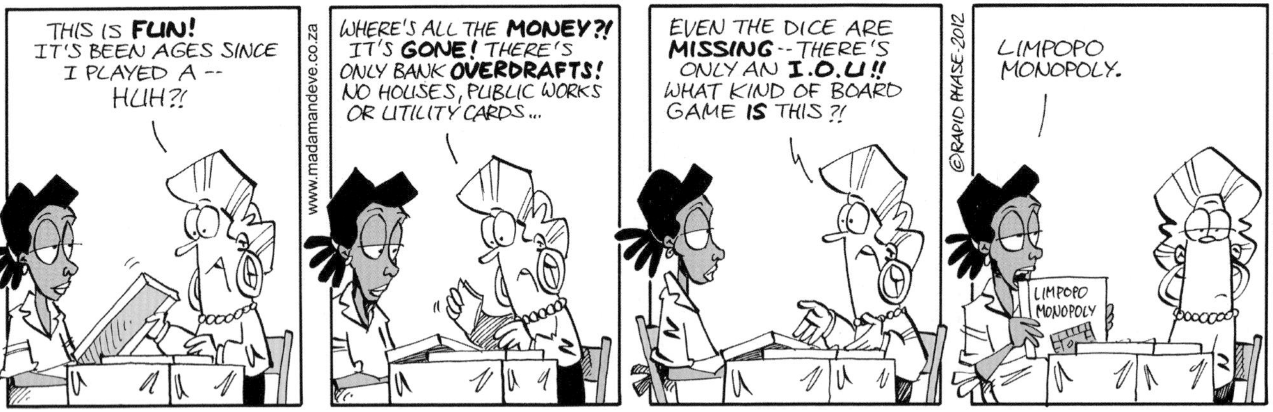
THIS IS FUN! IT'S BEEN AGES SINCE I PLAYED A -- HUH?!
www.madamandeve.co.za
WHERE'S ALL THE MONEY?! IT'S GONE! THERE'S ONLY BANK OVERDRAFTS! NO HOUSES, PUBLIC WORKS OR UTILITY CARDS...
EVEN THE DICE ARE MISSING -- THERE'S ONLY AN I.O.U!! WHAT KIND OF BOARD GAME IS THIS?!
©RAPID PHASE-2012
LIMPOPO MONOPOLY.
LIMPOPO MONOPOLY

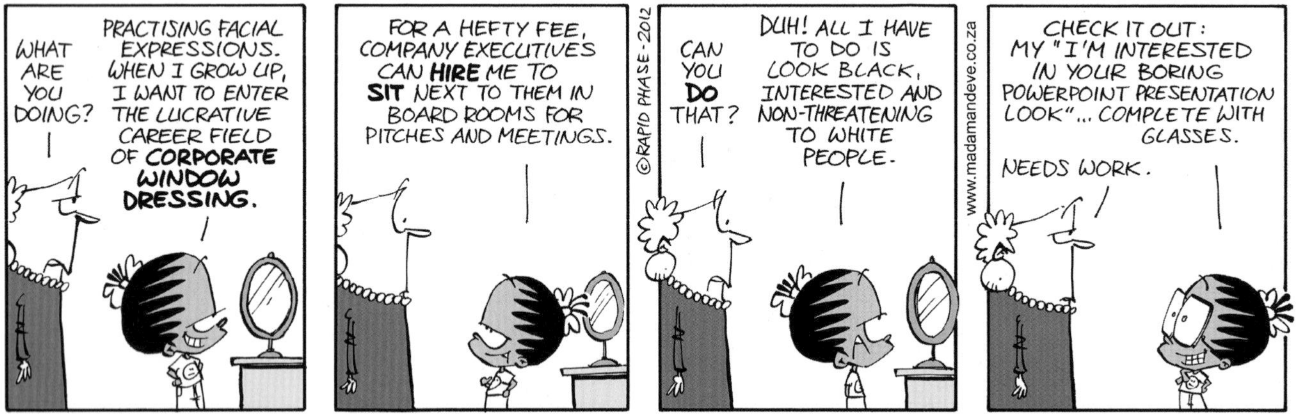
WHAT ARE YOU DOING?
PRACTISING FACIAL EXPRESSIONS. WHEN I GROW UP, I WANT TO ENTER THE LUCRATIVE CAREER FIELD OF CORPORATE WINDOW DRESSING.
FOR A HEFTY FEE, COMPANY EXECUTIVES CAN HIRE ME TO SIT NEXT TO THEM IN BOARD ROOMS FOR PITCHES AND MEETINGS.
©RAPID PHASE-2012
CAN YOU DO THAT?
DUH! ALL I HAVE TO DO IS LOOK BLACK, INTERESTED AND NON-THREATENING TO WHITE PEOPLE.
www.madamandeve.co.za
CHECK IT OUT: MY "I'M INTERESTED IN YOUR BORING POWERPOINT PRESENTATION LOOK"... COMPLETE WITH GLASSES.
NEEDS WORK.

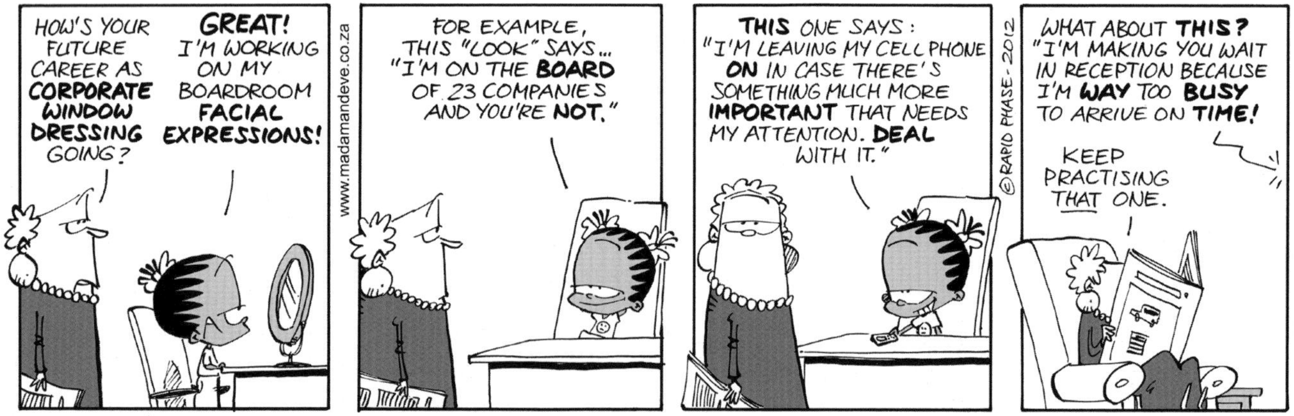
HOW'S YOUR FUTURE CAREER AS CORPORATE WINDOW DRESSING GOING?
GREAT! I'M WORKING ON MY BOARDROOM FACIAL EXPRESSIONS!
www.madamandeve.co.za
FOR EXAMPLE, THIS "LOOK" SAYS... "I'M ON THE BOARD OF 23 COMPANIES AND YOU'RE NOT."
THIS ONE SAYS: "I'M LEAVING MY CELL PHONE ON IN CASE THERE'S SOMETHING MUCH MORE IMPORTANT THAT NEEDS MY ATTENTION. DEAL WITH IT."
©RAPID PHASE-2012
WHAT ABOUT THIS? "I'M MAKING YOU WAIT IN RECEPTION BECAUSE I'M WAY TOO BUSY TO ARRIVE ON TIME!
KEEP PRACTISING THAT ONE.

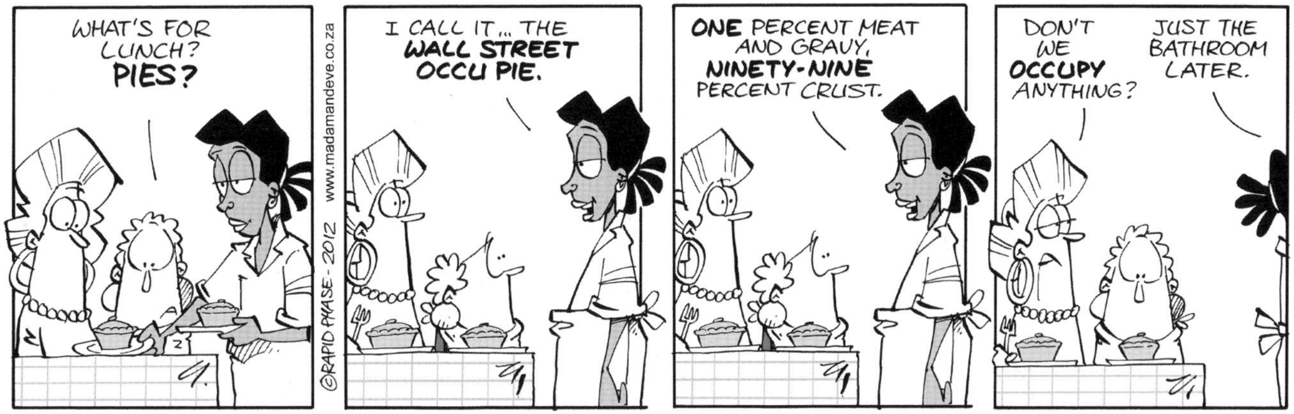
WHAT'S FOR LUNCH? PIES?
©RAPID PHASE · 2012
www.madamandeve.co.za
I CALL IT... THE WALL STREET OCCU PIE.
ONE PERCENT MEAT AND GRAVY, NINETY-NINE PERCENT CRUST.
DON'T WE OCCUPY ANYTHING?
JUST THE BATHROOM LATER.

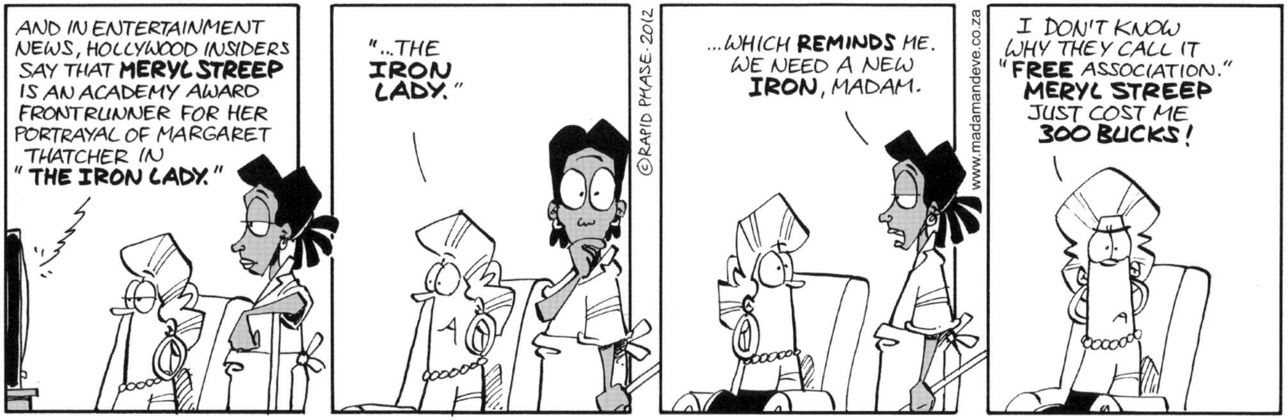
AND IN ENTERTAINMENT NEWS, HOLLYWOOD INSIDERS SAY THAT MERYL STREEP IS AN ACADEMY AWARD FRONTRUNNER FOR HER PORTRAYAL OF MARGARET THATCHER IN "THE IRON LADY."
"...THE IRON LADY."
©RAPID PHASE · 2012
...WHICH REMINDS ME. WE NEED A NEW IRON, MADAM.
www.madamandeve.co.za
I DON'T KNOW WHY THEY CALL IT "FREE ASSOCIATION." MERYL STREEP JUST COST ME 300 BUCKS!

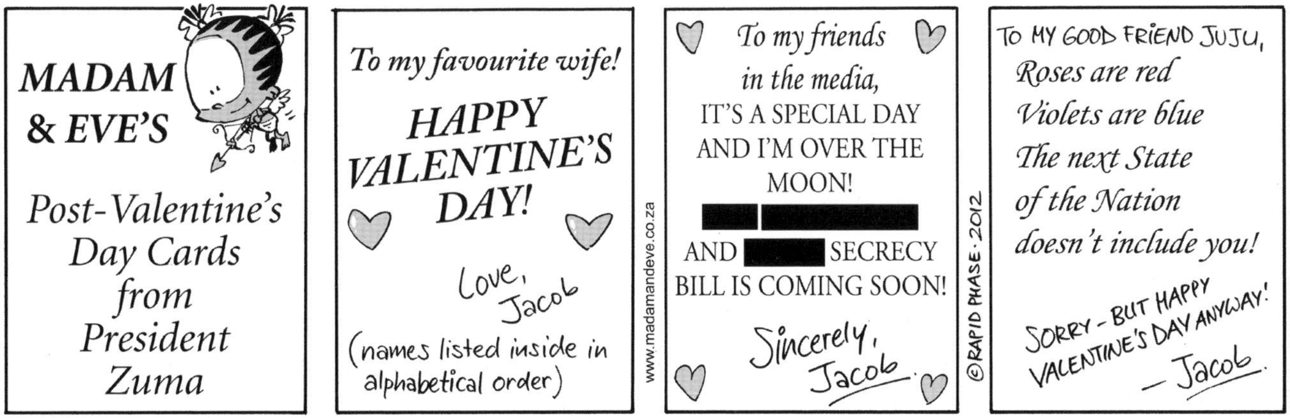
MADAM & EVE'S
Post-Valentine's Day Cards from President Zuma
To my favourite wife!
HAPPY VALENTINE'S DAY!
Love, Jacob
(names listed inside in alphabetical order)
www.madamandeve.co.za
To my friends in the media,
IT'S A SPECIAL DAY AND I'M OVER THE MOON!
[redacted]
AND [redacted] SECRECY BILL IS COMING SOON!
Sincerely, Jacob
©RAPID PHASE · 2012
TO MY GOOD FRIEND JUJU,
Roses are red
Violets are blue
The next State of the Nation doesn't include you!
SORRY - BUT HAPPY VALENTINE'S DAY ANYWAY!
- Jacob

Panel 1: IN HIS STATE OF THE NATION SPEECH, PRESIDENT ZUMA SAYS DEVELOPING A **STRONG INFRA-STRUCTURE** IS A TOP PRIORITY.

BIG DEAL.

Panel 2: I'VE KNOWN ABOUT THE IMPORTANCE OF A GOOD **INFRASTRUCTURE** FOR <u>YEARS</u>!

Panel 3: HERE'S YOUR **BRAN AND OAT** FLAKES.

Panel 4: LET ME KNOW WHEN YOU'RE DONE AND I'LL BRING YOUR **WEETBIX** AND **PRUNE JUICE.**

WANT SOME?

Panel 5: Daily News — ZUMA PROMISES THOUSANDS OF JOBS / The Star — ZUMA PROMISES ECONOMIC GROWTH

Panel 6: Daily News — ZUMA PROMISES THOUSANDS OF JOBS / The Star — ZUMA PROMISES ECONOMIC GROWTH

Panel 7: Daily News — ZUMA PROMISES THOUSANDS OF JOBS / The Star — ZUMA PROMISES ECONOMIC GROWTH

Panel 8: NO JOB NO MONEY. PLEASE HELP. / NO WORK. NO FOOD. PLEASE HELP.

Panel 9: THANDI! YOU **STILL** HAVEN'T DONE YOUR HOMEWORK?!

UH...

Panel 10: YOU KNOW, AT THE RATE YOU'RE GOING, YOU'LL NEVER PASS **MATRIC! THEN** WHERE WILL YOU END UP?!

Panel 11: CHIEF OPERATING OFFICER OF THE SABC?

Panel 12: AND MY FIRST REALITY TV SHOW? "PRIMARY SCHOOL SURVIVOR."

PRINCIPAL

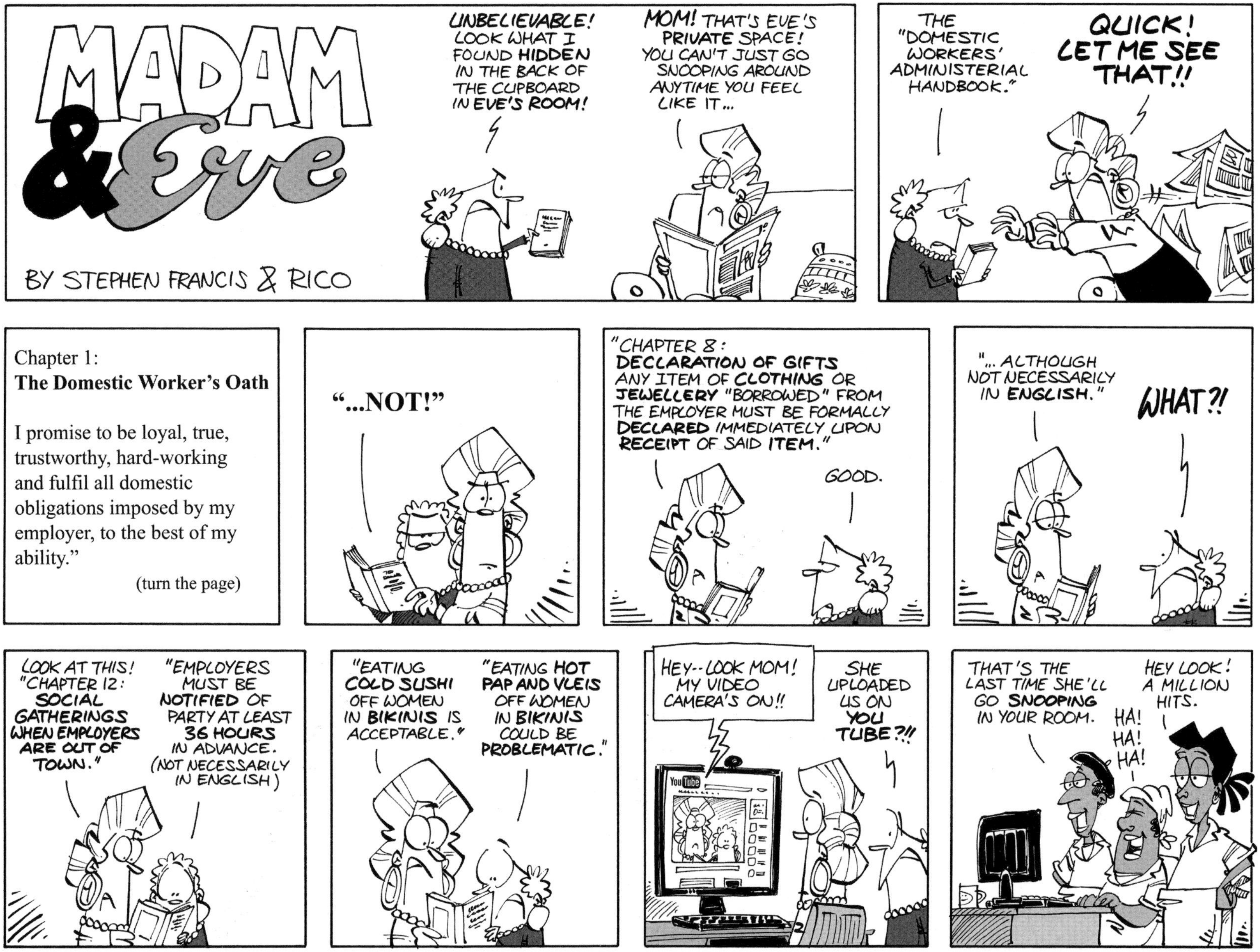
MADAM & Eve
BY STEPHEN FRANCIS & RICO
UNBELIEVABLE! LOOK WHAT I FOUND HIDDEN IN THE BACK OF THE CUPBOARD IN EVE'S ROOM!
MOM! THAT'S EVE'S PRIVATE SPACE! YOU CAN'T JUST GO SNOOPING AROUND ANYTIME YOU FEEL LIKE IT...
THE "DOMESTIC WORKERS' ADMINISTERIAL HANDBOOK."
QUICK! LET ME SEE THAT!!
Chapter 1:
The Domestic Worker's Oath
I promise to be loyal, true, trustworthy, hard-working and fulfil all domestic obligations imposed by my employer, to the best of my ability."
(turn the page)
"...NOT!"
"CHAPTER 8: DECLARATION OF GIFTS ANY ITEM OF CLOTHING OR JEWELLERY "BORROWED" FROM THE EMPLOYER MUST BE FORMALLY DECLARED IMMEDIATELY UPON RECEIPT OF SAID ITEM."
GOOD.
"... ALTHOUGH NOT NECESSARILY IN ENGLISH."
WHAT?!
LOOK AT THIS! "CHAPTER 12: SOCIAL GATHERINGS WHEN EMPLOYERS ARE OUT OF TOWN."
"EMPLOYERS MUST BE NOTIFIED OF PARTY AT LEAST 36 HOURS IN ADVANCE. (NOT NECESSARILY IN ENGLISH)
"EATING COLD SUSHI OFF WOMEN IN BIKINIS IS ACCEPTABLE."
"EATING HOT PAP AND VLEIS OFF WOMEN IN BIKINIS COULD BE PROBLEMATIC."
HEY--LOOK MOM! MY VIDEO CAMERA'S ON!!
SHE UPLOADED US ON YOU TUBE?!!
THAT'S THE LAST TIME SHE'LL GO SNOOPING IN YOUR ROOM.
HEY LOOK! A MILLION HITS.
HA! HA! HA!

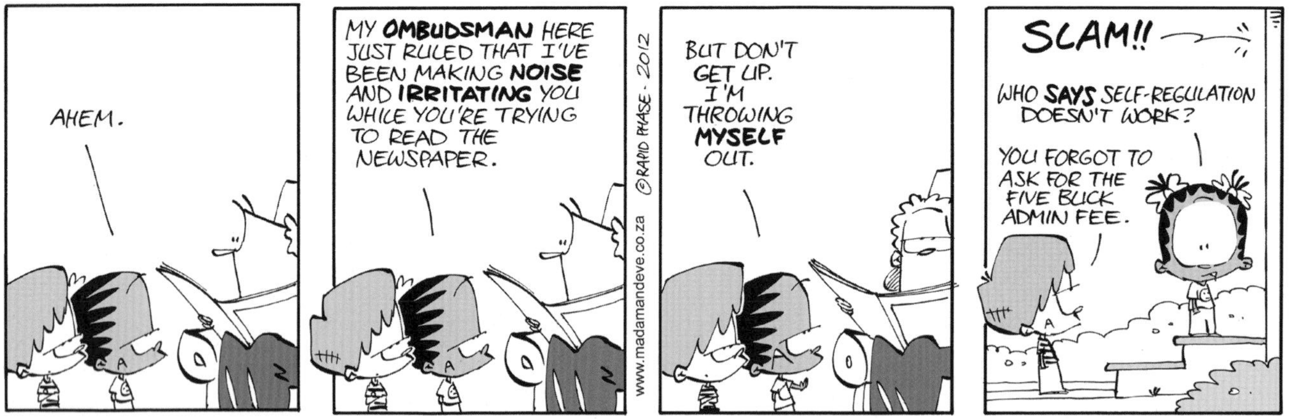
AHEM.
MY OMBUDSMAN HERE JUST RULED THAT I'VE BEEN MAKING NOISE AND IRRITATING YOU WHILE YOU'RE TRYING TO READ THE NEWSPAPER.
www.madamandeve.co.za ©RAPID PHASE · 2012
BUT DON'T GET UP. I'M THROWING MYSELF OUT.
SLAM!!
WHO SAYS SELF-REGULATION DOESN'T WORK?
YOU FORGOT TO ASK FOR THE FIVE BUCK ADMIN FEE.

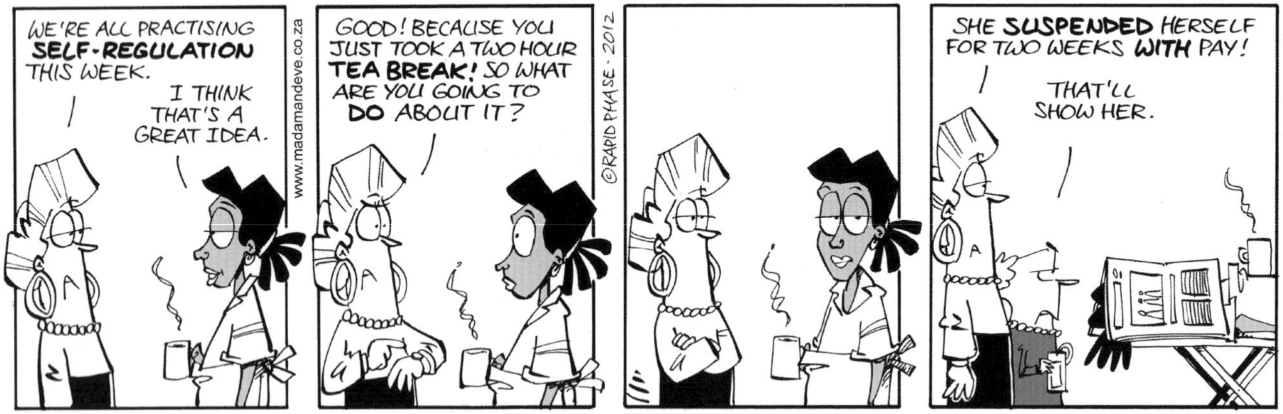
WE'RE ALL PRACTISING SELF-REGULATION THIS WEEK.
I THINK THAT'S A GREAT IDEA.
www.madamandeve.co.za
GOOD! BECAUSE YOU JUST TOOK A TWO HOUR TEA BREAK! SO WHAT ARE YOU GOING TO DO ABOUT IT?
©RAPID PHASE · 2012
SHE SUSPENDED HERSELF FOR TWO WEEKS WITH PAY!
THAT'LL SHOW HER.

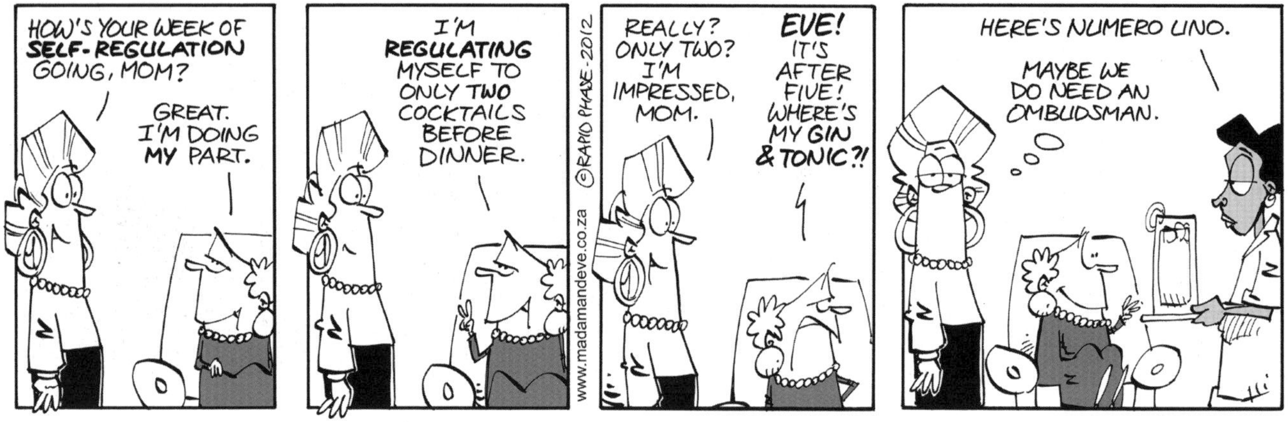
HOW'S YOUR WEEK OF SELF-REGULATION GOING, MOM?
GREAT. I'M DOING MY PART.
I'M REGULATING MYSELF TO ONLY TWO COCKTAILS BEFORE DINNER.
www.madamandeve.co.za ©RAPID PHASE · 2012
REALLY? ONLY TWO? I'M IMPRESSED, MOM.
EVE! IT'S AFTER FIVE! WHERE'S MY GIN & TONIC?!
HERE'S NUMERO UNO.
MAYBE WE DO NEED AN OMBUDSMAN.

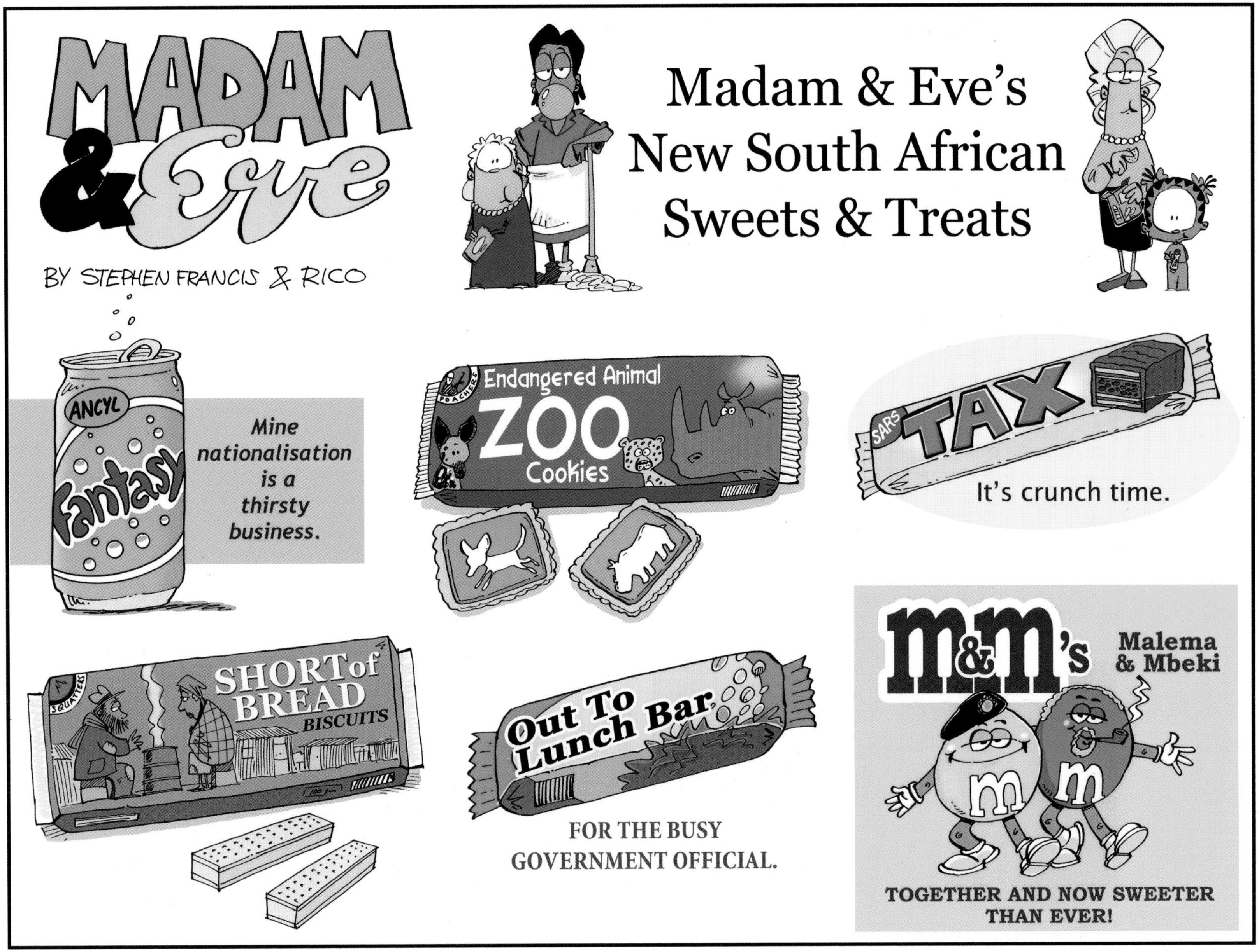
MADAM & Eve
BY STEPHEN FRANCIS & RICO
Madam & Eve's
New South African
Sweets & Treats
ANCYL
Fantasy
Mine nationalisation is a thirsty business.
POACHERS
Endangered Animal
ZOO
Cookies
SARS
TAX
It's crunch time.
SQUATTERS
SHORT of BREAD
BISCUITS
100 gm
Out To Lunch Bar
FOR THE BUSY GOVERNMENT OFFICIAL.
m&m's
Malema & Mbeki
TOGETHER AND NOW SWEETER THAN EVER!

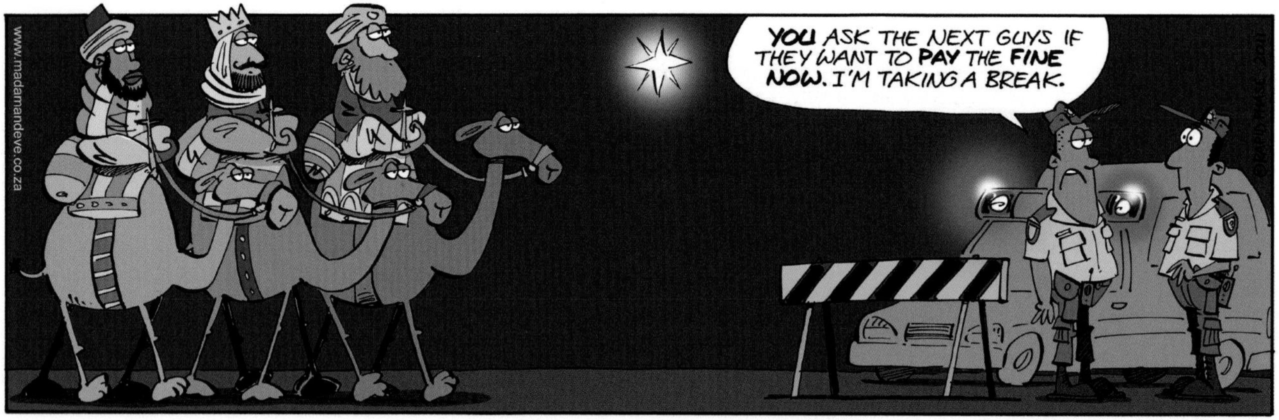
www.madamandeve.co.za
YOU ASK THE NEXT GUYS IF THEY WANT TO PAY THE FINE NOW. I'M TAKING A BREAK.

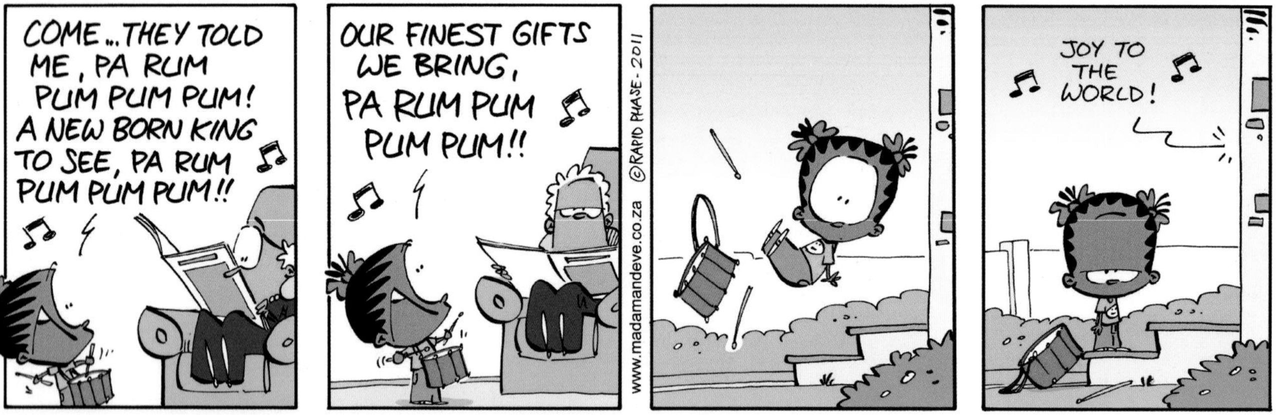
COME...THEY TOLD ME, PA RUM PUM PUM PUM! A NEW BORN KING TO SEE, PA RUM PUM PUM PUM!!
OUR FINEST GIFTS WE BRING, PA RUM PUM PUM PUM!!
©RAPID PHASE-2011
www.madamandeve.co.za
JOY TO THE WORLD!

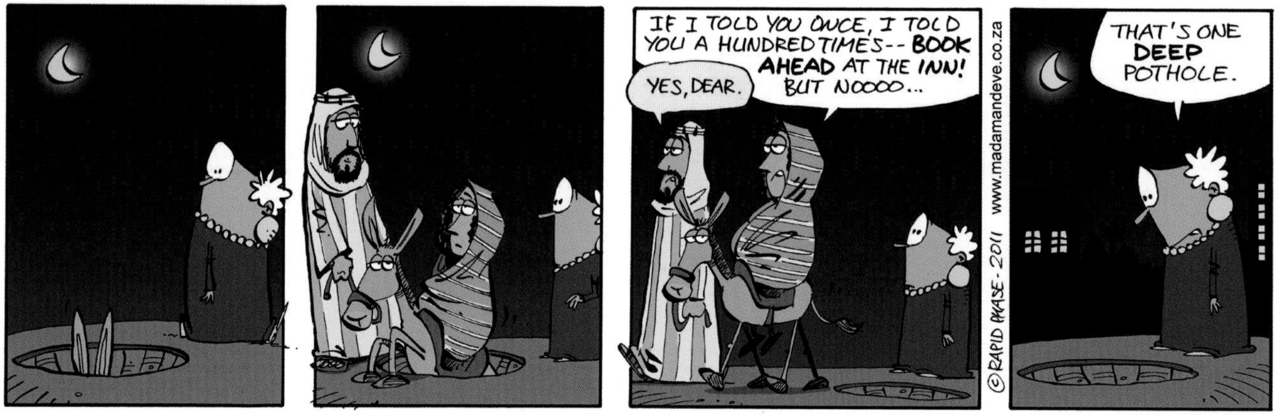
IF I TOLD YOU ONCE, I TOLD YOU A HUNDRED TIMES-- BOOK AHEAD AT THE INN! BUT NOOOO...
YES, DEAR.
www.madamandeve.co.za
©RAPID PHASE-2011
THAT'S ONE DEEP POTHOLE.

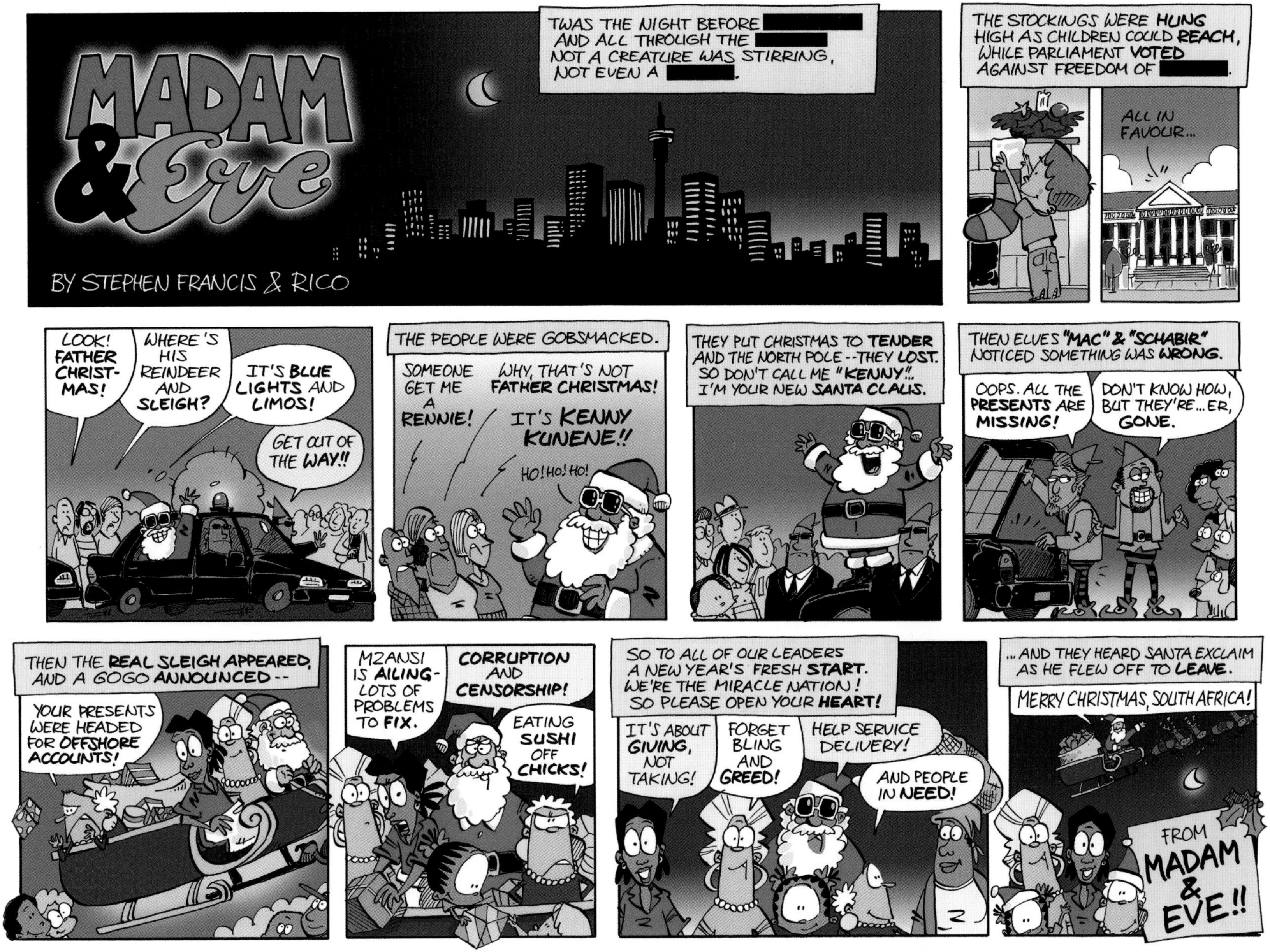
MADAM & Eve
BY STEPHEN FRANCIS & RICO
TWAS THE NIGHT BEFORE [redacted] AND ALL THROUGH THE [redacted] NOT A CREATURE WAS STIRRING, NOT EVEN A [redacted].
THE STOCKINGS WERE HUNG HIGH AS CHILDREN COULD REACH, WHILE PARLIAMENT VOTED AGAINST FREEDOM OF [redacted].
ALL IN FAVOUR...
LOOK! FATHER CHRIST-MAS!
WHERE'S HIS REINDEER AND SLEIGH?
IT'S BLUE LIGHTS AND LIMOS!
GET OUT OF THE WAY!!
THE PEOPLE WERE GOBSMACKED.
SOMEONE GET ME A RENNIE!
WHY, THAT'S NOT FATHER CHRISTMAS!
IT'S KENNY KUNENE!!
HO! HO! HO!
THEY PUT CHRISTMAS TO TENDER AND THE NORTH POLE -- THEY LOST. SO DON'T CALL ME "KENNY"... I'M YOUR NEW SANTA CLAUS.
THEN ELVES "MAC" & "SCHABIR" NOTICED SOMETHING WAS WRONG.
OOPS. ALL THE PRESENTS ARE MISSING!
DON'T KNOW HOW, BUT THEY'RE... ER, GONE.
THEN THE REAL SLEIGH APPEARED, AND A GOGO ANNOUNCED --
YOUR PRESENTS WERE HEADED FOR OFFSHORE ACCOUNTS!
MZANSI IS AILING-LOTS OF PROBLEMS TO FIX.
CORRUPTION AND CENSORSHIP!
EATING SUSHI OFF CHICKS!
SO TO ALL OF OUR LEADERS A NEW YEAR'S FRESH START. WE'RE THE MIRACLE NATION! SO PLEASE OPEN YOUR HEART!
IT'S ABOUT GIVING, NOT TAKING!
FORGET BLING AND GREED!
HELP SERVICE DELIVERY!
AND PEOPLE IN NEED!
... AND THEY HEARD SANTA EXCLAIM AS HE FLEW OFF TO LEAVE.
MERRY CHRISTMAS, SOUTH AFRICA!
FROM MADAM & EVE!!

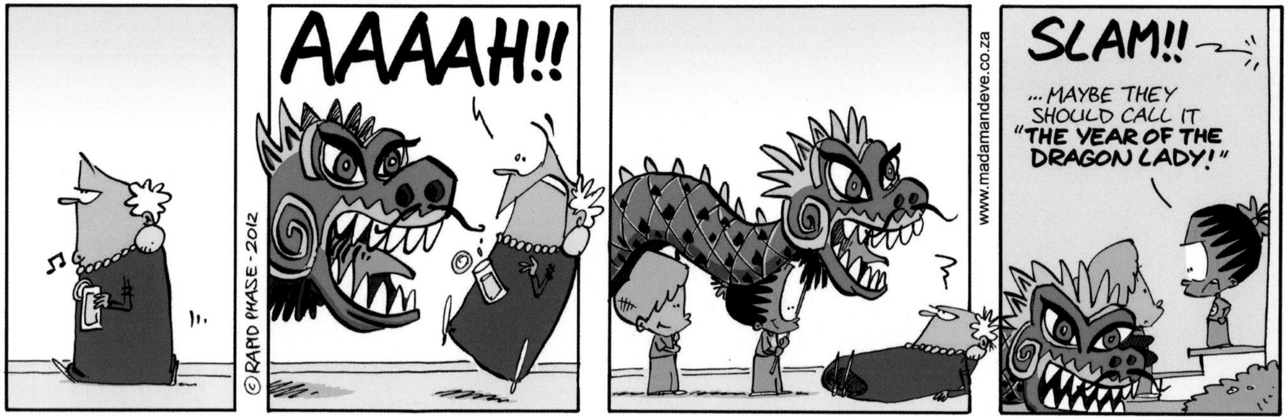
AAAAH!!
©RAPID PHASE - 2012
www.madamandeve.co.za
SLAM!!
...MAYBE THEY SHOULD CALL IT "THE YEAR OF THE DRAGON LADY!"

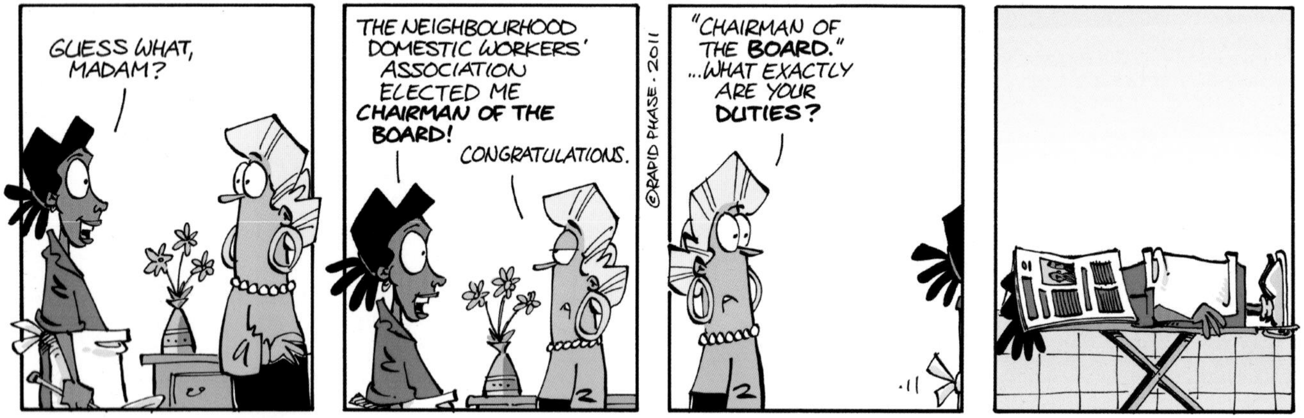
GUESS WHAT, MADAM?
THE NEIGHBOURHOOD DOMESTIC WORKERS' ASSOCIATION ELECTED ME CHAIRMAN OF THE BOARD!
CONGRATULATIONS.
©RAPID PHASE - 2011
"CHAIRMAN OF THE BOARD." ...WHAT EXACTLY ARE YOUR DUTIES?

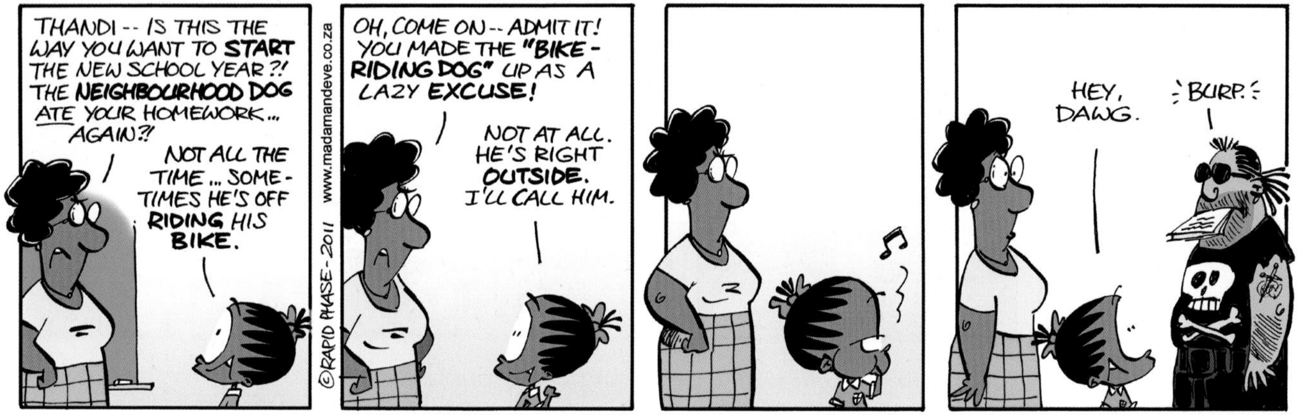
THANDI -- IS THIS THE WAY YOU WANT TO START THE NEW SCHOOL YEAR?! THE NEIGHBOURHOOD DOG ATE YOUR HOMEWORK... AGAIN?!
NOT ALL THE TIME... SOME-TIMES HE'S OFF RIDING HIS BIKE.
©RAPID PHASE - 2011 www.madamandeve.co.za
OH, COME ON -- ADMIT IT! YOU MADE THE "BIKE-RIDING DOG" UP AS A LAZY EXCUSE!
NOT AT ALL. HE'S RIGHT OUTSIDE. I'LL CALL HIM.
HEY, DAWG.
BURP.

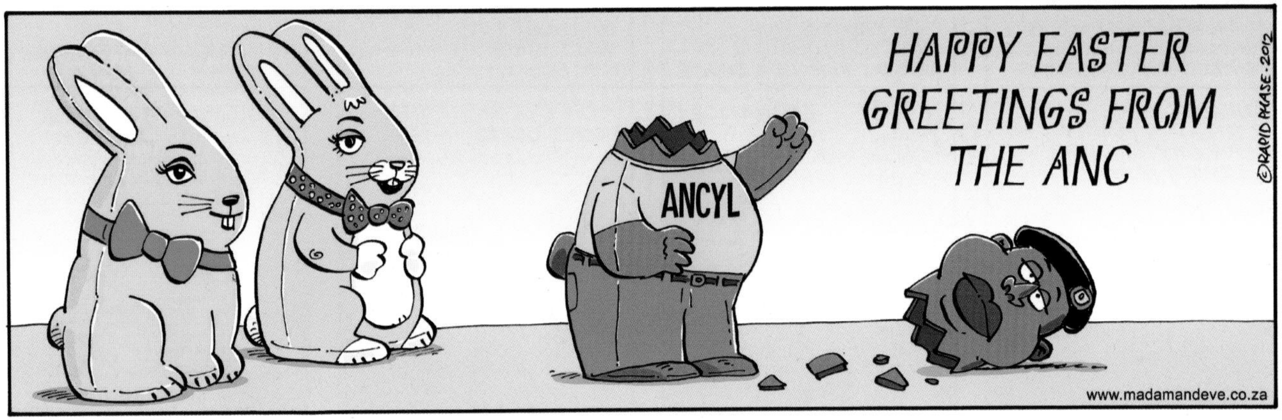
HAPPY EASTER GREETINGS FROM THE ANC
ANCYL
©RAPID PHASE-2012
www.madamandeve.co.za

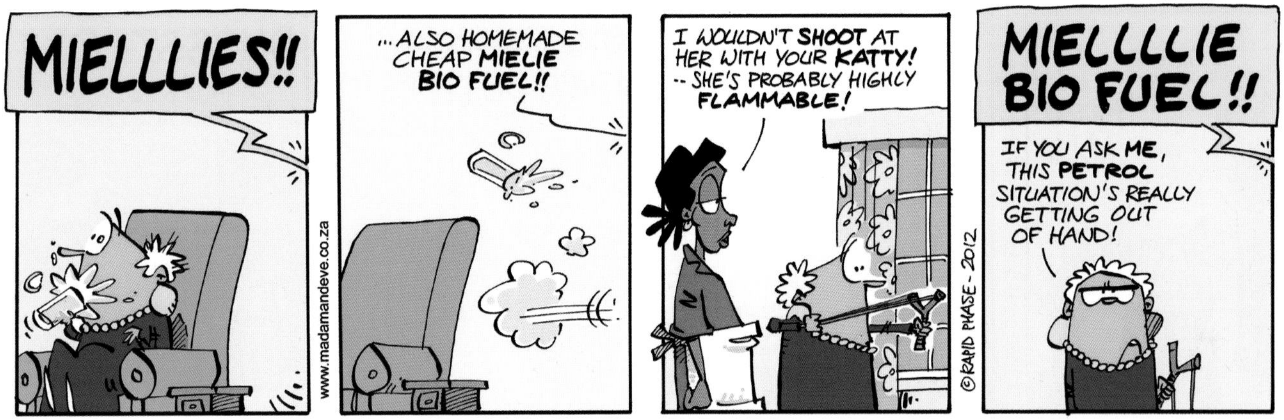
MIELLLIES!!
...ALSO HOMEMADE CHEAP MIELIE BIO FUEL!!
www.madamandeve.co.za
I WOULDN'T SHOOT AT HER WITH YOUR KATTY! -- SHE'S PROBABLY HIGHLY FLAMMABLE!
©RAPID PHASE - 2012
MIELLLLIE BIO FUEL!!
IF YOU ASK ME, THIS PETROL SITUATION'S REALLY GETTING OUT OF HAND!

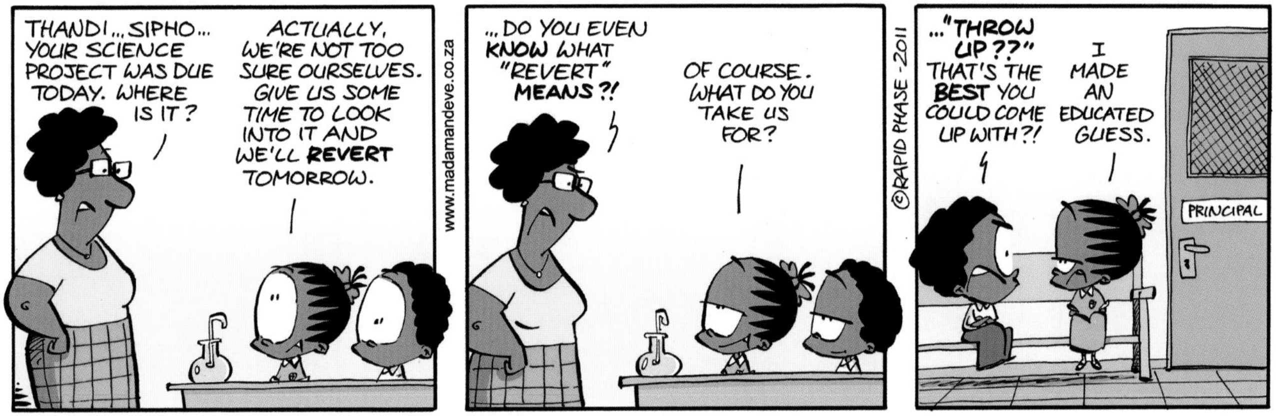
THANDI... SIPHO... YOUR SCIENCE PROJECT WAS DUE TODAY. WHERE IS IT?
ACTUALLY, WE'RE NOT TOO SURE OURSELVES. GIVE US SOME TIME TO LOOK INTO IT AND WE'LL REVERT TOMORROW.
www.madamandeve.co.za
...DO YOU EVEN KNOW WHAT "REVERT" MEANS?!
OF COURSE. WHAT DO YOU TAKE US FOR?
©RAPID PHASE - 2011
..."THROW UP??" THAT'S THE BEST YOU COULD COME UP WITH?!
I MADE AN EDUCATED GUESS.
PRINCIPAL

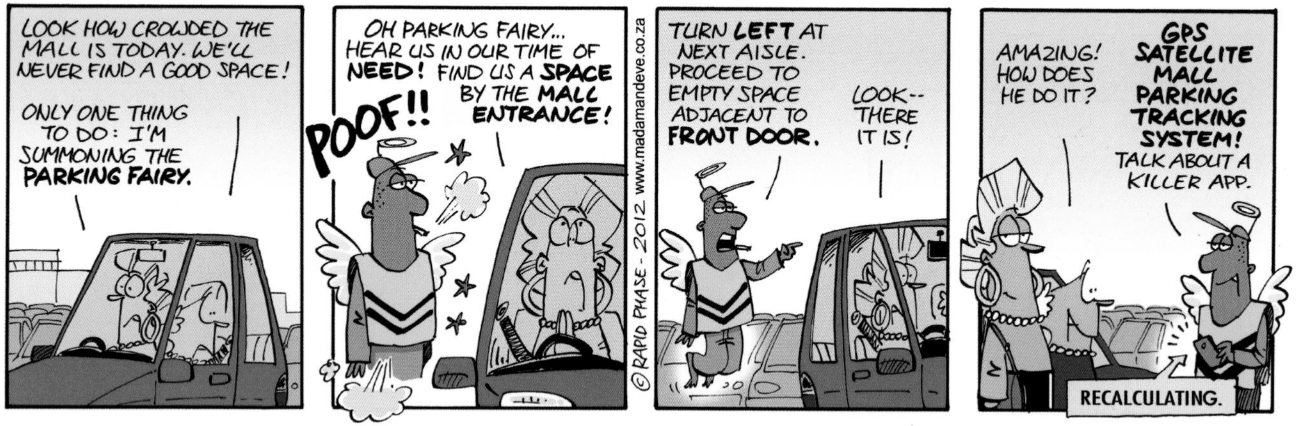
LOOK HOW CROWDED THE MALL IS TODAY. WE'LL NEVER FIND A GOOD SPACE!
ONLY ONE THING TO DO: I'M SUMMONING THE PARKING FAIRY.
OH PARKING FAIRY... HEAR US IN OUR TIME OF NEED! FIND US A SPACE BY THE MALL ENTRANCE!
POOF!!
www.madamandeve.co.za
©RAPID PHASE - 2012
TURN LEFT AT NEXT AISLE. PROCEED TO EMPTY SPACE ADJACENT TO FRONT DOOR.
LOOK-- THERE IT IS!
AMAZING! HOW DOES HE DO IT?
GPS SATELLITE MALL PARKING TRACKING SYSTEM! TALK ABOUT A KILLER APP.
RECALCULATING.

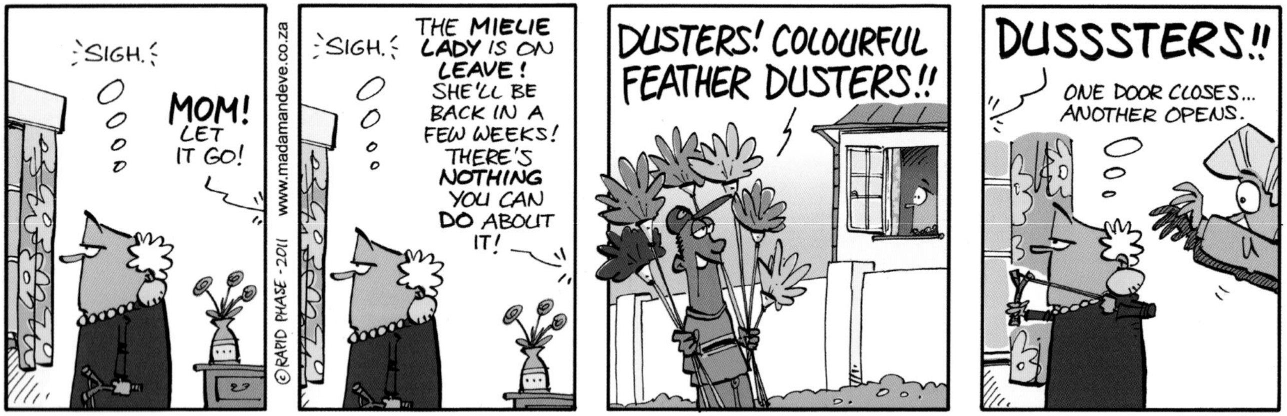
SIGH.
MOM! LET IT GO!
www.madamandeve.co.za
©RAPID PHASE - 2011
SIGH.
THE MIELIE LADY IS ON LEAVE! SHE'LL BE BACK IN A FEW WEEKS! THERE'S NOTHING YOU CAN DO ABOUT IT!
DUSTERS! COLOURFUL FEATHER DUSTERS!!
DUSSSTERS!!
ONE DOOR CLOSES... ANOTHER OPENS.

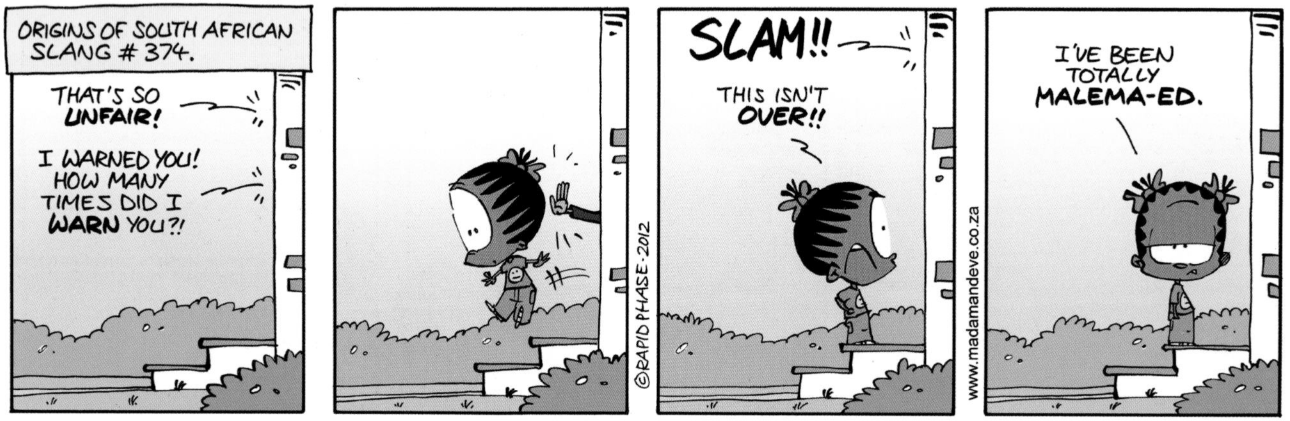
ORIGINS OF SOUTH AFRICAN SLANG # 374.
THAT'S SO UNFAIR!
I WARNED YOU! HOW MANY TIMES DID I WARN YOU?!
©RAPID PHASE - 2012
SLAM!!
THIS ISN'T OVER!!
www.madamandeve.co.za
I'VE BEEN TOTALLY MALEMA-ED.

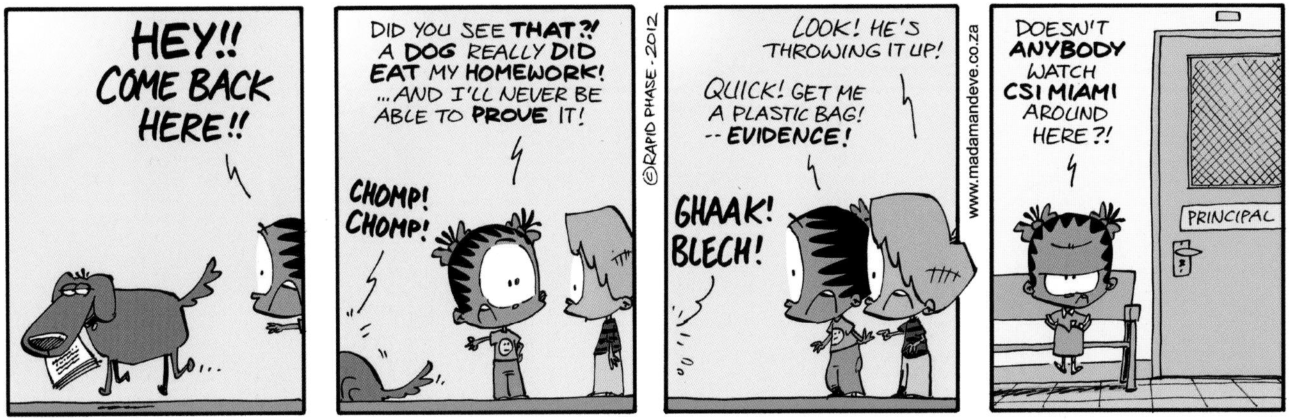
HEY!! COME BACK HERE!!
DID YOU SEE THAT?! A DOG REALLY DID EAT MY HOMEWORK! ...AND I'LL NEVER BE ABLE TO PROVE IT!
CHOMP! CHOMP!
©RAPID PHASE - 2012
LOOK! HE'S THROWING IT UP!
QUICK! GET ME A PLASTIC BAG! -- EVIDENCE!
GHAAK! BLECH!
www.madamandeve.co.za
DOESN'T ANYBODY WATCH CSI MIAMI AROUND HERE?!
PRINCIPAL

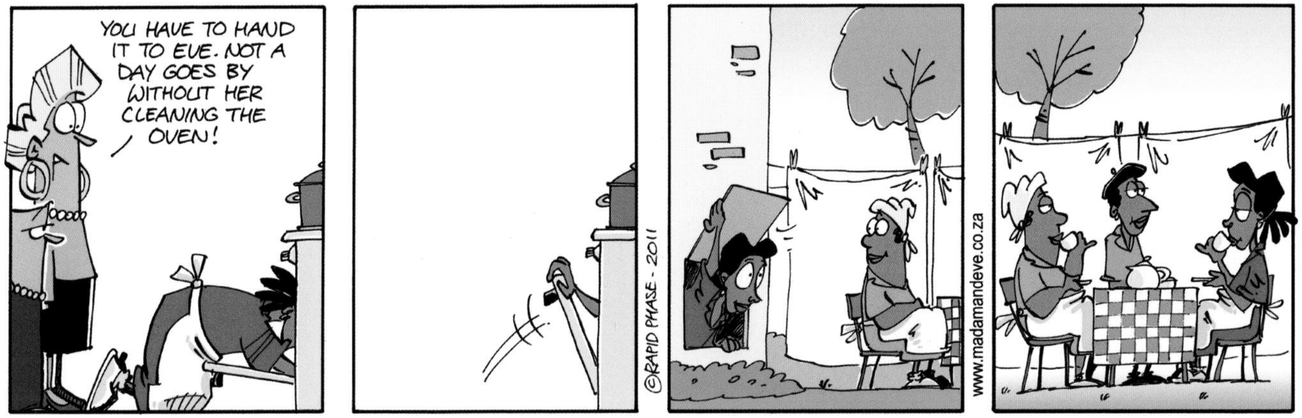
YOU HAVE TO HAND IT TO EVE. NOT A DAY GOES BY WITHOUT HER CLEANING THE OVEN!
©RAPID PHASE - 2011
www.madamandeve.co.za

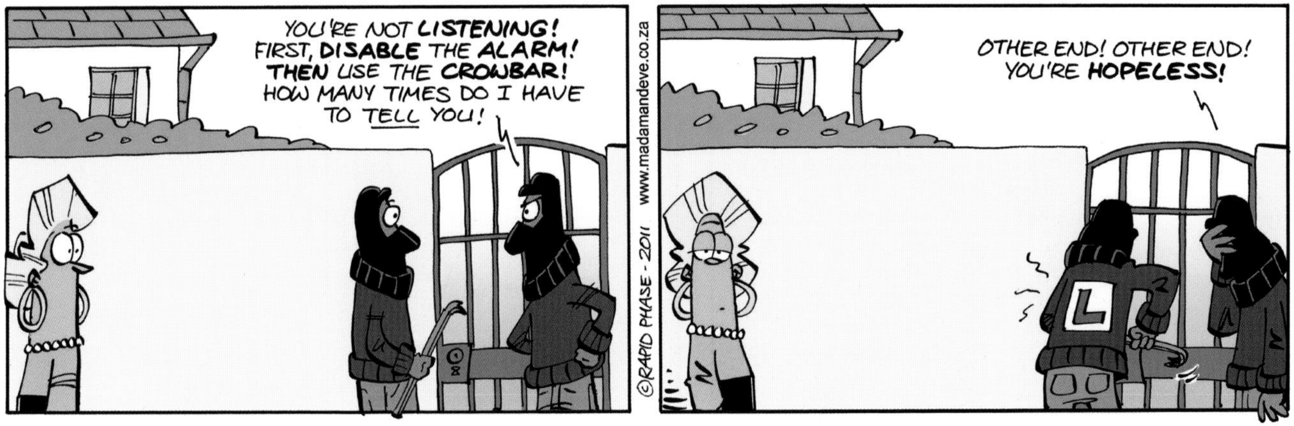
YOU'RE NOT LISTENING! FIRST, DISABLE THE ALARM! THEN USE THE CROWBAR! HOW MANY TIMES DO I HAVE TO TELL YOU!
©RAPID PHASE - 2011 www.madamandeve.co.za
OTHER END! OTHER END! YOU'RE HOPELESS!

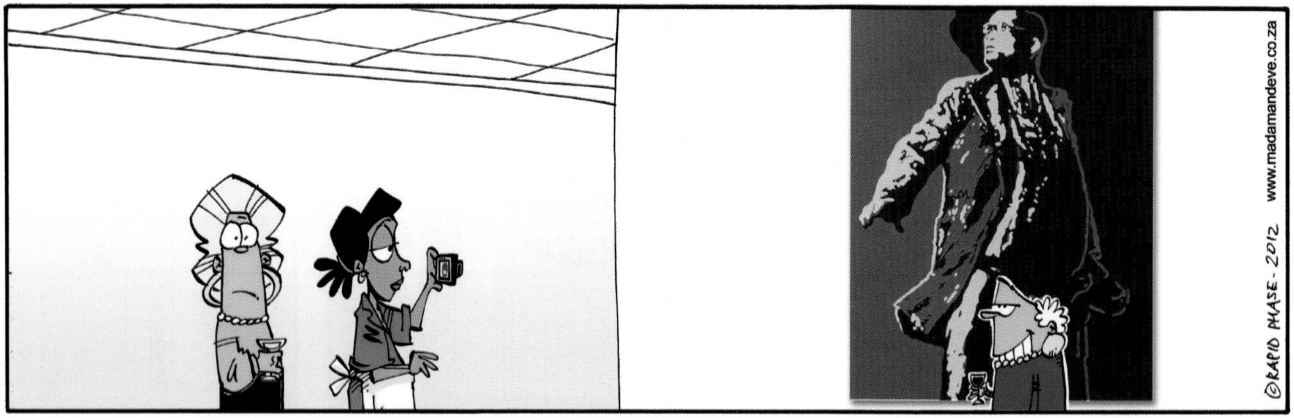

www.madamandeve.co.za
©RAPID PHASE - 2012

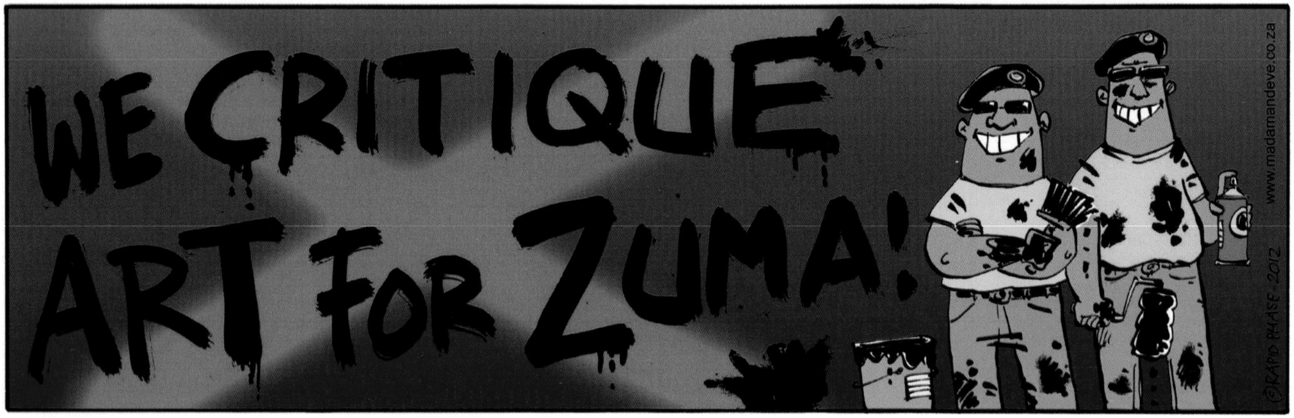

WE CRITIQUE
ART FOR ZUMA!
www.madamandeve.co.za
©RAPID PHASE - 2012

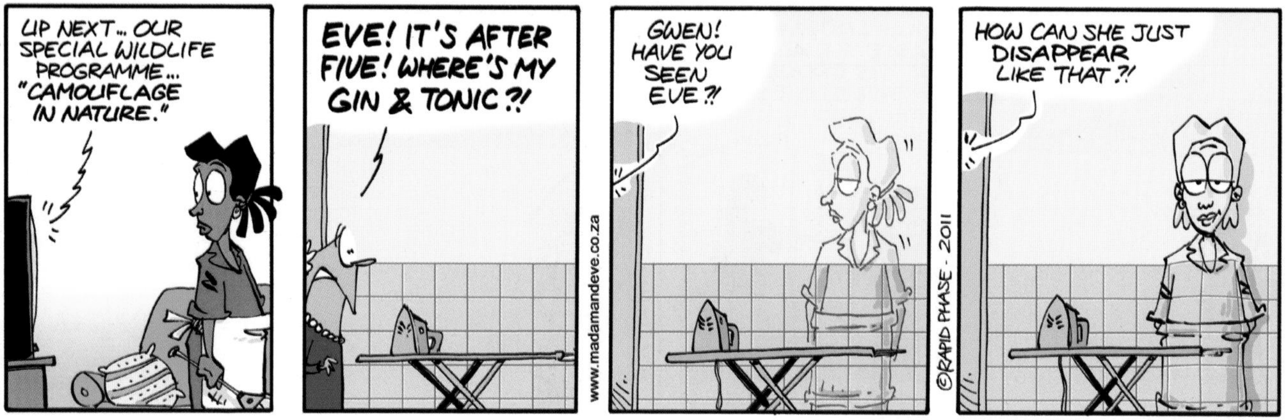

UP NEXT... OUR SPECIAL WILDLIFE PROGRAMME... "CAMOUFLAGE IN NATURE."
EVE! IT'S AFTER FIVE! WHERE'S MY GIN & TONIC ?!
www.madamandeve.co.za
GWEN! HAVE YOU SEEN EVE ?!
©RAPID PHASE - 2011
HOW CAN SHE JUST DISAPPEAR LIKE THAT ?!

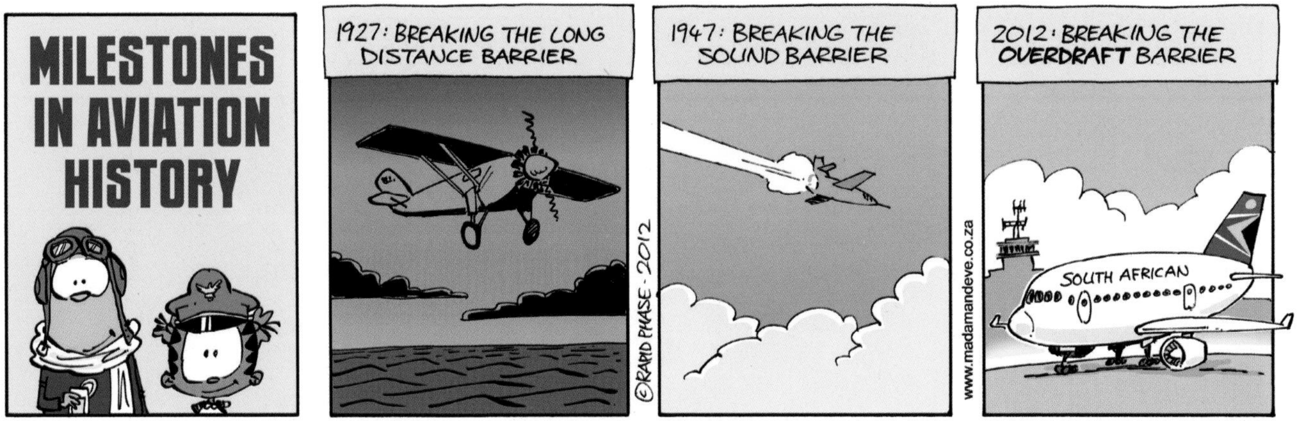
MILESTONES IN AVIATION HISTORY
1927: BREAKING THE LONG DISTANCE BARRIER
©RAPID PHASE - 2012
1947: BREAKING THE SOUND BARRIER
www.madamandeve.co.za
2012: BREAKING THE OVERDRAFT BARRIER
SOUTH AFRICAN

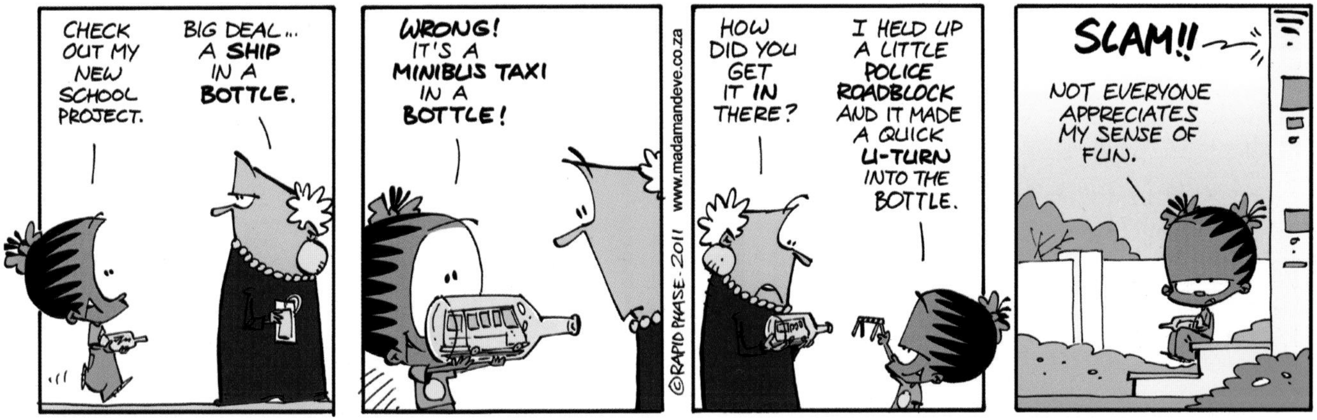
CHECK OUT MY NEW SCHOOL PROJECT.
BIG DEAL... A SHIP IN A BOTTLE.
WRONG! IT'S A MINIBUS TAXI IN A BOTTLE!
©RAPID PHASE - 2011 www.madamandeve.co.za
HOW DID YOU GET IT IN THERE?
I HELD UP A LITTLE POLICE ROADBLOCK AND IT MADE A QUICK U-TURN INTO THE BOTTLE.
SLAM!!
NOT EVERYONE APPRECIATES MY SENSE OF FUN.

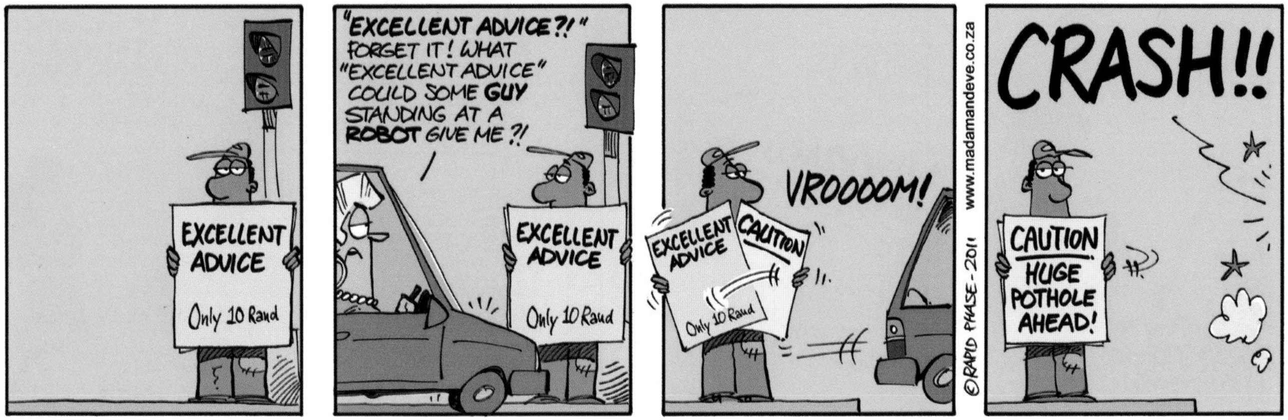
EXCELLENT ADVICE
Only 10 Rand
"EXCELLENT ADVICE?!" FORGET IT! WHAT "EXCELLENT ADVICE" COULD SOME GUY STANDING AT A ROBOT GIVE ME?!
EXCELLENT ADVICE
Only 10 Rand
VROOOOM!
EXCELLENT ADVICE
Only 10 Rand
CAUTION
www.madamandeve.co.za
©RAPID PHASE - 2011
CRASH!!
CAUTION HUGE POTHOLE AHEAD!

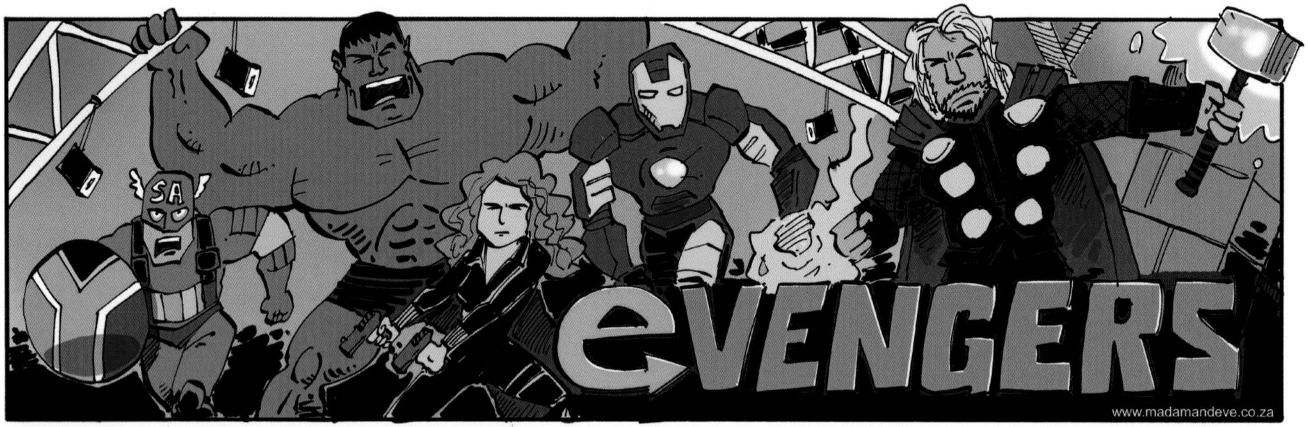
SA
eVENGERS
www.madamandeve.co.za

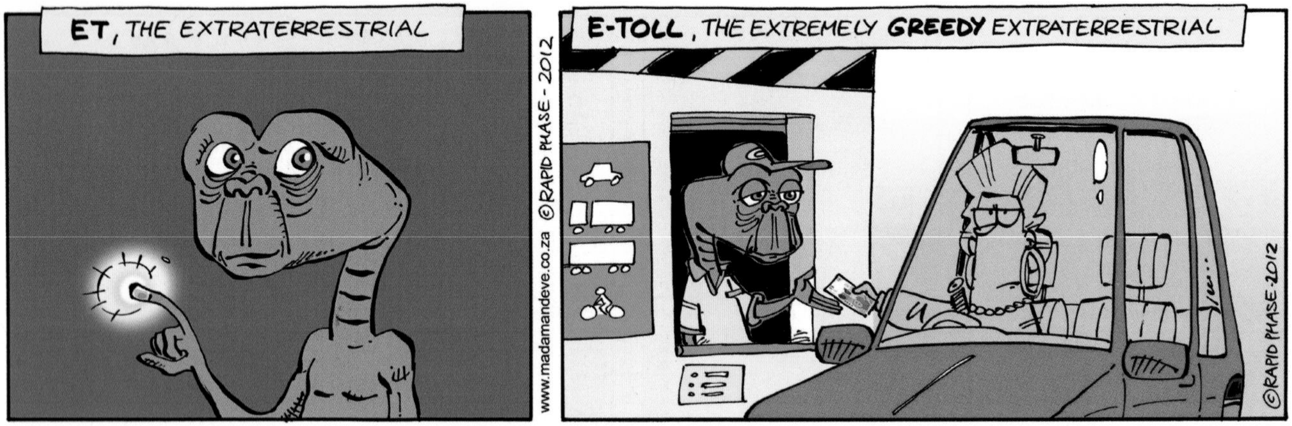
ET, THE EXTRATERRESTRIAL
E-TOLL, THE EXTREMELY GREEDY EXTRATERRESTRIAL
©RAPID PHASE - 2012
www.madamandeve.co.za
©RAPID PHASE·2012

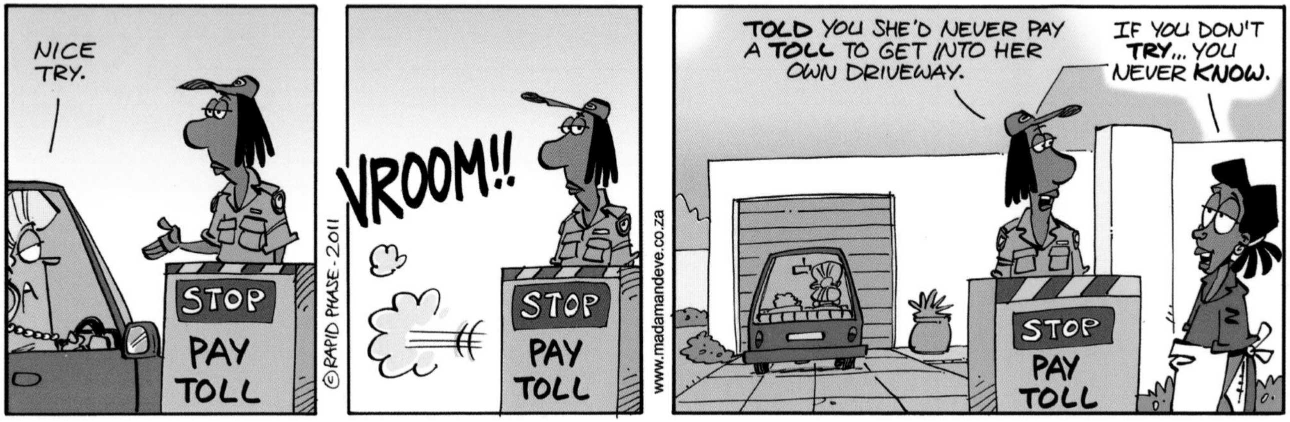
NICE TRY.
STOP
PAY TOLL
©RAPID PHASE - 2011
VROOM!!
STOP
PAY TOLL
www.madamandeve.co.za
TOLD YOU SHE'D NEVER PAY A TOLL TO GET INTO HER OWN DRIVEWAY.
IF YOU DON'T TRY... YOU NEVER KNOW.
STOP
PAY TOLL

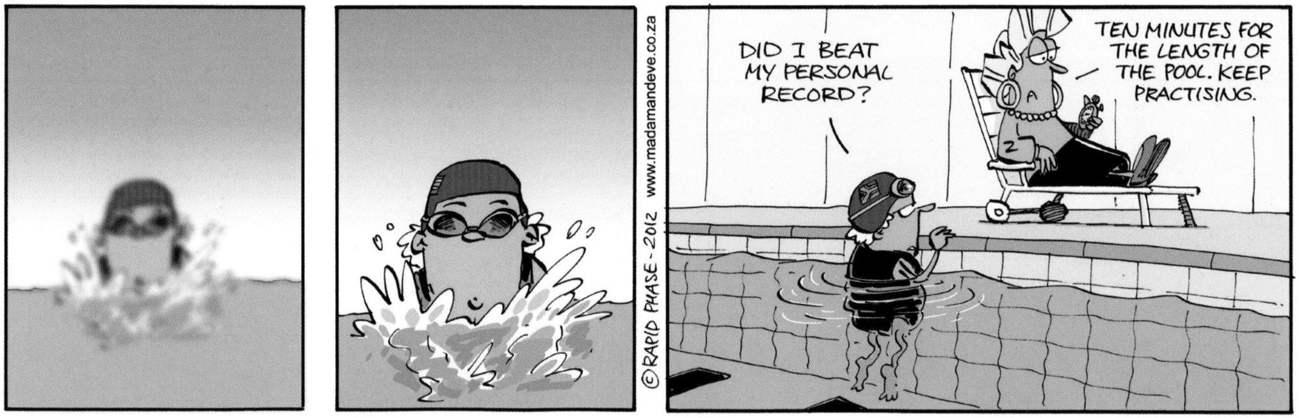
DID I BEAT MY PERSONAL RECORD?
TEN MINUTES FOR THE LENGTH OF THE POOL. KEEP PRACTISING.
© RAPID PHASE - 2012 www.madamandeve.co.za

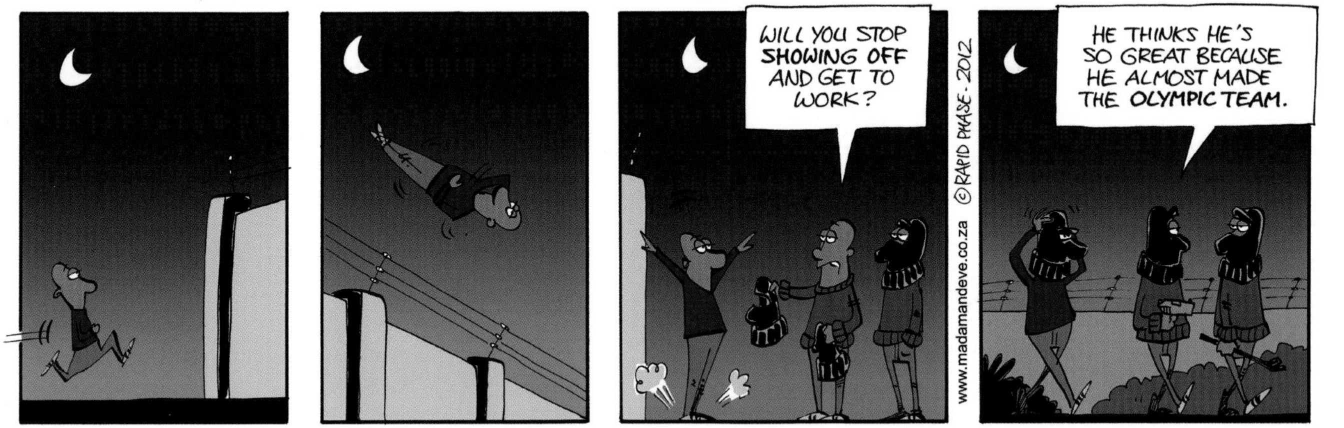
WILL YOU STOP **SHOWING OFF** AND GET TO WORK?
© RAPID PHASE - 2012 www.madamandeve.co.za
HE THINKS HE'S SO GREAT BECAUSE HE ALMOST MADE THE **OLYMPIC TEAM**.

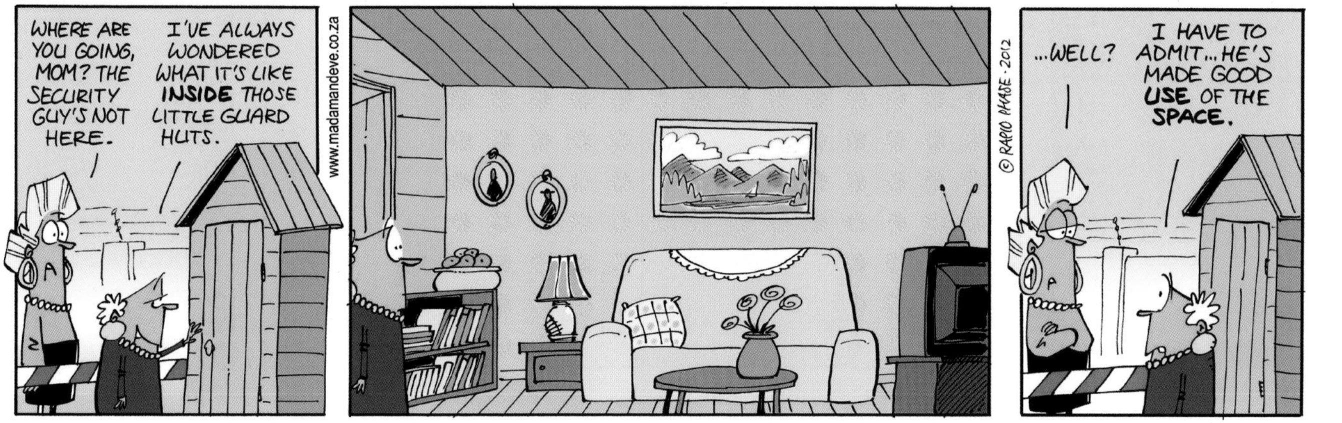
WHERE ARE YOU GOING, MOM? THE SECURITY GUY'S NOT HERE.
I'VE ALWAYS WONDERED WHAT IT'S LIKE **INSIDE** THOSE LITTLE GUARD HUTS.
www.madamandeve.co.za
© RAPID PHASE - 2012
...WELL?
I HAVE TO ADMIT... HE'S MADE GOOD **USE** OF THE **SPACE**.

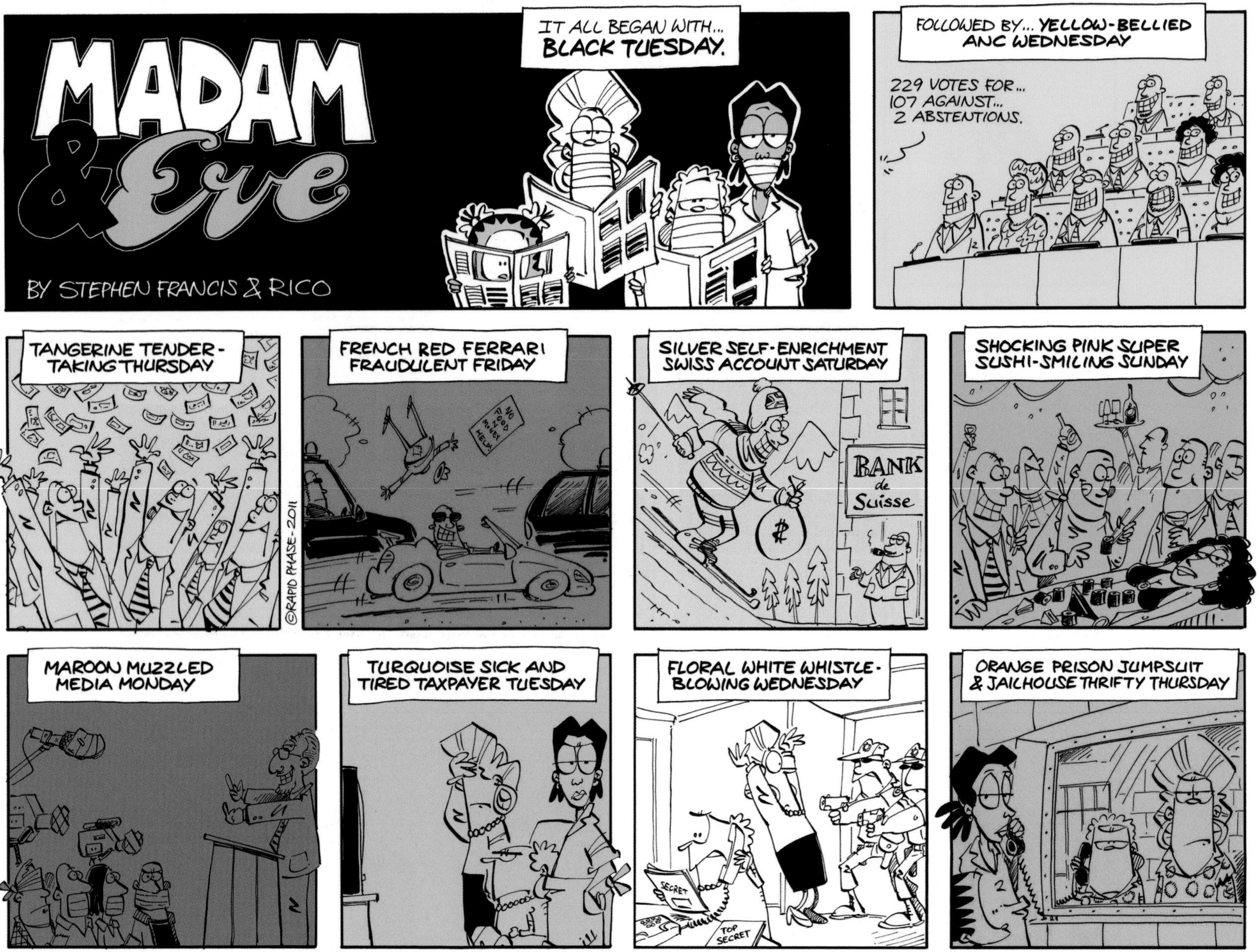
MADAM & Eve
BY STEPHEN FRANCIS & RICO
IT ALL BEGAN WITH... BLACK TUESDAY.
FOLLOWED BY... YELLOW-BELLIED ANC WEDNESDAY
229 VOTES FOR... 107 AGAINST... 2 ABSTENTIONS.
TANGERINE TENDER-TAKING THURSDAY
FRENCH RED FERRARI FRAUDULENT FRIDAY
©RAPID PHASE-2011
SILVER SELF-ENRICHMENT SWISS ACCOUNT SATURDAY
BANK de Suisse
SHOCKING PINK SUPER SUSHI-SMILING SUNDAY
MAROON MUZZLED MEDIA MONDAY
TURQUOISE SICK AND TIRED TAXPAYER TUESDAY
FLORAL WHITE WHISTLE-BLOWING WEDNESDAY
SECRET
TOP SECRET
ORANGE PRISON JUMPSUIT & JAILHOUSE THRIFTY THURSDAY

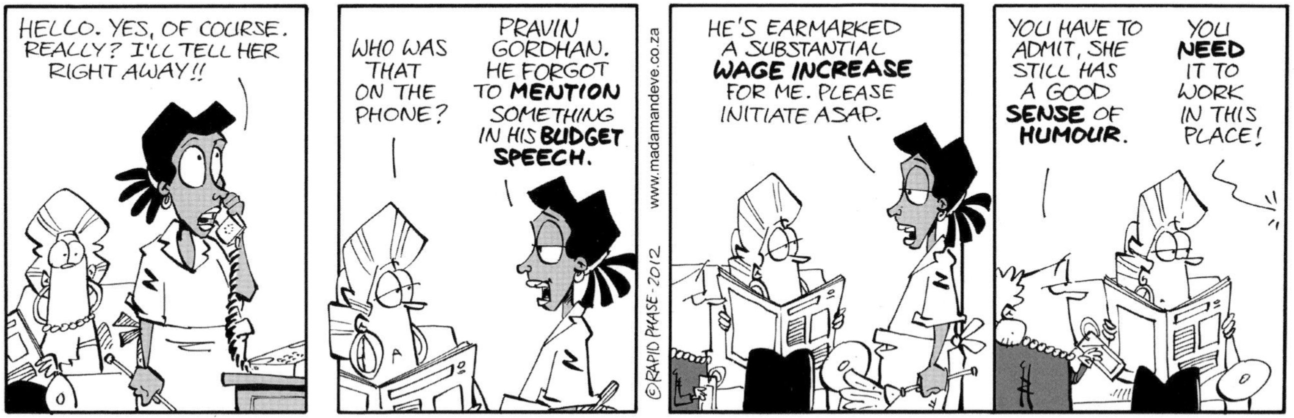
HELLO. YES, OF COURSE. REALLY? I'LL TELL HER RIGHT AWAY!!
WHO WAS THAT ON THE PHONE?
PRAVIN GORDHAN. HE FORGOT TO MENTION SOMETHING IN HIS BUDGET SPEECH.
©RAPID PHASE-2012 www.madamandeve.co.za
HE'S EARMARKED A SUBSTANTIAL WAGE INCREASE FOR ME. PLEASE INITIATE ASAP.
YOU HAVE TO ADMIT, SHE STILL HAS A GOOD SENSE OF HUMOUR.
YOU NEED IT TO WORK IN THIS PLACE!

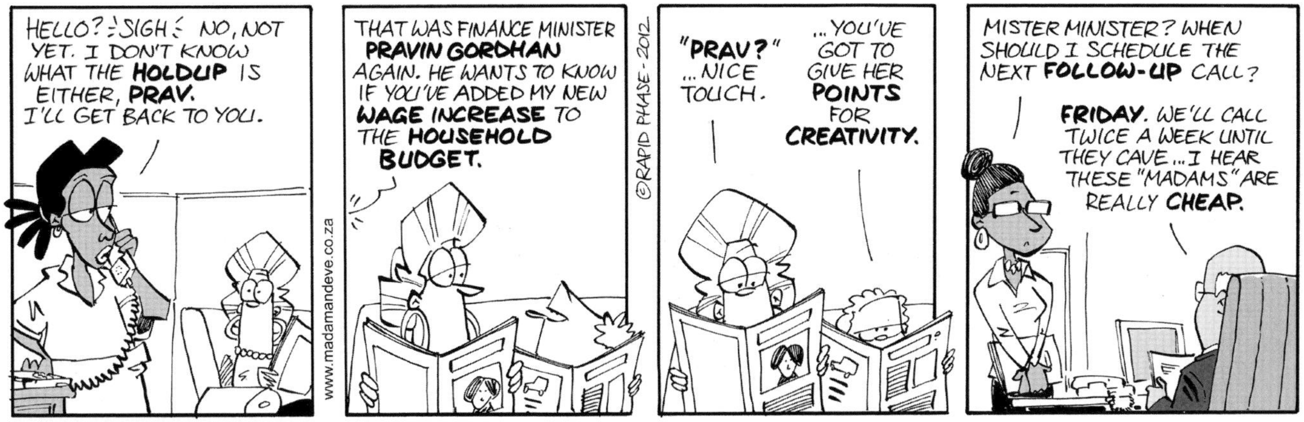
HELLO? -SIGH- NO, NOT YET. I DON'T KNOW WHAT THE HOLDUP IS EITHER, PRAV. I'LL GET BACK TO YOU.
www.madamandeve.co.za
THAT WAS FINANCE MINISTER PRAVIN GORDHAN AGAIN. HE WANTS TO KNOW IF YOU'VE ADDED MY NEW WAGE INCREASE TO THE HOUSEHOLD BUDGET.
©RAPID PHASE-2012
"PRAV?" ...NICE TOUCH.
...YOU'VE GOT TO GIVE HER POINTS FOR CREATIVITY.
MISTER MINISTER? WHEN SHOULD I SCHEDULE THE NEXT FOLLOW-UP CALL?
FRIDAY. WE'LL CALL TWICE A WEEK UNTIL THEY CAVE...I HEAR THESE "MADAMS" ARE REALLY CHEAP.

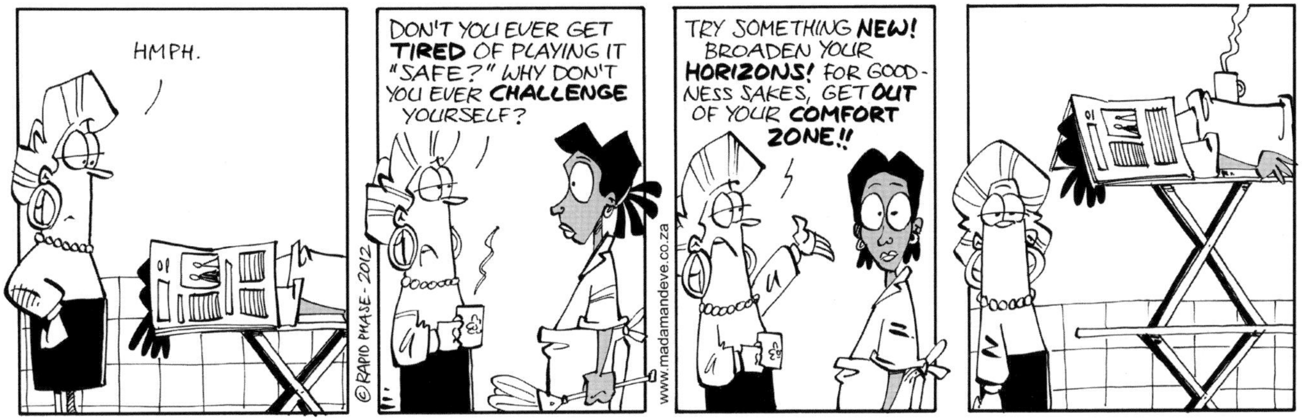
HMPH.
DON'T YOU EVER GET TIRED OF PLAYING IT "SAFE?" WHY DON'T YOU EVER CHALLENGE YOURSELF?
©RAPID PHASE-2012
www.madamandeve.co.za
TRY SOMETHING NEW! BROADEN YOUR HORIZONS! FOR GOODNESS SAKES, GET OUT OF YOUR COMFORT ZONE!!

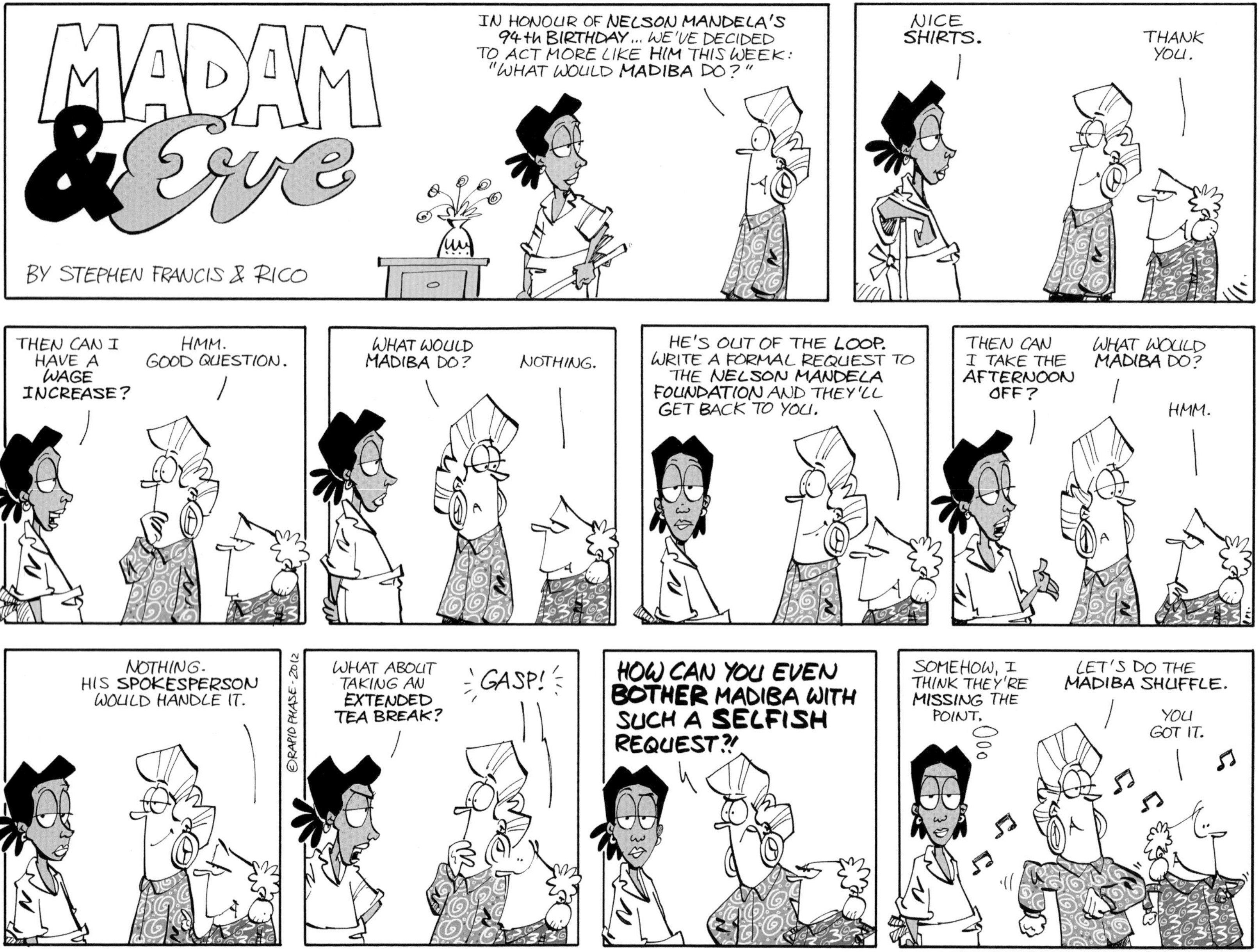
MADAM & Eve
BY STEPHEN FRANCIS & RICO
IN HONOUR OF NELSON MANDELA'S 94th BIRTHDAY... WE'VE DECIDED TO ACT MORE LIKE HIM THIS WEEK: "WHAT WOULD MADIBA DO?"
NICE SHIRTS.
THANK YOU.
THEN CAN I HAVE A WAGE INCREASE?
HMM. GOOD QUESTION.
WHAT WOULD MADIBA DO?
NOTHING.
HE'S OUT OF THE LOOP. WRITE A FORMAL REQUEST TO THE NELSON MANDELA FOUNDATION AND THEY'LL GET BACK TO YOU.
THEN CAN I TAKE THE AFTERNOON OFF?
WHAT WOULD MADIBA DO?
HMM.
NOTHING. HIS SPOKESPERSON WOULD HANDLE IT.
©RAPID PHASE · 2012
WHAT ABOUT TAKING AN EXTENDED TEA BREAK?
GASP!
HOW CAN YOU EVEN BOTHER MADIBA WITH SUCH A SELFISH REQUEST?!
SOMEHOW, I THINK THEY'RE MISSING THE POINT.
LET'S DO THE MADIBA SHUFFLE.
YOU GOT IT.

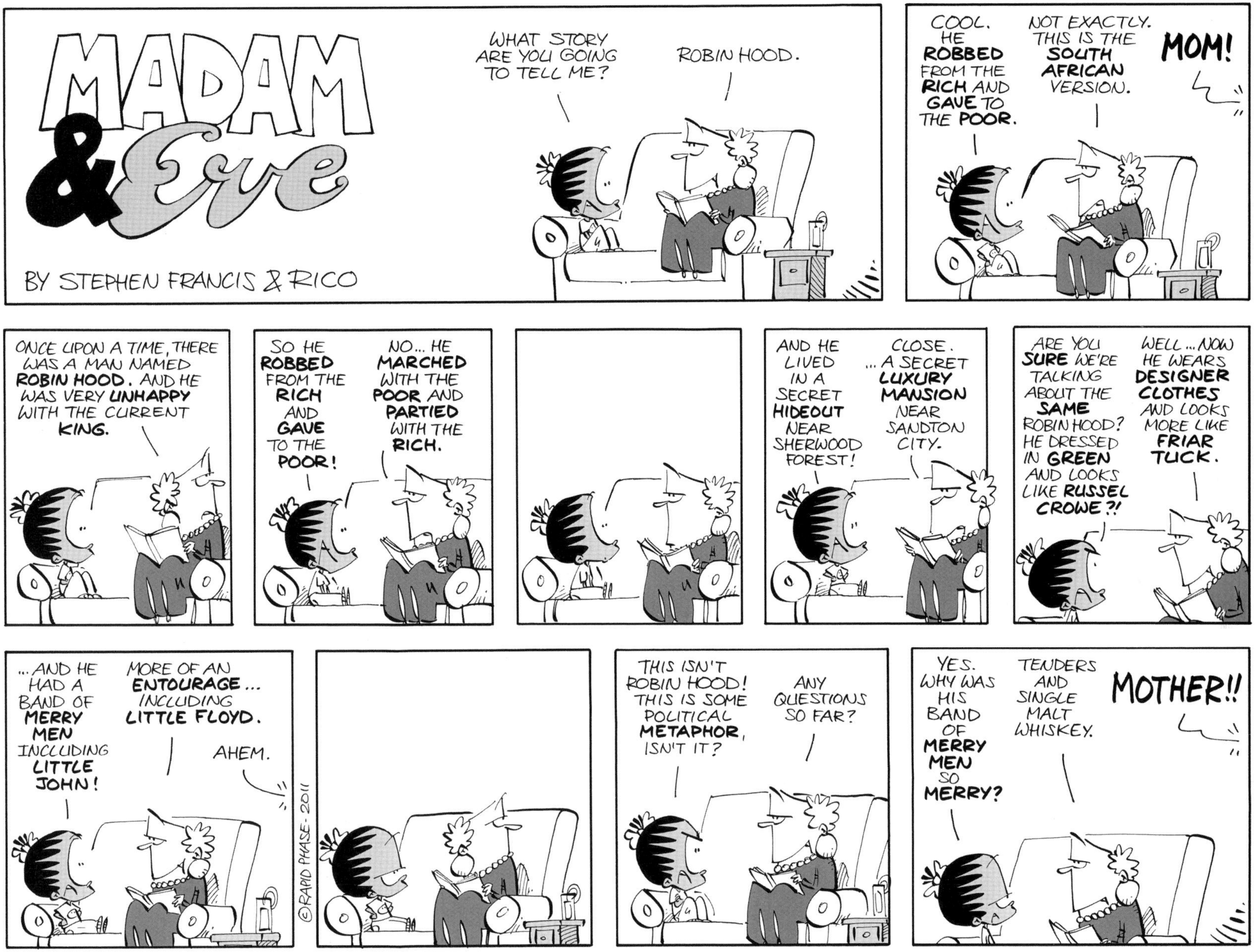
MADAM & Eve
BY STEPHEN FRANCIS & RICO
WHAT STORY ARE YOU GOING TO TELL ME?
ROBIN HOOD.
COOL. HE ROBBED FROM THE RICH AND GAVE TO THE POOR.
NOT EXACTLY. THIS IS THE SOUTH AFRICAN VERSION.
MOM!
ONCE UPON A TIME, THERE WAS A MAN NAMED ROBIN HOOD. AND HE WAS VERY UNHAPPY WITH THE CURRENT KING.
SO HE ROBBED FROM THE RICH AND GAVE TO THE POOR!
NO... HE MARCHED WITH THE POOR AND PARTIED WITH THE RICH.
AND HE LIVED IN A SECRET HIDEOUT NEAR SHERWOOD FOREST!
CLOSE. ...A SECRET LUXURY MANSION NEAR SANDTON CITY.
ARE YOU SURE WE'RE TALKING ABOUT THE SAME ROBIN HOOD? HE DRESSED IN GREEN AND LOOKS LIKE RUSSEL CROWE?!
WELL... NOW HE WEARS DESIGNER CLOTHES AND LOOKS MORE LIKE FRIAR TUCK.
...AND HE HAD A BAND OF MERRY MEN INCLUDING LITTLE JOHN!
MORE OF AN ENTOURAGE... INCLUDING LITTLE FLOYD.
AHEM.
©RAPID PHASE-2011
THIS ISN'T ROBIN HOOD! THIS IS SOME POLITICAL METAPHOR, ISN'T IT?
ANY QUESTIONS SO FAR?
YES. WHY WAS HIS BAND OF MERRY MEN SO MERRY?
TENDERS AND SINGLE MALT WHISKEY.
MOTHER!!

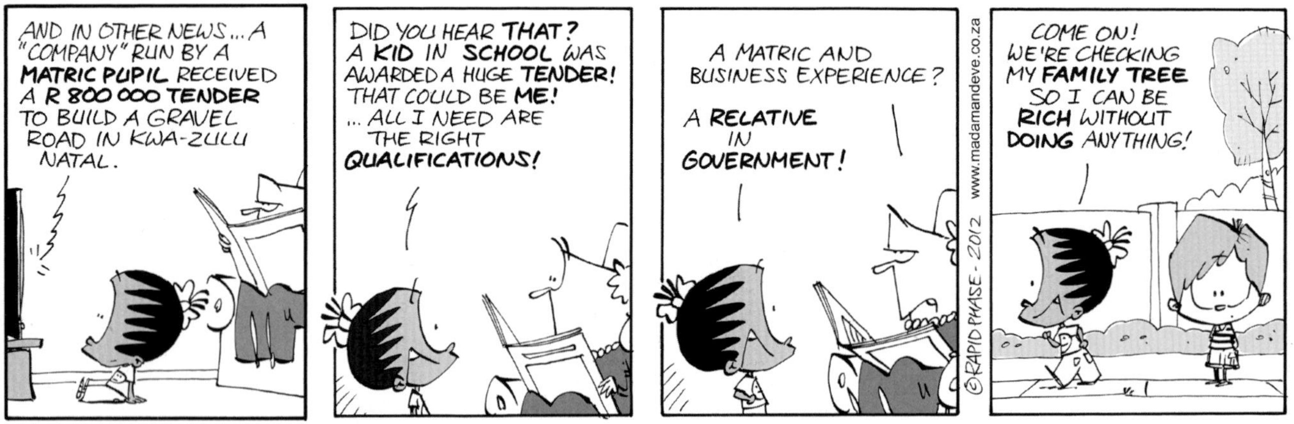
AND IN OTHER NEWS... A "COMPANY" RUN BY A MATRIC PUPIL RECEIVED A R 800 000 TENDER TO BUILD A GRAVEL ROAD IN KWA-ZULU NATAL.
DID YOU HEAR THAT? A KID IN SCHOOL WAS AWARDED A HUGE TENDER! THAT COULD BE ME! ... ALL I NEED ARE THE RIGHT QUALIFICATIONS!
A MATRIC AND BUSINESS EXPERIENCE?
A RELATIVE IN GOVERNMENT!
©RAPID PHASE-2012 www.madamandeve.co.za
COME ON! WE'RE CHECKING MY FAMILY TREE SO I CAN BE RICH WITHOUT DOING ANYTHING!

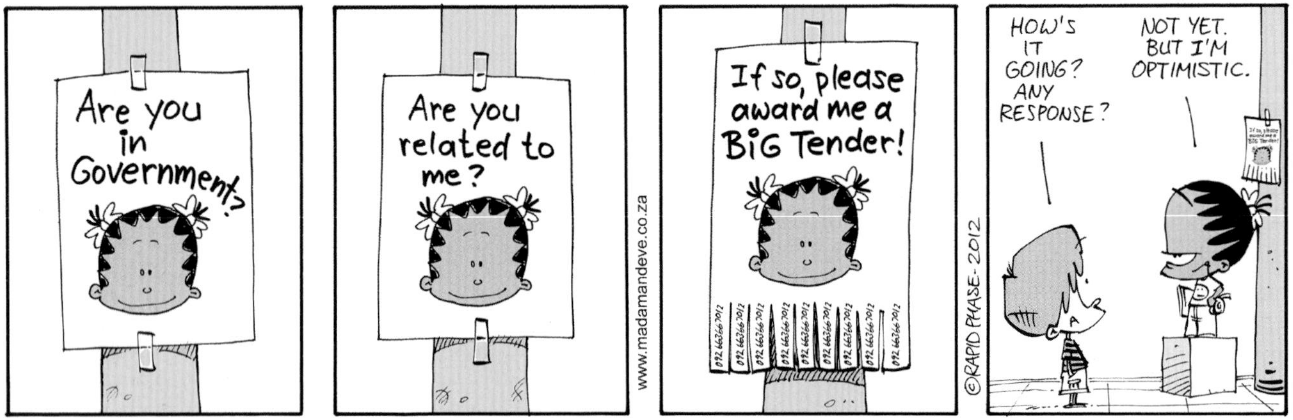
Are you in Government?
Are you related to me?
www.madamandeve.co.za
If so, please award me a BiG Tender!
©RAPID PHASE-2012
HOW'S IT GOING? ANY RESPONSE?
NOT YET. BUT I'M OPTIMISTIC.

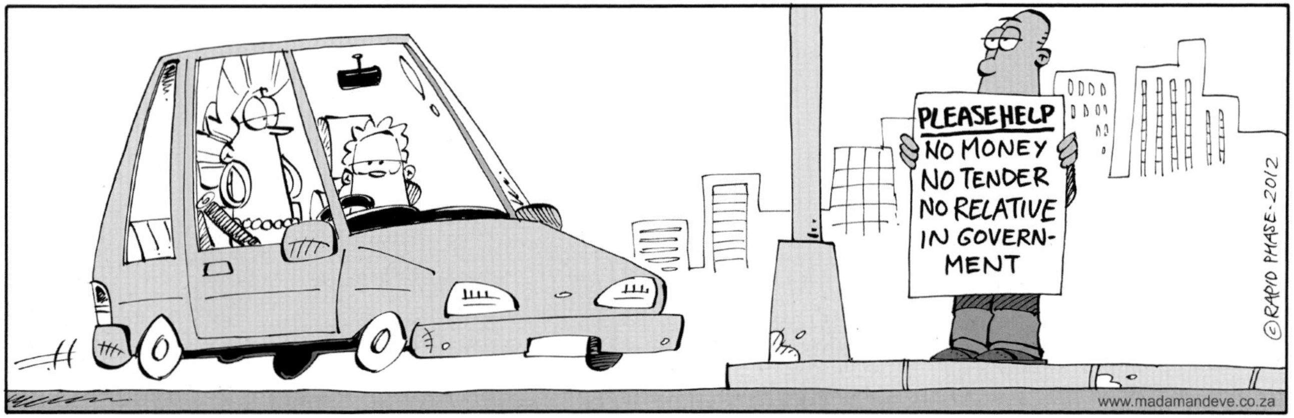
PLEASE HELP
NO MONEY
NO TENDER
NO RELATIVE IN GOVERNMENT
©RAPID PHASE-2012
www.madamandeve.co.za

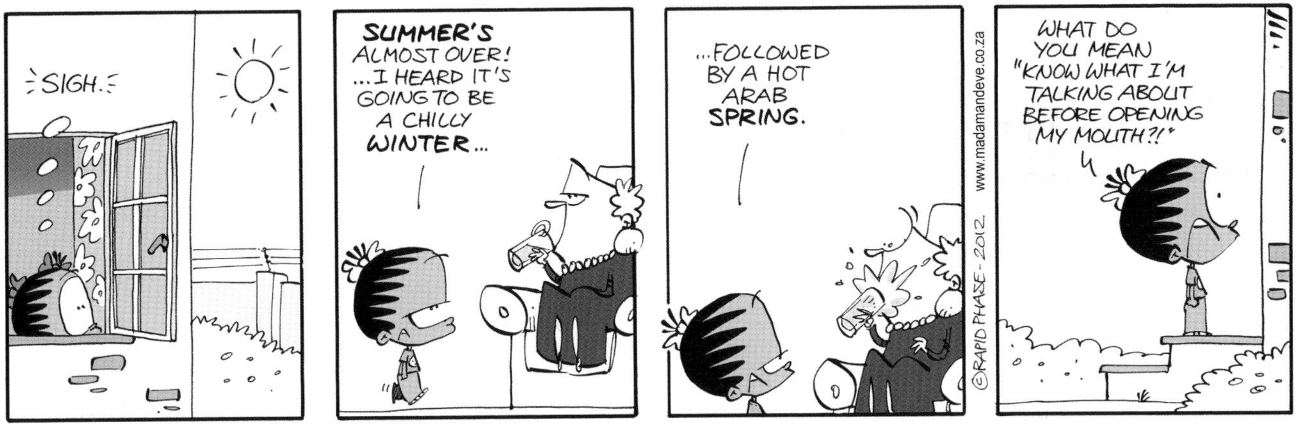
SIGH.
SUMMER'S ALMOST OVER! ...I HEARD IT'S GOING TO BE A CHILLY WINTER...
...FOLLOWED BY A HOT ARAB SPRING.
WHAT DO YOU MEAN "KNOW WHAT I'M TALKING ABOUT BEFORE OPENING MY MOUTH?!"
www.madamandeve.co.za
©RAPID PHASE - 2012

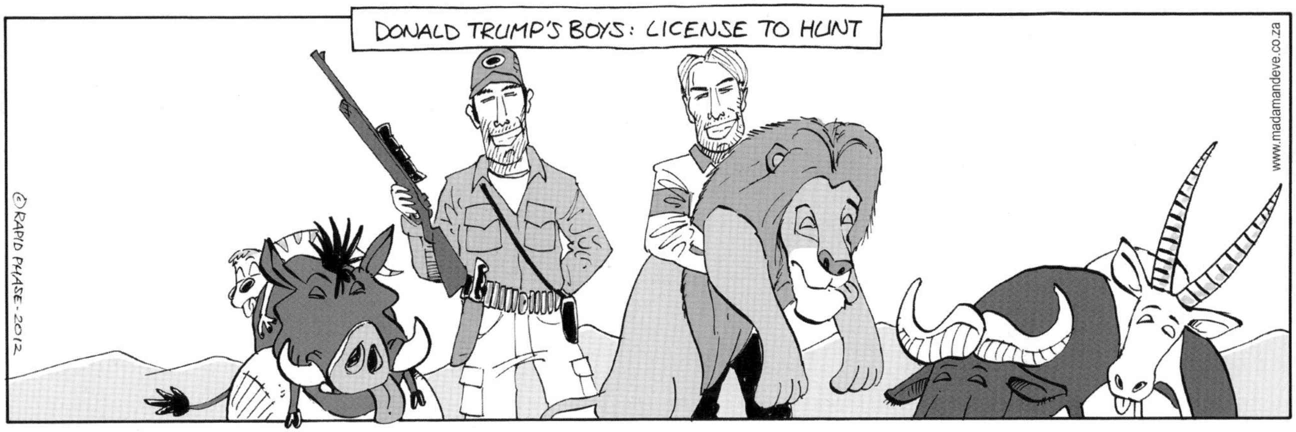
DONALD TRUMP'S BOYS: LICENSE TO HUNT
©RAPID PHASE - 2012
www.madamandeve.co.za

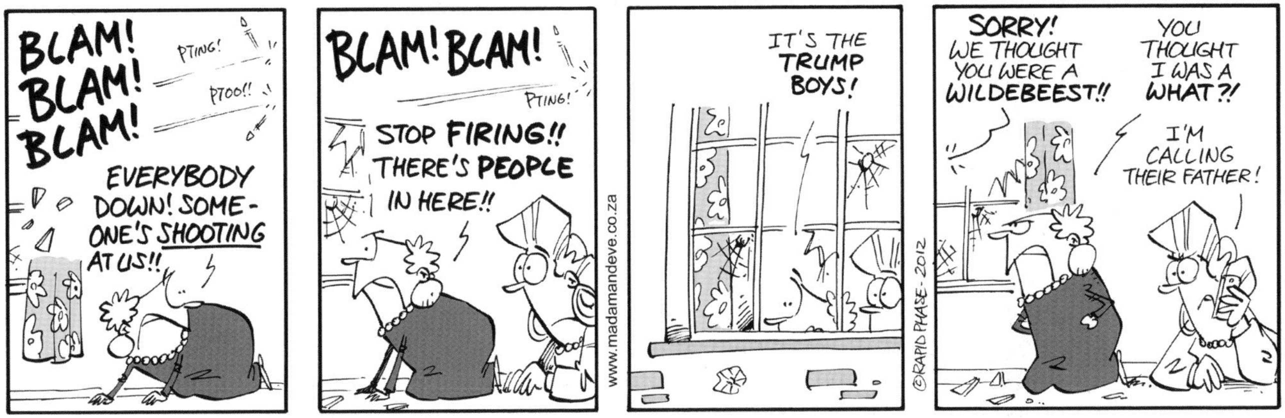
BLAM! BLAM! BLAM!
PTING!
PTOO!!
EVERYBODY DOWN! SOME-ONE'S SHOOTING AT US!!
BLAM! BLAM!
PTING!
STOP FIRING!! THERE'S PEOPLE IN HERE!!
www.madamandeve.co.za
IT'S THE TRUMP BOYS!
©RAPID PHASE - 2012
SORRY! WE THOUGHT YOU WERE A WILDEBEEST!!
YOU THOUGHT I WAS A WHAT?!
I'M CALLING THEIR FATHER!

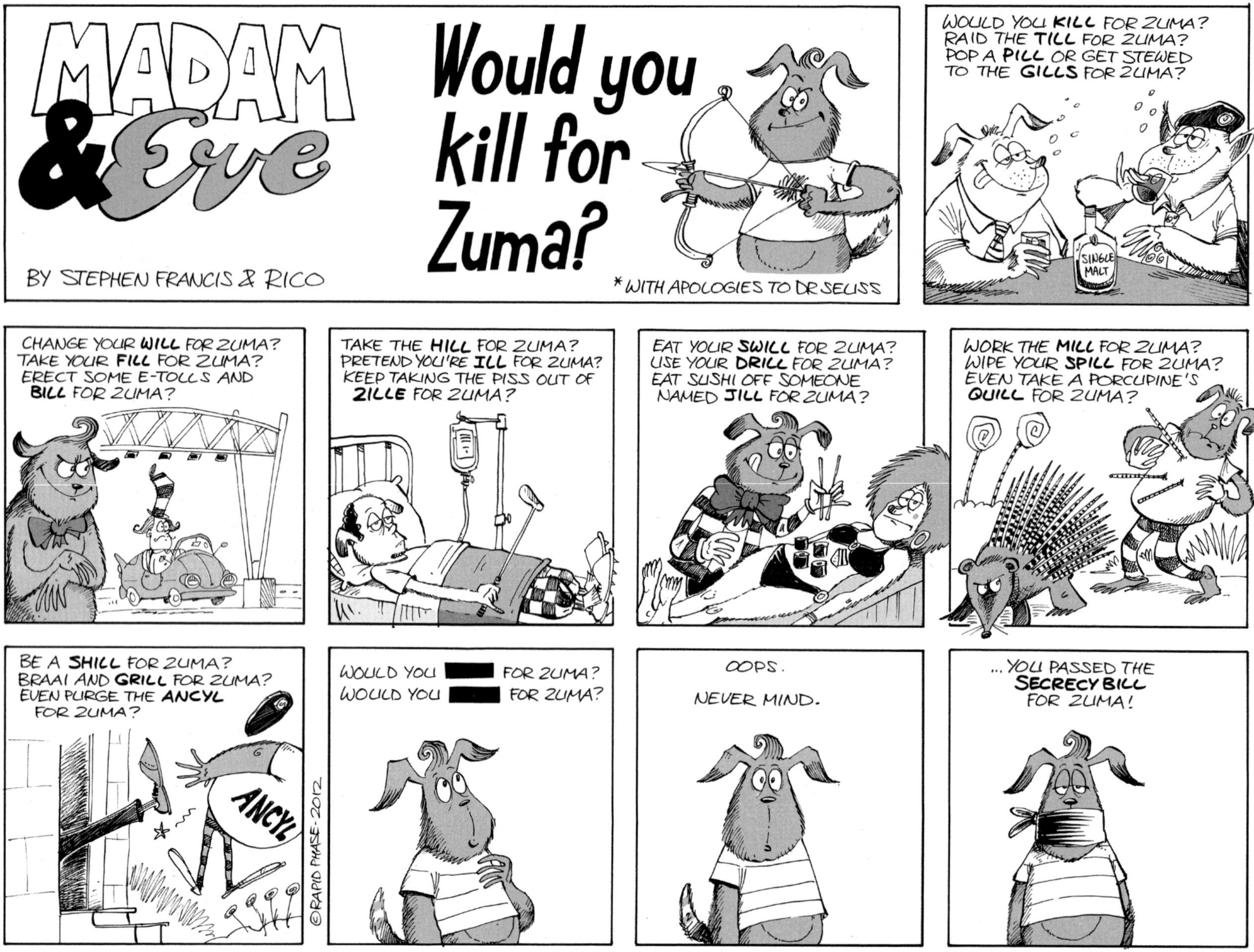
MADAM & Eve
Would you kill for Zuma?
BY STEPHEN FRANCIS & RICO
* WITH APOLOGIES TO DR SEUSS
WOULD YOU KILL FOR ZUMA? RAID THE TILL FOR ZUMA? POP A PILL OR GET STEWED TO THE GILLS FOR ZUMA?
SINGLE MALT
CHANGE YOUR WILL FOR ZUMA? TAKE YOUR FILL FOR ZUMA? ERECT SOME E-TOLLS AND BILL FOR ZUMA?
TAKE THE HILL FOR ZUMA? PRETEND YOU'RE ILL FOR ZUMA? KEEP TAKING THE PISS OUT OF ZILLE FOR ZUMA?
EAT YOUR SWILL FOR ZUMA? USE YOUR DRILL FOR ZUMA? EAT SUSHI OFF SOMEONE NAMED JILL FOR ZUMA?
WORK THE MILL FOR ZUMA? WIPE YOUR SPILL FOR ZUMA? EVEN TAKE A PORCUPINE'S QUILL FOR ZUMA?
BE A SHILL FOR ZUMA? BRAAI AND GRILL FOR ZUMA? EVEN PURGE THE ANCYL FOR ZUMA?
ANCYL
©RAPID PHASE · 2012
WOULD YOU [redacted] FOR ZUMA?
WOULD YOU [redacted] FOR ZUMA?
OOPS.
NEVER MIND.
...YOU PASSED THE SECRECY BILL FOR ZUMA!

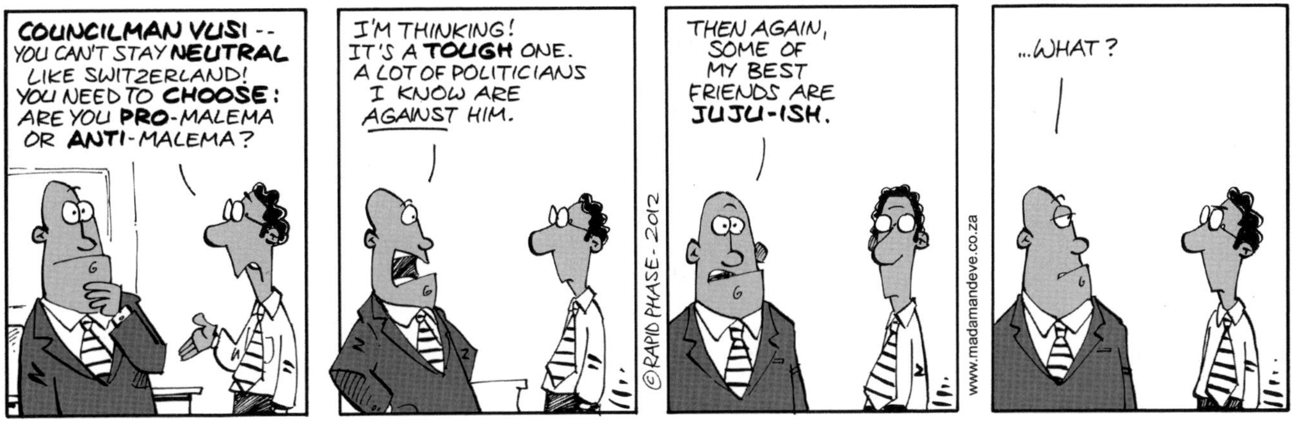
COUNCILMAN VUSI -- YOU CAN'T STAY NEUTRAL LIKE SWITZERLAND! YOU NEED TO CHOOSE: ARE YOU PRO-MALEMA OR ANTI-MALEMA?
I'M THINKING! IT'S A TOUGH ONE. A LOT OF POLITICIANS I KNOW ARE AGAINST HIM.
©RAPID PHASE - 2012
THEN AGAIN, SOME OF MY BEST FRIENDS ARE JUJU-ISH.
www.madamandeve.co.za
...WHAT?

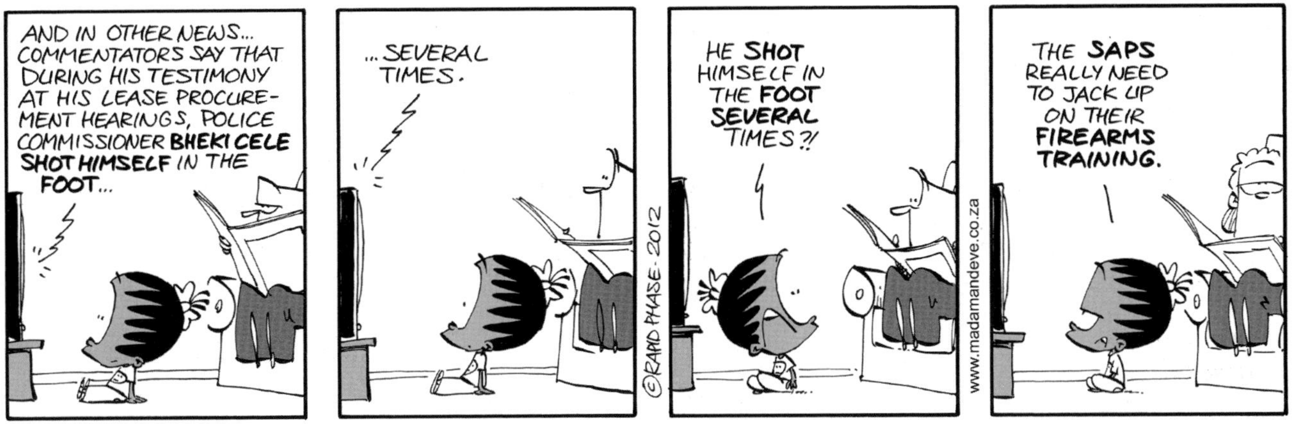
AND IN OTHER NEWS... COMMENTATORS SAY THAT DURING HIS TESTIMONY AT HIS LEASE PROCUREMENT HEARINGS, POLICE COMMISSIONER BHEKI CELE SHOT HIMSELF IN THE FOOT...
...SEVERAL TIMES.
©RAPID PHASE - 2012
HE SHOT HIMSELF IN THE FOOT SEVERAL TIMES?!
www.madamandeve.co.za
THE SAPS REALLY NEED TO JACK UP ON THEIR FIREARMS TRAINING.

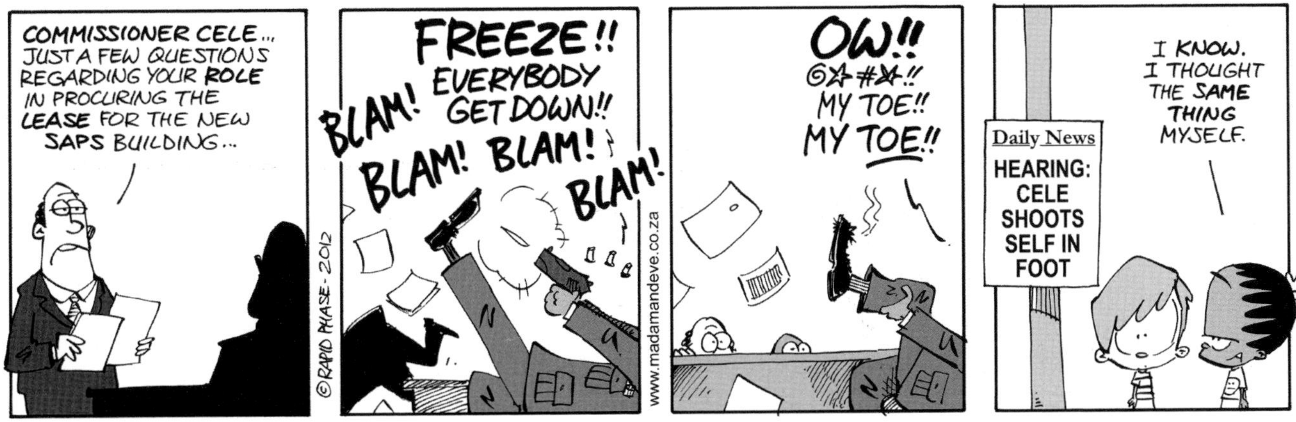
COMMISSIONER CELE... JUST A FEW QUESTIONS REGARDING YOUR ROLE IN PROCURING THE LEASE FOR THE NEW SAPS BUILDING...
©RAPID PHASE - 2012
FREEZE!! EVERYBODY GET DOWN!!
BLAM! BLAM! BLAM! BLAM!
www.madamandeve.co.za
OW!! ©☆#☆!! MY TOE!! MY TOE!!
Daily News
HEARING: CELE SHOOTS SELF IN FOOT
I KNOW. I THOUGHT THE SAME THING MYSELF.

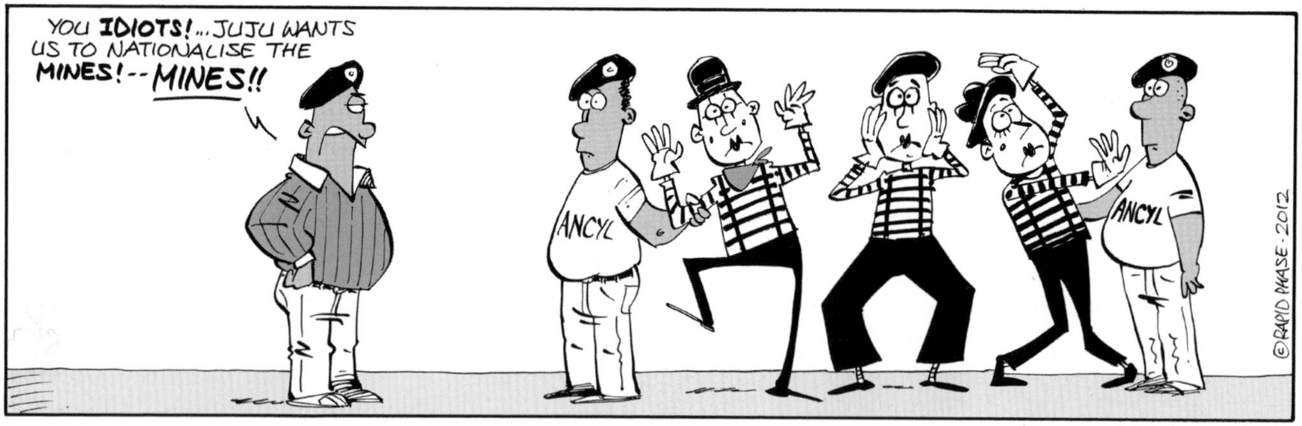
YOU IDIOTS!... JUJU WANTS US TO NATIONALISE THE MINES!-- MINES!!
ANCYL
ANCYL
© RAPID PHASE · 2012

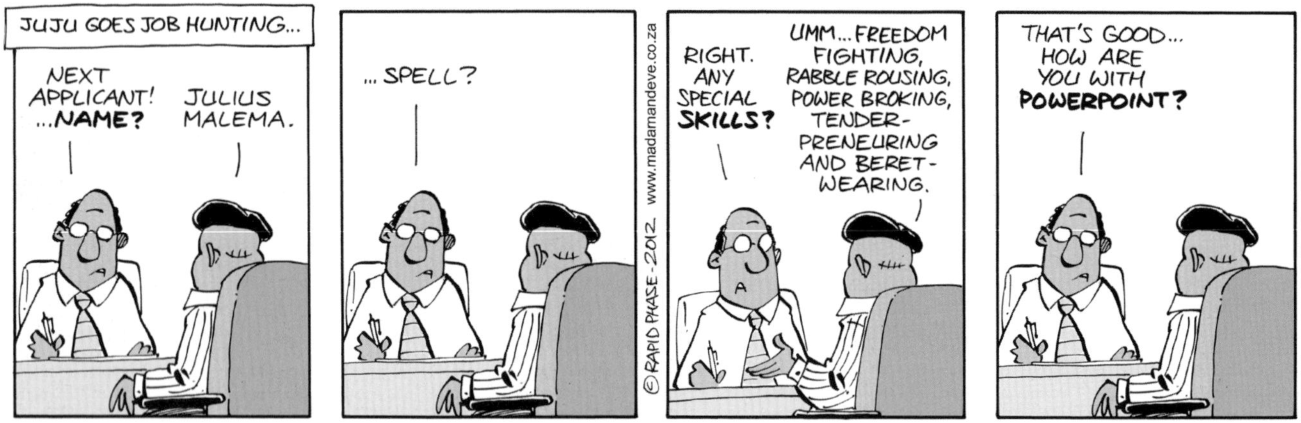
JUJU GOES JOB HUNTING...
NEXT APPLICANT! ...NAME?
JULIUS MALEMA.
... SPELL?
© RAPID PHASE · 2012 www.madamandeve.co.za
RIGHT. ANY SPECIAL SKILLS?
UMM... FREEDOM FIGHTING, RABBLE ROUSING, POWER BROKING, TENDER-PRENEURING AND BERET-WEARING.
THAT'S GOOD... HOW ARE YOU WITH POWERPOINT?

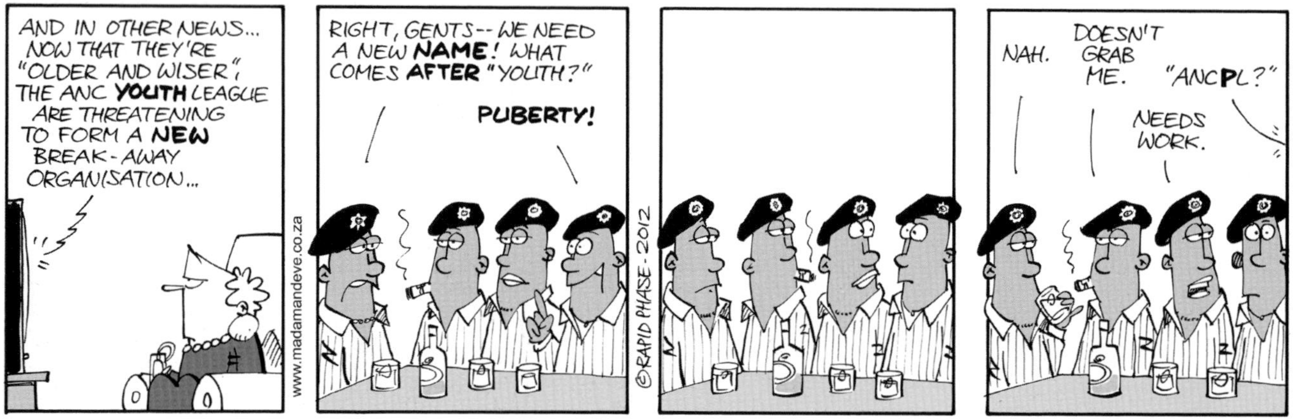
AND IN OTHER NEWS... NOW THAT THEY'RE "OLDER AND WISER", THE ANC YOUTH LEAGUE ARE THREATENING TO FORM A NEW BREAK-AWAY ORGANISATION...
www.madamandeve.co.za
RIGHT, GENTS-- WE NEED A NEW NAME! WHAT COMES AFTER "YOUTH?"
PUBERTY!
© RAPID PHASE · 2012
NAH.
DOESN'T GRAB ME.
"ANCPL?"
NEEDS WORK.

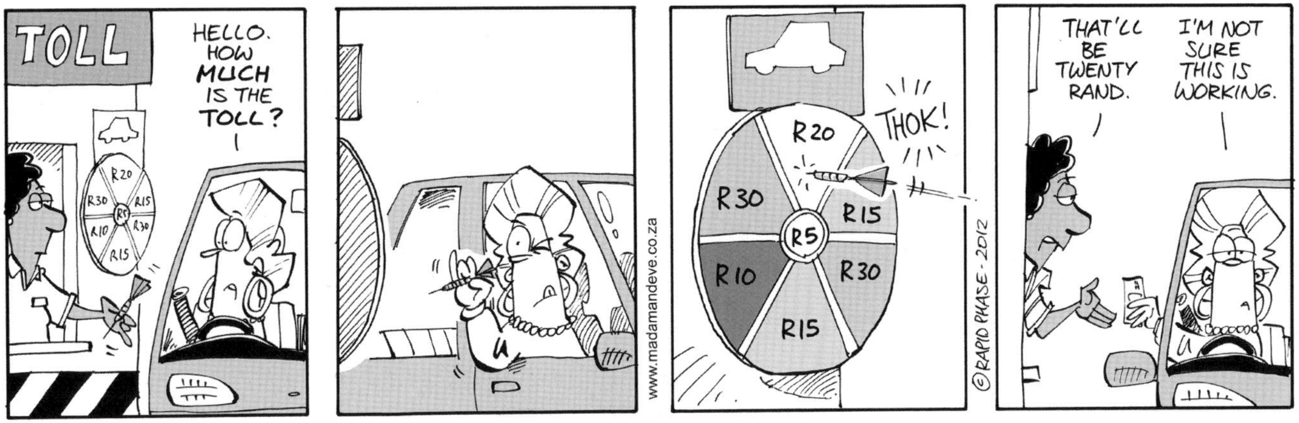
TOLL
HELLO. HOW MUCH IS THE TOLL?
R20
R30
R15
R5
R10
THOK!
www.madamandeve.co.za
©RAPID PHASE-2012
THAT'LL BE TWENTY RAND.
I'M NOT SURE THIS IS WORKING.

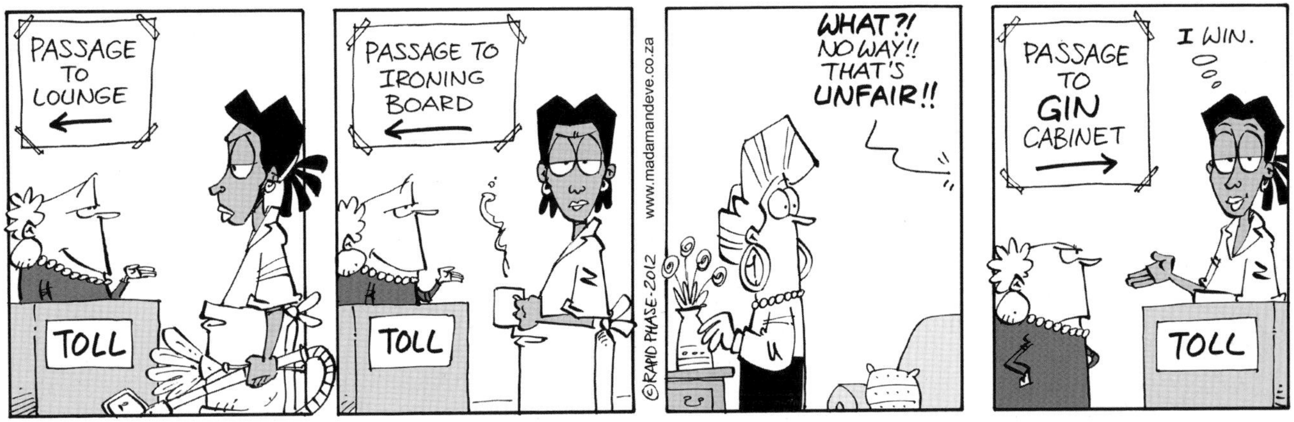
PASSAGE TO LOUNGE
TOLL
PASSAGE TO IRONING BOARD
TOLL
www.madamandeve.co.za
©RAPID PHASE-2012
WHAT?! NO WAY!! THAT'S UNFAIR!!
PASSAGE TO GIN CABINET
I WIN.
TOLL

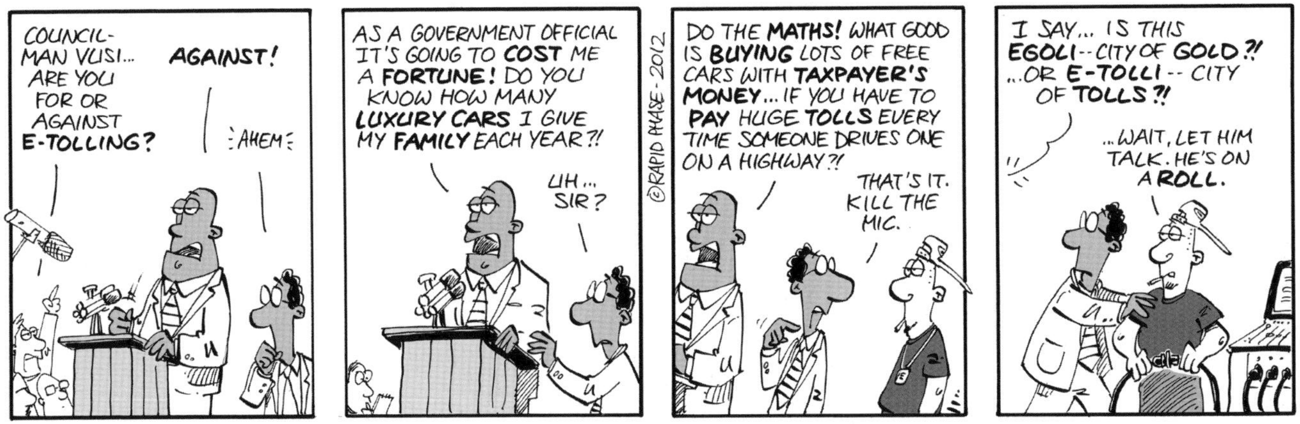
COUNCIL-MAN VUSI... ARE YOU FOR OR AGAINST E-TOLLING?
AGAINST!
AHEM
AS A GOVERNMENT OFFICIAL IT'S GOING TO COST ME A FORTUNE! DO YOU KNOW HOW MANY LUXURY CARS I GIVE MY FAMILY EACH YEAR?!
UH... SIR?
©RAPID PHASE-2012
DO THE MATHS! WHAT GOOD IS BUYING LOTS OF FREE CARS WITH TAXPAYER'S MONEY... IF YOU HAVE TO PAY HUGE TOLLS EVERY TIME SOMEONE DRIVES ONE ON A HIGHWAY?!
THAT'S IT. KILL THE MIC.
I SAY... IS THIS EGOLI -- CITY OF GOLD?! ...OR E-TOLLI -- CITY OF TOLLS?!
...WAIT, LET HIM TALK. HE'S ON A ROLL.

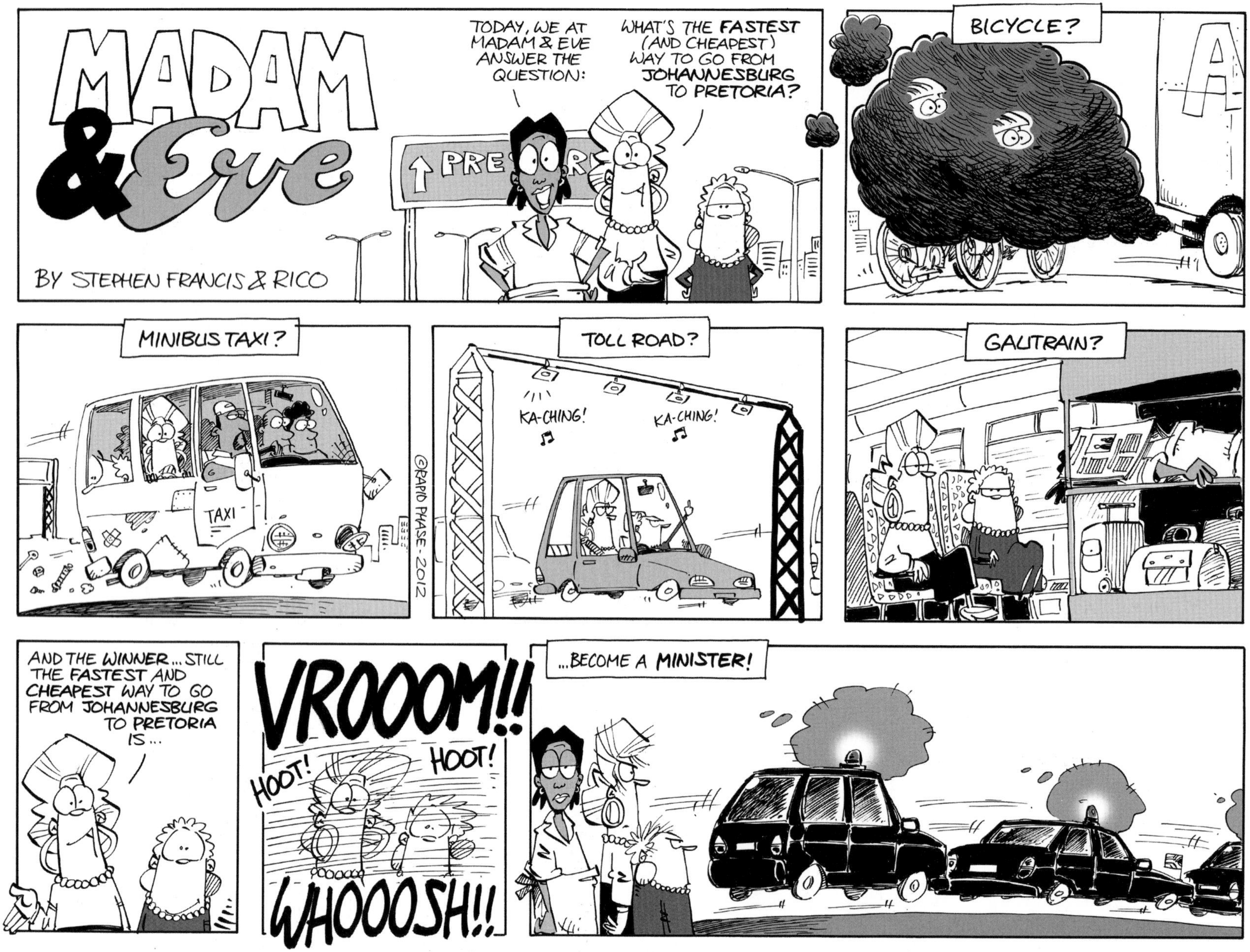
MADAM & Eve
BY STEPHEN FRANCIS & RICO
TODAY, WE AT MADAM & EVE ANSWER THE QUESTION:
WHAT'S THE FASTEST (AND CHEAPEST) WAY TO GO FROM JOHANNESBURG TO PRETORIA?
BICYCLE?
MINIBUS TAXI?
TAXI
TOLL ROAD?
KA-CHING!
KA-CHING!
©RAPID PHASE · 2012
GAUTRAIN?
AND THE WINNER... STILL THE FASTEST AND CHEAPEST WAY TO GO FROM JOHANNESBURG TO PRETORIA IS...
VROOOM!!
HOOT!
HOOT!
WHOOOSH!!
...BECOME A MINISTER!

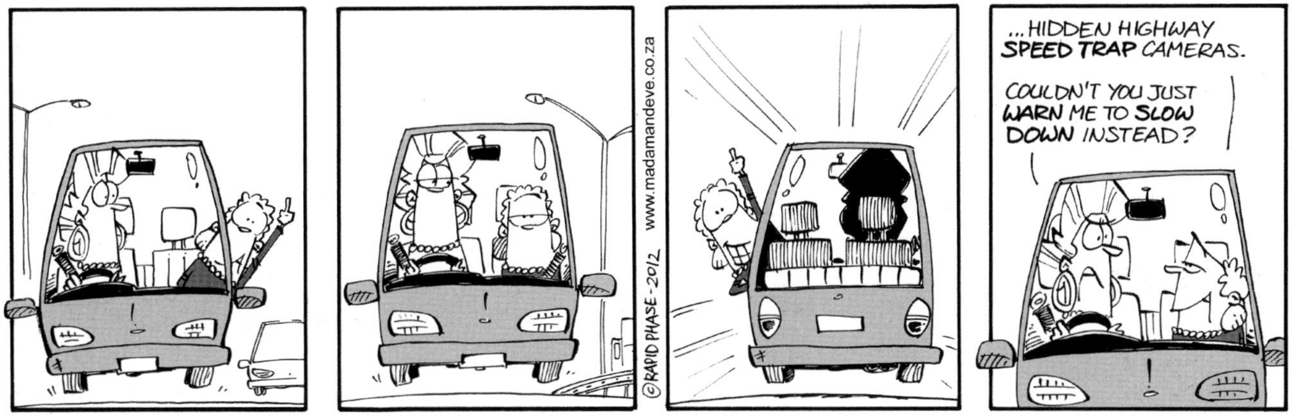
www.madamandeve.co.za
©RAPID PHASE-2012
...HIDDEN HIGHWAY SPEED TRAP CAMERAS.
COULDN'T YOU JUST WARN ME TO SLOW DOWN INSTEAD?

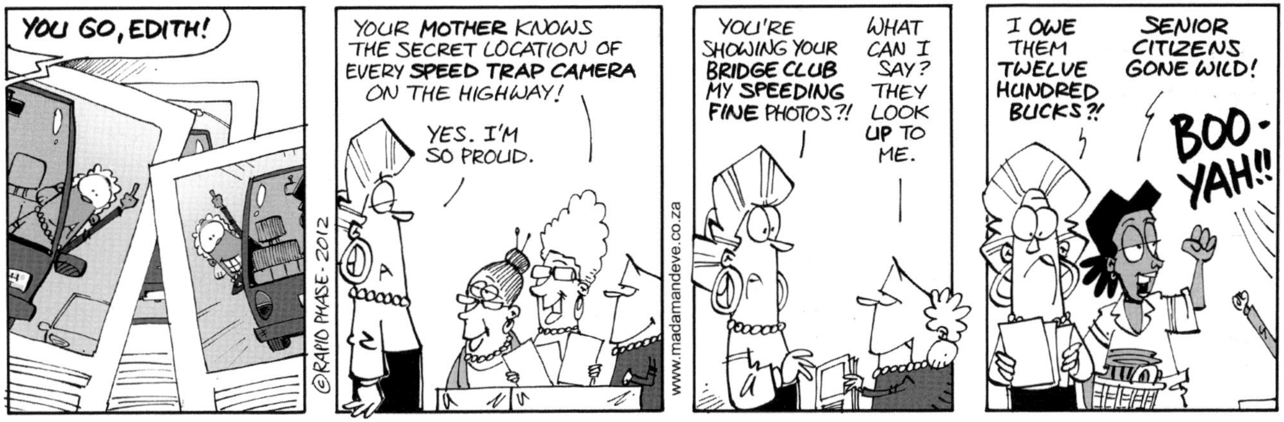
YOU GO, EDITH!
YOUR MOTHER KNOWS THE SECRET LOCATION OF EVERY SPEED TRAP CAMERA ON THE HIGHWAY!
YES. I'M SO PROUD.
©RAPID PHASE-2012
www.madamandeve.co.za
YOU'RE SHOWING YOUR BRIDGE CLUB MY SPEEDING FINE PHOTOS?!
WHAT CAN I SAY? THEY LOOK UP TO ME.
I OWE THEM TWELVE HUNDRED BUCKS?!
SENIOR CITIZENS GONE WILD!
BOO-YAH!!

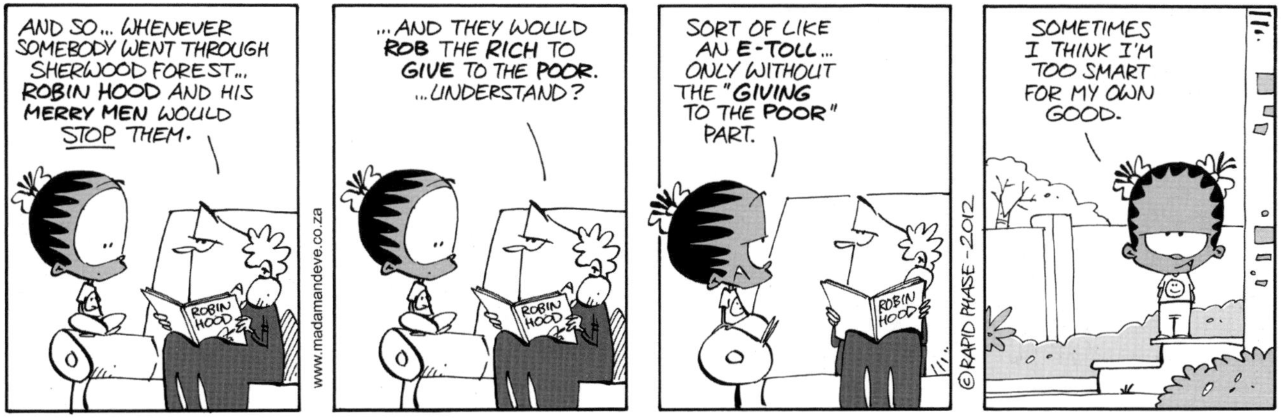
AND SO... WHENEVER SOMEBODY WENT THROUGH SHERWOOD FOREST... ROBIN HOOD AND HIS MERRY MEN WOULD STOP THEM.
ROBIN HOOD
www.madamandeve.co.za
...AND THEY WOULD ROB THE RICH TO GIVE TO THE POOR. ...UNDERSTAND?
ROBIN HOOD
SORT OF LIKE AN E-TOLL... ONLY WITHOUT THE "GIVING TO THE POOR" PART.
ROBIN HOOD
©RAPID PHASE-2012
SOMETIMES I THINK I'M TOO SMART FOR MY OWN GOOD.

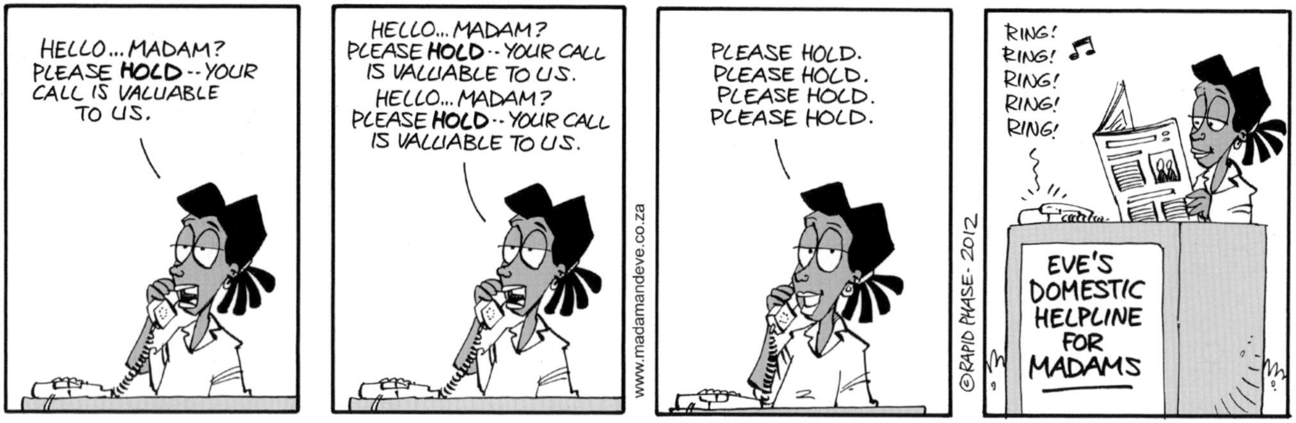
HELLO... MADAM? PLEASE HOLD -- YOUR CALL IS VALUABLE TO US.
HELLO... MADAM? PLEASE HOLD -- YOUR CALL IS VALUABLE TO US. HELLO... MADAM? PLEASE HOLD -- YOUR CALL IS VALUABLE TO US.
www.madamandeve.co.za
PLEASE HOLD. PLEASE HOLD. PLEASE HOLD. PLEASE HOLD.
RING! RING! RING! RING! RING!
EVE'S DOMESTIC HELPLINE FOR MADAMS
©RAPID PHASE·2012

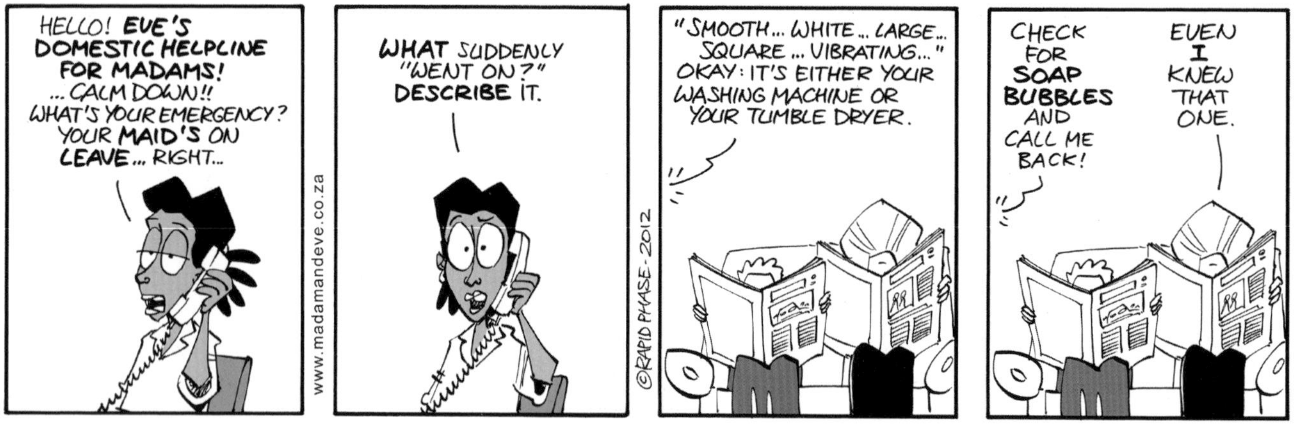
HELLO! EVE'S DOMESTIC HELPLINE FOR MADAMS! ... CALM DOWN!! WHAT'S YOUR EMERGENCY? YOUR MAID'S ON LEAVE... RIGHT...
www.madamandeve.co.za
WHAT SUDDENLY "WENT ON?" DESCRIBE IT.
©RAPID PHASE·2012
"SMOOTH... WHITE... LARGE... SQUARE... VIBRATING..." OKAY: IT'S EITHER YOUR WASHING MACHINE OR YOUR TUMBLE DRYER.
CHECK FOR SOAP BUBBLES AND CALL ME BACK!
EVEN I KNEW THAT ONE.

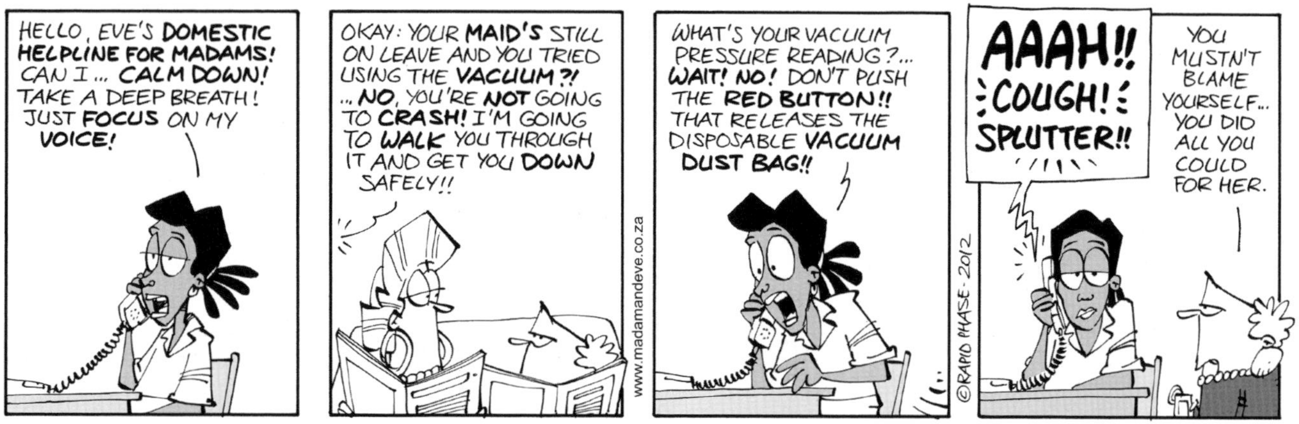
HELLO, EVE'S DOMESTIC HELPLINE FOR MADAMS! CAN I... CALM DOWN! TAKE A DEEP BREATH! JUST FOCUS ON MY VOICE!
OKAY: YOUR MAID'S STILL ON LEAVE AND YOU TRIED USING THE VACUUM?! ... NO, YOU'RE NOT GOING TO CRASH! I'M GOING TO WALK YOU THROUGH IT AND GET YOU DOWN SAFELY!!
www.madamandeve.co.za
WHAT'S YOUR VACUUM PRESSURE READING?... WAIT! NO! DON'T PUSH THE RED BUTTON!! THAT RELEASES THE DISPOSABLE VACUUM DUST BAG!!
©RAPID PHASE·2012
AAAH!! COUGH! SPLUTTER!!
YOU MUSTN'T BLAME YOURSELF... YOU DID ALL YOU COULD FOR HER.

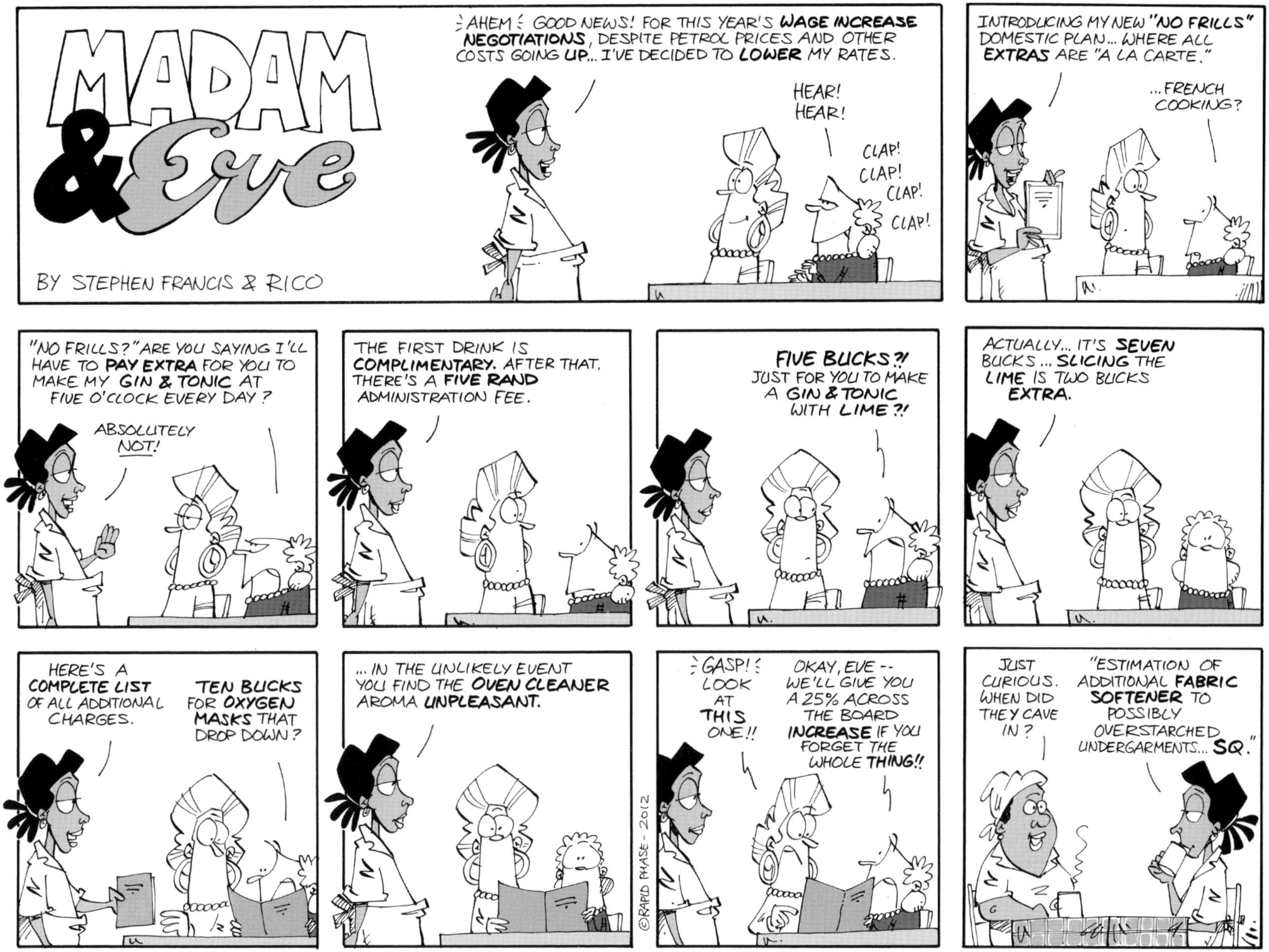
MADAM & Eve
BY STEPHEN FRANCIS & RICO
AHEM GOOD NEWS! FOR THIS YEAR'S WAGE INCREASE NEGOTIATIONS, DESPITE PETROL PRICES AND OTHER COSTS GOING UP... I'VE DECIDED TO LOWER MY RATES.
HEAR! HEAR!
CLAP! CLAP! CLAP! CLAP!
INTRODUCING MY NEW "NO FRILLS" DOMESTIC PLAN... WHERE ALL EXTRAS ARE "A LA CARTE."
...FRENCH COOKING?
"NO FRILLS?" ARE YOU SAYING I'LL HAVE TO PAY EXTRA FOR YOU TO MAKE MY GIN & TONIC AT FIVE O'CLOCK EVERY DAY?
ABSOLUTELY NOT!
THE FIRST DRINK IS COMPLIMENTARY. AFTER THAT, THERE'S A FIVE RAND ADMINISTRATION FEE.
FIVE BUCKS?! JUST FOR YOU TO MAKE A GIN & TONIC WITH LIME?!
ACTUALLY... IT'S SEVEN BUCKS... SLICING THE LIME IS TWO BUCKS EXTRA.
HERE'S A COMPLETE LIST OF ALL ADDITIONAL CHARGES.
TEN BUCKS FOR OXYGEN MASKS THAT DROP DOWN?
...IN THE UNLIKELY EVENT YOU FIND THE OVEN CLEANER AROMA UNPLEASANT.
©RAPID PHASE - 2012
GASP! LOOK AT THIS ONE!!
OKAY, EVE -- WE'LL GIVE YOU A 25% ACROSS THE BOARD INCREASE IF YOU FORGET THE WHOLE THING!!
JUST CURIOUS. WHEN DID THEY CAVE IN?
"ESTIMATION OF ADDITIONAL FABRIC SOFTENER TO POSSIBLY OVERSTARCHED UNDERGARMENTS... SQ."

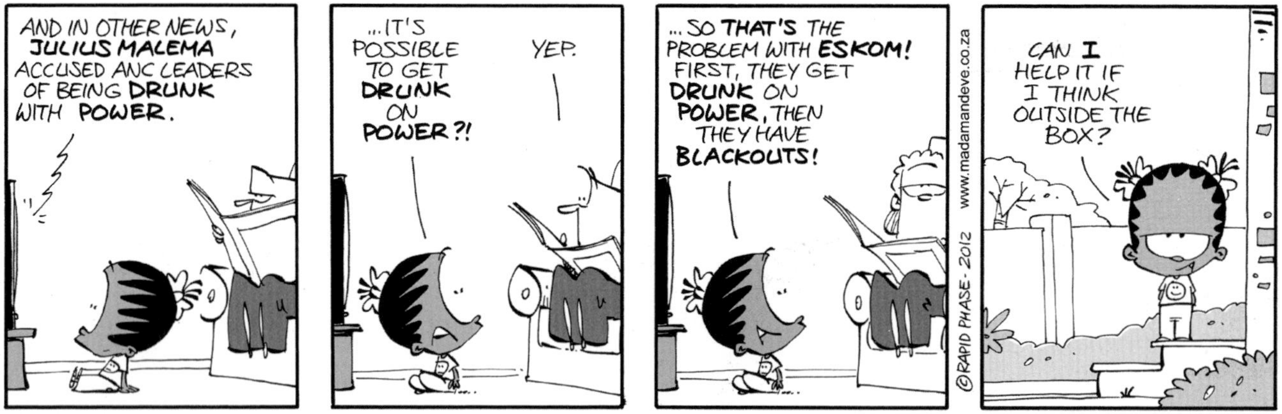
AND IN OTHER NEWS, JULIUS MALEMA ACCUSED ANC LEADERS OF BEING DRUNK WITH POWER.
...IT'S POSSIBLE TO GET DRUNK ON POWER?!
YEP.
...SO THAT'S THE PROBLEM WITH ESKOM! FIRST, THEY GET DRUNK ON POWER, THEN THEY HAVE BLACKOUTS!
©RAPID PHASE - 2012 www.madamandeve.co.za
CAN I HELP IT IF I THINK OUTSIDE THE BOX?

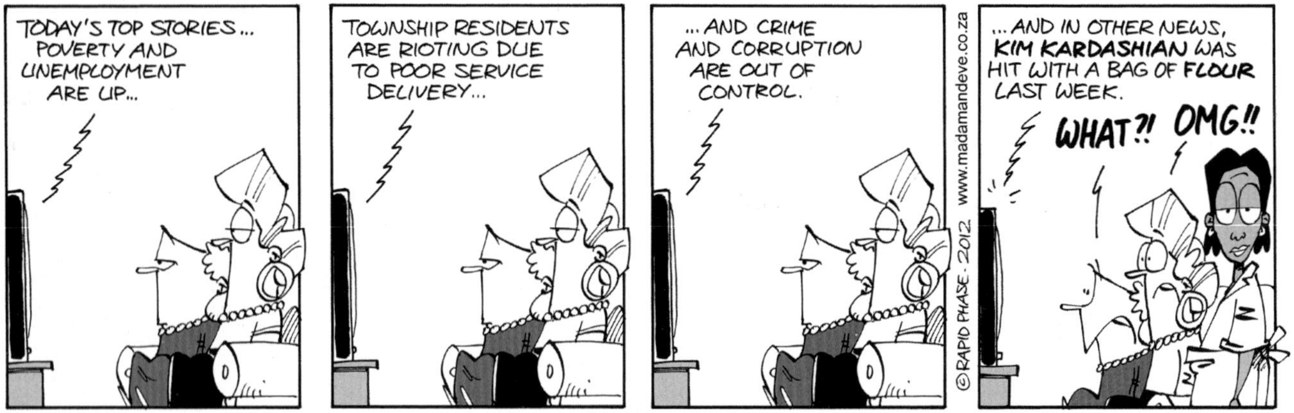
TODAY'S TOP STORIES... POVERTY AND UNEMPLOYMENT ARE UP...
TOWNSHIP RESIDENTS ARE RIOTING DUE TO POOR SERVICE DELIVERY...
...AND CRIME AND CORRUPTION ARE OUT OF CONTROL.
©RAPID PHASE - 2012 www.madamandeve.co.za
...AND IN OTHER NEWS, KIM KARDASHIAN WAS HIT WITH A BAG OF FLOUR LAST WEEK.
WHAT?!
OMG!!

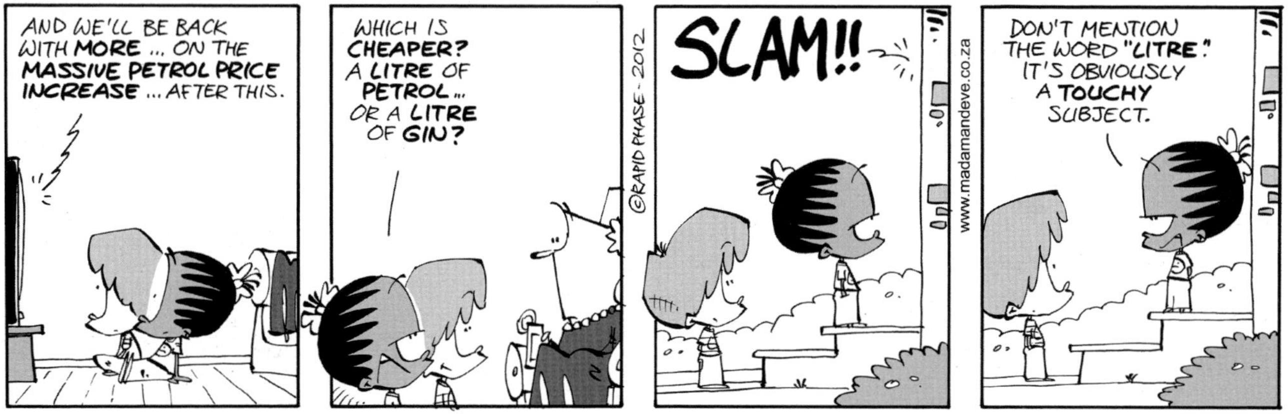
AND WE'LL BE BACK WITH MORE ... ON THE MASSIVE PETROL PRICE INCREASE ... AFTER THIS.
WHICH IS CHEAPER? A LITRE OF PETROL... OR A LITRE OF GIN?
©RAPID PHASE - 2012
SLAM!!
www.madamandeve.co.za
DON'T MENTION THE WORD "LITRE." IT'S OBVIOUSLY A TOUCHY SUBJECT.

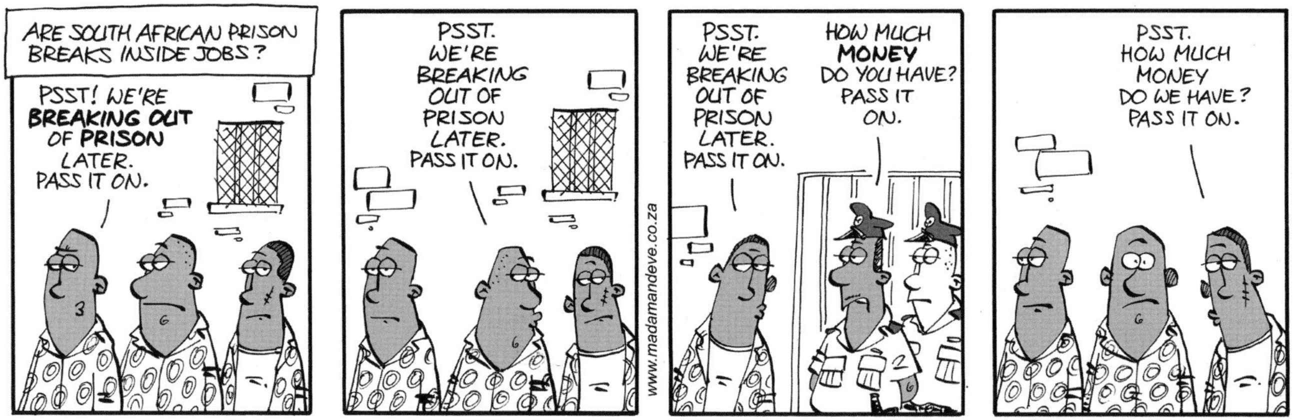
ARE SOUTH AFRICAN PRISON BREAKS INSIDE JOBS?
PSST! WE'RE **BREAKING OUT** OF **PRISON** LATER. PASS IT ON.
PSST. WE'RE BREAKING OUT OF PRISON LATER. PASS IT ON.
www.madamandeve.co.za
PSST. WE'RE BREAKING OUT OF PRISON LATER. PASS IT ON.
HOW MUCH **MONEY** DO YOU HAVE? PASS IT ON.
PSST. HOW MUCH MONEY DO WE HAVE? PASS IT ON.

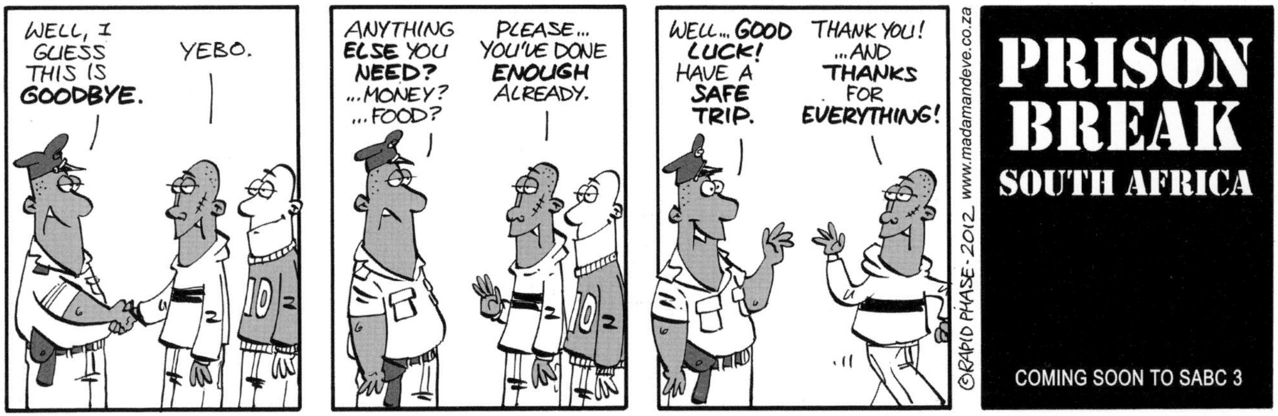
WELL, I GUESS THIS IS **GOODBYE.**
YEBO.
ANYTHING **ELSE** YOU **NEED?** ...MONEY? ...FOOD?
PLEASE... YOU'VE DONE **ENOUGH** ALREADY.
WELL... **GOOD LUCK!** HAVE A **SAFE TRIP.**
THANK YOU! ...AND **THANKS** FOR **EVERYTHING!**
©RAPID PHASE · 2012 www.madamandeve.co.za
PRISON BREAK
SOUTH AFRICA
COMING SOON TO SABC 3

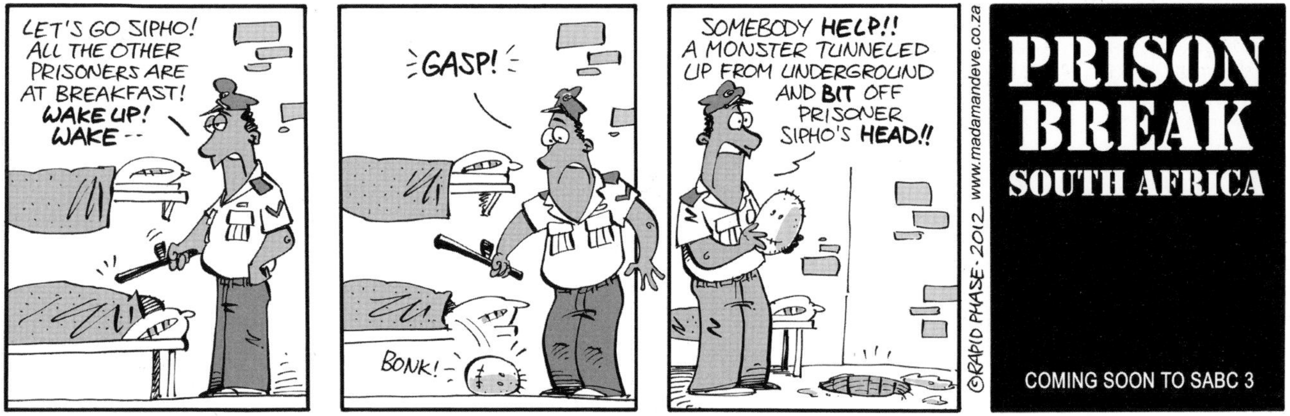
LET'S GO SIPHO! ALL THE OTHER PRISONERS ARE AT BREAKFAST! **WAKE UP! WAKE --**
GASP!
BONK!
SOMEBODY **HELP!!** A MONSTER TUNNELED UP FROM UNDERGROUND AND **BIT** OFF PRISONER SIPHO'S **HEAD!!**
©RAPID PHASE · 2012 www.madamandeve.co.za
PRISON BREAK
SOUTH AFRICA
COMING SOON TO SABC 3

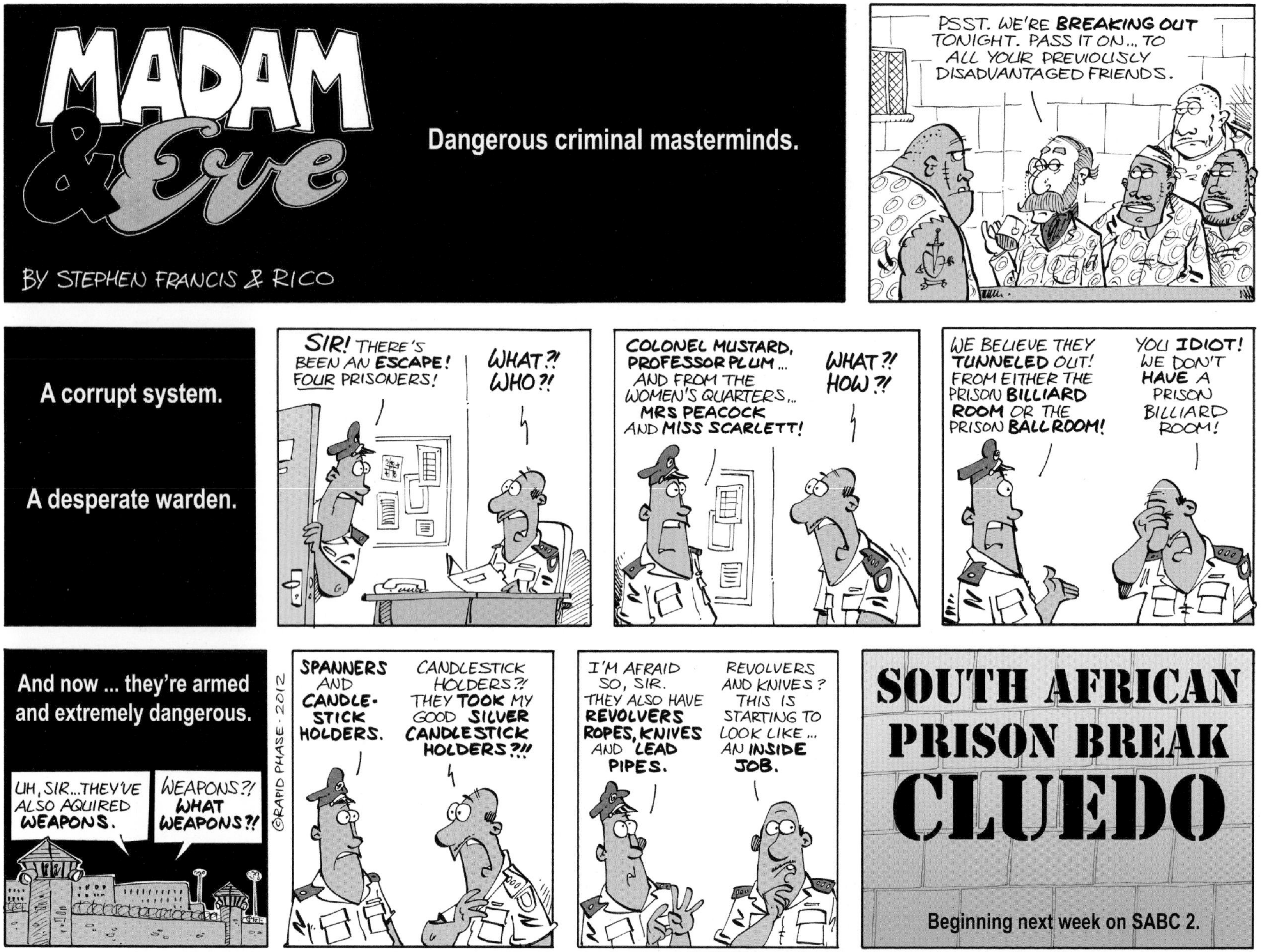
MADAM & Eve
BY STEPHEN FRANCIS & RICO
Dangerous criminal masterminds.
PSST. WE'RE BREAKING OUT TONIGHT. PASS IT ON... TO ALL YOUR PREVIOUSLY DISADVANTAGED FRIENDS.
A corrupt system.
A desperate warden.
SIR! THERE'S BEEN AN ESCAPE! FOUR PRISONERS!
WHAT?! WHO?!
COLONEL MUSTARD, PROFESSOR PLUM... AND FROM THE WOMEN'S QUARTERS... MRS PEACOCK AND MISS SCARLETT!
WHAT?! HOW?!
WE BELIEVE THEY TUNNELED OUT! FROM EITHER THE PRISON BILLIARD ROOM OR THE PRISON BALLROOM!
YOU IDIOT! WE DON'T HAVE A PRISON BILLIARD ROOM!
And now ... they're armed and extremely dangerous.
UH, SIR... THEY'VE ALSO AQUIRED WEAPONS.
WEAPONS?! WHAT WEAPONS?!
©RAPID PHASE · 2012
SPANNERS AND CANDLE-STICK HOLDERS.
CANDLESTICK HOLDERS?! THEY TOOK MY GOOD SILVER CANDLESTICK HOLDERS?!!
I'M AFRAID SO, SIR. THEY ALSO HAVE REVOLVERS ROPES, KNIVES AND LEAD PIPES.
REVOLVERS AND KNIVES? THIS IS STARTING TO LOOK LIKE... AN INSIDE JOB.
SOUTH AFRICAN PRISON BREAK CLUEDO
Beginning next week on SABC 2.

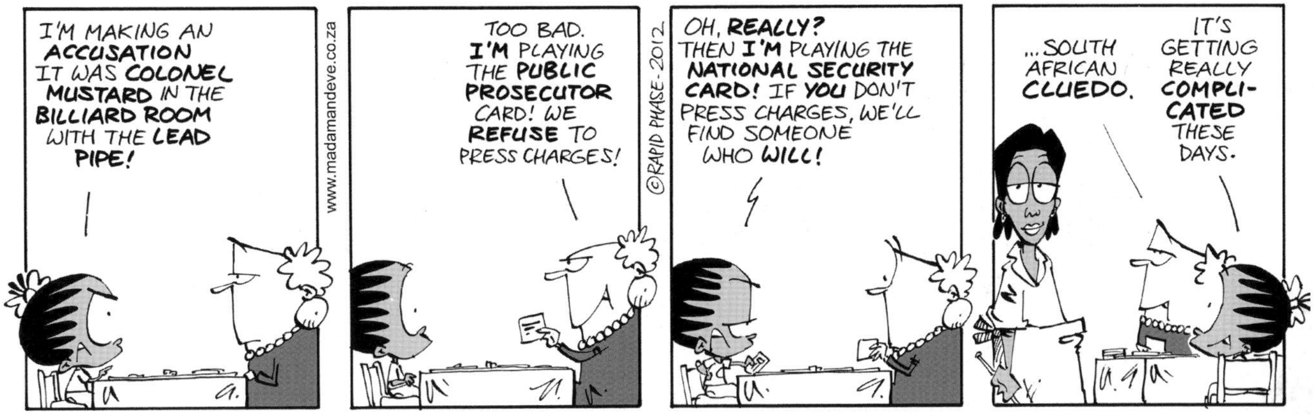
I'M MAKING AN ACCUSATION IT WAS COLONEL MUSTARD IN THE BILLIARD ROOM WITH THE LEAD PIPE!
www.madamandeve.co.za
TOO BAD. I'M PLAYING THE PUBLIC PROSECUTOR CARD! WE REFUSE TO PRESS CHARGES!
©RAPID PHASE·2012
OH, REALLY? THEN I'M PLAYING THE NATIONAL SECURITY CARD! IF YOU DON'T PRESS CHARGES, WE'LL FIND SOMEONE WHO WILL!
...SOUTH AFRICAN CLUEDO.
IT'S GETTING REALLY COMPLI-CATED THESE DAYS.

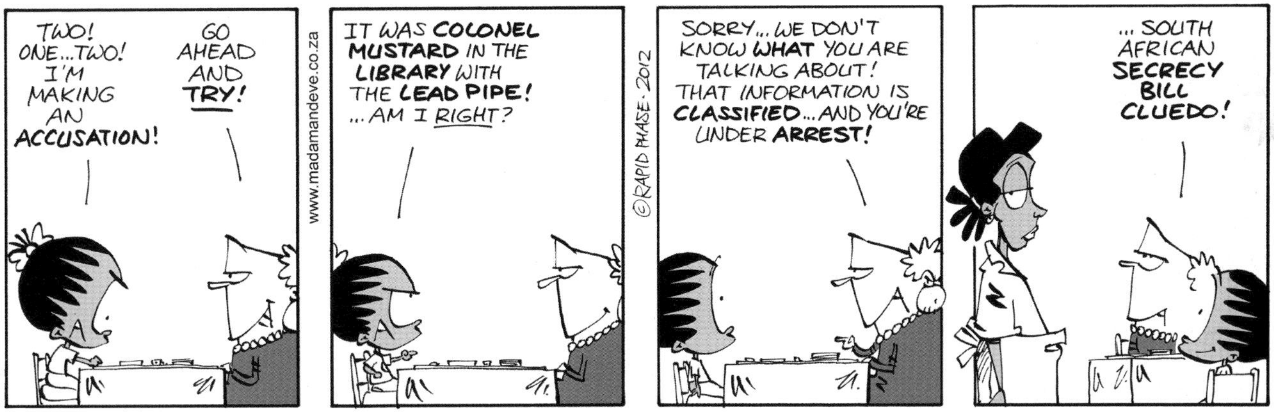
TWO! ONE...TWO! I'M MAKING AN ACCUSATION!
GO AHEAD AND TRY!
www.madamandeve.co.za
IT WAS COLONEL MUSTARD IN THE LIBRARY WITH THE LEAD PIPE! ...AM I RIGHT?
©RAPID PHASE·2012
SORRY... WE DON'T KNOW WHAT YOU ARE TALKING ABOUT! THAT INFORMATION IS CLASSIFIED... AND YOU'RE UNDER ARREST!
...SOUTH AFRICAN SECRECY BILL CLUEDO!

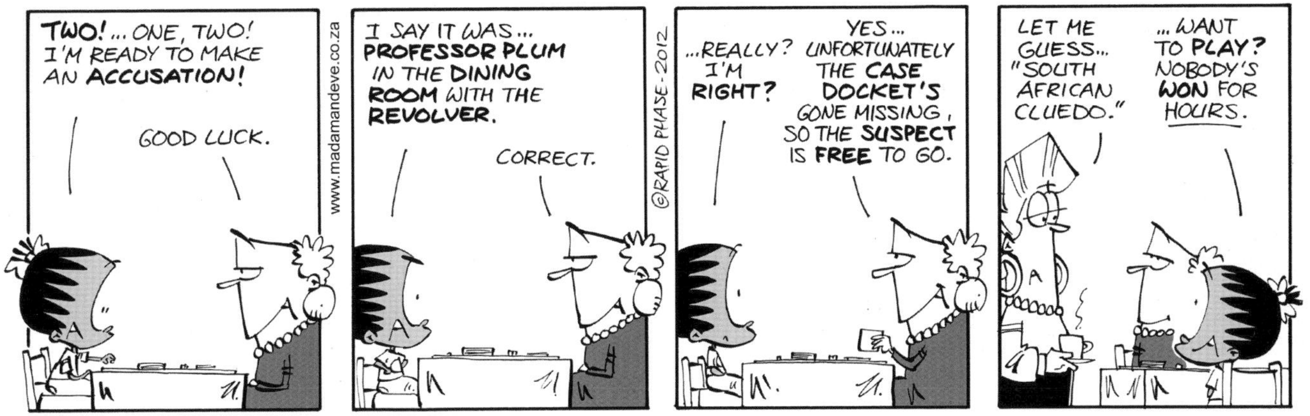
TWO!... ONE, TWO! I'M READY TO MAKE AN ACCUSATION!
GOOD LUCK.
www.madamandeve.co.za
I SAY IT WAS... PROFESSOR PLUM IN THE DINING ROOM WITH THE REVOLVER.
CORRECT.
©RAPID PHASE·2012
...REALLY? I'M RIGHT?
YES... UNFORTUNATELY THE CASE DOCKET'S GONE MISSING, SO THE SUSPECT IS FREE TO GO.
LET ME GUESS... "SOUTH AFRICAN CLUEDO."
...WANT TO PLAY? NOBODY'S WON FOR HOURS.

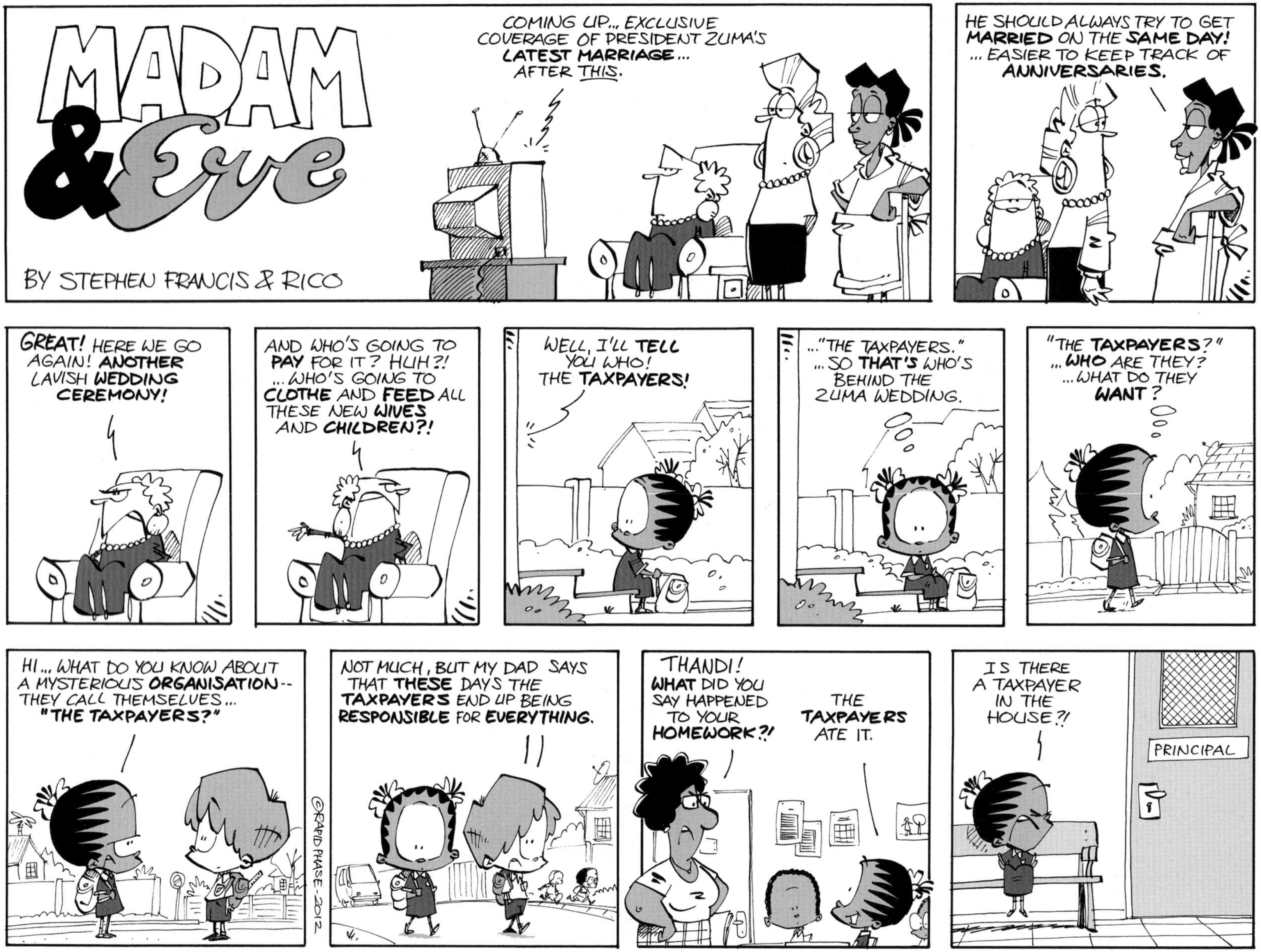
MADAM & Eve
BY STEPHEN FRANCIS & RICO
COMING UP... EXCLUSIVE COVERAGE OF PRESIDENT ZUMA'S LATEST MARRIAGE... AFTER THIS.
HE SHOULD ALWAYS TRY TO GET MARRIED ON THE SAME DAY! ... EASIER TO KEEP TRACK OF ANNIVERSARIES.
GREAT! HERE WE GO AGAIN! ANOTHER LAVISH WEDDING CEREMONY!
AND WHO'S GOING TO PAY FOR IT? HUH?! ...WHO'S GOING TO CLOTHE AND FEED ALL THESE NEW WIVES AND CHILDREN?!
WELL, I'LL TELL YOU WHO! THE TAXPAYERS!
..."THE TAXPAYERS." ...SO THAT'S WHO'S BEHIND THE ZUMA WEDDING.
"THE TAXPAYERS?" ...WHO ARE THEY? ...WHAT DO THEY WANT?
HI... WHAT DO YOU KNOW ABOUT A MYSTERIOUS ORGANISATION -- THEY CALL THEMSELVES... "THE TAXPAYERS?"
©RAPID PHASE-2012
NOT MUCH, BUT MY DAD SAYS THAT THESE DAYS THE TAXPAYERS END UP BEING RESPONSIBLE FOR EVERYTHING.
THANDI! WHAT DID YOU SAY HAPPENED TO YOUR HOMEWORK?!
THE TAXPAYERS ATE IT.
IS THERE A TAXPAYER IN THE HOUSE?!
PRINCIPAL

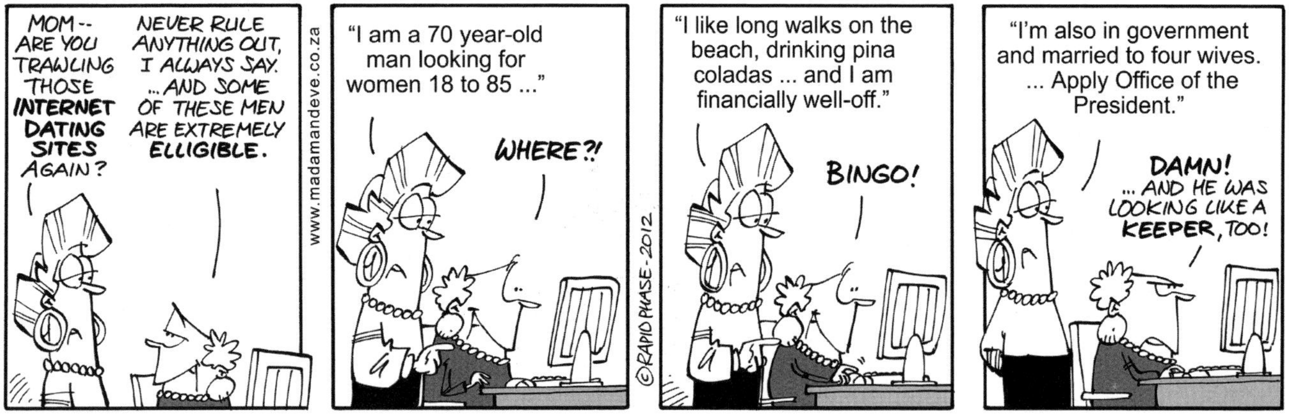
MOM -- ARE YOU TRAWLING THOSE INTERNET DATING SITES AGAIN?
NEVER RULE ANYTHING OUT, I ALWAYS SAY. ... AND SOME OF THESE MEN ARE EXTREMELY ELLIGIBLE.
www.madamandeve.co.za
"I am a 70 year-old man looking for women 18 to 85 ..."
WHERE?!
"I like long walks on the beach, drinking pina coladas ... and I am financially well-off."
BINGO!
©RAPID PHASE-2012
"I'm also in government and married to four wives. ... Apply Office of the President."
DAMN! ... AND HE WAS LOOKING LIKE A KEEPER, TOO!

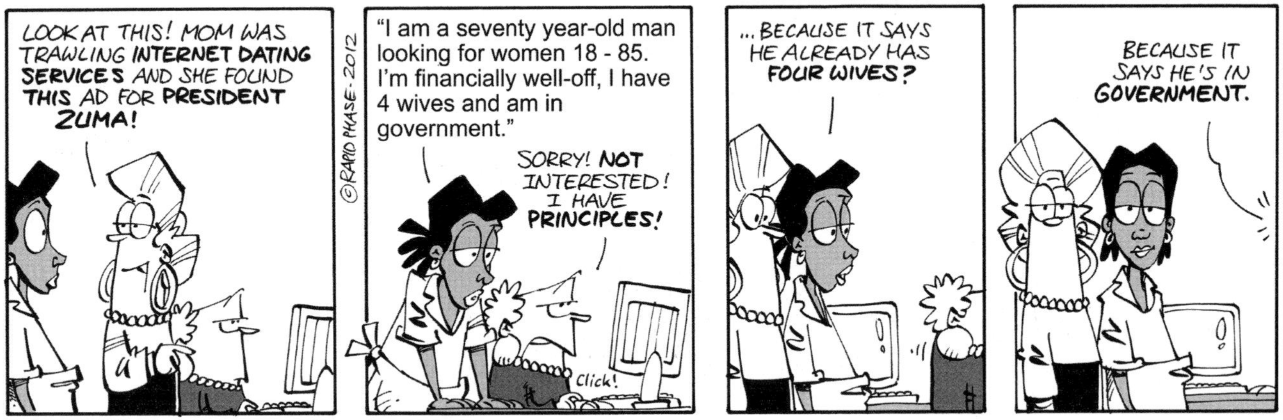
LOOK AT THIS! MOM WAS TRAWLING INTERNET DATING SERVICES AND SHE FOUND THIS AD FOR PRESIDENT ZUMA!
©RAPID PHASE-2012
"I am a seventy year-old man looking for women 18 - 85. I'm financially well-off, I have 4 wives and am in government."
SORRY! NOT INTERESTED! I HAVE PRINCIPLES!
Click!
... BECAUSE IT SAYS HE ALREADY HAS FOUR WIVES?
BECAUSE IT SAYS HE'S IN GOVERNMENT.

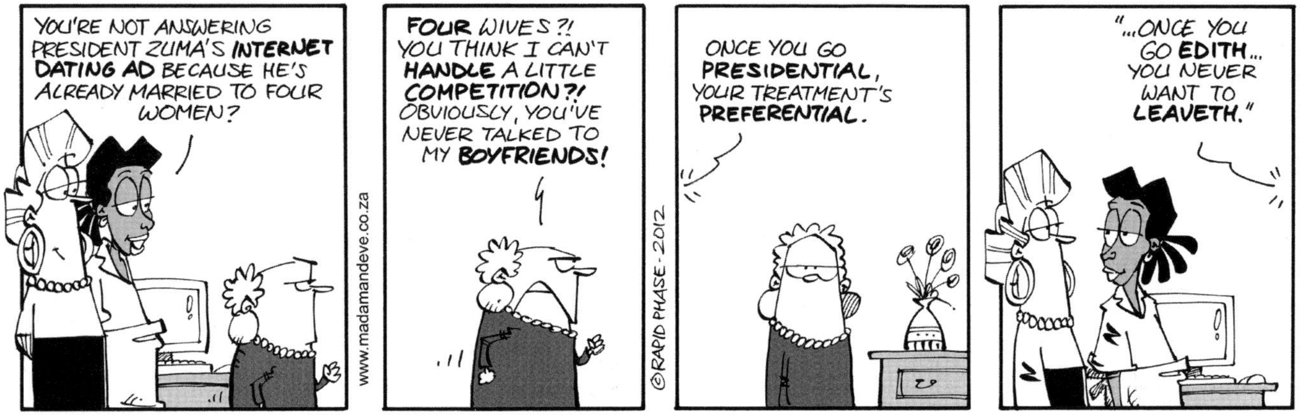
YOU'RE NOT ANSWERING PRESIDENT ZUMA'S INTERNET DATING AD BECAUSE HE'S ALREADY MARRIED TO FOUR WOMEN?
www.madamandeve.co.za
FOUR WIVES?! YOU THINK I CAN'T HANDLE A LITTLE COMPETITION?! OBVIOUSLY, YOU'VE NEVER TALKED TO MY BOYFRIENDS!
©RAPID PHASE-2012
ONCE YOU GO PRESIDENTIAL, YOUR TREATMENT'S PREFERENTIAL.
"... ONCE YOU GO EDITH... YOU NEVER WANT TO LEAVETH."

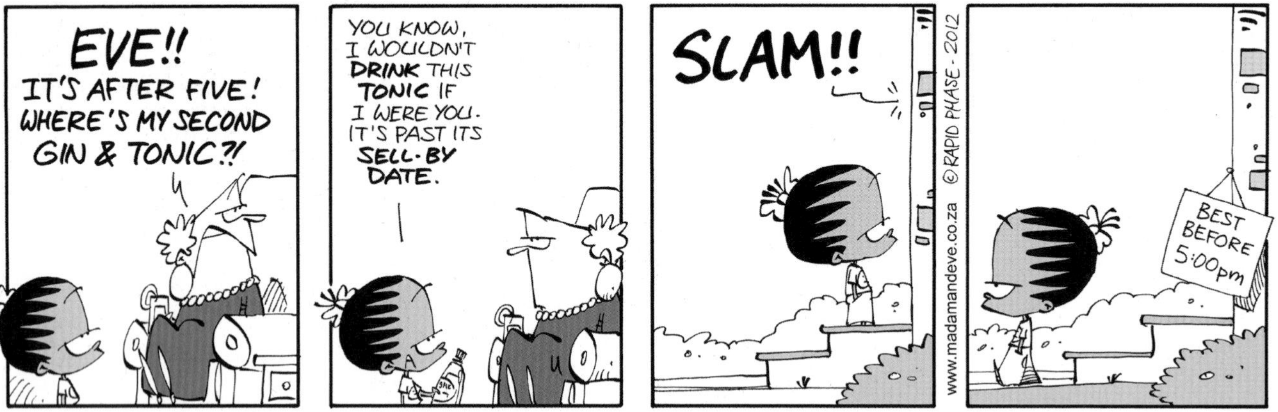
EVE!!
IT'S AFTER FIVE! WHERE'S MY SECOND GIN & TONIC?!
YOU KNOW, I WOULDN'T DRINK THIS TONIC IF I WERE YOU. IT'S PAST ITS SELL-BY DATE.
SLAM!!
© RAPID PHASE - 2012
www.madamandeve.co.za
BEST BEFORE 5:00pm

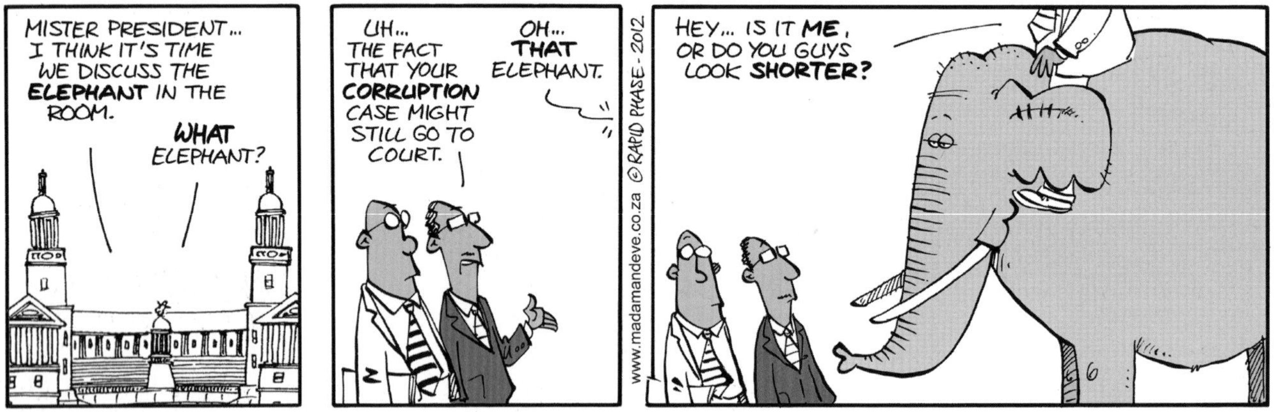
MISTER PRESIDENT... I THINK IT'S TIME WE DISCUSS THE ELEPHANT IN THE ROOM.
WHAT ELEPHANT?
UH... THE FACT THAT YOUR CORRUPTION CASE MIGHT STILL GO TO COURT.
OH... THAT ELEPHANT.
www.madamandeve.co.za © RAPID PHASE - 2012
HEY... IS IT ME, OR DO YOU GUYS LOOK SHORTER?

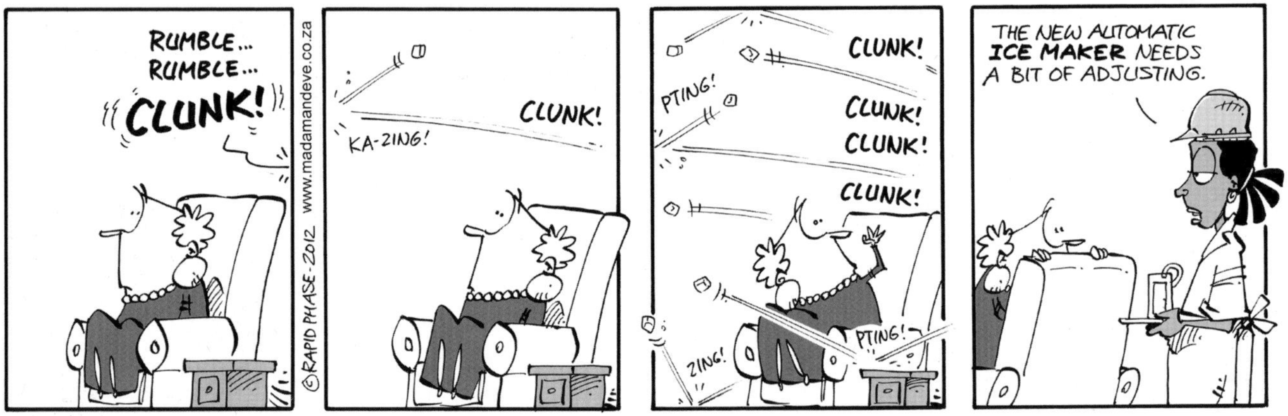
RUMBLE... RUMBLE...
CLUNK!
© RAPID PHASE - 2012 www.madamandeve.co.za
KA-ZING!
CLUNK!
CLUNK!
PTING!
CLUNK!
CLUNK!
CLUNK!
ZING!
PTING!
THE NEW AUTOMATIC ICE MAKER NEEDS A BIT OF ADJUSTING.

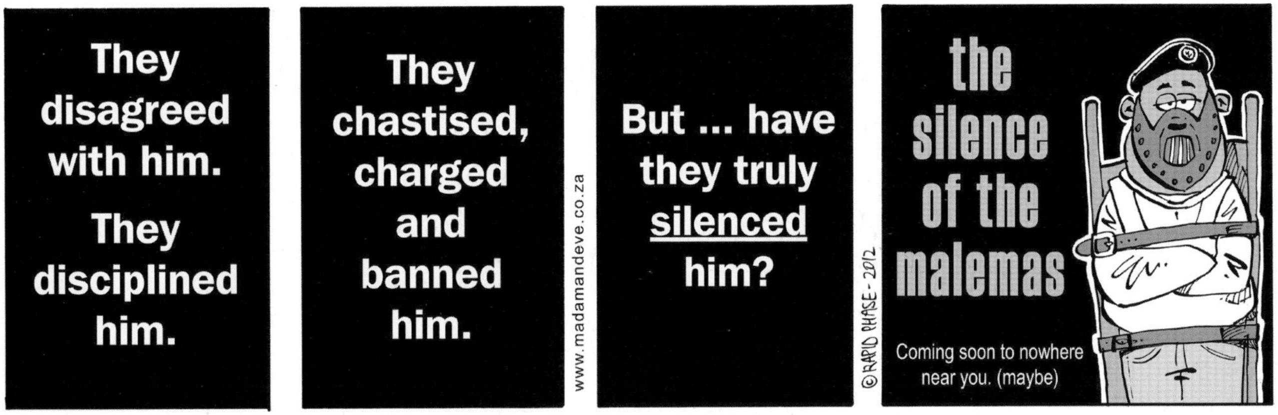
They disagreed with him.
They disciplined him.
They chastised, charged and banned him.
www.madamandeve.co.za
But ... have they truly silenced him?
© RAPID PHASE - 2012
the silence of the malemas
Coming soon to nowhere near you. (maybe)

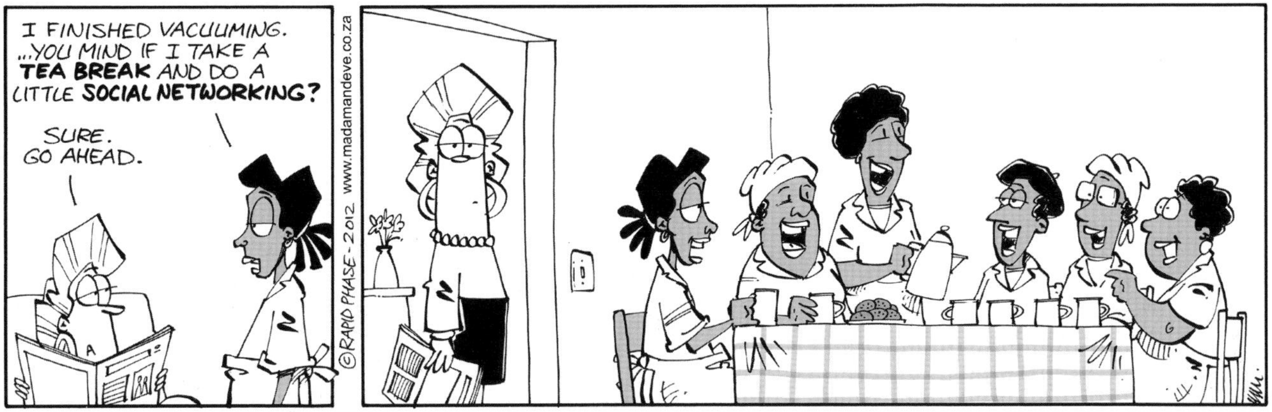
I FINISHED VACUUMING. ...YOU MIND IF I TAKE A TEA BREAK AND DO A LITTLE SOCIAL NETWORKING?
SURE. GO AHEAD.
© RAPID PHASE - 2012 www.madamandeve.co.za

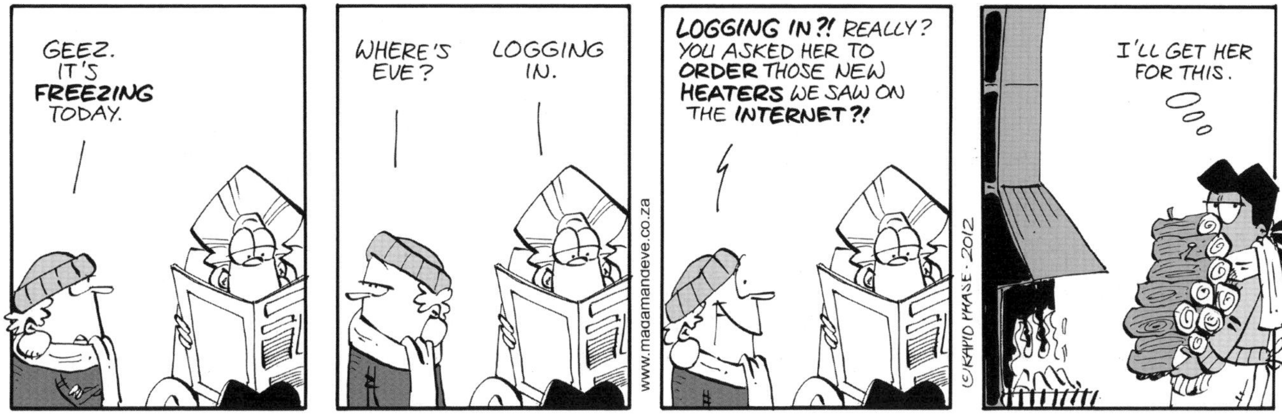
GEEZ. IT'S FREEZING TODAY.
WHERE'S EVE?
LOGGING IN.
www.madamandeve.co.za
LOGGING IN?! REALLY? YOU ASKED HER TO ORDER THOSE NEW HEATERS WE SAW ON THE INTERNET?!
© RAPID PHASE - 2012
I'LL GET HER FOR THIS.

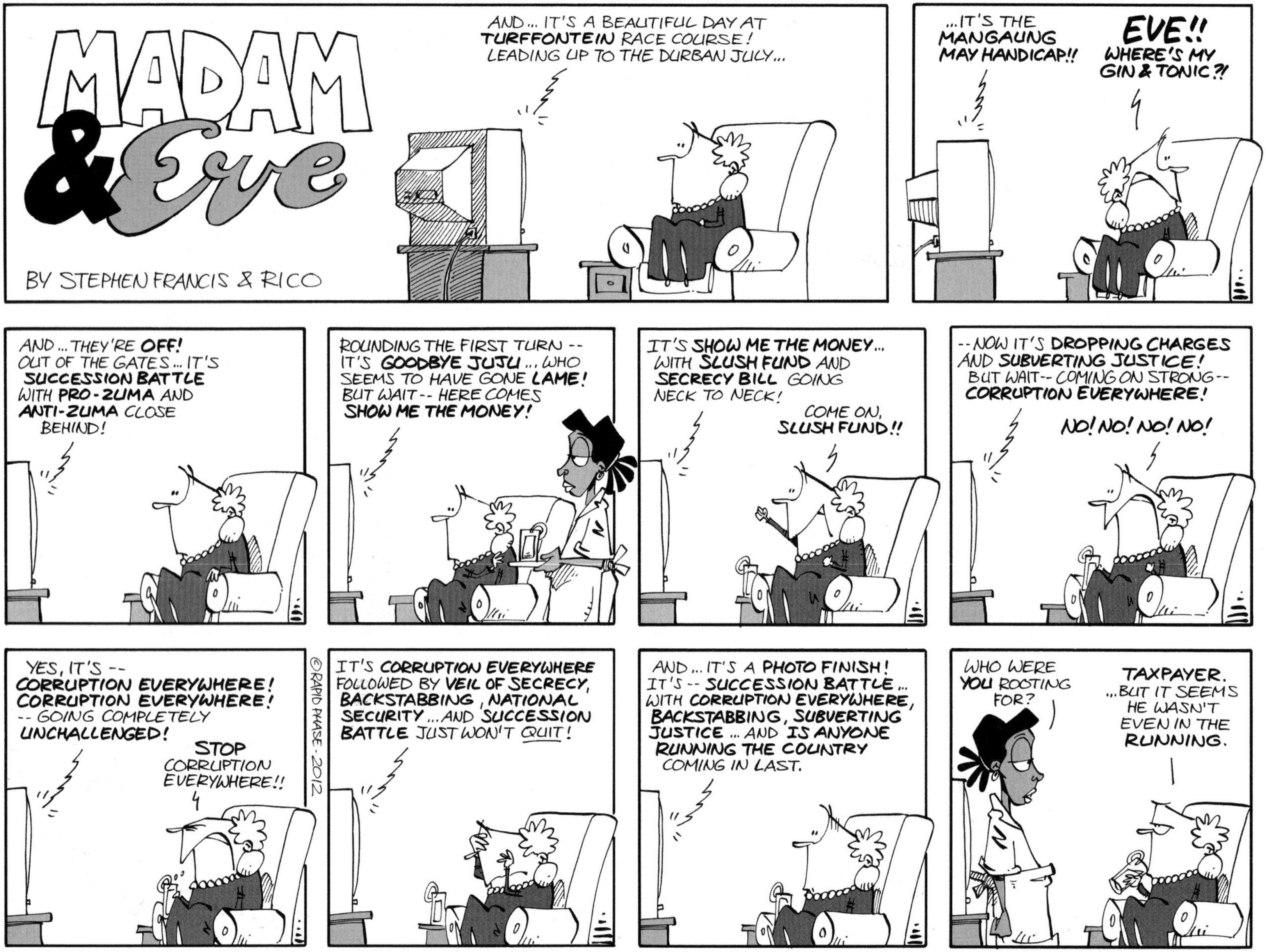
MADAM & Eve
BY STEPHEN FRANCIS & RICO
AND... IT'S A BEAUTIFUL DAY AT TURFFONTEIN RACE COURSE! LEADING UP TO THE DURBAN JULY...
...IT'S THE MANGAUNG MAY HANDICAP!!
EVE!! WHERE'S MY GIN & TONIC?!
AND... THEY'RE OFF! OUT OF THE GATES... IT'S SUCCESSION BATTLE WITH PRO-ZUMA AND ANTI-ZUMA CLOSE BEHIND!
ROUNDING THE FIRST TURN -- IT'S GOODBYE JUJU... WHO SEEMS TO HAVE GONE LAME! BUT WAIT -- HERE COMES SHOW ME THE MONEY!
IT'S SHOW ME THE MONEY... WITH SLUSH FUND AND SECRECY BILL GOING NECK TO NECK!
COME ON, SLUSH FUND!!
-- NOW IT'S DROPPING CHARGES AND SUBVERTING JUSTICE! BUT WAIT -- COMING ON STRONG -- CORRUPTION EVERYWHERE!
NO! NO! NO! NO!
YES, IT'S -- CORRUPTION EVERYWHERE! CORRUPTION EVERYWHERE! -- GOING COMPLETELY UNCHALLENGED!
STOP CORRUPTION EVERYWHERE!!
© RAPID PHASE · 2012
IT'S CORRUPTION EVERYWHERE FOLLOWED BY VEIL OF SECRECY, BACKSTABBING, NATIONAL SECURITY... AND SUCCESSION BATTLE JUST WON'T QUIT!
AND... IT'S A PHOTO FINISH! IT'S -- SUCCESSION BATTLE... WITH CORRUPTION EVERYWHERE, BACKSTABBING, SUBVERTING JUSTICE... AND IS ANYONE RUNNING THE COUNTRY COMING IN LAST.
WHO WERE YOU ROOTING FOR?
TAXPAYER. ...BUT IT SEEMS HE WASN'T EVEN IN THE RUNNING.

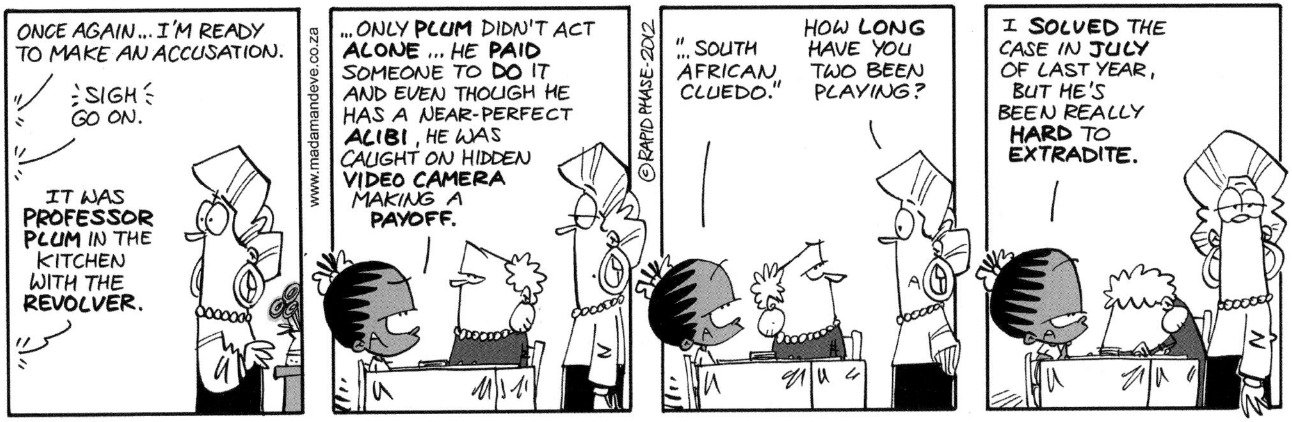
ONCE AGAIN... I'M READY TO MAKE AN ACCUSATION.
SIGH GO ON.
IT WAS PROFESSOR PLUM IN THE KITCHEN WITH THE REVOLVER.
www.madamandeve.co.za
...ONLY PLUM DIDN'T ACT ALONE ... HE PAID SOMEONE TO DO IT AND EVEN THOUGH HE HAS A NEAR-PERFECT ALIBI, HE WAS CAUGHT ON HIDDEN VIDEO CAMERA MAKING A PAYOFF.
© RAPID PHASE · 2012
"... SOUTH AFRICAN CLUEDO."
HOW LONG HAVE YOU TWO BEEN PLAYING?
I SOLVED THE CASE IN JULY OF LAST YEAR, BUT HE'S BEEN REALLY HARD TO EXTRADITE.

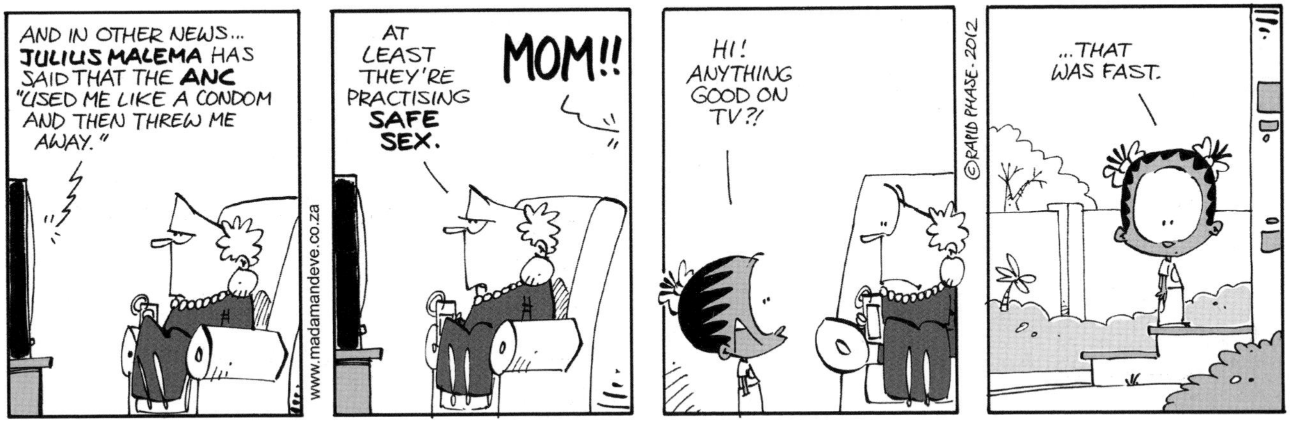
AND IN OTHER NEWS... JULIUS MALEMA HAS SAID THAT THE ANC "USED ME LIKE A CONDOM AND THEN THREW ME AWAY."
www.madamandeve.co.za
AT LEAST THEY'RE PRACTISING SAFE SEX.
MOM!!
HI! ANYTHING GOOD ON TV?!
© RAPID PHASE · 2012
...THAT WAS FAST.

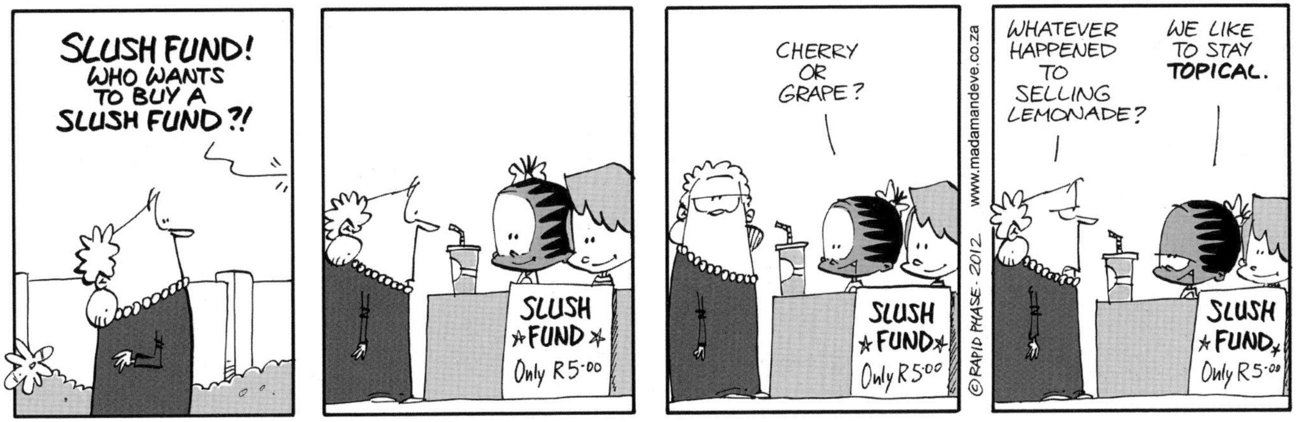
SLUSH FUND! WHO WANTS TO BUY A SLUSH FUND?!
SLUSH FUND Only R5·00
CHERRY OR GRAPE?
SLUSH FUND Only R5·00
www.madamandeve.co.za
© RAPID PHASE · 2012
WHATEVER HAPPENED TO SELLING LEMONADE?
WE LIKE TO STAY TOPICAL.
SLUSH FUND Only R5·00

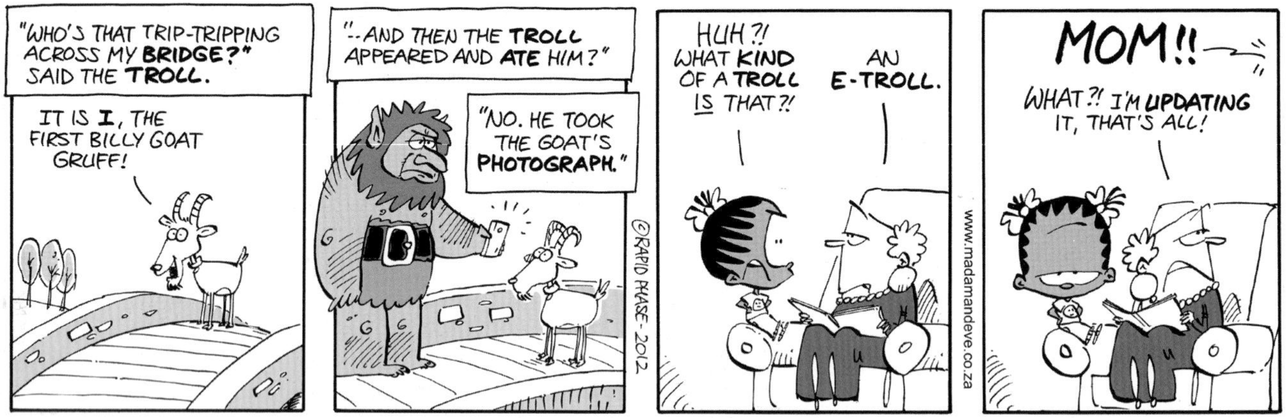
"WHO'S THAT TRIP-TRIPPING ACROSS MY BRIDGE?" SAID THE TROLL.
IT IS I, THE FIRST BILLY GOAT GRUFF!
"...AND THEN THE TROLL APPEARED AND ATE HIM?"
"NO. HE TOOK THE GOAT'S PHOTOGRAPH."
©RAPID PHASE - 2012
HUH?! WHAT KIND OF A TROLL IS THAT?!
AN E-TROLL.
www.madamandeve.co.za
MOM!!
WHAT?! I'M UPDATING IT, THAT'S ALL!

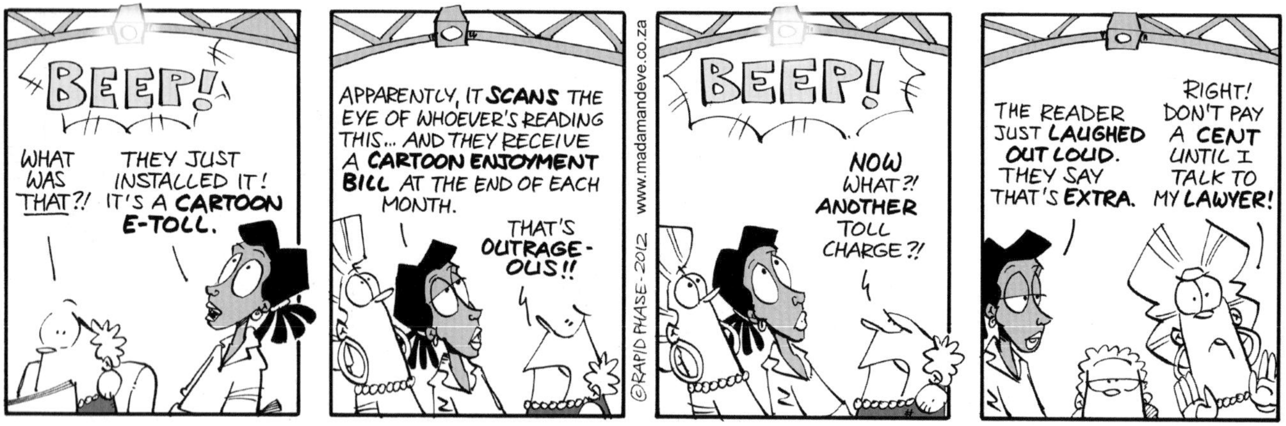
BEEP!
WHAT WAS THAT?!
THEY JUST INSTALLED IT! IT'S A CARTOON E-TOLL.
APPARENTLY, IT SCANS THE EYE OF WHOEVER'S READING THIS... AND THEY RECEIVE A CARTOON ENJOYMENT BILL AT THE END OF EACH MONTH.
THAT'S OUTRAGE-OUS!!
www.madamandeve.co.za
©RAPID PHASE - 2012
BEEP!
NOW WHAT?! ANOTHER TOLL CHARGE?!
THE READER JUST LAUGHED OUT LOUD. THEY SAY THAT'S EXTRA.
RIGHT! DON'T PAY A CENT UNTIL I TALK TO MY LAWYER!

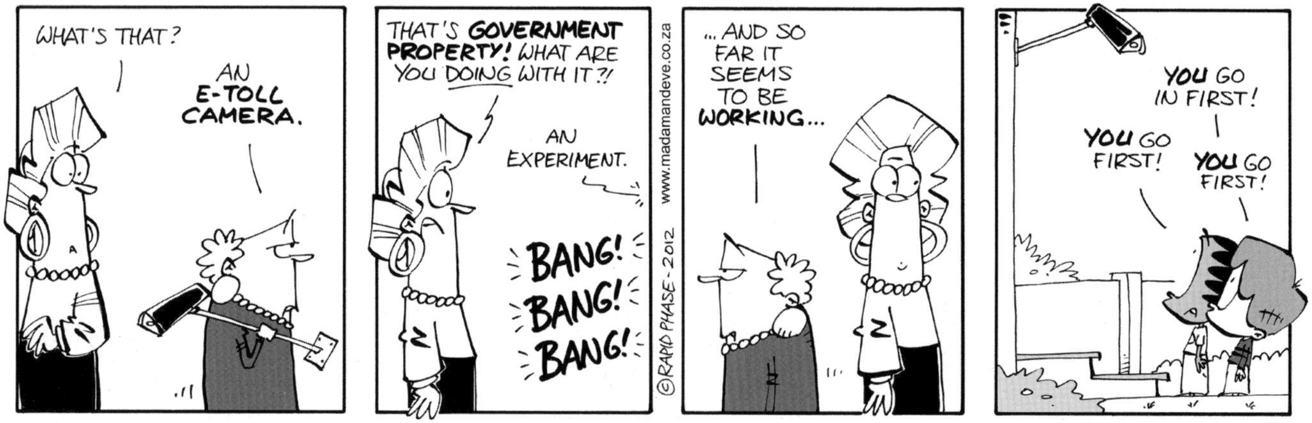
WHAT'S THAT?
AN E-TOLL CAMERA.
THAT'S GOVERNMENT PROPERTY! WHAT ARE YOU DOING WITH IT?!
AN EXPERIMENT.
BANG! BANG! BANG!
www.madamandeve.co.za
©RAPID PHASE - 2012
...AND SO FAR IT SEEMS TO BE WORKING...
YOU GO FIRST!
YOU GO IN FIRST!
YOU GO FIRST!

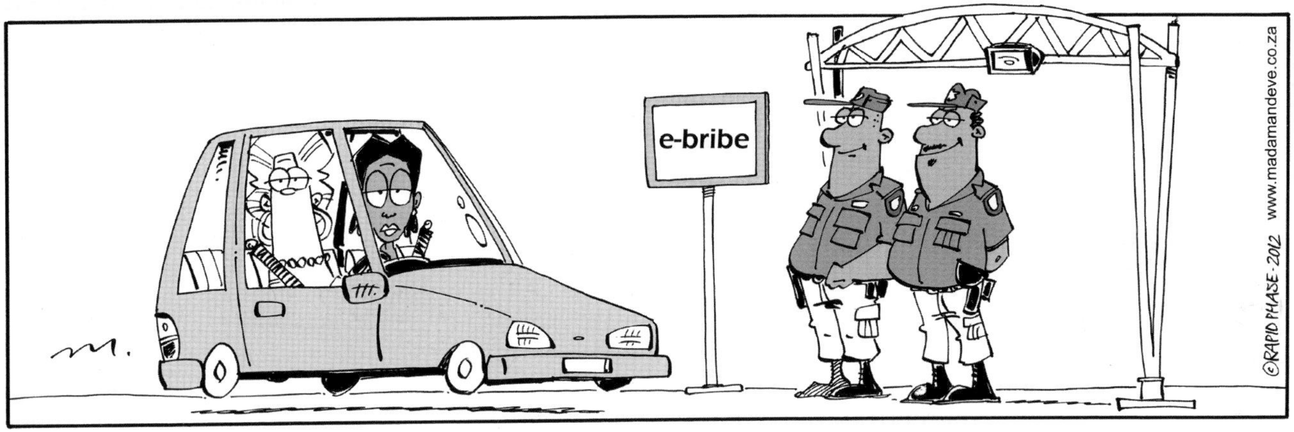
e-bribe
©RAPID PHASE · 2012
www.madamandeve.co.za

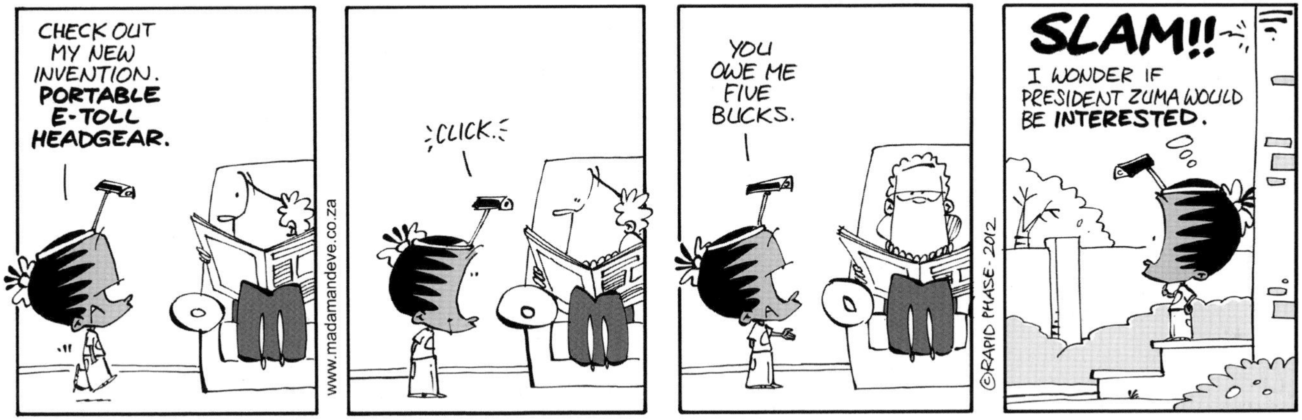
CHECK OUT MY NEW INVENTION. **PORTABLE E-TOLL HEADGEAR.**
CLICK.
YOU OWE ME FIVE BUCKS.
SLAM!!
I WONDER IF PRESIDENT ZUMA WOULD BE **INTERESTED.**
www.madamandeve.co.za
©RAPID PHASE · 2012

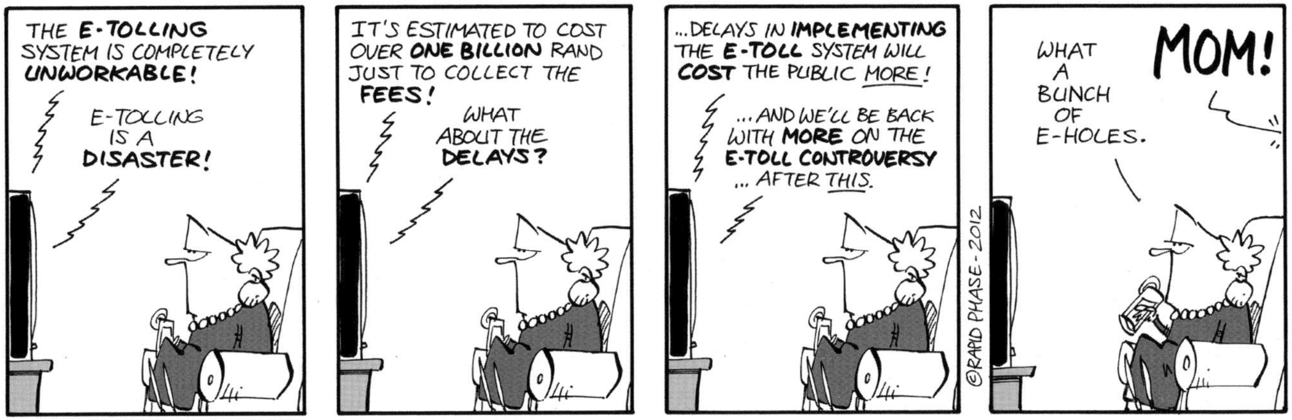
THE **E-TOLLING** SYSTEM IS COMPLETELY **UNWORKABLE!**
E-TOLLING IS A **DISASTER!**
IT'S ESTIMATED TO COST OVER **ONE BILLION** RAND JUST TO COLLECT THE **FEES!**
WHAT ABOUT THE **DELAYS?**
...DELAYS IN **IMPLEMENTING** THE **E-TOLL** SYSTEM WILL **COST** THE PUBLIC MORE!
...AND WE'LL BE BACK WITH **MORE** ON THE **E-TOLL CONTROVERSY** ... AFTER THIS.
WHAT A BUNCH OF E-HOLES.
MOM!
©RAPID PHASE · 2012

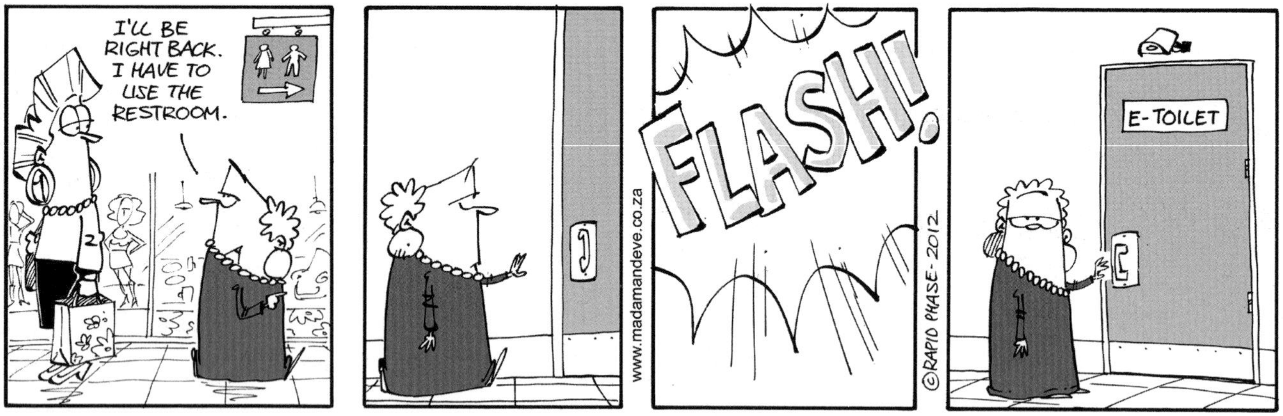
I'LL BE RIGHT BACK. I HAVE TO USE THE RESTROOM.
www.madamandeve.co.za
FLASH!
©RAPID PHASE - 2012
E-TOILET

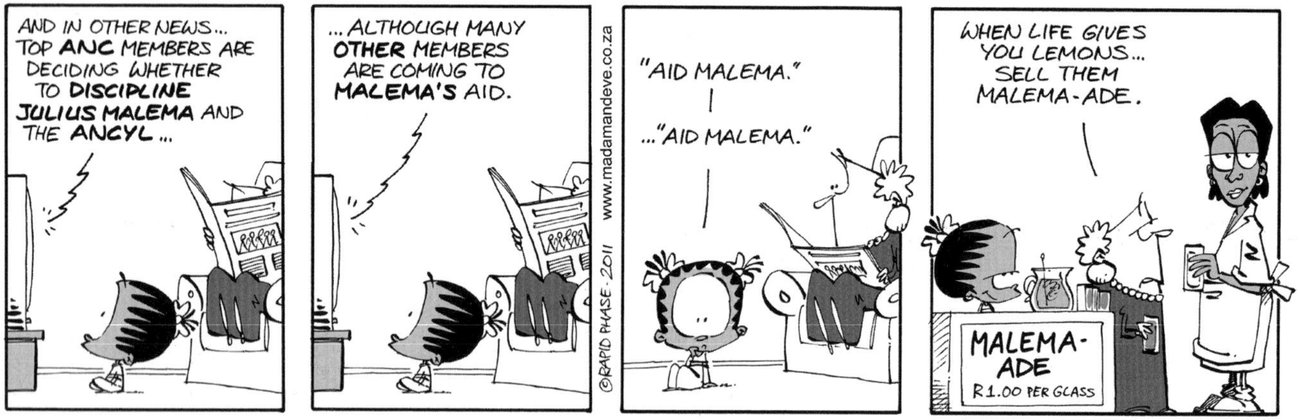
AND IN OTHER NEWS... TOP **ANC** MEMBERS ARE DECIDING WHETHER TO **DISCIPLINE JULIUS MALEMA** AND THE **ANCYL**...
...ALTHOUGH MANY **OTHER** MEMBERS ARE COMING TO **MALEMA'S** AID.
©RAPID PHASE - 2011 www.madamandeve.co.za
"AID MALEMA."
..."AID MALEMA."
WHEN LIFE GIVES YOU LEMONS... SELL THEM MALEMA-ADE.
MALEMA-ADE
R1.00 PER GLASS

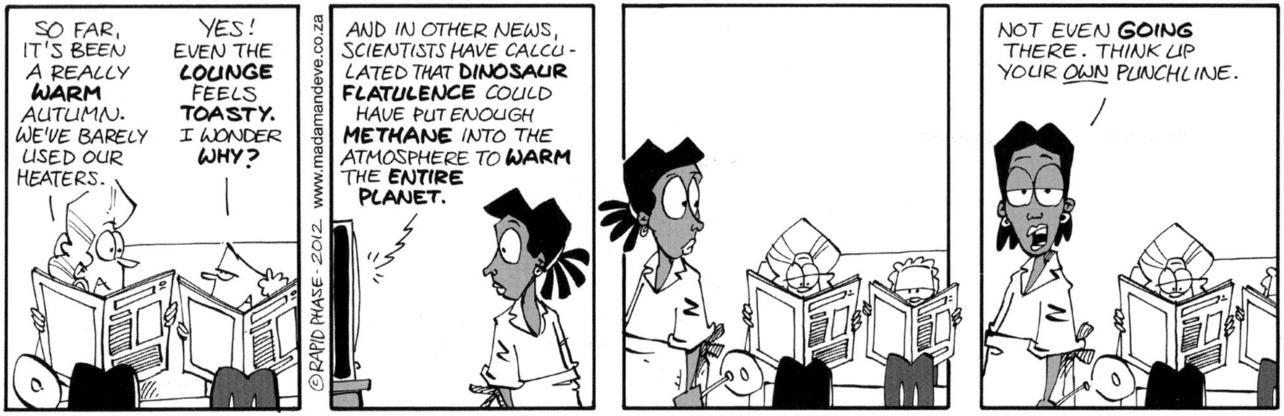
SO FAR, IT'S BEEN A REALLY **WARM** AUTUMN. WE'VE BARELY USED OUR HEATERS.
YES! EVEN THE **LOUNGE** FEELS **TOASTY.** I WONDER **WHY?**
©RAPID PHASE - 2012 www.madamandeve.co.za
AND IN OTHER NEWS, SCIENTISTS HAVE CALCU-LATED THAT **DINOSAUR FLATULENCE** COULD HAVE PUT ENOUGH **METHANE** INTO THE ATMOSPHERE TO **WARM** THE **ENTIRE PLANET.**
NOT EVEN **GOING** THERE. THINK UP YOUR OWN PUNCHLINE.

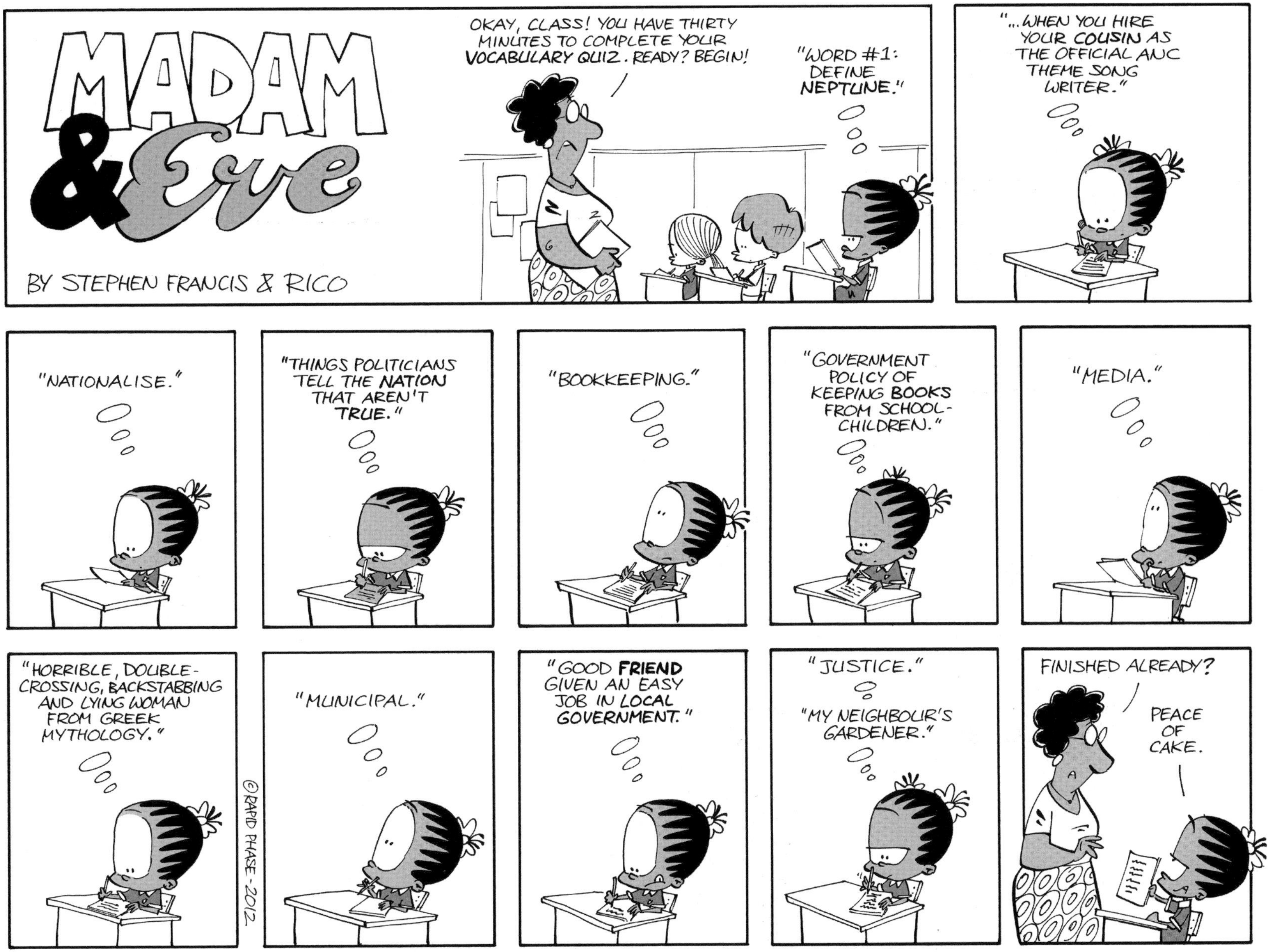
MADAM & Eve
BY STEPHEN FRANCIS & RICO
OKAY, CLASS! YOU HAVE THIRTY MINUTES TO COMPLETE YOUR VOCABULARY QUIZ. READY? BEGIN!
"WORD #1: DEFINE NEPTUNE."
"...WHEN YOU HIRE YOUR COUSIN AS THE OFFICIAL ANC THEME SONG WRITER."
"NATIONALISE."
"THINGS POLITICIANS TELL THE NATION THAT AREN'T TRUE."
"BOOKKEEPING."
"GOVERNMENT POLICY OF KEEPING BOOKS FROM SCHOOL-CHILDREN."
"MEDIA."
"HORRIBLE, DOUBLE-CROSSING, BACKSTABBING AND LYING WOMAN FROM GREEK MYTHOLOGY."
© RAPID PHASE - 2012
"MUNICIPAL."
"GOOD FRIEND GIVEN AN EASY JOB IN LOCAL GOVERNMENT."
"JUSTICE."
"MY NEIGHBOUR'S GARDENER."
FINISHED ALREADY?
PEACE OF CAKE.

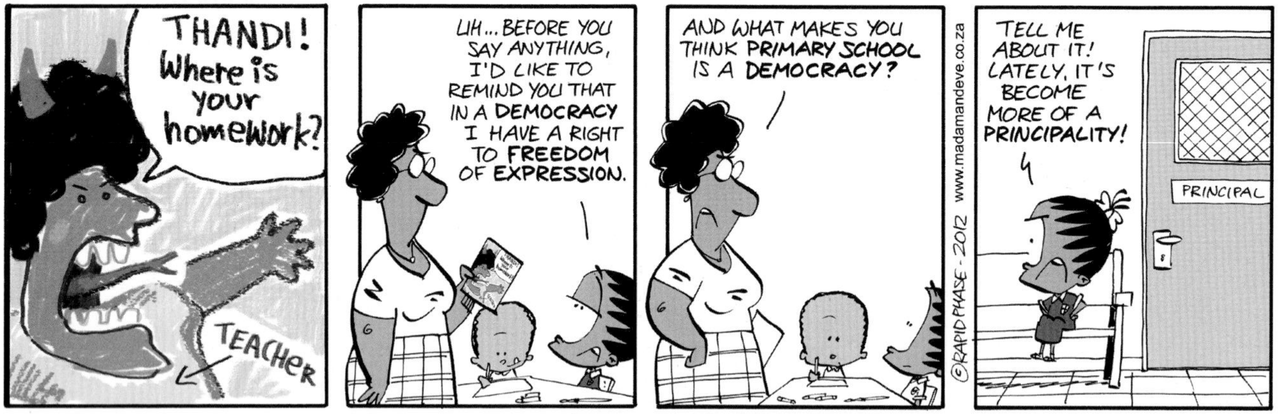
THANDI! Where is your homework?
TEACHER
UH... BEFORE YOU SAY ANYTHING, I'D LIKE TO REMIND YOU THAT IN A DEMOCRACY I HAVE A RIGHT TO FREEDOM OF EXPRESSION.
AND WHAT MAKES YOU THINK PRIMARY SCHOOL IS A DEMOCRACY?
©RAPID PHASE - 2012 www.madamandeve.co.za
TELL ME ABOUT IT! LATELY, IT'S BECOME MORE OF A PRINCIPALITY!
PRINCIPAL

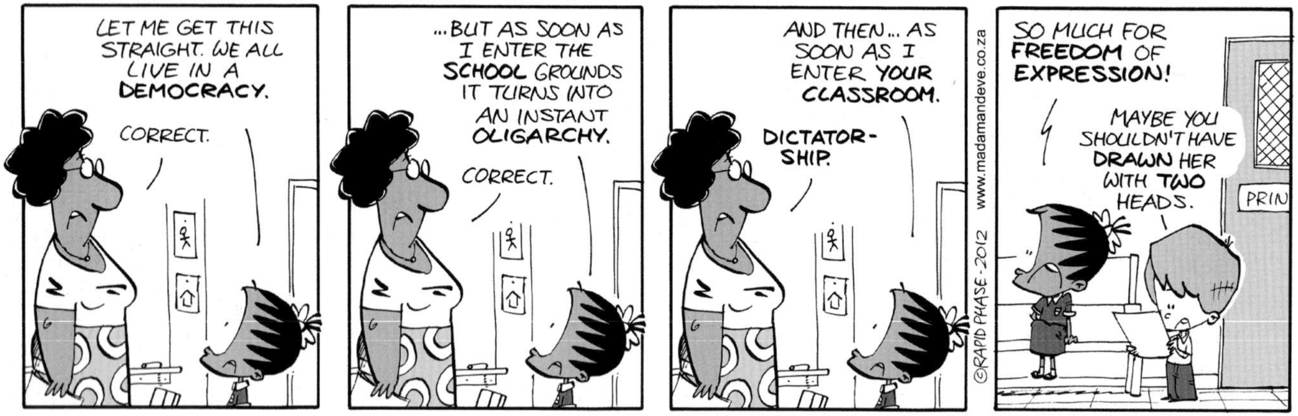
LET ME GET THIS STRAIGHT. WE ALL LIVE IN A DEMOCRACY.
CORRECT.
...BUT AS SOON AS I ENTER THE SCHOOL GROUNDS IT TURNS INTO AN INSTANT OLIGARCHY.
CORRECT.
AND THEN... AS SOON AS I ENTER YOUR CLASSROOM.
DICTATOR-SHIP.
©RAPID PHASE - 2012 www.madamandeve.co.za
SO MUCH FOR FREEDOM OF EXPRESSION!
MAYBE YOU SHOULDN'T HAVE DRAWN HER WITH TWO HEADS.
PRIN

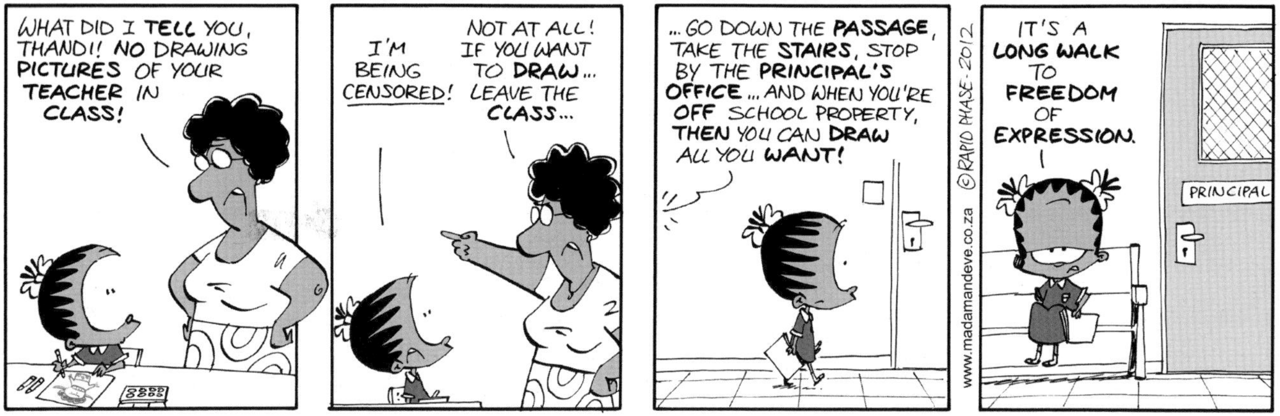
WHAT DID I TELL YOU, THANDI! NO DRAWING PICTURES OF YOUR TEACHER IN CLASS!
I'M BEING CENSORED!
NOT AT ALL! IF YOU WANT TO DRAW... LEAVE THE CLASS...
...GO DOWN THE PASSAGE, TAKE THE STAIRS, STOP BY THE PRINCIPAL'S OFFICE... AND WHEN YOU'RE OFF SCHOOL PROPERTY, THEN YOU CAN DRAW ALL YOU WANT!
©RAPID PHASE - 2012 www.madamandeve.co.za
IT'S A LONG WALK TO FREEDOM OF EXPRESSION.
PRINCIPAL

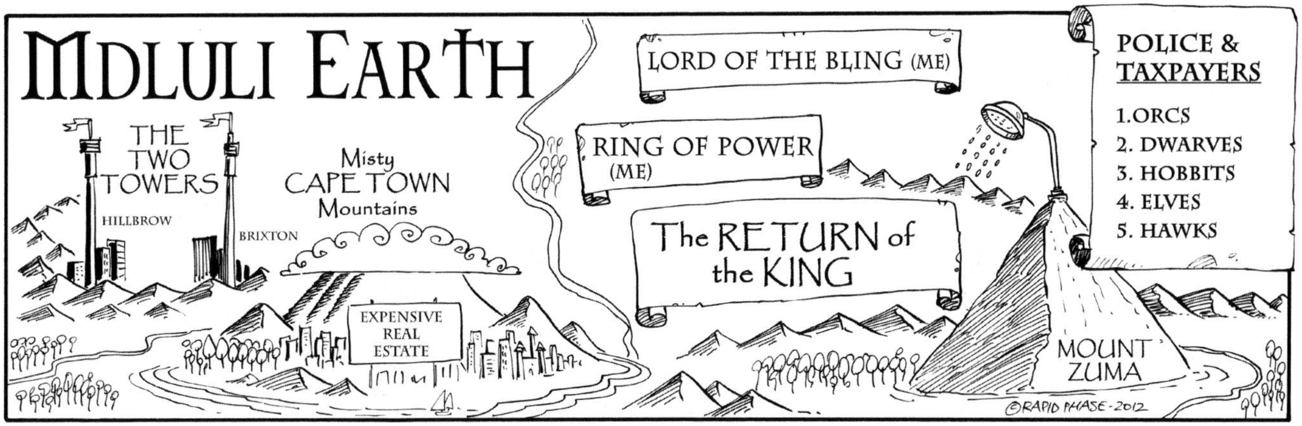

MDLULI EARTH
THE TWO TOWERS
HILLBROW
BRIXTON
Misty CAPE TOWN Mountains
EXPENSIVE REAL ESTATE
LORD OF THE BLING (ME)
RING OF POWER (ME)
The RETURN of the KING
MOUNT ZUMA
POLICE & TAXPAYERS
1.ORCS
2. DWARVES
3. HOBBITS
4. ELVES
5. HAWKS
©RAPID PHASE-2012

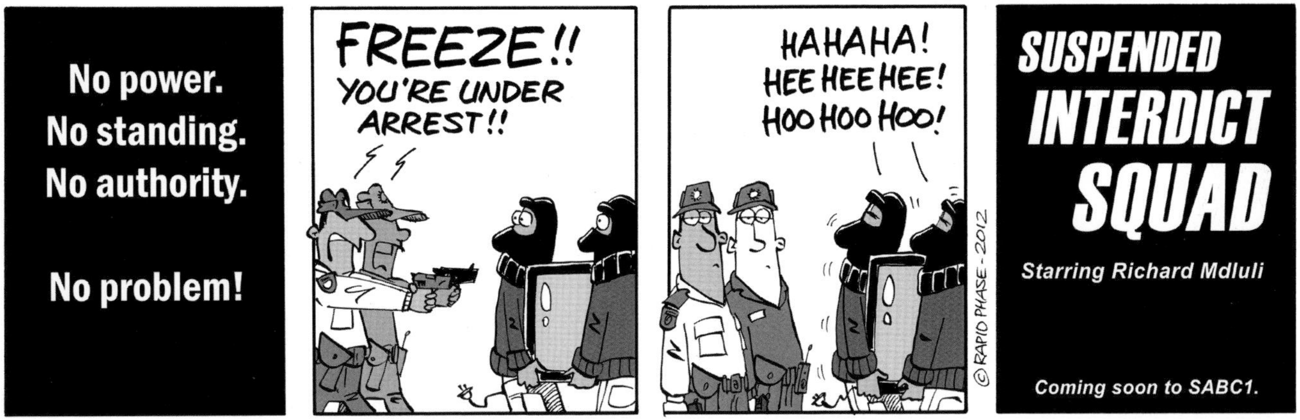

No power.
No standing.
No authority.
No problem!
FREEZE!! YOU'RE UNDER ARREST!!
HAHAHA! HEE HEE HEE! HOO HOO HOO!
© RAPID PHASE - 2012
SUSPENDED INTERDICT SQUAD
Starring Richard Mdluli
Coming soon to SABC1.

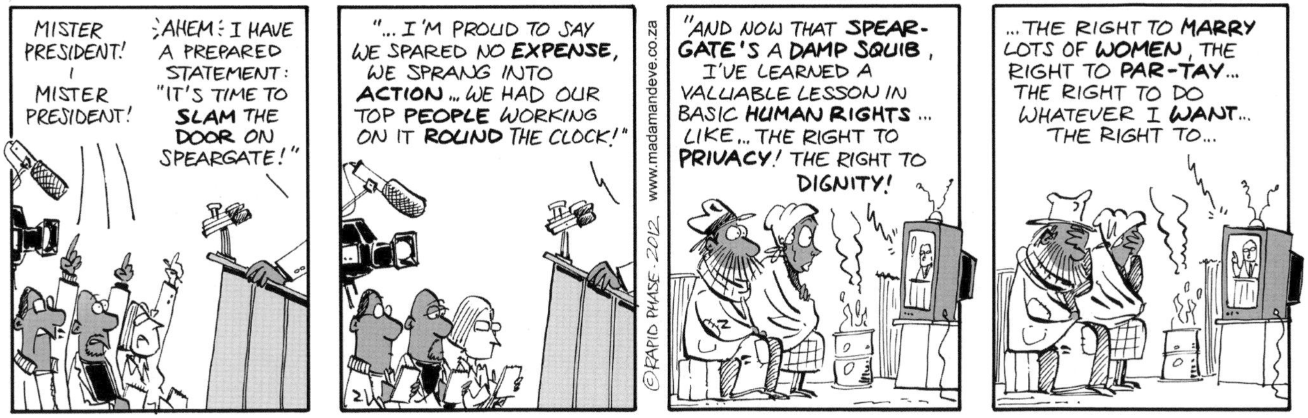

MISTER PRESIDENT! MISTER PRESIDENT!
AHEM: I HAVE A PREPARED STATEMENT: "IT'S TIME TO SLAM THE DOOR ON SPEARGATE!"
"... I'M PROUD TO SAY WE SPARED NO EXPENSE, WE SPRANG INTO ACTION ... WE HAD OUR TOP PEOPLE WORKING ON IT ROUND THE CLOCK!"
www.madamandeve.co.za
© RAPID PHASE - 2012
"AND NOW THAT SPEAR-GATE'S A DAMP SQUIB, I'VE LEARNED A VALUABLE LESSON IN BASIC HUMAN RIGHTS ... LIKE ... THE RIGHT TO PRIVACY! THE RIGHT TO DIGNITY!
... THE RIGHT TO MARRY LOTS OF WOMEN, THE RIGHT TO PAR-TAY... THE RIGHT TO DO WHATEVER I WANT... THE RIGHT TO...

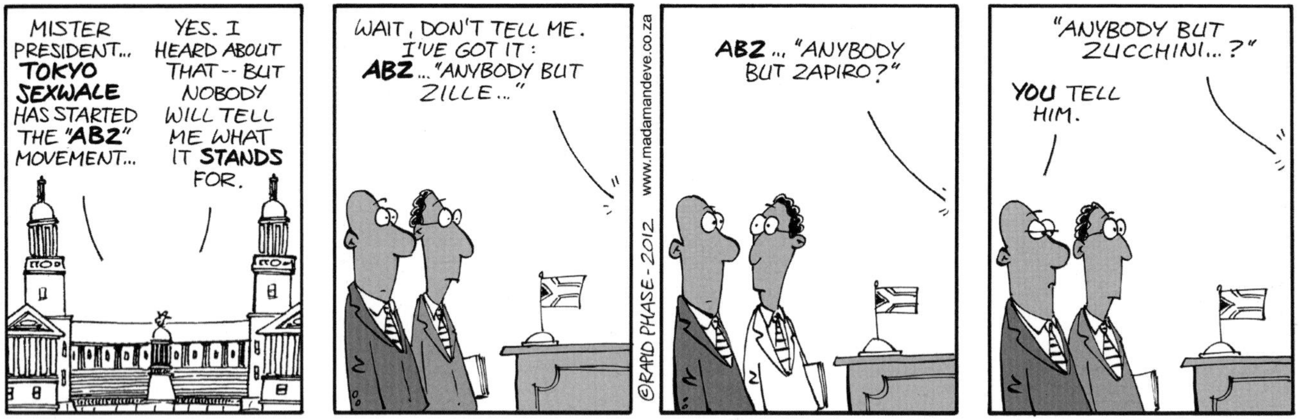
MISTER PRESIDENT... TOKYO SEXWALE HAS STARTED THE "ABZ" MOVEMENT...
YES. I HEARD ABOUT THAT -- BUT NOBODY WILL TELL ME WHAT IT STANDS FOR.
WAIT, DON'T TELL ME. I'VE GOT IT: ABZ... "ANYBODY BUT ZILLE..."
©RAPID PHASE - 2012 www.madamandeve.co.za
ABZ... "ANYBODY BUT ZAPIRO?"
"ANYBODY BUT ZUCCHINI...?"
YOU TELL HIM.

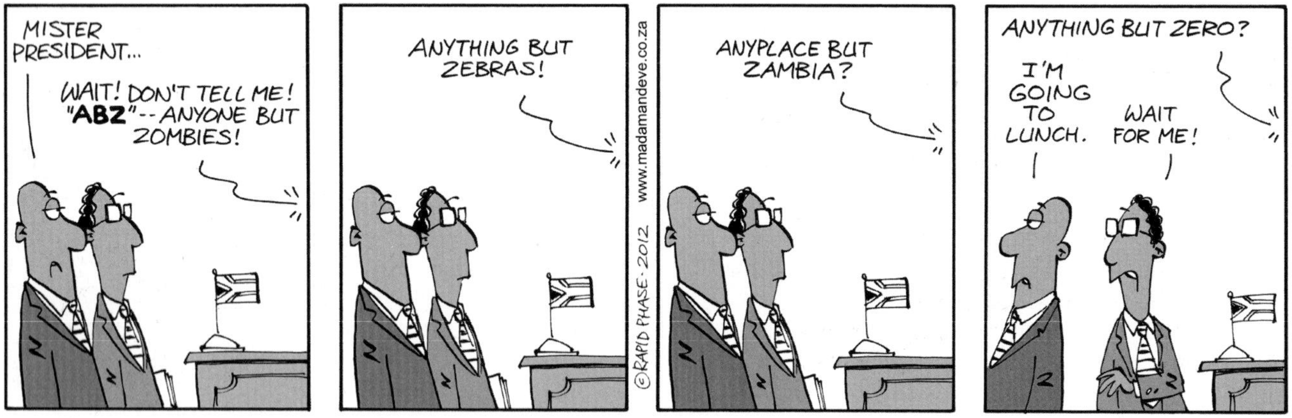
MISTER PRESIDENT...
WAIT! DON'T TELL ME! "ABZ" -- ANYONE BUT ZOMBIES!
ANYTHING BUT ZEBRAS!
©RAPID PHASE · 2012 www.madamandeve.co.za
ANYPLACE BUT ZAMBIA?
ANYTHING BUT ZERO?
I'M GOING TO LUNCH.
WAIT FOR ME!

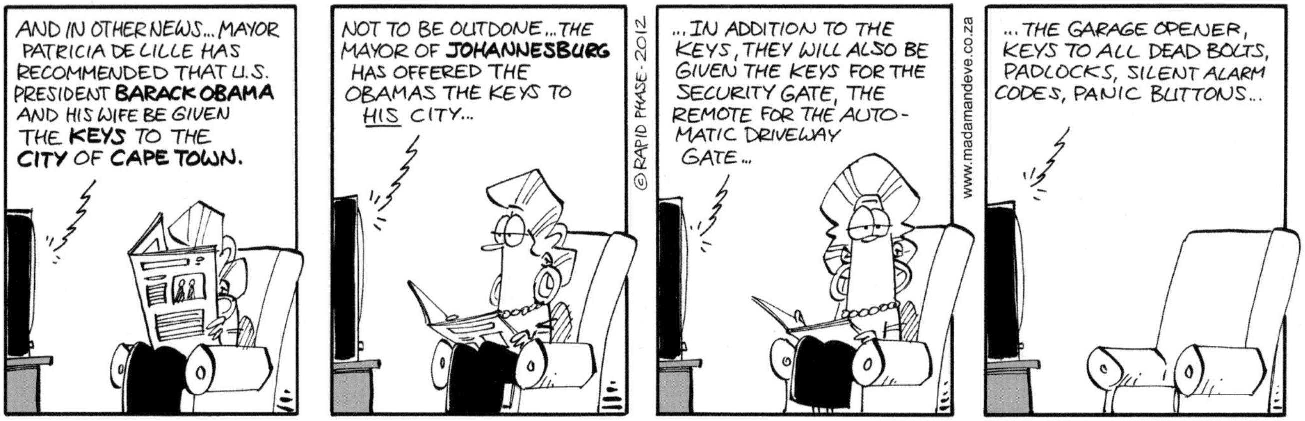
AND IN OTHER NEWS... MAYOR PATRICIA DE LILLE HAS RECOMMENDED THAT U.S. PRESIDENT BARACK OBAMA AND HIS WIFE BE GIVEN THE KEYS TO THE CITY OF CAPE TOWN.
NOT TO BE OUTDONE... THE MAYOR OF JOHANNESBURG HAS OFFERED THE OBAMAS THE KEYS TO HIS CITY...
©RAPID PHASE · 2012
...IN ADDITION TO THE KEYS, THEY WILL ALSO BE GIVEN THE KEYS FOR THE SECURITY GATE, THE REMOTE FOR THE AUTO-MATIC DRIVEWAY GATE...
www.madamandeve.co.za
...THE GARAGE OPENER, KEYS TO ALL DEAD BOLTS, PADLOCKS, SILENT ALARM CODES, PANIC BUTTONS...

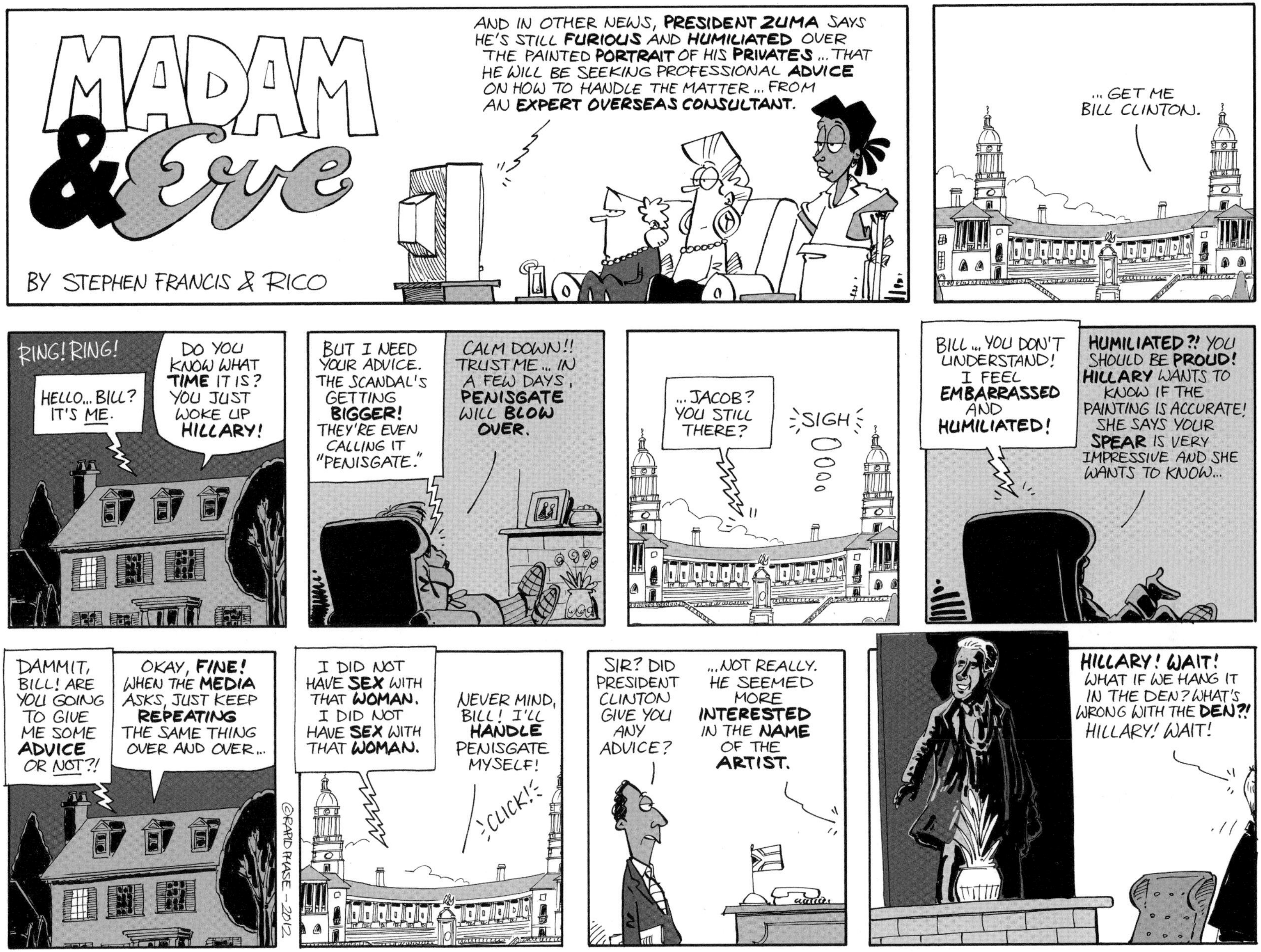
MADAM & Eve
BY STEPHEN FRANCIS & RICO
AND IN OTHER NEWS, PRESIDENT ZUMA SAYS HE'S STILL FURIOUS AND HUMILIATED OVER THE PAINTED PORTRAIT OF HIS PRIVATES ... THAT HE WILL BE SEEKING PROFESSIONAL ADVICE ON HOW TO HANDLE THE MATTER ... FROM AN EXPERT OVERSEAS CONSULTANT.
... GET ME BILL CLINTON.
RING! RING!
HELLO... BILL? IT'S ME.
DO YOU KNOW WHAT TIME IT IS? YOU JUST WOKE UP HILLARY!
BUT I NEED YOUR ADVICE. THE SCANDAL'S GETTING BIGGER! THEY'RE EVEN CALLING IT "PENISGATE."
CALM DOWN!! TRUST ME ... IN A FEW DAYS, PENISGATE WILL BLOW OVER.
... JACOB? YOU STILL THERE?
SIGH
BILL ... YOU DON'T UNDERSTAND! I FEEL EMBARRASSED AND HUMILIATED!
HUMILIATED?! YOU SHOULD BE PROUD! HILLARY WANTS TO KNOW IF THE PAINTING IS ACCURATE! SHE SAYS YOUR SPEAR IS VERY IMPRESSIVE AND SHE WANTS TO KNOW...
DAMMIT, BILL! ARE YOU GOING TO GIVE ME SOME ADVICE OR NOT?!
OKAY, FINE! WHEN THE MEDIA ASKS, JUST KEEP REPEATING THE SAME THING OVER AND OVER...
©RAPID PHASE - 2012
I DID NOT HAVE SEX WITH THAT WOMAN. I DID NOT HAVE SEX WITH THAT WOMAN.
NEVER MIND, BILL! I'LL HANDLE PENISGATE MYSELF!
CLICK!
SIR? DID PRESIDENT CLINTON GIVE YOU ANY ADVICE?
...NOT REALLY. HE SEEMED MORE INTERESTED IN THE NAME OF THE ARTIST.
HILLARY! WAIT! WHAT IF WE HANG IT IN THE DEN? WHAT'S WRONG WITH THE DEN?! HILLARY! WAIT!

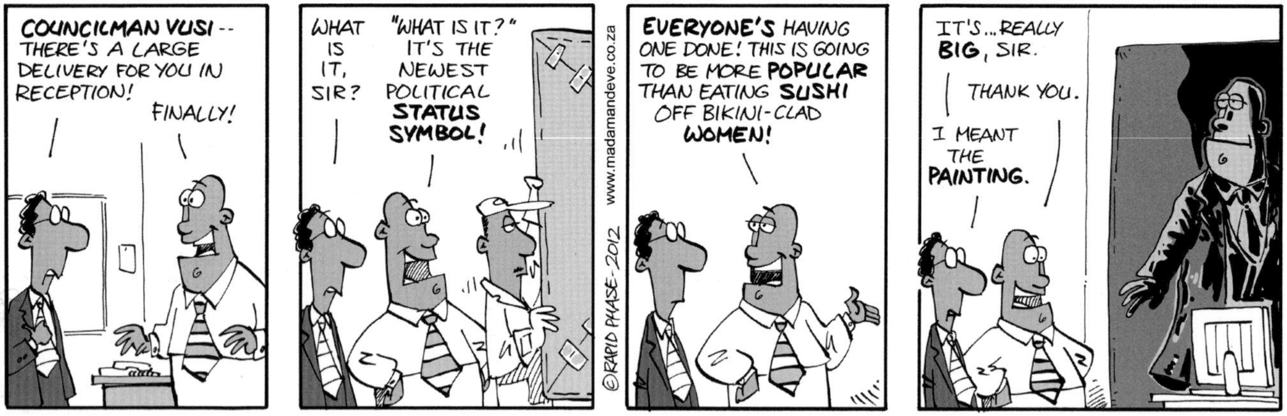
COUNCILMAN VUSI -- THERE'S A LARGE DELIVERY FOR YOU IN RECEPTION!
FINALLY!
WHAT IS IT, SIR?
"WHAT IS IT?" IT'S THE NEWEST POLITICAL STATUS SYMBOL!
EVERYONE'S HAVING ONE DONE! THIS IS GOING TO BE MORE POPULAR THAN EATING SUSHI OFF BIKINI-CLAD WOMEN!
IT'S ... REALLY BIG, SIR.
THANK YOU.
I MEANT THE PAINTING.
©RAPID PHASE · 2012 www.madamandeve.co.za

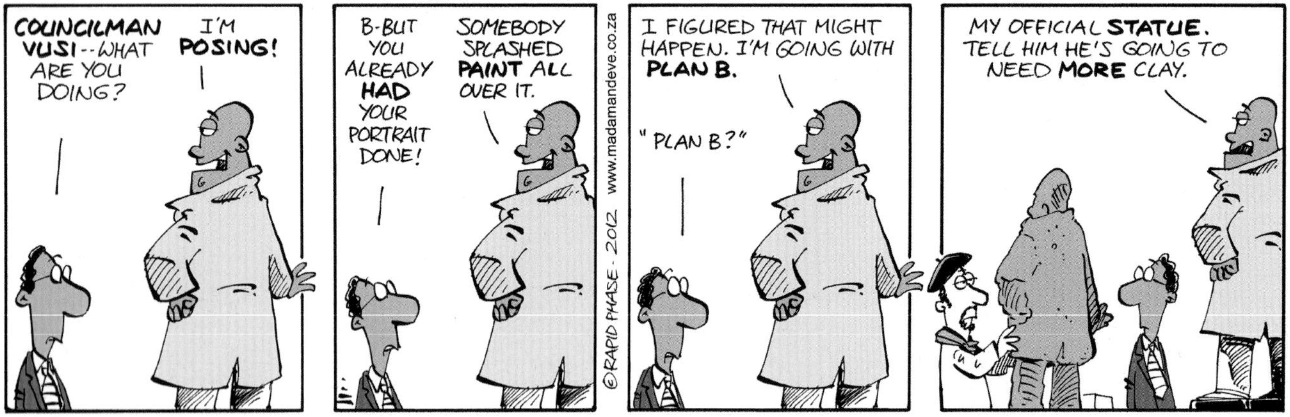
COUNCILMAN VUSI -- WHAT ARE YOU DOING?
I'M POSING!
B-BUT YOU ALREADY HAD YOUR PORTRAIT DONE!
SOMEBODY SPLASHED PAINT ALL OVER IT.
I FIGURED THAT MIGHT HAPPEN. I'M GOING WITH PLAN B.
"PLAN B?"
MY OFFICIAL STATUE. TELL HIM HE'S GOING TO NEED MORE CLAY.
©RAPID PHASE · 2012 www.madamandeve.co.za

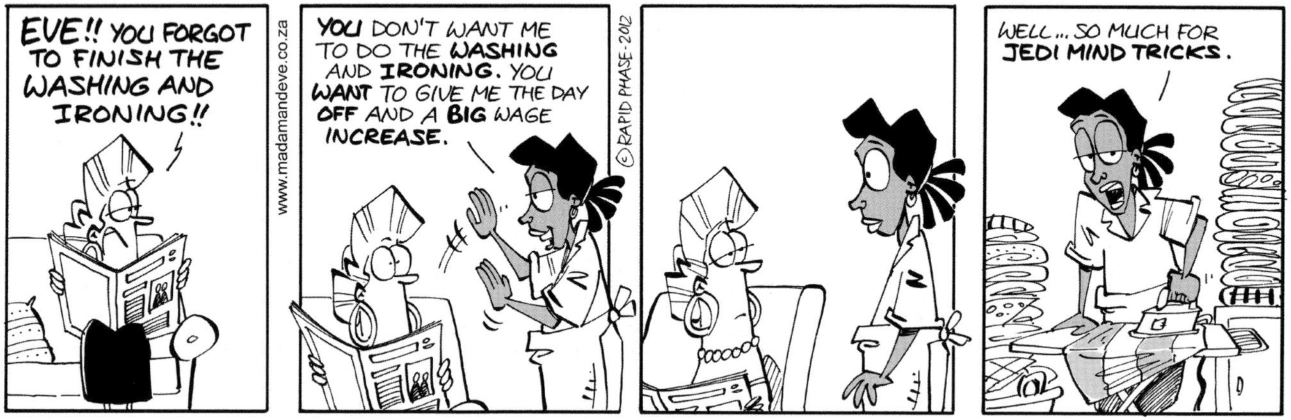
EVE!! YOU FORGOT TO FINISH THE WASHING AND IRONING!!
YOU DON'T WANT ME TO DO THE WASHING AND IRONING. YOU WANT TO GIVE ME THE DAY OFF AND A BIG WAGE INCREASE.
WELL ... SO MUCH FOR JEDI MIND TRICKS.
www.madamandeve.co.za
©RAPID PHASE · 2012

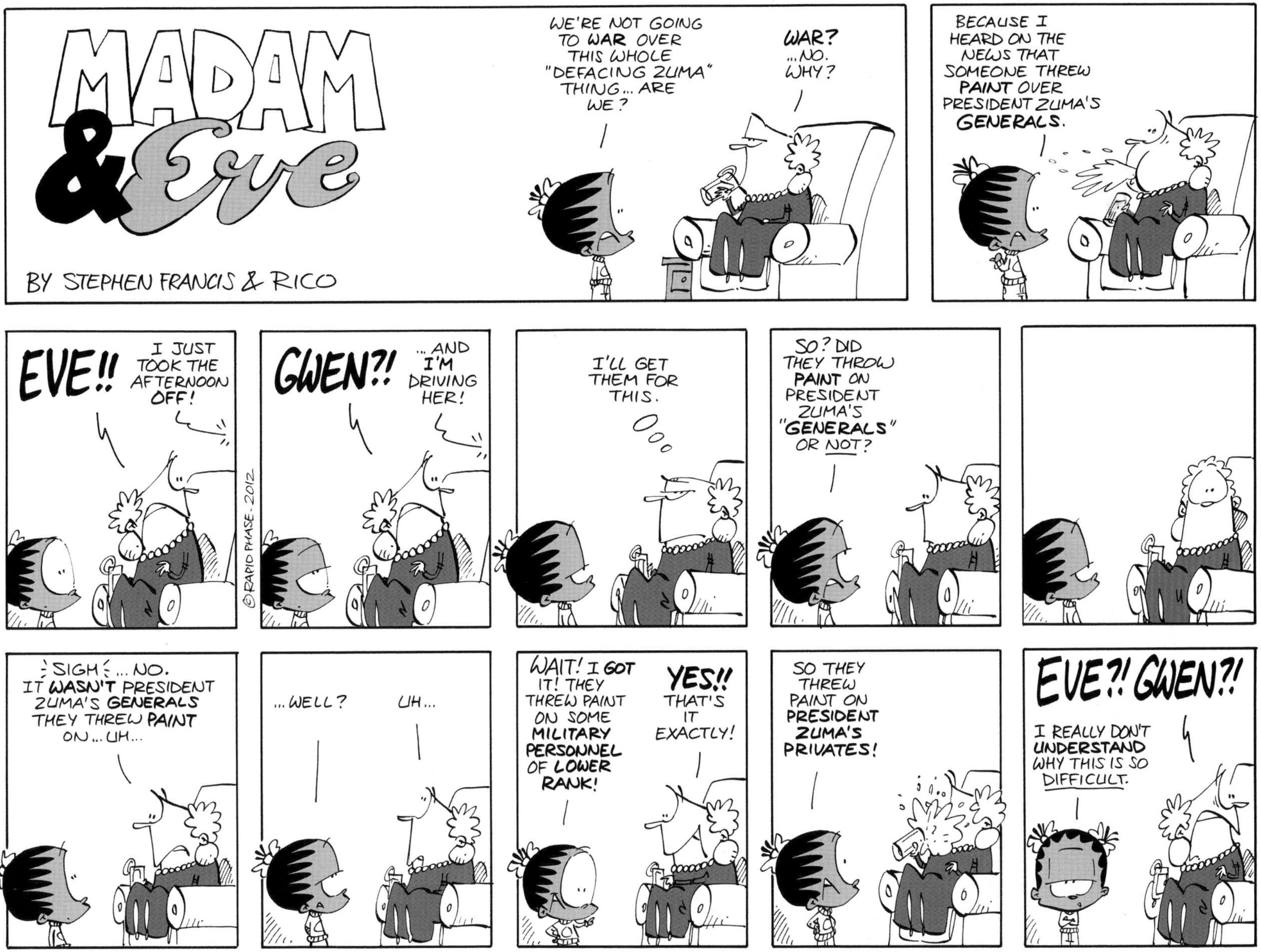
MADAM & Eve
BY STEPHEN FRANCIS & RICO
WE'RE NOT GOING TO WAR OVER THIS WHOLE "DEFACING ZUMA" THING... ARE WE?
WAR? ...NO. WHY?
BECAUSE I HEARD ON THE NEWS THAT SOMEONE THREW PAINT OVER PRESIDENT ZUMA'S GENERALS.
EVE!!
I JUST TOOK THE AFTERNOON OFF!
© RAPID PHASE · 2012
GWEN?!
...AND I'M DRIVING HER!
I'LL GET THEM FOR THIS.
SO? DID THEY THROW PAINT ON PRESIDENT ZUMA'S "GENERALS" OR NOT?
SIGH ... NO. IT WASN'T PRESIDENT ZUMA'S GENERALS THEY THREW PAINT ON... UH...
...WELL?
UH...
WAIT! I GOT IT! THEY THREW PAINT ON SOME MILITARY PERSONNEL OF LOWER RANK!
YES!! THAT'S IT EXACTLY!
SO THEY THREW PAINT ON PRESIDENT ZUMA'S PRIVATES!
EVE?! GWEN?!
I REALLY DON'T UNDERSTAND WHY THIS IS SO DIFFICULT.

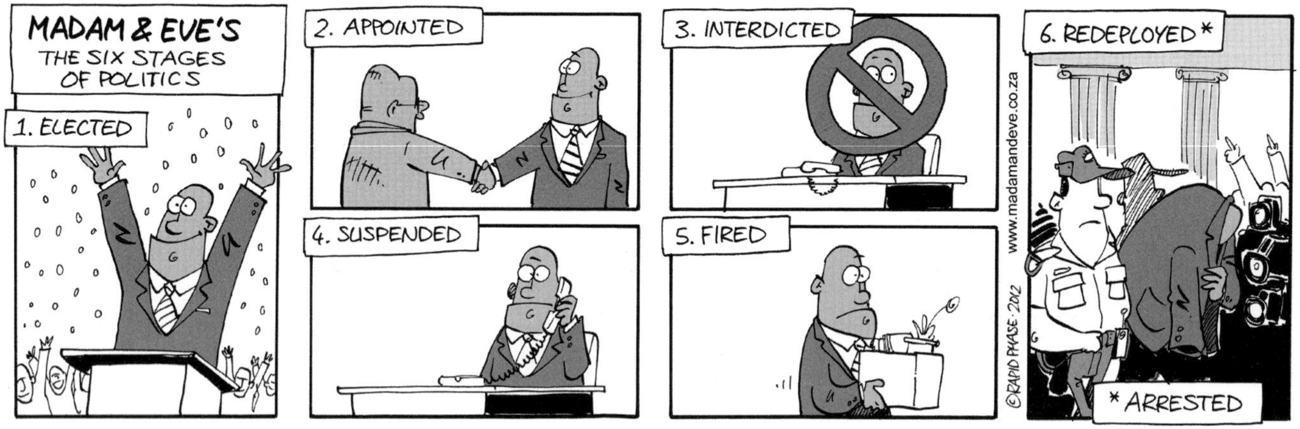
MADAM & EVE'S
THE SIX STAGES OF POLITICS
1. ELECTED
2. APPOINTED
3. INTERDICTED
6. REDEPLOYED *
4. SUSPENDED
5. FIRED
www.madamandeve.co.za
©RAPID PHASE · 2012
* ARRESTED

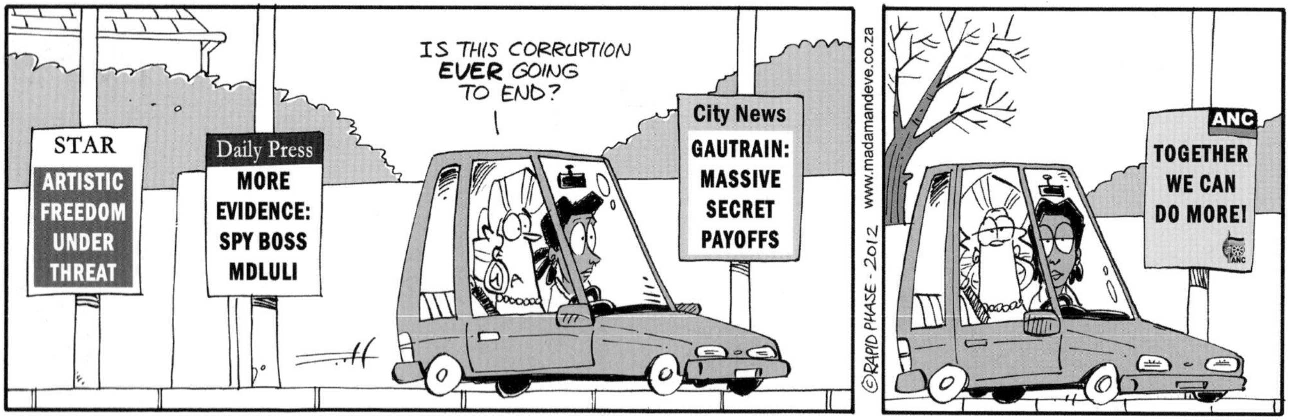
STAR
ARTISTIC FREEDOM UNDER THREAT
Daily Press
MORE EVIDENCE: SPY BOSS MDLULI
IS THIS CORRUPTION EVER GOING TO END?
City News
GAUTRAIN: MASSIVE SECRET PAYOFFS
www.madamandeve.co.za
©RAPID PHASE - 2012
ANC
TOGETHER WE CAN DO MORE!

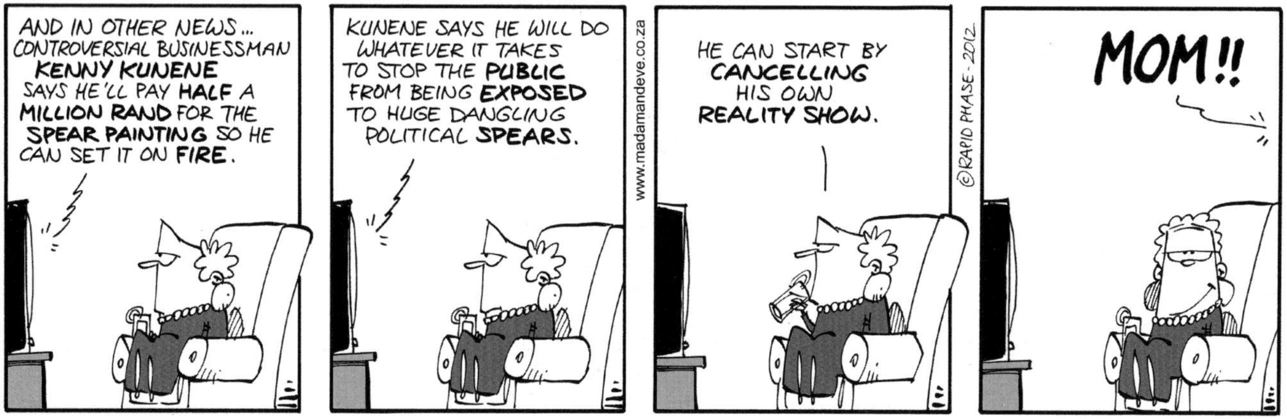
AND IN OTHER NEWS... CONTROVERSIAL BUSINESSMAN KENNY KUNENE SAYS HE'LL PAY HALF A MILLION RAND FOR THE SPEAR PAINTING SO HE CAN SET IT ON FIRE.
KUNENE SAYS HE WILL DO WHATEVER IT TAKES TO STOP THE PUBLIC FROM BEING EXPOSED TO HUGE DANGLING POLITICAL SPEARS.
www.madamandeve.co.za
HE CAN START BY CANCELLING HIS OWN REALITY SHOW.
©RAPID PHASE · 2012
MOM!!

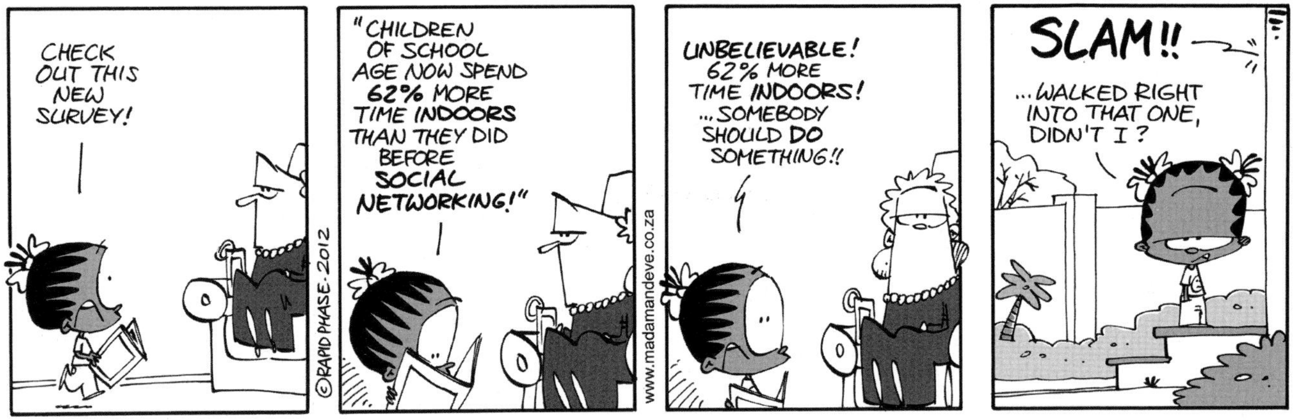
CHECK OUT THIS NEW SURVEY!
©RAPID PHASE · 2012
"CHILDREN OF SCHOOL AGE NOW SPEND **62%** MORE TIME **INDOORS** THAN THEY DID BEFORE **SOCIAL NETWORKING!"**
www.madamandeve.co.za
UNBELIEVABLE! 62% MORE TIME **INDOORS!** ...SOMEBODY SHOULD **DO** SOMETHING!!
SLAM!!
...WALKED RIGHT INTO THAT ONE, DIDN'T I?

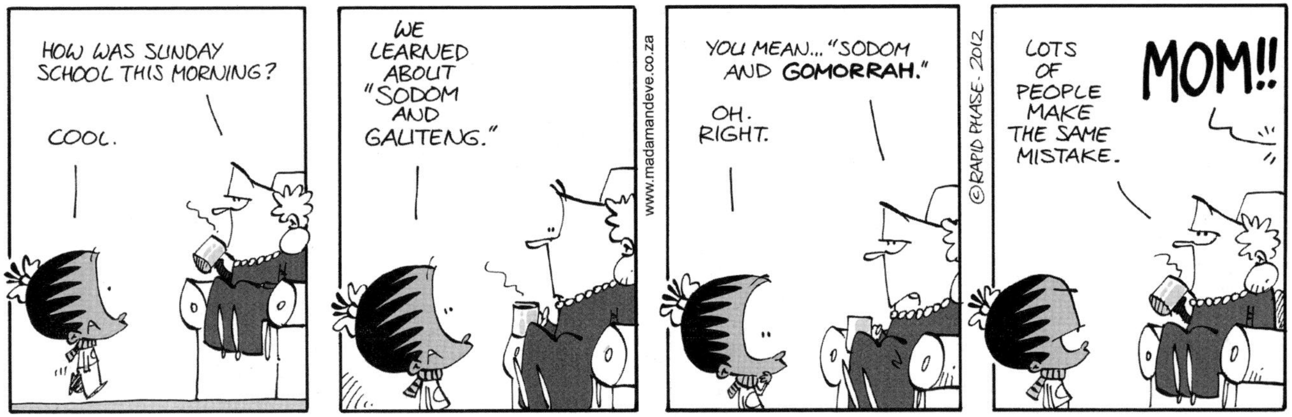
HOW WAS SUNDAY SCHOOL THIS MORNING?
COOL.
WE LEARNED ABOUT "SODOM AND GAUTENG."
www.madamandeve.co.za
YOU MEAN... "SODOM AND **GOMORRAH."**
OH. RIGHT.
©RAPID PHASE · 2012
LOTS OF PEOPLE MAKE THE SAME MISTAKE.
MOM!!

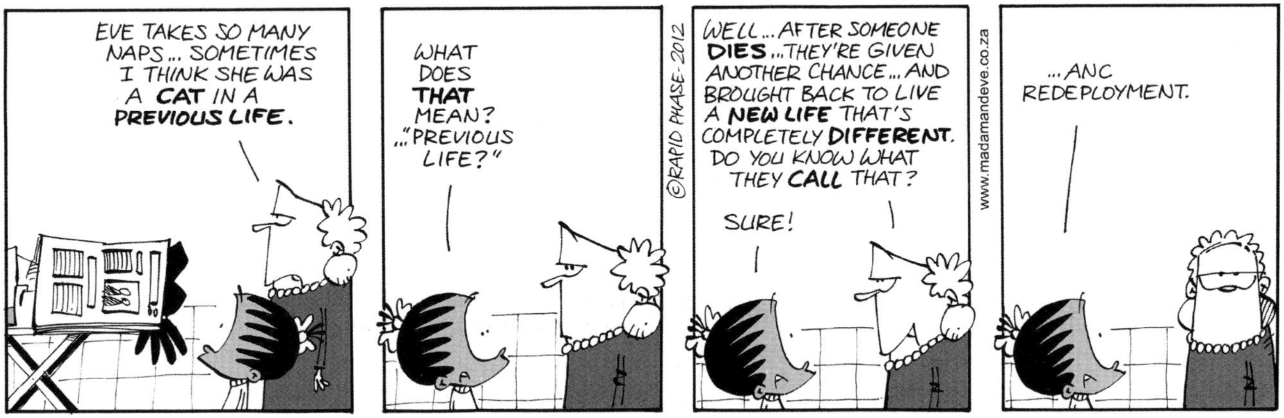
EVE TAKES SO MANY NAPS... SOMETIMES I THINK SHE WAS A **CAT** IN A **PREVIOUS LIFE**.
WHAT DOES **THAT** MEAN? ..."PREVIOUS LIFE?"
©RAPID PHASE · 2012
WELL... AFTER SOMEONE **DIES**...THEY'RE GIVEN ANOTHER CHANCE... AND BROUGHT BACK TO LIVE A **NEW LIFE** THAT'S COMPLETELY **DIFFERENT**. DO YOU KNOW WHAT THEY **CALL** THAT?
SURE!
www.madamandeve.co.za
...ANC REDEPLOYMENT.

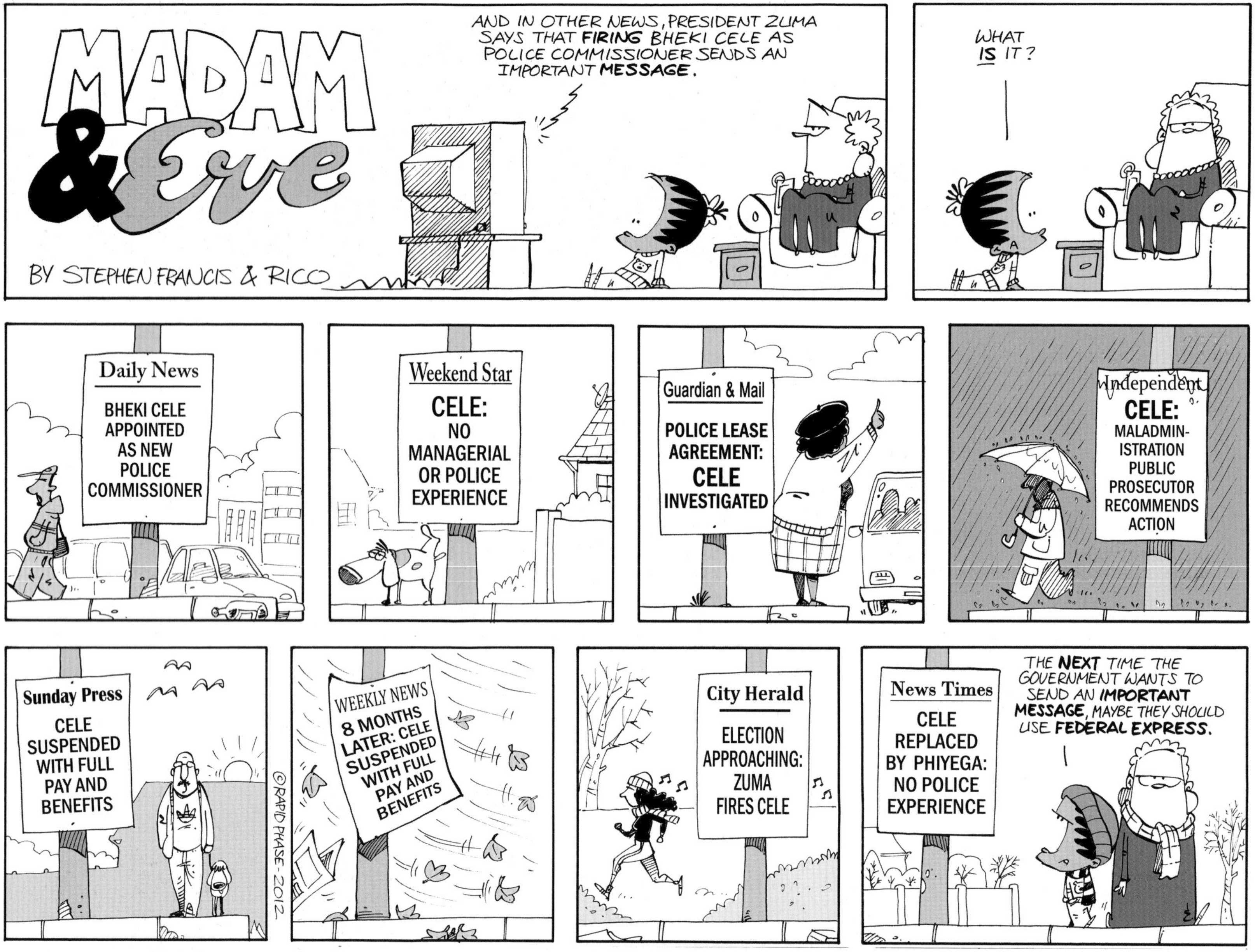
MADAM & Eve
BY STEPHEN FRANCIS & RICO
AND IN OTHER NEWS, PRESIDENT ZUMA SAYS THAT FIRING BHEKI CELE AS POLICE COMMISSIONER SENDS AN IMPORTANT MESSAGE.
WHAT IS IT?
Daily News
BHEKI CELE APPOINTED AS NEW POLICE COMMISSIONER
Weekend Star
CELE: NO MANAGERIAL OR POLICE EXPERIENCE
Guardian & Mail
POLICE LEASE AGREEMENT: CELE INVESTIGATED
Independent
CELE: MALADMIN-ISTRATION PUBLIC PROSECUTOR RECOMMENDS ACTION
Sunday Press
CELE SUSPENDED WITH FULL PAY AND BENEFITS
©RAPID PHASE-2012
WEEKLY NEWS
8 MONTHS LATER: CELE SUSPENDED WITH FULL PAY AND BENEFITS
City Herald
ELECTION APPROACHING: ZUMA FIRES CELE
News Times
CELE REPLACED BY PHIYEGA: NO POLICE EXPERIENCE
THE NEXT TIME THE GOVERNMENT WANTS TO SEND AN IMPORTANT MESSAGE, MAYBE THEY SHOULD USE FEDERAL EXPRESS.

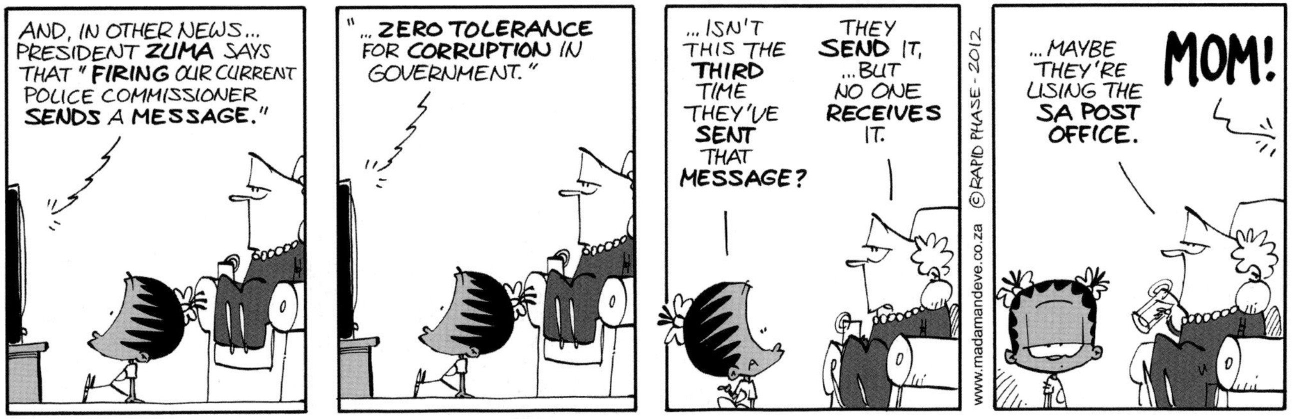
AND, IN OTHER NEWS... PRESIDENT ZUMA SAYS THAT "FIRING OUR CURRENT POLICE COMMISSIONER SENDS A MESSAGE."
"... ZERO TOLERANCE FOR CORRUPTION IN GOVERNMENT."
... ISN'T THIS THE THIRD TIME THEY'VE SENT THAT MESSAGE?
THEY SEND IT, ...BUT NO ONE RECEIVES IT.
© RAPID PHASE - 2012
www.madamandeve.co.za
... MAYBE THEY'RE USING THE SA POST OFFICE.
MOM!

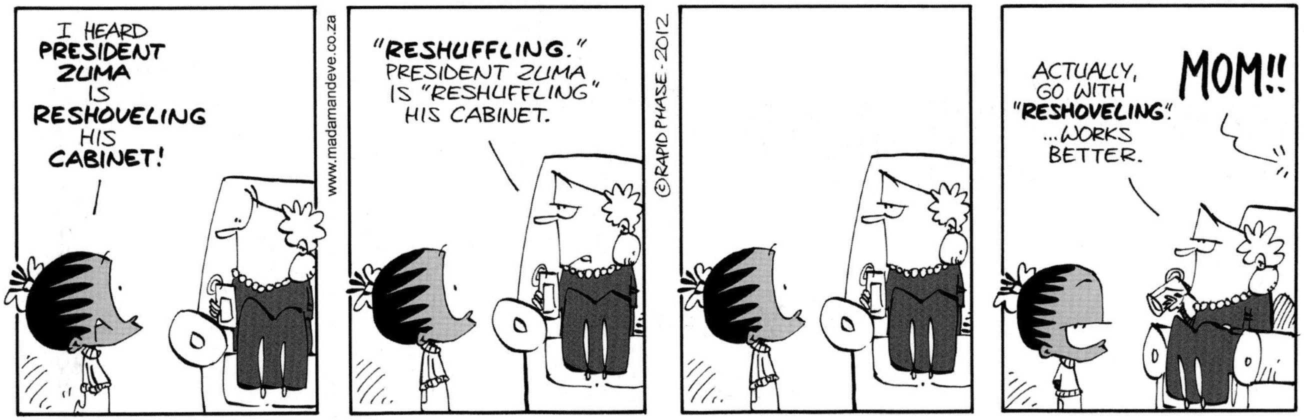
I HEARD PRESIDENT ZUMA IS RESHOVELING HIS CABINET!
www.madamandeve.co.za
"RESHUFFLING." PRESIDENT ZUMA IS "RESHUFFLING" HIS CABINET.
© RAPID PHASE - 2012
ACTUALLY, GO WITH "RESHOVELING". ...WORKS BETTER.
MOM!!

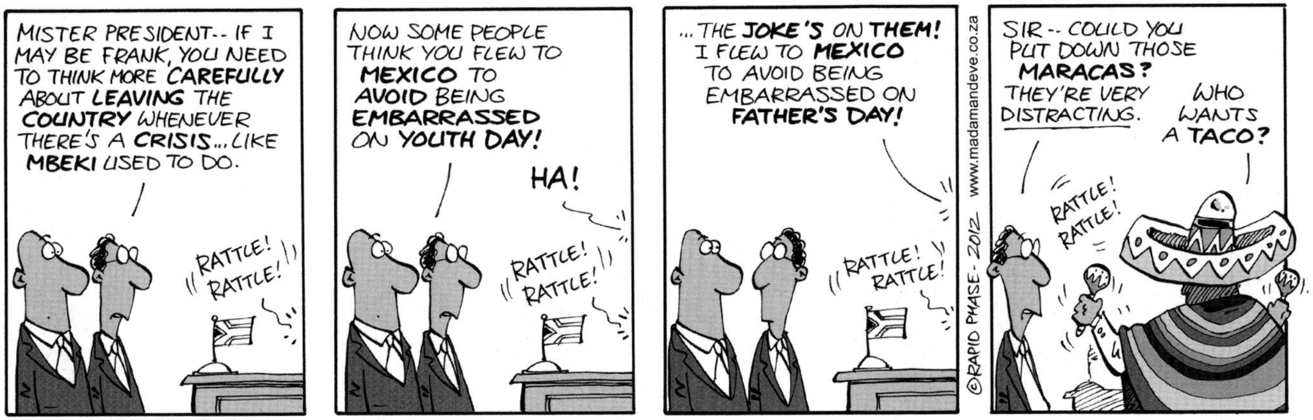
MISTER PRESIDENT-- IF I MAY BE FRANK, YOU NEED TO THINK MORE CAREFULLY ABOUT LEAVING THE COUNTRY WHENEVER THERE'S A CRISIS... LIKE MBEKI USED TO DO.
RATTLE! RATTLE!
NOW SOME PEOPLE THINK YOU FLEW TO MEXICO TO AVOID BEING EMBARRASSED ON YOUTH DAY!
HA!
RATTLE! RATTLE!
... THE JOKE'S ON THEM! I FLEW TO MEXICO TO AVOID BEING EMBARRASSED ON FATHER'S DAY!
RATTLE! RATTLE!
www.madamandeve.co.za
© RAPID PHASE - 2012
SIR -- COULD YOU PUT DOWN THOSE MARACAS? THEY'RE VERY DISTRACTING.
WHO WANTS A TACO?
RATTLE! RATTLE!

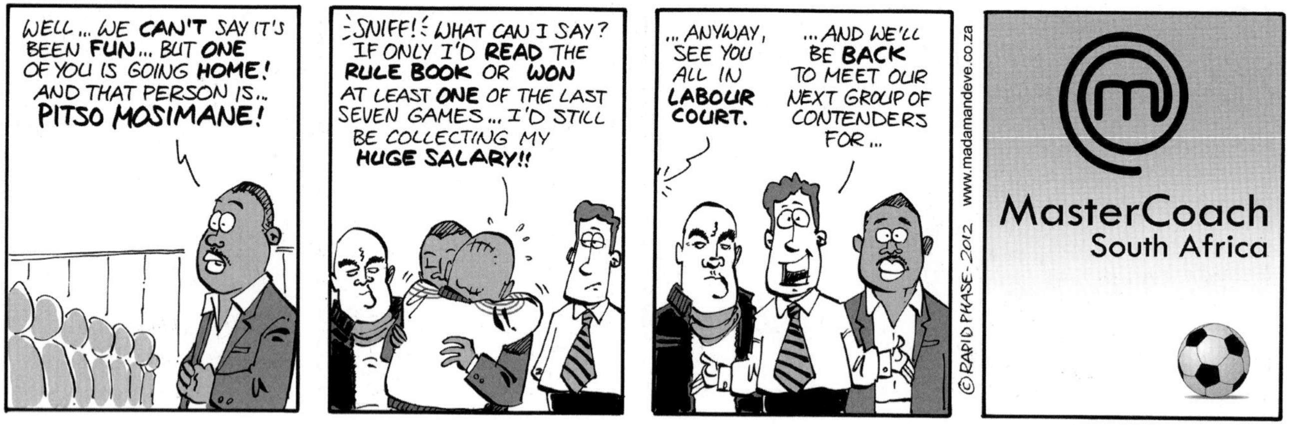
WELL... WE CAN'T SAY IT'S BEEN FUN... BUT ONE OF YOU IS GOING HOME! AND THAT PERSON IS.. PITSO MOSIMANE!
SNIFF! WHAT CAN I SAY? IF ONLY I'D READ THE RULE BOOK OR WON AT LEAST ONE OF THE LAST SEVEN GAMES... I'D STILL BE COLLECTING MY HUGE SALARY!!
... ANYWAY, SEE YOU ALL IN LABOUR COURT.
... AND WE'LL BE BACK TO MEET OUR NEXT GROUP OF CONTENDERS FOR...
©RAPID PHASE · 2012 www.madamandeve.co.za
MasterCoach
South Africa

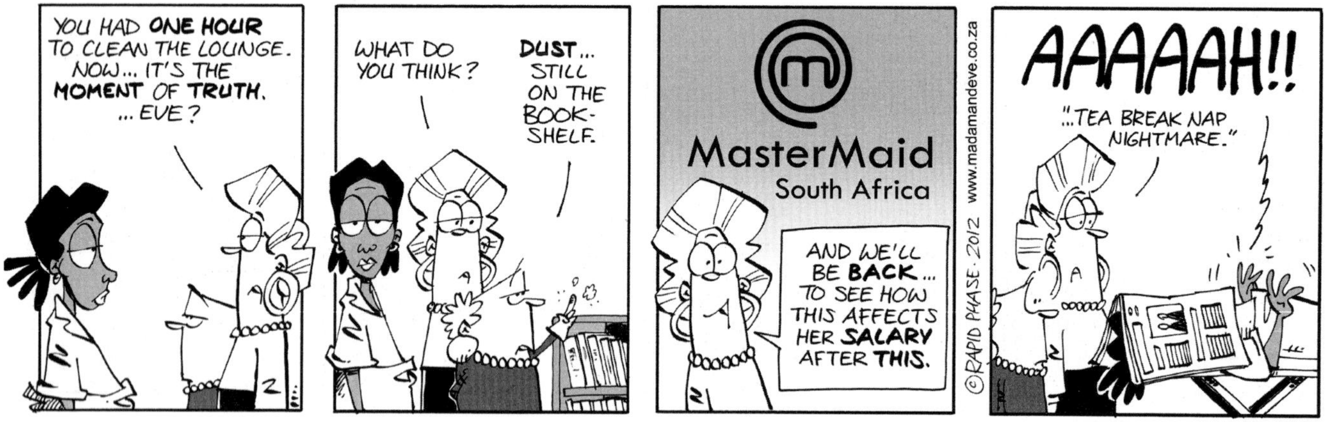
YOU HAD ONE HOUR TO CLEAN THE LOUNGE. NOW... IT'S THE MOMENT OF TRUTH. ... EVE?
WHAT DO YOU THINK?
DUST... STILL ON THE BOOK-SHELF.
MasterMaid
South Africa
AND WE'LL BE BACK... TO SEE HOW THIS AFFECTS HER SALARY AFTER THIS.
©RAPID PHASE · 2012 www.madamandeve.co.za
AAAAAH!!
"...TEA BREAK NAP NIGHTMARE."

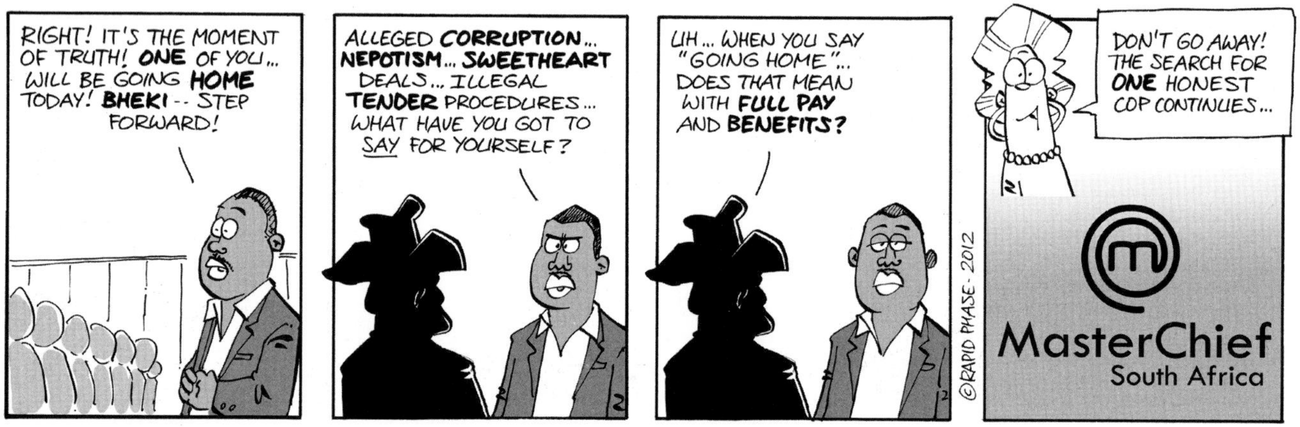
RIGHT! IT'S THE MOMENT OF TRUTH! ONE OF YOU... WILL BE GOING HOME TODAY! BHEKI -- STEP FORWARD!
ALLEGED CORRUPTION... NEPOTISM... SWEETHEART DEALS... ILLEGAL TENDER PROCEDURES... WHAT HAVE YOU GOT TO SAY FOR YOURSELF?
UH... WHEN YOU SAY "GOING HOME"... DOES THAT MEAN WITH FULL PAY AND BENEFITS?
©RAPID PHASE · 2012
DON'T GO AWAY! THE SEARCH FOR ONE HONEST COP CONTINUES...
MasterChief
South Africa

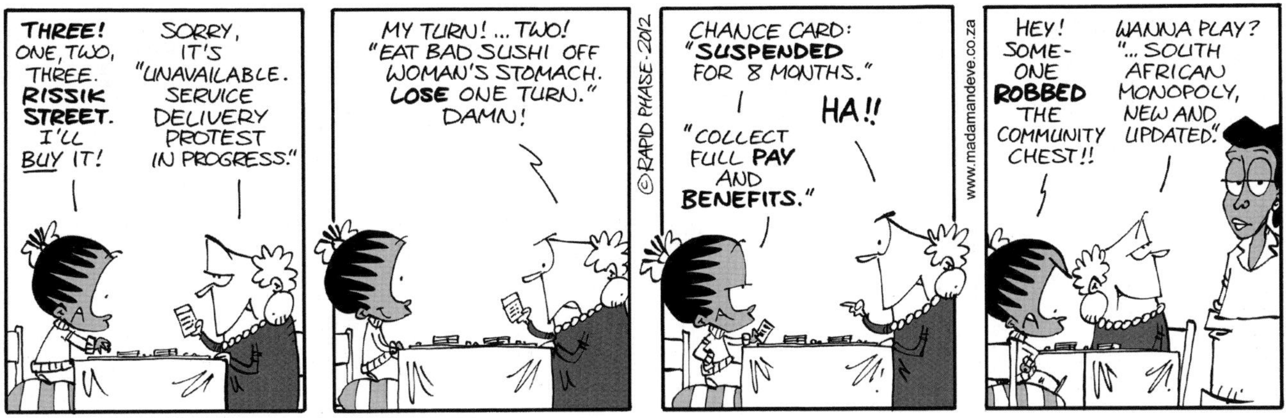
THREE! ONE, TWO, THREE. RISSIK STREET. I'LL BUY IT!
SORRY, IT'S "UNAVAILABLE. SERVICE DELIVERY PROTEST IN PROGRESS."
MY TURN! ... TWO! "EAT BAD SUSHI OFF WOMAN'S STOMACH. LOSE ONE TURN." DAMN!
©RAPID PHASE-2012
CHANCE CARD: "SUSPENDED FOR 8 MONTHS."
"COLLECT FULL PAY AND BENEFITS."
HA!!
www.madamandeve.co.za
HEY! SOME-ONE ROBBED THE COMMUNITY CHEST!!
WANNA PLAY? "... SOUTH AFRICAN MONOPOLY, NEW AND UPDATED."

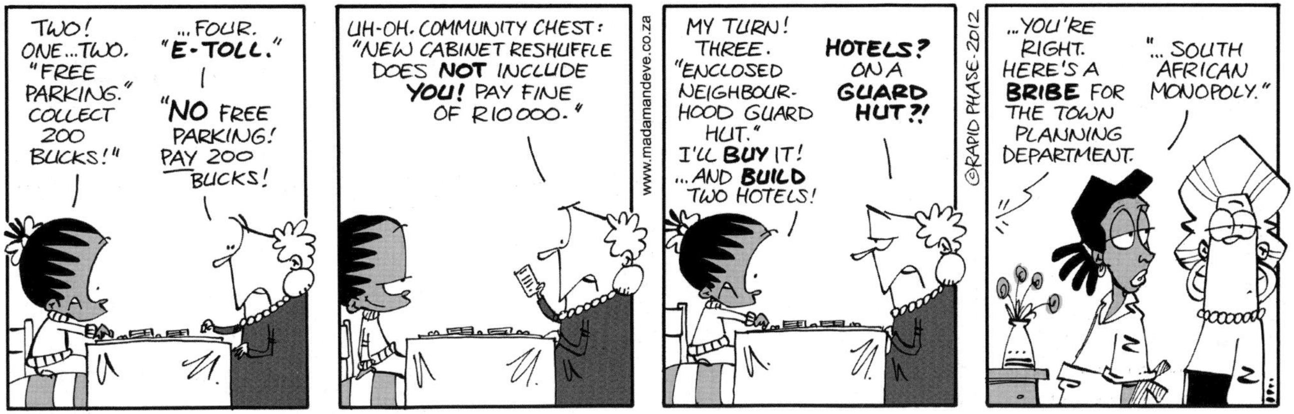
TWO! ONE...TWO. "FREE PARKING." COLLECT 200 BUCKS!"
...FOUR. "E-TOLL."
"NO FREE PARKING! PAY 200 BUCKS!
UH-OH. COMMUNITY CHEST: "NEW CABINET RESHUFFLE DOES NOT INCLUDE YOU! PAY FINE OF R10 000."
www.madamandeve.co.za
MY TURN! THREE. "ENCLOSED NEIGHBOUR-HOOD GUARD HUT." I'LL BUY IT! ...AND BUILD TWO HOTELS!
HOTELS? ON A GUARD HUT?!
©RAPID PHASE-2012
...YOU'RE RIGHT. HERE'S A BRIBE FOR THE TOWN PLANNING DEPARTMENT.
"... SOUTH AFRICAN MONOPOLY."

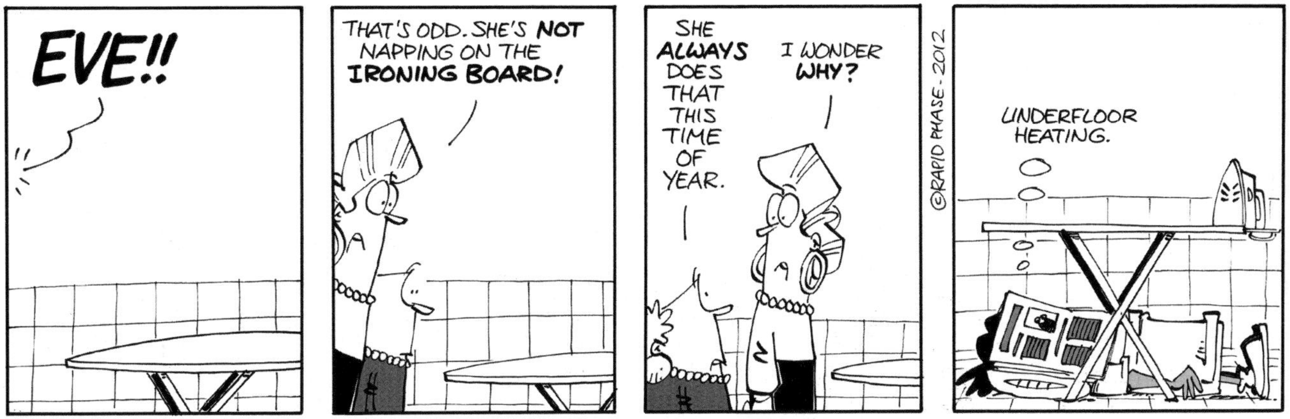
EVE!!
THAT'S ODD. SHE'S NOT NAPPING ON THE IRONING BOARD!
SHE ALWAYS DOES THAT THIS TIME OF YEAR.
I WONDER WHY?
©RAPID PHASE-2012
UNDERFLOOR HEATING.

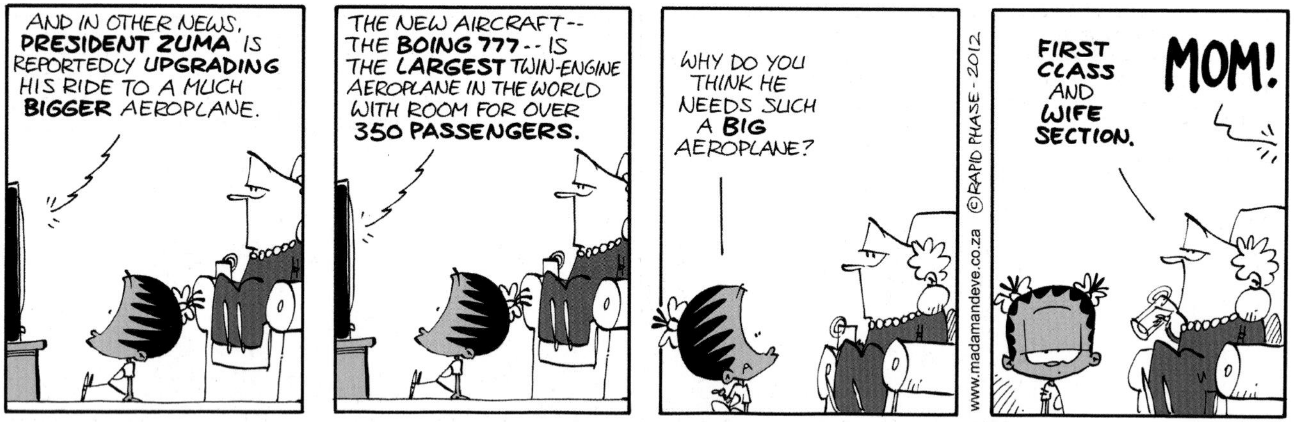
AND IN OTHER NEWS, PRESIDENT ZUMA IS REPORTEDLY UPGRADING HIS RIDE TO A MUCH BIGGER AEROPLANE.
THE NEW AIRCRAFT -- THE BOING 777 -- IS THE LARGEST TWIN-ENGINE AEROPLANE IN THE WORLD WITH ROOM FOR OVER 350 PASSENGERS.
WHY DO YOU THINK HE NEEDS SUCH A BIG AEROPLANE?
www.madamandeve.co.za ©RAPID PHASE - 2012
FIRST CLASS AND WIFE SECTION.
MOM!

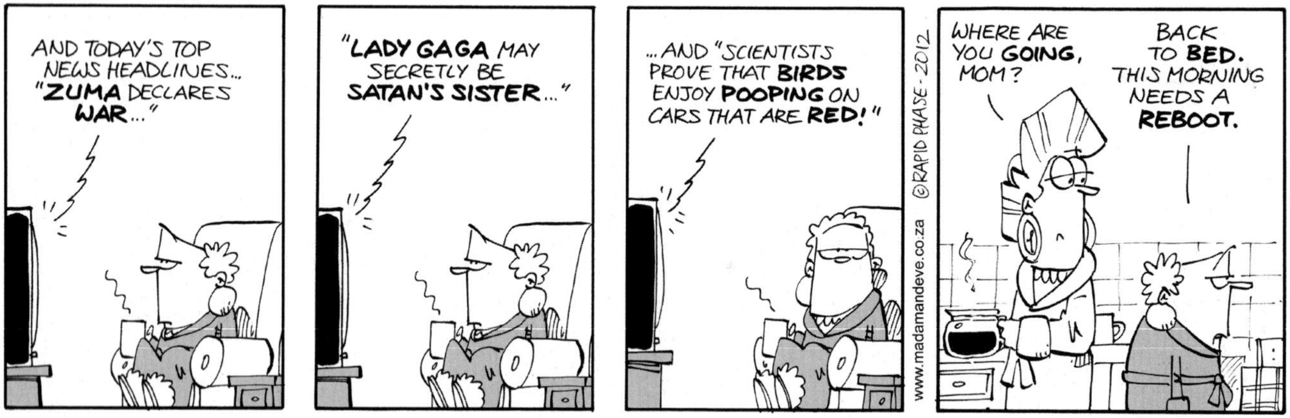
AND TODAY'S TOP NEWS HEADLINES... "ZUMA DECLARES WAR..."
"LADY GAGA MAY SECRETLY BE SATAN'S SISTER..."
...AND "SCIENTISTS PROVE THAT BIRDS ENJOY POOPING ON CARS THAT ARE RED!"
www.madamandeve.co.za ©RAPID PHASE - 2012
WHERE ARE YOU GOING, MOM?
BACK TO BED. THIS MORNING NEEDS A REBOOT.

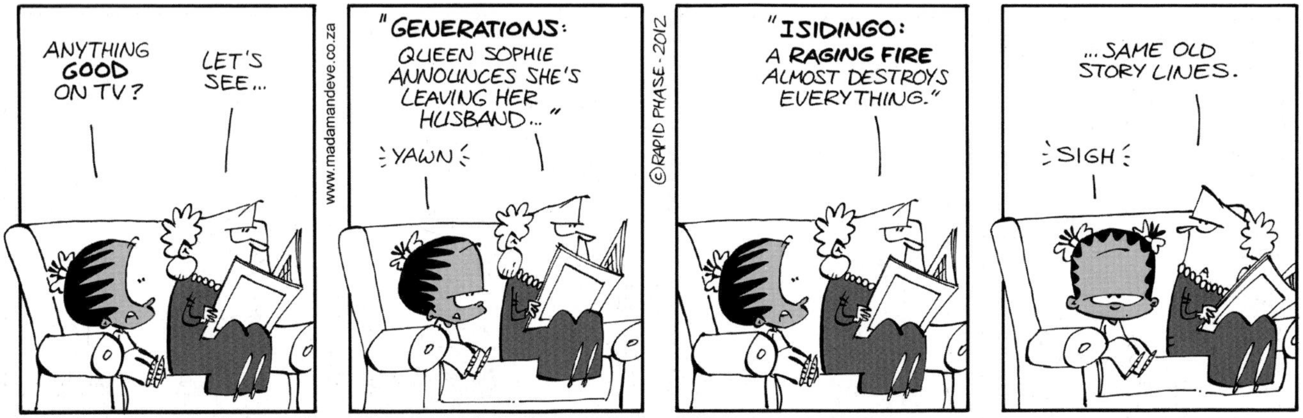
ANYTHING GOOD ON TV?
LET'S SEE...
www.madamandeve.co.za
"GENERATIONS: QUEEN SOPHIE ANNOUNCES SHE'S LEAVING HER HUSBAND..."
YAWN
©RAPID PHASE - 2012
"ISIDINGO: A RAGING FIRE ALMOST DESTROYS EVERYTHING."
...SAME OLD STORY LINES.
SIGH

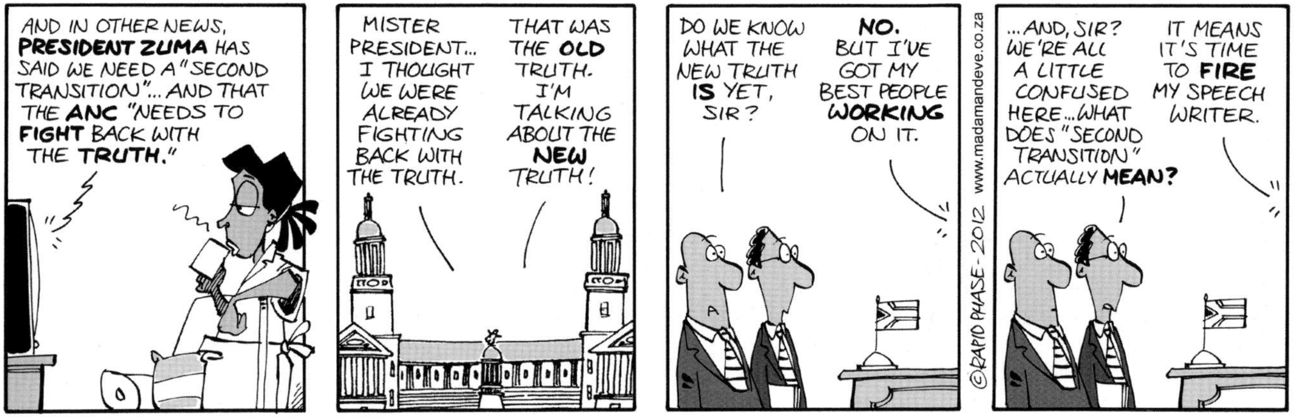
AND IN OTHER NEWS, PRESIDENT ZUMA HAS SAID WE NEED A "SECOND TRANSITION"... AND THAT THE ANC "NEEDS TO FIGHT BACK WITH THE TRUTH."
MISTER PRESIDENT... I THOUGHT WE WERE ALREADY FIGHTING BACK WITH THE TRUTH.
THAT WAS THE OLD TRUTH. I'M TALKING ABOUT THE NEW TRUTH!
DO WE KNOW WHAT THE NEW TRUTH IS YET, SIR?
NO. BUT I'VE GOT MY BEST PEOPLE WORKING ON IT.
©RAPID PHASE - 2012 www.madamandeve.co.za
...AND, SIR? WE'RE ALL A LITTLE CONFUSED HERE... WHAT DOES "SECOND TRANSITION" ACTUALLY MEAN?
IT MEANS IT'S TIME TO FIRE MY SPEECH WRITER.

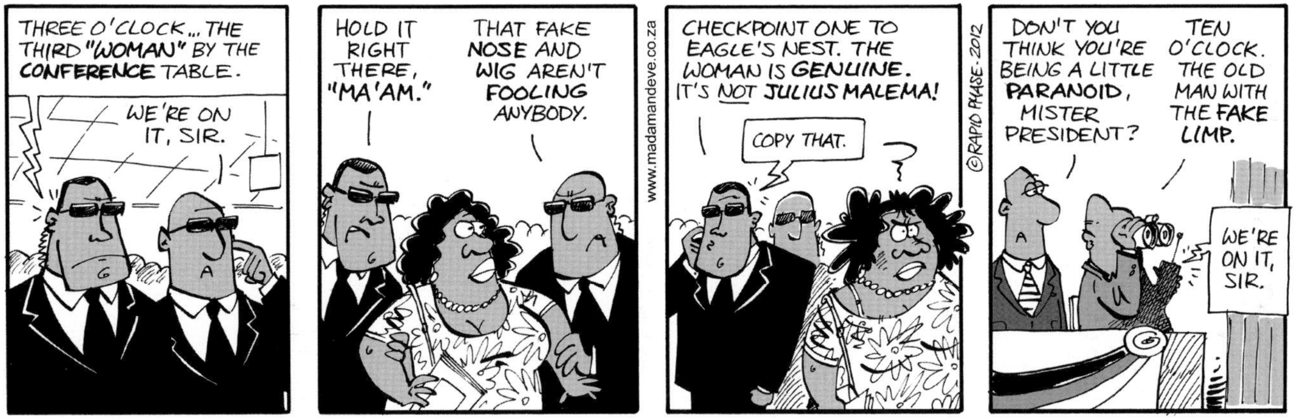
THREE O'CLOCK... THE THIRD "WOMAN" BY THE CONFERENCE TABLE.
WE'RE ON IT, SIR.
HOLD IT RIGHT THERE, "MA'AM."
THAT FAKE NOSE AND WIG AREN'T FOOLING ANYBODY.
www.madamandeve.co.za
CHECKPOINT ONE TO EAGLE'S NEST. THE WOMAN IS GENUINE. IT'S NOT JULIUS MALEMA!
COPY THAT.
?
©RAPID PHASE - 2012
DON'T YOU THINK YOU'RE BEING A LITTLE PARANOID, MISTER PRESIDENT?
TEN O'CLOCK. THE OLD MAN WITH THE FAKE LIMP.
WE'RE ON IT, SIR.

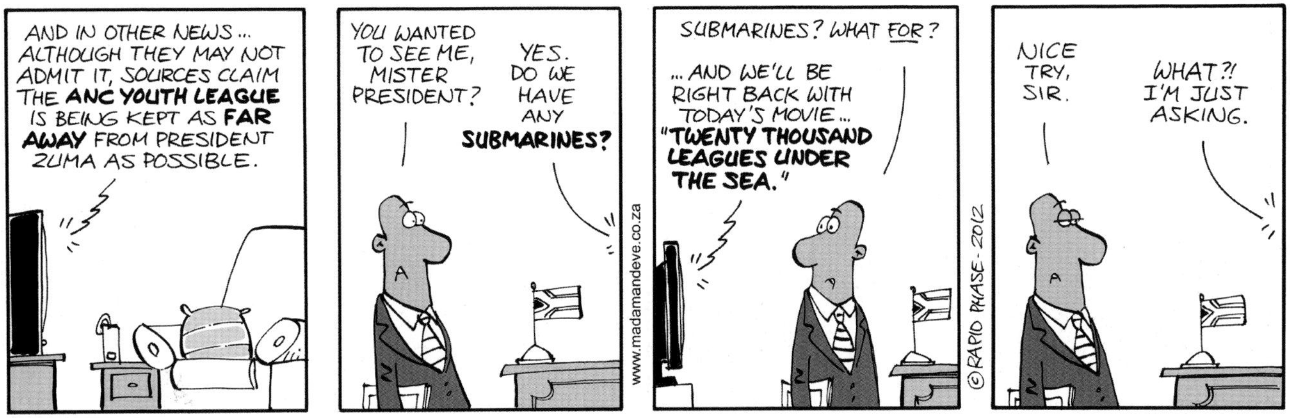
AND IN OTHER NEWS... ALTHOUGH THEY MAY NOT ADMIT IT, SOURCES CLAIM THE ANC YOUTH LEAGUE IS BEING KEPT AS FAR AWAY FROM PRESIDENT ZUMA AS POSSIBLE.
YOU WANTED TO SEE ME, MISTER PRESIDENT?
YES. DO WE HAVE ANY SUBMARINES?
www.madamandeve.co.za
SUBMARINES? WHAT FOR?
... AND WE'LL BE RIGHT BACK WITH TODAY'S MOVIE... "TWENTY THOUSAND LEAGUES UNDER THE SEA."
©RAPID PHASE - 2012
NICE TRY, SIR.
WHAT?! I'M JUST ASKING.

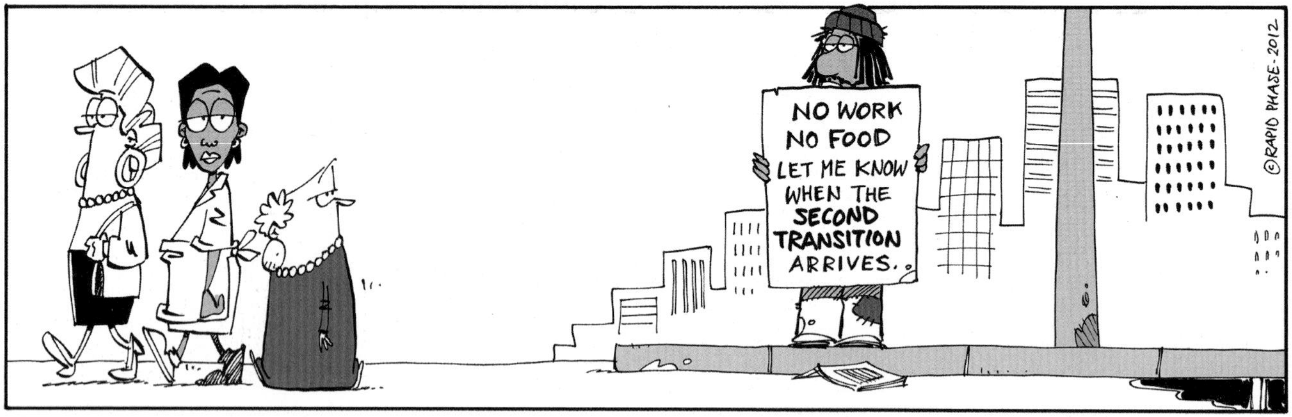
NO WORK NO FOOD LET ME KNOW WHEN THE SECOND TRANSITION ARRIVES.
©RAPID PHASE-2012

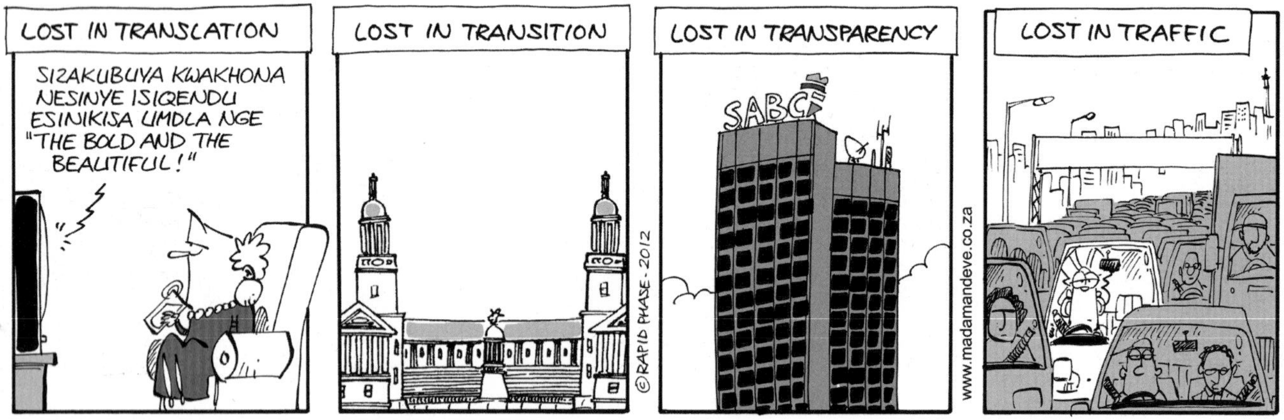
LOST IN TRANSLATION
SIZAKUBUYA KWAKHONA NESINYE ISIQENDU ESINIKISA UMDLA NGE "THE BOLD AND THE BEAUTIFUL!"
LOST IN TRANSITION
©RAPID PHASE-2012
LOST IN TRANSPARENCY
SABC
www.madamandeve.co.za
LOST IN TRAFFIC

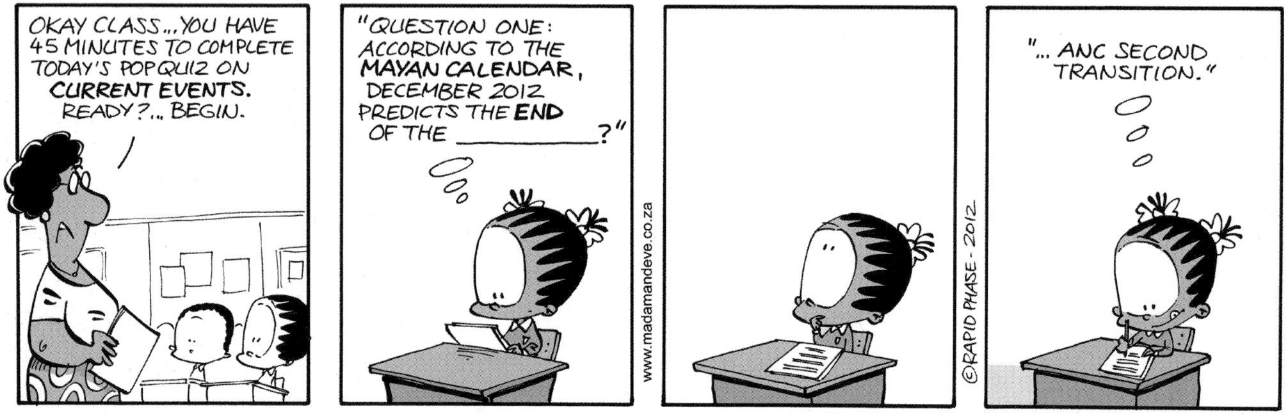
OKAY CLASS... YOU HAVE 45 MINUTES TO COMPLETE TODAY'S POPQUIZ ON CURRENT EVENTS. READY?... BEGIN.
"QUESTION ONE: ACCORDING TO THE MAYAN CALENDAR, DECEMBER 2012 PREDICTS THE END OF THE ________?"
www.madamandeve.co.za
©RAPID PHASE-2012
"... ANC SECOND TRANSITION."

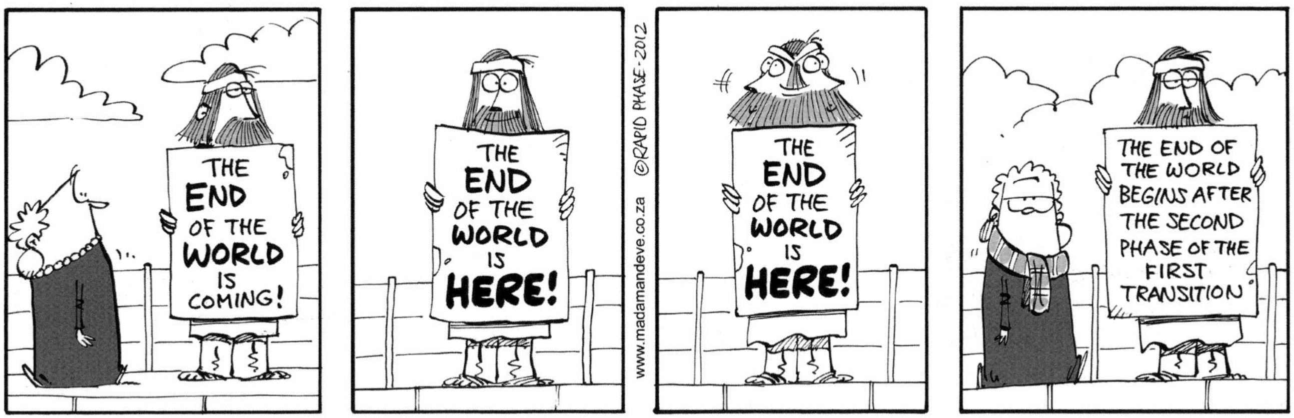
THE END OF THE WORLD IS COMING!
THE END OF THE WORLD IS HERE!
©RAPID PHASE·2012
www.madamandeve.co.za
THE END OF THE WORLD IS HERE!
THE END OF THE WORLD BEGINS AFTER THE SECOND PHASE OF THE FIRST TRANSITION

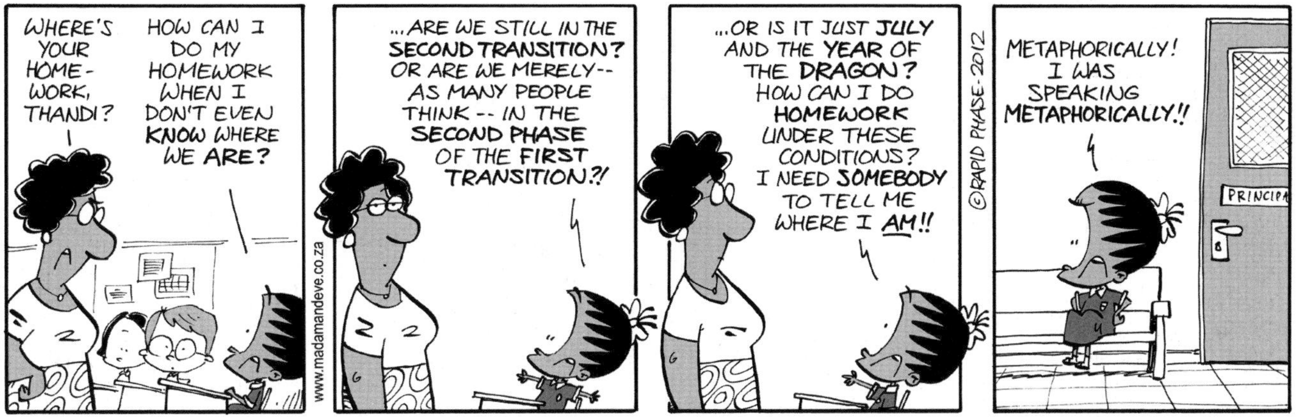
WHERE'S YOUR HOME-WORK, THANDI?
HOW CAN I DO MY HOMEWORK WHEN I DON'T EVEN KNOW WHERE WE ARE?
www.madamandeve.co.za
...ARE WE STILL IN THE SECOND TRANSITION? OR ARE WE MERELY-- AS MANY PEOPLE THINK -- IN THE SECOND PHASE OF THE FIRST TRANSITION?!
...OR IS IT JUST JULY AND THE YEAR OF THE DRAGON? HOW CAN I DO HOMEWORK UNDER THESE CONDITIONS? I NEED SOMEBODY TO TELL ME WHERE I AM!!
©RAPID PHASE·2012
METAPHORICALLY! I WAS SPEAKING METAPHORICALLY!!
PRINCIPA

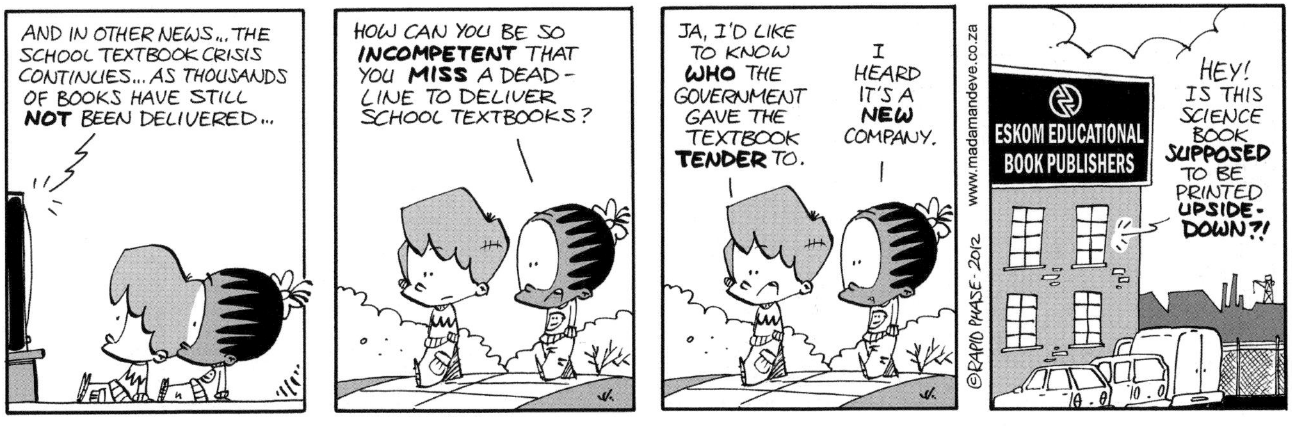
AND IN OTHER NEWS... THE SCHOOL TEXTBOOK CRISIS CONTINUES... AS THOUSANDS OF BOOKS HAVE STILL NOT BEEN DELIVERED...
HOW CAN YOU BE SO INCOMPETENT THAT YOU MISS A DEAD-LINE TO DELIVER SCHOOL TEXTBOOKS?
JA, I'D LIKE TO KNOW WHO THE GOVERNMENT GAVE THE TEXTBOOK TENDER TO.
I HEARD IT'S A NEW COMPANY.
www.madamandeve.co.za
©RAPID PHASE·2012
ESKOM EDUCATIONAL BOOK PUBLISHERS
HEY! IS THIS SCIENCE BOOK SUPPOSED TO BE PRINTED UPSIDE-DOWN?!

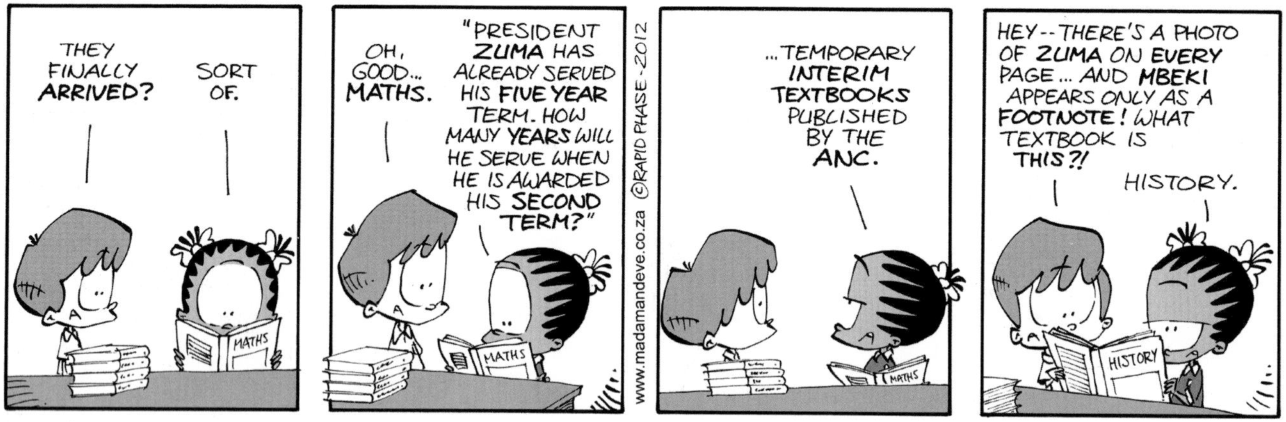
THEY FINALLY ARRIVED?
SORT OF.
OH, GOOD... MATHS.
"PRESIDENT ZUMA HAS ALREADY SERVED HIS FIVE YEAR TERM. HOW MANY YEARS WILL HE SERVE WHEN HE IS AWARDED HIS SECOND TERM?"
MATHS
www.madamandeve.co.za ©RAPID PHASE-2012
...TEMPORARY INTERIM TEXTBOOKS PUBLISHED BY THE ANC.
HEY--THERE'S A PHOTO OF ZUMA ON EVERY PAGE... AND MBEKI APPEARS ONLY AS A FOOTNOTE! WHAT TEXTBOOK IS THIS?!
HISTORY.
HISTORY

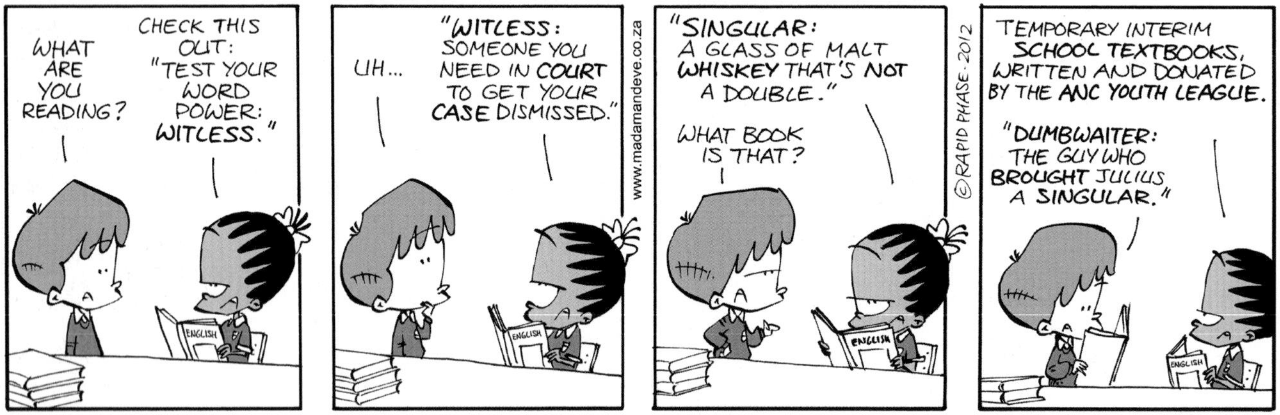
WHAT ARE YOU READING?
CHECK THIS OUT: "TEST YOUR WORD POWER: WITLESS."
ENGLISH
UH...
"WITLESS: SOMEONE YOU NEED IN COURT TO GET YOUR CASE DISMISSED."
www.madamandeve.co.za
"SINGULAR: A GLASS OF MALT WHISKEY THAT'S NOT A DOUBLE."
WHAT BOOK IS THAT?
©RAPID PHASE-2012
TEMPORARY INTERIM SCHOOL TEXTBOOKS, WRITTEN AND DONATED BY THE ANC YOUTH LEAGUE.
"DUMBWAITER: THE GUY WHO BROUGHT JULIUS A SINGULAR."

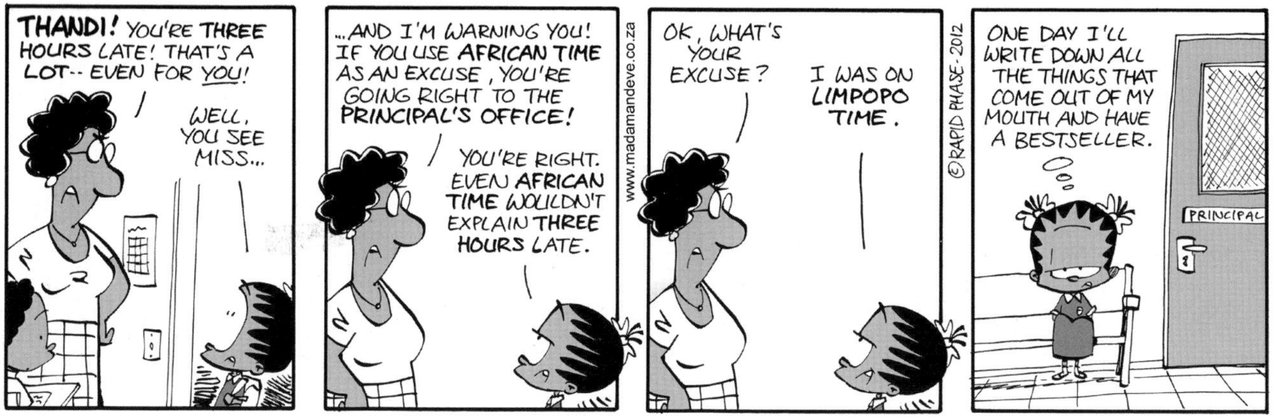
THANDI! YOU'RE THREE HOURS LATE! THAT'S A LOT-- EVEN FOR YOU!
WELL, YOU SEE MISS...
...AND I'M WARNING YOU! IF YOU USE AFRICAN TIME AS AN EXCUSE, YOU'RE GOING RIGHT TO THE PRINCIPAL'S OFFICE!
YOU'RE RIGHT. EVEN AFRICAN TIME WOULDN'T EXPLAIN THREE HOURS LATE.
www.madamandeve.co.za
OK, WHAT'S YOUR EXCUSE?
I WAS ON LIMPOPO TIME.
©RAPID PHASE-2012
ONE DAY I'LL WRITE DOWN ALL THE THINGS THAT COME OUT OF MY MOUTH AND HAVE A BESTSELLER.
PRINCIPAL

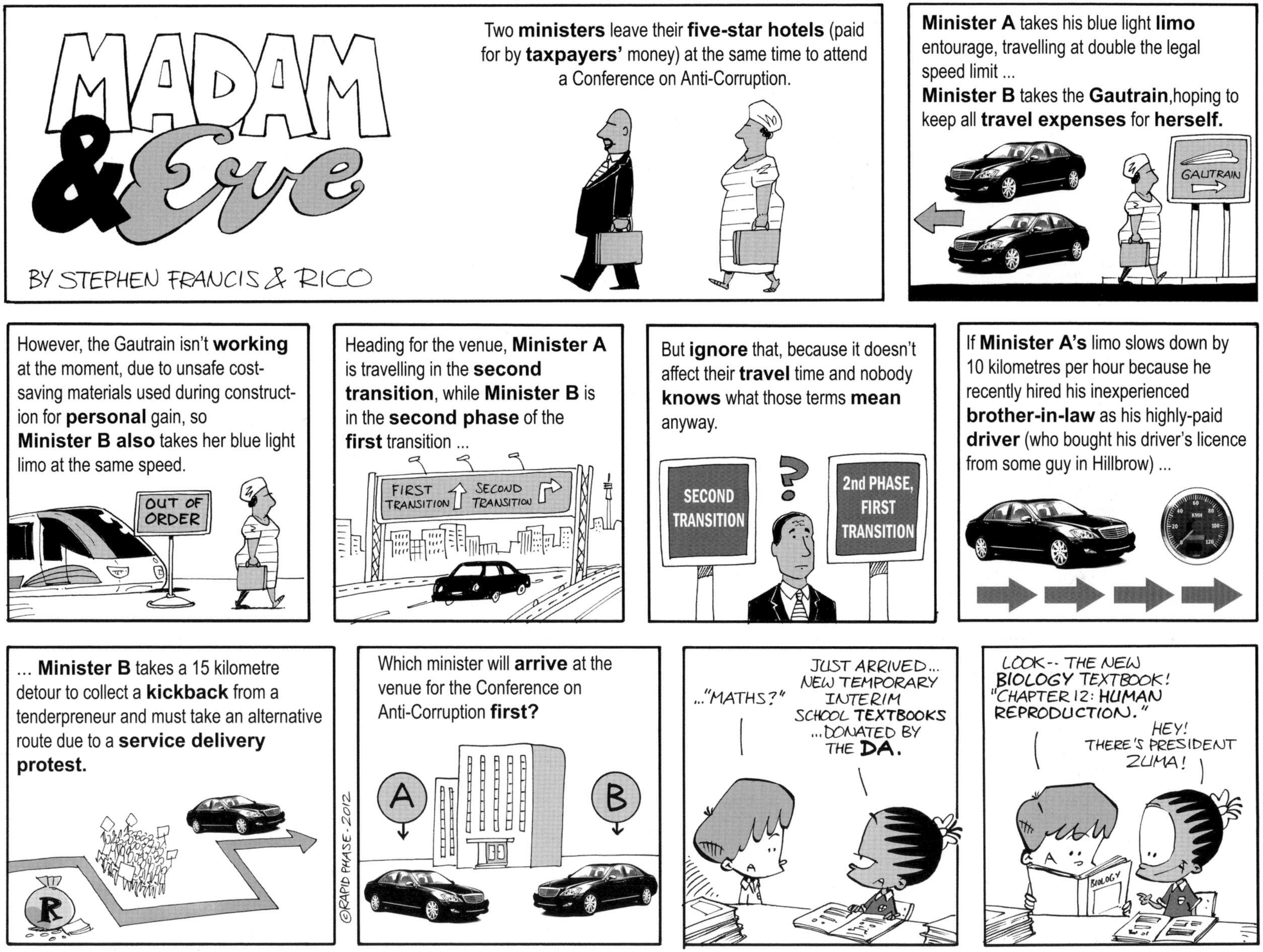
MADAM & Eve
BY STEPHEN FRANCIS & RICO
Two **ministers** leave their **five-star hotels** (paid for by **taxpayers'** money) at the same time to attend a Conference on Anti-Corruption.
Minister A takes his blue light **limo** entourage, travelling at double the legal speed limit ...
Minister B takes the **Gautrain**,hoping to keep all **travel expenses** for **herself.**
GAUTRAIN
However, the Gautrain isn't **working** at the moment, due to unsafe cost-saving materials used during construction for **personal** gain, so **Minister B also** takes her blue light limo at the same speed.
OUT OF ORDER
Heading for the venue, **Minister A** is travelling in the **second transition**, while **Minister B** is in the **second phase** of the **first** transition ...
FIRST TRANSITION
SECOND TRANSITION
But **ignore** that, because it doesn't affect their **travel** time and nobody **knows** what those terms **mean** anyway.
SECOND TRANSITION
2nd PHASE, FIRST TRANSITION
If **Minister A's** limo slows down by 10 kilometres per hour because he recently hired his inexperienced **brother-in-law** as his highly-paid **driver** (who bought his driver's licence from some guy in Hillbrow) ...
... **Minister B** takes a 15 kilometre detour to collect a **kickback** from a tenderpreneur and must take an alternative route due to a **service delivery protest.**
R
©RAPID PHASE · 2012
Which minister will **arrive** at the venue for the Conference on Anti-Corruption **first?**
A
B
JUST ARRIVED... NEW TEMPORARY INTERIM SCHOOL TEXTBOOKS ...DONATED BY THE DA.
..."MATHS?"
LOOK-- THE NEW BIOLOGY TEXTBOOK! "CHAPTER 12: HUMAN REPRODUCTION."
HEY! THERE'S PRESIDENT ZUMA!
BIOLOGY

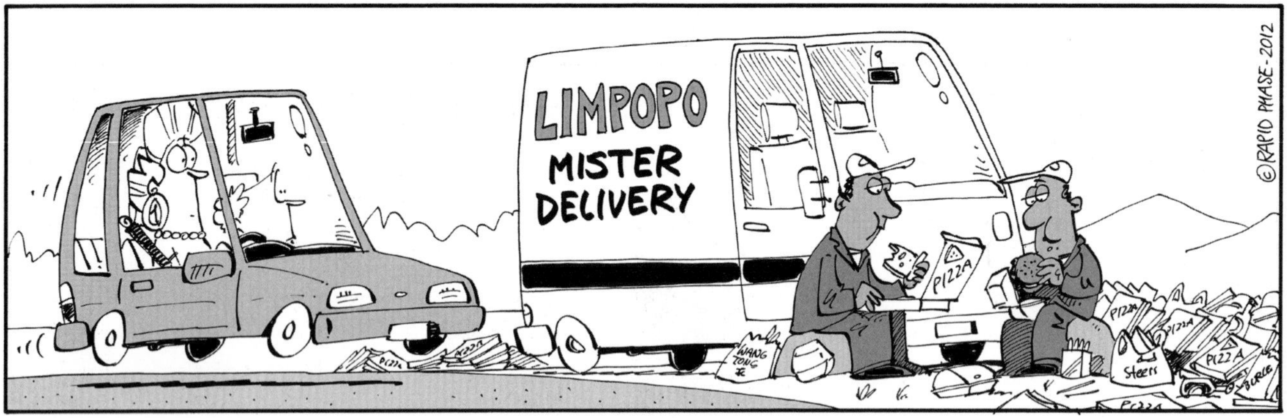
LIMPOPO
MISTER DELIVERY
PIZZA
©RAPID PHASE-2012

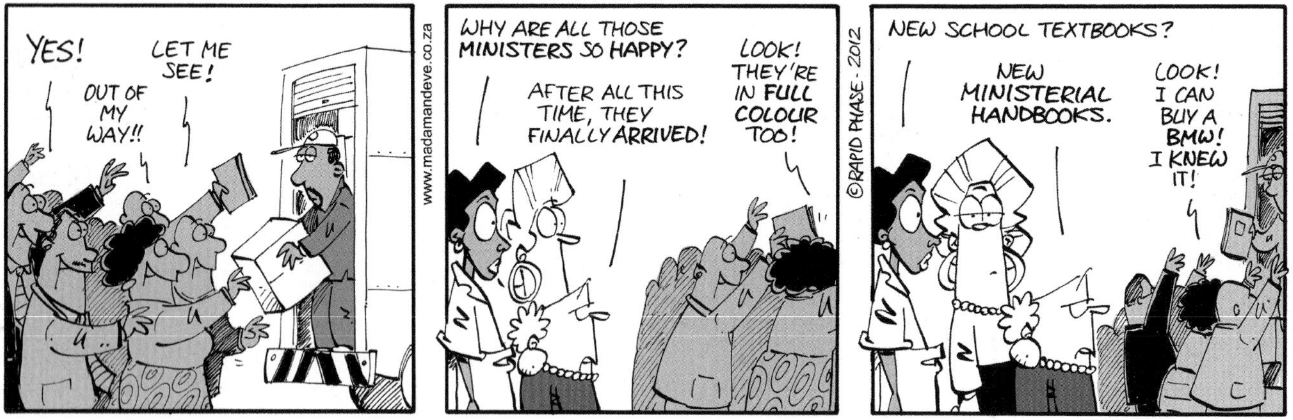
YES!
OUT OF MY WAY!!
LET ME SEE!
www.madamandeve.co.za
WHY ARE ALL THOSE MINISTERS SO HAPPY?
AFTER ALL THIS TIME, THEY FINALLY ARRIVED!
LOOK! THEY'RE IN FULL COLOUR TOO!
©RAPID PHASE-2012
NEW SCHOOL TEXTBOOKS?
NEW MINISTERIAL HANDBOOKS.
LOOK! I CAN BUY A BMW! I KNEW IT!

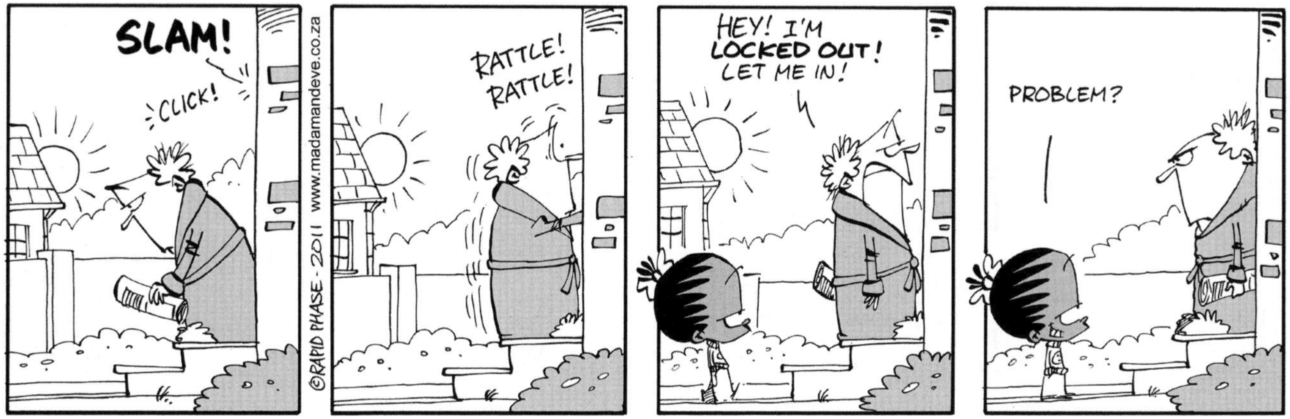
SLAM!
CLICK!
©RAPID PHASE-2011 www.madamandeve.co.za
RATTLE! RATTLE!
HEY! I'M LOCKED OUT! LET ME IN!
PROBLEM?

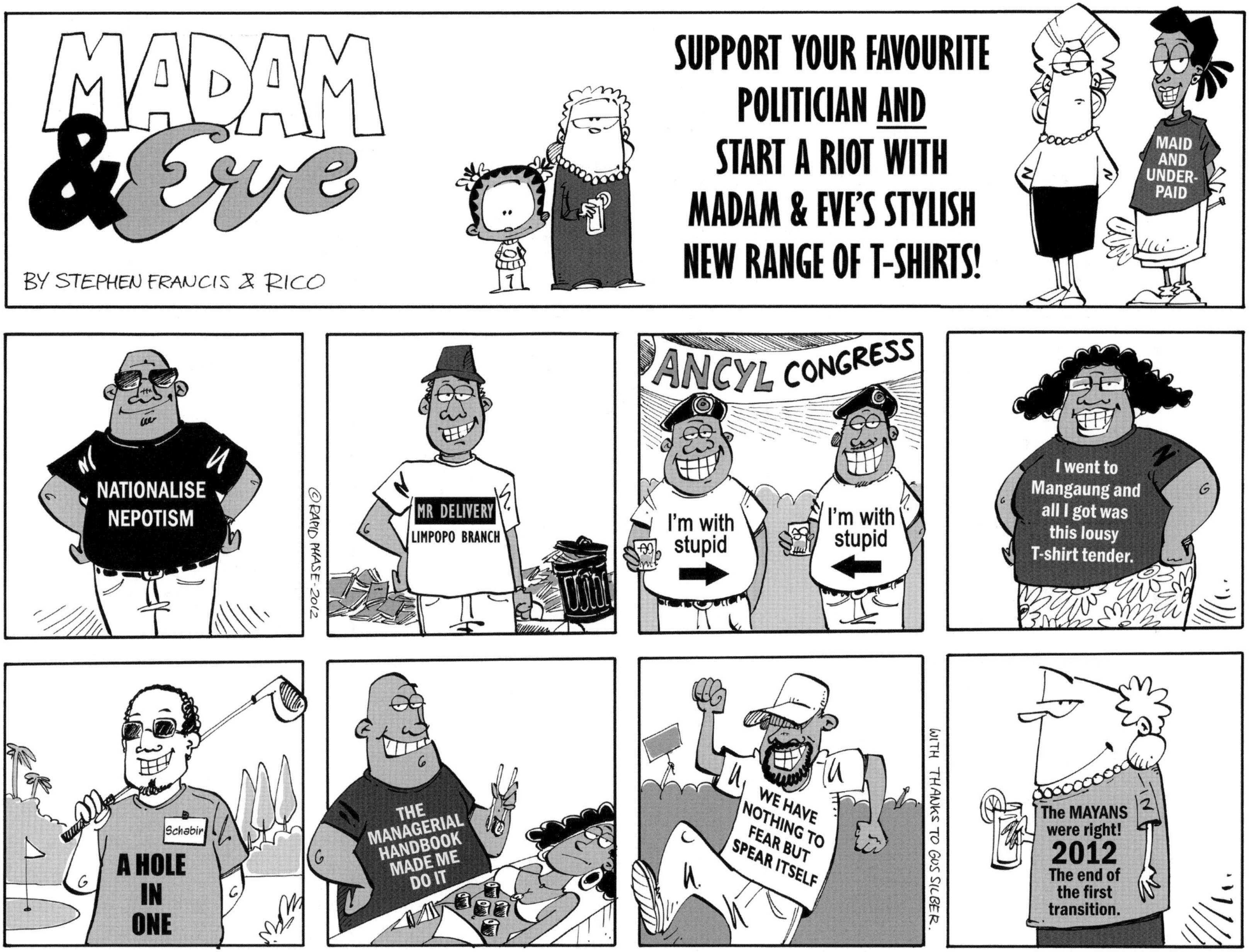
MADAM & Eve
BY STEPHEN FRANCIS & RICO
SUPPORT YOUR FAVOURITE POLITICIAN AND START A RIOT WITH MADAM & EVE'S STYLISH NEW RANGE OF T-SHIRTS!
MAID AND UNDER-PAID
NATIONALISE NEPOTISM
©RAPID PHASE-2012
MR DELIVERY
LIMPOPO BRANCH
ANCYL CONGRESS
I'm with stupid
I'm with stupid
I went to Mangaung and all I got was this lousy T-shirt tender.
Schabir
A HOLE IN ONE
THE MANAGERIAL HANDBOOK MADE ME DO IT
WE HAVE NOTHING TO FEAR BUT SPEAR ITSELF
WITH THANKS TO GUS SILBER.
The MAYANS were right!
2012
The end of the first transition.

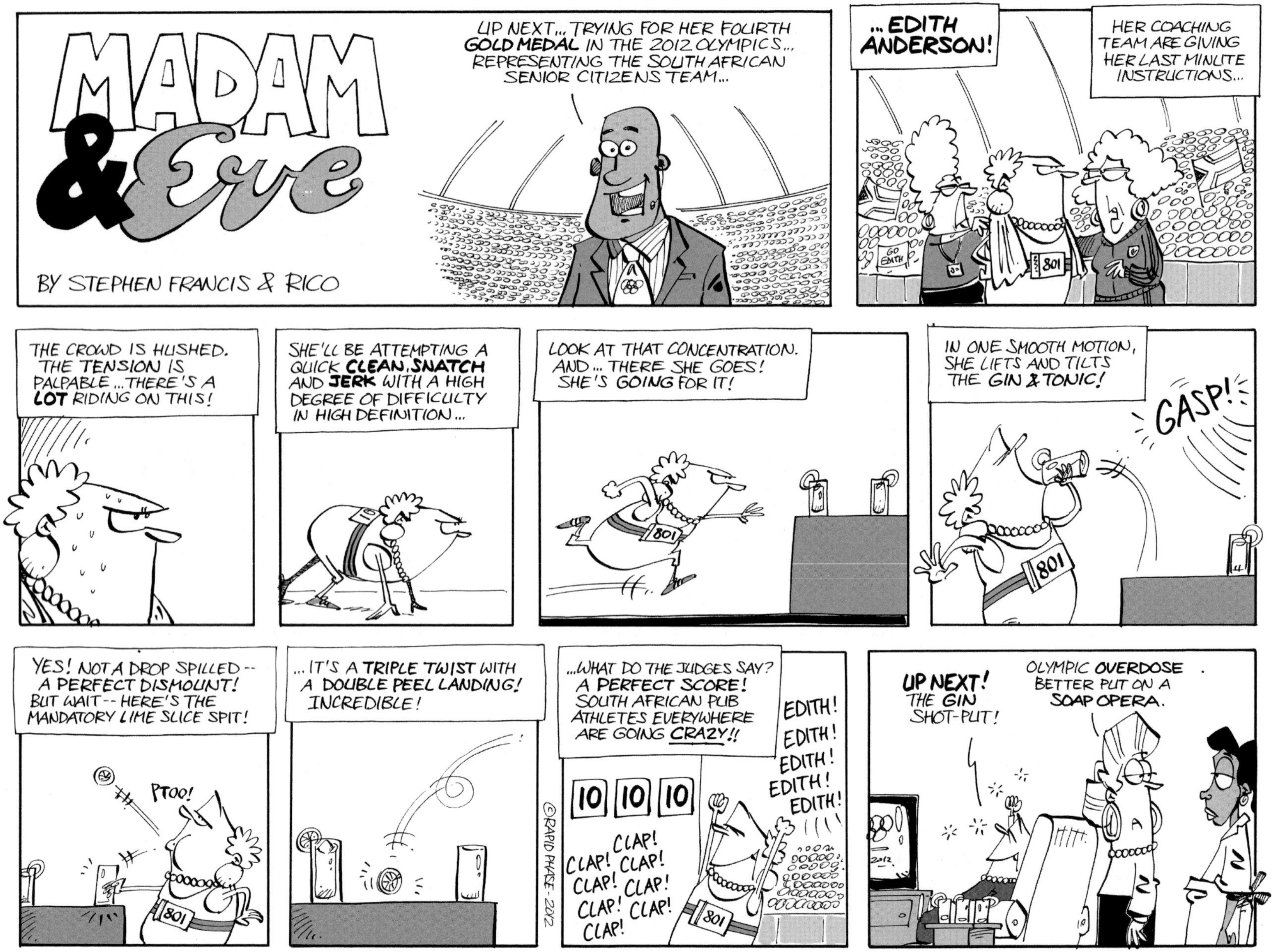
MADAM & Eve
BY STEPHEN FRANCIS & RICO
UP NEXT... TRYING FOR HER FOURTH GOLD MEDAL IN THE 2012 OLYMPICS... REPRESENTING THE SOUTH AFRICAN SENIOR CITIZENS TEAM...
...EDITH ANDERSON!
HER COACHING TEAM ARE GIVING HER LAST MINUTE INSTRUCTIONS...
GO EDITH
801
THE CROWD IS HUSHED. THE TENSION IS PALPABLE... THERE'S A LOT RIDING ON THIS!
SHE'LL BE ATTEMPTING A QUICK CLEAN, SNATCH AND JERK WITH A HIGH DEGREE OF DIFFICULTY IN HIGH DEFINITION...
LOOK AT THAT CONCENTRATION. AND... THERE SHE GOES! SHE'S GOING FOR IT!
801
IN ONE SMOOTH MOTION, SHE LIFTS AND TILTS THE GIN & TONIC!
GASP!
801
YES! NOT A DROP SPILLED -- A PERFECT DISMOUNT! BUT WAIT -- HERE'S THE MANDATORY LIME SLICE SPIT!
PTOO!
801
...IT'S A TRIPLE TWIST WITH A DOUBLE PEEL LANDING! INCREDIBLE!
©RAPID PHASE 2012
...WHAT DO THE JUDGES SAY? A PERFECT SCORE! SOUTH AFRICAN PUB ATHLETES EVERYWHERE ARE GOING CRAZY!!
EDITH! EDITH! EDITH! EDITH! EDITH!
10 10 10
CLAP! CLAP! CLAP! CLAP! CLAP! CLAP! CLAP! CLAP!
801
UP NEXT! THE GIN SHOT-PUT!
OLYMPIC OVERDOSE. BETTER PUT ON A SOAP OPERA.

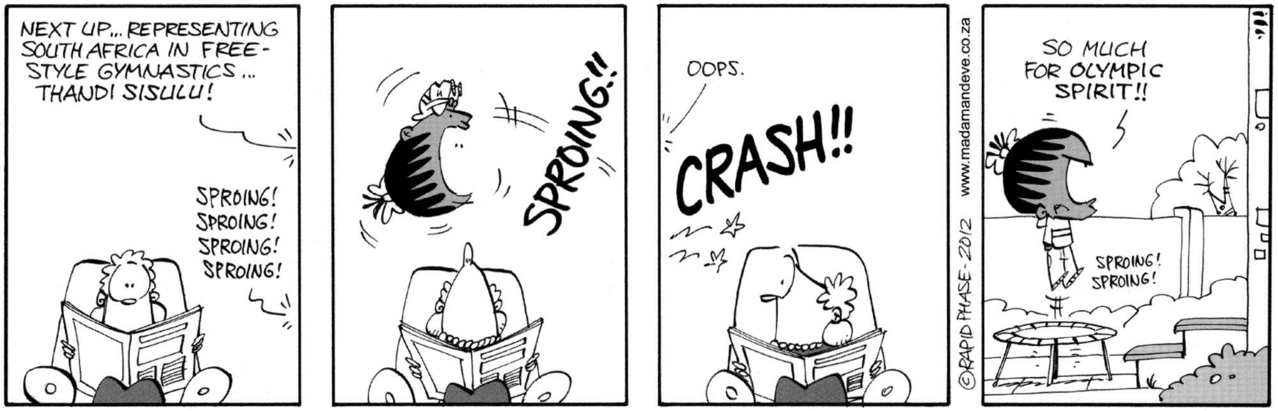
NEXT UP... REPRESENTING SOUTH AFRICA IN FREE-STYLE GYMNASTICS ... THANDI SISULU!
SPROING! SPROING! SPROING! SPROING!
SPROING!!
OOPS.
CRASH!!
www.madamandeve.co.za
©RAPID PHASE-2012
SO MUCH FOR OLYMPIC SPIRIT!!
SPROING! SPROING!

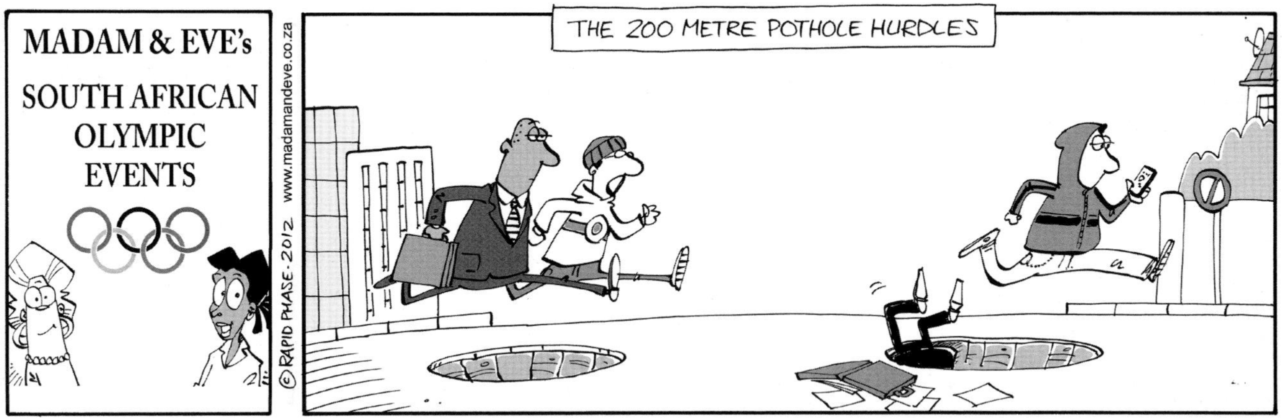
MADAM & EVE's
SOUTH AFRICAN OLYMPIC EVENTS
www.madamandeve.co.za
©RAPID PHASE-2012
THE 200 METRE POTHOLE HURDLES

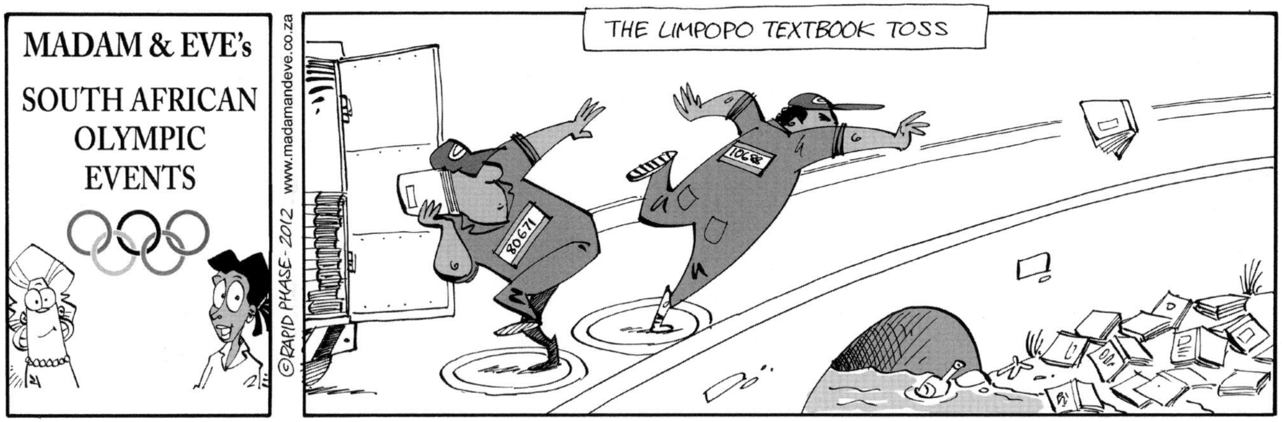
MADAM & EVE's
SOUTH AFRICAN OLYMPIC EVENTS
www.madamandeve.co.za
©RAPID PHASE-2012
THE LIMPOPO TEXTBOOK TOSS

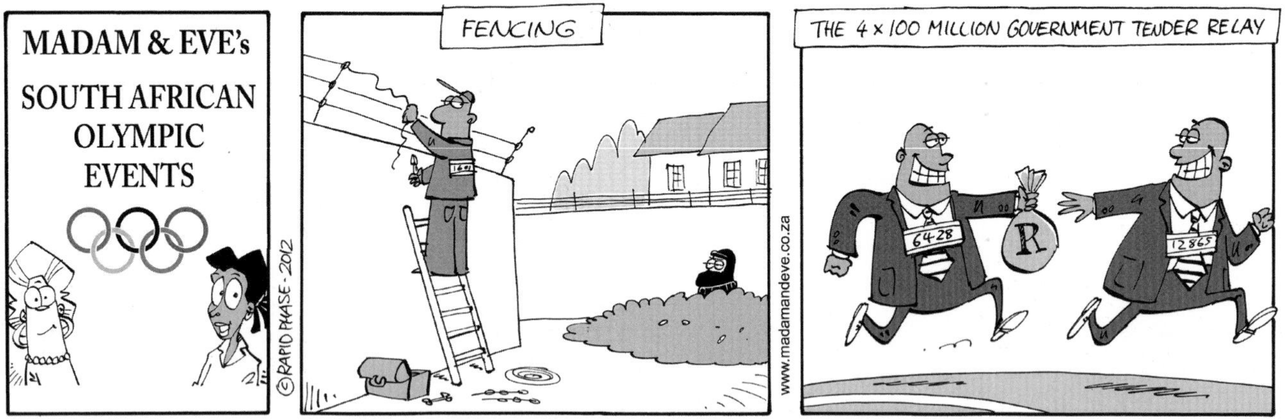

MADAM & EVE's
SOUTH AFRICAN OLYMPIC EVENTS
FENCING
©RAPID PHASE-2012
www.madamandeve.co.za
THE 4 x 100 MILLION GOVERNMENT TENDER RELAY
6428
R
12865

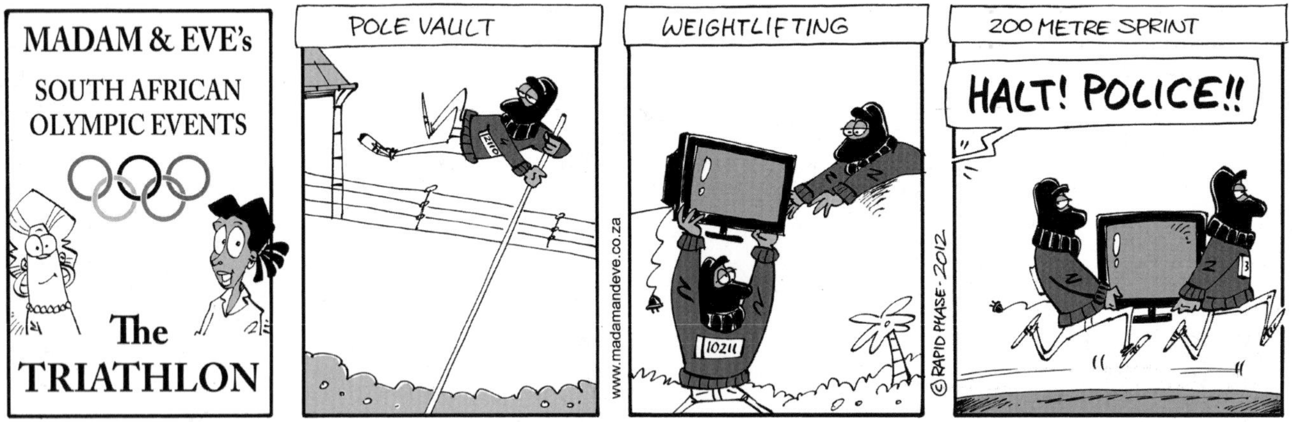

MADAM & EVE's
SOUTH AFRICAN OLYMPIC EVENTS
The TRIATHLON
POLE VAULT
WEIGHTLIFTING
10211
www.madamandeve.co.za
©RAPID PHASE-2012
200 METRE SPRINT
HALT! POLICE!!

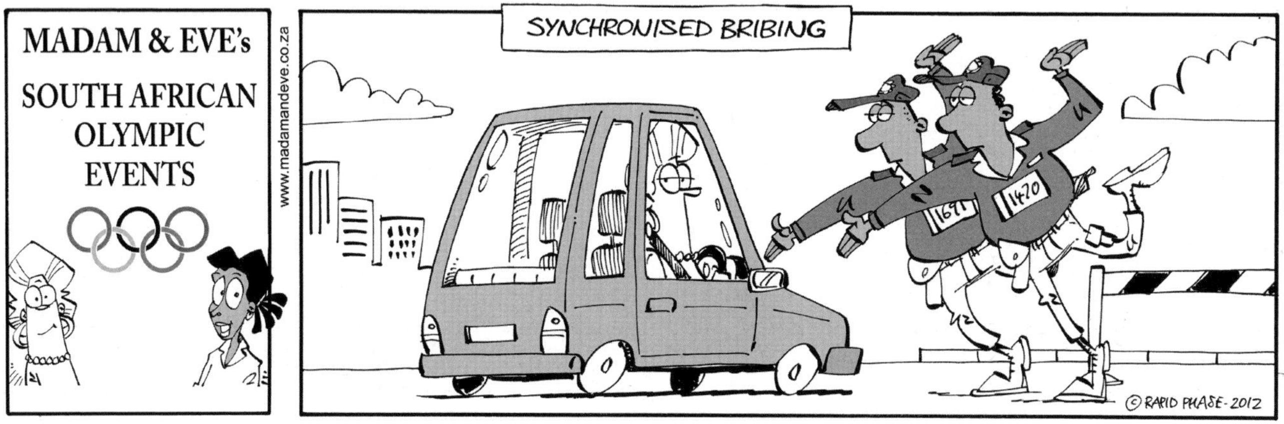

MADAM & EVE's
SOUTH AFRICAN OLYMPIC EVENTS
www.madamandeve.co.za
SYNCHRONISED BRIBING
1691
1420
©RAPID PHASE-2012

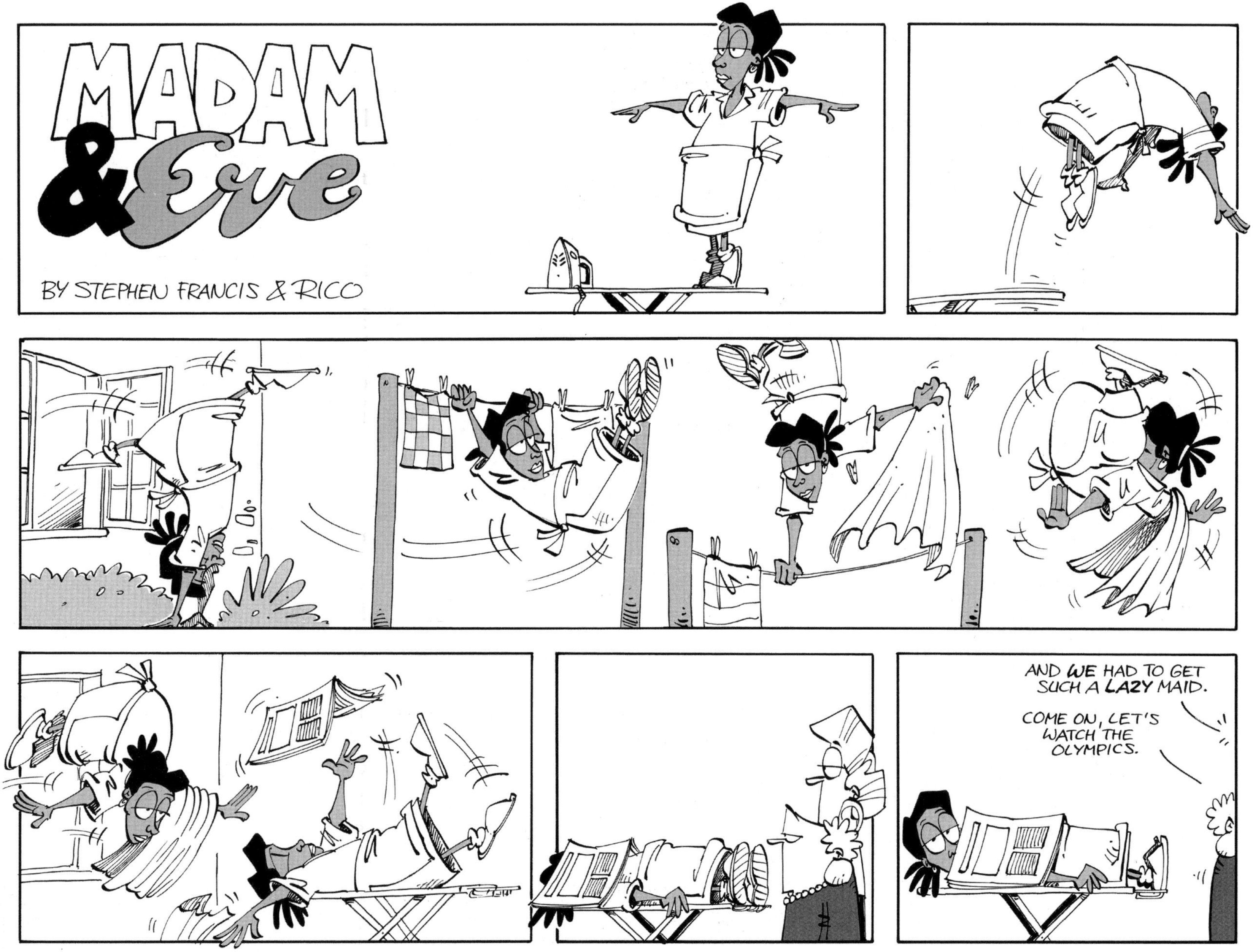
MADAM & Eve
BY STEPHEN FRANCIS & RICO
AND WE HAD TO GET SUCH A LAZY MAID.
COME ON, LET'S WATCH THE OLYMPICS.

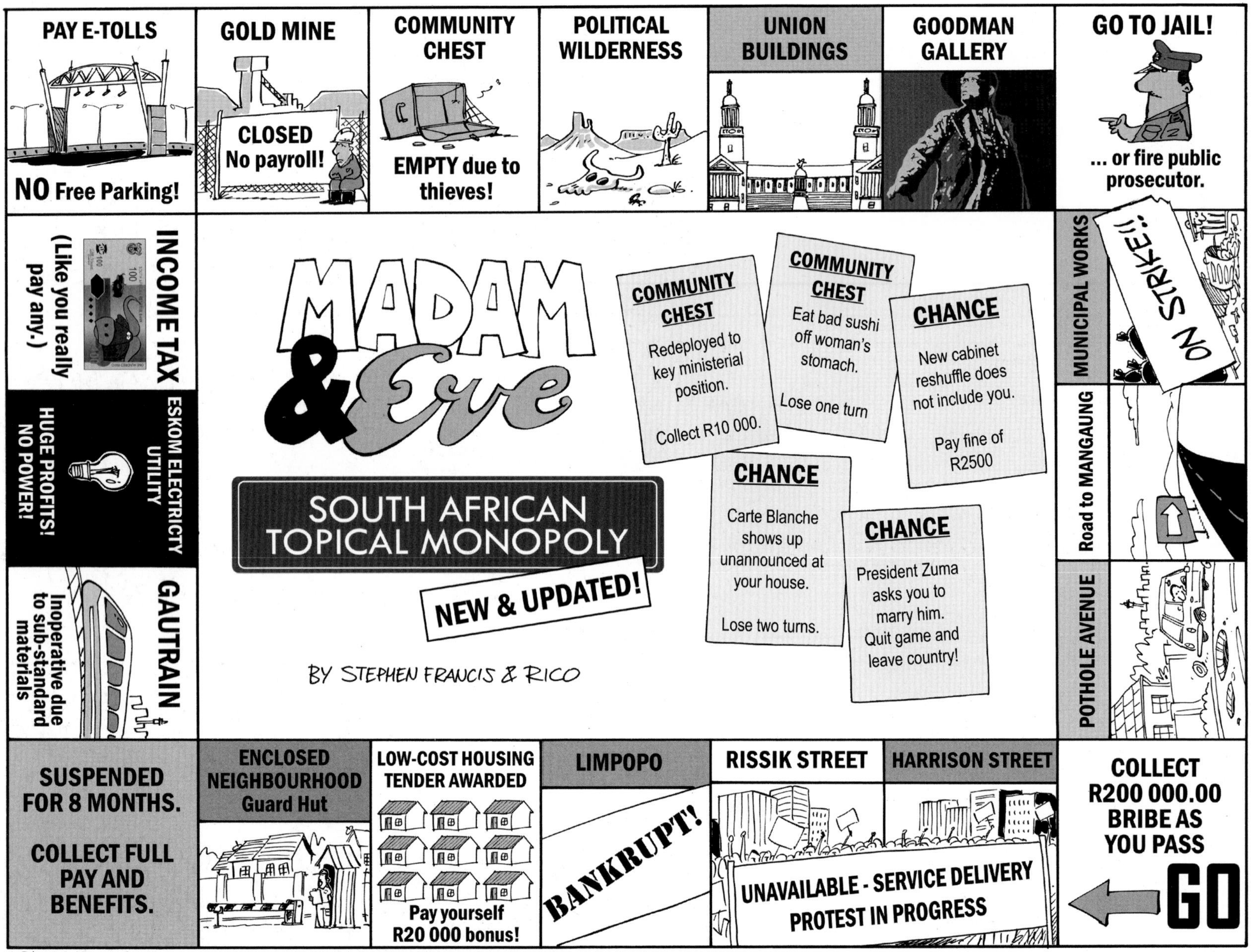
PAY E-TOLLS
NO Free Parking!
GOLD MINE
CLOSED
No payroll!
COMMUNITY CHEST
EMPTY due to thieves!
POLITICAL WILDERNESS
UNION BUILDINGS
GOODMAN GALLERY
GO TO JAIL!
... or fire public prosecutor.
INCOME TAX
(Like you really pay any.)
ESKOM ELECTRICTY UTILITY
HUGE PROFITS! NO POWER!
GAUTRAIN
Inoperative due to sub-standard materials
MADAM & Eve
SOUTH AFRICAN TOPICAL MONOPOLY
NEW & UPDATED!
BY STEPHEN FRANCIS & RICO
COMMUNITY CHEST
Redeployed to key ministerial position.
Collect R10 000.
COMMUNITY CHEST
Eat bad sushi off woman's stomach.
Lose one turn
CHANCE
New cabinet reshuffle does not include you.
Pay fine of R2500
CHANCE
Carte Blanche shows up unannounced at your house.
Lose two turns.
CHANCE
President Zuma asks you to marry him.
Quit game and leave country!
MUNICIPAL WORKS
ON STRIKE!!
Road to MANGAUNG
POTHOLE AVENUE
SUSPENDED FOR 8 MONTHS.
COLLECT FULL PAY AND BENEFITS.
ENCLOSED NEIGHBOURHOOD Guard Hut
LOW-COST HOUSING TENDER AWARDED
Pay yourself R20 000 bonus!
LIMPOPO
BANKRUPT!
RISSIK STREET
HARRISON STREET
UNAVAILABLE - SERVICE DELIVERY PROTEST IN PROGRESS
COLLECT R200 000.00 BRIBE AS YOU PASS
GO